Analytical Archaeologist

Collected Papers
of
DAVID L. CLARKE

This is a volume in

Studies in Archeology

A complete list of titles in this series appears at the end of this volume.

On behalf of the author, the editors
dedicate this book to Grahame Clark

David L. Clarke

Photo: Tim Frost

Analytical Archaeologist

Collected Papers
of
DAVID L. CLARKE

Edited by
his Colleagues

6933

1979

ACADEMIC PRESS

London   New York   San Francisco

A Subsidiary of Harcourt Brace Javanovich, Publishers

ACADEMIC PRESS INC. (LONDON) LTD.
24/28 Oval Road
London NW1

United States edition published by
ACADEMIC PRESS INC.
111 Fifth Avenue
New York, New York 10003

Library of Congress Catalog Card Number: 78–70512
ISBN: 0–12–175760–9

Printed in Great Britain by Butler & Tanner Ltd, Frome and London

List of Contributors

David L. Clarke, *formerly of Peterhouse, University of Cambridge*

Norman Hammond, *Department of Archaeology, Rutgers University, New Brunswick, New Jersey, USA*

Stella Clarke, *The Old House, Carmel Street, Great Chesterfield, Essex*

Glynn Ll. Issac, *Anthropology Department, University of California at Berkeley, California, USA*

Robert Chapman, *Department of Archaeology, University of Reading, Reading, Berkshire*

Andrew G. Sherrat, *Ashmolean Museum, Oxford*

Stephen J. Shennan, *Department of Archaeology, University of Southampton, Southampton*

Graham Connah, *Department of Anthropology, University of New England, Armidale, New South Wales, Australia*

J. E. Kerrich, *Department of Statistics, University of the Witwatersrand, South Africa*

Preface

At the time of his death in June 1976, David Clarke had agreed to publish a volume of selected papers, with a format similar to Lewis Binford's *An Archaeological Perspective*. In this highly successful work, Binford had interlarded some of his more important papers, reprinted from a variety of journals, with a personal narrative in which an assessment of the impact of the work was combined with a professional and intellectual autobiography. As with Binford, much of David Clarke's work had appeared in the form of relatively short journal articles, and although his personal life lacked some of the more picturesque episodes which Binford described with engaging frankness, his intellectual impact on the world of archaeology certainly justified the publication of a collected volume.

This book contains the articles which David had selected, arranged in the four sections which he had outlined in his single-page plan for the book. His plans had got no further, and none of the personal narrative had been written or even drafted. Although this was a serious loss, it was felt that the collected papers were themselves still worthy of publication, and that David's own assessment of his work and its impact could be, *faut de mieux*, replaced by the introductions and judgements of his colleagues. Each of the four major sections has been tackled by a different scholar, so that instead of the unity of David's self-appraisal we have diverse yet convergent views. Of the four, three (together with myself) were his pupils; one, Glynn Isaac, was a contemporary as a Research Student at Peterhouse. We all feel that we owe David a great debt, as a teacher and a friend, and our collaboration in the production of this, his last book, is a contribution to that now permanently debited account.

The selection of the five of us, from among the many who would willingly have made the effort, was mainly on the basis of particular qualification: Glynn Isaac had been a Visiting Fellow at Peterhouse for the last year of David's life, and knew more than most of us about the trend of thought which would have gone into David's own introductions to this book. Bob Chapman had been entrusted by David with the revision of his seminal book *Analytical Archaeology*, originally published in 1968: many of the battles that it fought have been long won, and much of the work cited has been overtaken by more recent scholarship (some of it directly or indirectly inspired by *Analytical Archaeology*). Bob Chapman's task was to slim down the text somewhat, so that the volume would still come within a student budget, and provide more up-to-date illustrations from the literature of the ideas and principles that David enunciated. As a result he is by now more familiar with the book than any of us, and his discussion of the two papers "Towards analytical archaeology" and "Analytical archaeology: epilogue" is greatly influenced by the absent presence of the more substantial work which they frame.

Andrew Sherratt has worked mainly on the prehistory of southeastern Europe, a region towards which, as he notes in an unpublished memoir, David Clarke was beginning to turn his thoughts as an area for field study, with "long-term plans perhaps for some Thessalian or Hungarian *tell* where the preservation of structured relationships could give full scope to his methods". His interests have retained the broad sweep that David instilled into all his pupils, and he remains in his current concern with the nature of prehistoric settlement and its relationship to environment, resources and communications, particularly close to the approach that David was taking in his major study of the Glastonbury Lake village. Of this work, discussed with many of us, only the preliminary sketch "A provisional model of an Iron Age society" ever reached publication, and no substantial manuscript for the developed study has been found, although there are hints of its existence in the sketch.

This paper apart, the section that Andrew Sherratt introduces contains material written over a seven-year period, from 1969, when *Analytical Archaeology* had just come out and *Beaker Pottery of Great Britain and Ireland* was in press, to 1976 when "Towns in the development of early civilization" was composed rapidly as an introductory address to a conference organized by a Petrean colleague, Tony Wrigley. Four of the five papers were unpublished at the time of David's death, so that many of their ideas have filtered through into the archaeological literature primarily in the work of his pupils, less afflicted by editorial costiveness. Only the Glastonbury paper had had wide circulation and, as a result, the European span of David's work remained unappreciated by most of his colleagues. These papers, and Andrew Sherratt's placing of them in an intellectual matrix in a way which I feel is especially close to that which David would have done, should belatedly correct that injustice.

The final section of David's outline for the book contains papers dealing with archaeological method, spanning more than a decade in their composition and coming mainly from the period before the publication of *Analytical Archaeology*. Three deal with beaker studies, preliminary findings in the course of thesis work and the subsequent publication of the *Beaker Pottery of Great Britain and Ireland*, volumes, and, as one of David's two pupils working on beaker problems (Bob Chapman being the other), Stephen Shennan was the obvious choice to place this work in perspective. In some ways he has had a more difficult task than Andrew Sherratt in the preceding section, since the European prehistory papers reveal an entirely new side of David's work to the world, while these "technical studies", as David termed them, are more restricted in their individual compass, worrying at single bones rather than attacking the whole skeleton. The exception, separated from the remainder of the group which were written and published before 1967, is the introductory chapter to *Spatial Archaeology*, brought to publication posthumously from page proof by Ian Hodder. In many ways, this is more of a philosophical disquisition than an essay on method *sensu stricto*, and might be thought to belong better in Glynn Isaac's section; but David thought otherwise.

Finally, why am I exercising editorial supervision over this book? I was asked to do so because I have had some experience of dealing with publishers, proofs and deadlines; I was more qualified to do this job than to write any of the sectional introductions, and I wanted to make some contribution towards salvaging anything possible for publication from the disaster of David's death. Although the book existed only as a list of titles divided into sections, all the papers were available, and their collective publication with appropriate commentary would complement the books already extant and round out more fully the future perception of an intellect and a personality now lost to us. David Clarke's place in the history of archaeological thought and endeavour remains to be assessed, as it will, by the lasting impact of his ideas, directly and through his pupils. We, his friends, offer this book as a contribution to that debate.

Norman Hammond

Contents

David Clarke: A Biographical Sketch

NORMAN HAMMOND

Any biography of David Clarke must be mainly intellectual rather than physical: his life was, by design, quiet and static, almost totally devoid of *éclat*, and devoted wholly to the pursuit of intellectual adventure by day and the enjoyment of his family at all other times. He did not revel in the heightened atmosphere of conferences, even the staid British variety, denied himself the solipsistic pleasures of reviewing the faults of others' work as far as possible, and concentrated on what he thought was worth doing in archaeology with a happy disregard for what others thought he ought to think. He was not a man of action, except in the mind, and was almost unique in being a major influence in archaeology without ever having directed a major excavation. He spent his entire academic life in Cambridge, in one of its smallest colleges and without any university post until he was nearly 36 years old, yet was one of a very few British prehistorians whose work was known across the world.

David came to Cambridge from one of England's best-known schools, Dulwich College, where he had studied the natural sciences and acquired thereby invaluable experience in understanding the structures and behaviour of complex entities; between school and university he had two years of obligatory National Service as an Army officer, spent in the Royal Signals Corps at Essen in Germany, and, whether this had any lasting influence or not, his attitude to archaeological problems was always European rather than insular.

In October of 1957, at 19, he came up to Peterhouse, already committed to reading for the Archaeological and Anthropological Tripos, and at the end of his first year obtained an Upper Second in Part I of the Tripos, which included papers in Social and Physical Anthropology as well as in Archaeology. In his second and third years, now reading Archaeology alone, he got a First Class, specializing in the later prehistory of Europe from the beginnings of farming to the Roman period. The Tripos course had a large "Greece-shaped gap" in it, since the Prehellenic Greeks and their ancestors were, at Cambridge as elsewhere,

1

within the purview of Classical Archaeology, and between Classical and Prehistoric Archaeology there was a great gulf fixed, with its origins in the Renaissance and its reality in two entirely different ways of regarding archaeological evidence. David saw no reason why this gulf should not be spanned, or indeed why it should exist at all, and promptly added Classics Department courses on Prehellenic Archaeology to his curriculum.

He graduated BA with First Class Honours in 1960, and was promptly accepted back at Peterhouse as a Research Student working for the PhD – at Cambridge, as in other English universities, consisting of the submission and defence of a dissertation after three years of independent study, without any of the course work or examinations required in American graduate schools. Being at Peterhouse, David was accepted as a supervisee by Grahame Clark, a Fellow of the College, Disney Professor of Archaeology in the University, and one of the most widely influential prehistorians of the century; if he did not already possess a broad mind and a willingness to read almost anything that might bear on his field, David certainly would have acquired such traits from Grahame Clark.

His declared subject of research was "the origins and development of British beaker pottery", and he was one of several research students who Grahame Clark had steered into examining the early ceramics of prehistoric Britain; others were working on urns and food vessels, typological distinctions set up decades earlier. In some ways the beaker *corpus* must have looked easier than some of the other themes available, in that Lord Abercromby had published a massive work early in the century that included a simple, sensible classification based on shape, in particular of the neck of the vessel.

David Clarke showed swiftly, however, that beakers were neither simple nor easy to analyse: many other characteristics apart from shape existed, including the motifs, combinations and disposition of decoration, and, far from falling into three large and clearly defined classes, these vessels possessed a bewildering range of similarity and difference from one to another. David's reaction was to turn to a sophisticated mathematical technique as yet unused in archaeology – matrix analysis – by which he could elucidate significant combinations of characteristics; the resulting matrix diagrams and the conclusions he drew from them were published in 1962 in the *Proceedings of the Prehistoric Society*, the world's leading prehistoric archaeology journal, edited, as it happened, by Grahame Clark. In historical perspective, it is fascinating to note that simultaneously, across the Atlantic, another paper had dropped a similar bomb into the complacent intellectual pond of orthodox archaeology: *American Antiquity* carried a short article, titled "Archaeology as anthropology", by Lewis R. Binford.

Archaeology in Britain may have been methodologically complacent, but in other ways it had undergone a dramatic transformation. The greatest impact had been in the field of chronology, where radiocarbon dating had begun to extend the time-scale of prehistory significantly during David's years as an undergraduate, albeit with some resistance from the establishment, who declared some of the dates "archaeologically unacceptable". David's view, shared by some others in his generation, but expressed with less clarity and courage, was that the cumulative impact of these new methods of investigation made much of establishment archaeology intellectually unacceptable. The expression of such views in memorable phrases like "the empty mind behind the floral waistcoat", capable of *ad hominem* interpretation, did little to endear him to archaeological Olympians.

David published two papers in major journals in 1962, good going for a second-year research student: the second, co-authored with Graham Connah, explored the possible use of remanent magnetism to set up a beaker chronology based on the vessels themselves, rather than on associated carbon. Here again the impact of his scientific schooling and his willingness to reach beyond the conventional methods of archaeology are exemplified. This work, and the progress made in his dissertation, were sufficient to earn him a William Stone Research Fellowship at Peterhouse; the competition for such fellowships at Cambridge has been described as "ferocious", and the successful candidates, in whatever field, are regarded as an intellectual *élite* among their contemporaries: the number of archaeologists who have made the grade is small.

The Fellowship meant at least three years of tenure and financial security, and in 1964 David made two momentous moves: he finished his dissertation, and he got married. Stella Moore was the Librarian of the Haddon Library in the Department of Archaeology and Anthropology, and David acknowledged her professional skill in aiding his work, as in *Models in Archaeology* for which Stella compiled the index. His marriage with Stella formed the background, the bedrock, on which the rest of his career stood.

My first memory of David, at the end of my first term at Cambridge, is of going into the cavernous room in which Peterhouse had installed him, in a Victorian terrace house, to ask for supervision in archaeology the following term: in the centre of the room was a sloping desk, at which a slight figure sat furiously drawing and inking-in formalized depictions of over-ornamented pots. Supervision was agreed on, and a shy inquiry elicited a short succinct disquisition on the pots, his beakers, and why they were interesting, and sent me away with a copy of the "matrix analysis" paper from *PPS*. The complexity of what David was doing, added to the incomprehension of the Palaeolithic acquired in the lecture room that first term, reduced me to despair: I had no idea that archaeology was like this. That I survived at all, not only in the second term but in the two succeeding years when I was again taught by David, was due largely to his encouragement. It was comforting to be taught by someone who would accept ignorance with patience, make coffee to accompany the weekly dissection of my attempt at an essay, and draw diagrams incessantly on the backs of old envelopes to illustrate his points. One of David's enduring monuments is the number of people he kept in archaeology through the encouragement of his teaching, when they might have fled to some less demanding discipline.

With the completion of his dissertation and the recognition of his work came invitations to speak at symposia, in Britain and abroad, on both his substantive work on beakers and on the underlying classificatory models: in 1966 at the Linnean Society in a symposium on "The classification of changing phenomena" and in 1964 in Gröningen at the Atlantic Symposium on his reclassification of British beakers. He had already visited all the major museum collections in the Netherlands and the Rhineland in pursuit of the Continental origins of British beakers, and knew the Dutch scholars in his field (with whom he maintained a deep, though friendly, disagreement on the interpretation of his material).

In 1966 Peterhouse elected him to an official Fellowship in place of his expiring Research Fellowship, and made him Director of Studies in Archaeology and Anthropology; henceforth, for the rest of his life, he was responsible for the teaching of undergraduates and the supervision of increasing numbers of research students. He was also made a Tutor in the College, with responsibility for the general well-being of a substantial number of undergraduates to whom he stood officially *in loco parentis*. This also was a duty he took seriously, entertaining his pupils generously with (and probably in excess of) the allowance made by the College; the pity is, in hindsight, that the amount of administration thus placed upon him held back the completion and publication of invaluable research.

In the following year he still managed to publish five pieces, three of them short notes on beaker materials from other peoples' excavations, his 1964 Gröningen paper, and a critique in *PPS*, co-authored with Professor J. E. Kerrich, on the pitfalls of using cumulative frequency graphs to compare the compositions of artefact assemblages. It seems to have been stimulated by two things: recent publications by Lewis and Sally Binford in the United States, and the earlier work of François Bordes and his school in the French Palaeolithic; and it is interesting as evidence of David's ability to criticize even the more complex theoretical notions in archaeology.

Ever since the completion of his dissertation, David had been working on a massive study of what archaeology was, and wasn't, and what it should be. It was, he concluded, "an undisciplined empirical discipline", and what it possessed was a soggy mass of intuitive and implicit governing assumptions; what it needed was a body of explicit and logical central theory, to provide the backbone of a true independent discipline, and a strong injection of ideas and methods from other disciplines which were conceptually more advanced. This was why, two years before Haggett's *Locational Analysis in Human Geography* appeared, David Clarke had begun to assemble, from an astonishing range of reading (he purposefully ploughed his way through every new issue of every journal to come into the Haddon Library), a synthesis of theories and applications that could be used to construct the framework for a discipline of archaeology and to show how scholars in other fields had evolved techniques for solving questions that archaeology was only just beginning to ask. His talk to the Perne Club at Peterhouse in October 1966, "Archaeology as a discipline", gave some idea of the independent status he thought the subject merited.

His study was completed in 1967, and published in the following year as *Analytical Archaeology*. It was heavy, and in those days expensive at £7 0s 0d, and many readers and reviewers found the contents heavy as well, especially in Britain, where

> his work was treated with reserve, verging on incomprehension: the enthusiasm of his written style, with its dense noun-clusters interspersed with vivid and striking metaphors and examples from an enormous range of reading . . . was the delight of the imaginative and the despair of the pedantic.
> (Andrew Sherratt, Obituary in *Nature*)

British archaeologists, on the whole, found the calibre of its ordnance too heavy, and retreated to shelter in their trenches; in America, where Lewis Binford had been softening up the opposition for some years both stylistically and intellectually, *Analytical Archaeology* was hailed as a classic work, and joined the Binfords' own book of that same year, *New Perspectives in Archaeology*, as a major intellectual force in remoulding archaeological thought. From Australia, the reviewer for *The Times Literary Supplement* declared it to be one of the most important archaeological books for decades.

In Cambridge, David Clarke had been made a "recognized lecturer", without a job but invited to give a course of lectures, and to give supplementary courses for members of the permament staff who were on sabbatical. He was not to be given a paid university appointment for another five years.

In 1970, the *Norwegian Archaeological Review* devoted an entire issue to a discussion of *Analytical Archaeology*, with comments by three North American scholars, Dell Hymes, William Mayer-Oakes and Irving Rouse, and one Scandinavian, Carl-Axel Moberg. David found the attitudes of Hymes, approaching archaeology from linguistics, and Moberg, approaching from a historical perspective, more illuminating and productive than he did the traditional archaeological pigeon-holing of Rouse. Mayer-Oakes's comments were politely acknow-ledged, but clearly not thought substantial. To their discussion David appended a reply, printed in this book, as an "epilogue" to *Analytical Archaeology*, in which he pointed out that the book was already "old-fashioned", and explained both his own mental preconceptions, which had moulded it, and the aims of the work – "stimulus", the creation of an "intermediate impossible" as a transition from an old to a new way of looking at the past. In describing the book as a "transient, pro-vocative model of a future class of archaeological textbook" he was pro-phetic, although the notion of transience is perhaps incompatible with the second edition of the book which Bob Chapman began to prepare under David's supervison, and which will appear a decade after the first. More than any other publication, *Analytical Archaeology* has institu-tionalized David Clarke as an important figure in the historiography of the discipline.

1970 also saw the final publication of David's dissertation, as two large volumes in the new Gulbenkian archaeological series from the Cambridge University Press. The presentation of the beaker *corpus*, in spite of the new methods used to reach its complex classification, appeared rather old-fashioned by comparison with his work of more recent genesis, but the interpretation of the material nevertheless aroused instant disagreement among fellow beaker specialists, as Steven Shennan details in his sectional introduction.

That year David allowed himself to be proposed for, and elected to, the Society of Antiquaries of London, the world's premier archaeologi-cal society. His feelings towards it remained always ambivalent – he was proud of the honour, but felt out of place in a group whose modal inter-est lay in the particularistic examination of historical archaeology, who would pack their lecture room for a talk on a Roman villa but leave it amost empty for news out of Africa or America. David resolved the ambiguity by never attending a meeting and never being formally admitted, and only occasionally putting "FSA" after his name.

He already had an idea for a new book, a successor to *Analytical*

Archaeology, in which its philosophy and the application of new methods which it advocated would be exemplified by a series of papers written by invited authors, who David felt to be in sympathy with his own ideas. The exemplar for the book was *Models in Geography*, edited by Chorley and Haggett (1967), which had similarly illustrated many of the approaches synthesized in Haggett's *Locational Analysis in Human Geography*. Those invited to contribute to *Models in Archaeology* in 1970 included some of David's students, including myself, some of his contemporaries as research students, and a number of like-thinking colleagues in the United States, including Lewis Binford and David Hurst Thomas. The resulting volume, published in 1972, literally spanned the world in its spatial coverage, and ran the gamut from simple chronological models to elaborate simulations of economies. David's own paper, apart from the synoptic introduction on "Models and paradigms in contemporary archaeology", was a preliminary essay on his next major project, a re-examination of the Glastonbury Lake Village, using the full range of modern concepts and theoretical techniques to reconstruct a society dead for two thousand years and dug up and published for over a half a century.

A further administrative burden had fallen upon him in late 1970, when he became Senior Tutor of Peterhouse, and apart from assembling and editing *Models in Archaeology* he was able to produce little for publication. He did undertake one of his few book reviews; at the invitation of Glyn Daniel, editor of *Antiquity*, he reviewed Watson, LeBlanc and Redman's *Explanation in Archaeology: An Explicitly Scientific Approach*, the most extreme archaeological application of Hempelian logical positivism. David felt that archaeology was its own discipline, and that the wholesale adoption of the intellectual approach of another field was stultifying; he was also well aware that the Hempelian approach was already considered outmoded by philosophers.

David's books were usually ignored by the most traditional-minded of British archaeologists, but when, at the invitation of Glyn Daniel, he wrote a piece for *Antiquity* of March 1973 titled "Archaeology – the loss of innocence", the provocation was too great for some of them. *Antiquity* was, after all, a respectable journal with discursive and witty editorials, substantial articles on subsantial discoveries, and satisfyingly bitchy book reviews, unlike its American homonym, which was now publishing computer printout as part of articles. As Glynn Isaac remarks in his sectional introduction, Daniel issued the invitation to "draw an exponent of the 'new archaeology' out into the open", presumably in continuation of the debate which had been rumbling on in *Antiquity* for several years, beginning with Jacquetta Hawkes's 1968 article "The proper study of mankind".

Several readers of *Antiquity* were moved to write rude letters to the Editor, excerpts from which were published in the June issue. By that time, however, David had other things on his mind: Grahame Clark was due to retire from the Disney Chair of Archaeology the following year, and David was a candidate; it was the only Chair he ever really wanted – he had already refused an approach from Harvard, and in 1975 was to do the same to Sheffield. The electors to the Disney Chair, however chose Glyn Daniel.

Later in the year a new junior post became available in the Department of Archaeology at Cambridge, and David, no snob, applied for that as well; I was a candidate for the same post, and it was not encouraging to be addressed throughout the interview by one senior figure as "Dr Clarke"; deservedly, and long past time, David was given a university post, an untenured Assistant Lectureship for three years, with the possibility of promotion to Lecturer (the promotion was notified on the day he died).

As Grahame Clark's retirement approached, the assembly of a *Festschrift* began, under the direction of two archaeologists at the British Museum, Gale Sieveking and Ian Longworth, the latter a contemporary of David's (who had in fact taken on urns for his dissertation in the division of British prehistoric ceramics). David, along with many of Clark's other pupils over his score of years as Disney Professor, was invited to contribute a paper. With characteristic wit he combined parts of the titles of two of the Professor's publications: "The Mesolithic Age in Europe" and "Prehistoric Europe: the economic basis", into "Mesolithic Europe: the economic basis?", (the ? was removed in proof, whether by David we know not), and produced a long critique of the meat-centred economic archaeology currently being done by members of one of the Professor's pet projects, the British Academy Major Research Project on the Early History of Agriculture. The paper itself is discussed by Andrew Sherratt in his sectional introduction; here it is perhaps sufficient to say that had it been published when it should, in 1974 instead of late 1976, its clarity of language and force of argument might have converted even some of the Clarkeophobes who complained to *Antiquity* about the more compressed style of his methodological arguments. It is, by consensus, the outstanding paper in a distinguished volume.

Although an excavation is not the environment in which any of us instinctively place David, he had had a wide range of experience "from workman to Assistant Director", as he put on his *curriculum vitae*. While an undergraduate he had taken part in excavations near his home in Kent, and participated in the departmental excavations at Cambridge. In 1959 he had travelled in Scandinavia and got himself on Mesolithic and Iron Age excavations in Denmark, and, the following year, after graduating, had carried out a field survey and test excavations in Greece with Robert Rodden. These excavations included the discovery and first sounding of Nea Nikomedeia, subsequently excavated by Rodden and noted in the 1960s as one of the earliest farming village settlements in Europe. While in Greece he also took the opportunity to experience a Classical excavation, working for the Greek archaeologist Petsas at Alexander the Great's capital of Pella.

In 1965, the only time that David and I ever coincided on a field project, he went to Greece again, to work on Eric Higgs's Epirus Palaeolithic sites; David arrived in the same vehicle as the novelist Hammond Innes, who subsequently immortalized Higgs in *Levkas Man*. David's main job was, it seems, to travel around the countryside with the geomorphologist Claudio Vita-Finzi examining sediments, and his figure can be seen in several of the photographs in the *PPS* report (1966) acting as a scale in eroded stream beds. His major discovery was the cave of Kastritsa, on the southern margin of Lake Ioannina, which Higgs excavated the following year and which proved to have a long Upper Palaeolithic sequence. Kastritsa and the Asprochaliko cave which Higgs dug in 1965, where David also worked briefly, together provided the basic sequence for the Palaeolithic of the southern Balkans, and David was always quite proud of having had a small part in the work.

Finally, in 1975, he began his career as a director, jointly with John Alexander, at a Neolithic "causewayed enclosure" near Cambridge. The site was intended to be the basis for a long-term departmental excavation, and its location on the junction of uplands and lowlands with adjacent waterlogged deposits looked likely to provide just the kind of evidence that David sought to explain the function and distribution of these sites: in a report of the first season's work in *The Times* David spoke of "a long-term research programme relating the site to its strategic position on the interface of chalk and fen country, and employing advanced analytical techniques to investigate the ecology and social context".

In 1975–6 David was beginning to move in new directions, as Andrew Sherratt makes clear in his introduction, beginning with his "emancipation from the cultural paradigm of Gordon Childe": he had abandoned the "hierarchies of entities" of *Analytical Archaeology* nearly a decade earlier, and moved into a more free-ranging examination of economic patterns, an early example of which is the "Mesolithic Europe . . ." paper, a later one the Oberried beaker symposium paper, discussed here by Steven Shennan, written and presented in 1974 but published only after David's death.

In addition, and I think significantly, he was becoming more prepared to spend time away from Cambridge. This was partly due to his children being old enough for Stella and they to come with him, but also reflected a growing confidence that his ideas were now well enough established for him to be a welcome and honoured guest, and no longer a voice crying in the wilderness. In 1974 he had been, briefly, a visiting lecturer at the Autonomous National University of Mexico, developing new archaeological analysis techniques in the computing department at the invitation of Jaime Litvak King, and he had a standing invitation to return which Litvak was beginning to press strongly enough for David to begin considering it seriously; he also fancied the idea of taking part in an excavation in the New World, and opportunities were being offered there.

He had an invitation to visit South Africa in the summer of 1976, and was preparing to depart thence, to join John Parkington's department for part of a term, when he fell ill. His illness, acute and dangerous though it was, left him very much alive and fairly cheerful; he could only walk a few steps to the end of his bed and back, but his conversation was characteristically wide-ranging. He had heard unofficially that his promotion was likely to come through by the end of June, and as a University Lecturer he would at last have a permanent academic position; he would also be able to remain a Fellow of Peterhouse, something which might have been doubtful had his university post been allowed to lapse. After years of doubt, his career now seemed set permanently in Cambridge, with the chance of competing for the Disney Chair again in 1980: typically, his conversation concentrated on teaching, and on the long-term plans he would now be able to put into operation.

He was anxious to get out of hospital and back to his family, and on 27 June he was discharged and returned home to Great Chesterford. Next day a blood clot, formed during the weeks of inactivity, detached itself, lodged in his lung, and killed him.

As Grahame Clark said in *The Times* on 8 July, "David is irreplaceable." The number of people who felt deeply about his death became apparent at the funeral service, held in the Long Vacation, when Cambridge is very empty: the Chapel of Peterhouse was crammed, especially with his pupils, so that people were sitting along the altar rails and in the sanctuary. The sense of loss was one I hope never to see again.

David was given, without choice, the option that Achilles took: a short life, but with fame while it lasted, a memory which will endure among his friends and pupils, and a reputation which will stand high in the history of his chosen discipline.

Bibliography of the Works of David L. Clarke, 1937–76

STELLA CLARKE

1962*a*   Matrix analysis and archaeology with particular reference to British beaker pottery. (*Proceedings of the Prehistoric Society*, N.S. XXVIII, 371–383)

1962*b*   With G. Connah: Remanant magnetism and beaker chronology. (*Antiquity*, XXXVI, 206–209)

1963   Matrix analysis and archaeology. (*Nature*, **199**, 790–792)

1965   Matrix analysis and archaeology with particular reference to British beaker pottery. (*VI International Congress of Prehistoric and Protohistoric Sciences, 1965*, II, Sessions I–IV, Rome, 1965)

1966*a*   Archaeological classification; symposium on the "Classification of changing phenomena", 18 March 1966. The Linnean and Classification Societies, London, 1966.

1966*b*   Review of *Beakers from Northumberland* by John Tait. (*Proceedings of the Prehistoric Society*, N.S. XXXIII, 365–367)

1967*a*   With J. E. Kerrich: Notes on the possible misuse and errors of cumulative percentage frequency graphs for the comparison of prehistoric artefact assemblages. (*Proceedings of the Prehistoric Society*, N.S. XXXIII, 57–69)

1967*b*   A tentative reclassification of British beaker pottery in the light of recent research. 2nd Atlantic Symposium, Gröningen, April 1964, 179–198.

1967*c*   With R. N. R. Peers: A Bronze Age beaker burial and Roman site at Broadmayne. (*Proceedings of the Dorset Natural History and Archaeological Society*, **88**, 103–105.)

1967*d*   Note to article by S. H. M. Pollard: Seven prehistoric sites near Honiton, Devon. (*Proceedings of the Devon Archaeological Society*, **25**, 19–39)

1967e Note to article by N. Thomas: A double beaker burial on Bredon Hill, Worcs. (*Transactions and Proceedings of the Birmingham Archaeological Society*, **82**, 69–70.)

1968a *Analytical Archaeology*, Methuen, London.

1968b Note to article by C. N. Moore: A beaker from Bulford. (*Wiltshire Archaeological Magazine*, **63**, 98–99)

1969 Note to article by D. A. White: Excavations at Brampton, Huntingdonshire. (*Proceedings of the Cambridge Antiquarian Society*, LXII, 10–11)

1970a Analytical archaeology: epilogue. (*Norwegian Archaeological Review*, **3**, 25–33)

1970b *Beaker Pottery of Great Britain and Ireland*, 2 Vols, Cambridge University Press, London.

1970c Note on the beaker from Bee Low in article by B. M. Marsdon: The excavation of the Bee Low Round Cairn, Youlgreave, Derbyshire. (*Antiquaries Journal*, **50**, part 2, 201–206)

1970d Review of *World Archaeology*, **1** (1–3), June 1969–February 1970, edited by C. Platt and F. R. Hodson. (*Proceedings of the Prehistoric Society*, N.S. XXXVI, 395–396.)

1972a (ed.) *Models in Archaeology*, Methuen, London.

1972b Models and paradigms in contemporary archaeology, in *Models in Archaeology* (D. L. Clarke, ed.), Methuen, London, pp. 1–60.

1972c A provisional model of an Iron Age society and its settlement system, in *Models in Archaeology* (D. L. Clarke, ed.), Methuen, London, pp. 801–869.

1972d Review of *Explanation in Archaeology: An Explicitly Scientific Approach*, by P. J. Watson, S. A. LeBlanc and C. L. Redman (New York, 1971). (*Antiquity*, XLVI, 237–239)

1973a Archaeology: the loss of innocence. (*Antiquity*, XLVII, 6–18)

1973b Review of *Automatic Artifact Registration and Systems for Archaeological Analysis with the Philips P1100 Computer: A Mesolithic Test Case*, by R. R. Newell and A. P. J. Vroomans (New York, 1972). (*Antiquity*, XLVII, 158–160)

1974 Note on three beaker sherds from Wiggonholt in article by K. J. Evans: Excavations on a Romano-British site, Wiggonholt, 1964. (*Sussex Archaeological Collections*, CXII, 26)

1975 Review of *The Explanation of Culture Change: Models in Prehistory* by C. Renfrew. (*Antiquity*, XLIX, 146–147)

1976a A beaker from Swalecliffe (found by Mr G. H. Wilby in October 1975). (*Canterbury Archaeology*, 1975/76, 12)

1976b The beaker network – social and economic models, in *Glockenbechersymposion Oberried, 1974* (J. N. Lanting and J. D. van de Waals, eds), Fibula-Van Dishoek, Bussum/Haarlem, pp. 459–477.

1976c Mesolithic Europe: the economic basis, in *Problems in Economic and Social Archaeology* (G. de G. Sieveking, I. H. Longworth and K. E. Wilson, eds), Duckworth, London, pp. 449–481. Reprinted by Duckworth, 1978 as a single bound article.

1977a (ed.) *Spatial Archaeology*, Academic Press, London and New York.

1977b Spatial information in archaeology, in *Spatial Archaeology* (D. L. Clarke, ed.), Academic Press, London and New York, pp. 1–32. Reprinted in *Revista Mexicana de Estudios Antropologicos*, XXIII, 1, 1977.

n.d.a Towards analytical archaeology; new directions in the interpretive thinking of British archaeologists. Symposium on Theory and Methodology in Archaeological Interpretation, Flagstaff, Arizona, 1968.

n.d.b (written 1969) The economic context of trade and industry in Barbarian Europe till Roman times, in *The Cambridge Economic History of Europe* (M. Postan, ed.), Cambridge University Press, Cambridge, to appear, Vol. II, Chapter 1.

The Philosophy of Archaeology

GLYNN LL. ISAAC

Archaeology in essence . . . is the discipline with the theory and practice for the recovery of unobservable hominid behaviour patterns from indirect traces in bad samples. [Consequently] . . . Archaeological logic should outline for us the theory of correct reason within our discipline, without making any unwarranted assumptions that the principles of logic and explanation are simple universals which may be transferred from one discipline and level to another. . . . [The critical scrutiny of patterns of archaeological reasoning] raises . . . problems of the nature of the logical relationship between archaeological conclusions and the grounds for those conclusions, . . .

This composite quotation from "Archaeology: the loss of innocence" (pp. 83–103 following) summarizes the subject matter of the three items in this part of the present volume. Each article, with differing thrust and emphasis, expresses the intensity of David Clarke's concern that the theoretical underpinning of archaelogical study be made both sound and explicit. The articles are prime sources for any student or scholar who asks the question: "Why do we need to bother with theory?" – and for those who go on to take an interest in the way in which theories of archaeological method can be developed.

It should be recognized that archaeologists need to concern themselves with theory in several different ways. As participants in the grand overall pursuit of understanding nature and man's place in nature, archaeologists should contribute to the development and revision of general theories of evolution, ecology and behaviour – especially as these relate to human evolution and to the dynamics of historic and contemporary cultural change and development. These are theoretical concerns which archaeologists ought to share with a combination of social scientists and natural scientists. However, archaeologists can only make their rightful contribution in this sphere if they handle their own peculiar kind of primary evidence effectively. In order to help elucidate culture growth and the interplay of social, ecological and economic factors in determining changing cultural configurations, archaeologists must be able to use the available evidence. Discarded artefacts, fallen-down houses, food refuse and so forth, provide a basis for making and testing models of economic, social and cultural systems which have existed in the past. How do archaeologists translate their relics into valid reconstructions of complex vanished systems of human life? Discussion of the theory of archaeological inference – "archaeological logic" in David Clarke's own phrase, is the central theme of each of the items in this section.

The brief review of the book *Explanation in Archaeology: An Explicitly Scientific Approach*, which had been written by Watson, LeBlanc and Redman, makes a good place to start acquiring a grasp of David Clarke's stance on this whole question. The book under review advocates the universal adoption by archaeologists of a set of procedures and criteria which had been developed by scholars such as Hempel and Oppenheim in other branches of science. Clarke is sympathetic, but argues strongly against archaeologists "attempting to force their studies into selected formats appropriate to quite different disciplines". He argues for an independent scrutiny by archaeologists of the peculiarities, limitations and opportunities intrinsic to their material and subject. He sees a multiplicity of different exploratory approaches as more promising than the adoption of one particular creed. Perhaps it is this stance more than anything else which epitomizes David Clarke's contribution to the development of the theory of archaeological method. Relative to the other great exponents of our times, he is an advocate of eclecticism rather than exclusivism or dogmatism – I shall return to this point.

The first item in this section, however, is a reprint of the opening chapter for a book compiled and edited by David Clarke. The volume *Models in Archaeology*, published in 1972, provided a rich *corpus* of examples of the practical implications of scrutinizing the theory underlying archaeological inquiry. The contributions sample the whole of archaeology – up and down two million years of time and across all the continents. The range of topics too is extraordinarily broad. David Clarke's chapter "Models and paradigms in contemporary archaeology", which is reprinted here, provides by far the best guide available to the great diversity of models which are currently being incorporated in archaeological writing.

At an early stage in the essay Clarke points out that "if explanation in general, and explanation in archaeology in particular, is viewed merely as a form of redescription which allows predictions to be made, then models as predictive forms of redescription are essential parts of archaeological explanation" (p. 22 following). This essay, he goes on to state, does not get embroiled with questions of "the role of hypotheses, theories and laws, or the problems of causality and indeterminism ...". Rather the essay presents a diversity of examples which illustrate aspects of the process of doing archaeology. It is made clear that there is a fundamental distinction between "controlling models" and "operational models". The former commonly embody the mental framework established by belief systems such as special creation versus evolution and so forth. Clarke goes on in the body of the chapter to show how diverse are the range of operational models already in use – and how much more diverse they are liable to become. He shows how some models are quasi-direct equivalents of archaeological phenomena; for example, experimental earth works or active replication of ancient technology. Other models are metaphors or mathematical abstractions. Towards the end of the essay (pp. 60–62 following), ethnographic and historic analogies are treated as yet another species of operational model. Although not explicitly discussed, David Clarke's observations on this point subsume the articulation of ethnoarchaeology with the system of models envisaged.

The essay closes with a section which picks out "four newly formulated, competing approaches" which Clarke chooses to style as "paradigms" in the sense of Thomas Kuhn. These are "morphological, anthropological, ecological and geographical paradigms". The essay shows that each of these involves particular preoccupations and emphases, rather than a claim to provide a complete framework that excludes other "rival" frameworks. The use of the Kuhnian term "paradigm" for this level may be debatable and distracting. However, in the final section, where Clarke asks the question, "Do these developments represent a 'New Archaeology'?", the question of the existence of a grand, overarching new paradigm is clearly under discussion. The admirable table of comparison between traditionalist and new archaeology documents such a paradigm shift without stating that it has definitely occurred. The key difference between the traditional and the new paradigms is the contrast between concern with particulars for their own sake, and the search for valid generalizations that transcend individual episodes. As the closing remarks of the essay show, the two paradigms can coexist and complement each other.

The second item in this section pursues the themes raised in the other two. "Archaeology: the loss of innocence" was commissioned by Glyn Daniel, the editor of *Antiquity*, apparently in order to draw an exponent of the "new archaeology" out into the open. David Clarke accepted the challenge and wrote this spirited and provocative essay, at which various readers and the editor himself did indeed snipe – providing in their comments and in the misunderstandings that these contain, good examples of some of the phenomena which had been discussed in the essay itself (see *Antiquity*, **42**, 93–95).

The "loss of innocence" essay opens with a brief characterization of the development of archaeology through stages of consciousness and self-consciousness to critical self-consciousness. It goes on to enumerate

and briefly discuss some of the developments which have transformed
archaeology during the past one or two decades, picking on the great
increase in numbers of practitioners, the development of effective physi-
cochemical dating techniques and on the use of computers as being
particularly significant. Clarke makes the cogent point that

> under the ultra-short chronologies [which prevailed prior to isotopic dating]
> archaeological time was confused with historical time . . . and seemed packed
> with data and events . . . [a] situation precisely equivalent to that under-
> lying the "catastrophe" theories of eighteenth century geology . . .

New paradigms, new philosophies and the rise of theories of concepts
are discussed as a part of the current movements in archaeology. As
in the models essay, the question is broached, "Do these developments
represent a 'New Archaeology'?" The answer is offered that it "does
seem difficult to sustain the view that the character, scale and rapidity
of recent change is of no greater significance than that experienced in
other 20-year spans of archaeological development".

The loss of innocence referred to in the title involves the replacement
of unstated, "common sense" evidence and inference, by carefully
scrutinized theories of concepts, information and reasoning – each of
which is discussed in turn. As Clarke shows, however much one may
bemoan the passing of the bold but elegantly simple opening phase in
the growth of archaeology, the discipline would be stifled if it did not
engage in introspection at this stage.

In the penultimate section, the important question of general theory
is discussed. The essay identifies a sequence of steps that intervene
between the life of the past and archaeologic perception of it. The steps
result in archaeologists having to work with a sample of a sample of
a sample. The message is clear: archaeologists must learn to assess and
correct for the effects of the sampling bias, which is both due to
"nature" and to their own procedures. This is a theme which has since
been taken up in recent years by Schiffer (1976) and by the most effective of the archaeological ethnographers (=ethnoarchaeologists),
Gould, Yellen, Binford, O'Connell and others.

Various critics of "Archaeology: the loss of innocence" all wrote to
the editor of *Antiquity* complaining of the style and form of the essay
(*Antiquity*, **42,** 93–95). I am inclined to feel that this was because they
were unable to assail the fundamental points in the message. As
readers will find, David Clarke had been at his gleeful best in choosing
ironic phrases; to pick out but a few: ". . . formerly adaptive, traditional
archaeological positions can evolve in the new environment into
. . . the attributes of a doomed race of disciplinary dinosaurs"; "Harnessing powerful new methodological horses to rickety old conceptual

carts has proved to be a ... drastic way of improving archaeological theoretical constructs, by elimination"; "The strength of the new archaeologies, or New Archaeology, is that it introduces a variety of questions where only answers were formerly proclaimed...". Finally there is this image of the state of inquiry,

> We must move from the traditional model of archaeological knowledge as Gruyère cheese with holes in it, to that of a sparse suspension of information particles of varying size, not even randomly distributed in archaeological space and time.

No wonder incensed and bewildered traditionalists attacked the form and style – it would be hard to quarrel with the substance. The essay is, in fact, packed with metaphors and must be read carefully. Some readers may find it helpful to read the opening section and then read the closing parts, starting at the section "general theory" before tackling the middle portions.

The comments of one of the correspondents in *Antiquity* presents a misunderstanding which serves to underscore the main point of the essay. He wrote,

> the meaning ... can be stated in one simple sentence: archaeologists now have access to more assistance of many kinds from other disciplines than was formerly the case, and properly used these aids are capable of adding greatly to our knowledge.

The main point of the essay is that the large volume of new information does not contribute simply to a more-of-the-same situation, on the contrary, it requires that the whole theoretical foundation of archaeology be re-examined. Archaeologists who had never stopped to consider whether the edifice in which they lived had any foundations found this incomprehensible!

These three articles join with other major writings on archaeological theory in their call for scrutiny of the basis of inquiry and in their advocacy that the conceptual basis of any study be made as explicit as possible. Clarke, however, differs from the position of many other prominent theoreticians, by not advocating any single approach as being universally prescribed. The formulation and testing of deductive hypotheses such as advocated by Binford and others is compatible with the alert and varied approach exhibited by Clarke, but is not demanded to the exclusion of other clearly stated and defensible procedures. The "covering law" approach of Watson, LeBlanc and Redman is acceptable where it is readily and usefully applicable, but it is not seen as the only form which scientific explanation can take. In *Analytical Archaeology*, David Clarke showed ably that systems theory could be a very powerful conceptual device in archaeology, but this approach is not represented in these essays as some kind of panacea. The reader of these essays on the theory of archaeological method may be inspired to seek "salvation" – but it would have to be a salvation that is individually constructed of elements chosen from a wide range of sources. As readers will see, the strengths that David Clarke brought to the writing of these essays were: first, keen originality of mind; second, an extraordinarily broad but effective knowledge of archaeological work being done on all time ranges and all continents; and third, an excellent grasp of developments in geography, ecology and anthropology. Add to this a lively sense of humour and it is easy to understand why these essays stand as important landmarks in the development of the theory of archaeological method.

Models and Paradigms in Contemporary Archaeology

DAVID L. CLARKE

INTRODUCTION

Models are undeniably fashionable and especially so in the primitive disciplines that range between the Arts and the Sciences – geology, geography, archaeology, anthropology, sociology, economics, psychology and aspects of biology. Indeed, in some quarters this vogue and this setting are, in themselves, taken as sufficient reason to dismiss the significance of the model-using approach. This repudiation only requires the additional evidence of the dangerous errors that have arisen from the mistaken use of bad models, an outline of their clear limitations and the assertion that scholars have in any event long known and tacitly used these procedures, and the case is complete.

The question is, however, not whether models are fashionable and dangerous toys of long standing, but *why* models are so fashionable in disciplines of this primitive kind, *why* are some models inadequate, and *why* do models generate such strong feelings if they are part of immemorial usage? If we have an old and dangerous component performing an important variety of tasks in a number of disciplinary machines, should we then ignore it because it is fashionable – or learn about it, improve upon it and explicitly develop its potential? Beach's (1957, p. 9) remark that "the history of economics could be thought of to a very large extent as a history of misapplied models" might be generalized for all academic disciplines but could also hardly be improved upon as a sufficient justification for a more explicit appreciation of models, their variety, their uses, abuses, capacities and limitations – fashionable or unfashionable (Harvey, 1969, p. 142).

What is a model? Models are pieces of machinery that relate observations to theoretical ideas, they may be used for many different purposes

Reprinted with permission from *Models in Archaeology* (D. L. Clarke, ed.), Methuen, London, 1972, pp. 1–60.

and they vary widely in the form of machinery they employ, the class of observations they focus upon and the manner in which they relate the observations to the theory or hypothesis. It is therefore more appropriate to describe models than to attempt a hopelessly broad or a pointlessly narrow definition for them. Models are often partial representations, which simplify the complex observations by the selective elimination of detail incidental to the purpose of the model. The model may thus isolate the essential factors and interrelationships which together largely account for the variability of interest in the observations: in this way the model may even share a similarity in formal structure with the observations.

If explanation in general, and explanation in archaeology in particular, is viewed merely as a form of redescription which allows predictions to be made, then models as predictive forms of redescription are essential parts of archaeological explanation. However, here we enter the domain of the Philosophy of Disciplines, more commonly miscast as the Philosophy of Science, and since this introductory chapter will make no extensive attempt to consider the essential background of patterns of explanation, the role of hypotheses, theories and laws, or the problems of causality and indeterminism, the reader is recommended to consult sources noted in references throughout this volume.

The relation between the model and the observations modelled may in general be said to be one of analogy, or in the case of logical and mathematical models more usually one of isomorphism (Clarke, 1968, pp. 59–60). The analogy implies similarity between the analogues in some respects and dissimilarity in others, since otherwise the analogy would amount to identity. The set of shared similar characteristics is conveniently called the positive analogy, the dissimilar characteristics the negative analogy, and characteristics about which it is not yet known whether they are similar or dissimilar, the neutral analogy (Hesse, 1963). In general, models serve as heuristic devices for manipulating observations and hypotheses; they may also act as visualizing devices, comparative devices, organizational devices, explanatory devices or devices for the construction and development of theory (Harvey, 1969, p. 141). Models are usually idealized representations of observations, they are structured, they are selective, they simplify, they specify a field of interest and they offer a partially accurate predictive framework. In this way a map will schematically present an idealized representation of a selected item and its distribution on a simplified projection of a map surface, or a classification system may provide a crudely predictive algorithm based upon the identification of selected key attributes, or a mathematical equation may symbolically express the interdependence of systems of selected variables from within an archaeological situation.

Why need the archaeologist concern himself with models? There are five main reasons, which may be briefly outlined:

1. Whether we appreciate it or not our personal archaeological opinions, approach, aims and selection of projects are *controlled* by largely subconscious mind models which we accumulate through time. We should realize that we are thus controlled.
2. Whether we appreciate it or not we always *operate* conceptual models in the interpretation of observations. We all resemble the Molière character who was delighted to find that all his life, unknowingly, he had been speaking prose. We should make these operational models explicit and testable.
3. The construction, testing, verification or refutation and modification of explicit models is the essence of the empirical and scientific approaches – providing the progressive cycle by means of which fresh information and insight are gained and theory is accumulated. Observations, hypothesis, experiment, conclusions, fresh hypothesis, fresh observations...
4. The existence of a model presupposes the existence of an underlying theory, since a model is but one simplified, formalized and skeletal expression of a theory – be it tacit or explicit – developed for a particular situation. A careful study of groups of models apparently expressing a common underlying theory for different situations may therefore help us to expose and articulate latent theory in a palpable and widely powerful form (Harvey, 1969, pp. 146–147). Model definition is a route to the explicit theory which essentially defines a vigorous discipline.
5. Finally,

   hypotheses are generated from the model expression of a theory;
   explanation comes from tested hypotheses;
   hypotheses are tested by using relevant analyses on meaningful categories of data.

Thus models are a vital element in all archaeological attempts at hypothesis, theory, explanation, experiment, and classification.

Model building is important in archaeology, therefore:

   because it is inevitably the procedure used;
   because it is economical, allowing us to pass on and exchange generalized information in a highly compressed form;
   because it leads to the discovery of fresh information and stimulates

the development and articulation of general theory of more than parochial importance (Haggett, 1965, p. 23).

However, we must be clear about the peculiarities and weaknesses of models. It is particularly important to realize that since models mirror only selected aspects of the observations then it is both possible, permissible and desirable to have more than one model of different aspects of a single situation – an economic model, perhaps, and a sociological model of the same set of assemblages, where a trivial observation under one model may become a central factor under another. Under this pluralist viewpoint there are many competing models for each archaeological situation, where none may be finally picked out as uniquely and comprehensively "true". The interaction between archaeologists and their material thus reflects a continuous flowering of models whose criteria are both internally and externally adapted to the contemporary climate of thought, and often between which no rational choice is possible. Let a million models grow (Hesse, 1963).

Very well, we may have more than one model at a time, all "true", and the devising of a new model does not necessarily mean that all others are wrong. However, this permissible pluralism only holds for models selecting different bases for analogy. Clearly there are good models and bad models, powerful models and restricted models. Bad models are most frequently misused models whose function has not been clearly specified and controlled, or where the model has been over-identified or unidentified with theory, or that display a lack of clarity about which are the positive, negative and neutral characteristics of the model analogy (Harvey, 1969, p. 160). Although some models simply present pluralist alternatives based on the varying selectivity of the analogy, others will offer successive approximations of greater power and in that sense may be ranked relative to one another for a given function upon a chosen field, and a choice may be made between rival models in such a way that successively more powerful models are employed. Even the exercise of this choice between models on the basis of relative power is complicated by the many dimensions of model power which combine comprehensive, predictive, efficiency and accuracy elements:

Comprehensiveness = the size of the set of situations to which the model is applicable;

Predictiveness = the number of bits of information that the model can predict about individual situations in that set;

Efficiency = the parsimonious capacity of the model to

make the most predictions using the fewest
statements and the most elegant structure;

Accuracy   = the quality of goodness of fit of the model predictions to the observations.

CONTROLLING MODELS

Amongst the reasons offered as justification for an archaeological concern with models it was implied that the archaeologist is the victim of a set of *controlling models* which affect his behaviour, including the discriminatory selection of the *operational models* which he chooses to deploy against archaeological observations. The nature of these cognitive or controlling mind models is both complex and composite. Through exposure to life in general, to educational processes and to the changing contemporary systems of belief we acquire a general philosophy and an archaeological philosophy in particular – a partly conscious and partly subconscious system of beliefs, concepts, values and principles, both realistic and metaphysical. These beliefs are then more consciously related to certain aims or goals by the mediating effects of our archaeological philosophy and its values, upon a series of alternative paradigms and methodologies. Thus, Kuhn (1970), in his fundamental work on the structure of changes in intellectual disciplines, has described the paradigm class of supermodel as implicit in the behavioural conventions held by a group of practitioners which delineate, focus upon and recognize a limited subset of data and experimental achievements, within their much wider disciplinary field, which for a time emphasizes the significant problems and exemplary solutions for that community of scholars.

The overall model of an archaeologist at work, therefore, may be represented as a set of controlling models which are embodied in the archaeologist's philosophy, the paradigms he chooses to align himself with, the methodologies that he finds most congenial and the aims that this system constrains. The controlling models encapsulate the archaeologist and his chosen operational models, although there is feedback between all these changing elements. In effect the archaeologist is operating in a plastic sack and from within it seeks to push selected operational models against the complex archaeological reality, constantly seeking for goodness of fit, but the constraints of the controlling models always remain to obscure his perception of the reality (Fig. 1).

Archaeologists, like most other practitioners, have the greatest difficulty in believing that their own perceptions are controlled to this degree – they may always apply to other archaeologists, of course. But the history of archaeology and science is full of examples. Archaeology has witnessed the successive difficulties engendered by controlling models that could not accommodate the acceptance of the human manufacture of stone tools, an antiquity of man before 4000 B.C., a Palaeolithic origin for cave paintings, or tool-using apes 2 000 000 years ago. Medieval man, with his theocentric and geocentric controlling model of the universe, similarly resisted the scientific and heliocentric model of Copernicus and Galileo even in the face of evidence that the old model did not fit the new observations. In the eighteenth century, observed eccentricities in the orbit of Mercury were accounted for, using Newton's model of the universe, by the presence of an unknown

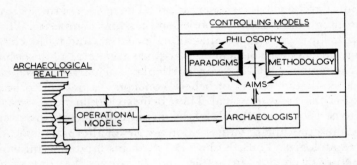

FIG. 1. A model of the archaeologist at work – the archaeologist enmeshed within a complex set of controlling models which constrain his conscious selection of operational models and interfere with his interpretation of archaeological reality. Contemporary changes in paradigms and methodology are the main stimuli that lead the archaeologist to adapt his views.

planet, which was promptly named Vulcan and sighted and described several times. The eccentricities are now accounted for in terms of other phenomena and the planet Vulcan has never been seen since. Even the direct photography of Mars has failed to convince observers who have spent a lifetime mapping the canals from low-power telescopes that the canals are not there. We observe what we believe and then believe in that which we have observed.

Since an archaeologist's philosophy changes, as a rule, very slowly and by infinitesimal steps, it is mainly the more rapidly fluctuating rival paradigm fashions and innovations in methodology that alter his aims, leading him to reject some as trivial and others as unattainable in the light of the new evidence. Paradigm literally means "example" and at any one time the prevailing paradigms within a discipline are best represented by those "exemplary" groups of experiments which are commonly held to enshrine the most progressive patterns of archaeological activity – the leading sectors of an expanding discipline. In this way, the contemporary archaeological scene might be roughly construed in terms of the emergence of four "new" paradigms:

1. Morphological paradigm – the detailed study of artefact and assemblage systems, especially in terms of the widely general regularities involving their intrinsic structures and relationships, mainly using computer techniques. Intimately involved with the numerical, statistical and taxonomic approaches (Clarke, 1968; Gardin, 1970; Hodson, 1970; Kolchina and Shera, 1970).
2. Anthropological paradigm – the study and identification of patterning and variability in archaeological data and its relationship to patterning and variability in the social structures with which it once formed an integral system; intimately linked with ethnological control experiments (Deetz, 1965; Longacre, 1970; Meggers, 1968; Whallon, 1968; Hill, 1970; McPherron, 1967).
3. Ecological paradigm – the detailed study of archaeological sites as an integral part of the mutually adjusting environmental and ecological systems in which they were once adaptively networked. Linked to ethology, economics and demography, and more deeply involved with faunal and floral contextual evidence, rather than with the artefacts (Coe and Flannery, 1964, 1967; Higgs, 1972; Higham, 1968; MacNeish, 1961, 1962).
4. Geographical paradigm – the study of sites as patterned systems of features and structures within systems of sites territorially distributed over landscapes in a mutually adjusted way. At the micro-level linked to architectural theory and settlement archaeology, at the macro-level with locational theory and spatial relationships; principally focused on sites and the spatial manifestations of activity patterns (Chang, 1968; Trigger, 1966; Ucko, Tringham and Dimbleby 1971; March and Echenique, 1971).

It is particularly diagnostic of the current state of archaeology as a developing discipline that we suddenly have a number of new, competing paradigms, that they are international, and that some individual archaeologists simultaneously embrace several of them or move uncertainly from one to another in the course of their work. In order to understand this contemporary state of flux it is necessary to look at the overall direction and pattern of development of archaeology.

The early history of the discipline of archaeology is a history first of individuals then of regional schools. Finding no established and common body of archaeological philosophy each archaeologist has felt forced to build his discipline anew from its foundations (Kuhn, 1970,

p. 13). These individual philosophies then emerged as pre-paradigm regional schools based on the inevitable involvement of localized groups of men confronting the same regionally peculiar range of archaeological phenomena within a common regional, national, linguistic and educational environment; increasingly separating themselves from other groups of archaeologists confronting the same range of phenomena but not in the same particular form or national context. Archaeology became a series of divergent regional schools with cumulatively self-reinforcing archaeological education systems and with regionally esteemed bodies of archaeological theory and preferred forms of description, interpretation and explanation.

The various archaeological schools have since become increasingly aware that they hold most of their problems in common and that these problems have been more effectively solved in some schools of archaeology than in others. Although national, linguistic and educational structures still support regionally focused schools of archaeology, horizons have been considerably widened by the emergence of internationally shared cross-school *approaches*, or proto-paradigms, and by the fruitful exchange of research students. These cross-cutting approaches now appear to be rapidly blossoming into the transient but full paradigms already noted and the convergence of the schools upon a common disciplinary code with regional variations now appears distantly perceivable (Clarke, 1970b).

The history of archaeology, then, is the history of its embryonic paradigms and their successive displacement – a history of "paradigms lost". However, paradigms are rarely lost altogether; instead they die very slowly as their substance is reincorporated in fresh patterns of research – new paradigms. Paradigms are thus successively augmented as the range of problems raised by them is solved and replaced by newer ones, and in this sense it is evident that some archaeologists are still content to work in terms of nineteenth-century paradigms where only the inevitable freshness of new material prevents them from actually writing nineteenth-century textbooks. There can be little harm in this activity but it can hardly be said to be a central contribution to the strength and widening powers of the discipline.

Kuhn (1970) has described the way in which paradigm changes are marked by periods of professional insecurity with the competitive emergence of a number of alternative paradigms, by practitioners oscillating between them, and by uncertainty about valid objectives and the most useful procedures. We are currently in the middle of just such an upheaval in archaeology as the result of the piecemeal integration of a large number of important new methodologies and approaches introduced over the last decade. This uncertainty is particularly apparent in the partisan competition between the paradigms and the differential importance they attach to faunal, floral, territorial and site evidence, as opposed to "implement-focused" traditionalist archaeology. The debate also extends to controversies about the appropriate or inappropriate nature of quantitative, numerical, statistical and nomothetic approaches to data traditionally handled on an ideographic and historically oriented basis (Trigger, 1968). These debates and arguments are widely shared by disciplines comparable to archaeology in their primitive development and ambivalent raw material, and comparable too in a renewed interest in the fundamental topics of theory, explanation and interpretation and their articulation within a disciplined approach (Harvey, 1969).

Once a comprehensive paradigm is fully established, the debate languishes through general acceptance and effort is concentrated upon squeezing the old lemon in the new way. Instead, research concentrates upon the determination of significant facts within the new paradigm frame, the testing of models appropriate to this new frame against those facts, and the consequent modification, extension and articulation of models within new theory. The ingredients for such a comprehensive new paradigm are (Chorley and Haggett, 1967, pp. 37–38):

1. It must be able to solve some of the problems that brought the existing paradigms into a patently unsatisfactory position.
2. It must be more general, powerful, parsimonious or accurate than the displaced paradigms.
3. It must contain more potential for development and provide an expanding rather than a contracting disciplinary field.

In summary, we can at least see that our archaeological philosophies are related to certain aims or goals by a series of fashionable or archaic paradigms and methodologies which together control what we select to study, how we choose to analyse it, and how and whether we test and reapply it. The types of study and model that are regarded as satisfactory at any given time are, then, a function of the individual's controlling models and the prevailing paradigms. There follows an unavoidably powerful chain of interdependence between the paradigm held, the aims of a particular study, the nature of the appropriate sample, the models and analyses suitable to these, the scale used, the patterns detectable given the scale and the methods of analysis, and the processes relevant for explanations at that scale (Nagel, 1961, p. 144; Harvey, 1969, pp. 382–384). Thus the paradigm is both a benefactor and a tyrant. The scrutiny of new categories and taxonomies brought into existence by paradigm shifts will define freshly relevant parameters, variables, attributes, relationships and entities, leading to the articulation of new theory. But surrender to a paradigm is the deliberate relinquishment of certain freedoms and an inevitable narrowing of intellectual focus. It often happens, paradoxically, that the paradigm-free research of lone, independent workers may provide the roots of future paradigms. The archaeologist must therefore learn not to surrender this freedom without careful thought; like the scientist, if he is completely a scientist, he must be unique among the users of models in that he should not become addicted to a particular way of perceiving (Rapoport, 1953, p. 306). Blind addiction to unspecified models of a limiting kind can only be avoided by a comprehensive knowledge and explicit understanding of their roles and weaknesses.

OPERATIONAL MODELS

For the purposes of discussion we have separated the class of operational models, which the archaeologist consciously and deliberately deploys, from the obscure set of controlling models, which subtly constrain his every move. This separation is, of course, an artificial one and many authorities would not extend the use of the term model to the controlling sets of philosophical constraints. However, there appears to be some value to be gained from noting the way in which archaeological controlling concepts influence the selection of particular operational models and that, conversely, the habitual use of particular operational models itself modifies our controlling concepts (feedback arrows, Fig. 1). The importance of this "inward" relationship of operational and controlling models is hardly less significant than the important "outward" constraint that the selected form of operational model imposes upon the kinds of information that can then be recovered. Not only does the decision to employ a particular operational model, technique or apparatus in a particular way carry with it an assumption that only certain sorts of circumstances prevail in the observations, but even in the results of the use of such a model the ideas of the operational procedure are inevitably absorbed into the statements of the experimental observations; nowhere more so perhaps than in excavation procedure in the field (Daniels, 1972, Fig. 5.1; Nagel, 1961, p. 83; Kuhn, 1970, p. 59).

Operational models, then, are the experimental analogues or the hypotheses produced from them, which the archaeologist pushes against a sample of archaeological reality to test the goodness of fit between the two. If the model hypotheses fit the archaeological sample accurately then we can speculate that the sample fulfils the preconditions assumed in the model – we may have recovered more information about the sample. If the archaeological sample deviates from the model prediction then this deviation is highlighted and provides a focus for further attention – this in turn reveals more information about the sample. By the repetition of this process in a continuous cycle of model building, testing, modification and retesting we can gain a continuously expanding set of information about the archaeological sample.

There are many schemes for the classification of operational models according to which of their many qualities one wishes to emphasize – classification in terms of their philosophical standing (*a posteriori, a priori*), by the stuff from which they are made (hardware, abstract, natural, artificial), the operating machinery that they employ (electrical, mechanical, mathematical, statistical), the field in which they operate (morphological, anthropological, ecological, geographic, demographic, economic) or the purpose for which they were designed (classification, simulation, reconstruction) and the dimensional qualities of the sample under investigation (static, dynamic, synchronic, diachronic). These and many other possible criteria allow a variety of classificatory arrangements for models in various multidimensional continua where model category overlaps and grades into model category in an "infinite" series of potentially useful schemes. It is this universe of interlinked concepts that makes model methodology both infinitely stimulating and fruitful but at the same time exceedingly dangerous (for the problems of model use, see Harvey, 1969, p. 158).

In practice, an archaeological segment of the real world is usually most fruitfully modelled by building up or building down groups of interlinked partial models, so harnessed together as to produce an output which begins to approach the real complexity of the data. These composite models hold the greatest potential for archaeology and many are illustrated in the chapters that follow. The pure metamodel classifications for models are therefore mainly of interest as simplified charts of archaeological activity using schematic map projections (Fig. 2).

The elementary map that we will take as our guide around the world of archaeological operational models is related to the analogous map of geomorphological models devised by Chorley (Chorley and Haggett, 1967, p. 59). In this particular portrayal a line is drawn between artificial models fabricated by the operator and natural real-life models extracted from physical, historical or ethnographic parallels; within each sector both material hardware analogues and abstract theoretical analogues are employed (Fig. 2). In fact the map may be conceptualized as a continuous surface with the hardware analogues from real-life to the east of the map merging into the artificial hardware analogues to the west. The spherical or cylindrical projection then has a longitudinal pole of model complexity, where artificial theoretical system

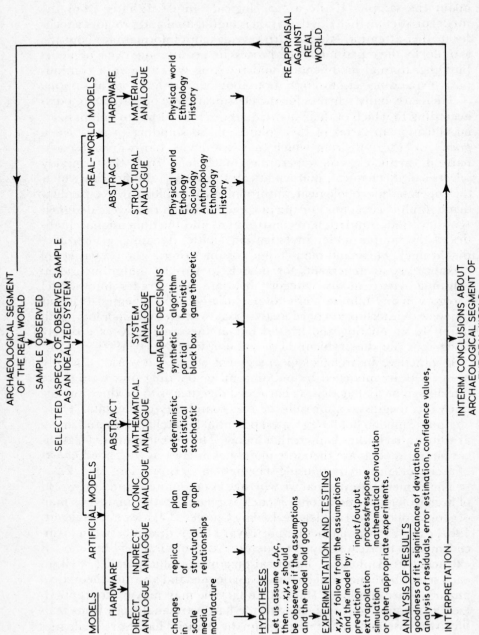

Fig. 2. A schematic view of the world of archaeological operational models, one of many alternating projections.

analogues converge upon real-life system analogues abstracted from historic-ethnographic situations, opposite a corresponding pole of simplicity where the simple hardware parallels and replicas meet.

In the simple region of artificial hardware models we encounter direct models of archaeological artefacts and sites with elementary predictive capacities – museum demonstration models, reconstruction models of buildings and structures, or direct replicas of artefacts. Of all operational models these are the best known to archaeologists at large – flint tools and projectile points have been copied and used, woodland has been cleared with stone, bronze and iron axes, ploughed with replica ards then planted and reaped with flint, bronze and iron sickles, facsimile houses have been built, burned and excavated, earthworks have been erected, storage pits tested, iron and copper smelted, pottery fired, all carefully reproducing archaeological prototypes (Ascher, 1961; Coles, 1966). These replicas are often full-size scale models, and even complete "prehistoric" farmsteads with fields, crops and domestic animals have been set up on the 30 ha site at Lejre in Denmark and at Butser Hill experimental farm, Hampshire, England, whilst a comparable scheme exists at Adesina Oja, Nigeria (see Daniels, 1972).

It is usually, but not always, the case that the artificial hardware model either changes the scale, modifies the medium of manufacture, or deviates from the technology used to produce the original and it is these distortions that must be carefully noted and controlled. However, selected distortions deliberately and carefully thought out enable us to compress the passage of time by reducing some factors and scaling up others, or to gain useful results without attempting total replication – for example the use of a 1/12 scale model has provided acceptable information on the erection of stones at Stonehenge (Stone, 1924). Nevertheless, such distortion in scale and production often leads to the formidable complications that arise from the differential consequences experienced by different variables – some will change together linearly with scale or material, others non-linearly and independently, and others even exponentially. It is at this point that the results from studying artificial hardware models produced by the workshop are often run against and compared with appropriately selected real-life ethnographic hardware parallels to control these aspects – a modern copy of an Iron Age smelting furnace against a comparable Sudanese furnace, for example (Coles, 1966, p. 5).

These hardware models enable us to learn by imitation, to estimate the original cost in time and labour and the efficiency and life-expectancy of the item – primitive steps in quantification which may also be matched from comparable ethnographic data. The models also allow predictive hypotheses to be formed relating the similarity of behaviour – or its artefact consequences – observed in the present to that preserved from the past. These hypotheses, or the models themselves, may then be tested by experiment and simulation and the results analysed and interpreted. A recent experiment illustrates this procedure. A full-scale earthwork was constructed at Overton Down, Wiltshire, in 1960 with various materials and artefacts embedded within it at exactly measured locations. This model then allows two different aspects to be simultaneously investigated, first of all providing an estimate of the labour time and methods required to build a massive bank and ditch with replicas of prehistoric artefacts, second to record the complex micro-geomorphological post-depositional processes of decay and collapse by sampling the earthwork, at appropriately estimated intervals of time, by excavation. The observations from this experiment are only just beginning but they have already contributed new information of great importance in modifying the traditional, erroneous and purely intuitive opinions previously held about silting and erosion processes on chalk soils (Jewell, 1963, 1966).

Here is an interesting example of an artificial hardware simulation model with a dynamic capacity. The drawback of having to wait 5, 10, 20, 50 and 100 years before being able to take the appropriate readings is a problem that might have been overcome by miniaturization in scale accompanied by changes in media and the simulation of erosional processes, but in this case the distortional consequences of such a procedure would probably have outweighed any convenience. An alternative might be the excavation of sections of a chosen series of historic earthworks of known date – perhaps ranging from Roman banks, through Medieval park boundaries to Recent railway embankments – but here again a degree of control on comparable media and erosional processes is lost; perhaps a composite procedure involving all three approaches and yet other possibilities might represent a solution.

In contrast with the direct artificial hardware models we may also distinguish an interesting category of indirect artificial hardware models, transitional between the imitative replicas and their consequences on one hand and the more powerful class of abstract, iconic or symbolic models on the other. The indirect hardware analogue imitates in concrete form not the direct external appearance of an archaeological artefact or site but instead provides a tangible replica of certain relationships noted and abstracted at a derivative and secondary level from primary and direct observations and analyses. The output of complex correlation analyses and cluster analysis studies may be expressed in this model form and it may be possible to consider to what extent aspects of the model thus visualized may be generalized to aspects of comparable situations.

A simple but effective example of an indirect artificial hardware model can be used, for example, to illustrate the dangers that follow from naïve comparisons of distribution densities plotted on flat map projections. Take a flat disc of silver foil and let it represent a large flat alluvial plain and mark upon it a dozen archaeological sites of a given period. Take an exact copy of this disc and the distribution over an identical area of silver foil, crush it into a ball and unroll it over an eggbox to give the effect of a mountainous terrain overriding complex small-scale relief; then compare the "flat" map projections of the two distributions of the dozen sites on the plain and the same sites, distributed in the same way, over an identical surface area (Fig. 3). It will be found that in practice the distribution of finds appears to be three to seven times more dense in the projection of the mountainous terrain than in the flat plain – although the density of sites per unit area is in fact the same in both cases. Now take the sparse distribution of Mesolithic sites in the Hungarian plain and compare it with the dense distribution in the map projection of the Alpine region, add in a multiplying factor for the differential loss of sites under considerable aggradation in the flat aluvial plain, and perhaps the degree of difference becomes less significant?

In any event this model reminds us that all archaeological distributions, artificially portrayed on flat map projections, were once distributed over complex surfaces – topographic, demographic, ecological surfaces, etc. – and what may appear to be a counter-locational analysis case of irregular distribution on one surface may provide a perfect case of evenly and regularly adjusted site distribution when mapped on another surface under a different transformation for the same area and material (Fig. 4) (Harvey, 1969, Chap. 14).

The class of indirect hardware models takes us some way from the elementary domain of simple artificial *hardware* analogues towards the complex realm of artificial *theoretical* models with its iconic, mathematical and system analogues. Iconic models merely represent observed properties as iconic symbols using a selective, distorted, simplified code distributed over an equally simplified field space of few dimensions – an elementary representational and demonstrative device but yet with some limited predictive and experimental capacities. Beyond these lie the symbolic mathematical and system models where properties and relationships in the archaeological sample are again represented by symbols, but which unlike the iconic codes are now explicitly integrated in a specified calculus of relationships or system of equations. Here we have an emerging capacity to cope with dynamic and diachronic

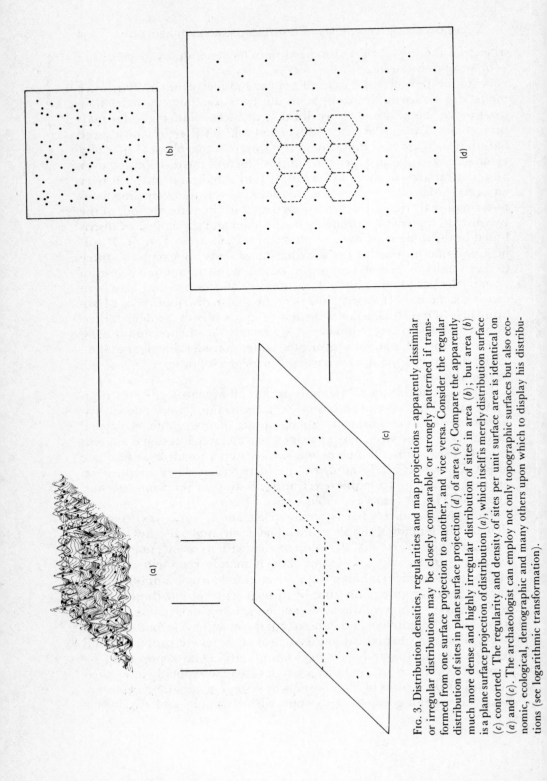

Fig. 3. Distribution densities, regularities and map projections – apparently dissimilar or irregular distributions may be closely comparable or strongly patterned if transformed from one surface projection to another, and vice versa. Consider the regular distribution of sites in plane surface projection (d) of area (c). Compare the apparently much more dense and highly irregular distribution of sites in area (b); but area (b) is a plane surface projection of distribution (a), which itself is merely distribution surface (c) contorted. The regularity and density of sites per unit surface area is identical on (a) and (c). The archaeologist can employ not only topographic surfaces but also economic, ecological, demographic and many others upon which to display his distributions (see logarithmic transformation).

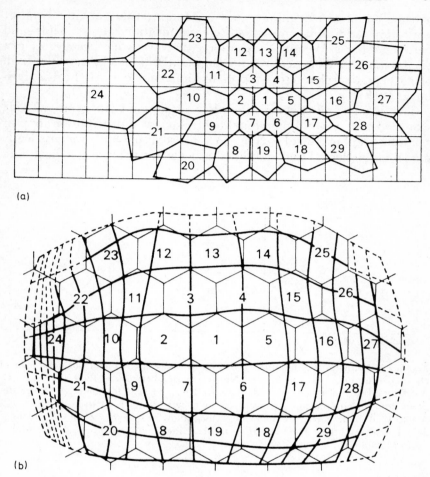

FIG. 4. Comparison between theoretical and actual map patterns by way of map transformations. (*a*) An approximation to Christaller's theoretical model in an area of disuniform rural population density. (*b*) A transformed map to produce even population densities and the superimposition of the theoretical Christaller solution (from Harvey, 1969).

developments, variables varying together and separately over large but nevertheless constrained ranges, with due allowance for stochastic elements and the complex sampling effects inherent in the archaeological data. Here we also meet the infinite variety of symbolic mathematical, numerical, algebraic, geometrical and statistical languages, amongst which we may choose, and which also have the unparalleled advantage of being both interdisciplinary in scope and international in meaning; important additional means of communication across fields and between schools. We must not suppose, however, that because we can display an archaeological relationship mathematically that it is itself of mathematical character – representation is not identity (Earl of Halsbury, 1968).

The iconic analogues frequently use a point distribution code scattered over a two-dimensional field – such as a distribution map or a simple graphical display (Fig. 5A). These displays characteristically model only selected and simplified aspects of the archaeological data

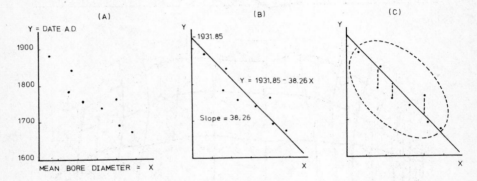

FIG. 5. (A) An iconic model of the relationship between the mean bore diameter of clay tobacco pipes from Europe and North America between *ca* 1600–1900 A.D. (B) A deterministic mathematical model ($Y=1931.85-38.26X$) for the relationships derived from the straight line regression formula best fitting the scatter of values. (C) A statistical model for the relationships which allows for the degree of scatter of the actual values and their deviation from the ideal line model (schematized from studies by Lewis Binford).

but they already allow the formulation of simple hypotheses about probabilities and expectations from analysis or extrapolation and thus provide a frame for testing such predictions. The statistical properties of the dispersion and the relationship between the points and the field space lead almost inevitably to the conversion of such iconic displays into statistical models which more succinctly account for the display pattern. In this way the iconic model demonstrating how the mean bore diameter of seventeenth–nineteenth-century clay tobacco pipes varied with their date and technology of manufacture (Fig. 5B) may be crudely but adequately expressed in a mathematical deterministic model derived from the straight line regression formula for the scatter of values – allowing the prediction of a date with a fair degree of accuracy, given a few hundred stem fragments such as are frequently found on European and Colonial sites (Walker, 1967):

let $x=$ the mean bore diameter of pipe stem fragment,
$y=$ the date of its manufacture;

then analysis shows that

$$y = 1931.85 - 38.26x \text{ for north European and American pipes.}$$

Such deterministic mathematical models are rare in archaeology since they assume that all the operating factors are known and are capable of exact expression. However, Carneiro (1960) offers a deterministic model relating shifting cultivation factors and length of settlement tenure for slash-and-burn agriculturalists under tropical forest conditions. Cook and Heizer (1968) have developed an allometric (loglog) model relating living floor area and population in aboriginal Californian settlements, where this approach might usefully be compared with another deterministic model for population estimates based on cemetery size and the age distribution of the skeletons therein (Birabon, 1971). All deterministic mathematical models, it may be noted, are only strictly applicable to a very limited field of data, although they may be very powerful over that range and at least suggest potential relationships beyond it.

Statistical models differ from deterministic models by including a capacity to cope with random effects, which may arise either from inherent fluctuations, from the effect that no two repetitions of an experimental test give identical results (C14 dating), or from variability within a sampled category. Statistical models can be derived from deterministic models by including an additional random component – thus the deterministic regression line model for clay pipes (Fig. 5B) could be modified to allow for the real cigar-shape scatter of points by estimating an appropriate error component (E):

$$y = 1931.85 - 38.26x + E \text{ (Fig. 5C).}$$

A precisely comparable random component is included in statistical models for analysing three-dimensional trend surfaces in order to distinguish significant residuals from localized small-scale fluctuations – an important technique for scrutinizing distribution maps of archaeological data for regional trends, and a reminder that the egalitarian dots on archaeological maps have differing quantifiable values (Clarke, 1968, p. 481).

Stochastic models differ from the ordinary statistical model in incorporating, in addition to the preceding considerations, a specific random process which replicates a sequence of changes on a probability

basis; reproducing net effects of myriads of differently directed infinitesimal factors – individually unspecifiable but jointly predictable. Stochastic models are thus especially suitable for simulating processes of
change, developmental sequences, and the consequences of randomly
impinging effects at a very small scale when compared to the level of
the study of the phenomenon as a whole. The particular process involved may be described in terms of successive chains of probabilities –
chains that may be classified as random walk, Monte Carlo, or Markov
chains, etc., according to the precise pattern of the transition probabilities. Archaeologists are currently discovering that the general theory
of stochastic processes provides a whole series of model formulations
in probabilistic languages very appropriate for certain archaeological
situations (Harvey, 1969, p. 266).

Thus random walk models describe processes in which the path or
sequence traced by an element moves or changes in steps, each step
or change being determined by chance in regard to direction, magnitude, or both. The cases most frequently considered are those in which
the element moves on a lattice of points in one or more dimensions
and at each step is equally likely to move to any of the nearest neighbouring points. The fluctuation and aimless wandering of the time trajectories of the majority of non-functional artefact and assemblage attributes, meandering within the range of their stable configurations, has
been compared with random walk models, and much of the stylistic
variation in Acheulean assemblages has been accounted for under such
a model (Fig. 6) (Clarke, 1968, pp. 448–449, 471, 575; Isaac, 1969,
p. 19). In this volume a random walk model has also been used to
represent the wanderings of discarded artefacts on the abandonment
of a site (Clarke, 1972, p. 806).

However, the mention of random walk movements in conjunction
with nearest neighbour points reminds us of their geographical implications and its potential significance for modelling the colonization,
movement or diffusion of archaeological artefacts and sites. For
example, if we wish to simulate the successive settlement site movements
of Danubian I slash-and-burn agriculturalists in fifth millennium B.C.
Europe, then a random walk model provides many interesting possibilities. Within a relatively homogeneous loess zone there will be an
infinite number of acceptable settlement locations stretching in all
directions to the limits of the loess band. So, when a settlement is to
be resited from time to time it will move on a lattice of points in two
dimensions and is equally likely at each transition to move to any of
the nearest neighbouring acceptable location points in any direction.
Such a movement typically arises in situations where the moves are
affected by a great many independently variable factors (Fig. 6).

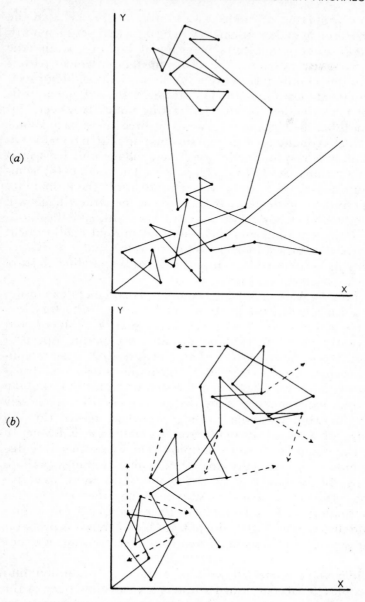

FIG. 6. (*a*) Random walk changes in which the path or sequence traced changes in steps, each step or change being determined by chance in regard to direction and magnitude. *X* and *Y* might be a pair of variables in an artefact study or geographical axes when the graph becomes a map. (*b*) Random walk changes in which the magnitude of each step remains the same, and which at every third move generates another element, also executing a comparable random walk pattern. This random walk and birth process may be applicable to settlement or population movements and fissioning and is related to the important general class of Yule Process models.

The general properties of random walk processes predict that the direction of movement of the settlement will be unbiased between north and south, east or west – other things being equal. Equally, because the Brownian motion or random walk is recurrent, the settlement path is almost sure to return infinitely many times to a small neighbourhood of former settlement locations, although the longer the settlement drifts the likelier it is to wander far from its starting point. However, this process will be intensified because every two or three moves each Danubian village will have generated enough surplus population both to continue itself and give rise to an additional new village unit by a kind of social binary fission (see Clarke, 1972, p. 843). The result of this compounding multiplication will endorse even more firmly the probability that some derivative settlements of any given ancestral village will remain in the general vicinity of the ancestral sites, although the multiplication of settlement units and their constant mutual readjustment will also ensure that over a long period of time the many derivative village units will become widely dispersed in an expanding mass of hunt-and-seek settlement pathways.

Now, this random walk model for Danubian I settlement expansion matches the archaeological observations in a far more satisfactory way than the east–west linear movement model customarily employed, and more significantly offers new explanations for some unique aspects of the Danubian I phenomenon – the characteristics that, despite continuous development through 600 years, and despite a dispersed distribution covering more than 1500 km of forested terrain, the Danubian I ceramic tradition remained remarkably conservative, relatively homogeneous in motif vocabulary, and everywhere passed through broadly comparable stylistic changes, from Romania to the Rhine. In the ensuing Danubian II phase these unique characteristics were dispersed in a mosaic of regionally diverse ceramic traditions, perhaps stimulated by the introduction of less mobile and more intensive agrarian and settlement systems, possibly including the development of plough agriculture. Many factors will have interacted to produce and maintain the ceramic uniformity of Danubian I, but it is probable that the pattern of settlement movements and relationships was one key factor.

The random walk model shows how settlement expansion into distant areas may be accomplished without loss of contact across the mass of mutually interacting settlement territories, constantly in motion, constantly colliding in fresh random associations with a constant interchange of inhabitants and artefacts updating every unit's behaviour patterns. Yet the same model reconciles this constant movement with the continuous occupation of regions by some descendants of villages that were formerly in that area hundreds of years previously. It also shows that at this scale the movement is only directional in so far as it is channelled within the loess bands and across the network of river and stream systems. When the universe under scrutiny is Europe as a whole and the scale half a millennium, then the Danubian I phenomenon may indeed be adequately represented by a linear movement model with a directed expansion along the loess "railway lines" from eastern to western Europe. If the boundaries of the loess represent the universe and the scale is the lifetime of a given village then a random walk model is more appropriate – once again reminding us that the scale of the study determines the level of model appropriate for its representation and the process appropriate for its explanation.

Above all else, the random walk model suggests one factor and one mechanism which would maximize the *opportunity* for the maintenance of common ceramic features changing in step across a vast distribution of widely dispersed communities. However, *opportunity* for such a homogeneity does not explain *why* this opportunity was in this case taken up, neither does it explain the conservatism of the tradition. Here we must consider other factors and perhaps suggest a mixed model upon the following lines.

1. Random walk of settlement communities, like the movement of gas particles, maximizes "collisions" and offers maximum opportunity for community interaction and homogeneous diffusion across a large area.
2. Ethno-economic models suggest that a characteristic social concomitant of shifting agricultural communities is the considerable inter-village mobility of families. This amounts to a random walk of family units between the random walking settlement communities – the family feuding with this group, moving to another, fissioning to a third and so on. This kind of social mobility would put the *opportunity* for interlinked parallel development into *practice*.
3. There is probably some additional factor needed to maximize ceramic homogeneity and conservatism in what still could have been a commonly held but rapidly changing ceramic tradition. This might probably involve social considerations of the kind modelled by Deetz (1965) and Longacre (1970):

   Matrilocality would favour ceramic conservatism but only bring males into the village;
   Patrilocality would exchange women between villages maintaining ceramic homogeneity but not necessarily conservatism;
   Village endogamy would favour ceramic conservatism but also between-site divergence;

Village exogamy would assist homogeneity but not conservatism.

The kinship solution with maximum within and between village *homogeneity and conservatism* would probably be some form of bilocal residence with 50% village endogamy and 50% exogamy, such as we see for example amongst the analogous Iban (Freeman, 1955). This speculation might be tested by comparing the variability of male-produced artefacts with associated female artefact variability, making certain assumptions.

4. Finally, one factor cited in the linear movement model remains significant in setting up an initial level of homogeneity over a large area – the comparative rapidity of the expansion, which will have been largely a consequence of demographic, ecological and swidden regime economic factors.

This thumbnail sketch may serve to illustrate this class of stochastic model at the macro-level of settlement movements whilst the similar model for discarded artefact movements serves a similar purpose at the micro-level (see Clarke, 1972). In a wider context the sketch illustrates the building up of composite models, the role of the model as a fountain of hypotheses for testing, the model as an explanatory device, the potential use of ethnographic data as a control on pure, theoretical models, and the importance of scale in the modelling and analysis of archaeological material.

Monte Carlo, Markov chain, Queueing Theory and Ergodic Theory represent other kinds of stochastic process models which are emerging or may emerge in archaeological contexts. The Monte Carlo technique suggests solutions to stochastic problems by employing sampling experiments upon a simulated model of the process under investigation (Haggett, 1965, pp. 58–60, 97–98). For example, the study of the surviving distribution of Körös Neolithic settlement sites along the river Tisza has produced a fragmentary but remarkably regularly adjusted lattice of settlement locations (Fig. 7); and yet how could locational analysis infer a regular inter-site adjustment of 2 km when we know the distribution to be a very fragmentary palimpsest of more than 500 years of occupation in this area? A simulation model was developed which assumed a random walk settlement movement within the suitable dry loess terraces close to running water but with the assumed constraint that two factors would lead to movement in the first instance to new locations about 2 km from the old.

1. An appropriate agricultural surface to support villages of this size on this terrain under the given technology would be a *ca* 1 km radius territory. Therefore, invoking the Law of Least Effort, the minimal move would be 2 km.

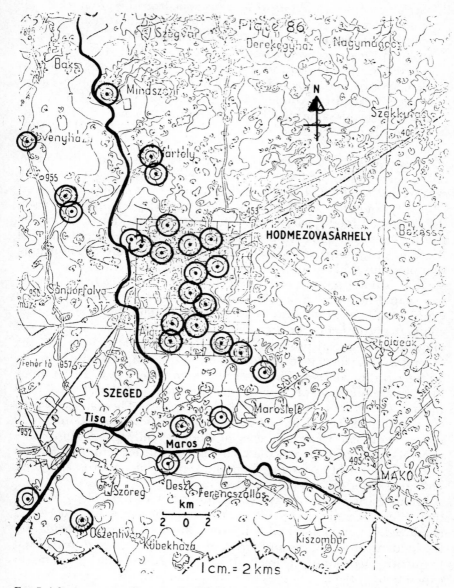

FIG. 7. A fragmentary palimpsest distribution of some 500 years of Körös Neolithic settlement along the river Tisza; the sites date between *ca* 5000–4500 B.C. radiocarbon. Sites within the amplitude of the river will in the main have been destroyed by its meanderings. (Based on original research by Dr John Nandris.)

2. However, disregarding the above considerations, a former village territory, although about to be abandoned on the grounds of soil exhaustion, will nevertheless include many residual resources and the results of much communally expended labour – cleared and drained areas, accessible water, pasture, residual tree crops, etc. Therefore, the old territory represents a valuable resource still to be exploited and thus requiring a move immediately adjacent to it yet ensuring fresh arable radius – therefore a move of 2 km. At the micro-level this same model accounts for the "lily pad" development of floors in some classes of settlement (Clarke, 1972, Figs 21.1–21.6).

These two factors may give a contemporary series of site adjustments on a 2 km modulus but how could this emerge from a fragmentary five century palimpsest? Well, a series of Monte Carlo samples taken at 2%, 10% and 50% levels of survival of detectable Körös sites upon the simulated model output for 500 years showed that, for complex reasons yet to be analysed, if the modulus of adjustment remained of the same order for that period of time then a false pattern enshrining that modulus is likely to be preserved, the pattern being "false" in so far as it is not a pattern of actually contemporary sites but a sample in a spatial-temporal cube. This example illustrates the way that such experiments may gradually develop a special and probably statistically complex set of theory for archaeological locational analysis that will allow for the special problems of the archaeological sample and the crucial way in which its distributions differ from superficially comparable geographical cases. The latter may then be seen as merely a limiting synchronic case of a more general spatio-temporal locational theory. There are other aspects of Geographical Theory, too, which current archaeological and ethnographic inquiries are suggesting may merely represent a partial theory of modern limiting cases in a more general theory yet to be articulated by taking into account the 2 million years of adaptively changing hominid settlement patterns and their changing determinants (see p. 61).

Monte Carlo models are especially important in archaeology because they offer a technique capable of reflecting the sampling procedures employed in excavation and field work, at the same time elucidating the hidden consequences and circularity that such procedures all too frequently incorporate (Daniels, 1972). The Körös village simulation experiment at the macro-scale may be paralleled, for example, by elementary Monte Carlo procedures at the micro-scale of assemblages and artefacts. Let us imagine that we have a multiple-layered site at which the repeated visits of the same group employed an identical assemblage in every layer of the site. Then let us suppose that a varying 60% sample was itself accidentally left for selective sampling by sondage excavation (Fig. 8). It will at once be perceived that, although the successive assemblages were in fact identical, the sampling effects are such as to make uncommon artefact types seem to appear and disappear in successive levels (this experiment is best simulated by successively drawing from a bag of coloured marbles, the assemblage in the bag remaining identical whilst the 60% of marbles successively grabbed varies). Now it is a well-known archaeological vice to nominate and classify assemblages by the presence or absence of rare "type fossils" – thus, imagine that

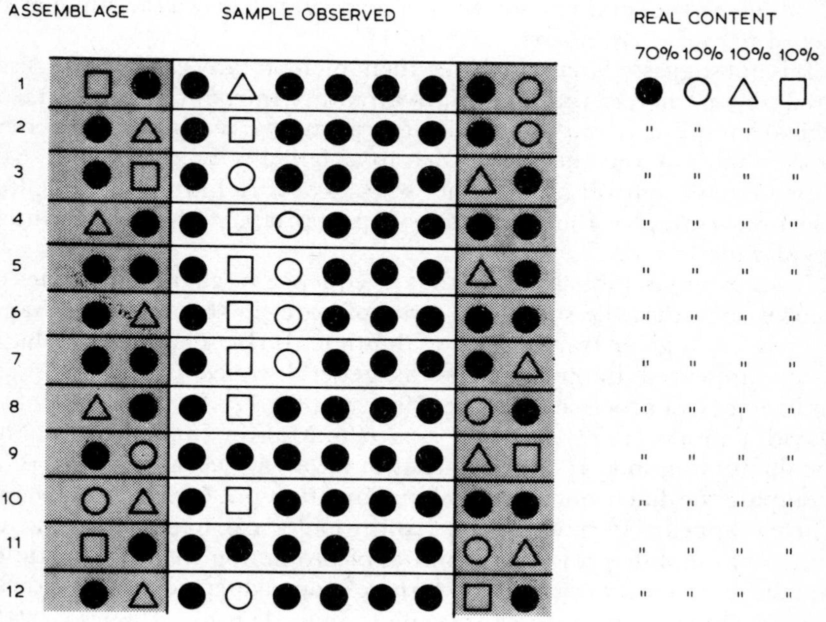

FIG. 8. The overriding consequences of variability introduced by sampling effects and the consequent dangers of "type fossil" nomenclature – a model of the interdigitation problem. The figure can be conceived as a stratified site at which the same artefact assemblage was repeatedly used (see "real content" of each horizontal assemblage). Sondate excavation or other sampling vagaries recover for classification and comparison only 60% of each assemblage – the selection in the vertical unshaded section ("sample observed"). If the triangle, square and unfilled circle are rare (infrequent) nominating type fossils, the column falsely appears to contain different assemblages coming and going in an irregular manner (interdigitation). If the triangles are handaxes, the squares scrapers, the open circles denticulates, and the filled circles "Typical Mousterian", then this model provides a crude simulation of the kind of interdigitation observed at Combe Grenal and other Mousterian sites.

In a more general setting the assemblage samples (1–12) could represent any set of incomplete assemblages from unstratified single sites widely distributed in space.

the most abundant artefacts in our model assemblage represent Typical
Mousterian, that each of the rare types represent, say, scrapers, hand-
axes or denticulates, then our model has at least partially simulated
the phenomenon of "interdigitation", where assemblage categories
appear and reappear in a random way in a stratigraphic column or
spatial distribution of assemblages. Famous cases of interdigitation involve not only Bordes's categories of Mousterian, but Upper Acheulean
and Hope Fountain assemblages, Late Acheulean and Developed
Oldowan, possibly the Acheulean and Clactonian phenomenon, and
certainly the Ceramic/Aceramic interdigitation of Çatal Hüyük levels
X–V, where the coming and going of pottery is clearly a sampling artefact of its rarity (Mellaart, 1966, p. 170).

It is not suggested that sampling phenomena totally explain the cases
cited above, merely that artificial variability introduced by archaeological sampling always overrides the particular variability inherent
in the material and that if we wish to isolate any one source we can
only do so by controlling the other sources of variability, by the skilful
selection of samples, the careful use of appropriate models and by intelligent experiment.

Markov chain models imply that a sequence of changes or series of
steps is such that the successive series of states in the chain or chains
are related by given transition probabilities. Markov chain models have
so far appeared in archaeology as general conceptual models for
archaeological processes (Clarke, 1968, pp. 63–77; Doran, 1970), but
David Thomas (1972) develops a specific Markov model to simulate
the fluctuating food resource output of an area over a period of time
(compare the diachronic model of similar situation, Fig. 15). Queueing
Theory appears in a number of anthropological papers relating to
individual mobility and probabilities of promotion to varying grades
and statuses within various patterns of social hierarchies and these
may yet have archaeological manifestations (Harvey, 1969, pp. 246,
266).

Ergodic models make the assumption that the statistical properties
of a set of observations in a time series are essentially the same as the
statistical properties of a set of observations of the same phenomenon
taken over a synchronic spatial ensemble (Harvey, 1969, pp. 128–129,
269–270). Models incorporating this special type of stationary stochastic process may have something to contribute to the modelling of spatio-
temporal distributions like that sketched above for Körös villages.
Curry (1967) has already applied such a model to central place systems
with the implication that the statistical properties of activity patterns
over *time* can be taken as implicit in the statistical properties of the *spatial*
pattern of site locations. It is interesting to note that an implicit ergodic

model must also underlie the frequent practice of using ethnographic-historic data from one area and period to model an archaeological situation in a "comparable stage of development" (stadial models), or when data from many such areas and periods are used to model some general historical process (Harvey, 1969, p. 129). Even the statistical properties of attributes, artefacts and assemblages may be modelled in ergodic terms on the assumption that the affinity between any such items in space is comparable to identical affinity between such items in time (Clarke, 1968, pp. 262–265). Thus two artefacts sharing a 75% affinity with a reference artefact may fall into this same category because they were both contemporary but made from a chain of copies effectively equidistant from the reference, or because they were both made equi-temporally from the reference, or because one was phenetically as far removed in space as the other was in time from the reference.

Thrown back by the glimpses of these mathematical mountains and dangerous precipices, our schematic map shows the archaeological explorer that beyond the diversity of stochastic process models lies a broad area of models with a comparable capacity to simulate complex processes – system models (Fig. 2). We are still within the realm of artificial theoretical models, but are beginning to approach the frontier with system models abstracted from real-life ethnographic, historical or physical situations.

System models are preoccupied with the flow of consequences between ensembles of interlinked components rather than with the detailed mathematical symbolism of particular elements. The particular components linked within the system are selected by the operator as his guess at the set which interacts to account for most of the variability of interest to him, in the frame of his particular study. The guess may be a bad one and it is therefore important to bear this in mind when first examining an impressive flow chart. Putting components in boxes in a system does not necessarily explain a process or even model it accurately; it depends what is in the boxes that are included and what is not in those boxes. All too often we may be presented with a flow chart that crisply formulates the obvious and only succeeds in modelling the satisfaction of the operator.

However, it has been repeatedly pointed out that these are universal criticisms of bad models and nobody is defending a case for bad models. The study of the interaction of components in systems is unavoidable because all situations may be conceived as systems of components and this is one of the ways in which dynamic processes may be modelled. The expression of such a system as a flow-interaction chart is both an explicit and potentially testable expression of a set of assumptions and hypotheses, and a vital step in setting up a computer simulation – this in itself accounts for the current popularity of the flow chart in some quarters and its vilification in others (Garvin, 1965).

System models may represent the flow of consequences between ensembles of interlinked variables or the flow of consequences between networks of decisions. The former class of system, systems of variables, is defined by sets of components such that changes in the values or states of some of these components can be shown to affect or alter with the value or state of some of their neighbours (Clarke, 1968, pp. 43–82). The overall state of the system therefore changes with the changing values, states, compositions and organizations of the components, and with the flow of correlation, energy, mass, commodity or information changes, according to the nature of the system being modelled. In general, such systems exhibit very common categories of "behaviour" brought about by their structural similarities and it is these general system properties that enable the operator to compare systems which may share elements of deep structure although quite dissimilar in surface structure. Thus two superficially very different systems are said to have "equivalence" when they transform the same inputs into identical outputs, opening up new realms of classificatory possibilities. Other common system properties may include – constraints, critical thresholds, stochastic oscillation, adaptive regulation and control by positive or negative feedback, convergence upon equilibrium states, replication and related concepts (Clarke, 1968, pp. 43–82; Chorley and Haggett, 1967, pp. 76–89).

System models have emerged at a range of levels of power and specificity in contemporary archaeological debate. At the lowest level the system approach has proved an extremely useful way of reconceptualizing archaeological problems ranging from general theory (Clarke, 1968) to models for food-collecting and food-production regimes in Mesoamerica 8000–200 B.C. (Flannery, 1968), and the Neolithic "revolution" in the Near East 10 000–5000 B.C. (Binford, 1968). By restricting the scope of the modelling, a more specific predictive or simulation power develops with the addition of qualitative information about the links and components in the system – the flow of consequences is specified and directions indicated, positive and negative feedback is identified and the nature of the inputs and outputs related. Finally, with an even more tightly defined frame of reference and still more information, it is possible to quantify the components and the input and output of the system and thus move towards quantified, measurable and testable predictions. These three levels of utility and capacity are aptly illustrated by Newcomb's models for Iron Age settlements in Cornwall (Fig. 9), the more powerful systems models of various forms (Figs 10–12), and Thomas's semi-quantified model of the Shoshone economic cycle (Thomas, 1972, Fig. 17.3). Many detailed verbal descriptions and quantitative estimations represent primitive archaeological movements towards the goal of an explicit, quantified, system display of the step-by-step logic of a problem which might then be susceptible to a powerful, testable computer simulation (Doran, 1970).

A particularly attractive feature of system models is their capacity to cope with very complex and unknown aspects of archaeological situations. Because of system closure, for example, models with infinite numbers of variables are in fact sometimes more tractable than models

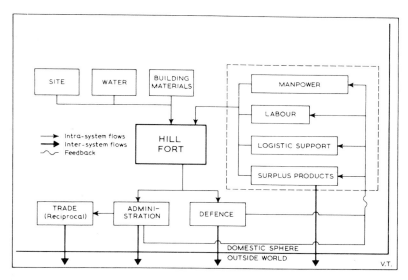

Fig. 9. A simple system model for a category of Iron Age hill fort in Cornwall (from Newcomb, 1968).

with a finite but large number of variables (Tobler, 1969). Similarly, where the details of the system components are known, it still remains possible to relate given system outputs (like demographic structure, perhaps) to preceding system inputs such as the population in the immediately preceding time period. Given the inputs and outputs, or estimates of them, it is possible to calculate the characteristics of the unknown system in the Black Box and thus infer the process (Fig. 13) (Clarke, 1968, pp. 59–62).

Black Box systems are the last of the three categories of models for systems of variables distinguished by Chorley (Chorley and Haggett, 1967, p. 85). The unknown subsystems of Black Box process-response models grade into the Grey Box of incompletely specified partial system models and the White Box of the completely specified but arbitrarily selected variables of synthetic models. Synthetic system models begin with the selective identification of key elements in a given archaeological complex, together with the adoption of some views about their interrelationship. A detailed study of the changing correlation patterns of

A SYSTEMS MODEL OF THE MEDIEVAL PARISH

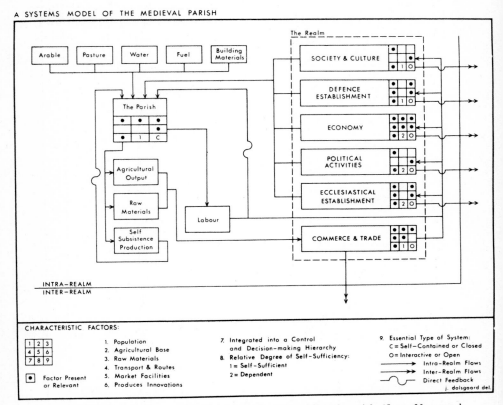

FIG. 10. A developed system model for a Danish medieval parish (from Newcomb, 1970).

these selected elements then allows the "variable system" to be mapped under successive conditions and its correlation structure examined by regression or cluster analysis for indications of yoked changes in groups of variables and scrutinized for cause and effect. When the variables are numerous and acting with composite effects it is useful to collapse the data matrix by factor analysis into a small number of idealized variables, which account for most of the observed variability of the data (see Binford, 1972, Figs 3.1–3.3). Synthetic system models have already proved especially valuable for the analysis of correlation patterns in attributes within artefact systems and artefact categories within assemblage systems (Binford and Binford, 1966; Clarke, 1968, pp. 541–542; Glover, 1969). However, synthetic system studies of trends in the values or states of mapped distributions, considered as "response surfaces", offer far wider applications of process-response models linking artefact or site distributions and ecological, environmental or demographic variability (see Clarke, 1972, p. 847).

However, the primitive flow-interaction chart which may model the flow of consequences between systems of variables may also model the

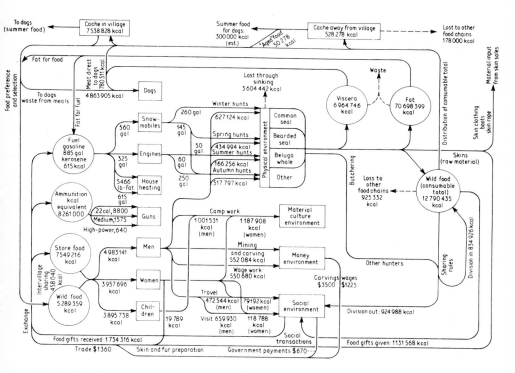

FIG. 11. The flow of energy in a hunting society; the system is outlined for two Eskimo households from direct observations over 13 months. The input of imported energy in the form of fuel and ammunition, along with the input of native game and imported foodstuffs (far left), enabled the four hunters and their kin to heat their dwellings and power their machines, and also join in many seasonal activities that utilized various parts of the environment in the manner indicated (right). The end results of these combined inputs of energy are shown as a series of yields and losses from waste and other causes (far right). The net yields then feed back through various channels to reach the starting point again as inputs. All figures are in kilocalories (from Kemp, 1971).

flow of consequences between systems of decisions – the realm of operational research and control and decision theory (see Daniels, 1972, Fig.
5.2). Decision systems and their models match the capacity of mathematical models in their range from the deterministic to the probabilistic, from algorithm models to heuristic, linear, combinatorial and
game theory models. These may seem remote areas of the world of
archaeological models but decision system models inevitably emerge
wherever complex processes of choice and decision are studied or simulated – whether simulating the complex routing of restricted manpower
and materials in a plan for a large excavation, or simulating and optimizing the economic schedule of the Shoshone or !Kung.

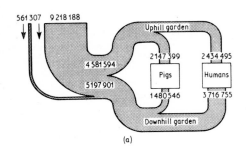

(a)

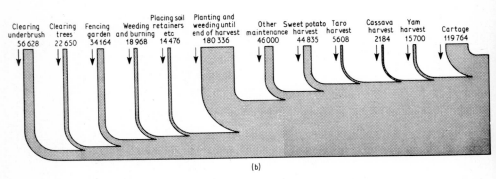

(b)

FIG. 12. The flow of energy in a slash-and-burn agricultural society; the system is outlined for 204 Tsembaga tribesmen from direct observations in New Guinea (from
Rappaport, 1971).

(a) The biomass of the crop yield in yams, cassavas, sweet potatoes and pigs, etc.,
measured in kcal. If this yield is compared with the major energy input (b), it gives
more than a sixteen to one return on the human energy investment, although this static
model would fluctuate over a run of good and bad years.

(b) The twelve major inputs of energy required in Tsembaga agriculture. The flow
diagram shows the inputs in terms of the kcal per acre required to prepare and harvest
a pair of gardens. Weeding, a continual process after the garden is planted, demands
the most energy; bringing in the harvest (right) ranks next.

Algorithm models present a precise set of instructions for solving a well-defined problem, whether the solution itself is imprecise or not. Many archaeological algorithm models are therefore key steps in computer studies like Gardin's reconstruction of early Assyrian trade networks (Gardin, 1965, Fig. 3). In practice no scheme of archaeological classification is really acceptable unless it is accompanied by an algorithm which will both instruct the novice how to employ the classification on real material and highlight the key attributes in the material (Fig. 14) (Lewis and Woolfenden, 1969).

Heuristic models, by comparison, involve successive approximations, often made on a probabilistic basis, sometimes adaptively changing with changing circumstances. These models can be used either where

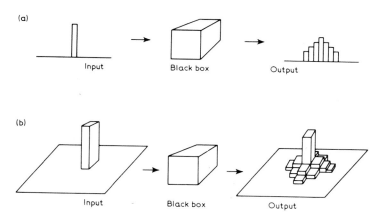

FIG. 13. Black Box system process and response models for complex unknown systems (after Tobler, 1969).

there is no algorithm available – playing chess, for example – or where the available algorithm is hopelessly uneconomic in use. Heuristics are rough formulations of systems of hypotheses; they have the advantage that they are flexible, especially suited to complex adaptive situations within changing circumstances, and they can cope with situations that cannot be quantified; they are therefore closely associated with probability theory, management information systems and heuristic non-numerical computer programming (George, 1970). Doran's use of a "HEURISTIC DENDRAL" technique to generate explanatory hypotheses within a simulation model for an Iron Age cemetery illustrates many of these qualities at work (see Doran, 1972, Figs 10.1–10.3).

Linear programming and combinatorial models develop further

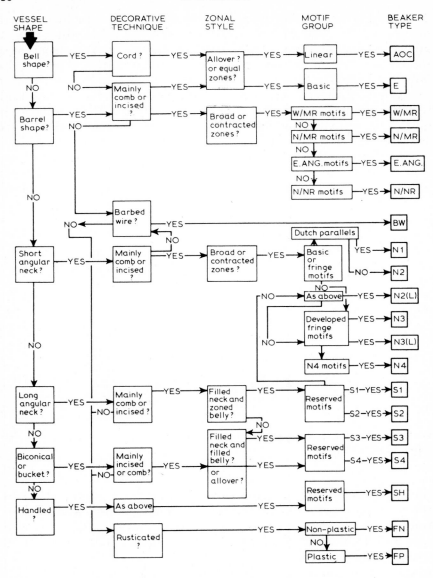

Fig. 14. A simplified algorithm model for the classification of British beaker pottery (Clarke, 1970a). Particular vessels are scrutinized and classified in terms of the covariation of their shape, decorative technique, zonal style and motif vocabulary. The partitioning of these sets of attributes produces twenty subsets or categories of vessel. A full algorithm would allow rapid and automatic computer classification of archaeological data.

aspects of decision systems. Linear programme models have been devised to solve and simulate situations that require the allocation of available resources to meet varying demands, indicating the optimal utilization of available resources in given circumstances (Vajda, 1960). The archaeological techniques of catchment area analysis and site system studies already produce data on utilization patterns and resource distribution especially suited to simulation in linear programme or game theory models (see Jarman, 1972), and Thomas has taken his model of the Shoshone economic system some way in this direction (see Thomas, 1972).

Game theory models further develop these possibilities by realistically introducing the uncontrollable but ever-present counter-optimal moves of the environing system or of competitor systems; thus many solutions that appear optimal under static and synchronic conditions turn out to be positively dangerous under dynamic and diachronic competition (Fig. 15). Decisions must often be taken where the chances of success rely not only upon the action of uncontrollable factors but also upon the interaction of moves made by other persons, entities or systems. It is for circumstances such as these that the theory of games has been developed. The theory demonstrates to each player the strategy he should choose to maximize his advantage and thus introduces the concepts of strategies, high risk and low risk moves, alternative outcomes, and minimax and other prudential solutions.

The application of the theory in archaeology and anthropology is usually based on the assumption that over long periods of trial and error cultural systems and subsystems adaptively shake down within a schedule of satisfactory if not optimal moves – resembling a player who may have to make his moves without precise foreknowledge of how his opponent will move but with a body of past experience which assists him to make a decision in such a way that, had he known his opponent's move, he would still have reached the same decision. The theory and its models are therefore potentially very well suited to simulating changes in economic systems operating within a changing environment and it may well prove possible to "game" the optimal or least-risk schedule of resource exploitation within the annual routine of a hunter-fisher-gatherer band or its adaptive "best moves" through a series of environmental changes – thus producing predictive models that could be tested by excavation and analysis in a specific context. Some elementary game theory models have already been used to simulate economic transactions and at the general level of archaeological theory (Clarke, 1968, pp. 94–96; Gould, 1969).

The richness and complexity of decision system and variable system models may be elaborated by building mixed models harnessing chains

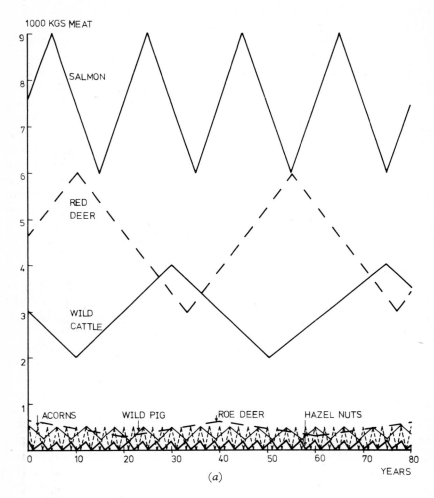

Fig. 15. A schematic model of the cumulative consequences of fluctuating food resources. The model has been devised for a population hunting-fishing-gathering a small inland territory of several kilometres radius, with a salmon river: perhaps a Mesolithic group in Britain or northern France after the oak/hazel maximum *ca* 5500–3000 B.C. The value of the oscillating resources has been taken from recorded pre-industrial annual game returns, assuming a culling factor which will allow the survival of the stock at a constant level. (*a*) gives the demographic and natural order of fluctuation of the key resources. (*b*) gives the summation of these fluctuating resources over eighty years and illustrates one reason why the demographic optimum capacity for such an

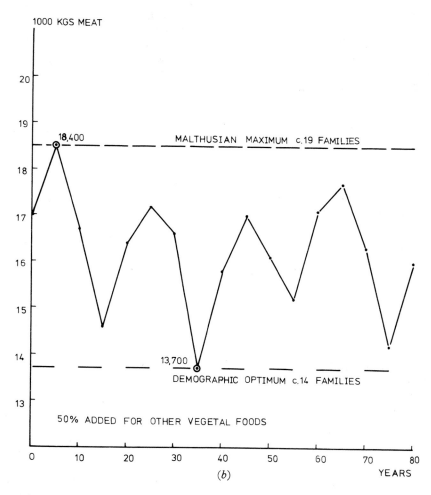

(b)

area is considerably lower than its hypothetical carrying capacity – the dynamic, dia-chronic model explains what a static synchronic study would find inexplicable.

The importance of resource oscillations and cycles as a source of population control and as an economic governor operates at three levels: (i) the annual cycle with a season of minimal resources; (ii) the successive annual oscillations with inevitable periodic 'bad years' when cycles in major and primary resources randomly coincide (as in this figure); (iii) occasional disastrous years or runs of years in which the factors above are accidentally exacerbated by bad weather or disease at crucial periods.

of decisions to networks of variables. At this level these artificial
theoretical models intergrade with system models abstracted from real-
world situations, past or present, used as analogies for archaeological
situations. Such real-world analogues may be selected with varying justification and skill from every aspect of the physical world and its
human record in history and ethnography. These analogues extend, of
course, from system models "built down" from particular real-life
cycles or generalized from world ethnographic data, to the humble level
of simple material analogies between artefacts.

Leaving aside models derived from the physical world for the
moment, we can now perceive that we have stumbled into the morass
of debate about the proper and improper use of historical and ethnographic "parallels" in archaeological interpretation. Extracting ourselves momentarily, it suddenly becomes clear that this ancient battle-
ground is merely a particular setting of the universal debate about
the proper and improper use of models in general. In this light, the
archaeological polarization into opponents and supporters of historic-
ethnographic models is seen as inappropriate – the book that has yet to
be written must instead distinguish and elucidate the valid procedures
for using these models and also define their inadmissible usage. Having
identified this front as but a part of the battle to clarify the proper use
of models, it is apparent that the dangers of historic-ethnographic analogues are simply those shared by all examples of model abuse, misuse
and profanation; the overwhelming justification for the need to explore
rather than ignore the use of models in archaeology (see Introduction
to this paper, pp. 21–25.

Models derived from historical and ethnographic situations may
range from simple material parallels to abstract systems of relationships,
and from metaphorical scene-setting to detailed predictive schemes. In
this complexity of levels and degrees of application lies one of the difficulties of generalizing rules for the proper use of all historic-ethnographic models in all archaeological situations. Nevertheless, we may
at least make some relevant observations.

1. We have learned that it is a general property of models that many
   different models will fit a given situation (see pp. 21–25). There are
   always many different historic-ethnographic models that could be
   found to fit an archaeological situation; it is no solution to stop looking after sighting the first. Therefore, goodness of fit is not sufficient
   justification for selecting one particular analogy – detailed if limited
   comparability must be established in terms of explicit criteria, which
   comparative ethnology must then confirm as functionally related to
   some constants shared by the archaeological case and the ethno-

graphic set (e.g., shellfish-gathering communities with a primitive technology, say) (Levine, 1969).

2. Historic-ethnographic analogies generate potential models for isomorphic archaeological observations – history and ethnology provide alternative models, only archaeology can test their applicability in a given archaeological context. Otherwise we perpetrate the circularity of using the same ethnographic data to derive *and* to support an interpretation, often tacitly on the first leg and then explicitly on the second leg of the argument (Clarke, 1968, pp. 59–60, 442–443, 646–648; Levine, 1969; Hill in Longacre, 1970, p. 51).

3. The exclusive use of historic-ethnographic models in archaeological interpretation must follow a tacit assumption that there has been no greater range of hominid behavioural and artefact variability over 2 million years than has been recorded in the minuscule sample of recent written histories and ethnographies – when surely we not only admit that the recorded variability is itself a tiny sample but that it is also the product of continuous adaptation from the infinitely greater set of fossil, now extinct, behaviour patterns that we wish to identify in order to trace and explain the disappearance of some and the survival of others. It would not only be poor science but it would be a scientific tragedy if we forced the social and economic life of *Australopithecus* into the recent pattern of either so-called modern "Primitives" or the highly evolved pattern of the modern apes. Uniformitarianism has proved a principle applicable at only the crudest level in interpreting the past, whether in geology or archaeology; certainly the patterns and processes of past hominid behaviour are related to those still observable to this day but the survivors are transformed relations, with many new additions and lacking many forms once existing (Binford, 1968).

Whether it is a bone with a hole in it from the Upper Palaeolithic and an Eskimo analogue, or the social pattern of the Arikara and Murdock's social structures extracted from the files of the Cross-Cultural Survey of 250 recent societies, goodness of fit is not enough. It must be supplemented by a case for comparability and must be tested against the archaeological record; even then, the historic-ethnographic model is no more than a powerful supplementary means of generating hypotheses to be added to the *a priori* models and hypotheses imagined, deduced or dreamed by the archaeologist from the direct scrutiny of the archaeological evidence. Only the latter procedure could possibly reveal to us that in Neanderthal society, say, the women did the hunting, clustered in bands of up to 300, each served by only a handful of males.

The great majority of real-world models employed in archaeology arise from historical or ethnographic contexts and their records and artefacts. However, no source is excluded as a means of generating models and hypotheses to be tested in archaeological settings – the analogy may come from the movements of molecules in a gas, the mutual adjustments of magnets floating in a bath, or the boundary patterns of bubbles in a soap film. Models derived from the physical world, in its broadest sense, may be as homomorphic with an archaeological situation as any "parallel" derived from ethnography or anthropology. Indeed, such a model is likely to be considerably more general and powerful than the latter class of analogy. The model derived from the physical world and the archaeological situation being modelled, upon closer investigation, may usually be shown to share latent structural similarities of a mathematical nature – the model from the physical world is but a particular representation, easily perceived, of a previously unnoticed and more general mathematical model. In this way, the molecular movements in a gas may model a situation in archaeological diffusion, but beneath both may lie the theory of probability and random interaction (see earlier sketch of Danubian I random walk settlement model). The polygonal territories of the floating magnets and the hexagonal patterns of bubbles in a soap film may illustrate the locational and territorial structures of archaeological settlement systems and geographical theory, but beneath both stretches the formal concepts of packing theory and optimized networks (Chorley and Haggett, 1967, Plates 17.8–17.13).

Physical hardware and theoretical models derived from the real world therefore take their place with artefact and structural models extracted from ethology, ethnology, sociology and anthropology. In their hardware forms these models approach the "pole" of simple material analogues to the far east of the chart (Fig. 2) in a meridian shared by the artificial hardware models on the far west and we have now completed our cursory glance at the model map. This chart of operational models is not an original one, it is badly copied from the work of a distinguished early cartographer (Chorley in Chorley and Haggett, 1967, Fig. 3.1). Neither is it the only possible map – other projections with different categorizations are both useful and desirable for plotting special courses. At least some of the monsters painted as lying in wait for the intrepid explorer may now be seen to be either avoidable or mythical and it may be admitted that a greater knowledge of model lands is preferable to navigation in ignorance. The fashionable nature of model cartography is then revealed not as a contemporary parlour game but rather as an important early elucidatory phase shared by primitive disciplines exploring their domains.

DISCUSSION AND SPECULATION

Archaeological interpretation changes generation by generation, and we are accustomed to interpret this succession as "progress". But is it? There is an uncomfortable suspicion that much of this change is directionless and that the changes we may wish to see as cumulative progress towards more exact knowledge are little more than a succession of contemporary mythologies. If there is some justice in this view, then the cause is clear – only the explicit construction and testing of archaeological models can provide the progressive cycle by means of which fresh information is gained, theory is accumulated and the cumulative knowledge within the discipline expanded. The development of powerful and explicit archaeological operational models, however, itself depends on the careful consideration of the cognitive models that frame *their* development, the controlling models generated by the system of philosophy, paradigms, methodology and aims of archaeologists and archaeology (Fig. 1).

Following Kuhn's philosophy of disciplines we have noted that contemporary archaeology exhibits all the characteristics of diverse and rapid change on an almost international front. After perhaps half a century of relatively steady change within a compartmented but broadly universal artefact-based, particularizing, qualitative, culture historical paradigm expressed in literary narrative clichés, we now have at least four newly formulated competing approaches, which we have crudely designated the morphological, anthropological, ecological and geographical paradigms. These new paradigms are clearly themselves transient phenomena, although that may mean a generation or more of independent existence; they share a wider philosophy than artefact classification, and a generalizing, quantitative, experimental attitude expressed in literary and symbolic jargon. They are also cross-cut by a number of new methodologies, which may change independently of the paradigms that share them (Fig. 16). This broad common basis to the group of currently rather partisan paradigms suggests at least the possibility that they will in due course merge within a new conformity. Nevertheless, at the moment each paradigm is intent on asserting its reasonable claims to existence and discarding the shackles that formerly bound it within the "traditionalist" paradigm. Since we have argued that the proper use of our operational models will be controlled by our preferred paradigm, let us take a brief look at the positions of these freshly polarized positions (Clarke, 1969, 1970b).

The position of the *morphological paradigm* embraces the expanding nucleus of studies whose main objectives are the cross-cultural definition of widely general regularities in the structural morphology of

NEW ARCHAEOLOGY	NEW PARADIGMS			
NEW METHODOLOGY	*Morphological Paradigm*	*Anthropological Paradigm*	*Ecological Paradigm*	*Geographical Paradigm*
New Field Methodology	Problem focused excavation, Area study and site system approach, Sampling considerations and methods, Pre-excavation and post-depositional model studies, Full use of scientific aids for location, processing and analysis of sites and deposits, including fine sieving, flotation and centrifuging, etc.			
	+	+	+	+
Model Methodology	Explicit development, borrowing and modification of appropriate models; thus Fig. 2: Observations, Models, Hypotheses, Experimentation and testing, Analysis of results, Interim conclusions and theory, Reappraisal of observations: repeat cycle.			
	+	+	+	+
System Theory Methodology	Cybernetic models for the pattern of system variables and their relationships, correlations, etc., or decisions and the flow of energy, mass, commodities, and information changes.			
	+	+	+	+
Quantitative Methodology	Counting and measuring *significant* variables and parameters to give values to the system models.			
	+	+	+	+
Mathematical Methodology	Natural languages and machinery for the expression of generalizations, especially quantifiable ones, Mathematical notation and expression, Statistical notation and analyses, Numerical taxonomic expression and measurements, Probability theory and methods, Error and confidence estimates, etc.			
	+	+	+	+
Computer Methodology	Analog and digital techniques for experimentation, simulation, analysis, visual display and graphics.			

FIG. 16. An earlier diagram suggested that changes in contemporary paradigms and methodology are the main stimuli that lead to new archaeological views (Fig. 1). This figure defines the "New Archaeology" as a bundle of such newly focused paradigms (pp. 26–27), bound by a related ideology and cross-cut by new developments in methodology. In reality, the discrete orthogonally intersecting categories must be conceived as irregular, blurred and mutually intersecting complex sets.

archaeological entities, as defined in terms of their components, the integration of these entities in yet higher organizations, and the exposition of the grammar of their development transformations (Clarke, 1968, Fig. 40; Deetz, Fig. 17). The studies within this nucleus are much concerned with the basic common particles of "implement-focused archaeology – attributes, artefacts, types, assemblages, cultures, culture groups and other complexes of material artefacts – together with their static and dynamic configurations. The basis upon which this approach is founded seems to be an explicit modern reformulation of the Montelian Principle that every artefact entity is related to every other artefact entity, but near entities are more related than distant entities, where "nearness" is a three-dimensional measure of nearness in space and time distribution, nearness in associations, and nearness in taxonomic affinity.

The advocates of this approach are perhaps more intimately concerned with the mathematical, statistical and computing machinery of the "new methodology" than any other group, but not exclusively so. This concern obviously follows the attempt to quantify and measure "nearness" in the relationships observed in the data and may perhaps lead to some kind of "taxonometrics".

The critics of this developing polarization suggest that it is too much concerned with crude, generalized regularities and that it is merely an abstract and sterile revival of the old typological and classificatory approaches of the last century, decked out in borrowed finery. These accusations imply an unduly atomistic approach with a tendency to treat complex entities as billiard balls, without sufficient regard for the social and ecological environments of the once living contexts. The partisans would dismiss these charges as romantic misrepresentations of the initial treatment of empirical data – claiming that the individual sources of variability sought by the other paradigms may *only* be recovered and identified when separated from the despised general regularities shared by structurally comparable entities. They would further point out that archaeological classification has remained a contentious and intuitive skill because its purposes and procedures have never been subjected to explicit discussion, measurement and quantitative tests. Indeed, the morphologists have succeeded in establishing that behind the seeming first-order information on the presence–absence and dimensions of attributes, once thought to have been the prime factors in archaeological classification, lies a second order in which every attribute itself has attributes of space and time distribution, association patterns, and affinity with other attributes. Thus the gap between taxonomic classification and intuitive classification is not fundamentally altered by differing purposes, but only separated by the difficulty of putting into explicit practice procedures that may be furtively half-accomplished in the brain (Clarke, 1970a, Chaps 3 and 4).

The *anthropological paradigm* reflects the interesting nucleus of studies that focus on the relationships between patterning and variability in archaeological data and patterning and variability in the social structures behind that data. The philosophy involved seeks a probabilistic mean path between the usual archaeological positions, which either assert that nothing can be deduced about the social attributes of archaeological entities, or tacitly assumes a naively simple equivalence at the other extreme. The partisans point out that social conventions and organizations, although weird and wonderful arrays of strange stochastic elements, nevertheless represent important and successful adaptive mechanisms. Where they are adaptively useful they will rise again and again and we then note them as an anthropological regularity or pattern. Where they are or become adaptively neutral they remain idiosyncratic, unlikely to be repeated and therefore not a recurrent pattern; where a social structure becomes disadvantageous and non-adaptive it dies out. Thus social conventions and organizations such as kinship and taboo systems possess important adaptive qualities, they vary with environment and as such are an interesting source of archaeological variability.

However, the anthropological approach goes further than a restricted interest in social structure. The proper use of anthropological and ethnological evidence and models in archaeological interpretation is a central concern. Here, too, there are clear emergent attempts to introduce quantification and measurements from anthropological analogues, if only to produce archaeological discussions in terms of appropriate orders of magnitude – the sizes of social units, crop yields under various conditions, the numbers of pots a household smashes in a year, the number of axes a man uses in a lifetime – crude improvizations in "ethnometrics".

The critics of this paradigm find its practitioners anthropologically under-equipped and over-naïve (Allen and Richardson, 1971). The machinery for expressing the relationships between archaeological and social entities are thought to be inadequate, and doubt is expressed about the possibility of separately distinguishing the archaeological variability arising from social sources and variability arising from other sources. The partisans react by pointing out control cases where variability in social structure is undubitably correlated with variability in material artefacts. Then, it is argued, although your specialist material may not appear to preserve this category of variability – in stone artefacts, perhaps – at least it is a potential source of variability which must be sought for and allowed for.

The practitioners within the *ecological paradigm* follow a contrasting theme, which may be epitomized by the comment of Reed (1963, p. 205): "who – except possibly archaeologists – would dig for artefacts when there are bones to be salvaged", where seeds, pollen and other floral, faunal and environmental evidence might be substituted for "bones". They would see their sphere as the study of the relationships between configurations of archaeological material and the environmental context in which it was once set, the mutual relations between such systems and their local ecology, together with the temporal and regional adaptive changes of these systems. This bold band talks of habitats, demes, clines, niches, trophic levels, biomes and ecosystems, and would see archaeology as a biological science connecting hominid behaviour with the variety in the environment of the globe in terms of energy exchange systems.

The cultural ecologists point with disdain to the infinitesimal pedantry of the archaeological taxonomist and to the contradictory conclusions of decades of dusty categorization more akin to philately than to the study of the unique 2-million-year-deep record of hominid behaviour patterns. They would contrast this with their increasingly quantified catchment analysis studies and the potentially fundamental measurements of energy flow and activity efficiency in energetics and thermodynamics.

Unabashed by these gibes, the critics of the ecological paradigm claim that the study has simply elevated the bathwater to a greater level of importance than the baby. The approach is improperly equipped to formulate biological statements, it is currently naive in its understanding of the samples that constitute its own raw material and anachronistically determinist in making insufficient allowance for the idiosyncratic degrees of freedom permitted to human activities in even the most constrained conditions. At its worst, the ecological paradigm merely substitutes the differential minutiae of bone or seed measurements for those of typology and transfers doubtful behavioural generalities from medieval peasants and song birds to prehistoric hominids, whilst its reports often regress to the level of the nineteenth century, simply illustrating a few archaeological *belles pièces*.

The *geographical paradigm* concentrates instead on the evidence relating within-site and between-site activity patterns with spatial patterning in artefact, feature, structure and site distributions; the study of archaeological sites as systems within systems of sites territorially distributed over landscapes. Starting with the within-site approach of architectural locational theory, sites are seen as encapsulating complex sets

D. L. CLARKE

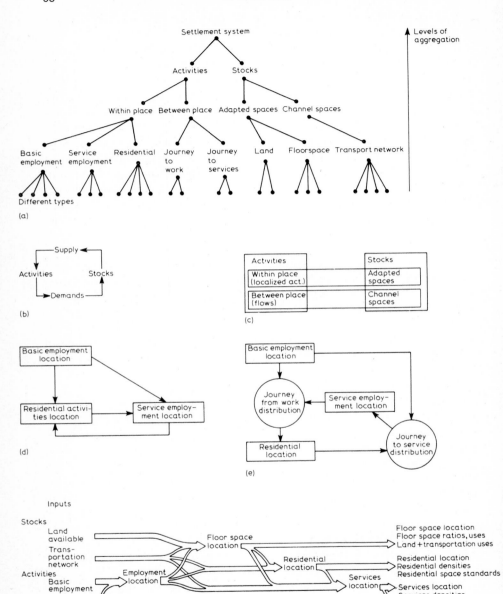

(a)

(b)

(c)

(d)

(e)

(f)

of man–man relationships in a spatial system in which activity patterns demand a building stock infrastructure, which, once built, itself restricts the further location of activities (Fig. 17) (March and Echenique, 1971). This model may then be extended to the scale of between-site relationships within settlement systems or hierarchies. Space and surface then become relativistic notions so that camp sites, farmsteads, villages, hill forts, *oppida,* and other extinct and contemporary settlement forms, influence the properties of the space around them; varying patterns of human activity thus form fields of influence which distort the properties of space (Harvey, 1969, p. 209). The relationships of a site system or artefact distribution become relative to some surface – it may be a two-dimensional map, a three-dimensional topography, or a demographic, environmental, economic iso-cost surface; regularities and patterning may appear if an appropriate surface is mapped and necessary transformations employed (Fig. 4) (Harvey, 1969, pp. 219–229).

Archaeologists working in this area can make use of the great body of locational theory and the well-established methods of measuring spatial relationships or quantifying site utilities (Cole and King, 1969). Thus Zipf's principle that the volume of activity over distance declines as a function of the distance from the reference site provides a frame for archaeological catchment area analysis and the Chinese Box territorial models. Even gravity models may be employed to simulate interaction between activities within sites, or between sites within systems (Fig. 18). These techniques have already been used with great success to model and predict the relative locations of 33 pre-Hittite towns in Bronze Age Anatolia, for example (Tobler and Wineburg, 1971). These and many other theories and measures are fundamentally relevant to the spatial information enshrined in archaeological observations.

The critics of this approach are vociferous (Taylor, 1970). They rightly criticize the unthinking transference of geographical models derived from perfect information and modern world situations to fragmentary time-palimpsest archaeological samples, imperfectly known

---

FIG. 17. Some elementary architectural models for the analysis of within-site structures and activity patterns (Echenique, 1971). (*a*) Levels of resolution of settlement models. (*b*) Relationship at the first level of disaggregation, by which activities demand stock of infrastructure; once built it restricts the further location of activities. (*c*) Relationships between the elements at the second level of disaggregation. (*d*) The structure of the Lowry within-place location model. (*e*) The Garin–Lowry activity location model in which the interactions of within-place activities are expressed as flows (between-place activities). (*f*) The simple static model contains the interaction of all the elements of the settlement spatial structure at the third level of disaggregation (stocks and activities).

and in prehistoric contexts. However, the partisans observe that this is simply a criticism of the improper use of models, and claim that it is nevertheless possible to adapt and adopt geographical models, after

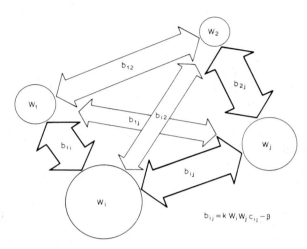

Fig. 18. Gravity model to simulate interaction between activities within sites, or between sites within systems (Echenique, 1971). The interaction (b_{ij}) between two within-place activities (W_i and W_j) is directly proportional to the product of the within-place activities and inversely proportional to some power of the cost of travel $(c_{ij} - \beta)$ separating them.

$$b_{ij} = k \frac{W_i W_j}{c_{ij} \beta},$$

where b_{ij} = traffic between zone i and j, k = constant of proportionality, W_i = within-place activity (e.g., residents) at zone i, W_j = within-place activity (e.g., residents) at zone j, c = cost of travel between zones i and j, β = parameter.

carefully rethinking them from the base upwards. In their more excited moments the partisans suggest that the locational theory of the geographers is a post-industrial, recent limiting case of an as yet latent and more general locational theory. Thus geographers regard settlement location, and therefore the central place theory describing it, as an economic process to which non-economic processes contribute a "noise" or error-term element (Harvey, 1969, pp. 118–120, 128, 139). However, archaeological and ethnographic data rather suggest that central place theory is the limiting case – observed for modern, Western communities in which the economic factor has been deliberately and especially intensified – of a more general locational theory in which site

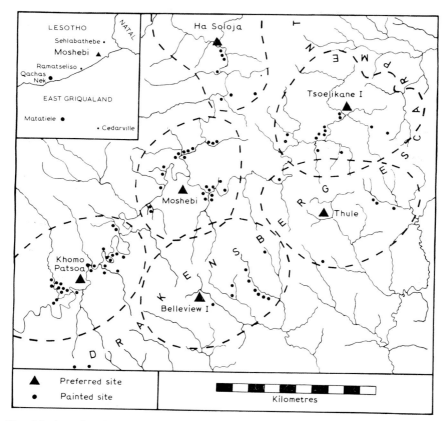

FIG. 19. A study of the site categories, site systems, base camps and satellite painted sites of prehistoric hunter-fisher-gatherers in eastern Lesotho (from Carter, 1970).

location is a multifactor process, which in different contexts may have differently weighted and selected variables.

   Thus aspects of central place theory appear to work where they ought not to work, in contexts where optimalization, rationalized planning, even towns and villages are not found, in systems of base camps, cemeteries, communal tombs, and hill forts (Fig. 17, 19) (Clarke, 1968, Figs 113–115; Carter, 1970, Fig. V). The more general theory seems to stem from the complex operation of packing theory upon mutually adjusted populations and their material insignia, in which a certain range of proximity of certain elements, sites or resources is essential for the system's functioning. In this view, long-term adaptive human behavioural, demographic, social and environmental processes dominate the satisfaction of mere economic requirements. If there is any truth in these partisan thoughts, and they at least make stimulating speculation, then the 2 million years record of archaeology and recent ethnology must have a major role to play in the elucidation of this important general behaviour and locational theory.

At the minimal level, the geographical paradigm in archaeology would rest its case on three salient points.

1. Even if it may not be possible to recover the contemporary elements in an archaeological site system, at least it must be admitted that different kinds of site existed in systems of relationships over landscapes and must be so hypothesized.
2. It should be possible to postulate an "idealized site system" from the integration of the fragmentary evidence of neighbouring regions; like an "ideal gas" this model then becomes predictive and allows itself to be tested and refined against evidence and experiment.
3. Indeed, inter-site adjustment across landscape *is* observed in complex archaeological data and *must* be explained; although the explanations may in many cases discover the distribution to be a sampling artefact.

Now, if we make the vain attempt to detach ourselves from the tyranny of the particular paradigms, some interesting common elements emerge from this explosion of anti-traditionalist views.

1. The new paradigms mark the full recognition that the domain of archaeology is greater than the realm of material implements. They show that there is a wider information pool than simply observations on material culture, and even material culture is seen to contain more and different kinds of information than previously assumed. The material equipment must be put in perspective as only *one* category of the artefacts of hominid behaviour – all of which preserve for us some overlapping information on the activities of our ancestors.
2. The new paradigms individually represent the exploitation of particular new spheres of information – morphological, social, environmental and spatial. They are preoccupied with the patterning and variability of their own limited information pool; indeed one would have a greater confidence in the claimed identifications of particular

sources of variability if each researcher had taken into account the variability sources sought by the others, and other than the one he was determined to find. Most archaeological data embrace many sources of variability in a cumulative but non-additive pattern, including very gross sampling sources of imposed variability (see Daniels, 1972, Figs 5.1–5.3).

3. The preoccupation with single aspects of variability in the archaeological record is carefully justified in some cases, in others it is the accident of the exclusive interest of the observer – a victim of his own controlling models and the dimensions of variability peculiar to the material that he knows well and extrapolates to the rest of archaeology. In the Palaeolithic we have stone plus a little bone and a few sites; in the Neolithic we have stone plus pottery and more sites; in the Metal Age we have stone, pots, metals, many sites of many categories, and many house and settlement plans. It is not surprising that each paradigm pursues its source of information in restricted archaeological contexts where temporal scale and observations are of a special kind.

4. Finally, we may note that each paradigm is struggling to produce a scheme of measurement and quantification in relation to its own dimensions – taxonometrics, ethnometrics, energetics, measures of utility, relative distance and interaction. Contrary to common opinion archaeology is made difficult by the very variety of potentially measurable elements and the choice which this presents.

Do these developments represent a "New Archaeology"? If so, how does it relate to "Traditionalist Archaeology"? Well, of course, it depends on the point of view of the observer. When viewed at a fine level all the strands of the "new" developments go back into the last century and beyond. When viewed at a coarse level what emerge are new configurations of old elements within a rather different philosophy, with different modes of expression and a different approach to those that preceded it and distinguished from them by a spasm of greatly increased rate of change and innovation, when compared with the preceding phase of development. Precariously trying to preserve our balance, these "new" developments would appear to be different but not necessarily better than their traditional antecedents, which continue in a flourishing form. They would, however, appear to have rapidly expanded into hitherto little-explored areas of the archaeological domain and to have infiltrated freshly available niches with a vigorous capacity to make fresh contributions to the discipline as a whole.

It is hardly surprising that when questioned some archaeologists would say that a "New Archaeology" does not exist – it does not exist for them; others would claim that it does exist but then differ about what it is, depending upon which of the new paradigms they espouse. It is clear, at least, that the term "New Archaeology" has been directly borrowed from the infant "New Geography". That prodigy seems to have been named by analogy with the Renaissance and in memory of Galileo's fundamental treatise on physics and mechanics, "Two New Sciences" (1610), and Bacon's "The New System" (*Novum Organum*, 1620). In terms of these analogies it is quite clear what "New" means – it implies a new philosophical position, an experimental, generalizing, theory-developing approach, with an empirical emphasis upon the formulation and testing of hypotheses, and following Bacon in his glorification of mathematics as "the Queen of the Sciences" and Galileo's dictum that "the book of Nature is written in a Mathematical language; without its help it is impossible to comprehend a single work therein".

Under this view there is a case for extending the nomenclature to the "New Archaeology", which may be represented by the bundle of newly focused paradigms bound by their new ideology and cross-cut by the new methodology, of which explicit model-using is a fundamental part (Fig. 16). It is then possible to set up a contrasting impression of the "New" and "Traditionalist" archaeology, which antagonists are quick to see as a new versus old confrontation. However, as we shall argue, both approaches have their vices and virtues, the new will become old and the old will continue and give rise to yet newer paradigms; their roles are complementary and mutually useful. For

	Traditionalist archaeology	New archaeology
Philosophy	Historical	Experimental
Approach	Qualitative	Quantitative
	Particularizing	Generalizing
Modes of expression	Literary	Symbolic
	Narrative	Jargon
Attitude	Isolationist and authoritarian	Condisciplinary and anarchic

example, the mathematical and model symbolism of the "New Archaeology" communicates to a wider audience of scientists and mathematicians, whereas the style of "Traditionalist" literature is more acceptable to the non-scientist. In other words, together they will draw upon a greatly enlarged pool of informants and information, and the artificial confrontation may be avoided by combining the elements from each column in many different ways for many different purposes.

NEW ARCHAEOLOGY

1. *Experimental* Let us assume (or if we assume) *a*, *b*, *c*, then *d*, *e*, *f* should follow. Question – do we observe *d*, *e*, *f*? Experiment – Answer. The development of a model with explicit assumptions – formation of hypotheses from the model – test the hypotheses experimentally, or test between the consequences thereof.

2. *Quantitative* Counting and measuring reduce vagueness, increase specificity, upgrade standards of argument, allow error estimates, numerical manipulation and explicit *testing* of model hypotheses.

3. *Generalizing* It is necessary to generalize in order to make probabilistic predictions about some class of items; we must generalize in order that we may particularize more powerfully. The inevitable use of classes of items requires appropriate classifications. In archaeology some information is more important than other information for certain purposes; therefore what is classificatory information depends upon the purpose.

4. *Symbolic* The use of mathematical, statistical and numerical languages in addition to prose. Symbolic languages are the natural model of expression for generalizations; in addition they are interdisciplinary and international means of communication over and above ordinary language, a series of *lingua franca*. Conveniently, mathematics solves puzzles even before a real-world example of the puzzle has been identified.

5. *Jargon* The use of condensed special-purpose code to express complex analogies; ugly and deplorable from the point of view of prose but aesthetics are not the prime criteria of communication within specialized disciplines; in any event, yesterday's jargon is tomorrow's prose (Clarke, 1970, p. 26).

6. *Overall attitude* Out-turned, across archaeological specializations and between disciplines, over paradigms, through regional schools and linguistic blocs (Kolchina and Shera, 1970); hence the role of interconnecting jargon, symbolic languages and the interdisciplinary exchange of isomorphic models (Clarke, 1968, p. 646). Although fraught with dangers this attitude allows the possibility that archaeology can make outward contributions to other disciplines, an essential feature if the discipline is to survive; this outward contribution has already begun on a small scale towards branches of mathematics, computer studies and classification, and to the social and behavioural sciences. Within the discipline a fresh freedom is allowed to choose alternative space scales, different mapping sur-

faces, varied geometries; we can use diverse process time-scales, alternative mathematical notations and variform symbolic languages; we can select different frames of reference, different sample spaces, classifications, entities, attributes, relationships and parameters. What may appear irregular under one view may emerge as a patterned and powerful regularity under another transformation.

CONCLUSION

It has already been suggested that the contemporary flowering of rival archaeological paradigms is a transient phenomenon and that these may, in due course, recombine within a new conformity founded on the broad common basis in methodology and ideology. However, this integration cannot take the form of a simple physical merging of views, or the tying together of a bundle of unrelated approaches with decorative ribbon, which so frequently stands for an integrated interdisciplinary approach. We have seen that preoccupation with a single paradigm leads to a dangerous preoccupation with a single set of sources of variability, leading only to an unbalanced interpretation and a new sectarianism. Instead we must turn to our advantage the many sources of archaeological variability and the many disciplinary domains that specially describe them. This can be achieved by using models from other disciplines to generate hypotheses about a particular archaeological situation and then using the archaeological evidence to test those hypotheses; similarly, archaeological models describing different sources of variability can be used to control and test one another. Thus non-artefactual data should be used to try and test hypotheses derived from other classes of data, and vice versa. In all this, the testing of models and hypotheses will be much enhanced by the embryonic developments in quantification, which we have already noted within all the separate paradigms.

In so far as there might be said to be a New Archaeology with a New Methodology and a New Ideology, we can see that it is a composite but convergent development of much older ideas – it is only new in terms of the particular patterning and integration of older elements, and in its quite proper attempt to explore the boundary possibilities of archaeology and to open up new ground. It does not replace Old Archaeology but rather augments it, as we learn from the theory of the cumulative development of paradigms. However, neither may these new developments simply be dismissed on the basis of their fashionable vogue and contemporary jargon; these are part of its outward connections. The New Archaeology has already begun to yield new kinds of information, to offer new solutions to some old problems and to show that other old problems were caused by attempting the impossible with the implausible. In addition, the strong theoretical content of the New Archaeology offers the beginnings for a strong and international body of explicit archaeological theory and methodology – where it should be remembered that a healthy discipline is defined not only by its particular body of observations but by the vigorous network of theory and methodology reticulating its parts. Indeed, it is the corpus of theory and methodology of greater than regional and sectarian importance that is the vital element that serves to coagulate those parts within the whole of one discipline – the theory that makes explicit how we do what we already do intuitively, and more, providing the basic tenets of the discipline in a form as appropriate in Peru as Persia, Australia as Alaska, Sweden as Scotland, on material from the twentieth millennium B.C. to the second millennium A.D.

It is clearly going to be very important to avoid needless and wasteful conflict of all kinds, between partisans of the various paradigms, or between the generations over the New Archaeology, much of which is unsound (intermediate imperfect), and Traditionalist Archaeology, much of which is equally unsound but which is nevertheless the foundation of much that is useful (complementary not rival elements in the same mosaic). Statistical, taxonomic and computer archaeology are here to stay, together with the morphological, anthropological, ecological and geographical approaches. But they will very rapidly fade into perspective as means towards ends, intellectual machinery, which, as always, may be employed usefully or stupidly. The shock and novelty of these innovations will surely be as incomprehensible to future archaeologists as the terror caused by the early motor cars is now incomprehensible to us. Non-numerical "old archaeologists" will be delighted to find that their potential is in no way diminished and that there will always remain scope for an infinite amount of valuable narrative synthesis, and high-level intuitive speculation – except that *now* their research students will test their professors' dicta and not simply accept them.

REFERENCES

Allen, W. L. and Richardson, J. B. (1971). The reconstruction of kinship from archaeological data: the concepts, the methods and the feasibility, *American Antiquity*, **36** (1), 41–53.

Ascher, R. (1961). Experimental archaeology, *American Anthropologist*, **63** (4), 793–816.

Beach, E. F. (1957). *Economic Models*, Wiley, New York.

Binford, L. R. (1968). Post-Pleistocene adaptations, in *New Perspectives in Archeology* (S. R. Binford and L. R. Binford, eds), Aldine, Chicago, pp. 313–341.

Binford, L. R. (1972). Contemporary model building: paradigms and the current state of Palaeolithic research, in *Models in Archaeology* (D. L. Clarke, ed), Methuen, London, Chap. 3.

Binford, L. R. and Binford, S. R. (1966). A preliminary analysis of functional variability in the Mousterian of Levallois facies, *American Anthropologist*, **68** (2), 238–295.

Birabon, J. N. (1971). Les méthodes de la démographic préhistorique, *International Population Conference, London 1969*, **4**, 2315–2320, Liège.

Carneiro, R. L. (1960) Slash-and-burn agriculture: a closer look at its implication for settlement patterns, *Men and Cultures* (A. F. C. Wallace, ed), University of Pennsylvania Press, Philadelphia.

Carter, P. L. (1970). Moshebi's shelter: excavation and exploitation in eastern Lesotho, *Lesotho*, **1**.

Chang, K. C. (ed.) (1968). *Settlement Archaeology*, National Press, Palo Alto, Calif.

Chorley, R. J. and Haggett, P. (eds) (1967). *Models in Geography*, Methuen, London.

Clarke, D. L. (1968). *Analytical Archaeology*, Methuen, London.

Clarke, D. L. (1969). Towards analytical archaeology: new directions in the interpretative thinking of British archaeologists, in Symposium on Theory and Methodology in Archaeological Interpretation, Flagstaff, Arizona, 1968. (See this volume pp. 145–179.)

Clarke, D. L. (1970a). *Beaker Pottery of Great Britain and Ireland*, Cambridge University Press, Cambridge.

Clarke, D. L. (1970b). Analytical archaeology: epilogue, *Norwegian Archaeological Review*, **3**, 25–33.

Clarke, D. L. (1972). A provisional model of an Iron Age society and its settlement system, in *Models in Archaeology* (D. L. Clarke, ed.), Methuen, London, pp. 801–869.

Coe, M. D. and Flannery, K. V. (1964). Microenvironments and Mesoamerican prehistory, *Science*, **143** (3607), 650–654.

Coe, M. D. and Flannery, K. V. (1967). *Early Cultures and Human Ecology in South Coastal Guatemala*, Smithsonian Press, Washington.

Cole, J. P. and King, C. A. M. (1969). *Quantitative Geography: Techniques and Theories in Geography*, Wiley, London.

Coles, J. M. (1966). Experimental archaeology, *Proceedings of the Society of Antiquaries of Scotland*, **99**, 1–20.

Cook, S. F. and Heizer, R. F. (1969). Relationships among houses, settlement areas and population in aboriginal California, in *Settlement Archaeology* (K. C. Chang, ed.), National Press, Palo Alto, Calif., pp. 79–116.

Curry, L. (1967). Central places in the random spatial economy, *Journal of Regional Science*, **7** (2), supp., 217–238.

Daniels, S. G. H. (1972). Research design models, in *Models in Archaeology* (D. L. Clarke, ed.), Methuen, London, chap. 5.

Deetz, J. D. F. (1965). *The Dynamics of Stylistic Change in Arikara Ceramics*, Illinois Studies in Anthropology No. 4, University of Illinois Press, Urbana.

Deetz, J. D. F. (1967). *Invitation to Archaeology*, Natural History Press, New York.

Doran, J. (1970). Systems theory, computer simulations and archaeology, *World Archaeology*, **1** (3), 289–298.

Doran, J. E. (1972). Computer models as tools for archaeological hypothesis formation, in *Models in Archaeology* (D. L. Clarke, ed.), Methuen, London, Chap. 10.

Echenique, M. (1971). A model of the urban spatial structure, *Architectural Design*, **41**, 278–279.

Flannery, K. V. (1968). Archaeological systems theory and early Mesopotamia, in *Anthropological Archaeology in the Americas* (B. J. Meggers, ed.), Anthropological Society, Washington, D.C.

Freeman, J. D. (1955). *Iban Agriculture*, Colonial Research Studies No. 18, HMSO, London.

Gardin, J. C. (1965). Reconstructing an economic network in the ancient Near East with the aid of a computer, in *The Use of Computers in Anthropology* (D. Hymes, ed.), Mouton, The Hague, pp. 378–391.

Gardin, J. C. (ed.) (1970). *Atchéologie et Calculateurs*, Centre National de la Recherche Scientifique, Paris.

Garvin, P. L. (1965). Computer processing and cultural data: problems of method, in *The Use of Computers in Anthropology* (D. Hymes, ed.), Mouton, The Hague, pp. 119–139.

George, F. H. (1970). Heuristics: short cuts to better use of computers, *The Times*, 26 June 1970, 25.

Glover, J. C. (1969). The use of factor analysis for the discovery of artefact types. *Mankind*, **7** (1), 36–51.

Gould, P. R. (1969) Man against his environment: a game theoretic framework, in *Environment and Cultural Behaviour* (A. P. Vayda, ed.), Natural History Press, New York, pp. 234–251.

Haggett, P. (1965) *Locational Analysis in Human Geography*, Arnold, London.

Halsbury, Earl of (1968). "Time's Arrow": an informational theory treatment, *The Human Agent*, edited for the Royal Institute of Philosophy Lectures, vol. 1, 1966–7, Macmillan, London.

Harvey, D. (1969). *Explanation in Geography*, Arnold, London.

Hesse, M. B. (1963). *Models and Analogies in Science*, Sheed & Ward, London.

Higgs, E. (ed.) (1972). *Cambridge Papers in the Early History of Agriculture*, Cambridge University Press, Cambridge.

Higham, C. F. W. (1968). Patterns of prehistoric economic exploitation on the Alpine foreland, *Vierteljahrsschrift der Naturforschenden Gesellschaft in Zürich*, **113** (1), 41–92.

Hill, J. N. (1970). *Broken K Pueblo: Prehistoric Social Organization in the American Southwest*, Anthropological Papers of the University of Arizona No. 18.

Hodson, F. R. (1970). Cluster analysis and archaeology: some new developments and applications, *World Archaeology*, **1** (3), 299–320.

Isaac, G. Ll. (1969). Studies of early culture in east Africa, *World Archaeology*, **1** (1), 1–28.

Jarman, M. R. (1972). A territorial model for archaeology: a behavioural and geographical approach, in *Models in Archaeology* (D. L. Clarke, ed.), Methuen, London, Chap. 18.

Jewell, P. A. (ed.) (1963). *The Experimental Earthwork on Overton Down, Wiltshire*, 1960, British Association for the Advancement of Science, London.

Jewell, P. A. and Dimbleby, G. W. (1966). The experimental earthwork on Overton Down, Wiltshire, England: the first four years, *Proceedings of the Prehistoric Society*, **32**, 313–342.

Kemp, W. R. (1971). The flow of energy in a hunting society, *Scientific American*, **224** (3), 105–115.

Kolchina, B. A. and Shera, Y. A. (eds) (1970). *Statistiko-kombinatornye metody v arkheologii*, Akad. Nauk SSSR, Inst. Arkheologii, Moscow.

Kuhn, T. S. (1970). *The Structure of Scientific Revolutions*, 2nd ed., University of Chicago Press, Chicago.

Levine, M. H. (1969) Interpreting Palaeolithic art: some methodological considerations, in Symposium on Theory and Methodology in Archaeological Interpretation, Flagstaff, Arizona, 1968.

Lewis, B. N. and Woolfenden, P. J. (1969). *Algorithms and Logical Trees: A Self-Instructional Course*, Cambridge Algorithms Press, Cambridge.

Longacre, W. A. (ed.) (1970). *Reconstructing Prehistoric Pueblo Societies*, University of New Mexico Press, Albuquerque.

MacNeish, R. S. (1961). *First Annual Report of the Tehuacan Archaeological-Botanical Project*, Phillips Academy, Andover, Mass.

MacNeish, R. S. (1962). *Second Annual Report of the Tehuacan Archaeological–Botanical Project*, Phillips Academy, Andover, Mass.

McPherron, A. (1967). *Jutunen Site*, Anthropological Papers No. 30, University of Michigan Press, Ann Arbor.

March, L., Echenique, M. *et al.* (1971). Models of environment, *Architectural Design*, **41**, 275–320.

Meggers, B. J. (ed.) (1968). *Anthropological Archaeology in the Americas*, Washington Anthropological Society, Washington DC.

Mellaart, J. (1966). Excavations at Çatal Hüyük, *Anatolian Studies*, **16**, 26.

Nagel, E. (1961). *The Structure of Science*, Harcourt, Brace & World, New York.

Newcomb, R. M. (1968). Geographical location analysis and Iron Age settlement in West Penwith, *Cornish Archaeology*, **7**, 5–14.

Newcomb, R. M. (1970). A model of a mystery: the medieval parish as a spatial system, *Skrifter fra Geografisk Institut ved Aarhus Universitet*, **23**.

Rapoport, A. (1953). *Operational Philosophy*, Wiley, New York.

Rappaport, R. A. (1971). The flow of energy in agricultural society, *Scientific American*, **224** (3), 117–132.

Reed, C. A. (1973). Osteo-archaeology, in *Science in Archaeology* (D. Brothwell and E. Higgs, eds), Thames & Hudson, London, pp. 204–216.

Stone, E. H. (1924). *The Stones of Stonehenge*, Robert Scott, London.

Taylor, C. C. (1971). The study of settlement patterns in pre-Saxon Britain, in *Man, Settlement and Urbanism* (P. Ucko, R. Tringham and G. W. Dimbleby, eds), Duckworth, London, pp. 109–113.

Thomas, D. H. (1972). A computer simulation model of Great Basin Shoshonean subsidence and settlement patterns, in *Models in Archaeology* (D. L. Clarke, ed.), Methuen, London, Chap. 17.

Tobler, W. R. (1969). A computer movie simulating urban growth in the District region, *International Geographical Union Commission on Quantitative Geography*.

Tobler, W. R. and Wineburg, S. (1971). A Cappadocian speculation, *Nature*, **231**, 39–41.

Trigger, B. C. (1966). Settlement archaeology: its goals and promises, *American Antiquity*, **32**, 149–160.

Trigger, B. C. (1968). *Beyond History: The Methods of Prehistory*, Holt, Rinehart & Winston, New York.

Ucko, P., Tringham, R. and Dimbleby, G. W. (eds) (1971). *Man, Settlement and Urbanism*, Duckworth, London.

Vajda, S. (1960). *Introduction to Linear Programming and the Theory of Games*, Methuen, London.

Walker, I. C. (1967) Statistical models for dating clay pipe fragments, *Post-medieval*

Whallon, R. (1968) Investigations of late prehistorical social organization in New York, in *New Perspectives in Archaeology* (S. R. Binford and L. R. Binford, eds), Aldine, Chicago, pp. 223–244.

Archaeology: The Loss of Innocence

DAVID L. CLARKE

The loss of disciplinary innocence is the price of expanding consciousness; certainly the price is high but the loss is irreversible and the prize
substantial.

Although the loss of disciplinary innocence is a continuous process,
we can nevertheless distinguish significant thresholds in the transitions
from *consciousness* through *self-consciousness* to *critical self-consciousness* and
beyond. Consciousness is perhaps achieved when the discipline is
named and largely defined by specifying its raw material and by pragmatic practice – archaeology is what archaeologists do. Thenceforth,
the practitioners are linked within an arbitrary but common partition
of reality, sharing intuitive procedures and tacit understandings whilst
teaching by imitation and correction in the craft style (Alexander, 1964,
pp. 1–60).

Gradually consciousness develops into *self-consciousness* and sophistication erodes the paradigms of innocence. Self-consciousness dawns
with explicit attempts at self-knowledge – the contentious efforts to cope
with the growing quantity of archaeological observations by explicit
but debated procedures and the querulous definition of concepts and
classifications. The discipline emerges as a restless body of observations
upon particular classes of data, between a certain range of scales, held
together by a network of changing methodology and implicit theory.
Teaching, now formalized in academies and universities, attempts to
condense experience within general principles and explicit rules; it is
no longer possible either to teach or to learn the vast body of data and
complex procedures by rote. Instead, classes of data and approaches
are treated in terms of alternative models and rival paradigms; inevitably, the comparison of classes introduces counting and measuring
which in turn entails a modest amount of mathematical and statistical
methods and concepts.

Reprinted with permission from *Antiquity*, XLVII, 6–18, 1973.

This process is also marked by the emergence of competitive individualism and authority, since the individual's living depends on the reputation he achieves as a focus in the media or by innovation and intensive work in a specialist field. The politics and sociology of the disciplinary environment increasingly develop this "authoritarian" state in which each expert has a specialist territory such that criticisms of territorial observations are treated as attacks upon personalities. This gradually becomes a seriously counterproductive vestige of a formerly valuable disciplinary adaptation by means of which authorities mutually repelled one another into dispersed territories, thus effectively deploying the few specialists over the growing body of data.

So, the new sophisticates industriously subpartition their discipline; each group deepens their specialist cells by concentrated research, thereby unconsciously raising barriers to communication between archaeologists within the expanding mass of period, regional, topic, methodology and paradigm cells. These individual cells are clustered within and crosscut larger regional partitions based on the convergent involvement of localized groups of men with the same regionally peculiar range of archaeological phenomena within a common national, linguistic and educational environment—increasingly separating themselves from other groups of archaeologists confronting the same range of phenomena but not in the same particular form or national context. Self-conscious archaeology has become a series of divergent and self-referencing regional schools with cumulatively self-reinforcing archaeological education systems and with regionally esteemed bodies of archaeological theory and locally preferred forms of description, interpretation and explanation, where the political and sociological characteristics of individualism and authority complement the narrow specializations within divergent academic traditions. The prevailing feeling is "look how much we know" and the general impression is that the discipline hardly exists as one subject at all.

These unsatisfactory developments culminate in the emergence of a new level of disciplinary consciousness, *critical self-consciousness*, in which attempts are made to control the direction and destiny of the system by a closer understanding of its internal structure and the potential of the external environment. Focus switches from the heap of data to the vast sample space and the prevailing feeling is now "look how little we know and how inappropriate are our models and explanations". The general impression moves towards the position that archaeologists hold most of their problems in common and share large areas of general theory within a single discipline with regional manifestations. If the first revolution from consciousness to self-consciousness is mainly technical then this second threshold is largely a philosophical, metaphysical and theoretical one brought upon us by the consequences of the first (Clarke, 1970, p. 27; 1972*b*, pp. 7–10).

In the new era of critical self-consciousness the discipline recognizes that its domain is as much defined by the characteristic forms of its reasoning, the intrinsic nature of its knowledge and information, and its competing theories of concepts and their relationships – as by the elementary specification of raw material, scale of study, and methodology. Explanation, interpretation, concepts and theory become central topics of debate and develop the essential significance of archaeological logic, epistemology and metaphysics. It is apparent that archaeologists need to know about knowing and the limits of what they can and cannot know from the data and to know this by critical appraisal, not simply by assertion. Demoralizing but fundamental questioning develops – given what we now know about the limitations of the data, concepts and methods, how do we know what we appear to know reliably? Given that many explanations, models and theories may all be simultaneously appropriate at many different levels and in different contexts, how do we choose between them? The astringent scrutiny of articles of faith and the burden of choice indeed represent an ordeal by fire – a painful refinement in the critical flame.

The needs of teaching emerge as one of the main disciplinary propellants into the space of expanding consciousness – student and amateur provide the fuel, research sparks ignition and the disciplinary elders monitor and direct in a series of contradictory instructions. A new environment develops as students and amateurs of an ever-widening background emerge in increasing numbers and archaeological units of all kinds multiply outside as well as inside the old Euro-American centres. From the Antipodes to Africa the old regionally self-centred "colonial" concepts are severely challenged and their weaknesses gravely exposed in the wider general debate. Question leads to unrest, freedom to further self-consciousness and thought about thought, as the unformulated precepts of limited academic traditions give way to clearly formulated concepts whose very formulation leads to further criticism and more debate (Alexander, 1964, p. 58). The rate of change becomes as disconcerting as the uncertainty, insecurity and general unrest – no one can deny the high price of expanding consciousness.

It is as unrealistic to ignore this contemporary context of debate as it is to portray these changes as painless moves from historic ignorance to archaeological enlightenment; each archaeology is of its time but since many deplore the time they will certainly be unhappy with its archaeology. The disciplinary system is after all an adaptive one, related internally to its changing content and externally to the spirit of the times. Past archaeological states were appropriate for past archaeological contexts, and past explanations were very much related to past archaeological states of knowledge (e.g., short chronologies) and our own are no better in these respects. However, formerly adaptive qualities frequently become disadvantageous vices in new environments and if archaeological development is not too closely to resemble genetic ageing, with its dramatic terminus, then there has to be a critical and continuous monitoring process to regulate development. Otherwise there is an accumulation of errors and a build-up of multiple failures which would demand a simultaneous spasmodic correction of global proportions. In the extreme case, formerly adaptive, traditional archaeological positions can evolve in the new environment into mono-focal, monodimensional and myopic specialization, conformist authoritarianism, academic regionalism and individualism, archaeological isolationism and chauvinism; the attributes of a doomed race of disciplinary dinosaurs.

THE NEW ENVIRONMENT

The transition of archaeology from noble innocence to self-consciousness and critical self-consciousness has been artificially condensed within such a spasm of an unusually abrupt and severe kind. Historical and technological developments have coincided in a remarkably rapid change in disciplinary environment and content in the decades following World War II, compressing these phases of transition within the span of a working life-time, from the 1950s to the 1970s. The World War itself was not without significance in this social and scientific revolution. Externally, neighbouring disciplines were transformed by interrelated spasms which erupted in the New Mathematics, New Biology, New Geology, New Geography, New Social Studies, and the New Architecture. Internally, the number and variety of archaeological amateurs, students, teaching-staff, university departments, research units and excavations have globally doubled or trebled in comparison with the 1930s. Simultaneously, the major technical developments of wartime introduced fresh archaeological potential, ranging from heavy mechanical excavators to new underwater and aerial equipment, through applied mathematics to operational research, computer electronics and atomic physics. A quantitative and qualitative technical and social revolution quietly transformed world archaeology in a series of almost imperceptible piecemeal changes.

These crucial decades have seen not only the emergence of new men, new methods and new equipment but more men, methods and equipment in a greater variety than ever before. New observations,

new ideologies, new philosophies and therefore new aims uncomfort-
ably jostle earlier ones – the new scepticism, uncertainty and insecurity
painfully chafe the traditional security of innocence and the comforting
confidence of habitual operations.

Many archaeologists will be unwilling to face the challenge of the
new situation and may either entrench themselves in traditional positions or retreat within the logically impervious bastion of the freely creative artist. However, although these reactions are understandable they
are based upon two quite mistaken beliefs; that we can indefinitely
avoid the challenge of new conditions by returning to primitive paradigms; and that the deployment of artistry and imaginative creativity
have no place amongst the new materials and new approaches. By
retreating within traditional forms it is always possible to alleviate but
never to banish the fresh burden of new decisions (Alexander, 1964,
pp. 10–60). A new environment develops new materials and new
methods with new consequences, which demand new philosophies, new
solutions and new perspectives.

New methodology

Old methods have not only been extended in new ways but a huge
range of new methodology has sprung up which either extends our
archaeological senses by detecting more, different and previously unknown data attributes, or extends our capacity for information recovery, manipulation and analysis. A new field methodology has
emerged with new techniques for site location, combining aerial recon-
naissance with a range of resistivity, magnetometer, gradiometer, elec-
trolocation and chemical location methods. New large-scale techniques
with heavy machinery for area excavation are complemented by small-
scale techniques for the processing and analysis of sites and deposits –
photogrammetry, fine sieving, flotation, centrifuging – which provide
data of a kind previously unknown. Physical, chemical and botanical
techniques amplify our information about the sources, properties and
movements of organic remains, fauna, flora, stones, clays, pottery, glass,
resins and metals – using chromatography, thin section methods, heavy
mineral analyses, optical and electron microscopy, electron micro-
probes, optical emission spectrometry, infra-red spectroscopy, X-ray
fluorescence, diffraction and microanalysis, beta-ray back scatter, neutron activation techniques, and many others.

Archaeological scales for measuring and counting, the key to comparative analysis, have been transformed. Chronological measurement
has been reformed by the many isotope methods, thermoluminescence,
fission track, archaeomagnetic, hydration, volcanic tephrachronology,

fluorine/nitrogen and many comparable developments – with profound consequences. Measures and counts now abound in a field traditionally devoid of comparative scales – taxonometrics, ethnometrics, energetics, thermodynamics, information indices of structural complexity, economic measures of utility, spatial measures of distribution (Clarke, 1972b, p. 53). The proper treatment of qualitative and quantitative observations has introduced a welcome precision and a proper appreciation of error, facilitated the testing of predictions and, above all, such measurement structures have revealed new empirical relationships and generated fresh theory – new problems.

The realization has also dawned in archaeology that mathematical methodology, a massive field in itself, provides many new possibilities. The appreciation that these methods are languages of expression and deal as much with order and relationships as magnitudes has introduced almost every branch of mathematics into archaeological contexts – from mathematical logic, to axiomatics, set and group theory, vectors, topology, probability, statistics, boolean algebra, matrix algebra, n-space geometry, numerical taxonomy, error and confidence estimates, combinatorics, linear programming, game theory, optimization methods, location-allocation techniques and many more (Clarke, 1968; Gardin, 1970; Kolchina and Shera, 1970; Hodson, Kendall and Tautu, 1971).

These reinforcing developments in excavation, analysis, measurement and manipulative machinery give added scope to the two other major fields of methodological innovation – explicit model-using and experimentation, and the comprehensive theory of systems and cybernetics (Clarke, 1972b, pp. 29–44).

Nevertheless, even amongst this explosive variety of new methodology two developments have emerged with repercussions which potentially dwarf the others – computer methodology and isotope chronology.

Computer methodology provides an expanding armoury of analog and digital techniques for computation, experimentation, simulation, visual display and graphic analysis. These sense-extending machine tools can either be used like the microscope to examine the fine structure of low-level entities and processes in minute detail, or like the telescope to scrutinize massive ensembles over vast scales. They also provide powerful hammer-and-anvil procedures to beat out archaeological theory from intransigent data – thus on one hand these methods can be used to construct models and simulate their consequences over a range of states, identifying test-conditions – on the other hand the computer may be used to analyse and test real data and measure our expectations under the model against the reality.

Whilst all thinking archaeologists must share severe reservations about what has *yet* been achieved with the aid of these tools, the fault is with the uncertain archaeologist and his shaky concepts, not with the machine; the new generation of archaeological craftsmen have yet to master the potential of the new tool. Indeed, a major embarrassment of the computer has been that it has enabled us to do explicitly things which we had always claimed to do intuitively – in so many cases it is now painfully clear that we were not only deceived by the intuitions of innocence but that many of the things we wished to do could not be done or were not worth doing and many unimagined things *can* be done; we must abandon some objectives and approach others in different ways. Harnessing powerful new methodological horses to rickety old conceptual carts has proved to be a powerful but drastic way of improving archaeological theoretical constructs by elimination.

The chronological consequences of isotope and other dating methods, especially the Carbon-14, Potassium-Argon, and Uranium series techniques, have infiltrated archaeological thinking in a manner which has largely concealed the significance of their repercussions. It has become increasingly apparent that the archaeologist must now think directly in terms of the kinked and distorted time surfaces of the chronometric scales which he actually uses – Carbon-14 time, Potassium-Argon time, and typological time – where the error factors are almost more important than the scale graduations. In another aspect, the transformation of archaeological time from ultra-short to very long chronologies has had unsuspected and little-discussed consequences for archaeological metaphysics, entity concepts, processes and explanations.

Under the ultra-short chronologies, archaeological time was confused with historical time and seemed packed with data and events; large-scale phenomena appeared to take place in swift interludes – hence the prevalence of "invasion" explanations. This situation is precisely equivalent to that underlying the "catastrophe" theories of eighteenth-century geology and we should note the connection between time-scale, explanation and theory, since it is now exceedingly doubtful that the archaeologist can continue to use the old stock of political, historical and ethnic explanatory models in this direct way. Thus, to interpret the French Mousterian sequence, of more than 30 000 years duration, in terms of the acrobatic manoeuvrings of five typological tribes is tantamount to an attempt to explain the Vietnam war in terms of electron displacements. Political, historical and ethnic entities and processes of these kinds cannot yet be perceived at that scale in that data, even if they then existed and even with our latest sense-extension and detection devices.

A fundamental lesson emerges – the *consequences* arising from the introduction of new methodologies are of far greater significance than the new introductions themselves. We must move from the traditional model of archaeological knowledge as a Gruyère cheese with holes in it to that of a sparse suspension of information particles of varying size, not even randomly distributed in archaeological space and time. The first thing we may deduce from this revision is that many of our taxonomic entity divisions are defined by lines drawn through gaps in the evidence and zones of greatest ignorance; this does not make these taxa invalid but it does gravely alter what constitutes meaningful manipulation and explanation of such entities. Now although these problems become less severe with later material they tend to become more subtle and they never entirely disappear. We must face the fact that although they may with care be mapped on to other disciplinary domains, archaeological observations, entities, processes and explanations remain archaeological animals and they are all scale, context, sample, paradigm and ultimately metaphysics dependent.

The huge content of the new and newly extended methodologies is self-evident. However, it has not been sufficiently grasped that, numerous as they are, these methods form only one new component in the new environment and that they are less important in their own right than the new information they provide and its cumulative intellectual consequences. Certainly new ancillary methods do not alter the intrinsic nature of the discipline and we must not suppose that because we can display an archaeological relationship mathematically and analyse archaeological data scientifically that the discipline itself necessarily assumes a mathematical or scientific status. But equally neither may we assume that, because we describe archaeological observations in a literary form and interpret our data imaginatively, the discipline is a free creative art (Clarke, 1968, pp. 635, 663; 1972b, p. 18).

New observations

The array of new and old methodologies have also combined over the same 20 years to produce a multitude of "surprising" new observations and to detect previously unrecognized sources of variability. Only the adaptive stability of the highly cellular structure of traditional archaeology has successfully disguised and dissipated what might have been a fundamental shock to the entire system by confining each disconformity to a localized compartment. However, effectiveness cannot be indefinitely sacrificed to stability, and archaeological explanations, models and theories have yet to accommodate – a broad area and multilinear origin for tool-using hominids spanning more than 2 600 000 years, man in Australia and America before 25 000 B.C., Japanese ceramics by 8000 B.C., Southeast Asian food production before 6000 B.C., and bronze technology by 2500 B.C., radiocarbon. Once again, epistemological adaptation to the empirical content of the new observations is of no less significance than the explanatory and conceptual adaptation now required to understand them. Even those most complete and finished accomplishments of the old edifice – the explanations of the development of modern man, domestication, metallurgy, urbanization and civilization – may in perspective emerge as semantic snares and metaphysical mirages.

New paradigms

In this information explosion it is hardly surprising that groups of practitioners have broken free from traditional conformity and realigned themselves around the study of the special problems of limited dimensions of the new evidence. Although their roots are old, we suddenly have a number of vigorous, productive and competitive new paradigms which have condensed around the morphological, anthropological, ecological and geographical aspects of archaeological data (Clarke, 1972b, pp. 6–53). Nevertheless, diverse though they may be, they are significantly international and share much of the new methodology, philosophy and experimental ideology.

A temporary new sectarianism may be the price for the dissolution of the old disciplinary fabric but this anarchic exploitation of freedom is symptomatic of the rethinking of primary issues. It is now at least refreshing to find archaeologists of one specialist interest, one regional school and one ideology making major if controversial contributions in other archaeological specialisms and fields; cellular isolation is no longer possible even were it desirable.

New philosophies

The threshold of critical disciplinary self-consciousness is currently being traversed as the inevitable consequence of the social and technical revolution in archaeology. The old disciplinary system could not indefinitely contain, suppress, or accommodate the accumulation of discordant new information within its structure, so the system has adapted by exploring a range of new philosophies and ideologies from which will slowly emerge, after due debate, those most capable of accommodating both the old and the new information and aspirations compatibly.

The new ideologies and philosophies therefore present no simple new orthodoxy but heterodox diversity; the strength of the new archaeologies, or New Archaeology, is that it introduces a variety of questions where only answers were formerly proclaimed and disciplinary exhaustion a certitude. The era of critical self-consciousness has therefore dawned with the explicit scrutiny of the philosophical assumptions which underpin and constrain every aspect of archaeological reasoning, knowledge and concepts; some of the possible developments of these aspects will be touched upon below (New Consequences).

THE NEW ARCHAEOLOGY

Do these developments represent a "New Archaeology"? Well of course it depends on the point of view of the observer and what the observer wishes to see. However, it does seem difficult to sustain the view that the character, scale and rapidity of recent change is of no greater significance than that experienced in other twenty-year spans of archaeological development. We seem rather to have witnessed an interconnected series of dramatic, intersecting and international developments which together may be taken to define new archaeologies within a New Archaeology; whether we choose to use these terms or avoid them is then mainly a personal, political and semantic decision.

We can define a postwar quantitative and qualitative revolution in the numbers and variety of archaeological amateurs, students, departments, excavations, equipment and methods. At first, it seemed these were merely numerical and technical changes which could easily be assimilated. However, the new methods produced new observations and fresh potential which could not be reconciled with the existing disciplinary system. New paradigms emerged as a response to this situation and now new ideologies and philosophies are being developed to reset the new archaeological information within an appropriate disciplinary frame and metaphysical field space.

The New Archaeology is an interpenetrating set of new methods, new observations, new paradigms, new philosophies and new ideologies within a new environment. It is not virtuous simply because it is new; many elements are unsound, inaccurate or wrong but that is equally true of much of traditional archaeology. Nevertheless, some of the new developments are unassailable and all of them are explicit, experimental attempts to grapple with, rather than avoid, the fundamental problems of archaeology; a critical self-consciousness which healthily extends to self-critical self-consciousness, the new archaeology monitoring and controlling the new archaeology (LeRoy Johnson, 1972, p. 374).

The financial and intellectual cost of these developments is severe and interposes rather subtle dangers. Traditional confidence and habitual disciplinary security crumble into the insecurity of critical self-consciousness and professional uncertainty, posing the heavy burden of choice within a vastly enlarged conceptual arena. Authority seems challenged by anarchy as familiar concepts collapse under testing, traditional guidelines dissolve and decisions become more difficult. New questions are asked but not always answered. Disreputable old battles, long fought and long decided in other disciplines, are imported into archaeology to be needlessly refought with fresh bloodletting. Even the new methods subtly threaten to redefine our basic concepts, entities and processes for us; sometimes for the better, sometimes for the worse, emphasizing the essential need for clear logical, epistemological and metaphysical control of archaeology by archaeologists – the price of freedom is eternal vigilance (Clarke, 1972*a*).

THE NEW CONSEQUENCES
Theory of concepts

It has become clear that every archaeologist has thoughtfully or unthinkingly chosen to use concepts of a certain kind – thus committing himself to a metaphysical position, restricting himself to certain paradigms, to use certain methodologies, to accept certain modes of explanation and to pursue certain aims; at the same time explicitly or tacitly rejecting other metaphysical positions, paradigms, methods, explanations and aims. In each era archaeologists represent the temporary state of their disciplinary knowledge by a metaphysical theory which presents appropriate ideals of explanation and procedure. But metaphysical systems are not systems of observations but invented systems of concepts without which we cannot think (Harré, 1972, pp. 100–139).

Archaeological metaphysics is the study and evaluation of the most general categories and concepts within which archaeologists think; a task long overdue (Clarke, 1972*a*). Unknowing devotion to one metaphysical system prevents the recognition of those of other archaeologists, and critical self-awareness is therefore the first step to the comprehension of the position of others and the bursting of the bonds tied by one's own metaphysical assumptions. Metaphysical systems may be invented ensembles and the archaeologist may be free to choose according to whim, since the choices are not between right and wrong; but judgement can still be exercised in terms of the validity of the concepts selected, the appropriateness of the ensuing explanation for the scale of concept selected and then the adequacy and power of that explanation thereafter.

This approach reveals that archaeologists, old and new, have adopted many quite different analytical concepts. The "historical" school have preferred the imagined historical individual, or group of individuals, acting at the personal scale within events of a comparable level; appropriate explanation has therefore been in terms of the states and reasons attributed to these actors laid out in rational and dispositional explanations. The "physical" school have preferred models ranging in scale from particle clouds to networks and billiard balls, thus diversifying causal and probabilistic explanations from diffusion waves in media, to systemic interaction and invasive displacement. It is amusing to note that just as "invasion" explanations were conditioned by the metaphysics of the short chronologies and produced a reaction towards "autonomous" explanations, so "autonomous" explanations become meaningless amongst networked communities. Indeed the capacity of archaeology to reinvent for itself archaic explanation structures long abandoned in other fields is remarkable – invasion "catastrophism" can be joined by the currently fashionable autonomous "spontaneous generation" explanations and that mysterious "phlogiston" civilization.

Archaeological entities, processes and explanations are bound by metaphysical concepts of time and space. So we may expect chronological and spatial revisions to be followed by profound disciplinary consequences. But, the very great importance of time and space measurement scales has often led the archaeologist to confuse the scales used for measurement with that which is being measured. Space and time are conceptual terms relative to the existence of complex phenomena; they exist because of the observed phenomena and not vice versa. Time and space are relative to some observed system, and a key step in archaeological interpretation is a model approach towards the meaning of time and space for the inmates of particular systems. The mobile Palaeolithic band moving on foot with limited external contacts and an extremely rapid generational turnover presents a very different time and space surface from the Iron Age society with elaborate transport, extensive international contacts and a slower generational turnover, even when occupying the same territory over a similar time-span. The measurement scale must not be confused with the relationships being measured and, in particular, forms of explanation should not be inappropriate to the error and graduation range of particular time and space scales.

The exposure of archaeological metaphysics to critical appraisal allows us the self-conscious capacity to consider the possibilities of altering or rejecting current disciplinary concepts in favour of some alternative forms. Thus, at the moment, archaeology is still a discipline in which artefacts, assemblages, sites and their contents are identified and related as relics of communities in accordance with rules formulated in terms of artefact taxonomies – the traditional Montelian paradigm. But these artefact taxonomies are merely systems of *a priori* rules whereby the relation or identification of the archaeological configurations that are to bear taxonomic labels is guided and controlled by taxonomic postulates. So some practitioners within the ecological and geographical paradigms might suggest that we abandon artefact taxonomy as the primary system for organizing, classifying and naming archaeological entities and devise some other system of classification, perhaps in terms of landscape and activity units of some kind. Now, although there is a Neo-Montelian response to this suggestion, the main point is that fundamental speculation at this level is exceedingly important if only because the more fundamental the metaphysical controlling model, the less we are *normally* inclined to rethink it.

Theory of information

The problems of information processing and nomenclature bring us into the field of archaeological epistemology – the theory of archaeological information (Clarke, 1972a). This will entail a critical and self-conscious concern with the kinds of information which archaeological methods might yield about the past, together with the limitations and obscurities imposed on the one hand by the nature of the record and on the other by our languages of expression.

Archaeologists have certainly failed to acknowledge the degree to which the nature of the archaeological record has imposed itself upon archaeological concepts. To a very large extent it now appears that many archaeological processes and groupings are "artefacts" of the nature of the elements in the samples and their aberrant distributions – the nature of the entities arising in the main from the information characteristics of archaeological channels than from differing kinds of ethnic units, for example. This becomes readily apparent if we contrast the sparse density of Lower Palaeolithic finds in space and time with their few artefact categories and limited numbers of attributes severely constrained by function and material, against the abundant later finds of many categories in many materials, with large numbers of attributes and a great range of stylistic variability. It is hardly surprising that the Palaeolithic complexes which we "detect" emerge as largely equifinal, functional groupings, many thousands of years deep and hundreds of miles in radius – whilst the later units appear to be socially constrained stylistic groupings, several hundred years deep by tens of miles in diameter. The units we perceive are defined as much by the intrinsic limitations of the record as by the technology of perceiving.

Any consideration of "Montelian" archaeological hypothetical entities – whether types, cultures, culture groups or varieties, traditions, cotraditions – introduces a number of epistemological problems. Whatever their status, we certainly use these theoretical terms to make reference and to relate observations. Now some hypothetical entities may prove to be real things, qualities, or processes and may be partially or completely demonstrated in due course (the "virus" was just such a concept) but others are merely summarizing terms-of-convenience employed to simplify complex expressions (the mechanical concept of "force" for example) (Harré, 1972, pp. 91–99). Now archaeology has been much vexed by the problem of whether its hypothetical entities are "real"; it had been intuitively assumed that they were so but the technical revolution which has allowed us to test for their existence reveals that they are structurally very complex and their "reality" is still a matter of debate. However, even should the *reality* of our hypothetical entities turn out to be of the latter merely referential form, their *utility* need not diminish. Although the Montelian paradigm was only a hypothetical mechanism which offered an account of the nature of archaeological data and explanations of its relationship to hominid behaviour, to be a Montelian under traditional archaeology was certainly to view this structure not just as a plausible model but as a reality. This is no longer possible or necessary and to be a Neo-Montelian within the new morphological paradigm is only to assume that it may still be a valuable way of thinking about the data (Clarke, 1972*b*, pp. 6, 45).

This focuses attention upon a fundamental duality in archaeological data. Site, settlement and cemetery archaeology has recently and productively reasserted the special richness of the information which may be extracted from the complex, integrated relationships encapsulated within such sites. However, something approaching 95% of the archaeological data that we have is not of this integrated form at all – it is disconnected, stray, collected, unprovenanced, pillaged or rescued material. Now, it was mainly for the purposes of extracting the maximum amount of useful information from this most abundant and very complex data, through comparative taxonomy, typology and distribution mapping, that the old hierarchies of archaeological entities were evolved.

Thus in practice we have two different but related dimensions of archaeological information which have to be reconciled and mutually exploited in an appropriate way. After all, since it is admitted that we will never be able to excavate the sites of a contemporaneous site system or, what is more to the point, given our chronological scales we would not be aware of the fact even if we had the luck to do so, it is apparent that what logically articulates sites within site system reconstructions is the repeated recurrence of sets of site categories and their mutual assemblage affinities. What allows us to speculate that in ninth-millennium B.C. Palestine there *may* already have existed complex site systems is that the concept "Natufian" relates large supersites like Jericho, to villages like Beidha, hamlets like Nahal Oren and specialized hunting and fishing sites of many kinds, like Mugharet-el-Wad.

Theory of reasoning

Whether the last sentence expresses a reasonable speculation depends partly on the data, partly on the concepts and partly on the reasoning involved. The critical scrutiny of patterns of archaeological reasoning immediately exposes the basic importance of archaeological logic within archaeological philosophy and theory. Archaeological logic should outline for us the theory of correct reasoning within our discipline, without making any unwarranted assumptions that the principles of logic and explanation are simple universals which may be transferred from one discipline and level to another (Clarke, 1972a). These matters introduce the other side of the problems of "explanation" and suggest why some reasoning may be appropriate at one scale, in one context, but inappropriate at another. It raises the problems of the nature of the logical relationships between archaeological conclusions and the grounds for those conclusions, between archaeological hypotheses and the reasons for their rejection or modification, the nature of predictions and postdictions and the dangers of correlations as explanations or causes of archaeological observations. The slippery nature of the logical aspects of archaeological explanation becomes apparent in the frequent confusions between the direct causes of archaeological observations and the explanation of the mechanism which brought about those causal stimuli at a yet deeper level. A proper scrutiny of such problems might allow archaeology to escape from the self-imposed paradoxes and tautologies which currently plague its arguments. Not the least interesting area in this respect would be some clear identification of the characteristics of "pathological" explanations – those which are rejected and yet which appear to use normally acceptable reasoning on sound data.

At least part of the confusion about explanation in archaeology arises from the mistaken belief that there is one universal form of archaeological explanation structure appropriate at all levels, in all contexts. Attempts have been made to say something which would logically characterize all archaeological explanations but which simply succeed in describing, with varying success, certain modes of explanation used at certain scales, in certain contexts to answer certain archaeological questions. After all, the explanation of the recurrence of a certain house plan may have a logical structure of one kind, whilst the explanation of the collapse of the Maya or Mycenaeans may have quite another; the explanation of complex events in sophisticated systems is an especially important and ill-understood area (Tuggle, Townsend and Riley, 1972, p. 8).

If archaeological explanations exist for many different purposes, and are of many different logical forms at varied levels in differing contexts, the appropriate procedures for judging and testing their accuracy, relevance and logical adequacy have yet to be explicitly uncovered; we must therefore resist an ill-fitting determination to force the patterns of archaeological reasoning within those supposed to hold for other disciplines (Clarke, 1972a). Nevertheless, we can anticipate some bases for such judgements. It has already emerged that one test of the relevance and adequacy of an archaeological explanation is the relevance and adequacy of its hypothetical elements. If the hypothetical is not relevant to the particular scale or context, as in the "tribal" explanations of the Mousterian, then the explanation fails. Second, several different explanations may still compete for attention and here, amongst other criteria, it is the explanation which derives from or implies the existence of the more powerful *theory* which is to be preferred. At the last, even when an explanation is proven not to be trivial, tautologous, circular, redundant or statistically accidental it always remains "conventional" – relative to the state of contemporary knowledge, a particular paradigm view and a given metaphysical position.

General theory

One of the prizes denied to us by the partitioned regionalism and specialism of the Old Archaeology is the explicit realization that there is or could be a comprehensive archaeological general theory. The difficulty with this intriguing possibility has never been a lack of forms which this theory might take and areas within which it might fulminate but rather the converse – the infinity of kinds of theory which might conceivably be appropriate for archaeology and the familiar problem of choice, where to search in the infinity? An earlier response was either to import the Historicism of Spengler and Toynbee, the Determinism of Ellsworth Huntington, the modified Marxism of Childe and others, or to react by rejecting the possibility of general archaeological theory and to disappear into the depths of particular research problems with the rapidity of hot stones on snow.

Now, this prize may not yet be within our grasp but a possibly emerging theoretical form does now seem distantly perceivable. We have seen that the rising interest in archaeological philosophy naturally leads to necessary metaphysical theories of archaeological concepts, epistemological theories of archaeological information and classification and logical theories of archaeological reasoning. Here is certainly a body of necessary but unfulfilled theory which overlies and permeates a series of other levels of archaeological theory that translate and explain the relationships between classes of archaeological phenomena; it is these unspecified steps which underly the critical leaps in archaeological reasoning. Without such a body of theory these critical leaps do indeed take-off and become a free-flight of creative fancy – an irresponsible art form.

These other levels of archaeological theory may be crudely expressed as the steps latent in any archaeological interpretation, relating:

1. The range of hominid activity patterns and social and environmental processes which once existed, over a specified time and area;
2. The sample and traces of these 1 that were deposited at the time;
3. The sample of that sample 2 which survived to be recovered;
4. The sample of that sample 3 which *was* recovered by excavation or collection.

The pairwise relationships between these levels generates the essential set of predepositional, postdepositional, retrieval, analytical and interpretive models and theory which all archaeologists intuitively employ in the interpretive leaps from the excavated data to the written report, covering the interpretive process from the grave to publication.

Predepositional and depositional theory – covers the nature of the relationships between specified hominid activities, social patterns and environmental factors, one with another and with the sample and traces which were at the time deposited in the archaeological record; largely a social, environmental and statistical theory relating behavioural variability to variability in the record, linking levels 1 and 2 above.

Postdepositional theory – the nature of the relationships between the sample and traces as initially deposited and their subsequent recycling, movement, disturbance, erosion, transformation or destruction; largely a micro-geomorphological and statistical theory linking 2 and 3.

Retrieval theory – the nature of the relationships between the surviving sample 3 and the characteristics of the excavation or collection process which selectively operated upon it to produce 4; largely a theory of sampling, field research design and flexible response strategies linking 3 and 4.

Analytical theory – the nature of the relationships between the observations 4, which become the data, and their subsequent operational treatment under selective modelling, testing, analysis, experimentation, storage and publication; largely a theory of information retrieval, selection, discarding, evaluation, compaction and decision costs, linking 4–1 via the interpretive theory.

Interpretive theory – the nature of the relationships between archaeological patterns established by analysis and verified by experiment, and predictions about the directly unobservable ancient behavioural and environmental patterns; largely a theory of prediction, explanation and model evaluation linking 4–1 by testing expectations derived by analogy against observations manipulated by analysis, given 2, 3, and 4.

These are, of course, not the only areas of archaeological theory but with archaeological metaphysical theory, epistemological theory and logical theory they clearly together constitute the nucleus of that theory – currently intuitive or unsatisfactory but gradually being specified – which makes archaeology the discipline it is and not merely the discipline of its operations, whether artistic, mathematic or scientific.

Certainly, part of archaeological theory, an important part of the predepositional and interpretive theories, may be reduced to social theory and might conversely be derived therefrom; emphasizing the great significance of social as well as environmental studies for the archaeologist. However, this is but a small part of archaeological theory and even in this restricted but important area the primitive terms and correlated concepts of social theory will require an appropriately specified transformation to conform with the space, time and sample characteristics of the equivalent archaeological data. The wider area of archaeological theory either treats relationships of a purely archaeological kind, or processes with space and time-scales for which there is no social terminology, or patterns which nowhere survive within the sample of recent human behaviour. Archaeology in essence then is the discipline with the theory and practice for the recovery of unobservable hominid behaviour patterns from indirect traces in bad samples.

THE NEW PERSPECTIVE

In the later postwar decades (1950s–1970s) the boundaries of archaeological consciousness and potential receded with great suddenness. Not surprisingly, archaeologists have been left perplexed by this phenomenon and its uncertain consequences. They have a choice – to continue to operate within the limited field space of traditional archaeology, in which case the New Archaeology does not exist for them, or they can step outside their former habitat and meditate upon its unsatisfactory nature and problems which that system could not ask or answer. For there exists, mathematically and philosophically, a class of problems for any language system which cannot be explained in that system's current form and we therefore move to new languages and new disciplinary systems not only to answer former questions which could not be answered but also to abandon former questions and answers which had no meaning. Nevertheless, by the same proposition we can predict the transience of the New Archaeology itself – but we should not confuse transience with insignificance.

New Archaeology represents a precipitate, unplanned and unfinished exploration of new disciplinary field space, conducted with very varied success in an atmosphere of complete uncertainty. What at first appeared to be merely a period of technical re-equipment has produced profound practical, theoretical and philosophical problems to which the new archaeologies have responded with diverse new methods, new observations, new paradigms and new theory. However, unlike its parent, the New Archaeology is as yet a set of questions rather than a set of answers; when the questions are answered it too will be Old Archaeology.

The renewed concern with theory is refreshing after the furtive treatment that this crucial aspect widely received (except in the American school) after the scientism and historicism of the 1920s–1930s. It re-emphasizes that such theory exists, in however unsatisfactory a form, in everything that an archaeologist does regardless of region, material, period and culture, although certainly requiring different particular values for particular problems. It is this pervasive, central and international aspect of archaeological theory, multiplied by its current weakness, which makes the whole issue of major importance in the further development of the discipline.

However, there are perhaps three groups of archaeologists who may be expected to be especially unwilling to welcome both the new developments and their theoretical consequences – amateurs, historical archaeologists, and practical excavators. The feeling that the vital and expanding corps of amateur archaeologists will be deflected by a new academic gulf is, however, largely a misconception based on a professional model of the amateur as an agricultural hayseed or a military buff; we risk forgetting that amateur archaeologists (the New Amateur?) embrace professions in laboratories, electronics industries, computerized business departments and technical factories and may have a better grasp of science, mathematics, computers and electronics than their temporary archaeological overlords.

For the archaeologist of later, text-aided and traditionally historically scaled periods the repercussions of the New Archaeology are more subtle than drastic. The new developments insist that the historical evidence be treated by the best methods of historical criticism and the archaeological evidence by the best archaeological treatment and not some selective conflation of both sets of evidence and their appropriate disciplines. The severe problems and tactical advantages which arise from integrating archaeological and historical evidence emerge as no more and no less than those arising between archaeological and physical, chemical, biological and geographical evidence. Indeed, work in text-aided contexts will increasingly provide vital experiments in which purely archaeological data may be controlled by documentary data, bearing in mind the inherent biases of both.

Finally, the practical excavator should appreciate more than any other archaeologist the degree to which his practice is controlled by his theoretical expectations, and these should accordingly be appropriate (Clarke, 1972b, pp. 5–10). Thus with a more explicit theoretical awareness the practical excavator may contribute to a qualitative increase in understanding rather than simply a quantitative increase in data. In any case, practical men who believe themselves to be quite exempt from any intellectual influences are, as Lord Keynes pointed out, usually the unwitting slaves of some defunct theorist (Keynes, 1936, p. 383).

Archaeology is, after all, one discipline and that unity largely resides in the latent theory of archaeology – that disconnected bundle of inadequate subtheories which we must seek to formulate and structure within an articulated and comprehensive system; a common theoretical hat-rack for all our parochial hats.

REFERENCES

Alexander, C. (1964). *Notes on the Synthesis of Form*, Harvard University Press, Cambridge, Mass.
Clarke, D. L. (1968). *Analytical Archaeology*, Methuen, London.

Clarke, D. L. (1970). Reply to comment on Analytical Archaeology, *Norwegian Archaeological Review*, **3**, 25–34.

Clarke, D. L. (1972a). Review of *Explanation in Archaeology*, *Antiquity*, XLVI, 237–239.

Clarke, D. L. (1972b). *Models in Archaeology*, Methuen, London.

Gardin, J.-C. (ed.) (1970). *Archéologie et Calculateurs*, CNRS, Paris.

Harré, R. (1972). *The Philosophies of Science*, Oxford University Press, London.

Hodson, F. R., Kendall, D. G. and Tautu, P. (eds) (1971). *Mathematics and the Archaeological and Historical Sciences*, Edinburgh University Press, Edinburgh.

Johnson, LeRoy (1972). Problems in *avant garde* archaeology, *American Anthropologist*, **74** (3), 366–375.

Keynes, J. M. (1936). *The General Theory of Employment, Interest and Money*, MacMillan, London.

Kolchina, B. A. and Shera, Y. A. (eds) (1970). *Statistiko-kombinatornye Metody v Archeologii*, Akad. Nauk SSSR, Inst. Arkheologii, Moscow.

Tuggle, H. D., Townsend, A. H. and Riley, T. J. (1972). Laws, systems and research designs: a discussion of explanation in archaeology, *American Antiquity*, **37** (1), 3–12.

Review of *Explanation in Archaeology: An Explicitly Scientific Approach*

DAVID L. CLARKE

There are many archaeologies, old and new, and there are many philo-sophies of science in whose terms the logical structures of these divers archaeologies might be examined. This volume relates the particular procedures and explanations pursued in one brand of New Archaeology to the framework of the logical positivist philosophy of science. Within this particular view archaeology is seen as an aspect of anthropology and since anthropology is a social science, then it is thought appropriate to use the positivist philosophy of science to outline the principles of reasoning, the theory of knowledge and the general concepts which archaeologists should follow. Hence the pennant flown proudly at the title head – "an explicitly scientific approach".

The six chapters of the book are grouped into three parts. The first deals with the nature of explanation in archaeology in the sense that it assumes explanation in archaeology to be identical with the positivist summary of explanation in the physical sciences. This leads to a highly specialized use of the term "explanation" and a focal belief that lawlike generalizations play a primary role in archaeological explanation. The second part of the book lays out two frameworks for archaeological explanation – the broad frame of systems theory operating around a sys-temic model of culture and culture process explanations of system change, followed by a detailed frame in which culture systems are seen as articulated within ecological systems. The final part of the book then discusses the incorporation of the logic of science within archaeological method.

The text attempts the philosophical articulation of the positivist logic of Fritz and Plog (*ex* Hempel and Oppenheim) with the epistemology

Reprinted with permission from *Antiquity*, XLVI, 237–239, 1972 of Deetz, Hill, Longacre, Spaulding, Struever and Whallon and the metaphysics of Binford and Flannery. This may serve to identify the particular brand of New Archaeology under discussion, although the authors are very careful to point out that they alone are responsible for the pattern within which these Protean sources have been cast. The volume that has emerged is an interesting and useful formulation, stimulating in some parts but irritating and too superficial in others. Nevertheless, it is to the overall credit of the work that whatever one's views it does raise fundamental issues.

One such issue is the relationships of Philosophy of Science to Archaeology. Now the main aim of philosophies of science is to clarify the logical, epistemological and metaphysical principles implicit in what scientists do. Any philosophy of science is thus merely a series of generalizations made by philosophers about the pattern of logical structures and concepts which relate the assumptions, observations, hypotheses, explanations and interpretations such as they observe in the work of natural scientists. It is therefore a fundamental mistake to impose *any* philosophy extracted from this limited set of disciplines upon a wider set of studies, which were not included within the initial set from which the generalizations were made. Since the principles of reasoning employed in mathematics do not hold good for chemistry, then there is little reason to suppose that the positivist philosophy of physics is especially appropriate for archaeology – not least if, for example, it appears only weakly applicable even for biology.

The error centres around the confusion of the philosophies of analytical disciplines with those of disciplines of other kinds and the further confusion within the class of analytical disciplines of the philosophies of the developed disciplines (Natural Sciences, etc.) with those of a more primitive configuration and less structured raw material (Social Sciences, etc.). The cycle of error then takes the general form sketched below.

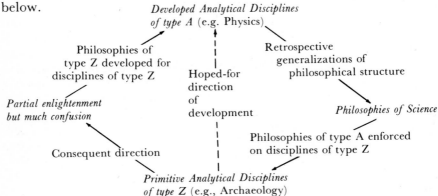

Developed Analytical Disciplines
of type A (e.g. Physics)

Philosophies of
type Z developed for
disciplines of type Z

Retrospective
generalizations of
philosophical structure

Hoped-for
direction
of
development

Partial enlightenment
but much confusion

Philosophies of Science

Consequent direction

Philosophies of type A enforced
on disciplines of type Z

Primitive Analytical Disciplines
of type Z (e.g., Archaeology)

Philosophers of Science are perennially horrified to see psychologists, social scientists, anthropologists, archaeologists, geographers and others, attempting to force their studies into selected philosophical formats appropriate to quite different disciplines; as in most areas of life, discipline is to be achieved by understanding and internal organization, not by coercion from without. However, such coercive studies are not entirely without value, although they mainly tell us to what extent the non-existent but latent philosophy of archaeology could be made to resemble the pre-existing, retrospective philosophy of a particular science.

Nevertheless, these widespread attempts to misapply the philosophies of the natural sciences and their pattern of development have led to a gradual shift in the "Philosophy of Science" to fulfil these very clear needs. There is thus a growing tendency for philosophers to conceive a multidimensional spectrum of "Philosophies of Disciplines", of which the Philosophy of Science is merely a particular area of early interest related to the extreme importance, abundant documentation, relative clear structure and mature growth of the Natural Sciences. Philosophers point out that if a Philosophy of Disciplines is to be developed then its very existence depends upon the explicit development of the philosophy of *each* discipline in its own terms, in order that the relationships between the philosophies of disciplines should become apparent and not imposed on the basis of unwarranted universal assumptions.

In short, there are many related forms and many linked ideals of explanation at many levels, all of which refer to the particular logic, epistemology and metaphysics of particular disciplines. What is currently required is the internal analysis (with external aid) and explicit development of valid principles of archaeological reasoning (archaeological logic), the specification of the general nature and special qualities of archaeological information (archaeological epistemology) and the careful clarification of archaeological concepts and their limitations (archaeological metaphysics). The many philosophies and theories of archaeology may then usefully take their place with and be assessed against the philosophies and theories of other disciplines, to produce a generally powerful Philosophy of Disciplines.

Such a goal is not simply of philosophical interest since the growth of archaeology depends on the vigorous and explicit development of archaeological philosophy and theory. For the path of development is a process of randomly searching serendipitous theoretical hops leapfrogging a more linear myopic accumulation and testing of observations. It is the duty of theoretical hypotheses to outrun fact so that speculation o'erleaps the present information state and points the way, then careful accumulation of tested data will revise the validity of the theoretical position, which may then leap ahead again.

"Analytical Archaeology" and After – Introduction

ROBERT CHAPMAN

Archaeology is an undisciplined empirical discipline. A discipline lacking a scheme of systematic and ordered study based upon declared and clearly defined models and rules of procedure. It further lacks a body of central theory capable of synthesising the general regularities within its data in such a way that the unique residuals distinguishing each particular case might be quickly isolated and easily assessed. Archaeologists do not agree upon central theory, although, regardless of place, period and culture, they employ similar and distinctive entities – the attributes, artefacts, types, assemblages, cultures and culture groups. Lacking an explicit theory defining these entities and their relationships and transformations in a viable form, archaeology has remained an intuitive skill – an inexplicit manipulative dexterity learned by rote. (Clarke, 1968, p. xiii)

In the opening paragraph of the preface to *Analytical Archaeology*, David Clarke stated concisely and forcefully his main criticism of archaeology's performance as a discipline in the mid-1960s. His avowedly ambitious attempt to provide archaeology with a "body of central theory" took up nearly 700 pages of print and introduced the reader to concepts and analytical techniques drawn from hitherto largely unexplored corners of the disciplinary universe: these included general systems theory, biology, geography, information theory, games theory and applied statistics. The style in which the book was written varied from general speculation to more detailed argument and from clarity to obscurity, as a plethora of strange concepts was presented. Reactions to the message, contents and style of *Analytical Archaeology* have also varied: "new frontier work", "too narrow", "artefact-oriented", "too ambitious", "messianic" and "brash methodological mystique" have all been used to describe the volume. Personal, as opposed to published, comments oscillated wildly from the avid enthusiasm of David Clarke's students and friends, through the lack of comprehension of many field archaeologists to the horror of the entrenched, classically educated British archaeological establishment: to the first he was a continual source of fresh insight and stimulus, to those in the middle he was an irrelevant mystery and to the last he was a dehumanized "bogey-man".

Indeed I find it difficult not to draw the conclusion that personal feelings about the man and his work more often took the place of reasoned debate within British archaeology. The "great debate" about archaeological methodology in Britain which *Analytical Archaeology* should have initiated has never really been pursued in depth. It is interesting to note that it was a Norwegian rather than an English journal which devoted an entire issue to discussion of the book, and that in a recent English book on the history of archaeology (Daniel, 1975) neither *Analytical Archaeology* nor *Models in Archaeology* were included in the chronological table of "main" events.

In writing this introduction to the articles "Towards analytical archaeology" and "Analytical archaeology: epilogue", my general aim is to place David Clarke's work within the context of the development of archaeological thought in the 1960s and 1970s. To accomplish this I shall start by relating "Towards analytical archaeology" to the book as a whole. Then attention must be directed towards the context in which the book was written and David Clarke's objectives, as expressed by him in "Analytical archaeology: epilogue". On this basis we can move forward to place both British and American reactions to *Analytical Archaeology* in perspective. Finally, it is of the utmost importance to outline the important conceptual and, to a lesser extent, analytical changes which have taken place in archaeological thought since 1968. In some cases, suggestions for rethinking and reanalysing archaeological problems have been pursued, if not always with success; in other cases, David Clarke's thoughts have fallen on deaf ears or stony ground.

From the reader's point of view it is most important to grasp that David Clarke's thinking and interests were not static. Already in 1970 he was referring to *Analytical Archaeology* (hereafter referred to as *AA*) as "an old-fashioned book". His active interests had moved from the "cultural morphology" of *AA* to the development of a specific philosophy of archaeology which was more than a pale imitation of the positivist approach drawn from the work of Carl Hempel by "law-and-order" archaeologists (for an amusing but thoughtful discussion see Flannery, 1973). While he still maintained his belief in the development of "a body of central theory capable of synthesizing the general regularities within its data", his perceptive and incisive intellect was always open to reconsideration of his previously published thoughts.

"TOWARDS ANALYTICAL ARCHAEOLOGY"

This is a conference paper prepared in 1968. It illustrates the main themes, but cannot act as a substitute for careful study of *AA*. The central concern with specifically archaeological theory is stated and the rationale behind the development of "cultural morphology" is presented:

> ... archaeology continues to remain a contentious and intuitive skill largely because it lacks a sufficiently explicit theory defining its entities and their modes of operation; the central theory which should synthesize the regularities of the data uniquely peculiar to the discipline, the ancient artefacts. (p. 146).

It is argued that this approach is neither better nor worse than the ecological approach (i.e., *cultural ecology*/the ecological paradigm in Clarke, 1972, pp. 46–47) or the anthropological approach (i.e., *cultural ethnology*/the anthropological paradigm in Clarke, 1972, pp. 45–46. Rather, each approach should be pursued according to its own kinds of evidence and analyses and then the results compared and contrasted (p. 153). However, linking all these fields of inquiry are the mathematical and statistical methods of analysis, associated with the use of electronic computers, which are grouped together under the title of the "new methodology". This is vital to the archaeologist if he is to understand the nature of his data samples and to isolate the complex relationships, degrees of affinity, correlations and trends present within his data. Furthermore the new (increasingly international) methodology requires that "archaeology must adaptively reorganise, reorientate, remodel and resymbolise itself in order to more effectively communicate with the potential of the computer systems" (p. 150).

The second part of the paper presents an outline of the three models which define much of the structure of the cultural morphology approach in *AA*. In order of presentation these are:

1. *a polythetic population model for archaeological entities:* derived from Sokal and Sneath's *Principles of Numerical Taxonomy* (1963);
2. *a dynamic system model for archaeological processes:* derived in the main from Ross Ashby's *An Introduction to Cybernetics* (1956) and presented in much greater detail in Chapters 2–3 of *Analytical Archaeology*;
3. *a nested hierarchical model for archaeological taxonomy:* the application of 1 and 2 to a model of archaeological entities increasing in complexity from the attribute through the artefact, type, assemblage, culture and culture group to the technocomplex (*AA*, Chapters 4–8).

As to the actual existence of these entities defined by material culture distributions, there is logical support in the nature of human behaviour:

> Archaeological entities exist because the network of links between people are not evenly distributed across an homogeneous mesh; the network of acquaintance, relationship and encounter is much more richly reticulated amongst some nodes in the mesh than amongst others, and furthermore this separation is reinforced by the uneven nature of the node distribution and by the uneven quality of the surface of the globe. (p. 162).

The general aim of this hierarchical classification is to isolate *regularities* (i.e., the entities) in and among the archaeologist's data which might eventually be shown to correlate in a broad but significant way with social (e.g., families, tribes, etc.), linguistic (e.g., dialect, language) and genetic (e.g., race, sub-race) entities. The basic assumption involved here is that the degree of interaction between human communities will be reflected in material culture, social organization, language and racial composition and that different levels in each of these aspects of human societies can be roughly correlated one with another (pp. 176–177; see also *AA*, p. 361, Fig. 61). This point is not developed in depth in "Towards analytical archaeology", but Chapter 9 in *AA* looks in particular at ethnographic evidence to support this line of argument.

The third section of the paper presents summary discussions of three of the archaeological entities, the subculture (developed more fully in *AA*, pp. 235–244), culture group (*AA*, pp. 287–320) and, more fully, the technocomplex (*AA*, pp. 321–357). Greater structural complexity makes these entities a challenge to the archaeologist who may be tempted, in the absence of detailed analysis, to deny their existence (p. 164). The author's answer to this scepticism is that:

> ... it seems more probable that the uncertainty about the grosser archaeological entities stems from their real complexity, as against their naive interpretations, from the lack of analyses, and above all from *the wholesale use of the term "culture" for every category of assemblage population whatever their structure or time and space dimensions.* (p. 164), (my emphasis)

This is a specific example of the loose terminology applied by archaeologists to all these basic entities and which provided David Clarke with one of the main stimuli towards the rigorous definition of entities seen in Chapters 4–8 of *AA*. This can be seen by reference to the first chapter of the book in which he condemns the ambiguity present in the archaeologist's usage of these different entities: for example the use of the term "culture" to apply to entities ranging in content, time-depth and spatial distribution from the Wessex bronze age "culture" to the supra-continental palaeolithic Acheulean "culture" (*AA*, p. 31; below pp. 168–169).

The last part of the paper draws together three main points or groups

of points. First, there is the attempt to relate the hierarchy of archaeological entities to social, linguistic and racial units which has already
been noted above. Second, the *raison d'être* for the hierarchical model
is presented in a slightly different form. Taking the "culture" as his
example, David Clarke argues that:

> ... to classify a series of assemblages as a culture is to predict a number
> of things about the limits of the population involved, of its area, its social
> and linguistic associations, its potential development patterns and its in-
> herent "behaviour". To classify a series of assemblages as part of one specific
> culture is to predict a further quantity of specific information; quite different
> information from that which would have been inferred for a different
> culture, and different again from that which would have followed its identifi-
> cation as a subculture, culture group or technocomplex. *The purpose of the
> hierarchical taxonomy is to organize our empirical knowledge in a way which will
> enable us to make reliable predictions.* (p. 177), (my emphasis)

Last, many of the same points about the need for the reorganization
of archaeological methodology as a response to the adoption of techniques from other disciplines are reiterated from the preface to *AA*.

CONTEXT AND OBJECTIVES

In 1970, the journal *Norwegian Archaeological Review* devoted an entire
issue to discussion of *Analytical Archaeology*. Comments were published
by Irving Rouse, William Mayer-Oakes, Dell Hymes and Carl-Axel
Moberg and a reply (reproduced here) by David Clarke. In this reply,
he stressed the exploratory nature of the book and again placed the
development of a general archaeological theory as the main objective:

> *Analytical Archaeology* is therefore a frame for the continuous endeavour to-
> ward the precipitation of an explicit and vigorous corpus of general theory
> which attempts to resolve the relationships that permeate archaeological
> data in its widest sense, everywhere in the world – as explicable and applic-
> able in Peru as Persia, Australia and Alaska, Sweden and Siam. (pp. 183–
> 184)

Archaeology was identified as an international discipline with a tacit
general theory which required elaboration and reconceptualization if
the subject was to make a significant contribution to knowledge (Objectives 1–5, below, pp. 185–187).

At the same time, David Clarke's unique and most stimulating contribution to British archaeology in the 1960s was to open our eyes to
the rapid changes taking place in other relevant disciplines (see Objective 6, below, p. 187). Changes in personnel, concepts and techniques

had accelerated to such an extent in some disciplines since World War II that the term "revolution" could legitimately be applied (see Kuhn, 1962, for discussion of disciplinary change). Thus, by the 1960s it was possible to identify, among others, a "new" geography, a "new" mathematics and a "new" biology.

In this context, it seems a worthwhile exercise to give brief consideration to the ways in which David Clarke came into contact with these changing disciplines and recognized their relevance and potential for changing the structure and content of archaeology as a discipline. First there was contact with the "new" biology, in the form of Sokal and Sneath's *Principles of Numerical Taxonomy* (1963). These authors were highly critical of the nature of classification as practised by their colleagues:

> ... the taxonomy of today is but little advanced from that of a hundred or even two hundred years ago.

> Biologists have amassed a wealth of material, both of museum specimens and of new taxonomic characters, but they have had little success in improving their power of digesting this material. The practice of taxonomy has remained intuitive and commonly inarticulate, an art rather than a science. (Sokal and Sneath, 1963, p. vii)

The accumulation of data in the absence of productive or meaningful analysis and synthesis was a feature which David Clarke immediately identified in archaeology (e.g. *AA*, p. 3). So also was the practice of defining clusters or groups on the basis of a few attributes or "typical" characters (e.g., type-fossils in archaeological cultures). This led Sokal and Sneath to contrast two models of the ways in which taxonomists defined classes of object. These were the *"monothetic"* model, in which "the possession of a unique set of features is both sufficient and necessary for membership in the group" (Sokal and Sneath, 1963, p. 13) and the *"polythetic"* model, by which the taxonomist

> places together organisms that have the greatest number of shared features, and no single feature is either essential to group membership or is sufficient to make an organism a member of the group. (Sokal and Sneath, 1963, p. 14)

Monothetic groups were regarded as artificial, while polythetic ones were thought to be more natural. The implications for archaeological classification were immediately clear to David Clarke (e.g., *AA*, pp. 35–38).

The last main criticism offered by Sokal and Sneath was that taxonomists should not confuse classification and estimates of similarity with interpretations of ancestral relationship: just because units A and

B were closely similar to one another did *not* require the interpretation that they were genetically related. In the words of Sokal and Sneath "phylogenetic speculations should not be involved in the classificatory process" (Sokal and Sneath, p. 8). In another way this was the same point as Lewis Binford was making in archaeology about the traditional equation of cultural differences and similarities with "cultural relationships" (Binford, 1965 – for further discussion see below).

In Sokal and Sneath's opinion, taxonomy had to become more *objective* and the methods employed should be *repeatable*. Estimations of resemblance between entities or attributes should be based on *numerical* methods (e.g., cluster analysis) and involve as many characters/attributes as possible. None of these characters should be "weighted" more than any others and the result should be the creation of a series of "natural" taxa.

The degree to which David Clarke adopted and adapted the main points of numerical taxonomy into his view of archaeology can be clearly seen (*AA*, pp. 512–549). In addition to the general conclusions which he drew from Sokal and Sneath, he also pursued a series of matrix and cluster analyses on the British beaker pottery studied for his PhD thesis (*AA*, pp. 592–594; also Clarke, 1962, 1970). Although these analyses have never been fully published, it is clear that he was the first British archaeologist to recognize and *fully* present the significance of Sokal and Sneath's work to his own subject (a point omitted from Doran and Hodson, 1975, pp. 158–186).

Indeed it is also important to note that David Clarke's initial experiments with matrix analysis, undertaken while he was a research student (Clarke, 1962), were carried out *before* the publication of Sokal and Sneath's seminal work. In this respect, he again revealed his gift for looking outside both his own subject and his own country in search of useful concepts and techniques. This refusal to be restricted to parochial interests led him to follow up the early attempts at statistical manipulation of artefacts published in America in the 1950s (Robinson, 1951; Brainerd, 1951; Spaulding, 1953; Tugby, 1958).

The use of quantitative analyses had also permeated through into geography by the early 1960s. The greater rigour applied to analyses of spatial interaction between human communities was also reflected in the methodology employed. Haggett (1965), in his book *Locational Analysis in Human Geography*, argued that geographers must be more concerned with the search for *regularities* in human behaviour and less preoccupied with its unique aspects. To this end they must recognize that order or regularity depends "on the organizational framework into which we place" our data (Haggett, 1965, p. 2). This led naturally to a discussion of the central importance of theory and the use of models "as a source of working hypotheses to test against reality" (Haggett, 1965, p. 19). Different kinds of models were outlined, as were the main methods of model-building (Haggett, 1965, pp. 19–22). Finally the role of models is justified on three counts:

(i) Model building is inevitable because there is no fixed dividing line between facts and beliefs.... Models are theories, laws, equations, or hunches which state our beliefs about the universe we think we see.

(ii) Model building is economical because it allows us to pass on generalized information in a highly compressed form ...

(iii) Model building is stimulating in that, through its very overgeneralizations, it makes clear those areas where improvement is necessary ... (Haggett, 1965, p. 23)

The influence on David Clarke of this discussion of the importance of theory in geography can be clearly seen in Chapter 1 of *AA* (especially pp. 32–35 and pp. 441–451) and more explicitly in *Models in Archaeology* (Clarke, 1972).

On a more practical level, Haggett's book provided a source for quantitative studies of human interaction which might be of use to the archaeologist. These included studies of diffusion processes (based primarily on the work of Hägerstrand in Sweden – see *AA*, pp. 464–469), human territorial behaviour (e.g., the relation of territory size and shape to such factors as population density, the need to minimize movement and exploitation "costs" – e.g., *AA*, p. 503–506), colonization and settlement diffusion (*AA*, pp. 469–473) and settlement hierarchies (*AA*, p. 507). The methods employed in these studies included computer simulations (e.g., Monte Carlo, Random Walk), set theory (*AA*, pp. 473–476), trend surface analysis (*AA*, pp. 427–431, 480–490), game theory (*AA*, pp. 490–491, 492–496), nearest-neighbour analysis (*AA*, pp. 507–509) and Thiessen polygons (*AA*, pp. 509–510). In all cases, it was argued or assumed that the "new" geography could be a productive source of models and techniques to be adapted to the study of spatial patterns in the archaeological record. Their potential was the focus of interest, rather than the presentation of actual case studies from archaeology: the only examples of the latter were those worked up in a summary form by David Clarke himself (e.g., the trend analysis of the diffusion of Early Neolithic painted wares in the Balkans, *AA*, pp. 429–431; and of the distribution of different neck-angles on Southern British Beaker pottery, *AA*, Fig. 100, p. 484).

One aspect of the "new" geography which has not been mentioned so far is the use of *general systems theory*, which has spread through many disciplines since the early 1950s. Credit for its definition is given to von Bertalanffy (1950):

He proposed this "new basic scientific discipline" and described it as a "new scientific doctrine of wholeness". By a system he meant any large assemblage of intercommunicating elements which can reasonably be regarded as a unit in itself: components forming a machine, neurones forming the brain, cells forming a living organism, employees forming an organisation. He stressed the desirability of finding the general laws which applied directly to systems, rather than attempting to understand their complex and sometimes mysterious behaviour by studying the properties of their constituent elements. (Doran, 1970, p. 290)

Associated with systems theory were a range of concepts such as homeostasis, feedback and different kinds of equilibrium. In geography it was first introduced into geomorphology and physical geography (e.g., Chorley, 1962) and then into human geography by Haggett (1965, pp. 17–19).

David Clarke's extension of systems theory into archaeology seems to have derived from a combination of influences, principally Haggett's book and Ross Ashby's *An Introduction to Cybernetics* (Ashby, 1956). As we have already seen above, a system was the model used for archaeological processes such as change in artefacts or cultures. This was intended to replace the usual analogies drawn between archaeological entities and machines or organisms (*AA*, pp. 38–39) when changes in distribution or content were being explained. But the systems model was *not* intended to be just a new *analogy:*

It would be all too easy at this stage to take systems theory as our model for archaeological processes and the cultural entities that generate them, without isolating precisely the kind of system these entities represent. This would simply extend systems theory and its terminology as yet another vague analogy of no practical potential.... We must try and understand what kinds of system exist in archaeology, what are their roles, limits and inherent properties as systems, how are they networked by subsystems and within what setting can these systems be conceived as existing. (*AA*, p. 39)

This demonstration of the nature of cultural systems was attempted in Chapters 2 and 3 of *AA*. Cultural systems were shown to be related to each other and to their environments. In addition, various concepts from information theory were integrated into this model (e.g., *AA*, pp. 88–101). It was then applied to the analysis of change, not only in cultures, but in all the other archaeological entities from attribute to technocomplex.

These, then, are the main constructive influences which went into *AA*: numerical taxonomy and the efficiency of the electronic computer; quantitative geography; systems theory; and above all a concern for the use of these concepts and techniques in a more generalizing study of archaeology which laid greater stress on the central role of theory.

In his own uniquely ambitious and experimental way, David Clarke was recognizing the need for archaeology as a discipline to adapt its concepts and procedures to the changing academic environment of the 1960s. The question we must now ask is how the archaeological world received this new synthesis and what factors governed their reactions? We will begin by considering the reaction in Britain and then move on to consider the American "school" of Lewis Binford.

THE BRITISH REACTION

Although it would be misleading to characterize British archaeology in the 1960s as possessing a unified consensus of opinion as to the aims, concepts and proper procedures of the discipline, it is possible to distinguish a few recurrent beliefs and opinions which found expression after the publication of *AA*. The reactions were not always expressed in print and when they were they more often took the form of summary condemnation rather than reasoned debate. Five fairly common reactions were as follows:

1. The book is a prime example of the decreasing ability of the younger generation of archaeologists to communicate their ideas and research in a clear literary style. Instead the archaeological "Mr Everyman" is baffled by a welter of cumbersome, incomprehensible *jargon*.

Like its fellow works on the other side of the Atlantic it is written in "obscure jargon" or "gobbledygook gibberish" (Daniel, 1973, pp. 93, 95). Rather than "new" archaeology, "it is merely *Newspeak* Archaeology, tricked out in a whole wardrobe of new vocabulary apparently designed more to impress than to enlighten" (Hogarth, 1972, p. 301). This "new vocabulary" is frequently derived from mathematical or scientific concepts and runs the risk of driving away from archaeology those people who are blessed with "humanist" or "historical" imagination (Hawkes, 1968).

2. The jargon which permeates *Analytical Archaeology* and other volumes such as *New Perspectives in Archaeology* (Binford and Binford, 1968) conceals the fact that there is nothing really "*new*" about their approach to archaeology (e.g., Hogarth, 1972). They still do fieldwork and use typology. Archaeologists have been aware of geographical studies since the pioneer works of Fox and Crawford and scientific studies such as pollen analysis and general Quaternary studies have been increasingly used since the earlier part of the century. Similarly the relationships between cultural systems and their

environments have been studied, albeit without the systems terminology, for at least the past thirty years (Higgs and Jarman, 1975,
p. 3).

This series of viewpoints has a common foundation in the belief that
archaeology changes in a continuous, cumulative way, with no radical
breaks or transformations. The present builds on the past, as archaeology moves "to newness by discovery and interpretation every decade"
(Daniel, 1973, p. 93).

3. British archaeologists should be cautious about the adoption of concepts and techniques from (a) other disciplines and (b) America.

As far as other disciplines are concerned, it is argued that their concepts may not be suitable to archaeological data or that their techniques
may have to be radically altered to fit the archaeological context (e.g.,
the use of statistical analyses on small samples of data). Alternatively
the concepts may only have the value of general *analogues* in archaeology
and may not be able to be operationalized (Doran and Hodson, 1975 –
see below for discussion regarding systems theory). A similar argument
applies to the influence of developments in American archaeology.
Hogarth (1972) cautions the reader that

There is a great risk that in incautious acceptance of American methods
the predispositions of American archaeologists may be adopted along with
them. (Hogarth, 1972, p. 303)

A contrast is drawn between American archaeology, which is specifically designed to study exclusively prehistoric societies, and European
archaeology which concentrates on the vivid interplay between its own
prehistoric "barbarian" societies and the literate civilizations of the
Near East (Hogarth, 1972, pp. 303–304). Daniel (1975, p. 371) also
seems wary of recent developments in America when he writes that
theory and methodology are the logical refuge of transatlantic archaeologists who have no solid monuments to study!

4. *AA* is simply a "handbook for potential [computer] users" (Hogarth,
1972, p. 302). Thus if one's concern is not with computers/statistics
but fieldwork and excavation, then the book is irrelevant.

5. *AA* is solely "artefact-oriented" and thus fails to open up any new
perspectives on long-term human behaviour patterns. Little note,
if any, is taken of the economic contexts in which those artefacts
were used. Statistical studies of material culture distributions will
add little to our knowledge of human behaviour while seasonal differences in tool-kits between economically complementary sites are
not taken into account as relevant variables. This essentially is the

response of the "cultural ecologists", as outlined in "Towards analytical archaeology".

At one time or another, David Clarke had answered all of the above
criticisms, either in print (e.g., see the papers that follow this introduction) or in his Cambridge lectures. He defended the use of new con-
cepts/jargon and numerate as well as literary methods of communication (e.g., below, p. 182; Clarke, 1972, p. 55). He arguued that a "New
Archaeology" did exist and defined its salient characteristics (Clarke,
1972, pp. 54–55). As far as the need for caution in the introduction
of concepts and techniques from other disciplines is concerned, the
views expressed in AA nowhere contradict this. Indeed it is freely acknowledged that the book consists of "anticipations, rash and premature" (AA, pp. xiv, 664) and that the analytical techniques derived,
for example, from geography, had *potential* applications in archaeology.
In this respect, the book's outlook was experimental and provocative –
a source of stimulus and not a dogmatic statement of research procedure.
    The last two viewpoints (4, 5) reveal more about their authors than
they do about AA. Hogarth's view of the book as a "handbook for potential [computer] users" reveals that he has missed the whole point about
the central role of theory in archaeology. A similar reaction is inspired
by the view of the "cultural ecologists" (point 5): they would have
made a more productive contribution to debate by recognizing the aim
of AA to look for regularities in material culture and arguing whether
these (a) actually existed or (b) were meaningful in terms of human
behaviour.
    The nature of the American influence (point 3) also inspires doubts
about its authors. To take Hogarth's views as an example, it is initially
unfortunate that he should be presenting a highly generalized view of
European prehistory which was being discarded as his article was being
published. Even if it *were* now a productive model, it would still be
the case that the archaeologist's specific domain is over *material* culture,
whether the societies concerned were prehistoric or historic. Again, it
was specifically stated in AA that the book was aimed at discovering
the regularities underlying archaeological data (i.e., material culture)
wherever in the world the past was being studied. As before, one wonders
whether the author has read the book he is criticizing and, further,
whether his published views reveal more about his own cultural feelings
towards Americans than anything of constructive academic content!
    Of course, it is all too easy to take up polemical positions for or against
AA, but much more difficult to explain *why* these positions have been
adopted. Before the 1960s, mainstream British archaeology consisted

largely of practitioners educated in the Classics, ancient and modern history – in short in the Humanities. A commonly held view was that prehistory was simply the backward extension of history into more uncertain periods in which we lack the written evidence to put flesh on the bare bones of material culture. Or, put another way, history reveals the "superstructure" (e.g., intellectual/spiritual achievement) as well as the "foundations" (economy/technology) of human life (Dymond, 1974). Archaeology was the "handmaiden of history". In this context, it is not surprising that it is the archaeology of the Roman and Medieval periods which aroused the greatest professional (and indeed public) interest. In turning his conclusions into "historical synthesis", the archaeologist was bound to express himself in a concise, *literate* way, comprehensible to professional, amateur and layman.

In one of his Cambridge lectures, David Clarke characterized the philosophy underlying this approach as *cultural idealism*. Central to this philosophy was the empathy approach: in order to pursue effectively both historical and archaeological studies, one had to rethink the thoughts and motives in the minds of people in the past (e.g., Collingwood, 1939). Furthermore, artefacts provided the archaeologist with direct contact with the thoughts and actions of people in the past. How often have we heard archaeologists and historians refer to the "appeal" of physical evidence (e.g., Dymond, 1974) and the role of "historical *imagination*" (e.g., Hawkes, 1968) in the study of the past?

The period after World War II saw many cultural and social changes within Britain and these came to be reflected within archaeology. The boost given to the sciences and technology both in the public and private sectors, the rapid upsurge in numbers undergoing full-time education, the consequent increased social mobility and the change in Britain's status from a colonial power to a European offshore island all had important consequences. British archaeology had to cope with a rapid influx of scientific concepts and techniques, the consequent overthrow of some of its most cherished models (e.g., colonialism giving way to independent development) and the staggering increase in professional opportunities in universities, museums and field archaeology bringing archaeologists of a much wider and more mobile social background than the Oxbridge core of the 1940s and 1950s. Many (for example, David Clarke and Colin Renfrew) had also been educated in the Natural Sciences as opposed to the Humanities.

The outcome of all these changes was the mutually incomprehensible clash of different archaeological approaches, educational backgrounds and social values which occurred in the 1960s. *AA* crystallized the "new" tradition in a provocative manner and laid down a direct challenge to mainstream British archaeology. So far there has been no answer from the latter group in an equally impressive publication. This partly reflects the willingness of archaeologists to accept some (or less commonly, all) of the changes outlined in David Clarke's work. But it also suggests that the educational and cultural gulf is so wide that there is no common ground on which productive debate can be maintained (cf., Kuhn, 1962). This certainly appears to be the case when one reads Professor Alcock's obituary for Sir Mortimer Wheeler:

> ... his approach was *too humane* to play the computerized numbers game, and he was altogether *too literate* to stand for *sociologese* and other kinds of *gobbledegook*. In the final pages of *Archaeology from the Earth* asking "what are we digging up and why?" he does indeed address himself to social problems; but *his grounding in ancient history was too sound* for him ever to have joined the rush to the New Geography or to systems analysis in the search for models and hypotheses. (Alcock, 1976, p. 12), (my emphases).

If this educational and cultural gulf is one factor behind British reaction to David Clarke's work, then the lack of detailed concern with methodology is almost certainly another. Before 1956 there was no book published in Britain which gave full attention to methodology, although there were occasional demands for its closer study. For example, Daniel wrote that:

> It remains painfully true that writings on prehistoric methodology are astonishingly few ... we must pay more attention to methodology, we must review again all our facts, check all the early generalisations and set our subject firmly on true foundations. (1943, p. 60)

But as far as one can judge from other publications in the 1940s and early 1950s British archaeologists did not feel the need to analyse or formalize their own methodology. When the American Walter W. Taylor produced his now famous book *A Study of Archaeology* (1948), there was little evidence that it had any effect on the thinking archaeologists on this side of the Atlantic.

In the preface to *Piecing Together the Past*, V. Gordon Childe acknowledges the need for a book which presented methodology in an *explicit* way (1956, p. v). He described the processes by which "artefact-types", "assemblages", "cultures" and "industries" were defined by the archaeologist. In particular, the "culture" was selected for discussion as the key entity, with its *possible* social, ethnic and linguistic correlations (see also Childe, 1963, p. 47). Childe also criticized the usage of loose terminology, such as the application of the same name to a *chronological period* and to a *cultural entity* (e.g., the Hallstatt period/culture of the European Early Iron Age – see Childe, 1956, pp. 84–110). Lastly, Childe looked at the processes by which cultures change from one form to another; these included cultural convergence/divergence, acculturation and diffusion (1956, pp. 135–158).

It is important to note that David Clarke took *Piecing Together the Past* as the starting point for his own work on archaeological methodology. Indeed I think it very likely that some British archaeologists would assert that Childe had said all that one could reasonably say and that many elements of *AA* were already present in incipient form in *Piecing Together the Past*. Doran and Hodson have noted (1975, pp. 161–163) how Childe (1956, p. 33; also 1963, p. 41) hinted at a polythetic model for archaeological entities such as the culture. However, at the same time, they point out that his definition of "types" was what we would now call monothetic and that he was prepared to admit to an "arbitrary element" in their definition (Childe, 1956, p. 162). In this respect, David Clarke made *explicit* and *consistent* usage of the polythetic model where Childe had been implicit and inconsistent. He also developed the hierarchy of entities beyond the level of the culture to include the culture group and the technocomplex (see above): this was a matter of clarification and amplification aimed at reducing the confusion which resulted from applying Childe's "culture" to a variety of entities of different timespans and spatial distributions.

What about the quantitative aspects of entity definition? Did not Childe write (1956, p. 34) that "the archaeological concept of culture is largely statistical"? Therefore what advances, beyond the filling-in of detail, are made in *AA*? To put it quite bluntly, Childe's concept of "statistics" was simply in terms of numbers or percentages: what was of interest was whether an assemblage had 10 artefact-types or 40 artefact-types. This was a conception which was then common among British archaeologists (see Collingwood, 1939, p. 134). Statistics of correlation, association or covariation which are now used in archaeology (Doran and Hodson, 1975) had not been developed in the subject in Britain in the mid-1950s. As far as Childe was concerned, statistics were "supplements" to more traditional typological methods (1956, p. 82). Thus his use of the word, as of "adaptation" and "equilibrium", cannot be taken to illustrate his development of all the techniques and concepts which we now associate with it and which were fully expressed in *AA*.

Although Childe's book was one of the formative influences on David Clarke's approach to methodology, *AA* was written in a different disciplinary environment. It was designed to integrate the significant aspects of this environment (e.g., statistics, quantitative geography, systems theory) into the archaeological methodology which Childe had formulated. This inevitably resulted in the need for more explicit and consistently rigorous definition of entities such as the artefact and the culture, and the use of a quantitative approach to the study of archaeo-logical processes, such as cultural change (as in *AA*, Chapters 10–11). This resulted in a volume on methodology which not only had the dis-tinction of being a rare event in British archaeology, but of being expressed in totally different concepts, language and techniques from those in which most professional and amateur archaeologists had been educated. The resulting gulf between these and the position taken by *AA* could not have been greater.

THE AMERICAN REACTION

It is significant that many of the examples of new statistical and com-puter analyses referred to in *AA* had been carried out in America in the early 1960s. These were a source of stimulus to David Clarke and an example of the way his outward-looking interests reached beyond purely insular British archaeology. I have already presented and dis-cussed reaction to *AA* within Britain, so it is now fitting that we turn our attention to America.

American archaeology is no more a totally unified discipline than is British archaeology. Not only are there divisions according to period and areas of interest (e.g., Classical, Mesoamerican, Palaeo-Indian) but also more personal divisions such as "new" and "traditional" archaeologists – and now even "young fogeys" (Flannery, 1973). So we should expect *AA* to have received a variety of reactions according to subject specialization and theoretical orientation. What do we actually find? From this side of the Atlantic it seems as if there is little in the way of published comment from the "traditionalists", whereas the "new archaeologists" acknowledge its analytical rather than its theoretical aspects. Thus it is referred to as a "guide to scientific tech-niques" (Watson, 1972) or an "impressive compendium of analytical procedures" (Watson, LeBlanc and Redman, 1971, p. xi). There is no doubt that David Clarke's discussion of systems theory and simulation has had a direct influence on some areas of research in American (e.g., Judge, 1970; Thomas, 1972). With the earlier development of a sys-temic perspective present in the publications of Lewis Binford and others (e.g., Binford, 1962, 1965; Flannery, 1968), there was clearly a receptive audience for this aspect of *AA*.

But what of the central aim of the book, the definition of an archaeo-logical theory dealing with specifically archaeological entities – "cul-tural morphology" as defined by David Clarke (see above)? The most widely held reaction to this is that the book's outlook is limited and traditional – it is "artifact-oriented" (e.g., Rouse, 1970). It ignores ecological factors and non-artefactual data and takes insufficient notice of *variability*, both in archaeological entities and human societies.

The concern with variability is one of the key features of the school of thought developed by Lewis Binford during the 1960s (see Binford, 1972). From its roots in the evolutionary anthropology of Leslie White, Binford has developed the view that culture should be studied as a whole *system* and that its primary function is an adaptive one:

> ... as archaeologists we are faced with the methodological task of isolating extinct sociocultural systems as the most appropriate unit for the study of the evolutionary processes which result in cultural similarities and differences. If we view culture as man's extrasomatic means of adaptation, we must isolate and define the ecological setting of any given sociocultural system, not only with respect to the points of articulation with the physical and biological environment, but also with points of articulation with the sociocultural environment. It is suggested that changes in the ecological setting of any given systems are the prime causative situations activating processes of cultural change. (Binford, 1972, pp. 159–160)

Given the systemic perspective, it is argued that the archaeologist's attention should be directed towards understanding the relationship between systems and subsystems. The basic premise is that all human culture is inherently variable as a result of such factors as differential social interaction, environmental differences and the need to undertake different tasks with different material equipment at the same or different locations. This variability should be reflected in the attributes, artefacts and sites which are the archaeologist's exclusive data. Therefore we should employ taxonomic procedures and statistical analyses which enable us to define this variability and then try to explain it (Binford, 1965; reprinted in Binford, 1972, p. 199). The processes of research and explanation by which systemic variability is investigated should depend on *deductive* reasoning, using hypotheses which must be tested against relevant data (also see Hill, 1972). Inductive reasoning is castigated as unrealistic and unscientific because it does not incorporate the testing of hypotheses on independent data. The use of this reasoning procedure, accompanied by the systemic perspective on culture, the denial of "limitations" on our knowledge of the past and the use of appropriate statistical techniques constitute the essence of the "Binfordian" school of American archaeology.

Binford's published reaction to *AA* must be understood in this context. He regards the use of Sokal and Sneath's numerical taxonomy as a "rigid inductivist approach to taxonomy" (1972, p. 248) and thinks that in spite of the use of statistics, systems theory and the new geography, the basic view of culture was traditional:

> Assemblage types, artifact types, etc., were to be arranged into a systematics based on measured degrees of similarity as a basis for reconstruction of culture history. Culture is patterned; patterning is cultural. Degrees of similarity in patterning, measured primarily in terms of associations, are a measure of cultural affinity. *What progress had been made?* (Binford, 1972, pp. 330–331), (my emphasis)

Thus we have the strange situation of Binford coming to the same general conclusion about *AA* as many traditional British archaeologists, but from a totally different perspective!

Although he does not explicitly say so, it is clear that Binford regards the book as a further example of the "normative" view of culture. His description and criticism of this view is best presented in "Archaeological systematics and the study of culture process" (Binford, 1965; reproduced in Binford, 1972, pp. 195–207). The essence of the normative approach is that similarities between cultures or artefacts reveal relationships (e.g., "migration", "influence", "trade") between their makers:

> Learning is the recognized basis of cultural transmission between generations, and diffusion is the basis of transmission between social units not linked by regular breeding behaviour. The corollary of this proposition is that culture is transmitted between generations and across breeding populations in inverse proportion to the degree of social distance maintained between the groups in question . . . as Caldwell . . . has said "other things being equal, changes in material culture through time and space will tend to be regular". Discontinuities in rates of change or in the formal continuity through time are viewed as the result of historical events which tends to change the configuration of social units through such mechanisms as extensions of trade, migration and the diffusions of "core" ideas such as religious cults . . . (Binford, 1972, p. 197)

As a result of this basic belief, the "normative" archaeologist uses taxonomic methods designed to group together attributes or artefacts by their similarities with each other: attributes are grouped together into artefacts, artefacts into assemblages, assemblages into cultures and so on up the hierarchy of entities. Binford argues that this approach masks the important variability *within* culture: thus using the examples of pottery, he argues that more emphasis in taxonomies should be placed on the complex relationships between "primary" (e.g., design, morphology) and "secondary" functional variation (e.g., context of use/production) than on the usual classification into a standard type series which is interpreted in terms of cultural relationships (Binford, 1972, pp. 199–202).

Drawing these aspects together, one may conclude that the Binfordian view of *AA* is that it contains traditional normative theory concealed behind a quantitative methodology. Similarity or shared traits are the basis for the creation of the hierarchy of entities which conceal important and more meaningful cultural variability. It is inductive in approach and is out of step with the problem-oriented research which the Binfordian school has done so much to propagate in the last 15 years.

These views are, I think, something of a misunderstanding and even a misrepresentation of the aims and philosophy behind *AA*. As has been stated above, the specific aim of the volume was to develop our understanding of material culture (the archaeologist's primary data) as a behavioural system. The emphasis was placed upon the search for regularities or patterning in the data which had been brought about by such factors as varying degrees of spatial interaction, similar environmental stimuli and the employment of similar technologies. Then the patterning in the material culture was compared with that in linguistic, social or racial data in order to isolate any potential overlap or relationships between these different sources of evidence on human behaviour. It is interesting in this respect that Binford makes no comment on the ethnographic studies on the suggestive relationships between material culture and other data which David Clarke presented (Clarke, 1968, pp. 365–388).

But it is a mistake to argue that the definition of patterning in material culture was the *sole* aim of David Clarke's approach to archaeology. On the contrary, it is the aspect which was *selected* for critical study in *AA*. He certainly did not deny the existence of variability in human behaviour and the archaeological record. He accepted sources of variability such as the environment, technology, social organization, population, economy and various stochastic factors. Indeed it was made quite clear that the definition of patterning in material culture was also intended to help isolate important sources of variability. This is a point which has been made recently by Plog:

> Clarke's message is that in formulating types, assemblages, or whatever, we must be careful to avoid reading variability out of existence. More attention must be given to the polythetic nature of types and continuous variation in our data because, while variation may make classification difficult and categories untidy, it is also the most important information for understanding any behavioural system. (Plog, 1975, p. 211)

According to *AA* the definition of regularity and variability are complementary analytical procedures and sources of information, but it is the regularity which receives greater stress *in this volume*. The roots of the regularity lie in human culture's capacity to act as an information system. Indeed, rather than simply polarize "normative" and "systemic" viewpoints, David Clarke saw that cultural transmission between human groups and localized systemic change were not mutually exclusive processes: the information system concept avoided the naive excesses of the "normative" model (e.g., vague "influences", doctrinaire diffusionism) and the unreality of a systemic model which played down human communication.

Lastly, it is an opinion worthy of consideration that nowhere do the American "new" archaeologists, and Binford in particular, acknowledge the thought given in *AA* to models and the generation and testing of hypotheses (e.g., *AA*, pp. 32–35, 441–451, 638–647). It is true that David Clarke did not beat the drum of Hempelian positivism, but in his work he was clearly exploring the use of models (later developed in Clarke, 1972 – see this volume), stressing the need for problem formulation and presenting different methods of hypothesis generation and testing. As with variability, these topics were not central to *this* volume as he conceived it. Thus, to dismiss the volume as "inductivist" and "traditional" does a disservice both to David Clarke and to those who have expressed these views. As with reaction among a section of British archaeology, summary dismissal has taken the place of more reasoned debate.

CHANGING ANALYTICAL ARCHAEOLOGY

It remains to make an assessment, however selective, of the degree to which David Clarke achieved his expressed aims of *exploration* and *stimulation*. How far and with what success have his suggestions for the development of archaeological theory and analysis been pursued since 1968? Given the rapidity of change within archaeology, we must also ask whether the book still has a relevant position in the subject in the late 1970s. In this way I hope to place *AA* in perspective as both a seminal work and a classic statement of a theory which was more at home in the archaeology of the 1960s than of the 1970s. As examples of changing views and developments I will discuss briefly quantitative analyses, the polythetic model for archaeological entities, the systems model for archaeological processes and in more detail, the emerging debate over the utility and validity of the "culture" concept.

Quantitative analyses

An indication of the rapidity of change in the application of mathematical and computer analyses in archaeology may be obtained by consulting the most recent syntheses by Doran and Hodson (1975) and Hodder and Orton (1976). In *AA*, David Clarke brought together examples of analyses already published (e.g., *AA*, Chapters 12 and 13) and suggested areas where further applications might be profitable. These included the analyses of spatial patterns derived from the "new" geography (e.g., nearest-neighbour analysis, Central Place Theory), the use of set theory, game theory and of random walk models. Now stimulus is often hard to define unless explicitly acknowledged, but in these three areas there have been attempts to pursue the lines of approach suggested by David Clarke. Spatial analysis has been developed beyond all recognition (see Hodder and Orton, 1976) especially with regard to the analyses of settlement patterns and artefact distributions (e.g., use of regression analysis, trend surface analyses, gravity models, simulation models, tests of association and significance). Archaeologists are also much more aware of the sampling factors which may affect our knowledge of spatial patterning in either sites or artefacts (Mueller, 1975; Schiffer, 1976) and the relationship between *pattern* and *process* is now being more explicitly formulated and analysed (e.g., Hodder and Orton, 1976, pp. 126–154).

As far as the use of techniques such as set and game theory and simulation studies using random walk models are concerned, the reader should consult Doran and Hodson (1975, pp. 285–316) and note especially the studies by Litvak King and Moll (1972), Thomas (1972) and Ammerman and Cavalli-Sforza (1973). The current success of these applications is a matter of debate (see Doran and Hodson, 1975) but the stimulus for their development was present in *AA*. Even if substantial application eventually proves impossible in some or all cases, at least the attempt will have been made.

The polythetic model for archaeological entities

As with some aspects of analysis, it seems that there have been few polythetic studies in archaeology above the level of the artefact or the assemblage (and in one case, the settlement – see Williams, Thomas and Bettinger, 1973). Taxonomic methods for clustering artefacts and assemblages are fully discussed in Doran and Hodson (1975), who also consider and reject the arguments against polythetic methods proposed mainly by Whallon (1972 – see Doran and Hodson, 1975, pp. 177–180). But at the levels of the culture, culture group and technocomplex, the suggestions advanced in *AA* do not appear to have been pursued in any depth. Within European prehistory analyses of cultures and culture groups have made little or no reference to polythetic classification. The entity at the top of the hierarchy, the technocomplex has been mentioned by a few authors (e.g., Gorman, 1971, p. 300; Tringham, 1971, pp. 37–38; Isaac, 1972) but little seems to have been added to the discussion presented in *AA*.

It is not immediately clear why there should have been this failure to develop the polythetic classification above the assemblage level, but I think that there are two possible reasons. First there is the *scale* of the entities involved, incorporating more complex patterning in the data over an increasing spatial network (e.g., from a few hundred miles radius for the culture and culture group up to some 3000 miles for technocomplexes). The time-span of these higher entities also increases from some 100 years to half a million years. This presents the researcher with a daunting task of both analysis and synthesis.

The second reason may be equally important. This is that among many European prehistorians interest in defining entities such as the "culture" has given way to the pursuit of social and economic goals (e.g., Higgs, 1972, 1975). "Culture studies" are viewed as sterile exercises which do little to advance our knowledge of long-term human behaviour. If not economic or bio-archaeologists, then we are exhorted to pursue "social archaeology" (Renfrew, 1973). It is no longer fashionable to pursue cultural morphology in the way set out in the middle chapters of *AA*.

The systems model for archaeological processes

If the *definition* of archaeological entities is no longer a fashionable exercise, their analysis and description in terms of dynamic systems is still an article of faith among younger archaeologists. The impetus provided by both Lewis Binford (e.g., 1965) and David Clarke has stimulated a succession of publications ranging from theoretical elaboration to practical application. In an important review article, Plog (1975) has shown how archaeologists have employed general systems theory as a theory of archaeology (specifically David Clarke), as a series of concepts (e.g., Flannery, 1968), as a source of models (e.g., Thomas, 1972) and hypotheses, and as an approach to explanation (see Renfrew, 1972). These applications extend from analyses of artefact-types, such as Judge's (1970) work on Folsom and Midland projectile points, through to more complex "big" problems such as the origins of agriculture (Binford, 1968; Flannery, 1968) and civilization (Renfrew, 1972).

This popularity of systems theory should not be allowed to obscure disagreement over its current success and potential in archaeology. Even among those researching in general systems theory there are reservations about the practicality of its application in other subjects, as it is claimed that there is still much intensive research to be undertaken (Klir, quoted in Doran and Hodson, 1975, p. 337). Within archaeology it has been argued that systemic concepts are not as revolutionary as some have claimed and that their application is limited by the nature of the archaeological record:

A severe limitation is placed on the efficacy of a systems approach by the necessity of tailoring the method so rigidly to the eccentricities of archaeological data. It is one thing to propose that human communities are best studied in terms of the forces and relationships between social, demographic, economic, ecological, technological and moral systems; the proposition loses something of its appeal when it is realised that in archaeology one can deal ineffectively or not at all with many of these aspects of human behaviour. These deficiencies result in an archaeology necessarily traditional in its basic concerns, although often expressed in misleadingly unfamiliar language. (Higgs and Jarman, 1975, p. 3)

The last sentence is part of the general argument about jargon which has already been mentioned above. The remainder of Higgs and Jarman's view seems confusing and self-defeating: as they do not say with *which* of these aspects "archaeology can deal ineffectively or not at all", they could be seen to be denying the validity of their own "palaeoeconomy" (Higgs and Jarman, 1975, p. 4) which deals with the relationship between population, technology and resources!!

On a more serious level, the disparity between systems theory and its practical application in archaeology is receiving increasing attention. Burnham (1973) questions whether such concepts as homeostasis and (in particular) adaptation can actually be applied to cultural processes:

. . . to my knowledge, no one has yet managed to specify processes operative in culture that are realistic "equivalent(s) of natural selection" or, for that matter, equivalents to any of the other key components of the biological evolutionary process. (Burnham, 1973, p. 94)

Even if one accepts the systems framework without Burnham's reservations, there still arises the following question: are we, and *should* we apply systems theory as a method of "asking old archaeological questions in new ways" (Plog, 1975, p. 213; cf., Doran, 1970, p. 294) or as a series of mathematical concepts in quantitative analyses on relevant archaeological data? Doran (1970) takes the view that studies such as those of Flannery (1968) and David Clarke simply use systems theory as a method for clearer thinking. This is accepted as a valid and productive exercise but a more rigorous approach is demanded:

> The terminology and concept framework within which facts and ideas are to be expressed seems dangerously vague. Although concepts such as dynamic equilibrium, positive feedback, Markov process, redundancy are all capable of mathematical definition, it is not these definitions which the proponents of systems theory have used, but rather the imprecise ideas which give rise to the definitions. *Without the rigorous definitions there is no mathematical theory, and without the mathematical theory there is no way of drawing objective conclusions from the evidence beyond what there has always been, the archaeologists own reasoning ability.* At best some degree of standardisation of argument might be achieved. (Doran 1970, p. 294), (my emphasis)

Doran and Hodson (1975, p. 339) reiterate this conviction and further argue that "archaeological data are insufficient for the mathematics of systems theory to be made to work".

Thus it seems as if the use of the systemic framework in archaeology may be at something of a crossroads in the late 1970s. From the optimistic days of Binford's early articles and David Clarke's substantial presentation in *AA*, we have come through a decade of many theoretical declarations of faith but few substantial applications, to a period of critical self-appraisal. There is little doubt that systems theory has enabled archaeologists such as Renfrew and Flannery to shed illuminating insights into important problems. With its emphasis on processes and complex interrelationships, it has enabled archaeologists to postulate mechanisms of change which no longer rely upon single explanations such as "diffusion" or "invasion". This emphasis was clear in *AA*, but ten years after its publication we have reached the point where more substantial research programmes are required if the systemic perspective is to retain a central role within archaeology (cf., Plog, 1975, p. 220).

Archaeological entities and the "culture" concept

While the systemic framework still remains fashionable among archaeologists in many areas, the use of the *full* hierarchy of entities presented in *AA* has enjoyed an adverse reaction. As has already been indicated, the definition of cultures, culture-groups and technocomplexes has received little attention. As far as British archaeology is concerned, the concept of a "technocomplex" has been largely ignored while "cultures" and "culture-groups" are now in decreasing use. Why has this change occurred? Are there any emerging research areas which might be of relevance to the culture concept? Lastly, how do these changes affect the content of *AA* and its position in the late 1970s?

The archaeological use of the culture concept was developed by V. Gordon Childe after earlier work by German prehistorians such as Kossinna. Childe defined the culture as follows:

> We find certain types of remains – pots, implements, ornaments, burial sites, house forms – constantly recurring together. Such a complex of regularly associated traits we shall term a "cultural group" or just a "culture". We assume that such a complex is the material expression of what today would be called a people. (Childe, 1929, pp. v–vi)

One of the central features of Childe's career, certainly in its early stages, was the systematization of European prehistory which resulted from his use of the culture as the organizing unit of analysis. Once cultures had been defined in time and space, their similarities were interpreted in terms of their degree of social interaction: movement of people, diffusion and influences were the processes most commonly suggested as being behind inter-cultural similarities. This is precisely the interpretation which Binford (see above) would now dismiss as "normative".

Through the writings of Childe and his contemporaries, culture-definition became one of the main foci of archaeological activity in the period from the 1920s to the 1950s. But in the last 20 years it has been relegated to the peripheries of research and some archaeologists have stated that the culture is no longer a relevant or useful concept in the last half of the twentieth century. For example, Daniel has written:

> Cultures, with their fine flavour of anthropology and anthropo-geography, replaced epochs and periods; but now we wish to describe prehistoric communities in their geographical, environmental and historical contexts without giving them cultural labels. The idea of a culture and cultures was a methodological device which helped us over the gap from the discrediting of the epochal idea to a time when exact dates were possible. Our aim now, surely, is to describe, as best we can with the material at our disposal at the time when we write, the life and times of prehistoric people without labels derived from technological and epochal models. (Daniel, 1971, p. 149)

It is at this point that we should ask why this change of interest has occurred after a period of some 30–40 years of practice and research. According to the argument presented above, the culture was merely a conceptual device for grouping together sites and artefacts in the absence of methods of independent absolute chronology. Such ordering is no longer necessary if we possess radiocarbon or other absolute dates which may tell us in which centuries or millennia particular sites were occupied. This view takes care of those areas where our knowledge of prehistoric chronology is dependent on stratigraphy, association and typology, but it ignores the spatial aspect of culture-definition: are there recognizable spatial patterns in the distribution of material culture which justify the creation of "cultures" and their equation with human social groups?

One point of view here is that "cultures" defined by material culture obscure the recognition of important variability in human behaviour. This is the essence of Binford's position (see above) and has also been espoused by Eric Higgs and his pupils at Cambridge (e.g., Higgs, 1972, 1975). In particular they have stressed the ethnographic observations of Donald Thompson, published in the late 1930s (Thompson, 1939) that the same group of Australian hunter-gatherers would use totally different material culture assemblages at different seasons of the year when they are exploiting animal and plant resources in different areas. The logical conclusion to be drawn from this was that the archaeologist might be giving cultural and even social status to differences which were in fact derived from economic practices. The converse might also apply: if the material culture assemblages from two or more sites were identical, it did not necessarily follow that their subsistence practices were also similar.

A further source of variability is the increasing recognition of exchanged or traded items in the archaeological record. This has been a feature of research employing characterization studies of raw materials using methods such as neutron activation analysis and optical emission spectroscopy drawn from the physical and chemical sciences. Within European archaeology, the initial impetus for this research came with the petrological studies of British Neolithic polished stone axes (e.g., Keiller, Piggott and Wallis, 1941 – for summary and further references see Shotton, 1969), and spectroscopic analyses of Copper and Bronze Age metalwork by Otto and Witter, as well as Pittioni in the 1930s and especially by the Stuttgart team of Junghans, Sangmeister and Schröder since 1949 (for early references see Britton and Richards, 1969). But it was not until the 1960s that these and allied techniques of analysis were extended to other raw materials such as pottery (well summarized in Peacock, 1970) and obsidian (e.g., Cann, Dixon and Renfrew, 1969).

Of all the materials which have been analysed in this way, it is the prehistoric pottery analyses which have proved the most thought-provoking. The often unwritten assumption that pottery was produced, used and discarded within the same social grouping, *in spite of* many ethnographic examples to the contrary, was widespread within European prehistoric studies. As pottery was also the most frequent artefact present on later prehistoric sites it is not surprising that it became an important diagnostic feature in the definition of cultures. Close similarities in forms, fabrics and particularly styles of pottery were thought to represent the tradition of a common social group.

One of the first challenges to these assumptions came with the publication of Jope's "The regional cultures of medieval Britain" (Jope, 1963). The main conclusion which he drew from the study of available medieval pottery distributions in Britain was that it was impossible to define regional cultures on this basis. Trading and marketing were demonstrated to be the main factors behind the distribution patterns, with "fine" wares having a wider distribution than more localized everyday "utility" wares. A few years later Peacock (1968) published the results of his petrological analyses of classes of Iron Age pottery found in the Herefordshire–Cotswold region of Western England. In his conclusion, he stated that:

> The evidence outlined above suggests that we are dealing with traded pottery, the distribution of which may have been largely determined by commercial rather than cultural factors. If this is the case, study of the origins of the styles . . . should lead to a greater understanding of the cultural heritage or influences affecting the potters *and not necessarily* the pot-users. (Peacock, 1968, p. 425), (my emphasis)

With the dissemination of Peacock's work, as well as other analyses mentioned above, British archaeology entered a period of uncertainty over the definition of prehistoric cultures (e.g., Cunliffe's (1974) use of "style zones" in the British Iron Age; Clark's (1975) definition of "home-base", "annual", "social" and "techno"-territories in studying the late- and post-glacial settlement of Scandinavia). This uncertainty was increased by a revival of interest in ethnographic studies of trade, stimulated in Britain by Grahame Clark's "Traffic in stone axe and adze blades" published in 1965. As a result, a point of view was emerging that some of the artefact distribution patterns which *had* been interpreted in cultural terms, were the result of processes of trade or exchange. Spatial patterns in material culture were *recognizable*, but should they necessarily be equated with social groups?

It is now argued that we should look very closely at the recognition of these patterns and employ tests of association to distinguish between random and non-random patterns. Hodder and Orton advocate that archaeologists should pursue the methods of culture trait distribution analysis as practised in social anthropology:

> In the case in which a number of distributions are located on a surface at random, there will be association groups (areas where a number of distributions overlap) which occur by chance. . . . "Random" association groups will be considered as "cultures" if the accepted archaeological definition is used. The tests for spatial association . . . allow us to determine whether

two distributions are intermingled in such a way that they are comparable to two random distributions. (Hodder and Orton, 1976, p. 200)

These tests of association are then applied to North German Early Bronze Age material and to the Middle Bronze Age in the Carpathian Basin (Hodder and Orton, 1976, pp. 211–223). Instead of the rather coarse definition of cultures there emerges a range of distributions from localized groups based on ornament types to much more widespread patterns formed by swords and axes. A social interpretation is suggested:

> The pattern, therefore, seems to be one of association groups of ornament types occurring in areas of higher densities of finds and perhaps of settlement. Outside a core area, a type is found with decreasing frequency as distance increased. In the peripheral area of its distribution a type may retain a low frequency even though other types occur densely. The maximum distance over which an artifact is found depends to some extent on the type of object. Thus, *types such as axes and swords probably had a comparatively low level of local demand*, and whether they were manufactured in one centre or not, these types are more widely spread than the ornaments. *They may relate to interaction at a high level in the social hierarchy*. (Hodder and Orton, 1976, pp. 219–221), (my emphases)

Not only does this suggest the need for care in the measurement of distribution patterns, but it also reminds us of Binford's point that important (in this case social) variability may be obscured by traditional "all-in" methods of culture-definition.

To summarize the arguments presented so far, it would be fair to say that Childe's concept of the culture has declined in usage as the complexities of material culture patterning and variability have received greater emphasis. Most archaeologists recognize the existence of spatial patterning in material culture, but the quantitative measurement of this patterning raises severe problems of interpretation. At the same time the combined evidence of characterization studies and ethnographic analogies strongly supports the argument that social and economic sources of artefact variability must be integrated into any analysis of material culture.

This brings us to an important aspect of current research into material culture. Clear distinction must be made between the actual *patterns* and the variety of possible *processes* that could have generated them. This point has been made recently by Rowlands and Gledhill (1977, p. 146) in discussing ethnographic analogy and is developed in a most stimulating way by Hodder and Orton (1976, pp. 126–154). The latter employ computer simulation studies to investigate the proposition that different spatial processes produce different spatial patterns in material culture. They demonstrate that this need not necessarily be true and that the same spatial pattern can be produced by different processes and vice versa. These observations are particularly relevant to the interpretation of artefact-patterns in terms of decreasing interaction with distance, as for example in the use of exchange or trade models.

The relationship between pattern and process has been pursued further by Ian Hodder (1977) in his study of artefact distributions among three tribes in the Baringo district of western Kenya. Between two tribes, the Tugen and the Njemps, there are clear distinctions in traits such as personal dress and compound plans and construction, and there is little intertribal movement of traits. In the archaeological record this evidence from the material culture would be interpreted as evidence for a *lack* of interaction between the two tribes. In actual fact, there is well-documented data on contact across the tribal boundaries (e.g., markets, reciprocal exchange, etc.). This observation runs contrary to one of the basic assumptions that stems from the use of the culture concept: the degree of interaction between communities or social groups is *not* necessarily directly reflected in material culture patterns.

On the other hand, Hodder notes that the methods of assemblage and culture definition presented in *AA* would be capable of distinguishing the three tribes and assessing which are more closely related to each other. But the reasons for these relationships could not be directly inferred. It is also argued that many different "cultures" could be defined in the Baringo district on the basis of the cultural traits *selected* (each with their own distributions) or *available* for study, due to the sampling problems associated with the preservation and recovery of material culture from the archaeological record. Again we come back to the problem of relating pattern and process: as Hodder writes,

> The simple definition of "cultures" tells us very little about the processes which produced artifact and trait distributions. (Hodder, 1977, p. 129)

Material culture studies such as those of Hodder in East Africa and Binford among the Eskimo (e.g., Binford, 1976) are part of an emerging research field which will contribute greatly to our understanding of the relationship between social interaction and cultural trait patterns. Similarly there is a need to develop our knowledge of the cultural and non-cultural factors that *distort* patterns in archaeological remains. Theoretical advances in this field have already been made, such as Schiffer's (1976) crucial distinction between *archaeological context* and *systemic context* and his classification of the various processes which might distort our view of patterns in the archaeological context. Factors such as differential disposal of artefacts in settlements or burials or in relation to their transportability, place of deposition (e.g., close to or distant from the context in which they were used), scavenging, redevelopment, erosion and recycling must all be considered here. Schiffer also presents examples of "behavioural chains" (Schiffer, 1976, pp. 49–53): for the cultivation and consumption of maize among the Hopi Indians he charts the sequence of activities related to the people involved, the technology used, the different locations and times of the activities and most important of all, the expected archaeological patterns which would result from them. This is in many ways analogous to Dennell's work (1972) on the deposition of botanical remains in different contexts within an archaeological site.

In Schiffer's work, as in a number of other publications, the theory for a study of the processes by which the archaeological record has been formed is present. This was also true of some of David Clarke's later publications (e.g., Clarke, 1973 – see this volume) in which he discussed "depositional" and "post-depositional" factors. However, what is now required is an attempt to put the theory into practice with some actual "test" cases. Hopefully such studies will soon emerge.

What effect do all these developments in the study of material culture have upon the relevance of *AA* in the late 1970s? It should be said initially that David Clarke was abreast of all the problems with the culture concept which research had raised. The importance of exchange in forming spatial patterns in material culture was fully recognized in his preference for the term "*network*" rather than "culture" in his last published work on the beaker problem (Clarke, 1976, especially p. 465). Similarly, he was quite clear that entities such as the "culture" need not necessarily have had any real existence in the past: but they could still be useful as "summarizing terms-of-convenience employed to simplify complex expressions" (Clarke, 1973, p. 14). In this way, "cultures" were seen as heuristic devices, bringing order into complex data as a necessary prerequisite to deeper analysis. The isolation of *regularity* was necessary in order to isolate important *variability* (see above).

In the light of the experimental research outlined above, it is clear that the methods of culture definition employed in *AA* may still have some validity in attempts to distinguish social groups on the basis of shared material culture. But what is equally clear is the need for quantitative measurement and association tests to be applied to spatial patterns in artefact distributions, the recognition of the complex relationships between spatial pattern and archaeological process, and an incisive attack on the relationship between material culture and social interaction. Further work on the relationship between material culture and social, ethnic or linguistic units, as outlined in *AA* (pp. 358–398), is also required. Meanwhile, as research in these fields develops within the next decade, we are left with the conclusion that the theory of entity definition proposed in *AA* is the yardstick against which the new research must be assessed. Even in the 1970s it remains the classic statement of one approach to the archaeological theory, and any new approach must be its equal in both logic of argument and depth of presentation.

CONCLUSION

Any attempt to discuss the development of themes and approaches in archaeology must be an essentially personal interpretation. As with material culture, we inevitably interpret in the light of our own theoretical perspectives: what we believe to be appropriate and productive methods, techniques, hypotheses and explanations. This introduction is no exception, but I have tried to present as objectively as possible David Clarke's general aims in writing *AA*. These were essentially threefold:

1. *Experimental* As he wrote at the end of the book, quoting Bacon, "truth comes out of error more readily than out of confusion". The experiment was designed to present the relevance of changes in other disciplines (the "New Studies") to archaeology, to propose an explicit central theory for archaeology and to pursue new techniques and apply new concepts to the study of the past.
2. *Stimulus* Difficult to assess in terms of success, but sufficient examples have been quoted in this introduction to show the effect which the volume has had on younger archaeologists since its publication.
3. *Outward/Forward-looking* Archaeology should not exist in splendid isolation. Developments in concepts and methods in other disciplines and other countries may be of relevance to the archaeologist. Exploratory studies may reveal potential applications which only more detailed case-studies can test. Archaeology is a rapidly developing, international discipline which requires its practitioners to look beyond their own parochial research interests to broader, deeper problems of common theory and methods.

Judged by these aims, I can only conclude that *AA* has justified its author's hopes. Of course techniques and concepts have continued to change since 1968, as I have tried to indicate, but the book's importance in the history of archaeology remains untouched. Alongside *New Perspectives in Archaeology*, published in the same year (Binford and Binford,

1968), it offered a direct challenge to "traditional" archaeology. In the words of David Clarke,

> Archaeology and these New Studies constitute a coupled system and therefore archaeology must adapt to the changing output of this context if it wishes to make the most use of these powerful arrivals. *Archaeology must be rethought, reorientated and rewritten* in order to facilitate these developments and in order to reciprocally contribute to the modern context. (Clarke, 1968, p. 664), (my emphasis)

I have tried to place this rethinking, reorientation and rewriting in the context in which *AA* was conceived, published and received, not only in Britain but also in America. The arguments for and against particular views and approaches have been presented. But as David Clarke would have wished, it is now up to the reader to look at the articles which follow, and at *AA* as a whole, and draw his or her own conclusions.

BIBLIOGRAPHY

Alcock, L. (1976). Sir Mortimer Wheeler, *Rescue News*, **12**, 10.

Ammerman, A. J. and Cavalli-Sforza, L. L. (1973). A population model for the diffusion of early farming in Europe, in *The Explanation of Culture Change* (C. Renfrew, ed.), Duckworth, London, pp. 343–357.

Ashby, W. R. (1956). *An Introduction to Cybernetics*, Chapman & Hall, London.

Bertalanffy, L. von (1950). An outline of general systems theory, *Brit. J. Phil. Sci.*, **1**, 134–165.

Binford, L. R. (1962). Archaeology as anthropology, *American Antiquity*, **28**, 217–225.

Binford, L. R. (1965). Archaeological systematics and the study of culture process, *American Antiquity*, **31**, 203–210.

Binford, L. R. (1972). *An Archaeological Perspective*, Seminar Press, London and New York.

Binford, L. R. (1976). Forty-seven trips, in *Contributions to Anthropology: The Interior Peoples of Northern Alaska* (E. S. Hall ed.), Archaeological Survey of Canada, Paper no. 49. Ottawa.

Binford, L. R. and Binford, S. R. (1968). *New Perspectives in Archaeology*, Aldine, Chicago.

Brainerd, G. W. (1951). The place of chronological ordering in archaeological analysis, *American Antiquity*, **16**, 301–313.

Britton, D. and Richards, E. E. (1969). Optical emission spectroscopy and the study of metallurgy in the European Bronze Age, in *Science in Archaeology* (D. Brothwell and E. S. Higgs, eds), Thames & Hudson, London, pp. 603–613.

Burnham, P. (1973). The explanatory value of the concept of adaptation in studies of culture change, in *The Explanation of Culture Change* (C. Renfrew, ed.), Duckworth, London, pp. 93–102.

Cann, J. R., Dixon, J. E. and Renfrew, C. (1969). Obsidian analysis and the obsidian trade, in *Science in Archaeology* (D. Brothwell and E. S. Higgs, eds), Thames & Hudson, London, pp. 578–591.

Childe, V. G. (1929). *The Danube in Prehistory*, Clarendon Press, Oxford.

Childe, V. G. (1956). *Piecing Together the Past*, Routledge & Kegan Paul, London.

Childe, V. G. (1963). *Social Evolution*, Fontana, London.

Chorley, R. J. (1962). Geomorphology and general systems theory, *United States Geological Survey, Professional Paper*, 500-B.

Clark, J. G. D. (1965). Traffic in stone axe and adze blades, *Economic History Review*, **18,** 1–28.

Clark, J. G. D. (1975). *The Earlier Stone Age Settlement of Scandinavia*, Cambridge University Press, Cambridge.

Clarke, D. L. (1962). Matrix analysis and archaeology with particular reference to British beaker pottery, *Proceedings of the Prehistoric Society*, **28**, 371–382.

Clarke, D. L. (1968). *Analytical Archaeology*, Methuen, London.

Clarke, D. L. (1970). *Beaker Pottery of Great Britain and Ireland*, Cambridge University Press, Cambridge.

Clarke, D. L. (1972). Models and paradigms in contemporary archaeology, in *Models in Archaeology* (D. L. Clarke, ed.), Methuen, London, pp. 1–60.

Clarke, D. L. (1973). Archaeology: the loss of innocence, *Antiquity*, XLVII, 6–18.

Clarke, D. L. (1976). The beaker network – social and economic models, in *Glockenbechersymposion Oberried, 1974* (J. N. Lanting and J. D. van der Waals, eds), Fibulavan Dishoek, Bussum/Haarlem, pp. 458–477.

Collingwood, R. G. (1939). *An Autobiography*, Clarendon Press, Oxford.

Cunliffe, B. W. (1974). *Iron Age Communities in Britain*, Routledge & Kegan Paul, London.

Daniel, G. E. (1943). *The Three Ages*, Cambridge University Press, Cambridge.

Daniel, G. E. (1971). From Worsaae to Childe: the models of prehistory, *Proceedings of the Prehistoric Society*, **37**, part II, pp. 140–153.

Daniel, G. E. (1973). Editorial, *Antiquity*, XLVII, 93–95.

Daniel, G. E. (1975). *150 Years of Archaeology*, Duckworth, London.

Dennell, R. W. (1972). The interpretation of plant remains: Bulgaria, in *Papers in Economic Prehistory* (E. S. Higgs, ed.), Cambridge University Press, Cambridge, pp. 149–159.

Doran, J. E. (1970). Systems theory, computer simulations and archaeology, *World Archaeology*, **1**, 289–298.

Doran, J. E. and Hodson, F. R. (1975). *Mathematics and Computers in Archaeology*, Edinburgh University Press, Edinburgh.

Dymond, D. P., (1974). *Archaeology and History: a Plea for Reconciliation*, Thames & Hudson, London.

Flannery, K. V. (1968). Archaeological systems theory and early Mesoamerica, in *Anthropological Archaeology in the Americas* (B. Meggers, ed.), Anthropological Society, Washington, DC, pp. 67–87.

Flannery, K. V. (1973). Archaeology with a capital S, in *Research and Theory in Current Archaeology* (C. Redman, ed.), Wiley, New York, pp. 47–53.

Gorman, C. (1974). The Hoabinhian and after: subsistence patterns in Southeast Asia during the late Pleistocene and early Recent periods, *World Archaeology*, **2**, 300–320.

Haggett, P. (1965). *Locational Analysis in Human Geography*, Edward Arnold, London.

Hawkes, J. (1968). The proper study of mankind, *Antiquity*, XLII, 255–262.

Higgs, E. S. (ed.) (1972). *Papers in Economic Prehistory*, Cambridge University Press, Cambridge.

Higgs, E. S. (ed.) (1975). *Palaeoeconomy*, Cambridge University Press, Cambridge.

Hill, J. N. (1972). The methodological debate in contemporary archaeology: a model, in *Models in Archaeology* (D. L. Clarke, ed.), Methuen, London, pp. 61–107.

Hodder, I. (1977). A study in ethnoarchaeology in western Kenya, in *Archaeology and Anthropology* (M. Spriggs, ed.), British Archaeological Reports Supplementary Series 19, Oxford, pp. 117–141.

Hodder, I. and Orton, C. (1976). *Spatial Analysis in Archaeology*, Cambridge University Press, Cambridge.

Hogarth, A. C. (1972). Common sense in archaeology, *Antiquity*, XLVI, 301–304.

Isaac, G. Ll. (1972). Chronology and the tempo of cultural change during the Pleistocene, in *Calibration of Hominoid Evolution* (W. W. Bishop and J. A. Miller, eds), Wenner-Gren Foundation, New York, pp. 381–430.

Jope, E. M. (1963). The regional cultures of medieval Britain, in *Culture and Environment* (I. L. Foster and L. Alcock, eds), Routledge & Kegan Paul, London, pp. 327–350.

Judge, W. J. (1970). Systems analysis and the Folsom-Midland Question, *Southwestern Journal of Anthropology*, **26**, 40–51.

Keiller, A., Piggott, S. and Wallis, F. S. (1941). First report of the sub-committee of the south-western group of museums and art galleries on the petrological identification of stone axes, *Proceedings of the Prehistoric Society*, **7**, 50–72.

Kuhn, T. S. (1962). *The Structure of Scientific Revolutions*, University of Chicago Press, Chicago.

Litvak King, J. and García Moll, R. (1972). Set theory models: an approach to taxonomic and locational relationships, in *Models in Archaeology* (D. L. Clarke, ed.), Methuen, London, pp. 735–756.

Mueller, J. W. (ed.) (1975). *Sampling in Archaeology*, University of Arizona Press, Tuscon.

Peacock, D. P. S. (1968). A petrological study of certain Iron Age pottery from western England, *Proceedings of the Prehistoric Society*, **34**, 414–427.

Peacock, D. P. S. (1970). The scientific analysis of ancient ceramics: a review, *World Archaeology*, **1**, 375–389.

Plog, F., (1975). Systems theory in archaeological research, *Annual Review of Anthropology*, **4**, 207–224.

Renfrew, A. C. (1972). *The Emergence of Civilisation*, Methuen, London.

Renfrew, A. C. (1973). *Social Archaeology*, University of Southampton.

Robinson, W. S. (1951). A method for chronologically ordering archaeological deposits, *American Antiquity*, **16**, 293–301.

Rouse, I. (1970). Classification for what? *Norwegian Archaeological Review*, **3**, 4–12.

Rowlands, M. J. and Gledhill, J. (1977). The relation between archaeology and anthropology, in *Archaeology and Anthropology* (M. Spriggs, ed.), British Archaeological Reports Supplementary Series 19, Oxford, pp. 143–158.

Schiffer, M. B. (1976). *Behavioural Archaeology*, Academic Press, New York, San Francisco and London.

Shotton, F. W. (1969). Petrological examination, in *Science in Archaeology* (D. Brothwell and E. S. Higgs, eds), Thames & Hudson, London, pp. 571–577.

Sokal, R. R. and Sneath, P. H. A. (1963). *Principles of Numerical Taxonomy*, Freeman, San Francisco and London.

Spaulding, A. C. (1953). Statistical techniques for the discovery of artifact-types, *American Antiquity*, **18**, 305–313.

Taylor, W. W. (1948). *A Study of Archaeology*, Memoir no. 69, *American Anthropologist*, **50**, Part 2.

Thompson, D. F. (1939). The seasonal factor in human culture, *Proceedings of the Prehistoric Society*, **10**, 209–221.

Tringham, R. (1971). *Hunters, Fishers and Farmers of Eastern Europe 6000–3000 BC*, Hutchinson, London.

Tugby, D. J. (1958). A typological analysis of axes and choppers from Southeast Australia, *American Antiquity*, **24**, 24–33. .

Watson, P. J., LeBlanc, S. A. and Redman, C. L. (1971). *Explanation in Archaeology: An Explicitly Scientific Approach*, Columbia University Press, New York and London.

Watson, R. A. (1972). The "new archaeology" of the 1960s, *Antiquity*, XLVI, 210–215.

Whallon, R. (1972). A new approach to pottery typology, *American Antiquity*, **37**, 13–33.

Williams, L., Thomas, D. H. and Bettinger, R. (1973). Notions to numbers: Great Basin settlements as polythetic sets, in *Research and Theory in Current Archaeology* (C. Redman, ed.), Wiley, New York, pp. 215–237.

Towards Analytical Archaeology – New Directions in the Interpretive Thinking of British Archaeologists

DAVID L. CLARKE

I

I think that it would be true to say that the murky exhalation which passes for "interpretive thinking" in British archaeology is currently showing signs of agitation. It would, perhaps, be a mistake to talk of absolutely new developments or an overall directional movement in so ethereal a body. Nevertheless, unusual agitation is apparent and the ceaseless partitioning and repartitioning which such disciplinary fields continuously undergo does inevitably reveal certain freshly polarized stances within the general field space. As is customary in such volatile effusions, the fresh concentrations seem to be incompatibly polarized with relation to one another and are accompanied by wholesale collision between their tenets and supporters, with the release of quite as much heat as light. But despite partisan feeling, and, indeed, because such clarifying polarizations and healthy interaction continue to develop, new light is indeed being generated.

The freshly polarized positions within this agitated body of interpretive thinking seem to have condensed around three main nuclei – cultural morphology, cultural ecology, and cultural ethnology. Each of these nucleated positions is associated with its group of vociferous and partisan advocates who are convinced that their particular approach is the primary route to archaeological advancement. These artificially separate and partisan nuclei are, however, partially interlinked by the fourth "new" factor in this ether – the important common language and philosophy of the "new methodology". Now I must hasten to add that neither these "new" positions nor the "new" metho-

Paper originally presented at the symposium on "Theory and Methodology in Archaeological Interpretation" at Flagstaff, Arizona, in September 1968. Not previously published.

dology are especially new in themselves or in their components; it is their cumulative condensation as integrated approaches with their own analytical grammars and their own predictive categorizations which is new. So, perhaps a short sketch of these "new" positions and their methodology may provide a suitable starting point.

Let us begin with cultural morphology. This position embraces the expanding nucleus of studies whose main objectives are the cross-cultural definition of the structural morphology of archaeological entities in terms of their components, the integration of these entities in yet higher organizations, and the exposition of the grammar of their developmental transformation. The studies within this nucleus are much concerned with the basic common particles of archaeology – attributes, artefacts, types, assemblages, cultures, culture groups and other complexes of material artefacts – together with their static and dynamic configurations. The advocates of this approach are perhaps more intimately concerned with the machinery of the "new methodology" than any other single group, but not exclusively so. The critics of this developing polarization suggest that it is an abstract and sterile revival of the old typological and classificatory approaches of the last century, decked out in borrowed modern finery. These accusations infer an unduly atomistic approach with a tendency to treat complex entities as billiard balls, without sufficient orientation towards the social and ecological environments of the once living contexts. The partisans would dismiss these charges as a necessary stage in the initial treatment of empirical data – claiming that archaeology continues to remain a contentious and intuitive skill largely because it lacks a sufficiently explicit theory defining its entities and their modes of operation; the central theory which should synthesize the regularities of the data uniquely peculiar to the discipline, the ancient artefacts.

The cultural ecologists would ignore such trivia. Cultural ecology they would see as the study of the relationships between the configurations of archaeological material and the ecological context in which it was formerly set, the mutual relations between such systems and their environment, together with the temporal and regional adaptive changes of these systems. This bold band talk of habitats, demes, clines, niches, biomes, and ecosystems and see archaeology as a biological science connecting hominid animal behaviour with the variety in the environment of the globe. The cultural ecologists point with disdain to the infinitesimal pedantry of the archaeological taxonomist and to the contradictory conclusions of decades of a dusty categorization more akin to philately than to an analysis of behaviour patterns. Unabashed by these gibes, the critics of cultural ecology claim that the study is only an outer periphery of the archaeological sphere, that it is currently naive in its understanding of the samples which constitute its raw material, and anachronistically determinist in making insufficient allowance for the idiosyncratic degrees of freedom permitted to human activities in even the most constrained conditions. At its worst, cultural ecology merely substitutes the differential minutiae of horn or bone measurements for those of typology, so that its reports often regress to the level of the nineteenth century, simply illustrating a few archaeological *belles pièces*.

Cultural ethnology reflects the small but interesting nucleus of studies which focus on the relationships between groupings in material culture and sociocultural regularities of all kinds – social, linguistic, or racial; the aim being to restore a realistic sociocultural predictive capacity to the many categories of archaeological entities. The philosophy involved seeks a probabilistic mean path between the usual archaeological positions which either assert that nothing can be deduced about the sociocultural correlates of archaeological entities, or tacitly assumes a simple one-to-one equivalence at the other extreme – tribe equals culture equals language, and so on. The advocates of cultural ethnology see the sociocultural interpretation of archaeological data as the central purpose of archaeology, the time–depth extension of anthropology. The critics of cultural ethnology find the machinery for expressing the relationships between archaeological and sociocultural entities still quite unsatisfactory even in its less naive forms, and doubt whether the sociocultural possibilities are sufficiently limited for the construction of viable interpretations. Nevertheless, with the current demise of ethnology in academic circles it is interesting to note that archaeology is taking on many of the tasks and problems formerly left to the ethnologist. Indeed, the archaeologist might soberly reflect that any failure of archaeology to establish itself as more than a popular opiate will surely consign the discipline to the same limbo plumbed by museum ethnology in the Old World.

So much for an oversimplified view of the currently rival partitions in British archaeology, now we can take a look at the "new methodology", the important but embryonic common language which increasingly unites the work of even the most partisan partitionists. The "new" methodology is not one method but an array of methods joined by a common philosophy of approach – an empirical approach seeking to utilize the wider general powers of numerical, mathematical and statistical models and formulations for building symbolic machinery capable of simulating archaeological phenomena; the digital and analog computer are, of course, integral parts of this methodology.

One of the prime concerns of this fresh ideology is to emphasize the intimate penetration and inseparable role of the mathematical concepts which secretly interlace even the most tacit and furtive archaeological models, analyses, and procedures. It is especially stressed that the moment the archaeologist excavates the peculiar content of a selected site he is already involved in sampling the preserved sample, of a site sample which is itself an accidentally deposited sample, of a former particular regional assemblage sample, of a localized prehistoric cultural assemblage population. The data from any archaeological project is a sample – a sample drawn from site, assemblage, and cultural target populations which remain unknown. The archaeological samples vary enormously in their relationship to these unknown target populations, as well as varying in the purposes for which they were obtained, the conditions of the sampling, and in the uses to which they are ultimately submitted.

The new ideology also directs attention to the observation that archaeological samples differ amongst themselves and, indeed, should be made to differ for the different purposes of each experiment upon the data – since the archaeologist's conceptual model of his data defines the population of interest, the variables to be measured, and the kinds of variability that need be considered. This conceptual model is ideally converted into a symbolic mathematical model accommodating the variables and structure of the mind model. Then, and only then, can a sampling plan be devised to seek out from the infinite range of kinds of samples the best category to test that particular model and situation. The samples may be intended to test for archaeological trends over a given area, alternatively they may be required to estimate the affinity of the sample to known cultural assemblages, or again the available population may be so large that the archaeologist may wish to take samples from which a reliable estimation may be made of the parameters of the unknown target population containing the sample; this latter estimate is usually based on a random sample. These are all categories of samples within the extensive universe of possible sample categories.

This philosophy reveals that from the very first instant, the archaeologist is grappling with the problems of samples of populations, populations of subpopulations, the definitions of their ranges of variation, their distribution of states and values, and the relations of the samples to once existing populations. In addition, the archaeologist will wish to progress from the methods of descriptive statistics and quantification to the realms of inductive statistics and the problems of relationship, seeking evidence of affinities and dissimilarities, trends and correlations, whilst expressing such findings in synthesizing probability propositions. Finally, the archaeologist may try to model the characteristics and relationships of his data in structured systems of hypotheses, preferably organized in the powerful and abstract terminology of symbolic models, where mathematical symbolism may provide a great variety of methods for arranging and expressing such hypotheses in static or dynamic forms. In this respect, the knowledge of new branches of mathematics constantly opens up new possibilities for the organization of such systems.

The ideological relevance of mathematical concepts and the new methodology to archaeology may therefore be crudely reduced to the requirements of – entitation, quantitation, computation and statistification. More specifically:

1. The provision of sampling systems for the testing of appropriate models, emphasizing the importance of the model in deciding the suitable sample before any sample has been taken; the development of samples in relationship to the model and data.
2. The need for entitation and quantification – the need to define and handle population concepts adequately and accurately using quantification and descriptive statistics.
3. The need to handle relationship concepts adequately and accurately using analytical inductive statistics for covariation, variance, correlations and trends, and including the study of affinities using numerical taxonomy.
4. The need to handle the regularities in complex data in terms of isomorphic systems of symbols arranged in axiomatic schemes, models, or calculi.

The computer, in this context, is merely the multipurpose power tool of the new methodology and, therefore, provides the varied capacity necessary for the tougher problems. Thus, the computer may be understood as the magnifying lens of the twentieth century, which, by means of varying arrangements, can be used like the microscope, to analyse the microstructure of complex entities in minute detail, or like the telescope to examine the integration of such entities within systems of a far greater scale. If the challenging problem in other disciplines in earlier centuries was the exponentially increasing mass of data released by the experimenter's lens and the explorer's new discoveries, then today archaeology is faced with a similar release of information from equally rich new sources. But whereas Linnaeus and the other great taxonomists faced this chaos with Aristotelean logic and the lens, we now face a similar situation armed with statistical and probability theory and the relentless energy of the computer.

The new methodology and its philosophy are being rapidly propagated by the ever-widening distribution of computer facilities and training, together with the exciting development of simple language

programming, dynamic simulation models, graphic oscilloscope outputs and direct scanning inputs. At the same time, analytical archaeology is itself tentatively beginning to put forward more and more
archaeological hypotheses in increasingly explicit and accurate symbolic
models. One cannot but remark upon the rapidity of this international
convergence which is beginning to diminish the gap between archaeological theory and computer practice. As analytical archaeology painfully perfects its symbolic models and makes more use of deterministic,
statistical, stochastic and dynamic model forms, so will it more directly
and effectively employ such powerful tools as the analog and digital
computer. The archaeologist must, however, remember that the
archaeology⇌computer coupling provides a two-way relationship;
archaeology must adaptively reorganize, reorientate, remodel and
resymbolize itself in order to communicate more effectively with the
potential of the computer systems. This is especially the case with
archaeological general theory. At the same time, this coupled system
is in a dynamic context and as the computers develop and change so
will the models of analytical archaeology.

In parenthesis, and perhaps to redress the balance of detached
moderation against ideological enthusiasm, we must still repeat the
axiom expressed by the first of all digital computer programmers – Lady
Lovelace, only child of Lord Byron, program writer to Charles Bab-
bage's "analytical engine" at Cambridge in 1843: "The analytical
engine has no pretensions whatever to originate anything. It can do
whatever we know how to order it to perform" (Wilkes, 1957, p. 289).

This preamble brings us roughly abreast of the currently fashionable
positions within the more experimental sectors of British archaeology.
One must not ignore the fact that the greater part of British archaeological activities, like those in other national schools, is continuously
engaged in the well-known literary exercise of running-on-the-spot: the
ceaseless descriptive rhapsody on the endless flow of new material, perfectly expressed in the notation of the last-generation-but-one, to the
glossy counterpoint of the narrative psalmody of archaeological, imitation history books. Equally, one cannot ignore the marked similarities
between the concentrations in current British archaeological interpretive thinking and the closely connected positions in the output of
the other national schools of archaeology, but more of that later. Perhaps it would first be worthwhile to try and understand the interrelationship and origins of the three "new" foci of analytical activity,
together with the significance of their "new" methodology.

The current problems and positions in archaeology are closely akin
to the analogous problems and positions of modern linguistics. In the
latter context, few people would deny that the study of grammar was

as valid a pursuit as the study of the literature on which it is based, and yet in archaeology the corresponding position often denies the possible existence of the equivalent of an archaeological grammar, or at least dismisses the possibility that any such construct might enlighten archaeological "literature". But grammar simply comprises the organized and ordered body of the relationships of words, as abstracted from a very large number of literary contexts – the condensation of a large number of observed regularities. It seems clear, however, that the outcome of the "new methodology" within the three fields of cultural morphology, cultural ecology and cultural ethnology will be some equivalent body of just such archaeological grammar, similarly condensing a large number of observed cross-cultural regularities in archaeological data.

However, there seem to be not one archaeological grammar but three "rival" archaeologies, with three separate grammars based on what may appear to be mutually contradictory approaches and propositions. These partitioned propositions of modern archaeology seem to exhort us to take totally opposed views of the same data.

Cultural morphology   Archaeological data is now detached from its contemporary sociocultural and environmental contexts. Archaeological data may therefore best be studied empirically as a material phenomenon with observable regularities. Artefacts and their assemblages should be studied in terms of their own attribute systems, away from the distortions of bias and loose presuppositions about their former contexts.

Cultural ecology   Archaeological data was formerly an integral part of mutually adjusted environmental and ecological systems in which the artefacts and their assemblages were elaborately networked. Archaeological data cannot, therefore, be meaningfully studied as an artificially discrete subsystem separated from the whole circuitry of interaction which was its physical context.

Cultural ethnology   Archaeological data is the relict product of human activity and behaviour. Such data was formerly an integral part of an internally adjusted sociocultural system in which the artefacts and their assemblages were elaborately networked. Archaeological data cannot therefore be meaningfully studied as an artificially discrete subsystem separated from the whole circuitry of interaction which was its social context.

The apparent conundrum is that all of these propositions seem true and, certainly, the rival archaeologies that they have given rise to have each made most useful contributions in recent years. If this is the case, how are these positions to be reconciled and what are the respective roles and mutual connections of these rival approaches, each with its own domain and partisan supporters.

The answer to this riddle of modern archaeology can best be sought in the elementary structure of the discipline's raw material. Thus, artefacts and their assemblages can be studied in terms of their relationships to three sets of references – their relationships to other artefacts and assemblages, their relationships to groups of people, and their relation-

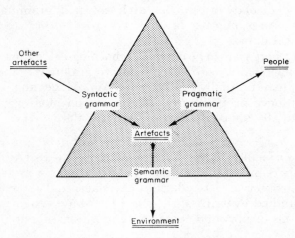

FIG. 1. Artefacts and interpretation. The three grammars of archaeological interrelationships and their three domains – the consequences of the three outputs of material culture communications. (Clarke, 1968, Fig. 169.)

ships to environmental regularities (Fig. 1). These three interfaces are certainly interrelated facets of the same data but nevertheless each interface opens onto a different operational domain with its own dimensions and therefore with its own grammar. The linguistic equivalent of this situation then makes it apparent that we need a syntactic grammar of cultural morphology, a semantic grammar of cultural ecology, and a pragmatic grammar of cultural ethnology, wherein:

1. *syntactics* synthesizes the relations between attributes, artefacts and assemblages at every level of their organization;
2. *semantics* synthesizes the relations between artefacts and their roles against the physical world;
3. *pragmatics* synthesizes the relations between artefacts and their users and observers – an important bifurcation.

In reality, therefore, there is no contradiction between the separate pursuit of each of these three "new" fields and its appropriate synthesizing grammar. These three contemporary partitions are mutually essential and are indispensable aspects of the same study rather than rival camps. However, the integration of the evidence from these three domains is most accurately accomplished if the archaeologist is aware of these separate sets of relationships and systematically sets about the independent construction of the different domain grammars, each in terms of its appropriate evidence. The equally essential need to integrate the findings and categorizations of these separate domains must be accomplished after the evidence of each has been treated separately – otherwise the attempt at a single all-purpose grammar of archaeological relationships will promote confusion between procedures and introduce too many dimensions for effective control.

The role of the new methodology in this analytical manipulation is a vital one. The ideal is to organize and order the synthesizing observations into symbolic models of ascending capacity. The grammar developed from such an approach may ultimately hope to achieve a calculus of relationships based upon observations of countless particular archaeological systems and might possibly achieve the symbolic representation of such systems. This would allow the manipulation and transformation of these general symbolic representations by means of a set of grammatical rules such that the consequences of a set of calculus operations would be isomorphic with the consequences of a parallel set of operations in the real world. These predicted consequences, or, strictly speaking, postdicted model formats, will not of course specify a detailed "result" of a given situation, merely defining that part of the outcome which would be the general structure associated with interactions of that particular category. It is just possible that the symbolic models of archaeological entities and processes may sufficiently share certain general classes of system organization that would enable them to be used as representational formulae – rather in the manner of chemical equation notation – within symbolic calculi. In the same way, it is conceivable that the homotopic relationships uniting cultural assemblages and artefact-types as transforms within distinct phylogenies may also one day be expressed by quantitative indices of "distortion" relating one phenotypic state to another. But these are ultimate speculations and even in a somewhat simpler material such a transition took the natural sciences nearly two centuries of ceaseless endeavour to accomplish.

Now, of course British archaeological thought cannot be realistically divorced from the world archaeological context in which it flourishes and with which it is mutually adjusted. Indeed, one of the most important factors in the current "agitation" is the mutual impact of the hitherto rather separate interpretive traditions of the archaeological schools of the New World, Western Europe, Eastern Europe, Africa and Australasia. In former years, each of these schools worked in its own terrain with its own idiosyncratic interpretive machinery – an inherited *corpus* adapted to local conditions. Each archaeological tradition knew of the existence of the others but the array of locally adapted features, the individual political tinctures, and the predominance of each school in its own area, together combined only to impress each school with the obvious astigmatic imperfections of its contemporary rivals. Nowhere has this process been more apparent than in the national "Histories of Archaeology" in which archaeology seems to have been developed entirely by the efforts of Americans, Marxists, Frenchmen, Scandinavians, or eccentric Welshmen, according to the unilinear mythology of the respective national schools.

The interpretive methodology of the regional schools of archaeology has been as much a part of strictly local colouring as the inevitably distinctive archaeological sequences of the same regions. Until recently it was largely ignored that, although the "archaeology" of each area was a unique mosaic, nevertheless the tacit interpretive methodology of archaeology as a discipline must either be valid beyond a local sphere of interest, or it fails to qualify for the purposes of general theory. Of course, the regional schools of archaeology have long exchanged personnel, and the wise itinerant archaeologist has always paid the obligatory, polite lip-service to the regional juju's and taboos of the alien territory that he has passed through; but polite phraseology and an inscrutable contempt do not constitute a real interaction. No, the new situation is one of real, large-scale, multidirectional and multidimensional interaction between the formerly discrete regional schools – with a consequently severe reappraisal of much of the localized dogmas and a real move to integrate the best interpretive machinery from all the schools within a single coherent empirical discipline of archaeology.

The main agents in this healthy interaction on an unprecedented scale are the young research students and their increasingly international language – the "new methodology". The younger research workers now regularly work for long periods in the territories of alien intellectual schools, they are seizing these opportunities to inspect, borrow, adapt, reject and integrate their own school ideologies with those of the local traditions within which they are encysted – the spores of contagion – like so many Lenins in so many railway trucks! This process is strengthened by the increasing numbers of these hybrid archaeologists appointed to teaching posts at foreign universities, where their compounded learning is rapidly passed to the eager young iconoclasts of their own age-groups – a process of communication made a thousand-fold more effective by the other main agent of their success, the inter-national "new methodology". Although this methodology is still as yet an embryonic formulation, it is nevertheless already revolutionizing the capacity for the rapid communication and teaching of the basis of archaeology, and this is one reason why it is so successful in short-cir-cuiting the "traditional" schooling of the regional faculties. The new methodology begins to offer an explicit central theory of archaeological entities and processes capable of superseding the tacit, unanalysed, local procedures and models, inherited regionally and learned by rote. This approach ultimately promises, in the distant future, to elucidate the relationships which permeate archaeological data by means of disci-plined procedures directed towards the precipitation of a body of general theory – the birth of "analytical archaeology".

The processes of interaction and ferment that have just been de-scribed are still at a very early stage of development, and it cannot be assumed that the current transient manifestations of those move-ments, with all their obvious imperfections, yet represent in any way a major breakthrough. Nevertheless, when asked to contemplate the new directions in interpretive thinking in British archaeology, one can hardly avoid the impression that the local agitation is but a part of a much wider effervescence and that cumulatively this is a movement of very great importance in the development of the discipline. Although it may be said with validity that this process of interaction has been going on for some time and that the "new" developments integrate old and tried components, nevertheless, it is the rate of change and the scale of the interaction which define this, like so many other, thresholds in archaeology.

II

The remainder of this paper will, therefore, focus on examples of some of the more interesting models currently developing in British archaeo-logy which may be of interest within the context defined by the title of this symposium. Some of these developments will have long been familiar to the reader and can therefore be rejected as redundant, others will turn out to be "anticipations, rash and premature" following Bacon's renaissance conception of the necessary developmental path of empirical studies, yet others can only be justified by the same great scholar's further dictum – "truth comes out of error more readily than out of confusion" (*Novum Organum*, 1620).

The particular approach followed here has been to select three related models developed within the field of cultural morphology and then to illustrate the powerful interaction and mutual enlightenment which even these imperfect formulations contribute to the domains of cultural ecology and cultural ethnology. The particular three models are:

1. a polythetic population model for archaeological entities;
2. a dynamic system model for archaeological processes;
3. a nested hierarchical model for archaeological taxonomy.

There is nothing particularly new about these models but they do have interesting implications and consequences.

A polythetic population model for archaeological entities

Most archaeological entities consist of populations or aggregates of entities of lower taxonomic rank. We are concerned with groups, groups of groups, and groups of groups of groups of attributes based on observational data. Culture groups are clusters of cultures, cultures are clusters of assemblages, assemblages are clusters of artefact-types, types are clusters of artefacts and artefacts are clusters of attributes. To the archaeologist the process of grouping objects within "sensible" groups, clusters, or populations has been a normal activity for decades. The nature of these groupings seemed to be quite clear; one made a list of attributes, intuitively prejudging that it encompassed the "best" grouping, and then placed entities in the group if they possessed the attributes and outside if they did not. The intended nature of these groups was transparently clear, they were solid and tangible defined entities like an artefact-type or a cultural assemblage, each possessed a necessary list of qualifying attributes and they could be handled like discrete and solid bricks. This class of group is well known to taxonomists and is called a monothetic group – a group of entities so defined that the possession of a unique set of attributes is both sufficient and necessary for membership (Fig. 2) (Sokal and Sneath, 1963, p. 13). The prevailing model for archaeological entities was a monothetic model.

The monothetic box of bricks model is still the prevailing concept tacitly underlying the definition of most archaeological entities. Archaeologists still seem to think that in order to define groups it is necessary that every member within the group must possess all the qualifying attributes. In practice, this ideal has never been demonstrated in archaeology; no group of assemblages from a single culture ever contains, nor ever did contain, all of the cultural artefacts; no groups of artefacts within a single type population are ever identical in their lists of attributes. Instead, we are conscious that these groups are defined by a range of variation specifically distributed between defined limits, by populations of attributes or types of which a high proportion are variously shared between individual members of the group and some are shared with members of yet other groups. This situation is not a monothetic grouping at all but belongs to the other great class of taxonomic groups – the polythetic groups (Fig. 2) (Sokal and Sneath, 1963, pp. 13–15).

A polythetic group is a group of entities such that each entity possesses a large number of the attributes of the group, each attribute is shared by large numbers of entities and no single attribute is assumed both

Attributes or artefacts	*Entities* A	B	C	D	E	F	G	H	I	J	K	L	
1	×	×	×	×	×	×							Monothetic group
2	×	×	×	×	×	×							
3	×	×	×	×	×	×							
4	×	×	×	×	×	×							
5	×	×	×	×	×	×							
6							×	×	–	×	–	–	Polythetic group
7							–	×	×	–	–	×	
8							×	–	×	×	×	×	
9							–	×	–	×	×	–	
10							×	–	×	–	×	×	

FIG. 2. General model (*b*), a model for archaeological entities. A model suggesting that archaeological entities are structured as polythetic group populations and may not be treated as monothetic group populations. ×, Present; –, absent. (Clarke, 1968, Fig. 3.)

sufficient and necessary to the group membership. There are obviously many varieties of polythetic population grouping according to the number of shared attributes, the maximum and minimum number of attributes shared between any pair, and the number of attributes possessed by each individual. One of the most interesting future tasks will probably centre around the definition of the precise nature of the distinctive polythetic formats underlying the behaviour of the various categories of archaeological entities and the clarification of how much of that behaviour may be understood as a general consequence of particular structural formats.

The fundamental implications of the realization that archaeological entities are polythetic populations, or partially polythetic groups of various kinds is beyond simple statement. For the first time one can honestly admit the wide variation in attribute content of artefacts

within types, types within assemblages, assemblages within cultures and
cultural assemblages within culture groups, without having to abandon
them as defined entities. The foolhardiness of emphasizing a single criterion or type-fossil as the initial requirement for group membership
can easily be recognized. For the first time it is possible to see that it
is this awkward variety and range of variation of our entities and their
attributes which underlies their original potential to change by mosaic
and multilinear development, based on the scattered but connected network of human populations. Indeed the consequences of the polythetic
model for the geographical analysis of archaeological distributions
are manifold. The polythetic model displaces the older "cultural brick"
and "radial contours" models of attribute and artefact distributions,
with a commensurate emphasis upon the stochastic factors in the area
distributions and an increased significance for the application of distribution statistics to the element samples plotted (Clarke, 1968, pp. 463–
490).

In conclusion, then, this work will proceed on the assumption that
the best available model for most archaeological entities is a polythetic
population model of some kind; we do not assume, however, that this
model is more than a temporary and approximate convenience. The
remaining sections will attempt to relate this static model to the various
kinds of archaeological population by means of the hierarchical model
(see Fig. 3) and give it a dynamic capacity by means of the system
model for archaeological processes.

A dynamic system model for archaeological processes

Archaeological literature frequently describes cultural situations in
terms of analogies with machinery obeying mechanical principles,
with biological superorganisms and their ontogeny, or with a cosmos
model of dynamic constellations. A little thought about these favourite
analogues for cultural entities will reveal that they are only linked by
a limited set of common characteristics which otherwise unite very dissimilar situations. These shared characteristics emphasize that the analogues are all dynamic complex wholes, formed of intercommunicating
networks of mutually adjusting entities – they are all dynamic systems.
The component attributes or entities are said to be "intercommunicating" in that changes in the values or states of some of these components
can be shown to alter with the value or state of some of their neighbours.
Any such change in value or state is customarily called a "transformation" and a sequence of transformations following a particular course
is then called a "trajectory". The general and inherent properties of
different kinds of systems are the field of cybernetics and it is clearly

in aspects of this field that useful models for cultural entities can best be sought.

It is all too easy at this stage to take systems theory as a model for archaeological processes and the cultural entities that generate them, without isolating precisely the kinds of system these entities represent. This would simply extend systems theory and jargon as yet another vague analogy of no practical potential. One can readily appreciate that artefact-types changing in terms of their fluctuating attributes, within an assemblage context, represents a system situation rather different from a culture changing in terms of its varying assemblages, within an environmental context; both situations involve coupled systems and their mutually adjusting trajectories but otherwise very different structures are involved. The archaeologist has yet to analyse sufficient numbers of archaeological situations in sufficient detail before he can hope to nominate and categorize the many different kinds of system within his data, each with similar but different intrinsic properties.

However, we can mark out some of the more elementary shared properties of our varied systems. Briefly, one can anticipate that culture groups, cultures, assemblages, types, and artefacts changing with time can be thought of as varieties of dynamic systems with certain inherent characteristics stemming from the general structure of the systems, rather than from their unique specific attribute, or entity states and values. It will therefore be necessary to define the limiting values of the systems' states and, ultimately, to specify the inherent properties of the systems according to their structural categories. The more general system properties that will be involved probably include – constraints, regularities, stability, equilibrium, adaptive feedback, apparent goal-seeking, stochastic oscillation, regulation and control, replication, and directive correlation concepts; of these we have only space to glance at the implications of oscillation.

System attributes and states vary contemporaneously within a territory and fluctuate their modal values through time, and in this sense oscillation in system states and values can be said to occur. A part of such oscillation in archaeological systems can be accounted for as directly adaptive feedback adjustment towards the requirements of successively changing conditions. But an equally significant part of the oscillation of such systems is not directly connected with movement towards a stable consensus; instead, it represents the aimless stochastic oscillation that can occur when the permissive boundaries of the successively stable sets of component values allow many equally viable trajectories. The idiosyncratic stochastic oscillations between acceptable poles is the basis of "fashions" in material artefacts and constitutes a peculiarly distinctive marker of particular phase states.

The apparently aimless wandering attribute states and values of archaeological systems has subtle advantages in that the multiplicity of aimlessly oscillating components may chance upon an arrangement or structure with emergent and latent potentialities. This will lead to exploitative development by retaining the advantageous changes and continuing to oscillate neutral ones. Fashion fluctuations of this kind may be thought of as "scanning" through variety "in search of" useful transformations – an efficient inherent tendency in this kind of system, maximizing random discovery. This "searching" capacity may be found in artefact-type systems of attributes, in assemblage systems of types, or in cultural systems of assemblages.

This multiplication of oscillating and searching trajectories, permitted within overall culture system trajectories, amounts to a randomized and mixed strategy advantageously pursued by multilinear development, promoted by the mosaic pattern of the interconnected but dispersed units of the system's generators. It is because human societies have such elaborate dispersed yet networked structures and such cumulative information systems that they develop not along chance lines but by convergently exploiting successively revealed chains of potentials. Sufficient reason in itself to explain many of the sequential regularities found in quite separate cultural system trajectories, especially the large-scale convergence of unrelated cultures towards limited similarities in "deep structure" when constrained by similar factors in environment, ecology, and technology; convergences which are all too often interpreted by the heavy-handed use of invasion model hypotheses (see the Mousterian versus Upper Palaeolithic controversy and, in this paper, the technocomplex concept).

A nested hierarchical model for archaeological taxonomy

The overall model most frequently adopted for categorizing archaeological entities has been a nested hierarchical model; this model can be conveniently adapted here to incorporate the polythetic entities arranged in ascending order of system complexity – where complexity is taken to register the degree of internal networking (Fig. 3). This organization of archaeological data is a purely arbitrary conception, but it is adopted here because it has certain virtues: it is concise; it suits polythetic entities; it is appropriate to archaeological affinity distributions; it breaks down the field of inquiry into successively smaller areas of uncertainty in an empirical manner; and, as a "natural" system, it possesses a general predictive capacity. Nevertheless, the fact that such a model is an arbitrary organization of data, which in reality exists in dimensions of greater complexity, should not be obscured.

CULTURE
A polythetic set of specific and comprehensive artefact-type categories which consistently recur together in *assemblages* within a limited geographical area. Levels: culture group, culture, subculture.

CULTURE GROUP
A family of transform cultures; collateral cultures characterized by assemblages sharing a polythetic range but differing states of the same *specific multistate artefact-types*.

ASSEMBLAGE
An associated set of contemporary artefact-*types*.

TYPE
Specific artefact-type; an homogeneous population of *artefacts* which share a consistently recurrent range of attitute states within a given polythetic set. Levels: type group, specific type, sub-type.

TECHNOCOMPLEX
A group of cultures characterized by assemblages sharing a polythetic range but differing specific types of the same *general families of artefact-types*, shared as a widely diffused and interlinked response to common factors in environment, economy and technology. The material manifestation of cultural convergence within a common stable environmental strategy.

ARTEFACT
Any object modified by a set of humanly imposed *attributes*.

ATTRIBUTE
A logically irreducible character of two or more states, acting as an independent *variable* within a specific artefact system. An epistemically independent variable.

Fig. 3. A schematic hierarchical model of the major archaeological entities arranged in ascending order of system complexity. The higher the entity in the classificatory scheme, the greater its predictive information content. (Modified from Clarke, 1968, Fig. 40.)

There are other kinds of model which might have been and could be adopted for the same data – branching dichotomous models or multi-dimensional models offer two such alternatives. Indeed, it is clear that archaeological entities do not really exist in simple hierarchical levels and that many of the most tantalizing archaeological problems are false conceptual dilemmas arising from the aspects of this model which are not entirely adequate. The difficulties of cross-correlating the "hier-archical" sets of social, cultural, linguistic and racial classifications is a case in point. The evidence rather more closely approximates with a continuous multidimensional model of some kind.

The hierarchical aspect of the present model (Fig. 3) must therefore be taken as a temporarily acceptable expedient with some dangerous properties. The philosophy behind the hierarchical model might be glossed somewhat along the following lines. Archaeological entities exist because the network of links between people are not evenly distributed across an homogeneous mesh; the network of acquaintance, relation-ship, and encounter is much more richly reticulated amongst some nodes in the mesh than amongst others, and furthermore this separation is reinforced by the uneven nature of the node distribution and by the uneven quality of the surface of the globe. Archaeological entities of varied complexity and structure exist because there once existed net-works of links between people of a corresponding variety, constraints which "incidentally" generated links between their artefacts. Archaeo-logical entities are, therefore, for the most part compounded of many other entities clustered in certain ways and in these respects they are all "populations".

The general impression emerges that archaeological entities are cate-gories of complex system manifestations represented by populations of elements generated by related but unspecified categories of social units. The systems have a polythetic structure based upon constrained varia-tion of sociocultural and environmental variety. Although there is con-tinuous clined variation on a regional basis there is nevertheless a cor-relation between the distribution areas of the different artefact-types and the demes producing them – although this correlation is neither the boundary of the cultural brick theory nor the concentric contours of the radial diffusion theory. If one accepts that archaeological entities are complex rather than simple then one need not capitulate to the healthy revulsion of the "anti-entity" school.

If we follow the premises of the hierarchical and the system models, then the time and space "behaviour" of the complex systems represent-ing archaeological entities can be separated into two aspects. One aspect reflects the regularities inherent in a particular entity system as a member of a category of similar systems. The other aspect of entity "behaviour" reflects the idiosyncrasies arising from the particular and unique values and states of the elements in a specific system, which then give rise to the peculiar behaviour of the particular entity as opposed to the general behaviour shared by that entity with every other entity within a general category. One purpose of the whole hierarchical model approach is, therefore, to try and categorize or classify archaeo- logical data in a scheme which will draw together material with analogous properties, in order that these properties might be predic- tively specified and might thus allow the unique residual properties of the particular case to be the more accurately outlined. Such an organ- ization becomes of vital importance when one seeks to cross-relate the class properties of different dimensions of the same systems, for example, when the archaeological artefact-type, assemblage, culture, culture-group systems have to be related to dialect, language, and language groups; to roles, kin-groups, tribes, and tribal groups; and to demes, subraces, races and racial groups.

The nested hierarchical model of polythetic entities simply provides a convenient representation of archaeological categories to which, if accurately defined, we should be able predictively to link a limited range of social, linguistic, racial, geographical and temporal behaviour. This objective is, however, far from the scheme's current capacity: partly because the hierarchical model is not entirely appropriate and partly because archaeologists have abandoned defining their terms. It is not assumed for one moment that the definitions adopted in this paper are wholly accurate or will be widely accepted. On the contrary, it has been assumed throughout that widely useful and accepted defini- tions for archaeological entities and processes will only come about after a prolonged period of terminological anarchy. The definitions sug- gested here (Fig. 3) are to be understood as a positive step towards this healthy anarchy in that they may provoke modifications and alternatives from amongst which a satisfactory terminology may ulti- mately be selected. The history of other empirical disciplines suggests that such a period of clashing views and concepts is to be infinitely pre- ferred to the prevailing complacency within archaeology.

III

So brief an outline of these current models in cultural morphology hardly develops the implications which follow from them. The best that can be managed within the scope of the present paper is the selective appraisal of three of the more interesting and therefore controversial entity categories – the subculture, the culture group, and the technocomplex. It is perhaps some measure of the progress of cultural morphology that the structural formats of the lower entities – attributes, artefacts, types, assemblages – are being defined with a convergent degree of agreement by different authors, following in the wake of the increasing numbers of detailed analyses at these levels. In contrast, it is the grosser archaeological entities which are least well understood – an inevitable consequence of the lack of empirical studies testing their detailed structure. It is even possible at the present time for a powerful reactionary current to support the hypothesis that cultural entities have no real existence in archaeological data and that in reality artefact and assemblage trends are a matter of irregular, uncorrelated clines in all directions. This agnosticism is a healthy development since it amounts to a "null hypothesis" which should considerably clarify the evidence for and against the culture concept.

However, it seems more probable that the uncertainty about the grosser archaeological entities stems from their real complexity, as against their naive interpretations, from the lack of analyses, and above all from the wholesale use of the term "culture" for every category of assemblage population whatever their structure or time and space dimensions. For this reason alone it may be useful to separate the specific cultural assemblage concept from the entities above and below that status, which are the main sources of confusion when packaged, labelled and interpreted as of cultural status. The isolation of entities of subculture, culture group and technocomplex rank immediately goes some way to disperse the confusion surrounding the archaeological "culture" and partially restores a useful predictive information content to the much battered cultural assemblage taxon.

Subcultures

The subculture or subcultural assemblage, or kit, has a number of very different forms and roles, represented in the archaeological record by different categories of artefact-type complexes. This intermediate level entity can be defined as a restricted specific artefact-type complex – a polythetic set of different specific artefact-types repeatedly found together within a population of assemblages. The detection of the component type complexes within cultural assemblages should play an important part in sociocultural analysis and the assessment of the roles played by various social segments and activity groups. To some extent a sociocultural system can be viewed as a system of interacting subcultures or subsystems – *some* of which are made apparent in material cultural assemblages. However, subcultural kits usually contain items polythetically shared with other subcultural kits in the same networks, one artefact-type being variously used in various kit contexts. The total cultural assemblage or site assemblage is, therefore, not a simple additive composite of various subcultural kits and, although attempts have been made to isolate these kits as statistical common factors, this approach only offers an analogy to their structural integration, unless proper attention is paid to the selection of an appropriate sample to test the particular model.

An archaeological subculture or subcultural assemblage might, therefore, be seen as an infra-cultural segment, or activity alignment, characterized by a specific type complex and closely related to the sociological concepts of the role and subculture but not identical therewith. Such subcultures and their type complexes are particularly interesting both as analytical concepts and by virtue of their variety and semi-independent existence. Some subcultures are non-exclusive social fractions, others are rigidly exclusive in the sense that an individual may not belong to this segment and to certain others as well. Some subcultures are interchangeable and transferable from culture to culture, together with their material trappings; although some sociological subcultures are not marked by any material equipment at all. As a broad scheme one might isolate five varieties of subculture which register in the archaeological record – ethnic residuals, regional, occupational/activity, social status, and sex subculture assemblages. Each of these categories has a different and distinctive format and, therefore, the correct identification of the subcultural structure of a particular case is a very important step towards predictively modelling the properties and behaviours appropriate to that class.

The nature and degree of subcultural segmentation within a given sociocultural system appears to mark a significant variable quality for comparative study. From the archaeological viewpoint the subcultural type complexes provide important information about former sociocultural structuring and make analytical interpretation more comprehensible. The archaeological subcultural assemblage must be carefully distinguished from the full cultural assemblage or "culture". In several cases in the past, subcultural complexes have been mistakenly given full cultural status with confusing results. Perhaps the most significant value of the subcultural entity is the appreciation that the processes that act upon this entity level are different from those that can act upon complete cultural units – each entity category has restricted behavioural models appropriate only to that entity level. In the case of subcultural interaction, truncation, substitution and insertion, the basic range of models has been sketched by Steward (1955). Ethnologically, the subculture correlates with certain regularities in linguistic dialect and with sociological role complexes, rather than with kin-based units – indeed, it serves an important cross-kin function within cultural enclaves.

Culture groups

Our intention in skipping from the infrastructure of the subcultural complexes to the suprastructure of the culture groups has already been explained as an attempt to clarify the intervening structure of the archaeological culture by defining the hole left for it, rather than taking another swipe at a much battered peg. Unless I am mistaken, the New World equivalent of the Old World culture group is the entity occasionally discussed under the heading of a "cotradition", but since the term "tradition" is the most ambiguous label in the armoury of the American archaeologist we will avoid it.

The culture group is a system of cultures, assemblages and artefact-types occupying a dispersed but interconnected group of territories over a certain period of time. The system is most richly networked within its component culture sybsystems which are then more loosely interconnected within the culture group entity. The "looseness" or relative simplicity of these intercultural connections and affinities may vary from unconscious and unorganized linkage to artificial and optimally organized networking. However, even at its most elaborate, the culture group remains more richly networked within the component culture subsystems than between culture and culture in the entity. It would, perhaps, in this light, be more accurate to see the culture group as a circuit of linked systems rather than as a system with subsystems; the culture is a more complex entity than the culture group.

Nevertheless, the culture group as a system or circuit of cultural entities does affect the "behaviour" of the cultures within it, and various important regularities arise from this field constraint. The culture group is maintained and exists by virtue of a common set of variety and the continued circulation of incoming variety at a certain minimal level. Should this variety cease to circulate, or should it fall below the minimal threshold, the culture in the circuit will diverge independently. If the variety continues to circulate within the group, then the time-trajectories of the component cultures are continuously interrelated by this shared constraint and a certain level of common regularity in their development. Since the local environments of the cultures within the group will not be identical, the culture group interconnection acts as a useful circulating pool of adaptive information – some of which may be useful against the background of changing circumstances. A successful strategy in one member of the group may induce similar stances in the other members.

In this way, the network of a pre-existing culture group acts as a pre-stamped circuit, offering a ready constructed set of channels and information linking a set of largely congruent sociocultural systems. The area format of an existing culture group may, therefore, act as a preferential acculturation or expansion network for fresh cultural penetration and infiltration – so that an expansive culture often preferentially infiltrates the areas of cultures within its own group, or within another homogeneous group, even when "logical" predictions might have favoured more obvious patterns. This preferential bias is not, of course, universally followed on every occasion, but it is sufficiently frequent to play an important part in the repeated appearance of the same kaleidoscope of area mosaics which are such a marked regularity in the culture history of a continent. It may be noted that it is important to differentiate culture area from culture group area, a distinction which allows the area concept to recover some of its lost validity.

A culture group entity can come into existence in three main ways, which in itself means that the social and linguistic correlates of this entity are no less complex than those of any other in the hierarchy. An expanding culture can tessellate into a group of collateral cultures; or a group of unrelated cultures may converge in affinity under the influence of shared constraints; or, finally, an existing culture group may be repatterned. It is the space–time bundle of temporarily related cultural assemblages which we are seeking to isolate. This aim is in part generated by the pursuit of clearer definition and more information, but is also in part prompted by the useful character of the culture group as a conceptual tool. This utility arises from the alternating cumulative requirements of taxonomic "splitting" and "lumping" and the periodic need to review the culture group "woods" as opposed to the analytical interest in the individual culture "trees". Although it may prove impossible to allocate an assemblage to a precise culture, it is usually much easier, requiring less information, to allocate the assemblage to a culture group – to one unknown member of which the assemblage primarily belongs. In this way, although the individual cultures of ancient Europe or North America remain myriad and ill-defined, the culture groups offer a broadly simplified pattern of bundles of related transforms. By alternating between the minutiae of incisive analysis and the broad pattern of overall development the archaeologist can grope his way forward to fresh information.

So far the culture group has been loosely portrayed as a group of generally similar, collateral cultures representing allied culture states from a single but multistate cultural assemblage system trajectory in time and space. The cultures are, therefore, necessarily related as transforms and not independent cultures and their assemblages will, consequently, polythetically share sets of transform types – numbers of type states from single multistate artefact-type trajectories. The individual assemblages will, consequently, not necessarily be closely similar in terms of various states of specific multistate artefact-types. This statement embodies the main morphological distinction between assemblages within a culture and assemblages within the broader culture group.

These are the general conditions which have to be reduced to a viable definition. As an effort in this direction, we might define a culture group as – a group of affinally related, collateral cultures characterized by assemblages sharing a polythetic range but differing states of the same specific multistate artefact-types. A low-level affinity, perhaps 30% or less, uniting the group in terms of shared sets of specific type states, but a residual high level affinity, perhaps 60% or more, uniting the group in terms of sets of multistate type families. The essence of the culture group, so defined, then becomes the polythetic set of multistate artefact-types which are variously shared by the culture group's members and which together express the culture group's integral identity. Ethnologically, the culture group correlates with regularities in language and language group patterns, and with tribe and tribal group formats.

Technocomplexes

It is probable that many prehistoric entities, particularly in Palaeolithic studies, are of the rank of culture groups at best, rather than of the status of true single cultures as defined here. It seems probable that most of the Lower and Middle Palaeolithic groupings are of this order, or of an even looser order, and that groups approaching true cultural rank are detectable at the moment only in parts of the Upper Palaeolithic – and even then only dubiously. This does not mean that cultural entities did not exist in these early times, but that we are only now beginning to have sufficiently detailed data and powerful analyses of stochastic trends to think about defining cultural and regional groups within such gross entities as the Mousterian and even in the Aurignacian. The entities that we have at present belong to much looser categories, as one might suspect from their huge space and time dimensions, their low predictive information content, and the tacit abandonment of the suffix "culture" by most Palaeolithic archaeologists. Palaeolithic specialists refer to the Mousterian and Acheulean and not to the Mousterian culture and Acheulean culture, as the old textbooks once did. Indeed, there is a growing widespread conviction that many Palaeolithic and Mesolithic groupings reflect diverse and unrelated communities sharing only certain common aspects of environment, economy, technology and stimulus diffusion.

Since it is extremely difficult to discuss an entity without a name, let us tentatively call these gross groupings – technocomplexes: a term intended to convey a certain kind of gross artefact complex as the vector of particular general sociocultural, technological, economic and environmental stances. The technocomplex is a larger and looser entity than the culture group; an entity of larger size but lower rank than either the culture, or the culture group (Fig. 3).

We have seen that the need to define such an entity stems from the dangerously loose application of "culture" or "tradition" to quite disparate levels of archaeological entity, or the alternative and equally irresponsible neglect to qualify entity labels with classificatory indicators – the Acheulean (blank). If the rank of the taxon is never stated, it becomes difficult to ensure that only interpretive models of an appropriate kind are being harnessed to appropriate and mutually comparable entities. The loose employment of such terms as Gravettian, Palaeo-Indian, and Tardenoisian probably reflect no more than widely convergent technologies linked by interdiffusion and in use in similar contexts, although undoubtedly subsuming true entities of cultural status. The Acheulean and the chopper–flake-tool complexes surely reflect huge and loose alignments of this rank, rather than those smaller, higher rank entities that we have already discussed. It would therefore seem that the Palaeolithic archaeologist is probably, with rare exceptions, dealing with entities of technocomplex and culture group status; whereas his later colleagues are preoccupied with entities of cultural and subcultural rank. The importance of comparative status is that these differences in rank carry quite different information and implications about the range of the ethnic, sociocultural and linguistic attributes to be inferred for the entity. To confuse entities of differing ranks is to confuse and impair the information content of the classification. Clearly we need to know something of the characteristics of the technocomplex entities and their behaviour in space and time.

It is not possible to use the simple dimensions of archaeological entities as the determinative factor in categorizing them and their properties because the essential scale of ranking is one of structural richness and complexity rather than size. But, nevertheless, size is connected with the differences in entity categories and their behaviour, and may at least be employed to show how singularly inappropriate it is to use the culture or tradition label for every kind of archaeological taxon. One may contrast in this respect the dimensions of technocomplex entities like the Acheulean, Mousterian and Gravettian with say 3000–700 miles radius by 500 000–10 000 years, against culture groups like the European corded ware or the American Woodland tradition say 700–200 miles radius by 1000–300 years, with culture entities like the European Cortaillod culture or the American Pueblo culture of from 200–20 miles radius by 1000–0 years – where these dimensions are guessed average ranges for the entity categories. It may indeed be argued that these entities are a continuously merging spectrum, but that is also true of the visual spectrum, which we nevertheless segment in terms of discrete colours. If the wavelength of light differs, its properties are different; if the dimensions and complexity of "cultures" are different, their properties are different. The convenience of the categorization is that it allows us to study the dynamic ontogeny of entities changing rank, configuration, and dimensions – cultures expanding into culture groups and then repatterning technocomplexes, or vice versa, or any oscillating course between the entity ranks.

Perhaps we should now turn to the more detailed structure of technocomplex entities and their ethnographic and ecological linkage. The group of cultural assemblages falling within a particular technocomplex will usually include ethnically and linguistically quite diverse groupings – any smaller, homogeneous units will form culture and culture group subsets within the more comprehensive technocomplex. Furthermore, the assemblages need not share any specific artefact-types or type states, suggesting at first sight a total lack of affinity between the assemblages within the complex. This dissimilarity may indeed be total at the type and type state levels, but the affinity relationship uniting the group does appear at the "deep structure" type group or type family level. The technocomplex assemblages may not share the same specific type or state of backed blade, burin, end-scraper, awl, or point, but they will share a polythetic range of differing specific types and states from within a common set of such artefact-type families. The technocomplex assemblages need only share a polythetic selection from a shared set of families of artefact-types – most of which are artefacts broadly grouped by common environmental roles and common technology.

It may be worthwhile to go a little further into the invaluable concepts of "deep structure" and "surface structure" which we have freely borrowed from modern linguistic analysis. By deep structure I intend to convey the regularities which exist as a low-level affinity between assemblage formats when analysed only at the lowest type family level – say, assemblages sharing skis, sledges, goggles, lunate knives, burins, biface points, harpoons, lamps, bow and arrow, axes, skin boats – within the polar and circumpolar technocomplexes. By surface structure I intend to highlight the very varied superstructure which can still richly diversify individual cultures and culture groups even when erected upon such a shared substructure. The surface structure therefore embraces the higher-level affinities between assemblage formats analysed at the intermediate level of specific multistate types for culture group clusters, or at the highest level of specific type state populations for cultural assemblages or cultures. Clearly, the surface structure of cultural morphology is intimately expressing the unique identity of social groups in terms of their shared whims and stochastic idiosyncrasies, whereas the deep structure is profoundly rooted in the constraining interstices of the englobing ecosphere – a set of constraints widely shared beyond individual cultures (Clarke, 1968, pp. 565–566).

The technocomplex entity begins to emerge as a comprehensive and low-level category uniting a complex of type complexes, widely diffused in space and time but linked together as the skeletal frame of a general sociocultural mixed strategy, adapted to the conditions of a broadly homogeneous environmental context – an ecosystem. A loose polythetic complex of artefact-type families associated with the implementation of a particular range of subsistence patterns within a particular range of ecological niches. Without further elaboration, we may attempt to define the technocomplex as – a group of cultures characterized by assemblages sharing a polythetic range but differing specific types of the same general families of artefact-types, shared as a widely diffused and interlinked response to common factors in environment, economy and technology. A negligible level of affinity, perhaps 5% or less, uniting the group in terms of shared specific types but a residual medium level affinity, perhaps 30–60%, uniting the complex in terms of shared type families.

The technocomplex is a huge system networking culture groups, cultures, assemblages and artefact-types. The richest reticulation in the network remains within the individual self-regulating culture units. The extracultural network is less complex, uniting only the general deep structuring of parts of the otherwise diverse culture systems; the linkage at this low level depending upon widespread diffusion and convergent development within a particular ecosystem. The technocomplex system is really an interlinked set of systems sharing a broadly similar material and technological substructure, but probably quite varied in the rest of their sociocultural superstructure. However, since the convergent factor is the operating ecosystem constraint, and since a racial group is a population that has been isolated sufficiently long to have developed characteristics that distinguish its members from those of the same species outside its ecosphere, it follows that in limiting cases there may occasionally be close relationships between technocomplex units and racial groups; the rather exceptionally constrained background of the Mongoliform peoples may provide such an example, before their wider dispersion, that is.

Particular technocomplex formats are metastable equilibrium basins into which a number of independent and variform culture trajectories have converged. The steady state of systems within a particular technocomplex basin is metastable, in so far as certain changes or sequences of changes in the coupled sociocultural and environmental systems will initiate displacement out of the stable configuration and towards another format. The particular technocomplex basin is thus both a metastable basin and a constrained set through which culture system trajectories must pass and momentarily pause, before they may move on to certain other technocomplex basins. The culture must, for example, move into the food-producing technocomplexes before its trajectory can move into the full urban or industrial technocomplex regions. Each technocomplex has a limited number of alternative trajectories into and out of its basin, each trajectory with differing potential in terms of its route through successive metastable formats. It is the serious constraints offered by successive technocomplex basins that give rise to the most general and striking regularities in cultural trajectory sequences – the regularities summarized in the modern versions of the "Three Age" model in which the categories are not rigidly successive levels but sequences of groups of technocomplex basins linked by various trajectories with various but limited "goals". The widespread convergent movement into the earliest food-producing configurations in the Old and New Worlds illustrates the nature and general regularities of these changes, which transcend particular culture boundaries.

The oscillating trajectories of culture systems approaching a new technocomplex basin "behave" as if they were homing or goal-seeking systems, the adjusted state or stable basin being the goal. This apparently directive factor in system trajectories we now see to stem from coupled feedback adaptive changes in the integrated system. An interesting feature of the trajectories into such stable format is the "trial and error" adaptive hunting of the system and all its stochastically oscillating components, all effectively scanning the available variety for suitable mutually stabilizing attributes and components. The individual culture systems, as semi-Markovian systems with semi-stochastic transformations, move from one state to one of a possible set of states, the selection being based on the limited range of possible states, and having certain differential probabilities. As systems of this general kind, cultural trajectories from basin to basin are not unique and, consequently, cultures within a technocomplex set do not form a wholly homogeneous category at the surface level, neither are their past or future trajectories necessarily identical, but as a significant common adjustment the technocomplex may channel many of these trajectories through the same succession of formats.

In most existing studies of material culture, entities of technocomplex rank are either unlabelled, mislabelled, or they remain delitescent. In American archaeology, the term "tradition" is sometimes used more consistently for entities of this general configuration, thus – the Palaeo-Indian tradition. However, since the term "tradition" is also widely and conveniently used for the time-depth or time-trajectory of every kind of archaeological entity, it falls into the same ragbag, multilevel, multipurpose category that robs a term of its possible information content, as we have seen in the case of the term "culture". The terminological situation is further complicated by the dynamic development of technocomplex phenomena in which the artefacts and technology defining a technocomplex may often first appear in a single culture, become widespread in its culture group expansion, and only terminally express a gross technocomplex entity. Indeed, it is, in reality, a procedural norm in modern archaeology simultaneously, tacitly and dangerously to apply a particular entity name to every level of the different sociocultural sets of which it is a member; thus, the term "Tardenoisian" is used to delineate the localized assemblages of a French Mesolithic culture, the less similar assemblages of a Franco-Cantabrian culture group, and the varied assemblages of a Eurasiatic technocomplex, without ever specifying the actual category under consideration.

A technocomplex basin is defined by an integrated strategy involving only a skeletal set of artefact-type families, a certain technology, a specific environmental range, with a similar blend of subsistence and resource exploitation methods. To analyse an example already mentioned, one can take the loose Tardenoisian technocomplex when used for assemblages from the Balkans to Britain and from Spain to Poland – the specific Tardenoisian culture group of France and Spain being a detailed subset within this gross set. In the Tardenoisian technocomplex, we have a certain set of geometric microlith and flint and antler artefact families, a conical core, micro-blade and burin technology, in the mixed forest zone of postglacial Europe, hunting small forest game with the bow and only marginally exploiting marine resources. This simple set of traits unites the various far-flung territories and diverse assemblages of many different sociocultural and presumably different ethnic and linguistic units.

The technocomplex units that we are about to list are usually heterogeneously designated cultures, culture groups, complexes, industries, traditions, phases, or horizons, or they simply remain labels for unclassified footballs. Their names variously refer to a type site of the group, the first culture discovered to show the particular technocomplex format, a "typical" culture within the group, or they refer to a single major aspect of the technological, economic, environmental, assemblage equilibrium polygon. If one takes into account the idiosyncratic micro-structure of the artefacts and the missing basketry, wood and bone arte-facts, and decorative motifs from cave painting to body paint – then the monolithic technocomplexes would reveal much smaller entities of culture and culture group levels with a greater complement of corre-lated linguistic and sociocultural information. One suspects that such a diversification would appear in the superficially monomorphous "cultures" of Australian prehistory, the American Palaeo-Indian tradi-tion, and in such Palaeolithic entities as the Acheulean, Mousterian, or Gravettian.

Like the culture group, the huge space–time dimensions of the tech-nocomplex have the great advantage of providing a much simpler and less "noisy" outline of prehistoric trajectories – expressing them not as individual culture system trajectories, which the sample can hardly yet support, but clustered in successive bundles. The European Palaeolithic sequence, for example, reduces to the interaction and transformations of the Acheulean, Clactonian, Mousterian, Aurignacian and Gravettian, or Perigordian, technocomplexes; where many of these entities in-tegrate subcomplexes and technocomplex transforms, like the many facies of the Aucheulean industries, or some of the five groupings within the Mousterian. Strongly localized and smaller time–space entities like the Franco-Cantabrian Chatelperronian, Solutrean, or Magdalenian, *sensu stricto*, or the Vézère Aurignacian, these may be isolated by de-tailed seriation and stochastic trend analyses and suggest culture or more probably, culture group transforms in time-depth. Characteristic-ally, the gross technocomplexes are strongly correlated with particular ecosystem zones – the Acheulean with Savannah woodlands or the Gra-vettian with the Steppes. However, one should remember that these ecosystems are defined by selected complexes of intersecting niches, dif-ferentially exploited, and will not usually be susceptible to definition as homogeneous areas, bands or zones – although subject to the usual horizontal constraints of the equatorial system. Indeed, the careful study of technocomplex areas is likely to tell us as much about the former boundary areas of ancient ecologies as vice versa.

Before leaving the European context one can hardly escape comment on the relevance of the technocomplex concept to the development of an acceptable model for the interpretation of the Neanderthal/Sapiens and Mousterian/Upper Palaeolithic confrontation and transformation. At the moment we seem stuck with the simplistic equation of these enti-ties which then necessitates an invasion hypothesis secretly modelled on the later arrival of the Neolithic in Europe – in other words modelled on an old model which Neolithic specialists have themselves just abandoned. Or, alternatively, we have a French nationalist model of an *in situ* transition from the Mousterian and Neanderthal man to the Upper Palaeolithic and *Homo sapiens*. Both of these models are unsatisfactory and both of these models are focused under the assumption that the appropriate entities and processes involved are of the culture category. However, the archaeological record tells us of a widespread technological change from making flint tools on flake blanks to making flint tools on blade blanks. This transition took many thousands of years and was accompanied by sweeping changes in European ecology; simple time change was certainly one factor, stimulus diffusion probably another and sociocultural adaptation perhaps a third. The physical anthropological record, as recently reinterpreted, tells us that Neanderthal man was *Homo sapiens neanderthalensis* and that at least some of the less specialized Neanderthals of Southeastern Europe were probably directly ancestral to the later Sapiens communities of the same area, although this may not be the case for the Atlantic Neanderthals in the extreme conditions of Outermost Europe.

The overall impression emerges that, given the space, time and content dimensions of the archaeological samples concerned, it is probably a mistake to employ a culture-tribal model in this context and that a technocomplex-racial group model would be more appropriate. In simple terms, we seem to have the local technological repatterning of diverse communities over a very long period of time, coupled with the cumulative adoption of fresh sociocultural strategies in a changing environment, and not implausibly connected with stimulus diffusion from small-scale population movements, convergently spreading useful innovations to already related groups facing closely related changing conditions; genetically a somewhat parallel development would satisfactorily account for the Neanderthal/Sapiens transformation.

In the same general way New World prehistory exhibits the same kinds of archaeological entities, each with a pronounced ecosystem adaptation – starting with the Palaeo-Indian (grasslands), Old Cordilleran (coastal and montane), Desert (desert plateau), Archaic (temperate forest), Northwest Microblade (Arctic and Subarctic), and the Arctic Small-Tool (Arctic) technocomplexes. The so-called Palaeo-Indian industries, for example, are united by the possession of large flint projectile points, some of them noted for their connection with the hunting of specific species – the Clovis point with the mammoth and the Folsom point with the bison. Recent attempts to rename the Palaeo-Indian complex as "big-game hunting traditions" amounts to an asymmetric recognition of their loose technocomplex basis. It follows that culture models are quite inappropriate for interpreting the changing configurations and contents of these New World technocomplexes, and to call their vast ecospheres "culture areas" merely adds to the crippling misinterpretation that this already naïve concept has to carry.

The Palaeolithic prehistory of Africa provides a similar breakdown into groups of many differing levels. The great technocomplexes provide the framework of the Oldowan, Chellean, Acheulean groupings (equatorial savannah), moving on multilinearly into the Sangoan (evergreen forest), Fauresmith (grassland), Levalloiso-Mousterian (plateau savannah), and Lupemban (evergreen forest) technocomplexes. Here again there are well-documented connections between the generalized artefact assemblages shared within the technocomplex and particular ecosystems met by a common mixed strategy – such links connect the Sangoan complex, with its heavy axe and pick-like tools, with its territories in the Congo forest lands. The short characterization of the ecosystems given in the brackets above is of course quite insufficient, for the reasons sketched earlier – different technocomplexes may simultaneously or successively occupy different selections and combinations of niches even within an homogeneous ecological zone. Nevertheless, these characterizations at least make it quite apparent that it is totally inappropriate to conceive either the sociocultural content or the entity dynamics of these vast systems in terms of the culturo-tribal model.

IV

It was the optimistic hope of this essay that the preceding section would outline, how ever sketchily and controversially, the way in which some current models in British cultural morphology contribute to the spheres of cultural ecology and cultural ethnology and vice versa. With all its atomistic drawbacks archaeological morphology still seems to contribute the only means by which the range of social, linguistic and racial variety of archaeological units can be guessed. If we reject the hypothesis that archaeological and sociocultural entities have a simple one-to-one equivalence, at one extreme, and the hypothesis that these entities have no mutual relationship, at the other extreme, then at least it seems possible to link:

subculture	– subculture	– dialect	– social/ ecological niche	– subcommunity
culture	– tribal band	– language	– culture area, multi-niched territory	– population subrace

culture group	– tribal group	– language group	– multi-territory habitat zone	– subrace or race
technocomplex	– groups of tribal groups	– multi-language groups	– a biome ecosystem	– race or race group

where it is emphasized that the connecting dashes indicate "related-to" *not* equivalence, and assuming that the context in question is prehistoric.

Whatever one may think of the adequacy of this particular classificatory scheme and its hierarchical model (Fig. 3), it is clear that archaeology requires some such means of reconstructing the range of probable social, linguistic and racial structures that relate to peculiarly archaeological entities – together with the processes appropriate to each category of entity. In the analysis of particular situations, the archaeologist needs to be able to isolate, identify and relate the operational taxonomic units to the appropriate operational sociocultural units acting within the field space; in jargon form, the OTU's must be related to OSU's. The best kind of classification is the one that allows most propositions to be made about its constituent entities – the taxonomy with the best predictive capacity. At the moment, our ranked entities are merely the generalizations involved in classifying things in various categories. Nevertheless, to classify a series of assemblages as a culture is to predict a number of things about the limits of the population involved, of its area, its social and linguistic associations, its potential development patterns and its inherent "behaviour". To classify a series of assemblages as part of one specific culture is to predict a further quantity of specific information; quite different information from that which would have been inferred for a different culture, and different again from that which would have followed its identification as a subculture, culture group, or technocomplex. The purpose of the hierarchical taxonomy is to organize our empirical knowledge in a way which will enable us to make reliable predictions.

Unfortunately, archaeology is still an undisciplined empirical discipline. A discipline lacking a scheme of systematic and ordered study based upon declared and clearly defined models and rules of procedure. It further lacks a body of central theory capable of synthesizing the general regularities within its data in such a way that the unique residuals distinguishing each particular case might be quickly isolated and easily assessed. Archaeologists do not agree upon central theory, although regardless of place, period and culture they employ similar tacit models and similar procedures, based upon similar and distinctive entities – the attributes, artefacts, types, assemblages, cultures, culture groups and technocomplexes. Lacking an explicit theory defining these entities and capable of modelling their relationships and transformations in a viable form, archaeology has remained an intuitive skill – an inexplicit manipulative dexterity learned by rote.

It seems likely, however, that the second half of the twentieth century will retrospectively be seen to mark an important threshold in the development of archaeology – a phase of transition towards a new disciplinary configuration. Since the 1950s, archaeologists have been made increasingly aware of the inadequacies of their own archaic formulations by the disjunctive comments of a whole new generation of techniques and procedures now widely used in the fields of interjacent social sciences. The adaptive repatterning of archaeology has been set in motion by the discipline's coupling with the study of systems, games theory, set and group theory, topology, information and communication theory, cultural ecology, geographical locational analysis and analytical and inductive statistics powered by those key innovations – the digital and analog computers.

A whole array of new studies has developed whose implications have diffused piecemeal into archaeology and which increasingly permeate its fabric in a somewhat disconnected fashion; a derivation, however, that does not necessarily make them peripheral to the organization of archaeology as a discipline in its own terms and dimensions. This new methodology is to be carefully distinguished from the scientific aids increasingly used by archaeologists. Scientific aids no more make archaeology into a "science" than a wooden leg serves to classify a man as a tree – isotope dating, chemical analyses, and proton magnetometers remain adjuncts. By contrast, the new primary attitudes are central to the whole structure of the discipline. Most of these primary attitudes contributing to analytical archaeology are mathematical rather than scientific and simply emphasize that the relationship between analysts and their data may be as much enlightened by simple changes in viewpoint as by direct augmentation of the quantity of data. Archaeologists have concentrated far too much upon increasing the quantity of their data and far too little upon increasing the quality of their conceptual apparatus.

One response to these new developments has been to avoid them by a nostalgic retreat into historiography; another response has faced these innovations and initiated a period of groping experiment, inevitable error, and constructive feedback; whilst yet a third response awaits the outcome, studiously inert within carefully encysted reputations – all of these reactions are concurrently in full development. However, merely to add these new techniques and approaches to the existing structure of archaeology, like so many lean-to extensions of a shabby and already rambling edifice, is no solution to archaeological amorphism. The implications of these developments must be integrated within a fully congruent and redesigned discipline – the feedback in all these new couplings is such that not only must these techniques be selectively modified to match archaeological dimensions but archaeology must itself adapt and change to gain the best advantage of this freshly emergent potential.

REFERENCES

Clarke, D. L. (1968). *Analytical Archaeology*, Methuen, London.
Sokal, R. R. and Sneath, P. H. A. (1963). *Principles of Numerical Taxonomy*, Freeman, San Francisco and London.
Steward, J. H. (1955). *Theory of Culture Change*, University of Chicago Press, Chicago.
Wilkes, M. V. (1957). *Automatic Digital Computers*, Methuen, London.

Analytical Archaeology: Epilogue

DAVID L. CLARKE

All communication systems, including written literature, display a number of characteristics which both enrich and complicate the transfer of stimuli. The messages which the source, in this case the author, wishes to communicate to an audience are severely constrained by the antecedent background of that author. In this way archaeological authors abundantly illustrate in their works the vices and virtues of their personality, their language, their national culture and its peculiar education pattern, the regional school of archaeology in which they have been trained and so forth. The messages are generated in the brain of the author within this context and are then selectively transmitted as a communication coded in literary form – a code in which the simple meaning of every word has an additional and varying emotive power for each and every recipient. Furthermore, the refractory nature of the literary channel and the whims of the author will also introduce those unselected attributes, random errors and mistakes which constitute the "noise" or "static" superimposed upon the original characteristics of the message. It is, then, this coded message plus "noise" that arrives at the individual receiver. However, the individual receivers themselves resemble the author in the respect that their reception is tuned in a manner biased by *their* personality, language, national culture, education and training. To the consternation of the author and the puzzlement of the receiver, the reader is presented not with the message conceived by the author but with that message, plus the distortion of the transmission, the noise of the channel and the bias effect of the receiver. If this message is a complicated one involving disputed matters of theory and the audience consists of receivers tuned in totally different manners, then one can hardly be surprised at the very diverse quality of the reception or at the difficulty experienced in receiving in certain quarters at all.

Analytical Archaeology is an old-fashioned book – it was written between 1963 and 1967 and went to press in 1968. The message that

Reprinted with permission from *Norwegian Archaeological Review*, **3**, 25–34, 1970.

the author wished to communicate was mainly one of stimulus rather than one embodying retrospective information describing established events, since the theory of archaeology nowhere exists in an integrated, sophisticated or comprehensive form (see objective 7 below). The main intention was therefore to sketch how such a theory was not only possible but essential and how such a theory might emerge from the disconnected and piecemeal arrival of a wide array of interdisciplinary techniques and procedures currently impinging upon archaeology. These messages were clearly modulated by the characteristic constraints of this particular author – an optimistic personality, a British education of a kind peculiarly specialized in the Natural Sciences and the insular characteristics of a general training in European archaeology simultaneously combined with a common membership of the trans-oceanic English-speaking schools of archaeology; doubtless it will amuse readers to detect yet other idiosyncratic features which serve to identify this particular source. The messages thus formed by the nature of the author were then transmitted in a specialized literary code called "jargon", with the liberal and deliberate use of redundancy and it was these coded messages, plus "noise", which arrived at the variously attuned receivers.

It may be noted, therefore, that the diverse reactions of the receivers have as much to do with the bias and tuning of their own backgrounds as with the quality of the information in the author's message. Some receivers have been stimulated; some, indeed, to oscillations so violent that one fears for their stability and wonders about the orientation of their tuning. Other receivers have baulked at the condensed special-purpose code called jargon, apparently on the assumption that so specialized a discipline can progress, and has progressed, with the vocabulary of everyday commerce and that the polite and genteel scholar has no place for quasars and quarks, quanta and cations, permafrost and photogrammetry, bacteriophages and helminths, morphemes and phonemes, tort and formulary, not to mention deoxyribonucleic acid (DNA) – there are other criteria of communication than the aesthetic. As for redundancy, the advantageous significance of this characteristic in the transmission of complex messages on a single, noisy channel has been discussed at length in the volume in question (pp. 91–92, 654–655). Thankfully, a number of readers appear to have received the gist of the intended messages without undue difficulty and some even admit the reception of stimulus, the main purpose of the transmission.

Books are consciously written towards limited objectives, for a particular audience; they are not written with the aim of total explanation of all aspects of a field, for all possible audiences. Unconsciously, however, authors write books to educate themselves by clarifying their own observations and by demonstrating to themselves that their tacit beliefs may be explicitly and logically linked together in a valid system of inference, whilst at the outermost fringes of his work the author is often semiconsciously exploring the reasonableness of the distant consequences of some of his more central, conscious thoughts. This conscious and unconscious procedure may produce an uncomfortable contrast in passages of comparative obscurity and lucidity but it may be noted that the few real areas of fresh insight and new exploration are often strongly correlated with the obscure passages, since authors tend to express with perfect lucidity only that which is already widely understood. On the whole, these semiconscious meanderings of the author are therefore valuable activities since they at least enable the limited audience to obtain from reading the book some portion of any understanding or insight that the author gained from writing it.

Perhaps it would be useful to specify how these very general points relate to *Analytical Archaeology*.

Analytical Archaeology was written for an audience with a balance of literacy and numeracy, with a wide interest in the changing scholastic universe of which archaeology is merely a small part, and a fervent concern in the exploration of the expanding possibilities of archaeology as a discipline. It may be thought that such an audience is vanishingly small but sales of the volume do not confirm that pessimism.

Analytical Archaeology assumes the artificial nature of the mosaic of academic disciplines and their temporary pattern of internal partitioning – the rival archaeologies (Chang, 1967, p. 137). It is also assumed, nevertheless, that such clusterings within the universe of knowledge come into being when they have a fresh contribution to make and fade like ghosts when that contribution is exhausted. The transient condensation which forms a discipline englobes in a fresh combination a particular body of observations and holds that body together by means of an organized network of theory and methodology; indeed, the strength of the corpus of theory and the vigour of its ramifying developments serve to coagulate the parts within the whole of one discipline. The strength of the theory and methodology is crucial. Archaeology is just such a transient discipline – an organized body of knowledge; *organized* in its emergent form with a tacit and complex body of central theory framing a series of schemes of systematic study; *knowledge* which in this case derives from collecting empirical observations concerned with events of a certain kind. *Analytical Archaeology* is therefore a frame for the continuous endeavour towards the precipitation of an explicit and vigorous *corpus* of general theory which attempts to resolve the relationships that permeate archaeological data in its widest sense, everywhere in the world – as explicable and applicable in Peru as Persia, Australia and Alaska, Sweden and Siam.

First, it may be expedient to note the "unconscious" objective of *Analytical Archaeology* before listing the work's main short-term objectives. It is now a commonplace that archaeology must attempt to recover and use *every* source of information which can tell us anything about hominid activities in the past. It now appears that tools and implements and their typology are only one such source of information and one which unfortunately became synonymous with the study of archaeology at an early stage. Now, we would recognize that much information on hominid activities is also preserved imprinted upon the fauna, flora, soils, sediments and other environmental records which constitute the context of the implements and is even fossilized in the spatial relationships between sites, structures and artefacts spread across particular loci or whole landscapes. The implements must certainly be put in perspective as only *one* category of the artefacts of hominid behaviour – *all* of which preserve for us some overlapping information on the activities of our ancestors.

The "discovery" that all such categories are artefacts under the broad definition usually adopted – any object modified by a set of humanly imposed attributes – has stimulated two reactions. One extreme reaction revenges itself upon the once dominant implement typology by itself ignoring the implements as a future source of useful information in a wave of productive palaeoecological fervour. A second reaction, perhaps also an extremist one, is stimulated by the great possibility that if every surviving relic of hominid activity is an "artefact", or assemblage of artefacts, from a cathedral to the bones of a flock of sheep, from the mechanically linked system of artefacts which form a machine to a settlement imprint in the pollen record – then, to what extent can the archaeological theory of artefacts and their assemblages be usefully extended towards a universal structural theory of culture, embracing linguistics and architecture, archaeology and food-production? A universal general theory based on the common conditions imposed on all artefacts by the similarly structured minds common to all hominids. *Analytical Archaeology* was partly written to explore, as a general extrapolation of its particular objectives, the extent to which the general rules describing "implement" artefact behaviour were adequate as general rules for all hominid artefacts, in the limiting case. My interim conclusion is appended in the notes on the comments upon *Analytical Archaeology* (below).

To resume, the short-term objects of *Analytical Archaeology* can be condensed under seven headings which embrace the consciously limited objectives pursued in relation to the limited frame of the book.

1. *Stimulus* When the positive aspects of traditional archaeological thought are brought together with the philosophy implied by the analytical approach the whole scope of archaeology becomes more vigorous and vital. New dimensions of thought become permissible in terms of theory and analysis; in which one may talk about an individual archaeological case or populations of entities against appropriate models, an illuminating freedom of choice depending on the particular resolution level or scale at which one chooses to work; in which one can generalize models and patterns and from them particularize in a more informative way (Harvey, 1969, p. vi).

2. *Identification* Archaeology is practised in such widely differing areas, for such widely differing special purposes that its practitioners become unaware that they hold most of their problems in common with some other archaeologists and that these problems have been more effectively solved in some schools of archaeology than in others. Even if archaeology is held to be simply the sum of what all archaeologists do, it would materially assist them in doing it if they could accurately identify the common material, the common questions, the common problems, the common procedures, the common solutions and the common objectives – if they could identify archaeology as a discipline.

3. *Role* If archaeology is identified as a discipline with its own special material, questions, problems, procedures, solutions, objectives and theoretical calculus then it ceases to be the reluctant source of information where no other is available (in prehistory), or the source of selected illustrations to decorate the arguments of other disciplines (in the overlap with written history and anthropology) – and becomes instead an immature but coherent source of unique information. Information which may then be compared with that independently gathered by other disciplines, with their different procedures, extracting different information about the same events; archaeology must be a separate and distinct study if its contribution is to be most enlightening. If the anthropologist or historian selectively uses archaeological data that conforms with his pre-existing arguments we reveal nothing, we learn nothing, we do not progress. By contrast, in this newer role archaeology requires a higher degree of self-definition in order that its contribution might be the greater – realistic separation for more effective co-operation, high specialization without partisan partitioning, awareness and knowledge right across the field, skill and specialization within a chosen part.

4. *Theory*   It is widely held in most disciplines that the best observers are also good theorists and that the best theorists are amongst the good observers, and archaeology is surely no exception:

> About thiry years ago there was much talk that geologists ought only to observe and not theorize; and I well remember someone saying that at this rate a man might as well go into a gravel-pit and count the pebbles and describe the colours. How odd it is that anyone should not see that all observation must be for or against some view if it is to be of any service. (Charles Darwin, 18 September 1861)

> I have an old belief that a good observer really means a good theorist. (Charles Darwin, 22 November 1860) (both quotations – Medawar, 1969, p. 11)

> You can't collect your evidence before you begin thinking ... because thinking means asking questions and nothing is evidence except in relation to some definite question. (Collingwood, 1963, p. 281)

The problem which the introductory axiom raises for archaeology is that the subject is said not to have any theory – at least, none that is of any use. *Analytical Archaeology* takes the philosophical view that the central theory uniting archaeology is implicit in what archaeologists do and constitutes a real central theory however weak and inadequate any written account of it may prove to be. Such general theory remains general even to partitioned rival archaeologies, the adequacy of which still depends upon the wider adequacy of the ideological assumptions which underlie the development of their arguments. The ideology which unites the studies within one discipline regardless of area, period, or culture.

5. *Archaeological models*   Perhaps one of the most important objectives of *Analytical Archaeology* is its attempt to demonstrate the fundamental importance of "model" making and using to the philosophy, practice and theory of archaeology. Even a very simple model can be a useful tool – not, it may be noted, in the low level of generalized information it predicts about a particular case but in the comparative degree to which a number of particular cases deviate from its common base line. Thus, the construction, testing, verification and modification of explicit models is the essence of the empirical and scientific approach. By repeating the cycle . . . question, observation, tentative model, test of model, modification in a fresh model, more observation . . . new information can be brought to light and an approach made to the disciplined procedure of the more exact sciences . . . question, observation, hypothesis, experiment, fresh hypothesis . . . etc. It is then apparent that model-testing is the major form of archaeological experiment – whether

one is testing a statistical model on a computer, a reconstruction model in the field or museum, or a conceptual model in an excavation.

6. *Models from other disciplines* In objective 3, "Role", the strongest emphasis was simultaneously laid upon the special and separate nature of archaeology as a discipline and the need for a more general outward awareness within the partitions of the discipline and beyond the discipline to other disciplines entirely. The reason for this separation and yet connectivity argument can now be carried. For, wherever possible, the appropriate specialized models from all other relevant disciplines – ethnology, anthropology, ecology, economics, geography, etc. – should be independently used to generate hypotheses about the events which have also been evaluated in archaeological terms. In this way non-arte-factual information and non-archaeological models may be used to test and control archaeological information, models and hypotheses relating to the same situation, or similar category of situations; data from one discipline can be used to test hypotheses derived from other disciplines and from other classes of data and vice versa, with illuminating results.

7. *General objective* In the closing pages of the volume it was suggested that archaeology must be rethought, reorientated and rewritten in order for it to adapt to the output of its greatly changed contemporary context. These changes are so diverse, so far-reaching and so recently upon us that this task cannot yet be accomplished in the communications of a single author. Usually an author communicates to describe something that has already happened and been clarified either historic-ally or logically; this is a matter of retrospective description, matching information to established events. However, one may also communicate to describe something of the immediate future; in this case the intention is not description but creative stimulus – provocation. It is sometimes necessary, using the latter technique, to accomplish the jump from an old disciplinary pattern to a new one, to pass through an intermediate pattern that is only partially satisfactory – where this state may be de-scribed as an "intermediate impossible". This is an important creative procedure in which the "intermediate impossible" format will suffice long enough for it to provide a stepping stone to a new disciplinary pattern which is more rigorously acceptable (De Bono, 1970).

Analytical Archaeology was conceived as just such an intermediate form, a transient, provocative model of a future class of archaeological textbook which will elaborate analytical archaeology on a more power-ful basis and thereby linked the national archaeologies of the world with an explicit international methodology and theory – a move not towards uniformity but towards diversity within a common framework. If this conception is thought to be a reflection of the author's undue optimism we may pause to recollect that a former archaeological model emerged from a similar period of rapid change and spread throughout the world between 1819 and 1850; where *Analytical Archaeology* is not thought to provide such a model but to indicate something of its possible nature.

NOTES ON THE COMMENTS UPON ANALYTICAL ARCHAEOLOGY

I would first like to say how grateful I am for the various comments—I only wish they had been available before I wrote the book. Given the six hundred and seventy pages of *Analytical Archaeology* and the preamble above, there is neither the space, the time, nor the necessity for a very lengthy response to the clear comments made by Hymes, Mayer-Oakes, Moberg and Rouse. I will make some brief points and concentrate on the positive conclusions which come out of the discussion.

For an author who does not mention linguistics, Hymes seems to have found an awful lot of it to comment upon in *Analytical Archaeology* (although missing the reference to "deep structure" and "surface structure" (p. 565)). The reason for this pattern will emerge towards the end of this comment. I think Professor Hymes is really accusing me of not having written his own excellent paper (Hymes, 1970) to the 1969 Marseilles Symposium on "Linguistic Models in Archaeology"—a forthcoming volume (Gardin, 1970) amongst several others, by the way, which will make the specialized language and mild numeracy of *Analytical Archaeology* seem the essence of simplicity. Professor Hymes' comments are therefore not really about *Analytical Archaeology* but form a stimulating treatise on the relationships of archaeological theory and structural linguistics based on his own paper and the work of Deetz; essentially the comments of a linguist who believes that the key to archaeological theory exists in the theory of structural linguistics.

I have pointed out that one of the subconscious objectives of *Analytical Archaeolology* was to explore the extent to which the general rules of archaeological artefact behaviour could provide a general set of rules capable of framing studies of all human artefacts or vice versa. This was a groping attempt towards the concept expressed by Hymes—"it seems likely that the human mind provides some commonalty, the materials considerable differentiation, and functions some commonalty, some differentiation both" and which then seems to lead him to comprehend linguistics as part of the key to a general understanding of the structure of culture. Thus we have a linguist believing that linguistic theory is a key to the structure of language and who sees the latter as one of the levers on the lock guarding a general understanding of the structure of culture. In addition, we have an archaeologist not believing but exploring the parallel possibility that archaeological theory, as the key to the structure of artefact assemblages, might be a decisive instrument for the same purpose. But, alas, the lock has as many guards and levers as there are disciplines and just as the archaeological key will only partly turn in the linguistic lock so vice versa and neither is sufficiently comprehensive to provide a single key to the general problem.

The reason for this failure is probably that despite the common basis of the human mind operating behind all its artefacts it is not a sufficient constraint, given the very great diversity of artefact materials and their myriad different purposes, to superimpose common regularities of more than the most elementary kind. That we should clarify and pursue even these crude regularities within a general theory of artificial culture is, I agree with Hymes, a most worthy aim but not one which will push the capacity of archaeology much further. By their general nature such common factors are likely to be interesting observations of limited utility; that one may define archaeological analogues of the phoneme and morpheme and call them factemes and formemes is very interesting, but what then (Deetz, 1967, pp. 83–92)? My own conclusion is that such common denominators provide an interesting but limited field for the further exploration of the common characteristics of an arbitrary class of items called "artefacts" in which the categorization is itself a perceptive artefact – artefacts for communication (language), artefacts for activities (sites and structures), artefacts for implementing activities (implements), artefacts for sustaining activities (plants and animals) or artefacts for multiple special purposes (kinship systems, religious systems, etc.). Indeed, even within archaeology the typological treatment of tomb plans or house plans or other remains of "artefacts integrated in mechanical assemblages" already illustrates the marginal collapse of an approach proper to implements. In contrast, the very special constraints shared by artefacts within these and similar common purpose categories does make them a useful focus for the study of appropriately specialized disciplines. *Analytical Archaeology* took just such a limited frame of reference for investigation, with these more general possibilities beyond its horizon and this is why the very obvious parallels with linguistics were allowed to emerge in their own but different way; they were not cited and taken from linguistics but were allowed to develop *in situ* to emphasize the limited analogy.

Mayer-Oakes produces some interesting comments on "problem formulation" and suggests that the general model for procedure presented in *Analytical Archaeology* is inadequate. I would accept this but beg to point out that all models are inadequate by definition, since all models are deliberately partial representations of a complex reality simplified for the limited purpose in hand. It also seems to me that to put "problem formulation" in a box in a flow chart does not explain the process itself. The second area of critical comment points out that I do not attempt a discrete analysis by dimensions such that some entities are space entities, some form entities, and some time entities. This approach seems to distort complex multidimensional entities and situations into a series of single dimensions whereas it seems preferable to attempt a multidimensional characterization rather than handle a large number of different projections independently, or clumsily in conjunction. I do not find this dimensional approach productive, at least in this particular form.

Moberg's comments are especially interesting as those of an author with an historical bias equivalent to the science bias of the author of *Analytical Archaeology* and in a way equivalent to the linguistic bias of Hymes. I think I agree with all of Moberg's comments but find that it is partly a semantic argument about the definition of "History" as a discipline and partly a misunderstanding of what I was trying to do in my simplistic discussion of ancient "peoples". In the main I was trying to test, using near-contemporary literature as an independent source, the general purpose classificatory model (culture, culture group, etc.) set up so that archaeologists could first identify and isolate the operational taxonomic units in the frame of their particular study and by this machinery crudely relate them to an appropriate scale of operational sociocultural unit; in jargon form the OTU's must be identified and then related to some OSU's if appropriate basal criteria from the archaeological evidence is to be made available to set up the fully appropriate predictive models from other disciplines. If the Mousterian and the Perigordian are technocomplexes rather than cultural assemblages then the appropriate scales for setting their social, linguistic, racial and technological interpretive models are not those that are usually employed for the discussion of the *Homo sapiens* and *Homo sapiens neanderthalensis* "confrontation" (i.e., non-confrontation).

I must confess that I find as much difficulty in understanding Rouse as most people have in reading Clarke—mainly, I think, because our philosophical frames are different and each has great trouble converting into the other's terminology (another good reason for an international methodology). For example, I find it exceedingly difficult to see anything but retrospective circularity in a scheme which distinguishes "projectile points" as historical-index types but views "tools" as functional-types. In general, Rouse is setting-up his own misinterpretation of my postulates and then demolishes these straw-men with tank-like logic – but it must be noted that the straw-men are his artefacts, not mine.

However, I accept Rouse's main point – his closing quotation from Brew – we certainly need many more special-purpose classifications appropriately designed for the dimensions of clearly specified problems. Although here Rouse has misunderstood the point of my classificatory scheme. The hierarchical model for the categorization of the major archaeological entities is a *general purpose* scheme to be used for the identification of OSU's from OTU's as explained above; in much the same way that the species, genus, family, order, class, division system provides a general purpose zoological classification. A *general purpose* classification is not an *all-purpose* classification and does not warrant or deny special-purpose classifications.

REFERENCES

Chang, K.-C. (1967). *Rethinking Archaeology*, Random House, New York.
Clarke, D. L. (1968). *Analytical Archaeology*, Methuen, London.
Collingwood, R. G. (1963). *The Idea of History*, Clarendon Press, Oxford.
De Bono, E. (1970). Playback 11 – analysis; a new functional word, *Science Journal*, **6** (1), 28–29.
Deetz, J. (1967). *Invitation to Archaeology*, Natural History Press, New York.
Gardin, J.-C. (1970). *Archéologie et Calculateurs: Problèmes Semiologiques et Mathématiques*, CNRS, Paris.
Harvey, D. (1969). *Explanation in Geography*, Edward Arnold, London.
Hymes, D. (1970). Linguistic models in archaeology, in *Archéologie et Calculateurs: Problèmes Semiologiques et Mathématiques* (J.-C. Gardin, ed.), CNRS, Paris.
Medawar, P. B. (1969). *Induction and Intuition in Scientific Thought*, Methuen, London.

Problems in European Prehistory

ANDREW G. SHERRATT

David's writings fall naturally into three periods. The first was centred upon his thesis work on British beaker pottery, and concentrated upon a specific topic of culture-history and the problems which arose from it. Its innovations were more in matters of technique than of basic approach. The second phase, which culminated in *Analytical Archaeology*, was in many ways a generalization of its arguments and methods. It added a much wider range of reading, and enormously increased archaeological awareness of what was happening in related fields, but the structure into which these insights were fitted was itself of a rather traditional character (Binford, 1972). The third phase, cut short by his untimely death, was a much more radical period of reappraisal. Rather than adding new elements to an existing design, the whole subject was being redefined. Its role in relation to the rest of the behavioural sciences was coming to be seen as one in which archaeology had as much to give as to receive. Insights from other disciplines were no longer to be plundered as paradigms to be imitated, but subsumed as special cases in an emerging body of integrated theory.

This fundamental step came about, not as the result of abstract speculation, but in the course of writing about prehistory. All the papers of this section belong to this third phase, and indeed cover the successive steps of its internal development. They range in time from the account of "The economic context of trade and industry in Barbarian Europe till Roman times", begun shortly after the completion of *Analytical Archaeology*, to the lecture on "Towns in the development of early civilization", given shortly before his death. They range in scope from a sketch of the nature of the beaker problem with which he started his research, to a review of the definition of urbanization in an archaeological perspective and on a world scale. The third phase was, like the first, a period in which David was actively engaged in writing about prehistory; but it is in sharp contrast to it, both in the breadth of problems with which he was concerned, and in the greater diversity of approaches which he brought to them.

While the first two periods of his writing have their structured syntheses in the form of *Beaker Pottery of Great Britain and Ireland* and *Analytical Archaeology*, the writings of the third period are inevitably more piecemeal. All of them are in some sense sketches (at least by the scale of the man who could produce those two comprehensive works in the few hours a week which could be kept free from extensive college responsibilities). Their general character, however, is clear. They are attempts to explore what he saw as the developing areas of archaeological research. Two elements stand out as particularly important to his new approach: a concern for the ecological basis of cultural development, and a particular attention to the social context of material transactions. These were expressed in studies of Mesolithic subsistence, Neolithic trade and exchange, and Iron Age community patterning. A common feature of many of these problems is the information contained in the relevant spatial distributions, whether at zonal, regional or household level. These explorations were thus supported by his theoretical investigation of the potential of spatial analysis. There is no doubt that the new synthesis which was emerging, and was written up in introductions and reviews (see the fifth, sixth, seventh and eighteenth papers in this volume), would eventually have led him to recast his theoretical and methodological views in a way which would make *Analytical Archaeology* seem as outdated as his early discussions on beakers now appear.

The papers on European prehistory are not essays in a single *genre*; although all were solicited papers for collections or symposia, they range from the long account of trade and industry, which was prepared from a mass of factual data over many months, to the short but concentrated presentation of his ideas on urbanization, which was written in the form of lecture-notes for immediate presentation at a conference in Cambridge. The study of Iron Age Glastonbury and its context stands out from the rest in being a measured account of his chosen research project in the years following *Analytical Archaeology*, written as his own substantive contribution to the volume which he himself edited, *Models in Archaeology*. Since the dates of publication (or non-publication) of these papers bear only a distorted relationship to the period of their composition, it is as well to bear both in mind. They are (in chronological order of writing):

"The economic context of trade and industry in Barbarian Europe till Roman times" – written 1969, not previously published;
"A provisional model of an Iron Age society and its settlement system" – written 1970–1, published 1972;

"Mesolithic Europe: the economic basis" – written 1972–3, published
   1976;
"The beaker network – social and economic models" – written 1974,
   published 1975;
"Towns in the development of early civilization" – written 1976, not
   previously published.

This succession demonstrates a pattern of development over the
crucial period of the later 1960s and early 1970s – arguably the most
exciting decade in archaeology for nearly a century. During this time,
very rapid changes took place, brought about by a variety of forces –
a widespread underlying dissatisfaction with the state of prehistory, a
dissolving of parochial concerns by wider world contacts, the spread
of anthropological ideas from America, the development of new techniques of analysis, and the progress of David's own thought. Together,
these brought to an end the long period of relative stability during which
archaeologists moved on a predictable cycle of excavation and typological analysis, and marked the shift to a new occupation with unfamiliar
sampling and recovery procedures, unfamiliar bodies of non-archaeological literature, and unfamiliar methods of statistical and spatial
analysis, which are now slowly settling down to become the accepted
orthodoxy of the 1980s. So rapid has been this shift that it is now hard
to think back to how different things were in 1965. Beginning with new
methods to cope with the rising tide of data, the reconsideration of
archaeology quickly spread to increasingly fundamental questions of
procedure, theory and even metaphysics.
   An important thread in David's own development, as evidenced by
these papers, was his emancipation from the cultural paradigm of
V. G. Childe and his espousal of alternative modes of explanation
rooted in economic anthropology and ecology. Some idea of how he
saw the new elements fitting together may best be gained from his study
of Glastonbury; while the implications which a new, behavioural
archaeology has for the human sciences in general can be seen in his
lecture on urbanization. The following pages take the discussion of
these topics through the papers of this section.
   Analytical Archaeology, on its publication in 1968, had come as such
a novelty to Old World archaeology because it suggested that the subject involved more than intuitive skill, and demanded the application
of sustained analytical thought. British and European archaeology has
not in the twentieth century been particularly distinguished by the
power of its intellectual penetration: the subject has tended to serve
as a sump for the lowbrow ancient historian, or a respectable indoor
habitat for the explorer and field man, and to provide rationalization

for the activities of the antiquarian and collector. Even as taught in many universities, it has had a strongly anti-intellectual streak, emphasizing expertise in excavation and typological finesse at the expense of sustained inquiry into the development of human culture and society.

The exception to this, from the mid-1920s to the mid-1950s, was Gordon Childe, "for long the sole prehistorian to draw his subject from its rustic and academic backwaters and make it contribute to the main streams of thought" (Jaquetta Hawkes). By his outstanding intellect and grasp of the raw material, Childe dominated prehistoric archaeology with few rivals. His textbooks summarized what was known of the subject, while his "popular science" writings expounded what came to be the accepted revolutionary/diffusionist explanations of prehistoric development. These views had been essentially formed by 1930, largely on the basis of nineteenth-century anthropology and the continental ethno-archaeology of World War I; but his coherent and well-argued expositions continued to provide an unchallenged synthesis even for a decade after his death in 1957, and to this day have not been replaced for the general reader. The Childean concept of prehistory arose from the procedures needed to organize the archaeological record at a primary level – the typical problems of the "classificatory" stage in the development of a science. The ideas of "cultures", and their "contacts" and "relationships" were a direct outcome of the need to systematize archaeological evidence by dividing it into classes and making comparisons between them. Such had been the dominant concern of prehistorians since the late nineteenth century. Their problems characteristically arose directly from the evidence, rather than from theories which could be tested by reference to it. Their procedures were designed to establish multipurpose classifications which largely ignored the different sources of variability in their material; and their explanations, by reference to "cultural tradition", "diffusion" or "contact", were essentially reifications of their taxonomies. This rationale successfully sustained both the interwar and postwar growth of archaeology, down to the 1960s, when it was increasingly challenged on both sides of the Atlantic.

By this time, the uncritical use of diffusionist explanations by European prehistorians had long retarded the emergence of an appropriate functional understanding of phenomena such as megaliths, for example, and had been taken to absurd length in postulating contacts between communities on the strength of slight resemblances in material culture. Allied with evidence for cultural discontinuity (which was often no more than the fragmentary character of the archaeological record itself), this had tended to produce a prehistory full of invasions and migrations. The healthy reaction to this was led by American work, and especially the trenchant criticisms of Lewis Binford. Comparable doubts were expressed by Grahame Clark in his famous lecture on "The invasion hypothesis in British prehistory" (Clark, 1966), which was the signal for a general attack on prevailing modes of explanation.

Analytical Archaeology thus came at a critical point; and perhaps, with hindsight, too early. It looked both to the past and to the future. To a large extent it was still within the Childean paradigm, and was concerned to bring more powerful quantitative methods to the solution of Childean problems. It stressed the importance of forming multipurpose entities by numerical taxonomy, and of diffusion as a widely applicable explanation. But it brought in – albeit in a somewhat undigested form – seminal new ideas such as subsistence and locational strategies, trend-surface and network analysis, which were to become increasingly important elements: and it prefigured future developments for instance by an analysis of the variety of situations comprising "diffusion", with a series of spatial tests for distinguishing them (*Analytical Archaeology*, p. 418). Yet although full of penetrating insights and new observations, *Analytical Archaeology* stood at the beginning of the process of rethinking prehistory, not at the end.

It was at this point that "The economic context of trade and industry in Barbarian Europe till Roman times" was written. It was intended to replace Gordon Childe's chapter in a previous edition of the *Cambridge Economic History*, but it took on a much more ambitious form. The format offered the opportunity of writing an account of European prehistory which avoided the "counterfeit history" of which he complained. It also allowed a further exploration of the reasons for cultural similarity, hitherto lumped together as processes of diffusion, which resulted from the various kinds of trade and exchange. It thus not only attempted to summarize most of the relevant archaeological evidence from a vast and diverse period of time, but to consider it in the light of anthropological findings, and especially the work of Karl Polanyi on the social embeddedness of the primitive economy (Polanyi, Arensberg and Pearson, 1957). It was a great advance on previous work in its discussion of the social functions of artefact-types and its inference of the circulation-systems of which they are the fossilized remains; and it took further some of the arguments already used by Grahame Clark when writing on the stone axe trade (Clark, 1965).

The paper was written at a time when the reaction to the older style of prehistory was in full swing. A leading critic of diffusionism and all it stood for was Colin Renfrew, who in papers on "Colonialism and Megalithismus" and "The autonomy of the south-east European Copper Age" (Renfrew, 1967, 1969) offered a picture of local development in which European prehistoric societies seemed to operate as largely closed systems in relation to their neighbours. While acknowledging the principle that, in writing culture-history, contacts should not be multiplied beyond necessity. David nevertheless thought that the extreme insistence on local autonomy was a passing phase, which would be replaced by a more balanced view. In a sense, he bypassed the debate on "autonomy" (which he considered rather sterile) by investigating the kinds of network which actually linked often far-flung societies by exchange-cycles and trading caravans. In the "trade and industry" paper he began the move from explanations involving a debate over "tradition" and "influence" to models of networks of various kinds along which particular items were likely to travel and the distances they were likely to achieve.

An example of this approach, from five years later, is given by the paper on the beaker network, presented to an international symposium at Oberried in the Black Forest in 1974. The title is significant, for the network idea has increasingly taken on the role of the "culture" as the primary concept of the emerging orthodoxy. Unlike the idea of the culture, it allows for explanations which are not tautologies, by giving the archaeologist the opportunity to specify the kinds of contact which were operating and the forces which kept them in existence. In the case of beakers, David was concerned to stress the role of fine pottery as one of a series of prestige items with a characteristic range of distribution (cf., Sherratt, 1976). Such an expensive product, made in a restricted number of centres, would appear in different proportions on sites depending on their access to, and relations with, these centres. Such a model demands quantitative archaeological data to demonstrate it, and many more characterization studies than have been hitherto carried out; a ten-year programme of work opened up by approaching the problem in a new way.

More importantly, this approach goes beyond "culture-history" or "cultural change" – too often merely a chronicle of the artefacts themselves – towards a genuine archaeological concern with the social role of the artefact and thus with society itself. The congruence of archaeological interest in alliance and exchange with the current focus of social anthropology on similar ideas is an encouraging portent of their value to each other. What David would have been quick to point out, however, is that there is no simple mapping of one discipline's set of concepts on that of another. What emerges must be greater than both.

If Gordon Childe was outstanding in systematizing (and thereby partly on fossilizing) the structure of European prehistory in the first half of the twentieth century, then it was another English-speaking archaeologist, Grahame Clark, who has often pointed the way towards the kind of ecological prehistory which is increasingly gaining ground today.

Grahame Clark had moved early in his academic career from a dominant concern with typology to an interest in social organization and – more easily translated into archaeological practice – a concern with the ecological setting of prehistoric communities, not simply as an exercise in reconstruction but as a powerful element in the explanation of their behaviour. This message, along with the importance of anthropology, was a basic feature of his teaching in the Department at Cambridge, to whose Disney Chair of Archaeology he succeeded in 1952. David was curiously uninfluenced by this strand in his training, until long after his PhD research was completed, and *Analytical Archaeology* written in its aftermath. Only through the dialogue with Eric Higgs and his pupils did this aspect come fully to his attention, when it was characteristically absorbed, analysed, and turned inside out to produce the tribute to Grahame Clark of which the title was itself a conflation of two of the Professor's best-known books: "Mesolithic Europe; the economic basis".

Eric Higgs was a retired sheep-farmer who had come to archaeology as his second career. Grahame Clark, whose research assistant he became, saw the possibility of fostering in his own department an expertise in the study of faunal remains from an archaeological rather than a palaeontological point of view (Clark, 1952, p. 4). The instruction in faunal identification which Higgs provided proved to be a great attraction to potential research students, and in 1967 the environmental work of the Department was officially constituted as The British Academy Major Research Project on the Early History of Agriculture – though still, in more familiar parlance, known as the "Bone-Room".

Although on paper concerned with agricultural prehistory, the project also reflected Higgs' own interest in the Palaeolithic, and brought a characteristic long-term perspective to the problem (Higgs and Jarman, 1969). His earlier work in Epirus, interpreting Palaeolithic settlement in the light of recent pastoral groups in that area, gave him a special interest in seasonal changes and transhumant movements. These he saw as an optimal method of integrating resources under widely differing forms of exploitation. From this perspective, sites were no longer replicate components of the same "culture", but complementary elements of exploitation systems, each with its own special relationship to the area accessible from it. Claudio Vita-Finzi's apt phrase "site-catchment" neatly summed up this idea of a settlement and its economic territory.

The Higgsian approach was thus to ignore the nuances of material culture, with which he saw archaeologists (including David, then finishing his account of British beakers) as pathologically obsessed, and to concentrate instead on long-term trends in the economic record. This he did by means of improved methods of retrieval of animal and plant material from excavations, and by site-catchment analysis – walking out from prehistoric settlements to determine the differential accessibility of the various resources which surrounded them. Soon his research students were domesticating musk-oxen, interviewing shepherds on remote hillsides, and walking through Greek farmyards and Israeli minefields evaluating the terrain around well-known sites which had never been looked at in this way before (Higgs, 1972).

These rigorous activities were supported by a philosophy of extreme economic determinism in which population pressure constantly forced adjustment to environmental limitation, occasionally relieved by technical advance. The actual patterns of exploitation adopted by human groups were seen as rigidly specified by the intersection of technology and environment, which made them as predictable as those of any other animal. Territoriality was a basic component of such behaviour. On a short time-scale, the essential congruence between human society and economic necessity might be obscured by a mass of minor, meaningless variables; but, in the long-term, basic biological factors would assert themselves. An appreciation of the potential complexity of ecological systems was thus a hindrance to a true understanding of human development, which could only be approached by isolating the most powerful forces in the situation and dealing with these alone (Higgs, 1972, 1975).

While some aspects of this outlook were doubtless merely a reflection of the conditions under which their own research was conducted, the sense of priority which Eric Higgs and his followers conveyed was a most valuable contribution to the intellectual climate of Cambridge archaeology. Its stress on economic essentials, and the method of putting its ideas into practice through site-catchment analysis, helped to articulate the widespread dissatisfaction with conventional artefact-orientated approaches and at the same time suggested a realistic alternative. This programme attracted many of the most able students and produced a row of important case-studies in many different periods and areas. It was inevitable that this lively school of research within the same university department should influence David's own work: even though its very existence was in some sense a protest against the approach which was symbolized by *Beaker Pottery of Great Britain and Ireland* and *Analytical Archaeology* (Higgs, 1970).

The two systems of archaeological thought represented by *Analytical Archaeology* and the work of the Early Agriculture Project stood at the end of the 1960s in friendly academic rivalry. Not only was the raw material of their researches different, but their professed philosophies clashed on issues of determinism, scale and etiology. Loyalty to both seemed impossible. In fact, however, a continuing dialogue was in progress, and the lively discussions in David's seminars frequently centred on this clash of views. His own witty characterization of the debate forms part of the fifth paper in this volume: but by the time those words were written, in 1971, he had already absorbed the methods, if not the philosophy, of the Higgsian approach.

In the paper on Glastonbury, which appeared in the same volume, the catchment model is brilliantly applied. It is both firmly tied to a yearly cycle of activities in the immediate neighbourhood of the site (Fig. 10 on p. 420) and also generalized into a whole "Chinese box" of catchment systems on different scales. Equally importantly, artefactual evidence (and especially the characterization of raw materials) is used as a positive demonstration of the movement of resources within these zones. Such methods may help to transform the catchment model from a heuristic assumption to a falsifiable hypothesis; though its use in the former mode is still valuable with a large sample of unexcavated sites, especially where it is combined with appropriate tests of significance (Flannery, 1976).

From the economy of a single site, David turned to the economic basis of a whole period, the Mesolithic. This occupied much of his attention from 1972 to 1974. It was to be a study in integrated bio-archaeology, covering both artefactual and biological evidence within the perspective of the Holocene vegetational succession. It is a classic example of the way he was able to rise above the immediate categories of material evidence to assess the contribution of each and to correct for their biases. Taking the Higgsian premise of economic priority, he set out to demonstrate how an uncritical use of any class of evidence could miss the point, and produce a misleading picture. The over-emphasis on animal-products which characterized much of the work of the "Bone-Room" was an obvious target; and indeed one passage actually describes the personnel of that institution – the reindeer man, the red-deer man, and the cereal girl (though the caricature is balanced by the inclusion of the misguided beaker man). But polemic was succeeded by practice: and in succeeding sections he took up the related processes of postglacial adjustment – sea-level changes, obliteration of morainic lakes, and forest succession – and showed by reference to ethnographic studies in New Zealand and South Africa how the opportunities of the early Holocene might have been grasped. His conclusions ranged from a new explanation of the use of microlithic assemblages to a postulated root- and nut-based temperate horticulture – a *tour de force* of reinterpretation in which an ecological archaeology transcended each of its narrowly based sections. It was the answer to a challenge; not to validate artefactual studies against the criticisms of bio-archaeology, but to change both into something better.

The study of Glastonbury has already been cited as an example of David's application and extension of Higgsian models. In fact, it is this and more. In the introduction to the *Models in Archaeology* volume in which it appeared (the fifth paper in this volume) David discussed the four major areas of science which archaeologists had sought to emulate – the morphological paradigm of numerical taxonomy, the ecological paradigm of environmental explanation, the anthropological paradigm of social reconstruction, and the geographical paradigm of spatial analysis. His integration of the last two is as notable an achievement of the Glastonbury paper as his use of the first and second.

While the bodies of theory to which they relate – social patterning and settlement layout in one case, architectural space-structure and locational theory in the other – have distinct origins and associated literatures, they are in practice closely related. Indeed, as David pointed out in "Spatial information in archaeology" (the eighteenth paper this volume), they are parts of a continuum, dominated at one end by social factors and at the other by economic ones. The potential of studying ancient settlements from an anthropological point of view had been demonstrated by Longacre's analysis of the Carter Ranch Pueblo (Longacre, 1968). Stimulating work on the utilization of space on a small scale was also being carried out by Cambridge architects such as March, Martin and Echenique. These gave the impetus to his study of settlement layout and function.

The Glastonbury study began with a typological study of the buildings on the site and a structural analysis of their interrelationships. This was controlled by a study of the contents of the buildings. This procedure resulted in the recognition of a replicated system of modular units, which contain both male and female domestic and working space. Contrasts between these units emerged both in wealth, and in the orientation of their external connections, as indicated by raw materials. These suggested a social system composed of exogamous lineages, three generations of which would occupy one of the modular settlement units. At this point, the evidence of Old Irish traditions was introduced for comparison with the results of archaeological analysis, and the analysis was extended in terms of Murdock's observations on the role of the patrilocal extended family, fraternal polygyny and the levirate to provide detailed insight into the structure and function of an Iron Age society.

From this micro-scale, the study expanded to consider the site in its regional context. Its economic role was identified as that of a seasonally supplemented marshland outlier dependent on the Maesbury "hillfort", offering autumn grazing to complement the limestone uplands. More generally it can be seen as a typical segment of the pattern of settlement in southwest England, characteristic of the Iron Age Dumnonii but surviving in many aspects through into Medieval times. Such an arrangement of "hillfort" centre, farmsteads and hamlets is interpretable in terms of a settlement hierarchy, arranged on Christaller's administrative principle $(k=7)$ rather than a market model. The whole settlement-system should therefore be seen as a relatively underdeveloped area of southern Britain immediately before the Roman conquest, preserving many archaic features. The contrast between this and the more advanced parts of southeast Britain which already had more differentiated and partly market-based economies was appreciated by the Romans themselves who drew their first frontier to exclude the more self-sufficient and politically resilient tribesmen of the west.

This wholly original pioneer study used with outstanding effect the 70-year-old records of the Glastonbury excavations to demonstrate the wealth of inferences which can be drawn from highly structured settlement material. In putting together such a variety of evidence with clearly formulated theory, David produced a classic piece of work which will be imitated for many years to come.

The final paper in this group, "Towns in the development of early civilization", is also David's last piece of written work. It was addressed, not to archaeologists, but to a conference on towns organized by the historical magazine *Past and Present*. It is therefore significant in two ways; as an indication of his thinking on later periods, and as an expression of his views on the contribution of archaeology to the social sciences in general.

David's contacts with historians were especially frequent since they were well represented on the high table at Peterhouse. He never believed, like some of the more fanatical protagonists of the archaeological point of view, that archaeological evidence is superior to that of history because of its lack of bias – indeed, he was foremost in pointing out the evident biases of the archaeological record. But he firmly held that, when each was considered in its own terms without making an unhappy attempt to match the two prematurely, the different facets illuminated from separate sources – each with its own properties and bias – could produce a more three-dimensional picture than either alone. Although archaeological evidence does have a vastly greater (though yet scarcely tapped) reservoir of potential information, in contrast to the well-thumbed body of textual evidence, the value of this information can be multiplied many times by conjunction with the relevant texts.

What is more important, however, is the range of situations which are only evidenced archaeologically and not in any other way. Theories based upon observation or written evidence alone must consider only a fraction of relevant human behaviour. Many extinct societies and extensive patterns of pre-literate behaviour can only be recovered by archaeological means. Moreover, the kinds of society which produce written records or are accessible to be recorded in this way are in many respects unusual and atypical; and a comprehensive theory requires the integration of information from history, anthropology, and archaeology. Approached in this way, well-studied historical or contemporary situations appear as the bases for subtheories which must themselves be tested in a wider context and integrated into theories of more universal validity.

Thus the bodies of locational and central-place theory used by modern geographers, for instance, represent special cases of human spatial behaviour with roots deep in the Pleistocene, with a comparably extended variety in which a more general set of regularities should be discernible. It is thus imperative to rise above the constraints of disciplines based upon particular classes of evidence to achieve a fully comparative analysis of all the situations relevant to the aspect of behaviour in question. Paradoxically, such a comparative science of society is predicated upon the achievement of maturity in each of its constituent disciplines, so that each can fully evaluate the biases of its own subject-matter.

A further contribution of the final paper is the good example which it gives of the shift from monocausal to processual models. As Kent Flannery has often insisted, social processes can rarely be reduced to simple correlations, but can more profitably be described as regular sequences of development which can be triggered in a variety of ways. This is well exemplified by urbanization, and this approach provides a paradigm which can be extended to other important developments in human ecology and social organization. It is an enduring sadness that its author did not live to pursue such researches, with his characteristic breadth of knowledge and imagination.

David Clarke was particularly suited by his intellectual temperament to the needs of his subject after 20 years of post-war data-accumulation and with new winds blowing through the social and biological sciences. Indeed, in longer perspective, archaeology as a whole is at last in the second half of the twentieth century in a position to make a major contribution to the mainstream of intellectual achievement. The facts which nineteenth-century social evolutionists had to speculate about or to reconstruct from the range of contemporary societies are being increasingly revealed by archaeological research. Evidence on the "early history of mankind" accumulates daily. It is vital at this stage to look beyond the mass of individual observations to the body of ideas which they support. Sir Peter Medawar has written:

> The factual burden of a science varies inversely with its degree of maturity. As a science advances, particular facts are comprehended within, and there-fore in a sense annihilated by, general statements of increasing explanatory power and compass . . . In all sciences we are being progressively relieved of the burden of singular instances, the tyranny of the particular. We need no longer record the fall of every apple. (Medawar, 1969, p. 128)

David saw this in terms both of a more mature discipline of archaeo-logy and a wider comparative social science to which this discipline would make a major contribution. It is an ambitious conception. Will archaeology respond to the challenge? The man who most clearly pro-claimed these potentialities is no longer here to see their realization. We are left with his vision, and his example.

REFERENCES

Binford, L. R. (1972). *An Archaeological Perspective*, Seminar Press, New York and Lon-don.

Clark, J. G. D. (1952). *Prehistoric Europe: The Economic Basis*, Methuen, London.

Clark, J. G. D. (1965). Traffic in stone axe- and adze-blades, *Economic History Review*, **18**, 1–28.

Clark, J. G. D. (1966). The invasion hypothesis in British prehistory, *Antiquity*, **40**, 172–189.

Flannery, K. V. (1976). *The Early Mesoamerican Village*, Academic Press, New York.

Higgs, E. S. (1970). Review of *Analytical Archaeology*, *Proceedings of the Prehistoric Society*, **36**, 396–399.

Higgs, E. S. (ed.) (1972). *Papers in Economic Prehistory*, Cambridge University Press, Cambridge.

Higgs, E. S. (ed.) (1975). *Palaeoeconomy*, Cambridge University Press, Cambridge.

Higgs, E. S. and Jarman, M. R. (1969). The origins of agriculture: a reconsideration, *Antiquity*, **43**, 31–41.

Longacre, W. A. (1968). Some aspects of prehistoric society in east-central Arizona, in *New Perspectives in Archaeology* (S. R. Binford and L. R. Binford, eds), Aldine, Chicago, pp. 89–102.

Medawar, P. B. (1969). *The Art of the Soluble*, Methuen, London.

Polanyi, K., Arensberg, C. M. and Pearson, H. W. (1957). *Trade and Market in the Early Empires*, Collier-Macmillan, London and Free Press, New York.

Renfrew, A. C. (1967). Colonialism and Megalithismus, *Antiquity*, **41**, 276.

Renfrew, A. C. (1969). The autonomy of the south-east European Copper Age, *Proceedings of the Prehistoric Society*, **35**, 12.

Sherratt, A. G. (1976). Resources, technology and trade, *Problems in Economic and Social Archaeology* (G. de G. Sieveking, I. H. Longworth and K. E. Wilson, eds), Duckworth, London, pp. 557–581.

Mesolithic Europe: The Economic Basis

DAVID L. CLARKE

Archaeologists usually base their interpretations on particular sets of data – pots, flints, bones, seeds, sites – or on observations based on those data; the interpretations are, in a sense, the pendent consequences of the chosen data. Widely accepted interpretations then become the conventional framework for further discussion and research, and the conventional interpretation becomes traditional. Now, although in such a rapidly changing discipline all interpretations must remain transient conventions, there are nevertheless dangers that arise from working only within a set of data towards dependent conventional interpretations. These limitations arise from the observation that the analyses and interpretations of any data are constrained and distorted by missing information, inherent biases, sampling aberrations and persistent stereotypes (traditional misinterpretations) and by the fundamental difficulty that the results of any analyses will usually fit a very large number of different interpretative models. Inevitably, the concern with the explicit formation and testing of alternative hypotheses and their models emerges; in particular, there is the need to compare the interpretative models that arise as a consequence of the analysis of data, with models of expectation derived from other sources and which take account of the sampling problems of the data under analysis.

The conventional interpretation that depicts the displacement of the European meat-eating Mesolithic hunter-fishers by Neolithic cereal farmers has indeed become traditional; a satisfactory evolutionary picture of the displacement of lower cultures and economies by higher ones – what one might call Social Darwinism in action. Satisfactory as this model may once have been in terms of the philosophy and ideology then prevalent, this conventional picture begins to look less likely in

Reprinted with permission from *Problems in Economic and Social Archaeology* (G. de G. Sieveking, I. H. Longworth and K. E. Wilson, eds), Duckworth, London, 1976, pp. 449–481.

the light of more recent thought and work (Wilkinson, R. G., 1973; Higgs, 1972; Lee and DeVore, 1968). Characteristically, the traditional picture largely emerged from the typological analysis and interpretation of artefacts and site data with little or no consideration for the technical and sampling difficulties of that data and but scant attention to organic, social and ecological considerations, before the pioneer work of Professor Clark at Star Carr. A particular interpretative model, based on one interpretation of a limited set of data, became at first conventional and then traditional, and still remains deeply entrenched, without due consideration for alternative interpretations of the same data and a proper evaluation in comparison with the expectations on ecological, environmental, ethnographic, economic and theoretical grounds.

A first step in any such study should at least attempt to assess and allow for the range of inherent assumptions, limitations, biases and sampling problems that will constrain and orientate both the set of data under analysis and the interpretations that seem to arise inexorably and conclusively from that analysis. Although this essay makes no pretence of being a formal study of the European Mesolithic, it is perhaps worth summarizing what seem to be the major biasing factors in the traditional interpretation in order to foresee their interpretative consequences.

The objective in this essay is, first, to outline the biases, sampling problems and stereotypes that currently seem to distort the interpretation of European Mesolithic material (Part I). Then, an attempt is made to put the artefact and site data on one side, so that a sketch model of the general ecological background of Europe *ca* 10 000–5000 b.c. may independently suggest expectations about the nature and distribution of the Mesolithic subsistence systems (Part II). Finally, the data, observations and the ecological predictions are brought together, in an effort to throw some light on the many different interpretations of the "transition" from regional Mesolithic economies to the Neolithic pattern of food production in Europe (Part III).

I. BIAS, SAMPLING PROBLEMS AND STEREOTYPES

Meat fixation: a cultural bias

It is a culturally induced assumption that hunted mammals were the main source of Mesolithic food supply and meat quantitatively the most important foodstuff. Modern North Europeans and North Americans come from cultures that especially esteem meat, partly because meat protein has always provided an important source of immediate body heat in cold wet northern climates. However, even in these extreme modern diets, meat *rarely* contributes one-third of the diet by weight and *rarely* more than half of the daily protein intake. The partly illusory and partly modern emphasis on a meat diet and the animals that supply it has been compounded by the correlation between the area where this preference at present prevails, the area where archaeology as a modern discipline developed, and the area of local Late Glacial cultures in which, under tundra and steppe conditions, meat certainly did for a while constitute a major and visibly impressive part of the diet – the reindeer of the Magdalenian, the mammoth of the Gravettian and the buffalo of the Palaeo-Indian.

However, the hominids and primates are predominantly vegetarian omnivores, and this dietary flexibility has been one of the unspecialized characteristics that led to the great expansion of this mammalian order. The middle-latitude distribution of the earliest hominids was no accident: the middle latitudes of the globe are the richest in plant life, the prime regions for sunshine and photosynthesis. The dentition and skeletal structure of the early hominids clearly reflect the pursuit of an omnivorous diet with the emphasis on vegetable matter – basically leaves, shoots, roots, fruits, seeds, flowers, buds, nuts supplemented by insects and small animals. It is only in the photosynthetic deserts of near-Arctic or Antarctic conditions that man must rely predominantly on animal and marine foods, and substitute the moss from reindeer stomachs and the algae from fish gullets for missing vegetal elements. Man therefore makes the best of incident solar energy by cropping the trophic pyramid at the primary, plant level; as an omnivore he advantageously avoids the limiting consequences of a specialized herbivorous or carnivorous diet (Jolly, 1970).

Certainly, one of the special characteristics that distinguished the early hominids from the other primates was the development of big herbivore hunting, but the quantitative significance of this activity for the diet is probably much over-emphasized. In any event, scarcely less important than the Pleistocene "meat revolution" must have been the "plant revolution" that followed the use of fire to roast plant foods, bursting the starch grains, making them more digestible and breaking down the cellulose cell-walls so that the gastric juices could reach the cell contents, thus greatly increasing the food value of plants and early focusing especial attention on the starchy roots, tubers, rhizomes and bulbs, with their simple vegetative reproductive system.

In short, modern studies and our vestigial soft anatomy confirm that man is a vegetarian omnivore whose diet and subsistence patterns are tightly correlated with latitudinal variations in sunlight and abundance of his primary plant foods. Since the abundance and species variety of plants decrease as one moves out of the tropical and temperate zones, and approach zero in the Arctic, the incidence of hunting, gathering and fishing is inevitably related to latitudinal ecology. However, the trend is not a simple linear one, since *edible* plant species form an irregular proportion of the total plant cover, and this proves to be an important feature in European ecology, where the edible plant species of the Temperate Forest zone, taken as a whole, were quantitatively as rich as or richer than the Mediterranean zone, for reasons relating to soils, rainfall, plant community density and structure. In the end, it is the nature and juxtaposition of local micro-variations in ecological structure which add crucial positive and negative residuals to the overall trend in food potential (Lee and DeVore, 1968, pp. 7, 42).

The so-called "hunters" of Temperate and Mediterranean Europe probably depended for most of their subsistence on sources other than hunted mammal meat, namely gathered wild plant foods, fungi, algae, shellfish and fish. It is probable that in these latitudes ($35°–55°$ N), gathered vegetable foods would have provided 60–80% of the diet by weight, and meat from all sources – hunted mammals and gathered land, sea and riverine molluscs, crustacea, insects, fish, amphibians and small reptiles – only 30–40% by weight, *in toto*. With the important exception of the northern coniferous and birch forest zone and the Arctic beyond, the European Mesolithic aboriginals were neither predominantly hunters nor mammal meat consumers but largely gatherers, with a substantially vegetal diet whose abundant sources are difficult to appreciate in the *degraded* ecology of modern Europe. They certainly hunted game and fished assiduously but these activities, however impressive in artefact equipment, however prestigious and time consuming, did not provide the greater part of the diet or protein by weight. The traditional misinterpretation rests on a series of biases which we should now examine critically.

Sampling aberrations – technical biases

The unbalancing effects of numerous cumulative unvoiced positive and negative sampling biases, over-representing some aspects and under-representing others, are for example:

1. *Faunal bias* The artefacts aside, the archaeological record is dominated by the bone evidence. Meat inefficiently leaves much inedible bone waste that preserves relatively well under many conditions; plant-foods are much less wasteful and their small unconsumed residue preserves badly and survives, if at all, transformed into unrecognizable and often microscopic forms (decomposed faeces, plant fibres, seed

spikelets, etc.). This disproportionate representation can suggest that mammalian fauna with large robust bones provided the bulk of the diet. Thus, in a series of unargued steps, we may slip from "80% of the bones were red deer" (how many individuals, 4 or 400, how many got away, how many hunters, how many man-hours?) to "80% of the diet was red deer" (on what basis?) to "deer formed 80% of the subsistence basis" (by weight, man-hours?) and, ultimately, to "red-deer economies" in which anything from salmon to acorns may have provided the staple food.

2. *Northern and Alpine bias* The great majority of wet Mesolithic sites with good organic preservation are in northern Europe or, more broadly, from the zone which at the time of occupation was within the northern edge of the northern forests and less than 500 miles from the contemporary Norwegian ice-cap. Star Carr, for example, was a winter site set in the sheltered fringes of the Northern pre-Boreal birch forest, facing the Norwegian ice-cap only 400 miles away across an exposed, ice-locked North Sea bay. In these settings and these contexts we would expect meat to be quantitatively well represented and vegetal foods difficult to substantiate; in fact, the evidence from the plant-remains and root-mattocks used at Star Carr shows how remarkably crucial were the lakeside and marsh plants in the northern subsistence pattern (Clark, 1972, pp. 10–26). The only other significant group of wet Mesolithic sites are the equally unrepresentative Alpine lake sites. We lack investigated sites with good organic preservation from lowland Temperate Forest and Mediterranean zones. However, it is clear that such sites exist and that we should be concentrating on the wet Mesolithic sites of southern Britain, France, south Germany and central Europe and on the vast potential of the arid desert sites of Almerian Spain with their basketry and wooden equipment (Clark, 1952, Plate XIII). The Mesolithic sites from which we have organic and vegetal material are confined to extremely limited peripheral areas that happen to be locationally atypical of the Temperate and Mediterranean ecology as a whole.

3. *Artefact bias* The asymmetric bias effects, which operate cumulatively on artefact production, use, preservation and interpretation, inevitably lead to an interpretative sump in which all surviving artefacts are assumed to be related to hunting and meat-processing.

(a) Asymmetric production and correlation with activities: large numbers of artefacts may be produced for particular tasks that are of short duration and little significance for subsistence whilst, conversely, major activities of staple subsistence-value may be represented by few or unspecialized artefacts. There is no one-to-one correlation between numbers of artefacts and the extent or value of the associated activity pattern. Vegetable and other gathered foods often need little more than dextrous hands and specialized teeth with the addition of a few wooden sticks and points, whereas a variety of specialized stone artefacts is necessary for the particular tasks of killing, skinning, gutting, butchering and otherwise processing animal carcases – especially those of large mammals. Vegetal and gathered food requires little artefact equipment and that largely in perishable materials.

b) Asymmetric preservation: much of the organic equipment associated with vegetal and gathered foods will fail to survive whilst, conversely, a much greater proportion of the stone equipment associated with hunting and butchering will readily survive.

(c) Asymmetric interpretation: the final barrier – the little equipment associated with vegetal food-gathering and processing that does survive may often be blindly misinterpreted in terms of hunting and butchering: the throwing-stick for nuts becomes a boomerang for small game; the Clacton digging-stick(?) becomes a spear-point; the antler mattock, a dispatching weapon; and the microlithic sickle armature, a projectile barb. There is a presumption that because some flint artefacts are associated with hunting and butchering, then others must be similarly associated, thus extending a weak probability to the status of an untested and sweeping general proposition (Clarke, 1968, p. 18); whereas a significant and possibly, in certain cases, a major proportion of flakes, blades, bladelets and microliths may have been associated with vegetal and other food-gathering and processing, as recent evidence suggests (Fig. 1; see below).

4. *Method and technique bias* Archaeological techniques of excavation and methods of analysis partly decide what information will or will not be recovered. There has been insufficient large-scale excavation of Mesolithic open and cave sites and too few of these have been accompanied by the fine sieving, flotation, coprolite analysis, centrifuging and horizontal pollen studies that are necessary to discover the subsistence pattern in general and the role of plant foods in particular. Strangely, these techniques have been used on later open sites and mounds so that, paradoxically, wild plant foods often first "appear" in Neolithic to Iron Age contexts. However, the first appearance of a wild plant food in a Late Neolithic deposit is more likely to represent the statistically sporadic discovery of an erratically preserved and, by Neolithic times,

marginally present constituent, rather than the first use of the plant in the area. Much indirect evidence for the wild plant potential of Mesolithic Europe comes, therefore, from Neolithic and even later sites. In addition, many of the existing flotation techniques discriminate in favour of carbonized seed material and against microscopic fibres from roots, tubers and foliage; this bias for seed-recovery and against root-data may turn iout to be of crucial importance in our interpretation of the development of food-production in Temperate Europe. Finally, some compensation for the lack of suitably processed sites, and the lack of sites with good preservation, may yet be achieved by the locational analysis of Mesolithic sites in relation to the vegetal and other resources of their catchment area (Fig. 6) (Cassels, 1972).

Stereotypes: traditional misinterpretations

Strictly speaking, stereotypes are fixed mental impressions, but we are here concerned with those that are supported more by convention than by evidence.

1. *Mesolithic = microlithic = bow-and-arrow hunting; therefore Mesolithic equipment equates with a meat diet*   This stereotype is one of the most entrenched and most misleading of all conventional assumptions. Microlithic flints are rarely the most numerous flint artefact class in European postglacial industries *ca* 10 000–4000 B.C.: some industries have none at all and many have merely a few snapped trapezes. Even where they do appear, microliths were used in many different ways and there is growing evidence that a high proportion of these elements was employed in composite tools for plant-gathering, harvesting, slicing, grating, plant-fibre processing for lines, snares, nets and traps, shell openers, bow-drill points and awls; where they were employed as barbs in any number was most probably in a small amount of equipment not associated with hunting mammal meat (fish hooks, bird arrows, fish arrows and leisters). The evidence suggests that with the light Mesolithic bow the arrows used were also light, with a small penetration capacity and therefore encumbered with, at most, one or two armatures on mammal-hunting points; for example, the widely standardized single-point and cutting-side-barb Loshult type known from Scandinavia, Switzerland and Spanish Levantine art, or the narrow trapeze transverse arrow (Fig. 2).

The survival of microlithic-armatured knife-hafts at Shanidar (Iraq), Columnata (N. Africa), Murcielagos (Spain) and Bienne (Switzerland) opens up a rather different picture (Solecki, 1963; Camps-Fabrer, 1966; Vayson, 1918). It is now clear that the ancestry of the

Neolithic sickles lies in a wide variety of contemporary Mesolithic/
Upper Palaeolithic composite cutting and harvesting knives in wood,
bone and antler, either set with blades or microblades in line to give
a straight cutting edge (Fig. 2) or set with slanting blades, microblades,
broad trapezes, notched and serrated blades in line, or lunates or
triangles set vertically, to give varieties of saw-edge (Fig. 1). It would

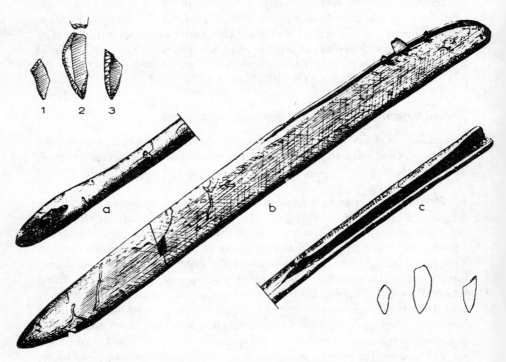

FIG. 1. The harvesting knife from Columnata (North Africa), after J. Tixier. (Apart
from the microliths 1, 2, 3, the scale is one-third.)

appear that the ancestry of these types is very ancient, possibly extending into the Middle Palaeolithic, and that they are on the whole contemporary and associated functional variants with different duties,
rather than a simple typological sequence. What those functions were
we can only guess, but those from the Mediterranean zone are often
accompanied by seed-grinding stones and the lighter, pointed-toothed
varieties would be very suitable for comb-cutting light edible herbage,
shoots, buds, small fruits, fragile legumes and grass seeds. The straight-
edged or denticulate forms would be more suitable for sawing through
thicker edible stems, roots and fruit-stalks, while the heavy oblique-

edged settings of blades and trapezes could hack bunches of tough-stemmed grasses and plants with firmly attached seeds.

These implements would answer a pressing requirement for efficient "mechanization" of laborious hand-plucking procedures, since small vegetal elements must commonly be gathered in vast numbers, thousands of seeds and hundreds of leaves, if they are to be of subsistence value. Such equipment would greatly increase the yield per unit of time and energy-expenditure, thus decisively raising highly abundant, nutritious but small-unit vegetal foods to more-than-marginal economic value by technological means; one more vital step in the increasingly intensive exploitation of vegetal foods.

The short harvesting knife from the Capsian levels at Columnata *ca* 6000 B.C. is particularly informative (Camps-Fabrer, 1966, pp. 147–148). In its present short form, with a total half-length of 21 cm and slotted section of 9 cm, it once held five microliths of which three broken stubs survive – two broken lunates and one triangle (Fig. 1). This single artefact raises in a particularly trenchant way a number of fundamental and interesting points. Here we have microlithic elements, of the forms conventionally interpreted as projectile barbs, patently hafted in a cutting-tool. Since the broken triangle is virtually the same as the Løshult arrow side-barb, we have visible proof that homogeneous morphological types may have more than one use. Conversely, the triangle was hafted in line with lunates, showing that different morphological types may have been used together for identical purposes and that the makers did not necessarily distinguish in their own ethno-classification between triangles and lunates; maybe they saw a single spectrum of "micro-units" in which spurred triangles merged into triangles into lunates as, indeed, they visibly do. An archaeological classification based on total morphology provides only one taxonomy – a classification based only on the functional edges and points would produce another (White, 1969). Many basic problems of Palaeolithic flint-artefact classification emerge here, but perhaps the immediate lessons are that microliths are not exclusively projectile barbs, that one artefact-type may have many different haftings and uses, and *vice versa*.

The Shanidar hafts, and others from Europe, confirm the implications of the Columnata knife. The slotted length of these harvesting-knives averages 20–40 cm with provision for some 5–30 microliths. Besides this diverse class of artefact for gathering vegetal foods, there were probably others for processing them – many of them equipped with blades, microblades and microliths. Some probably fall into the "bean-slicer" class – one or more sharp flint units set in a small hand-grasped haft over which stems, roots and fruits could be quickly drawn in one motion to produce sliced or shredded elements suitable for

FISHING   &   FOWLING

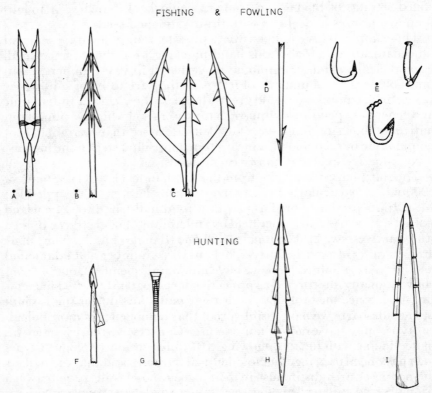

HUNTING

Fig. 2. Hafted composite artefacts set with microliths and microblades. A, B, C, D, E, J, K are based on ethnographic models.

A – bident leister
B – fishing arrow
C – trident
F – Løshult type barbed arrowhead
G – Eising type narrow trapeze
    arrowhead

D – razor shellfish dart
E – barbed fishhooks

H – Trørød type projectile point
I – Tarvastu type thrusting spear

cooking and digestion. Artefacts of precisely this type have been recovered from Switzerland, North Africa and Nubia, set with single blades, lunates or triangles (Clark, 1971, p. 45).

A most important related class of artefacts with microlithic units, of which we have at the moment only ethnographic evidence, is the composite grater board – a rectangular wooden board into which large numbers of microlithic flint points, microflakes, or transverse rows of straight, notched or serrated blades have been fitted (Fig. 2). Varieties

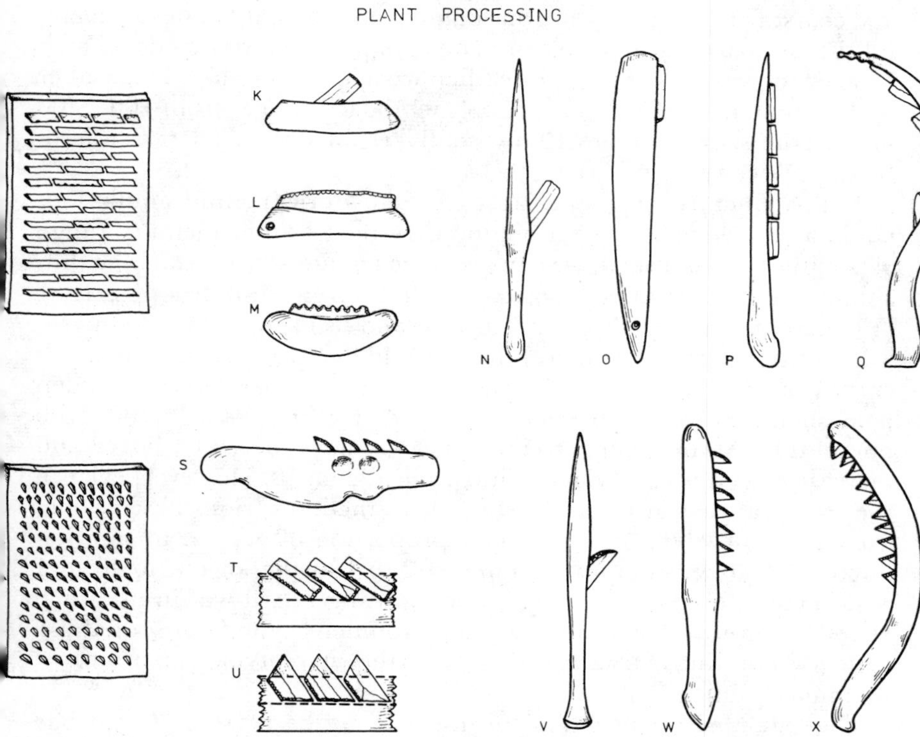

PLANT   PROCESSING

FIG. 2. (continued)

J – grater (blade set)
K – Obermeilen type slicer knife
L – Nussdorf type slicer knife
M– Wangen type saw knife

R – grater (point set)
S – Bienne type saw knife
T – saw-edge achieved with
      oblique blades
U – saw-edge achieved with
      broad trapezes

N – Lucerne type slicer knife
O – Shanidar type slicer knife
P – Baikal type harvesting knife
Q – Karanovo type harvesting sickle

V – Qadan type slicer knife
W– Columnata type harvesting knife
X – Murcielagos type harvesting sickle

of this implement are used throughout the surviving forest zones of
South America, Africa and southeast Asia as the chief means of preparing many different species of roots, nuts and fruits; the grater is usually
held face upwards like a washboard and the peeled or processed root
or vegetable is rubbed up and down the surface to produce a coarse
meal or mash. The universality of this simple and obvious instrument
and its correlation with processing forest produce, especially roots, nuts

and coarse fruits, suggests that one might well expect it to appear in any subsistence pattern similarly based on comparable forest foods. If such an artefact was in prehistoric use, then we might note that the number of flint or stone elements in just *one* such board ranges from 100–2700 micro-points, or from 6 to 40 rows of flakes, blades, flakelets or micro-blades (Yde, 1965, p. 35).

At this juncture we might pause to make a brief mental simulation, not of any particular Mesolithic industry but of an elementary range of possibilities. As a start, we can visualize an industry in which, within a family unit, each hunter possesses half a dozen Løshult-type arrows (12 microliths in all), three or four bird and fish arrows (12–30 micro-liths) and a leister (6–30 microliths); he and four other family members carry varieties of harvesting knives (40–60 microliths) and two women hold slicing knives (2–6 microliths) and a grater board (100–2700 microliths). At the other extreme, we can remove the grater board and increase the number of microlithic projectile barbs. However, even in the crude range that we have established, the industries still vary only from those in which the dominant proportion of vegetal to hunting microliths moves from approximately 2 to 1 at the lowest, to 40 to 1 and beyond, if any kind of composite grating board was in use, such as we might expect in a wet-forest environment. The figures establish little except the extreme position of the stereotype: microliths = mammal hunting.

The extended discussion of this aspect may be tiresome but it has wide repercussions. In Australia, microlithic industries are associated with the extensive exploitation of vegetal foods on a continent in which there is no evidence at all for the use of the bow in the aboriginal present, the extensive rock art or the archaeological deposits. In the Wilton and other "microlithic" industries of Southern Africa, modern evidence suggests a correlation between the increased production of microlithic elements and the more intensive exploitation of vegetal foods, particu-larly seeds, roots and bulbs (Deacon, 1972). India and southeast Asia similarly possess microlithic industries associated with environments in which wet-forest and riverine vegetal foods were exploited. Perhaps then, it is not too outrageous to invert the old stereotype: not micro-liths = hunting but microliths = vegetal foods. Both statements are, of course, extreme forms, but it now seems perfectly reasonable to see the wider variety and use of microlithic elements in Postglacial woodland and forest situations as partly correlated with an increasingly mechanized interest in, and more efficient gathering and processing of, vegetal foods. This would form a suitable prelude to the rise of more intensive man/plant relationships.

Microlithic flintwork was a technical extension of the Middle and

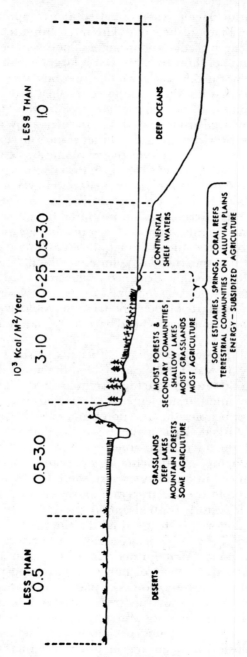

FIG. 3. World distribution of primary ecological production in various sectors (after Odum).

Upper Palaeolithic development of hafted and composite tools, served by the flake and blade techniques. The microlithic technique enables the maximum length of edge and number of points to be extracted from a minimal volume of flint, so that even a large leaf-shaped thrusting-spear blade can be quickly, easily and more robustly made out of wood, bone or antler with only the working edges sheathed in flint (Fig. 2). Thus, the technique allows the regular exploitation of small, nodular pebbles for even large artefacts and this, in turn, allows the permanent occupation of territories without any other stone source. The procedure incidentally allows the more effective exploitation of small sources of extremely hard, or extremely sharp, materials for special purposes – obsidian, chalcedony, agate or cornelian. However, not the least economy of the technique was its construction of composite tools in terms of small, rapidly replaceable and interchangeable, standardized and mass-produced units, manufactured in advance and kept in readiness for inevitable wear-and-tear – a pull-out and plug-in construction. A broken Solutrean spearhead or splintered Magdalenian harpoon required a complete, specially designed replacement. In most composite tools the breakage would be localized to one or two elements and, in many cases, a standard bladelet or triangle could equally replace a reaping knife tooth or an arrowhead barb (see Columnata and Løshult; Figs 1, 2).

If this microlithic technique is so efficient, possibly the ultimate in flint technology, how did it die out? Given the many different advantages of the technique and given the extremely diverse and interchangeable functions of microlithic elements, clearly no single, simple answer is universally applicable; the question is none the less a legitimate one and not to be shirked. Part of the answer is that in many areas, for many purposes, the microlithic stone technique was *not* displaced until cheap and satisfactory metal technology prevailed locally: flint microliths were produced in quantity even in some European Early Bronze Age contexts, and in India, Africa and southeast Asia they survive, not surprisingly, into historic contexts and recent times. However, it seems that an earlier factor was the gradual development of more powerful bows that could give a large heavy arrowhead very deep penetration, so that light composite points for maiming and poisoning were replaced by large leaf-shaped, tranchet or barbed-and-tanged projectile points for killing. At the same time, domestic plant and animal foods increasingly displaced the need for the great variety of composite tools for gathering and harvesting many different kinds of vegetal foods on one hand, or the need for numerous specialized bird and fish arrows, leister barbs and shellfish equipment on the other; the increasingly standardized heavy hacking-sickle and grinding-quern replaced the variety of specialized harvesting knives, slicers, cutters, graters and, probably, wooden food-mortars. A highly specialized and diversified composite tool-kit, based on small replaceable units variously hafted, gave way to a less diversified tool-kit based on a few, standardized and specially designed shapes, with a broad capability over a much more limited and focused range of faunal and floral tasks. In Europe, the steady development of farming and metallurgy between 4000 and 3000 B.C. quickly completed the transition, although microlithic flint drill-bits and lathe-tools continued to be made.

2. *Man-the-hunter*   This stereotype partly relates to the northern meat fixation and partly to the more widespread cultural emphasis on meat, animal magic, hunting prowess and stock numbers, all of which bear either an inverse or no relationship to the dietary importance of meat in the cultures concerned. Until the work of Lee and DeVore (1968) there was a general archaeological failure to grasp the dietary actualities of man the omnivore, a failure to comprehend the quantity, quality, stability and variety of highly nutritional plant foods widely available throughout most of the year in the forests of Temperate Europe and scarcely less abundant in the undegraded Mediterranean woodlands. Figures are misleading and to emphasize one particular plant species is to miss the very significance of the composite abundance and inter-locking seasonality of large groups of plant food-species, which meant that there was hardly a month in which a new combination of edible gums, saps, barks, shoots, stems, buds, flowers, fruits, nuts, roots, tubers, rhizomes, corms, bulbs, mosses, seaweeds, water-plants or fungi was not available, waiting immobile, predictable, for the plucking, even signalling their presence with coloured flowers and distinctive foliage; insignificant perhaps species by species but, gathered in diversified bulk, they provided an impressive and stable subsistence basis.

At most seasons in the year, any child over four could gather sufficient to feed itself and others, and in the lean seasons there were always the efficient and nutritious natural storage organs – the roots, seeds and nuts designed to over-winter without further treatment. It is easy to forget that the steady plucking of four Temperate-forest gatherers could at will pick the edible carcase weight of an adult red deer in less than four hours; whilst, in the Mediterranean park-lands, one worker with a harvesting knife could gather enough wild grass seed to produce 1 kilogram of clean grain with twice the protein value of domestic strains. In three weeks of such work a family unit could gather more grain than it could consume in a year. The same Mediterranean woodlands in Italy alone yield some 400 tonnes of Stone Pine nuts in an average year with the protein equivalent of more than 600 tonnes of lean round steak, making these pine kernels the most nutritious of all European nuts, richer even than the mongongo nuts of the !Kung (Howes, 1948: mongongo 27% protein; *Pinus pinea* nut 33.9% protein, 48.2% fat). Cooler Mediterranean woods will also yield a tonne of hazel nuts to the hectare, 3 tonnes of chestnuts a hectare and 10–20 tonnes of edible bulbs for each square kilometre of fertile woodland (Howes, 1948; Hill, 1952).

The temperate oak/hazel forests are no less productive and commonly yield 700–1000 litres of edible acorns for each mature oak tree, half a tonne of hazel nuts a hectare, 20–50 tonnes of edible bracken root per square kilometre, 5000–10 000 kilograms of fungi and 13–15 kilograms of blackberries a day in season. These figures are themselves dwarfed by the huge quantity of protein directly available in a wide range of edible herbaceous leaves and plants, consumed as cress, salad, spinach and asparagus meals. Even the less rich northern Boreal forests will regularly yield 137 000–273 000 litres of edible berries rich in sugars and vitamins (Howes, 1948; Hill, 1952).

To restore perspective, man-the-vegetarian will have been almost as rare as man-the-carnivore. What we have to compare and contrast is the complementary, but competitive, balance of energy-expenditure and energy-return from plant-gathering and meat-hunting, integrated as they always were within omnivorous seasonal schedules and skilful combinations – the high-risk, high-yield, high-energy-expenditure and dangerous pursuit of hunting against the low-risk, moderate yield, low-energy-expenditure and reliability of gathering. There are, after all, few plants that can escape the determined gatherer, but even the archaeological record widely documents the escaped aurochs, elk, reindeer, seal and pike; the mute testimony to the many wasted man-hours of patient travelling, waiting and stalking by one or more hunters – hours and equipment lost with no return.

Amongst the !Kung Bushmen, for example, Lee (1968, p. 40) records that seven active men spent 78 man-days hunting but achieved only one successful kill for every four man-days' effort. Even in this rather moderate area for vegetal foods on the fringes of the Kalahari desert (85 edible plant species), one man-hour of hunting produced only 100 edible calories, whilst equivalent gathering produced 240 calories return; gathering was thus 2.4 times more productive than hunting. But even this must surely have been a low ratio in favour of vegetable foods for the warm wet Temperate European deciduous forest (*ca* 250–450 edible plant species), or the warm dry grassy Mediterranean woodlands (*ca* 200–350 edible plant species), around 7000–5000 B.C. If the stereotype "man-the-hunter" has any basis, then it would appear to be that the less predictable, more expensive food-source has gathered a greater accretion of cultural interest, myth and ritual than the routine staples of life, which rarely if ever fail (Lee, 1968, p. 40).

3. *Gathering-hunting-fishing — the primitive and marginal economy*   The traditional stereotype of the land-to-mouth existence and continuous, leisureless food-quest, once thought to characterize gatherer-hunter-fishers, has been completely demolished (Lee and DeVore, 1968; Wilkinson, R. G., 1973). Indeed, the collapse has been so complete that the revelation that the average gatherer-hunter-fisher works fewer hours for his food than the average peasant or factory-worker has combined with the pressing contemporary interest in ecological pollution to threaten a nostalgic renewal of the convention of the "affluent innocent exploiting his everfruitful undegraded environment with infinite ingenuity", the "noble savage" no less; a model which makes it even more awkward to account for the adaptive development and successful spread of plant and animal domestication.

It is difficult to establish a fresh conventional position on this topic; so much depends on different cultural scales of values and our own ignorance of long-term cultural and environmental process. However, perhaps we can say that it is unlikely that Mesolithic man was less intelligent or ingenious than ourselves; that he was technologically restricted but not primitive, and that his subsistence patterns were probably productive, fragile and inelastic but rarely marginal. Gathering-hunting-fishing subsistence strategies have clearly existed in a great variety of varying patterns, in a great variety of environments of varying productivity and hazard. Clearly, there will have been a range of subsistence effort, diet adequacy, population stress, leisure time, health, security and stability and this range will have fluctuated over time, even in given environments, to varying degrees. The "fragility" of these subsistence strategies will also have varied, but this inherent fragility rests upon the relatively direct effect of environmental oscillations upon these intricate and delicately scheduled economies, with their relatively short and simple food chains and their restricted capacity for environmental control. Food-producing communities are no less subject to environmental changes and periodic disasters but, by and large, their reciprocally specialized and more elastic economies, with longer and more complex food chains, give them a better chance of stability and control of at least the smaller peaks and troughs of environmental fluctuations, without decreasing their local populations.

In the artificially polarized discussions of gathering-hunting-fishing and food-producing subsistence economies, the most neglected point is perhaps the most important: that food-production with maintained, controlled and stored domestic plant and animal species *supplemented* revised gathering-hunting-fishing in the new economies. The change was an additive one with a net increase in social and economic variety, diversity, complexity and stability.

4. *Gathering-hunting-fishing into food-production: the artificial dichotomy* The work of Higgs and Jarman has emphasized the artificiality of this over-simple economic division and clearly demonstrates that many of the problems surrounding this "transition" circularly arise from the stereotyped division itself (Higgs & Jarman, 1969; Higgs, 1972). Man, plant and animal relationships are seen as complex and adaptively flexible so that patterns of exploitation will have varied recurrently in space, time and structure over the last two million years. Even the fluctuating trend towards increasingly complex and close relationships between man and certain species is seen as essentially analogous to comparable trends involving species associations other than man over similar time-spans. The evidence shows that gatherer-hunterfishers exist in complicated interrelationships with their plant and animal resources, amongst which some practices of herd and crop control and management and resource storage were seldom unknown, and patterns of exploitation resulting in the husbanding of plant and animal resources were a not uncommon feature. Hardly any Postglacial group will have been unaware of the potential of the simple control of vegetation by fire-setting, the elementary consequences of seed planting or root reproduction, animal taming and herd culling, or food storage by drying, freezing or pickling in vinegars or honey. This latent knowledge, like the knowledge of converting clay into fired ceramics, was not seriously exploited until circumstances demanded it.

These views emphasize the artificiality of the simple bipolar division into gathering-hunting-fishing and food-producing economies and they underline the great dimensional variety and complexity of their development and interrelationships. Although no single criterion may, therefore, be usefully employed to differentiate these states one from another it is perhaps useful to have some basic gauge of the level at which the husbandry of nutritional resources begins to constitute food-production. All economies expend energy in the maintenance and control of food supplies on the one hand and the detection and pursuit of food supplies on the other. Perhaps it might be said that husbandry moves into food-production when the energy expended in the maintenance and control of food supplies first expands beyond that expended in the detection and pursuit of plant and animal food sources. Such an energy cost threshold might then provide a useful quantitative basis for our conventional division between gathering-hunting-fishing and food-producing systems (Lawton, 1973).

Gathering, hunting and fishing easily satisfied the demands for fresh food under normal conditions and food is rarely accumulated beyond possible need – a need which arises amongst hunting and gathering societies only if there is a part of the year not covered by the successive ripening of fresh wild crops as, for example, in winter in the deciduous forest zone. The lack of storage reflects conditions of plenty rather than scarcity and, in many ways, resource husbandry and food-production may be seen as possible economic responses amongst several alternatives to poorer conditions and population stress, a response that would recur stochastically wherever and whenever such conditions might develop, but a response that would prevail and spread only when such conditions became permanent and widespread and where technology would allow; food-production is perhaps the economy of a degraded environment (Wilkinson, R. G., 1973, p. 47).

For Europe, the upshot of the dissolution of the extreme Mesolithic-man-the-hunter and Neolithic-man-the-food-producer stereotype has yet to be fully explored and tested by carefully designed research and excavation projects. However, it would appear that many areas of the European Temperate forests *ca* 7000–4000 B.C. were areas of very high edible productivity, as rich in wild foods as any areas in the world at that latitude: areas in which it was not so much a matter of the late arrival of advanced food-production, diffused from distant sources, as of local continuance of rich wild-food resources and stable population pressure. Here, Temperate-forest husbandry had probably developed over the millennia in a rather different direction, of which we are only now beginning to catch glimpses. The northward spread of the productive species of hazel-nut, apple, pear and other food species in the oak/hazel forest, although part of an ecological and climatic succession, may well have been extensively and deliberately assisted by fire-clearance and even planting (Waterbolk, 1968). The nut-bearing beech trees and some edible-root species seem to have made a similarly suspicious preliminary advance into northwestern Europe.

There is also growing evidence of forest fire-setting in European pollen-sequences – a practice that opens up the forest canopy, fertilizes the forest floor and directly stimulates the growth and yield of out-shaded trees like hazel: this multiplies the proportion of edible herbaceous plants and especially develops the root and tuber growth of vegetatively reproducing forest-floor species like the edible bracken root. The artificial forest glades so created, directly open to the limited northern sunlight, then become important grazing and browsing resources for wild deer, cattle and boar, a hunters' trap until the forest succession reasserts itself. The food potential of fire-controlled oak/

hazel/bracken associations is particularly large and a forest husbandry based on this elementary technique and a basic knowledge of vegetatively reproducing forest root-staples would be difficult to improve upon, until population pressure, climatic or ecological changes, or all three together, might combine with the availability of alternative forest swidden regimes to supplant it.

Summary

This discussion has tried to highlight the major biasing factors and the main conventional stereotypes that have channelled the analysis of European Mesolithic data. If one takes the more recent and carefully gathered information and combines it with the older sources of information, bearing in mind the inherent sampling biases and reinforcing stereotypes, then it would seem that several alternative interpretations of the same data are possible. At one extreme, it is still possible to accept the traditional model and assimilate the new evidence to it. At the other extreme, the evidence will allow the inversion of almost every step in the traditional argument: hunting was the main European Mesolithic food source (plants . . .); mammal hunting was the main role of microlithic equipment (plant gathering . . .); advanced food-producing societies and economies displaced hunter-fisher-gatherers (productive gathering-hunting-fishing societies and economies were increasingly forced, in adverse circumstances, to develop intensively food-productive techniques that they had long practised marginally). In between these positions are others that have no inherently greater probability by virtue of their median position alone.

There would seem to be, in the study of European Mesolithic industries between *ca* 7000–4000 B.C. and latitudes 35°–55° N:

1. A current over-emphasis of the quantitative and general subsistence significance of mammal meat in the diet and the role of land-mammal hunting in the subsistence pattern.
2. A corresponding under-emphasis of the quantitative significance of gathered and vegetal foods in the diet of the gatherer-hunter-fishers of the ecologically rich European coastline, Temperate forests, Mediterranean wood and grasslands, and a neglect of the consequences of this for the social and economic organization and territorial sizes and schedules of the Mesolithic groups.
3. A general under-estimation of the overall productivity and probable sophistication of the diverse and subtly integrated gatherer-hunter-fisher societies and economies of this area and period.

The contemporary archaeological development of the ecological paradigm has been an important factor in redressing the biased conclusions that emerged from earlier studies restricted to artefact data (Clarke, 1972, p. 47). However, there has been a disconcerting tendency for essays in this new field to repeat the worst sins of the artefact typologist in a new dimension, merely substituting the different minutiae of bone or seed measurements and statistics for those of typology and substituting doubtful generalizations, based on eccentric faunal and floral samples, for those once committed upon artefact assemblages. Perhaps the outstanding example of this has been the emphasis on single species studied in isolation from subsistence assemblages; clearly, this practice is in part a consequence, as was its artefact counterpart, of a misguided attempt to understand complex, interrelated systems by allocating research to one dismembered element at a time, by one man at a time – the reindeer man, the red-deer man, the cereal girl and so forth. It was on this basis that we long ago developed the specialized halberd man, the dagger man and the beaker man, which brings us no nearer understanding Early Bronze Age assemblages, and their social and economic correlations.

Specialized study of components is, to some extent, necessary, but cultural assemblage systems or economic subsistence systems cannot be reconstituted merely as a list of their miscellaneous parts, in which certain elements are declared "staple" or "key" elements *ab initio*. Indeed, the whole emphasis on single elements – vegetal as opposed to meat foods, this species as opposed to that – is almost certainly yet another anachronistic, mono-focal, mono-cultural extrapolation of the present into the past. There is considerable evidence that plant species, at least, not only grew together but were also gathered together, planted together, cooked together, eaten together and perhaps classified together in complex associations and not in pure, single Linnaean species crops and meals (Renfrew, 1973). Obviously, meat and vegetables are complementary resources for the omnivore and the specification of any subsistence system must deal with the relative balance of energy-expenditure in their intake and the relative values of their output at a particular time and place.

Real economies are integrated: only a fraction of their structure is represented by the list of resources exploited; indeed, only a small fraction if such a study is restricted to vegetal or animal sources alone, and less still if restricted to a single species, however dominant. The vital missing half of the systemic structure is contrained in the specification of the *relationships* of the elements in the structure: their relative seasonal fluctuations, their relative energy-input/output, their relative contributions to the whole economy. Man/resource relationships are not simply the sum of the resource attributes but depend upon the competitive yields and demands – in time and labour – of other activities, both economic and non-economic, of different cultural priorities; the relationships depend not only on the "mix" and the "weighting" but also are relative to particular environmental and cultural states. Thus, the archaeologist's construction of an "expected model" of subsistence behaviour in a given environment cannot treat each resource independently but must reconcile the hypothesized pattern of exploitation with the presence and abundance of other resources (organic and inorganic) and technologies at the same site and at complementary sites within the annual site system or network; an integrated approach is necessary (Wilkinson, P. F., 1973).

The second part of this essay will therefore attempt to sketch, in a schematic form, a series of very general "models of expectation" for European Mesolithic subsistence patterns derived from the ecological, biological, behavioural and economic attributes of the food resources of Mesolithic Europe. These gross expectations can then be compared with the direct archaeological observations, and areas of good fit or deviation from expectation can be highlighted. Finally, these "sketch models" allow some further speculations to be made about the local nature of the transition from the Mesolithic to the Neolithic in Europe.

The framework for these speculations and hypotheses is provided by the conclusions of the preceding analysis of the biases, stereotypes and assumptions prevailing in European Mesolithic studies; those tentative conclusions provide our new conventions. It follows that special emphasis will be placed on the basic role of "wild" vegetal foods within integrated subsistence patterns. Although the passing references to faunal food resources is a deliberate part of this attempt to redress a former unbalance, nevertheless it will be clear, from what has already been said, that in detailed studies the animal food sources must be properly balanced within the integrated patterns.

In conclusion, the grand synthesis attempted here is conjectural; in our own terms of reference the simulation of regional Mesolithic economies could be carried out realistically only at a far more restricted scale and in reference to regional and environmental factors tightly specified in time and space. The gathering-hunting-fishing potential of the Rhône delta, or in the English Weald, *ca* 7000–4000 B.C., would indicate a more useful scale of unit for detailed studies, comparable to that of Yarnell's "aboriginal relationships between culture and plant life in the Upper Great Lakes region" (Yarnell, 1964). A more generalized study can only be justified by its value as a stimulus and focus for further research.

II. EUROPE: THE GENERAL ECOLOGICAL BACKGROUND

According to our model, Mesolithic man in Temperate and Mediterranean Europe probably derived the greatest proportion of his food supply directly from plant sources, supplemented by wider gathering and by hunting herbivorous mammals who themselves relied upon, and competed for, many of the same plant resources; conveniently, where the edible roots, grasses, seeds, foliage, nuts and fruits were in season there, too, would be the wild pig, ovicaprids, cattle and deer. Wherever the productivity of a wide variety of plant foods was exceptionally high, there we would expect to find gatherer-hunter-fishers harvesting the vegetal abundance both directly and indirectly by culling the more efficient herbivores. Although man could directly utilize only a proportion of the plant resources, nevertheless that proportion was also certainly the favoured food of some other herbivorous animal. In short, if we wish to arrive at some expectation of where and when Mesolithic communities might be expected in Europe, then we must discover where the productivity and variety of edible plant foods was highest within European ecology. We need an elementary grasp of prehistoric European ecological energetics and food cycles, from the gross trends of the ecological and climatic zones to the productivity of particular catchment-areas, and ultimately the net edible yield, nutritional and utility value of key associations and their individual species.

In food cycles, non-living and living elements are bound together in a pyramidal system through which energy cascades and matter recycles – the ecosystem. Plants, the primary producers, use incident solar energy, minerals and water to make living tissue, later eaten by herbivores, which in turn are eaten by carnivores – the trophic levels of the trophic pyramid (*trophikos* = nourishment). As living tissue dies at each stage, it is decomposed and recycled, and in many productive food chains the decomposers form an important part of the system. The fungi in the deciduous forest are one example of nutritional importance.

The limitations of ecological efficiency predict that for every 1000 plant calories consumed by herbivores only 100 are passed to carnivores and only 10 calories to top carnivores; the energy pyramid thus produces the related pyramids of biomass and numbers. Man, however, escapes some of these limitations by means of his omnivorous diet, feeding at all levels but roughly in proportion to their abundance. Thus, man makes the best use of solar energy by cropping the trophic pyramid directly at the plant level. Above this, the aims of converting as much solar energy as possible into protein for human use may be served best by cropping first those cold-blooded molluscs, crustacea and fish that waste no growth energy in maintaining body temperature, and then by cropping those herbivores with the highest growth efficiencies. In this way a gathering-hunting-fishing diet, omnivorously consuming conveniently gathered and gregarious plant foods, fungi, molluscs, crustacea, fish and herbivores best approaches a high subsistence efficiency (Phillipson, 1966).

The direct connection between solar energy and primary productivity introduces a number of latitudinal constraints. Roughly speaking, the solar energy entering the atmosphere in the Mediterranean zone is about 6×10^8 cal m^{-2} year^{-1}; in the Middle Temperate zone, about 4.7×10^8 cal m^{-2} year^{-1}; and in the cloudy Northern Temperate zone around Britain, only about 2.5×10^8 cal m^{-2} year^{-1}. Under natural conditions the Mediterranean zone therefore has a greater *potential* productivity, a greater variety of species and a heavier standing crop than the Temperate forests, and the Temperate forests a similar potential advantage over the northern coniferous forests and tundra; it is this latitudinal variation that is behind the tightly correlated proportion of vegetal foods in gatherer-hunter-fisher diets (Lee and DeVore, 1968, p. 43).

However, although the gross trend of this latitudinal variation in potential productivity does directly influence human dietary variability, it is seriously modulated by a number of more localized factors. First of all, it is only a *potential* level of productivity and local productivity will be extensively modified by local-sector conditions in terms of regional water supply, altitude, location, geomorphology, soil fertility and ecological structure; thus a stand of hazel trees on good soils in southern Britain will produce more than some comparable stands on thin, dry, poor Mediterranean soils, although the *average* productivity would be half a tonne of hazel-nuts in Kent, as opposed to one tonne per hectare in Catalonia. It follows that, other things being equal, plant and animal species distributed widely in Europe will usually be significantly more productive at the southern margins of their distribution; a skewed productivity pattern. This turns out to have been an important factor in the super-productivity of deciduous forest species on the Mediterranean margins of their distributions and of the mixed deciduous/coniferous forests on the southern margins of the northern climatic zones, just as the Late Glacial tundra and steppe of Upper Palaeolithic France will have been much more productive than under present northern conditions.

The second modifying factor is that, from the human point of view, what is important is not the gross productivity of the environment but the edible productivity. Only a proportion of the biomass is directly edible and we therefore need to know where high primary productivity coincides with a high proportion of edible yield. For example, the coral animals that produce reefs are amongst the world's greatest primary producers but their productivity has not been directly tapped by man for food, although the indirect consquences of this colossal productivity are culturally important (Fig. 3).

Bringing these factors together, we see that even in crude terms the dietary potential of an area relates to its latitudinal position, the attributes of each catchment sector, the edible proportion of the total productivity and its seasonality, the output return for energy-expenditure in harvesting the sector produce and the location of that sector in relation to other productive sectors. These factors must coalesce to make up a viable catchment-area productivity for a site and to ensure its ease of access to reciprocally productive site sectors and catchment areas within an economic annual schedule.

In the European context, the zones with the highest directly edible productivity are shown in descending order in Table 1 (Whittaker, 1970).

TABLE 1. *Edible productivity in the European zones*

	Relative edible proportion of nett productivity	Number of edible species	Nett primary productivity (dry gm^{-2} year^{-1})
Temperate deciduous forest	Very high	*ca* 250–450	600–3000
Mediterranean mixed woodland	High	*ca* 200–350	200–2000
Boreal mixed deciduous and coniferous forest	High	*ca* 200–350	400–2000
Boreal coniferous forest	Low	*ca* 100–200	400–2000
Tundra and Alpine	Low	*ca* 50–150	10–400

The warm damp Temperate deciduous forests and glades best combine a high nett productivity with a very high proportion of edible output, spread over a wide variety of plant and fungal species, exploited by a similarly wide range of productive herbivorous mammals and birds. The Mediterranean mixed woodland with sclerophyllous and xerophytic evergreens, stands of grassland and some interpenetrating deciduous communities produces a quantitatively high yield of edible plant foods and dependent fauna but, despite the latitudinal advantage, the average yield is lower than from much of the deciduous forest because of the long dry season, the high proportion of coarse and evergreen foliage, the simple wide-spaced forest structure and the large areas of poor soils. Nevertheless, in this zone in particular, exceptional sectors with unusually rich alluvial soils, plentiful local water supplies and suitable locations would produce edible yields greater than those of most of the deciduous zone.

The mixed deciduous and coniferous Boreal forest of the northern zone centred on the Baltic ranks next to the Mediterranean in edible productivity because of the advantageous mixture of species, the reliable rainfall and the rich glacial soils. The pure Boreal coniferous forests further to the north also show a surprisingly good nett primary productivity based on the adaptive efficiency of the evergreen coniferous species; however, very little of this productivity is directly edible by man and the edible elements are few and scattered in different communities. Naturally, these trends (few edible species and a low productivity) are continued in the northern tundra and, to some extent, in true Alpine peak areas to the south. Here we must be careful to distinguish cold-restricted true Alpine heights over 1500 metres, from the rich, highly productive sub-alpine damp forested slopes and high alluvial valleys that flank and intersect the Pyrenean, Alpine, Carpathian and Balkan mountain systems.

Within and across these latitudinal trends, we have the additive effects of particularly productive geomorphological and ecological sectors – the swamps, marshes, deltas, estuaries, lagoons, littoral zones, lakes, river and stream valleys, alluvial plains, and marine shallows (Fig. 3). The productivity of individual sectors will vary with latitude and ecology but, by the very nature of their general structure, these sectors normally introduce limited areas of unusually high productivity combined with an unusually high edible portion (see Table 2).

The great freshwater marshes and swamps of Europe (British fens, the Hungarian marshes, Pripet marshes, and the extinct Mediterranean and Balkan lake marshes) and the deltas, estuaries and lagoons of the major rivers (Danube, Po, Rhône, Guadalquivir, Tagus, Rhine–Thames, Vistula deltas) have a nett primary and edible productivity probably greater than any other sector or zone. This is due to the extremely high productivity overall and because whole plant-communities, from the shore marginals to the floating flora, are directly edible by man, whilst incidentally supporting a wealth of mollusc, crustacean, fish, mammal and wildfowl life. In general, all the water-related sectors have the especial advantage of stealing water and nutrients from vast land-drainage surfaces – often crucial in dry Mediterranean or sparse northern conditions (Birdsell, 1957).

Some inkling of the prodigious potential output of these waterlogged environments can be suggested by the 21.56 productivity measured for

TABLE 2. *Productivity of individual sectors, in descending order of edible output (Phillipson, 1966; Whittaker, 1970)*

	Edible proportion of nett productivity	Nett primary productivity $(\text{g m}^{-2} \text{ year}^{-1})$
Swamps, marshes, deltas, estuaries, lagoons	High	800–4000+
Littoral zones, alluvial plains, eutrophic lakes, river and stream valleys	High	500–2000
Marine shallows, continental shelves, forested mountain slopes and high valleys, oligotrophic lakes, grasslands	Moderate	200–1500

a temperate European grass swamp, of which a substantial proportion was the nutritious and easily gathered *Glyceria fluitans*, a wild rice-like plant (Hedrick, 1972). Perhaps of equal importance is the extraordinary productivity, in the same temperate marsh environment, of the club-rush (*Scirpus lacustris*) which has the remarkable capacity to produce 46 tonnes ha^{-1} year^{-1}) (dry weight) outstripping the most productive cereals including maize (*Zea mays*, 34 tonnes ha^{-1} year^{-1}) (Phillipson, 1966, p. 37). This rush has a high edible yield, including large tubers, the lower stems and seeds; traces of *Scirpus* have been recovered from several archaeological sites (Renfrew, 1973). Only slightly less productive are the totally edible watercresses that, together with the other water-plants, provide valuable green foodstuffs long after northern land species have been cut back by late-autumn and early-winter frosts.

Altogether, the edible productivity of the water-related plant communities is remarkable, ranging from the reed, water-lily, watercress and water-chestnut communities (*Scirpus, Typha, Phragmites, Nuphar, Trapa*, etc.) to the long list of edible waterside grass, clover and herb associations (water-plantain, water-gladiolus, water-parsnip, water-speedwell, etc., marsh mallow, marsh samphire, marsh marigold, marsh cress, bog moss, swamp potato, etc.). This abundance is partly accounted for by the constant supply of water, alluvium and rich nutrients, and partly by the important role of meandering and flooding steams, rivers, lakes and swamps in creating openings in the forest cover (Fig. 4). Similar factors account for the equally productive littoral communities of important edible plants, together with their preference for somewhat open, saline conditions and the frost-repelling winter warmth of the sea (sea holly, sea rocket, sea bindweed, sea fennel, sea parsnip, sea kale, etc.).

A survey of the list of the highly productive edible-plant sectors stresses the underlying importance of damp montane, waterside and water borne habitats. This correlation, in turn, introduces a number of consequences for Mesolithic Europe.

1. The waterside effect: the connection between Mesolithic sites and the flanks of freshwater swamps, marshes, rivers, streams and lakes has long been noted. The conventional explanation has been to stress the seasonal importance of the shellfish, crustacea, fish, wildfowl and mammal sources of meat in these abundant environments. However, significant as those secondary food sources must always have been, we can now see that they themselves relate to the much greater primary edible-plant productivity of these sectors, covering an abundance of roots, rhizomes, tubers, stems, leaves and fruits that can hardly have been of lesser importance. A secondary sampling consequence of this effect has certainly been the constant destruction of waterside sites by erosion, dredging, flooding and meandering watercourses, or their burial under the accumulated alluvium of 600–10 000 years. The Mesolithic levels in the lower Po delta, for example, are now buried at a depth of more than 10 metres and the comparable deposits of the other major delta systems must lie at a similar depth, where they have survived at all. However, sporadic but invaluable sites are occasionally preserved in these situations, when set on hard hilly deposits that extrude above the accumulating alluvium, or when set at the hilly margins of the delta environment (e.g., Châteauneuf-les-Martigues) providing residual fragments of once extensive site systems.

2. The coastal effect: the correlation of Mesolithic sites and middens with deltas, estuaries, lagoons, salt marsh and littoral sectors has led to a similar tendency to stress the visible contribution of the fish, shellfish and mammals, and to forget the much greater primary productivity of the wide variety of directly edible maritime plant-species and communities. The *Brassica*, *Beta*, *Crambe* and *Echinophora*, edible root ancestors of the beets, kales, turnips, cabbages and parsnips are all extremely important natives of these coastal areas, along with many other productive species and all the edible seaweeds (*Zostera*, *Atriplex*, *Lathyrus maritimus*, *Scirpus maritimus*, etc.).

In terms of the productivity of the marine coastal zone itself then, once again, we must emphasize the greatly superior edible productivity of the Atlantic-shelf littoral, as opposed to the Mediterranean shallows, although both were certainly major resource zones. The tidal Atlantic littoral has the advantage of a higher oceanic and tidal energy system, a range of inter-tidal habitats, more complex estuarine and deltaic ecology, the productive intermixture of cold Arctic and warm gulf streams and the upwelling of the nutrient-laden deep ocean waters against the shelf. These factors combine to make the Atlantic coastal zone prodigiously productive in seaweeds, shellfish, crustacea, fish, seals and other marine mammals. The tideless, enclosed Mediterranean has a poorer ecology although its southern latitudinal advantage does once again produce large yields of particular species in limited locations. The one European area that has the unique combination of a Mediterranean latitude and an Atlantic coastline is Portugal, where shellfish gathered by hand and rake annually exceed 10 000 tonnes and the coastal interests of the local Mesolithic are widely evident; although, once again, one must also remember the abundant vegetal resources of the same highly productive alluvial littoral in this southern latitude.

The Galician and Tagus middens remind us of another major sampling consequence of this coastal correlation – the destruction of littoral sites by complex marine and land fluctuations. Most of the Mesolithic coastline and most of its littoral and associated sites are irretrievably lost. The only exceptions are the fragmentary Baltic areas of isostatic coastal recovery (Ertebølle phase), the uplifted patches of western Britain and Galicia and the coastal sites accidentally preserved where located high on the point or island remnant of a coastal hill range, well above the local inundation level. It is now apparent that, throughout the Atlantic and Mediterranean, we have only the "stubs" of once extensive Mesolithic littoral systems, fortuitously preserved for us only in these few fragments – the Ertebølle, Obanian, Portland Bill, Téviec and Hoëdic, the Galician and Asturian, and the Tagus middens. The strikingly similar location, dietary evidence, bone harpoons, shellfish picks, scoops and Mesolithic flint-work that once led to speculation about Azilian movements from Iberia to Scotland can now be, more reasonably, associated with the common exploitation pattern of the same once widespread rich resource zone. In the Mediterranean, isolated sites like the Franchthi cave on the tip of the Argolid peninsula have been preserved only sporadically and for the same reasons; they serve to remind us of the gross sampling distortion imposed by the lost littoral sites and provide us with the limited means to reconstitute the probable forms of the missing evidence.

The general rise in Postglacial sea levels after *ca* 10 000 B.C. was certainly important as a contemporary environmental factor as well as for its present sampling consequences. In the Mediterranean in particular, the structural morphology of the northern Mediterranean coastline is such that for most of its length the mountainous or hilly interior rises abruptly behind the narrow littoral. This has nearly always been the case but the rapid Postglacial rise in Mediterranean sea-level between *ca* 10 000–5000 B.C. reduced an already attenuated littoral band to some half or two-thirds of its total area, simultaneously removing two-thirds of the most productive coastal alluvium sector and its directly edible plant resources, and cutting to a critically low level the already restricted winter and spring browsing and grazing of the herbivorous mammals.

In the one or two extensive low-lying Mediterranean plains such as the Rhône and Po deltas, the small rise in sea-level resulted in dramatic losses of fertile and very productive Mediterranean areas of alluvium, marsh and swamp. The Danube delta also lost about 10 000 square miles of highly productive land surface in 5000 years, a scale broadly equivalent to the losses in the northern Adriatic. On the Atlantic coast an even more dramatic process took out some 20 000 square miles of comparably productive North Sea Basin alluvium and marsh, drowning one of the biggest estuaries in Europe – the joint estuary of the united Rhine, Thames, Meuse and Scheldt. British and Dutch studies have recently suggested that widespread Mesolithic territorial adjustments and other consequences followed the creeping inundation of the North Sea Basin and one might anticipate similar results for the circum-Adriatic/Ionian Sea complexes of the Mediterranean and the Danube/Dnestr/Crimean complexes of the Black Sea (Jacobi, 1973; Kooijmans, 1972).

The drowning of extensive shallow shelf-areas of the Mediterranean and North Sea between *ca* 10 000–5000 B.C. and the breaching of the freshwater Baltic Ancylus Lake in the north *ca* 7000–6500 B.C. were not entirely negative in their results. In all three cases productive littoral lost to land-plants and mammals became new, rapidly colonized coastal shallows even more richly productive in edible molluscs, crustacea and fish than the earlier marine zone. Thus, in the Mesolithic sites of the Adriatic, Portugal and probably in those of the Maglemose/Ertebølle transition in the north, we have some stratigraphic evidence for the growing importance of mollusc against red-deer meat in the period *ca* 8000–3000 B.C. Naturally, the development of the new marine habitats to a productive climax took many centuries after the initial drowning but, since the drowning was a semi-continuous process, high-productivity shallows were developed continuously, successive bands coming into and going out of peak productivity until marine conditions stabilized somewhat *ca* 5000 B.C.

This "climax" effect", in which a new resource took many centuries after its initiation before it reached an ecologically productive peak, is also found in the development of the Postglacial rivers and lakes left behind by the glacier melt waters and multiplied by the havoc imposed by glaciers on ancient drainage systems. In the early centuries these fresh, primitive, cold lakes – oligotrophic lakes, poor in nutrition, with little organic matter and low productivity – were gradually colonized by water-plants, fish and waterfowl. After several more centuries, and as cold conditions receded, animal and plant species diversified and multiplied, as the pioneer *Salmonidae* were joined by the numerous and very productive eel, carp and perch families (carp, roach, bream, pike, perch). The rivers and lakes slowly matured into a mesotrophic or eutrophic ecology, rich in nutrition, until both nett and edible productivity reached a maximum. Subsequent silting and organic accumulation downgraded productivity until ultimately only peat bogs were left. This process was most pronounced behind the retreating skits of the northern glaciers, on a wide front from Yorkshire to the Polish Masovian Lakes, but it was also going forward on a smaller, but locally important, scale in the glaciated high valleys of the Pyrenees, Alps, Carpathians and the Balkan–Pindus chain. As they were released, myriads of now-vanished lakes were successively colonized and successively grew to peak edible productivity some centuries or millennia after their initiation; so a sequential pattern, from south to north, of high lake-productivity was released *ca* 8000–5000 B.C. as continental climatic improved. The Maglemose, Kunda, Ladoga and Onega sites eloquently testify to the speed with which the northern Mesolithic kept pace with the expanded plant, fish and wildfowl resources of the maturing northern lakes, and the large Alpine Mesolithic lakeside sites offer a similar testimony. In the Mediterranean, there is comparable, although less well-documented, evidence for the Mesolithic exploitation of Postglacial lake and swamp margins from Bulgaria, Albania, Epirus, Macedonia, Thessaly, at Lake Ohrid in Yugoslavia and on Lakes Fucino, Bolsena and Trasimeno in Italy. Significantly, in these damp plant-rich alluvial Mediterranean lake-basins, plant and animal husbandry were already well advanced by the seventh and sixth millennia B.C. and the preceding industries are either typologically indistinguishable or buried under earlier alluvium.

Summary

The distribution, territories and annual site systems of the Mesolithic communities of Europe must have been closely related to the edible productivity of their particular sectors and to the efficiency with which successively productive sectors could be linked within a continuous and convenient annual circuit. Under most European conditions, plant productivity provided the most abundant and most stable primary food supply for man and the herbivores. As the figures indicate, there are many natural ecosystems that have a greater edible productivity than many agricultural systems. This is because under natural conditions there is a full photosynthetically active plant-cover throughout most of the year, which traps the maximum amount of sunlight, water and nutrients in the complex layers of mutually adjusted foliage and roots; conditions rarely achieved with widely spaced, single-layer, single-species crops (Fig. 5) (Phillipson, 1966, pp. 45–47). The gatherer-hunter-fishers of Europe were not incompetent agriculturalists but employed different subsistence systems exploiting different, and sometimes richer, food resources in a different environment.

The ecological considerations discussed earlier identify the general areas in which we would expect to find relatively high concentrations of gatherer-hunter-fishers and their sites, together with some of the sampling problems that seriously modify those expectations. Thus, the close juxtaposition of the productive Mediterranean littoral wood and grasslands, with marsh and sea resources on one hand, and cooler higher foothills on the other, would lead one to expect a discontinuous, but relatively high, density of territorial occupation in the littoral band some 50 miles deep from the Black Sea to Iberia. The especially advantageous ecology of the Crimea/Danube delta, Adriatic/Po delta and Provence/Rhône delta sectors should have carried unusually high levels of occupation. On the Atlantic coast, the unique Portuguese combination of a Mediterranean climate, a mixed ecology and a tidal Atlantic littoral with major estuaries has already been stressed. Further north, the combination of the superior edible productivity of the southern margins of the Temperate deciduous forests with the rich Atlantic littoral and riverine resources more than compensated for the cooler climate. The great North Sea/Baltic plain, freshly colonized by the productive Temperate and Mixed forests, united a prodigiously productive littoral ecology with a recently glaciated zone, speckled with countless productive lakes and rivers and floored with a variety of glacial soils. This productive band sweeps round through lower Poland, losing its coastline but picking up the Vistula and Dnepr river-systems, the Pripet Marshes, and the variegated and glaciated north flanks of the Carpathians, running east to the Danube delta again.

The expected-density model of European gatherer-hunter-fishers and their sites then takes on a roughly saucer-like distribution with a relatively high-density annular coastal and glaciated "rim", probably of small, rich, closely packed orthogonal territories and a low-level, less-populated interior of larger, less-productive territories, with the exception of certain major montane and riverine inliers – principally the Alpine system, the Carpathian/Bohemian system and the Danube drainage system.

Not surprisingly, our expected model of Mesolithic site-distribution matches the actual distribution quite well, with certain important negative residuals. It should be remembered that we have offered a different ecological explanation of this distribution from the conventional correlation with meat food exploitation. The negative residuals are no less significant. The coastal Mesolithic sites are rich but extremely sparse, with the Ertebølle excepted. The Mesolithic sites expected from the rich-ecology area of the inland Danube/Tisza system are largely missing, as they are from the area of the Danube delta and the Bulgarian lowlands, even richer in natural resources. In all of these cases I would suggest, unless some special local circumstances prevail, that mainly sampling factors are intervening, e.g., lack of research, deep alluviation, heavy erosion, extensive coastal inundation.

In all of these cases we have some few, usually peripheral, sites that represent, once again, the mere "stubs" of the former Mesolithic territorial systems once centred in the lower riverine, deltaic or littoral sectors. In this light, we should perhaps see the Danube gorge sites of the Lepenski Vir complex as not so much a unique local adaptation but a restricted sample of the once extensive lower Danube riverine Mesolithic, preserved for us by its unusual location, where the deeply channelled and constrained Danube cuts high ground. In the Black Sea littoral and the Danube estuary we have already noted that the original delta and littoral covered 10 000 square miles now lost to the sea. Nevertheless, there is still the significant juxtaposition of the Crimean/Dnestr sites, which were probably a seasonal part of these littoral-deltaic systems from the time when the rivers Dnepr, Bug, Dnestr, Prut and Danube shared a united outflow of potential comparable to or greater than the contemporary Thames–Rhine–Meuse confluence. The enigmatic early development of the coastal Neolithic Hamangia culture may then represent merely the "ceramicization" and first visible traces of such a population. The situation would thus be analogous to the circum-Adriatic adoption of Impressed Ware by the divided but related gatherer-hunter-fishers of the drowned Adriatic basin and Po delta.

III. THE REGIONAL MESOLITHIC ECONOMIES AND THE NEOLITHIC TRANSITION

Naturally, no detailed exposition is intended here, but merely an extension of the implications of the general ecological model to the different resources available to regional Mesolithic subsistence systems and the possible consequences of such regional differences for different developments in the ensuing Neolithic. We now wish to identify some of the regional plant communities that concentrated an unusually high yield and a high proportion of edible constituents and, in particular, the species that yielded an exceptionally abundant and nutritious resource whose subsistence value could hardly have been ignored. With what seasonal schedules, exploitation strategies and existing husbandry practices would these food associations be linked, and in what way can they be related to the food-producing practices developed between *ca* 6000–4000 B.C.?

The gatherer-hunter-fisher subsistence system is usually a seasonal circuit or alternation of successive sites and their catchment-areas, which exploit varied combinations of productive ecological sectors. The annual length of the circuit is normally the minimum necessary to produce an adequate level of nutrition for the group, season by season, but especially in the season of greatest scarcity. In the lean season site location is critical and must ensure a catchment-area of the greatest and most reliable food productivity possible in the circumstances (Fig. 3). These critical sites are the weakest links in the circuit, the annual bottleneck through which the population must pass successfully, reduce its numbers or change its strategy. We have already emphasized that, in Temperate and Mediterranean European conditions, the most abundant, most diversified and most reliable food source will normally come from vegetal sources. It therefore follows that the catchment-areas of most critical sites will often have to combine the most highly productive sectors of edible plant productivity – springs, deltas, estuaries, marshes, swamps, lagoons, sea coasts, lake and river margins or montane valleys (Fig. 3).

In a theoretically optimal situation, the annual circuit length would be zero and the annual subsistence strategy be accomplished by short expeditions from a permanent base site. Many advantages and some disadvantages accrue from a sedentary base but, in general, a successive range and variety of fresh food gained by periodic movement would take precedence over the mere advantage of a static residence – except in those unusual circumstances where a successive range of abundant fresh food *could* be gathered throughout the year from one site. Were there any such locations in Mesolithic Europe? We are not certain but, on ecological grounds, one can begin to point out where they might be and what their subsistence spectrum might embrace. However, even for the "average" group there was no mobile/static dichotomy – if local conditions were exceptionally fruitful and exceptionally attractive then a static base might exist for a number of years until more variable conditions returned, and then a seasonal circuit might once again become the sounder strategy (Thomas, 1972).

The annual schedules and territorial schemes that we might expect in Mesolithic Europe are likely to have covered a very wide range of flexible arrangements, altered sensitively from one year to another, oscillating back and forth around short- and long-term social and environmental trends. Higgs (1966) and Flannery (1969) have stressed the generality of vertical, transhumant economies, especially in mountainous zones in dry climates. When the lowland vegetal and animal resources are restricted by summer drought, then movement by men and game to higher altitudes allows the exploitation of the differing seasonal developments and the higher rainfall: an extended yield of spring vegetation and earlier autumn seeds, fruits and nuts can then be obtained by moving at a carefully judged speed through the ecological zones and communities. The tightly packed and variegated montane communities will also usually return a high and diverse yield for short-distance movements. Combined with a littoral or lacustrine winter base, such systems were ideally suited to Mediterranean and Alpine conditions and are frequently indicated by the transportation of mountain resources to lowland sites and vice versa. We have this kind of evidence, for example, linking the Peloponnesian mountains and littoral; the Pindus with the Thessalian lakes and Epirote coast; the Dalmatian Alps and the Adriatic coast; the Apennines with the Tyrrhenian and Adriatic littoral; the Ligurian Alps and the Ligurian coast; the Meseta rim and the Spanish Levantine coast; the Pyrenean and Cantabrian mountains with the Bay of Biscay and Golfe du Lion. Comparable inland regimes probably prevailed in the Swiss Alps, and very possibly in the Balkan and Carpathian systems and wherever productive lakes, marshes or littoral were closely adjacent to productive mountain foothills and uplands.

However, there is growing evidence that there were other and more complex movements, where differences in altitude and rainfall were insignificant or, where there was a scheduling conflict between the seasonal requirements of several productive resources, or special local, ecological or climatic conditions offered better alternatives. Such annual territories would probably include lateral coastal, orthogonal coastal, upper/lower riverine, deltaic and estuarine territories as well as forest/swamp, forest/delta, forest/lake and even alkaline/acid soil-combinations, all of which offer the possibility of reciprocal seasonal yields. In the deltaic marshes for example, winter flooding forces man, deer, pig and cattle into the upper delta or foothills but, in the summer, the greatly extended area of freshly productive lower delta is once more available to man and beast. It may be suggested that the subsistence relationship between the Dnestr/Crimea sites and the old Danube delta, the Alpine/Istria sites and the Po delta and between the Provence/Languedoc sites and the Rhône delta were, for some period, of this later type. Across the flat Great North European Plain vertical economies could not be practised except at the extreme Pennine margin, in the form documented by Professor Clark (1972) at Star Carr, or at the extreme Bohemian and Carpathian margin. Over the great plain the territorial systems must have oscillated instead between varying combinations of coastal, deltaic, estuarine, riverine, swamp and lake-focused site networks.

What these speculations suggest is that if a sector is too homogeneous ecologically, too extensive or of low "edible productivity", it will either be taken up only marginally or be virtually unoccupied. Thus, parts of the deep interior of the Spanish Meseta, and even the core of the larger loess areas of Central Europe, seem to have carried a sufficiently low-density Mesolithic population for their presence to be currently undetectable. In contrast, we may note the special importance of the so-called "marginal" dissected mountains, deltas, swamps, marshes, estuaries and abundant forests for the gatherer-hunter-fisher economies. Marginal is a relative term and the distribution of Mesolithic sites may be marginal to the preferred terrain of modern agriculture but it was never marginal in terms of its own subsistence patterns.

Mediterranean Mesolithic

The Mediterranean is a climatic and ecological buffer-zone in which proximity to the Equator is set against distance from the ice-cap and reinforced by the ameliorating influences of the sea itself, so that development within the zone is marked by a continuity of species and associations, with fluctuations mainly in distribution and density. The same continuity is witnessed in many of the flint industries and it is a matter of preference whether we label the regional complexes of *ca* 10 000–5000 B.C. Mesolithic, Epipalaeolithic or Protoneolithic. They are all of these things taxonomically, but about their subsistence status we are less clear. On ecological and flint-taxonomic grounds, divisions can be made between the characteristics of the Eastern Basin, the Western Basin and the North African littoral, but for our purposes we will concentrate on the European shores of the twin basins; although the great significance of Northern and Atlantic African interconnections for Iberia, and Anatolian and Steppe interconnections for the Balkans, should not be underestimated.

The regional pollen sequences for the Mediterranean countries will, in due course, provide the only sound basis for the detailed local studies that must ultimately frame the mosaic of Mesolithic developments. However, it would seem, in general, that between *ca* 10 000–7000 B.C. the cool and temperate zone at the head of the Adriatic and the Franco-

Ligurian seas was gradually colonized by warmer species from the south. Birth and pine gave way to juniper, pines and oaks, as the residual Mediterranean evergreen and drought-resisting flora gradually expanded from major pockets in southern Iberia, southern Italy, southern Greece and the South Balkans (although many deciduous tree species, such as hazel, survived inland at higher altitudes). In consequence, part of the ecological difference between the east and west Mediterranean basins, at this period, arose from the differing communities of local mixed deciduous woodland displaced from the littoral bands – pine/oak/hazel in the west and oak/elm in the east basin; and part from the differing remnants of Late Pleistocene flora left in the residual southern reservoirs to recolonize the north.

In this first complex phase, *ca* 10 000–7000 B.C., the northern half of the Mediterranean was partly occupied by a mixed Temperate woodland, distributed well to the south of its present area above the Pyrenees and Alps. It has already been noted that the Temperate deciduous forest had an extremely high "edible productivity" and that this would have been greatly multiplied by the increased productivity of this southern climate and the variety provided by intermixed Mediterranean flora. The abundant deciduous browsing and grazing seems to have supported a prolific range of deer, aurochs, horse and boar, and both resources supported a flourishing Mesolithic population such as we see in the Spanish Levantine art – sufficiently numerous to give rise, perhaps, to the territorial skirmishes of the paintings. Further south, in the southern Iberian, Italian and Greek peninsulas the lower "edible productivity" of the entrenched Mediterranean evergreen flora supported rather different regimes, in which coastal resources were critically important from an early phase.

Between *ca* 7000–5000 B.C. the Mediterranean vegetation gradually established itself throughout the peninsulas at least in the warm, dry littoral band. Perhaps in Iberia, and possibly in Italy, it now seems probable that this relict vegetation already included stands of some wild cereal grasses, legumes and the important wild olive, wild grape-vine, strawberry tree association with its high edible rating (*Olea oleaster, Vitis silvestris, Arbutus unedo*); the grass and legume seeds, such as *Secale dalmaticum*, were summer staples and the fruits of the trees and their associated creepers were important autumn and early-winter staples. Other commonly associated plants with edible elements included the cistus, myrtle, juniper and evergreen oaks with edible acorns (*Cistus* spp., *Myrtus communis, Juniperus phoenicea, Quercus suber, Quercus ilex*). High-yielding hazel-nut trees were also available at cooler altitudes, but more important than any other winter staple must have been the highly nutritious and very abundant "pignolias" – the pine-kernels of the ubiquitous Stone Pine (*Pinus pinea*) with one of the highest protein yields of any known nut (Howes, 1948, p. 17).

The characteristics of the expanding Mediterranean climatic regime established the remainder of the ecological pattern. A moderate annual rainfall and a late summer drought of severe proportions at sea-level limited coastal woodlands to mainly xerophytic and evergreen tree species growing in widely spaced communities, interspersed with stands of flowers, grasses, legumes and herbs. Much of this predominantly annual herbaceous vegetation was directly edible as salads, and could be harvested throughout the year, thanks to the warm, wet, frostless littoral winters, or provided seeds that could be gathered in April and May before pursuing the same harvest slightly later at higher altitudes inland. Many of the herbaceous plants are drought-adapted, including the extremely important and numerous range of Mediterranean bulbs that remain dormant for long periods, commencing growth as soon as rain falls again. This "bulb flora" includes many edible species, some famous for their easily recognizable flowers – *Iris sisyrinchium*, Grape Hyacinth (*Muscuri racemosum*), Orchids (*Orchis* spp.), Star of Bethlehem (*Ornithogalum umbellatum*), Lilies (*Liliaceae*), Crocuses (*Irideae*) and, above all, the important wild leek, shallot, garlic, onion family (*Allium* spp.). These edible bulbs and a number of comparably adapted edible-root plants (*Apium, Asphodel, Arum, Carum* spp., *Cyperus esculentus, Peucedanum graveolens*, etc.) were widely distributed, but especially abundant in damper montane valleys, coastal clearings, marsh and swamp edges.

The early mixed Temperate and Mediterranean woodlands were very productive with a high quantitative yield and probably some 350–450 edible species, of which perhaps 100–150 would have been important locally. The later, more extensive, development of the full Mediterranean xerophytic ecology along the coastal strip substantially reduced the overall quantitative edible yield and reduced the range and density of edible plants to some 200–350 species. It is at this stage that an increased exploitation of productive rabbit, ovicaprid, shellfish and marine foods seems to have augmented the decreasing abundance of red deer and other herbivores and, to some extent, the decreasing variety of vegetal foods. It is also against this context that a more intensive exploitation of the restricted food-species associated with the spreading southern flora may have led to more careful husbandry of the long-exploited wild olive, wild vine and many species of grasses and legumes over a wide area embracing southern Iberia, Italy and the Balkans.

Early Mediterranean ecology makes it likely that the vegetal basis of many of the Mesolithic subsistence systems on the European littoral will have been a pulses/bulbs/grass-seeds and nuts combination, balanced by coastal gathering, fishing and fowling, and inland hunting of ovicaprids, deer, aurochs and equids. The pulses provided protein, oil and carbohydrate; the bulbs and fruits produced water, carbohydrate and some protein and vitamins; whilst the nuts and grass-seeds contained a good supply of proteins, fats and carbohydrates. The very high water-content provided by bulbs, roots, leaves, shoots, buds, flowers, fruits and berries will have been a useful feature in the Mediterranean summer drought, with most of the concentrated nutrition coming from the seeds, fruits, nuts, fish and meat sources. The Mediterranean nuts were of particular importance as storage winter sources of calories and protein, at a season when game would have been more widely scattered. In general, over-wintering should have been little problem in the Mediterranean mild wet winters with a fairly constant basic supply of edible green salad plants, bulbs, roots and nuts. The critical period will have been late summer, when drought scorched the withered vegetation and game animals moved to fresher pastures at higher altitudes. Apart from the special alternatives based on marine, delta or marsh ecologies, many of the Mediterranean Mesolithic schedules seem to have followed the vegetal and faunal harvest into the hills.

This model suggests the basic and early importance of the pulse/bulb/grass-seed and nuts combination throughout the Mediterranean; probably acorns, hazel nuts and pine nuts were universally important with perhaps walnuts, almond or pistachio in the Balkans and sweet chestnuts in the western Mediterranean. The traditional nutritional Mediterranean "salep" meal of ground bulbs of many species may have supplemented the pounded mash of pulse and grass seeds reaped with composite harvesting knives (Hedrick, 1972, pp. 264, 560). The early familiarity with the edible seeds of a very large range of legumes and grasses will certainly have included some ancestors, or at least close relations of the later Neolithic range of fully domesticated legumes and cereals and the possibility of an indigenous southern Mediterranean and Balkan pre-Asiatic pulse and grass husbandry from at least the eighth millennium looks not implausible (Clarke, 1971). As we shall see, from about that time the northward spread of the limited Mediterranean xerophytic vegetation correlated with other changes that, perhaps, intensified the increasing exploitation of the olive/vine/arbutus, grass/legume and ovicaprid associations of the developing littoral *maquis*.

Temperate forest Mesolithic

North of the Alps and Pyrenees, the zone later occupied by the expanded Temperate forest was initially a cool or cold corridor bounded by the northern Baltic ice-cap and the southern glaciers of the Alps and Pyrenees, a zone of tundra, open steppe and forested steppe warmed only at the juxtaposition of the Atlantic currents and the warm Mediterranean, one on either side of the Dordogne isthmus. As conditions ameliorated, this area of low biomass, exploited by large migratory herbivores and containing wide human territories, was increasingly colonized from the south by pioneer Temperate deciduous forest *ca* 10 000–9000 B.C. and gradually became an area of high biomass, with a very high edible productivity exploited by numerous herds of small herbivores and probably broken up into a mosaic of small, productive Mesolithic territories. The "reindeer" economies, which had dominated the French plain and the German Wald as far north as the Hamburg swamps, either migrated or adapted in the face of the advancing pine and birch mixed forest and the growing potential of the maturing Postglacial landscape and forests. Whatever form the coastal seal and salmon hunting facies of the Magdalenian took, it must have contributed to the later coastal economies exploiting the rapidly growing marine and littoral potential of the Atlantic zone.

The pioneer birch and pine woodland quickly gave way to a thicker Late Boreal mixed forest with increasing hazel and oak communities, reaching a climax in a dense oak, hazel, alder, lime and elm forest in the warm, wet phase of the Postglacial climatic optimum between *ca* 6000–4000 B.C. (Fig. 4). This canopy, of many deciduous species and of great structural complexity, covered most of the Atlantic and Northern European plain and extended as far as southern Sweden and the mixed deciduous and coniferous stands east of the Baltic. The structure of this entire forest was determined by the annual loss of leaves in the autumn and the cessation of fresh green growth for a long snowy winter of three to five months. The colossal annual rain of leaves and organic detritus produced a dense ground-layer of damp humus and dead rotting and decaying trunks, dominated by large quantities of fungi, mosses and liverworts, many of them edible and available the year through. Above this enriched ground-layer rose the field-layer of abundant herbaceous plants and small sparse stands of grasses, dominated by perennials and vegetatively spreading root and tuber plants like bracken (*Pteridium aquilinium*). Bracken spreads by means of long rhizomes that grow horizontally to produce dense and continuous stands, often extending over many acres in the field-layer, where its large leaf area makes it the most efficient interceptor of the limited amount of light that penetrates the upper forest layers (Fig. 5) (Riley and Young, 1968, p. 13).

This productive field-layer of bulbs, roots, rhizomes and tubers was shaded by a shrub-layer of hazel, berry-bearing bushes, brambles and

Fig. 4. Deciduous woodland, Doubs, France. Note the break in the canopy caused by the river and its seasonally flooded margins.

248

Fig. 5. Broadleaf woodland, Hampshire, England. Note the complex structure of the deciduous forest layers, and the extensive

shrubs up to 15 feet high. Above this the tree-layer completed the structure in which the oak, elm and ash crowns formed an almost continuous shady canopy at between 25–100 feet, broken only by artificial herbaceous glades or natural ones around lakes, rivers, swamps and outcrops (Fig. 4). The complex ecological structure of two to four layers and diverse associations of tree and plants, bound by climbers and brambles, utilized every gleam of sunlight at every level in minutely integrated schedules of fruition and leaf-shedding, which differ slightly from one species to another. The detailed structure of the forest was spatially correlated with the varying dampness, acidity and nature of the underlying soils and, since these were highly varied across the old glacial terrain, this provided a great horizontal diversity of communities to be seasonally exploited, as well as the vertical one through the forest layers.

It is quite apparent, from the European Temperate forest structure, that Mesolithic man must have lived in and through the englobing forest habitat and its richly productive ecology. The humus-enriched soils provided ample browsing and grazing for an equally abundant wild life of deer, aurochs and boar, limited, in the main, by the annual constraint of the long cold European winter. However, for most of the year, the complex deciduous forest produced a great quantity and variety of seasonal vegetal foods, especially roots, foliage, fruits and nuts, supported by a vast range of ancillaries, from the important fungi to edible barks, sap-sugars and mosses, the variety of Atlantic seaweeds, and the special littoral root and herb associations of the coastal estuaries and shores. Throughout the forest, the abundant Postglacial lakes, swamps and many major rivers and streams added a rich network of additional resources on a scale quite unknown in the Mediterranean.

The contrast between the established Temperate forest and its resources and even the undegraded Mediterranean woodlands and their associations must always have been rather striking. The number of Temperate forest edible vegetal species is nearly one-third richer (250–450 species): edible perennials, roots, tubers and rhizomes dominate the resource spectrum together with the edible leaves, shoots, buds, flowers, berries, fruits and nuts. In contrast, the edible seeds of the sparse stands of grasses and the few pulses seem to have been insignificant: there were far fewer indigenous pulse and grass species; they occurred widely scattered, or in limited glades; they were comparatively unpredictable and low-yielding in the tiered wet-forest context; and ripened late in a short season, to be hotly competed for by grazers and abundant bird life. Although the Temperate forest provided fewer and noticeably less nutritious edible nut species, nevertheless varieties of acorns and hazel-nuts provided a very abundant but fluctuating and moderately nutritious background, with Swiss Pine (*Pinus cembra*) kernels and beech-nuts in southern areas.

The major problem for the gatherer-hunter-fisher in the Temperate forest zone will have been that of over-wintering in an ecology that had effectively shut down for several months. Marine, littoral, river, marsh and lake resources offered one winter-base solution with the combination of the still-productive green water-plants and rhizomes of the reed associations (*Scirpus, Phragmites, Menyanthes*) or the seashore root and leaf communities (*Atriplex, Beta, Crambe, Echinophora, Brassica, Eryngium*); waterside solutions to which many of the forest mammals also resorted. The alternative was to mimic the squirrel by storing roots, nuts, dried berries and dried fruits such as the crab apple; this, in turn, meant an intensive period of communal autumn gathering, preparation and storing in pits and baskets, which then must serve as a base-area for the rest of the winter. There is growing evidence that in especially advantageous sheltered areas, with freshwater springs and catchments that produced large quantities of storable resources within a small radius, extensive winter base-camps were established for large groups on this basis – including the expected range of irregular storage pits, root-roasting pits, nutting stones, winter huts (perhaps of turf), access to water and, perhaps, originally the composite slicers, graters, wooden mortars, throwing-sticks and digging-sticks discussed earlier.

Putative winter base-camps of this type, marked by large flint-scatters, pits and structures, are found from Britain to Poland and southern France, mainly in sheltered southerly locations on light or sandy soils, once thought to have been thinly forested. However, the tight correlation of these large Mesolithic sites and particular loamy sands, sandy gravels or greensands is very reminiscent of the Danubian I interest in the loess soils. It is well illustrated by the important Horsham group occupying the Wealden ridge linking Britain to France, between the warming Atlantic to the south and the North Sea (Fig. 6). Radial territories from this common core could conveniently run across several ecological zones, north to the Thames valley marshes and estuary, or south to the lost Sussex and Hampshire coastline on the sheltered South Channel bay.

The modern evidence suggests that these sandy gravels and comparable soils in adjacent Europe, in fact, carried varieties of oak/hazel/bracken associations. Indeed, these warm light soils provide both ideal growth conditions for bracken, and the richest and most productive soil conditions for hazel-nut production, in Western Europe (Riley and Young, 1968, Fig. 6; Howes, 1948, pp. 182–183; Masefield *et al.*, 1971, p. 26). This immediately emphasizes the unique importance of the great edible productivity of the oak/hazel/bracken/bramble/fungus

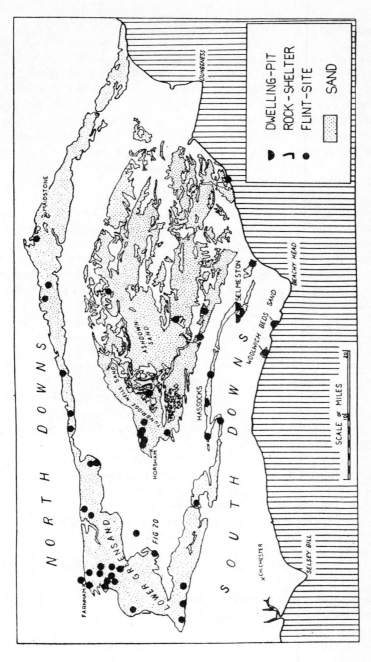

Fig. 6. Distribution map of sites of the Horsham group *ca* 6000–4000 B.C. showing the strong correlation between the site locations and the sandy-loam soils with the most productive combination of bracken, acorns and hazelnuts, along the freshwater spring line. The Horsham sites are now far more numerous but although sites have significantly been found outside the sandy-loam terrain the overwhelming correlation with these soils remains and is reinforced. The coastline indicated is modern (map after Clark and Rankine (1937–8), *Proceedings of the Prehistoric Society*, **5**, 93).

associations on these soils – producing a vast localized and storable autumnal yield of edible acorns, hazelnuts, bracken rhizomes, blackberries and edible fungi. The average annual productivity of brackenroot alone (*Pteridium aquilinum*) ranges between 20–50 tonnes km^{-2} and it is edible, after treatment, throughout the year; it stores well and formed the major subsistence basis of the Maori gathering economy (Shawcross, 1967; Hendrick, 1972, p. 470). The annual productivity of edible acorns, hazelnuts, berries and fungi must also be calculated in tens of thousands of kilograms in this environment (Howes, 1948; Brothwell and Brothwell, 1969, p. 86).

The key contribution, however, will have been the easy storage and complementary nutritional value and reliability of nuts and roots. In a forest economy based on nuts and roots the cycle of low nut-productivity years may be counterbalanced by root reserves, especially if several different species of nut and root are gathered. The roots are naturally rich in carbohydrates, some sugars and a little protein, whilst acorns and hazelnuts provide valuable fat, protein and other elements. The fungi, too, may be dried and stored to provide important protein and vitamin resources; for example, laboratory animals fed on mushrooms as their protein put on 30% more weight than those fed on cheese (Brothwell and Brothwell, 1969, p. 90). Particularly important after a lengthy winter diet of roots, nuts and fungi will have been the vital antiscorbutic value of the many early herbaceous spring greens widely available in the deciduous forest. Naturally, over and above this bulk of vegetal diet will have been the mammal meat, fish, shellfish and wildfowl resources that would be taken whenever and wherever the opportunity offered.

In warm wet temperate shady forests a major proportion of the total edible productivity is locked up in the large subterranean growth of many varieties of roots. The natural subsistence emphasis would fall therefore, on forest root perennials and vegetatively reproducing tuberous plants, as opposed to the Mediterranean prominence of the annuals and sexually reproduced seeds. The superabundance of Temperate forest edible roots demanded exploitation and simultaneously solved three subsistence problems:

1. They provided the most reliable minimally fluctuating staple, the year through and year by year, and bridge the critical winter gap;
2. they filled the carbohydrate and protein gap left by the low availability of grass and pulse-seeds in the Temperate forest;
3. they stored easily, harvested easily and reproduced speedily and simply, requiring little special effort or equipment.

Hardly any gatherer-hunter-fisher group that has exploited vegetatively reproducing roots and tubers can have been ignorant of the superficial basis of that reproduction and its simple control – the broken tip
of the rhizome normally growing again to produce a new plant. A
similar broad knowledge may be assumed for the elementary control
of forest ecology by fire-setting, to open up the canopy for grazing,
allowing the hazel and other shrubs to nut and fruit effectively, making
the herbaceous plants flourish and stimulating the root growth of
bracken and related root-plants in a prototype of slash-and-burn agricultural practice (Simmons, 1969). In short, the probability is that the
late Mesolithic exploitation of the Atlantic Temperate deciduous forest
already closely approached varieties of asexual horticulture and forest
husbandry based on limited fire-setting, pruning and clearing, long
before slash-and-burn agriculture centred on annual grass-seeds was
able to penetrate this habitat.

The Mesolithic/Neolithic transition

The discussion, so far, has attempted to show that traditional interpretations of the archaeological data from Mesolithic Europe between
ca 10 000–4000 B.C. have been artificially limited by the complexities
of weak conventional assumptions, inherent sampling biases and reinforcing stereotypes. Following the work of Higgs and Jarman, man,
plant and animal relationships may be seen as intricate and fluctuating
rather than as a single progressive sequence from simple to advanced,
from hunting to domestication. There is increasing reason to believe
that a very wide range of plants and animals have been associated with
man in complex and changing subsistence interrelationships in the past,
in which some measure of crop and herd control and resource management, manipulation and husbandry were already practised. In middle
and southern European latitudes, ecological inference and an alternative interpretation of the data would suggest that the great bulk of gatherer-hunter-fisher diet would be drawn from the natural abundance
of reliable and diverse vegetal sources. In the Mediterranean, it would
naturally embrace a pulse/bulb/grass-seed and nuts dietary base, supplemented by hunting and marine gathering. The pulses and grass-
seeds were probably harvested together, using the various forms of
microlithic-toothed reaping-knives, and amongst this wide range of
productive grass and pulse species were probably some of the ancestors
of later intensively domesticated strains in the process of closer control
and selection. Amongst the animals culled, it appears that in some
areas the red deer and in others the ovicaprids, cattle, pigs and even
rabbits may already have occupied a specially controlled relationship

amounting to elementary husbandry; supplementary props to a gathering-hunting-fishing economy.

By contrast, in the European Temperate forest zone, the subsistence basis was probably focused on various root/foliage/fruit and nut combinations exploited in techniques which perhaps in some areas already approximated to simple forest horticulture. The genetic traces of the early husbandry of these root staples are less dramatic, because asexual reproduction gives rise to a limited variability and gene interchange; whilst the sexually reproducing seed crops have a relatively free gene interchange and, therefore, a naturally high plasticity, variability and rate of change, leading to the appearance of complex hybrids, novel crosses and new forms with no wild parallel. An abundant mammal fauna probably provided ample meat supplies with less need for advanced husbandry techniques, except in winter; in the north the scavenging dog had been domesticated early, perhaps as an over-wintering resource; and perhaps, in similar circumstances, the omnivorous pig may already have been closely controlled around its abundant natural marsh habitat in the Crimean/Dnestr/Danube delta. Otherwise, meat and vegetal resources were widely drawn from the abundant littoral and marine resources of the Atlantic coast and from the productive network of Postglacial lakes and rivers.

However, a series of environmental changes brought wider influences to bear on these two, rather differently based, subsistence patterns in which the developing instability of the Mediterranean systems *ca* 7000–6000 B.C. ultimately impinged on the more stable Temperate forest regimes. The elements of this hypothesis can be sketched as follows, although once again we must stress the inevitability of local divergences relating to strongly localized conditions:

1. *Ca 8000–6000* B.C.*: Southern Mediterranean preadaptive and pre-Asiatic phase* The southernmost economies of coastal Iberia, Italy and Greece adapted to the expanding evergreen ecology, leading to a more intensive exploitation and husbandry of the remaining plant-foods, especially the grasses, legumes, vine and possibly the fig, olive and various bulbs (*Allium* spp., etc.). The diminishing herds of large herbivores were supplemented by increasing recourse to marine resources and more intensive exploitation and husbandry of the remaining small, gregarious and small-territory animals that were easier to manipulate (shellfish, dog, pig, rabbit, ibex/ammotragus/ovicaprids). The freshly inundated and colonized littoral, under warmer conditions than at present, provided optimal conditions for marine shellfish, crustacea and fish productivity. The overall trend was towards a more static population, strongly tied to littoral resources, exploited from more sedentary

critical sites that allowed direct manipulation of the small-range animal herds and year-through husbanding of the local trees, grasses, legumes and bulbs and possibly already included sporadic resowing.

2. *Ca 7000–6000* B.C.: *Northern Mediterranean transformation*   The subsistence patterns of the middle and northern parts of the Mediterranean peninsulas were transformed from south to north under the growing pressure of coastal inundation, which slowly reached a critical threshold, combining with the fall in edible productivity of the reduced littoral that remained. This collapse of the early Mediterranean mixed-forest transhumant systems in a chain reaction was initiated by the regionally critical loss of up to two-thirds of the already slender littoral with its high directly edible productivity, which provided the critical winter browsing and grazing areas for man and the hunted herbivores. This loss was doubled by the accompanying south to north displacement of the residual mixed deciduous and Mediterranean littoral woodland by the expanding sclerophylous and xerophytic ecology with a much lower edible productivity for man and beast. The combined result was a major quantitative decrease in primary vegetal resources and herbivore carrying capacity in the most critical "over-wintering" sectors of the transhumant schedules of man and mammals. Long-distance interior/coast transhumant systems were, therefore, increasingly replaced by littoral systems of the southern type, as southern ecology spread north, and the return for energy-expenditure on increasing marine foods, especially shellfish, for the first time compensated fully for the decreasing yield of hunted herbivores, especially red deer (Fig. 7). Since the summer and autumn exploitation of coastal marine resources was seasonally incompatible with the simultaneous inland montane exploitation of migrant herbivore herds, the earlier preference for the latter strategy gradually gave way to the former and the northward spread of a largely littoral system of semi-sedentary groups practising pre-Asiatic forms of Mediterranean plant and animal husbandry.

3. *6000–5000* B.C.: *Mediterranean interconnection and integration*   The rising importance of marine resources was probably responsible for the appearance of the first reliable sea-going canoes *ca* 6500–6000 B.C. This technological innovation was advantageously involved in the more extensive exploitation of marine resources and distant island and coastal resources (deep-sea and migratory fish, tunny, deeper shellfish beds; large fishhooks appear). In addition to its importance for population responses to potential resources, the sea-going canoe was instrumental in the rapid interchange of successful local, East Mediterranean and Asiatic plant and animal domesticates through the

networks between previously isolated communities. The unpopulated
Mediterranean islands were now reached and colonized and their raw
materials like obsidian widely distributed (Cyprus, Crete, Malta, Sardinia, Corsica, the Balearics). The domestic sheep and goat gradually
replaced the waning shellfish as a main protein source; emmer, einkorn
and barley similarly displaced less productive local cultivars. The widespread use of plain and impressed ceramics developed to handle sedentary storage and the regular cereal-gruel and stew basis of the newly

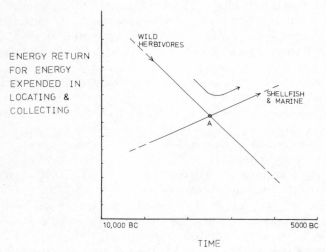

Fig. 7. Schematic model suggesting a cross-over point (A) at which Mediterranean
gathering-hunting-fishing coastal/inland strategies, with higher altitude summer
camps in the interior, gave way to littoral systems with coastal summer camps as the
return for energy expended on shellfish and marine food husbandry overtook the falling
return from diminishing deer, cattle and horse herds. Experimental ovicaprid and
cereal husbandry increasingly displaced the role of marine foods after *ca* 5000 B.C.

integrated and productive economy. Whether the "domesticated"
olive, vine and fig were part of the indigenous local development, as
it now seems they might have been, or whether they were among the
later exotics, has yet to be decided. A new and productive subsistence
pattern had been developed by the selective integration of a diverse
range of pre-existing husbandry practices and staples, drawn from a
wide pool of formerly different, disconnected, localized, gatherer-
hunter-fisher husband patterns.

4. *6000–5000* B.C. *Mediterranean expansion and northern penetration* A
single new strategy may, and usually does, solve different problems in

different places and the probability is that the causal factors behind the adoption of controlled food-production practices were very different from place to place, but not altogether unrelated. In the Balkan zone, especially in southern and coastal Bulgaria, it is doubtful if the pattern of littoral-loss and ecological change took the same form that it did in the Mediterranean peninsulas. However, the Balkan zone was certainly an area of high edible-food productivity under natural conditions. The eastern Balkans were exceedingly rich in edible plant species, partly because of the varied climate, the soils, the rainfall and the ecological diversity, but mainly because the area had always been a southern interglacial refuge for both European and Asiatic steppe species (see Newbigin, 1968, p. 212). On these grounds, we must suspect that a substantial early gatherer-hunter-fisher population underlies the momentarily more impressive Neolithic cultures. Given that the predominant terrain was a mixture of alkaline and acid outcrops, low alluvial swamps and high mountain plateaux, the ecology also ranged from deciduous oak/beech/elm forest through extensive grassy and lightly wooded steppe to a Mesomediterranean woodland with walnut and hazel trees. Against this context, the work of Dennell (1974) suggests a local development not unlike that of the southern Mediterranean with local gatherer-hunter-fishers developing increasingly complex forms of plant and animal husbandry based on the changing local grassland ecology and perhaps already embracing local legumes, fruits, cereals, pigs, ovicaprids and cattle.

It would seem that it was from the broad base of the Balkan peninsula, with its vegetal wealth and Mesomediterranean climate that a successfully integrated cattle/sheep/goat/cereal economy penetrated what, up till then, had been thinly occupied areas of Eastern Europe – the mixed oak, pine, hazel, elm, lime and birch woodlands of the Middle Danube plain. The new Starčevo/Körös/Cris subsistence pattern allowed the previously marginal dry loess soil bands to be taken into very productive exploitation for the first time. The restricted gatherer-hunter-fisher communities strung along the Danube and Tisza margins seem, on the Lepenski Vir evidence, to have been absorbed within a well-adapted composite economy utilizing both the old and the new resources and techniques.

Beyond the Balkan-type ecology and cultures of the eastern triangle of continental forested steppe conditions lay the mixed deciduous forest of the Baltic–Carpathian arc to the north and the fringes of the great Temperate maritime oak forest of the Atlantic plain to the west. Along the highly productive glaciated, river- and lake-dotted Northern plain lay a belt of interrelated and long-stabilized "Epi-Gravettian" gatherer-hunter-fisher communities. These already closely similar and closely linked forest economies are now brought into focus for the first time when they too develop their own, pointed-base, oval-bowl, ceramic assemblages from the Bug–Dnestr culture in the south, through the Polish Masovian, Zedmar, Narva to the Ellerbek and Ertebølle assemblages in the north. This chain of "ceramicized" gatherer-hunter-fishers continued their forest economy, with little change beyond some domestic pigs and their new pottery until, at a later date, they developed their own northern agricultural pattern in the indigenous and emergent TRB and corded-ware culture groups.

On the western frontier the highly successful emergent Danubian I economy and life style solved the initial problems of the fertile, but wetter and more heavily forested, loesses; and these, too, were brought into productive occupation before 4000 B.C. The low-density centre of the saucer-like Mesolithic population distribution had been finally and productively penetrated by subsistence methods based on a combination of exotic and traditional pursuits, techniques and staples, in which the low natural edible-productivity of the local glade communities were replaced by highly productive artificial associations. However, surrounding the new population expansion and infilling within this central core lay the encircling chain of long-established, well-adapted and, by the standards of the time, numerous gatherer-hunter-fisher populations of the Baltic–Carpathian belt to the north, the Temperate maritime forest to the west and in the Alpine valleys to the south. It was in these areas that a substantial continuity of population and subsistence practices persisted in a set of highly distinctive, regionally peculiar culture-groups, within which it may be suspected that a number of idiosyncratic practices are merely late and more substantial manifestations of very much earlier traditions.

Nevertheless, under the influence of environmental, ecological and demographic changes, the "new" techniques and resources gradually displaced some of the older and no longer competitively productive practices in the much changed environment of fourth-millennium Europe. The productive climax of the Maritime mixed-oak forest was lost and many of the Postglacial lakes, rivers and coasts were long past their productive maturity. The maximum growth of the forests had been reached before *ca* 4000 B.C. and the forest declined, and became more open, as the climate became more continental and as the cumulative result of four thousand years of human interference. The onset of sub-Boreal conditions presented the challenges of a changed European ecology to a new population structure, equipped with greatly modified technology and subsistence practices.

CONCLUSION

This frankly speculative and theoretical essay has attempted to avoid the prison of conventional interpretations of limited data samples, in order to explore alternative possibilities. Only when the range of alternative models has been defined may we usefully test between them in a series of carefully selected, detailed analyses on restricted data. It is, after all, the duty of speculation, hypothesis and theory to outrun current fact and thereby direct and focus the next stages of research. Speculation is both essential and productive if it obeys the cardinal injunctions that it must predict and that some of those predictions must ultimately be testable. As it happens, the hypotheses developed here are not utterly speculative. They rest on the theoretical implications of recent ecological, ethnographic, demographic, economic and archaeological work and fit the evidence available as effectively as more conventional interpretations, which are no less speculative. The basic assumptions and concepts upon which any study rests are ultimately metaphysical speculations, in the philosophical sense, and we develop new archaeological explanations as much by changing our metaphysical assumptions as from our changing data.

In conclusion, then, this essay identified a number of testable points. If microliths and blades were hafted in graters we might expect a transverse, as opposed to a longitudinal, wear pattern. If roots were important, we might expect certain distribution consequences for human communities (Fig. 6) and methods capable of recovering root and leaf fibre from decomposed faeces could provide a direct test. Suitable excavations in key areas like dry Almerian Spain and wet Temperate Atlantic Europe would also try the adequacy of the ecological and subsistence inferences. If the early coastal Mediterranean Mesolithic economies transformed from south to north, in the manner sketched, then carbon-dating should provide a direct test of this generalization.

Finally, the essay develops some interesting unconventional interpretations.

1. Mesolithic artefacts and subsistence patterns are not incompetent attempts at later Neolithic artefacts and patterns, or degenerate efforts at Upper Palaeolithic products; Mesolithic artefacts and subsistence patterns were well designed and well adapted for what could best be done to achieve an adequate food supply from certain environments, using that technology.
2. Microlithic equipment had many diverse and interchangeable functions but, taken globally, it is tempting to suggest that some especially abundant and diversified microlithic equipment may relate to

phases of intensive vegetal resource exploitation and therefore, by definition, to incipient phases of plant domestication.

3. Some of the subsistence economies of the Mesolithic in the western maritime oak mixed forest may have approached limited, fire-controlled *asexual* horticulture and arboriculture, based on vegetatively reproducing *root* staples, forest *perennials*, controlled nut and fruit trees, backed up by shellfish, dog and pig husbandry, rather than by "conventional" hunting, fishing and gathering routines: this wet Temperate forest economy would more closely resemble the root-based forest horticulture of South America, Central Africa, Australasia and New Zealand, complete with wooden pestles, mortars, bark-beaters and graters; recent forest horticulture surviving only where the forest itself has survived in a productive form.

4. One may contrast this with the *sexual seed-based* subsistence patterns of the broad Mediterranean zone from North Africa to Iran, centred on grass and pulse *annuals* with hard tough seed-cases that need to be reaped with microlithic harvesting knives, ground between stones and stored in pits. A contrast may thus be noted between the extremely early southern appearance of extensive microlithic equipment, grinding-stones, storage baskets and pits (as at Shanidar, by 15 000–10 000 B.C.) from Iran to North Africa in the dry Mediterranean grass and woodland zone, as opposed to the soft, fibrous root, nut and fruit grating and slicing equipment of the northern deciduous forest zone (Solecki, 1973; Clark, 1971).

REFERENCES

Birdsell, J. B. (1957). Some population problems involving Pleistocene Man, *Cold Spring Harbor Symposia in Quantitative Biology*, **22**, 47–69.
Brothwell, D. and Brothwell, P. (1969). *Food in Antiquity*, Praeger, New York.
Camps-Fabrer, H. (1966). Matière et art Mobilier dans la Préhistoire Nord-Africaine et Saharienne, *Mémoires du Centre de Recherches Anthropologiques, Préhistoriques et Ethnographiques (Algérie)*, No. V.
Cassels, R. (1972) Human ecology in the prehistoric Waikato, *Journal of the Polynesian Society*, **81**, 196–247.
Clark, J. D. (1971). A re-examination of the evidence for agricultural origins in the Nile valley, *Proceedings of the Prehistoric Society*, **37**, 34–79.
Clark, J. G. D. (1952) *Prehistoric Europe: the Economic Basis*, Methuen, London.
Clark, J. G. D. (1972) *Star Carr: a Case Study in Bioarchaeology*, Addison-Wesley Modular Publications No. 10, Addison-Wesley, Reading, Mass.
Clarke, D. L. (1968). *Analytical Archaeology*, Methuen, London.
Clarke, D. L. (ed.) (1972). *Models in Archaeology*, Methuen, London.
Deacon, H. J. (1972). A review of the Post-Pleistocene in South Africa, *South African Arch. Soc.*, **1**, 26–45.

Dennell, R. W. (1974). Neolithic and Bronze Age economies in Bulgaria, unpublished dissertation, Cambridge University.

Flannery, K. V. (1969). Origins and ecological effects of early domestication in Iran and the Near East, in *The Domestication and Exploitation of Plants and Animals*, (P. J. Ucko and G. W. Dimbleby, eds), Duckworths, London pp. 73–100.

Hedrick, U. P. (ed.) (1972). *Sturtevant's Edible Plants of the World*, Dover Publications, New York.

Higgs, E. S. (1966). The climate, environment and industries of Stone Age Greece: Part II, *Proceedings of the Prehistoric Society*, **32**, 1–29.

Higgs, E. S. (ed.) (1972). *Papers in Economic Prehistory*, Cambridge University Press, London.

Higgs, E. S. and Jarman, M. R. (1969). The origins of agriculture: a reconsideration, *Antiquity*, **43**, 31–41.

Hill, A. F. (1952). *Economic Botany*, Botanical Science Publications, New York.

Howes, F. N. (1948). *Nuts: Their Production and Everyday Uses*, Faber and Faber, London.

Jacobi, R. M. (1973). The British Mesolithic, unpublished dissertation, Cambridge University.

Jolly, C. J. (1970). The seed-eaters: a new model of hominid differentation based on a baboon analogy. *Man*, **5**, 5–26.

Kooijmans, L. P. L. (1972). Mesolithic bone and antler implements from the North Sea and from the Netherlands, *Berichten van de Rijksdienst voor het Oudheidkundig Bodemonderzoek*, **20–21**, 27–73.

Lawton, J. H. (1973). The energy cost of food gathering, in *Resources and Population* (B. Benjamin, P. R. Cox and J. Peel, eds), Academic Press, London, pp. 59–76.

Lee, R. B. (1968). What hunters do for a living, or, how to make out on scarce resources, in *Man the Hunter* (R. B. Lee and I. DeVore, eds), Aldine, Chicago, pp. 30–48.

Lee, R. B. and DeVore, I. (eds) (1968). *Man the Hunter*, Aldine, Chicago.

Masefield, G. B., Wallis, M., Harrison, S. G. and Nicholson, B. E. (1971). *The Oxford Book of Food Plants*, Oxford University Press, London.

Newbigin, M. I. (1968). *Plant and Animal Geography*, Methuen, London.

Phillipson, J. (1966). *Ecological Energetics*, Edward Arnold, London.

Riley, D. and Young, A. (1968). *World of Vegetation*, Cambridge University Press, London.

Renfrew, J. M. (1973). *Palaeoethnobotany: The Prehistoric Food Plants of the Near East and Europe*, Methuen, London.

Shawcross, K. A. (1967). Fern-root and the total scheme of 18th century Maori food production in agricultural areas. *Journal of the Polynesian Society*, **76**, 330–352.

Simmons, I. G. (1969). Evidence for vegetation changes associated with Mesolithic man in Britain, in *The Domestication and Exploitation of Plants and Animals* (P. J. Ucko and G. W. Dimbleby, eds), Duckworths, London, pp. 113–119.

Solecki, R. S. (1963). Two bone hafts from northern Iraq, *Antiquity*, **37**, 58–60.

Thomas, D. H. (1972). A computer simulation model of Great Basin Shoshonean subsistence and settlement patterns, in *Models in Archaeology* (D. L. Clarke, ed.), Methuen, London, pp. 671–705.

Vayson, A. (1918). Faucille préhistorique de Solferino, *L'Anthropologie*, **29**, 393–422.

Waterbolk, H. T. (1968). Food production in Prehistoric Europe, *Science*, **162**, 1093–1102.

White, J. P. (1969). Typologies for some prehistoric flaked stone artefacts in the Australian New Guinea Highlands, *Archaeology and Physical Anthropology in Oceania*, **4**, 18–46.

Whittaker, R. H. (1970). *Communities and Ecosystems*, Collier MacMillan, London.

Wilkinson, P. F. (1973). The relevance of musk-ox exploitation to the study of prehistoric animal economies, unpublished dissertation, Cambridge University.

Wilkinson, R. G. (1973). *Poverty and Progress*, Methuen, London.

Yarnell, R. A. (1964). Aboriginal relationships between culture and plant life in the Upper Great Lakes region. *Anthropological Papers*, 23, Museum of Anthropology, Michigan.

Yde, J. (1965). *Material Culture of the Waiwai*, The National Museum, Copenhagen, Roekke X.

The Economic Context of Trade and Industry in Barbarian Europe till Roman Times

DAVID L. CLARKE

INTRODUCTION

The antecedents of trade and industry in the European Continent extend continuously through time to the activities of the earliest hominids, a million years ago, in a Europe that we would now scarcely recognize; a Europe with an unfamiliar geography, a different climate, and an exotic fauna and flora. In Man's own knowledge and continuing experience there have been not one Europe, but a succession of Europes through time, each with its own distinctive character. Indeed, the minute penetration of the European environment which mapped the resources of later trade and industry was the cumulative consequence of this successive experience of every aspect of Europe, under every kind of condition, collectively stored in the cultural traditions of its inhabitants. It might almost be said that Man stayed still and let Europe fluctuate about him in its oscillating trajectory. But this of course is not true, for Man's ancestors continuously adapted both biologically and culturally in such a way as to intensify Man's branching penetration deep into the interstices of his environment. In this process, Man's cultural adaptations have increasingly insulated his populations from environmental fluctuations by means of the increasing regulatory variety of his material and social artefact assemblages.

It at once seems incongruous to take historical concepts of trade and industry back into a series of contexts in which ultimately Man is not even *Homo sapiens* and in which perhaps formalized speech itself may be doubted. Nevertheless, the most primitive tool-using hominids practised complex economies – elaborate time and role allocation strategies,

Prepared in 1969 to appear in *The Cambridge Economic History of Europe* (M. Postan, ed.), Cambridge University Press, Cambridge, in press, Vol. II, Chap. 1.

combining various subsistence methods and extraction processes with which to feed and equip the community and ensure its continuity. Even in these earliest contexts, commodities were gathered, shared and exchanged on a limited scale whilst a multiplicity of raw materials were regularly exploited by the repetitive employment of special technological skills. This much archaeology tells us with certainty.

The incongruity – the anachronism – is to imagine that in these ancient contexts the communities concerned viewed these economic activities in the highly peculiar, highly formalized way conditioned in us by our contemporary background. We may even legitimately talk about the economic strategy of a troop of baboons, but it would surely be unwise to attribute to them that selectively atomized perception of their activities which is indeed a peculiar product of our own minds. When we analyse the economies of ancient European societies and scrutinize their trade in commodities, or the organization of their industries, we must constantly recollect the retrospective astigmatism of our transient view, accustomed as it is to the peculiarly idiosyncratic and asymmetric emphasis of contemporary industrial economies. It is our own cultural astigmatism which seeks to polarize functional and nonfunctional transactions, to separate utilitarian from ceremonial activities and above all mistakenly seeks an "economic purpose" behind the cultural manifestations which are the multipurpose spicules of group activities. Although it is true that our astigmatism grows less as the activities approach our own times, it remains no less a distorting factor in attempts to understand study of a Neolithic village, perhaps four thousand years earlier. We must remember that in other sociocultural contexts the exploitation of resources, the processes of production, the distribution of commodities by exchange and the concepts of wealth are all pursued on a different scale, in terms of different philosophies and with the conscious emphasis on quite other facets of these activities. The cultural models that constrain the activities of other cultures differ from our own and, consequently, those activities are not entirely explicable in terms of our concepts of economics, trade and industry.

In order to understand the appropriate contextual dimensions of exchange and production in ancient Europe we must be careful to use reconstruction models closer to those of anthropology than to the more formal models of modern economics; indeed, it is probably necessary to use a mixture of models derived from animal behaviour, social anthropology, and economics. In the first three-quarters of a million years of European hominid activity, the primate behaviour factor will dominate the patterns fitted by the mixed model; in the last quarter of a million years, social anthropology will more extensively map the variations, until in the remaining millennium formal economic factors will dominate in modelling activities in which, nevertheless, the three factors still coexist. To these factors we should correctly add those accidental and stochastic elements which are the necessary ingredients of any realistic interpretive model. This approach suggests that it need not be inappropriate to use modern terms for ancient activities as a predictive analogue – an indication of hidden potential – nor is it entirely inapppropriate to use the mathematical methods of modern economic analysis upon primitive economies. These procedures simply serve to show what aspects of ancient activities can be immediately comprehended in the dimensions of our own modern minds, at the same time establishing those irreducible residual aspects for which explanations must be sought amongst the other factors in the context. The best that we can do is to stretch the data of prehistory over a conceptual framework incorporating behavioural, cultural, economic and stochastic models, using each factor in turn to control the others, thereby noting the most adequate model in the particular context and learning from the discrepancies between the models – a kind of mental regression analysis.

Since we are familiar with the contemporary conceptions of industry and trade it is mainly necessary to sketch some of the dimensions in which the elements of these activities differ in the contexts of other societies. It is not that our cultural network and its structure is substantially different from those of the ancient Europeans, merely that the selective emphasis of the bonds is rather different. In human societies, both past and present, the population is everywhere networked by the cross-cutting web of kinship relations and the superimposed mesh of social acquaintances. Groups of kinsmen may co-operate to produce, distribute and consume commodities, or join together in other activities, whilst at the same time the individual members will be variously inter-linked with non-kin groups in age sets, status classes, recreational cliques, ceremonial fraternities, religious bodies, military regiments, political factions and exchange partnerships. All of these linked lattices have the effect of extending special obligation relationships throughout a finite population, with advantageous reciprocal consequences. Production and consumption may be regulated in the network, famine or natural disaster may be co-operatively overcome and fresh advantages may be more effectively exploited by sharing their development with others – with a reciprocal gain in prestige status. Internal conflict will tend to run contrary to some relationships shared by various parties and these interested bystanders may therefore move to minimize and heal the disruption. In such an intricately adjusted web of relationships, economic activities and exchange partnerships are an integral part of the social, religious, psychological and material culture nexus and these latter factors can never be separated from any hypothetically "pure" economic considerations (Firth, 1967).

So much for the static network of social obligations, but cultures are dynamic systems with moving and circulating contents and changing internal and external relationships. A significant proportion of this dynamism is bound up with the circulation of commodities within the system and at any one time the relationships between individuals in the network is connected with the distribution state of the commodities within the network at that time (Harding, 1967). In many ways, culture systems run on the circulation of commodities within a distribution flow operated by the social machinery. In most communities, for example, the nodal regularities of the daily, weekly, monthly seasonal, annual and life-cycle activities of the individuals in the social group are selectively but strikingly marked out by appropriate ceremonies, in which special commodities are consumed, manufactured, or dispersed in a continuous cycle, conferring birth gifts, age-group and status insignia, maturity emblems, bride price, dowries, wedding feasts, gift exchanges, religious sacrifices and dues, communal levies, and the requisites for burial ceremonies. In this context, consumption and display of commodities is a conspicuous and outwardly meaningful communication serving many purposes other than strictly utilitarian ones; especially serving to restate in an intricate symbolism the mutual rank, status and roles of the individuals in the network at that time – a kind of decorated pecking-order. The commodities used in this symbolic decoration of values may be of any kind and represent an idiosyncratic and stochastic selection. Nevertheless, the continuous definition, maintenance and fulfilment of mutual roles within an elaborate machinery of status and prestige relationships is a factor in even the most modern economic activities.

The arbitrary units of exchange recognized by a society are a particularly important and selected subset of commodities within the larger set of commodities in circulation. Some commodities may be circulated freely in any direction and from amongst these are usually selected favourite staples as media of transaction – durable commodities with a certain scarcity value but not so scarce or capricious as to fail to keep a constant flow through the social machinery. These units of exchange may be utilitarian or non-utilitarian, consumable or non-consumable, manufactured or natural objects: favourite commodities are shells, teeth, tusks, furs, feathers, hides, beads, bracelets, torques, ingots, axes, mats and fabrics, or consumable staples such as pigs, cattle, sheep, tobacco, salt, yams, bananas and cereal grains. The use of foodstuffs as exchange media may at first seem surprising, but they are quite sufficiently durable and are only consumed when absolutely necessary; in this way, an active trade in foodstuffs may have no primary connection with nutritional requirements. The corn bins of the Neolithic chieftain, the horse herds of the Scythian prince, the cattle of the Celtic noble, and the *pithoi* of olive oil in the Minoan potentate's magazines represented actual capital wealth as well as potential food (Clarke, 1968; Clark, 1965).

However, apart from the commodities in free circulation and the media of exchange, there is usually a third set of commodities which on no account may be used as media of exchange – the symbolic insignia marking certain castes or *élites*, often intricately decorated and elaborately finished artefacts, conspicuously enshrining the consumption of much labour, food surplus, rare resources and rare materials. The existence of these exotic prestige insignia which cannot be obtained by free exchange, constitutes an important set of barriers marking subcultural castes or cliques into which it is not possible to "buy" oneself, however wealthy the individual may be. Nevertheless, prestige itself, whether symbolized by restricted regalia or by an impressive surplus of ordinary commodities, has the capacity to exert influence and is a source of power in the society at large. In all societies, prestige is a cashable commodity, a form of capital on whose account loans may be borrowed, expeditions financed and obligations and treaties secured. The New Guinea "big man" relies on his hoard of imported boars' tusks and shell lunulae not only to mark his rank and thus gain the proper deference appropriate to it, but as a means of gaining followers and the services of sorcerers and canoe masters. The Aunjetitz chieftain of Early Bronze Age Europe similarly relied on his hoard of imported amber nuggets, faience beads, bronze ingots and weaponry, to endorse his rank and gain specialists for his retinue, and the Mycenean princeling upon his treasury to gain the obeisance of his villagers and as surety for the expensive tackle and gear for his mercantile speculations.

The anthropological model of commodity production and circulation outlines the way in which extensive *"kula"* trade rings might be mainly circulating strange prestige kickshaws which primarily served to increase the local status of the exchange partners and strengthen their partnership, whilst almost incidentally and on sporadic occasions facilitating the additional circulation of some "useful" staples. All in all we can appreciate that commodities were exchanged, and raw materials were regularly exploited with special technological skills, in the most ancient societies of Europe, but that the context of those activities was very different from the contexts that we extrapolate to them when we think in terms of trade and industry. It is no longer surprising to find that commodities of many kinds circulated over vast areas of prehistoric Europe without long-range movements by individuals and involving not so much commodities of economic "utility" as decorative gewgaws or display weaponry. Commodities more congruent with our own ideas of utilitarian trade were produced and circulated in this context and clear memories of these later media of exchange are preserved in our European vocabularies – salt (salary), a handful of iron spits (drachma), ingots (aes), cattle (pecuniary), land (fee), and grain. These "useful" commodities were, however, only part of the system and would rarely be the cause of the exchange system coming into existence.

The history of trade and industry in barbarian Europe is therefore essentially the history of activities which have been transformed almost beyond recognition. In the anthropological model, the production and circulation of commodities is secondary to the proper functioning of the culture concerned and operates on a satisficer basis (Clarke, 1968, pp. 94–95). In the modern economic model, society is deliberately reorganized in an attempt to optimize its economic sector – a reorganization frequently to the detriment of large sections of the society's population but to the marked benefit of other sections. This aspect alone should be sufficient to help us resist the temptation to see this transformation in terms of a former primitive arrangement and a recent advanced configuration, with a steady, simple, onward and upward evolutionary trend linking one to the other; the overwhelming temptation to write the economic history of Europe in a few paragraphs – the farming villagers replace the hunters, metals replace stone technology, surplus supports the city, the city state becomes the nation and all the while the mines get deeper and deeper and society better and better. Alas, because archaeological information is such a peculiar sample and so difficult to interpret, some resemblance between this caricature and this chapter is almost inevitable.

Nevertheless, the economic development of Europe has been a good deal more complex and uneven than such an approach would suggest. Europe has always been an area with a great diversity of habitats, an intricate nested tessellation of different soils, routes, barriers, fauna, flora and climate, a varied mosaic of intersecting macro- and micro-environments. At the most crude level, we will repeatedly contrast the developments in the Mediterranean zone with the differing patterns of temperate middle Europe and coniferous northern Europe – a contrast stretching back to the primeval habitat requirements of the earliest hominids and primates.

European cultural development and diversification has followed a mosaic and multilinear pattern congruent with the diversity of the continent. The economic developments have been simultaneously interacting and cumulative, discrete and divergent, fluctuating and convergent. Former centres of development periodically became peripheral and frontiers became central; archaic survivals suddenly became advantageous bases for fresh development and elaborate economic formats periodically revealed an incapacity for further adaptive development. The pattern is one of repeatedly reticulating development hunting-and-seeking in many directions, in constantly changing environments; one can at best trace only the diverse trajectories of certain economic innovations and trade conditions, marking their successive contributions to particularly localized but critical thresholds.

It is a well-known property of complex systems that the successive introduction of unrelated factors may cumulatively approach a threshold beyond which the system cannot survive unchanged. At the same time, the introduction of new elements or conditions into such a context may result in the emergence of unforeseen consequences or capacities – the development of fresh potential. Now the cultural systems of prehistoric Europe may be approximately portrayed as dynamic information and activity systems locked in complicated processes of interchange with other changing societies and with their changing environing systems. The individual social, economic, religious and psychological configurations of these systems were certainly very diverse but they were all richly networked complex systems coupled within their territorial environments. It is not entirely surprising, therefore, that certain broad thresholds can be discerned in the developing economic pattern of prehistoric Europe, thresholds which have important implications for the growth of trade and industry (Clarke, 1968, pp. 77–81).

The elements which mark these putative thresholds in the archaeological record do not appear suddenly, together, at single points in time, neither are they simultaneously found all over Europe. The individual elements inevitably have long antecedent trajectories; it is, however, the cumulative effects of the successive introduction and integration of these elements and conditions that combine to mark the emergence of a fresh economic capacity, which particularly interests us here. Although often initially restricted to the Mediterranean zone of Europe, the contemporary and subsequent repercussions of many of these successive system repatternings was increasingly widely felt through the continent. The elements combining to define these broad economic thresholds necessarily include a great diversity of factors – environmental, social, religious, historical, political, economic and technological. It is the very comprehensive diversity of such a complex of changing factors which makes their reinforcing ramifications the more powerful. Unfortunately, the archaeological record gives us only an irregular sample of information on these diverse changes and, in some important aspects, no information at all. The archaeologist is still particularly prone to ignore the catalytic importance of the contemporary social, political and historical factors – how things came to be the way they were, the restrictive effect this had on further outcomes, and the advantageous or disastrous exploitation of successive situations organized by social, political, religious and military leaders.

The thresholds that we are going to use to segment the continuity of European development are, of course, determined by our present interest in trade and industry within the economic context. We know far more about the later thresholds from their greater mass of archaeological material and the enormous quantity of contemporary written records. For these later periods, we can make some clumsy attempt to assess the political and historical factors which are so conspicuously missing from the earlier phases. In contrast, the Palaeolithic epoch is so huge chronologically, so environmentally diverse, and so little understood that its appearance as a featureless monolith in the economic record is mainly a monument to our ignorance, to be passed over with great rapidity in the shortest possible space. Yet to assume any degree of economic or social homogeneity, or lack of change, over such a vast and diverse era is clearly absurd. Nevertheless, the apparently quickening pace of development with passing time does not appear to be entirely an illusion – the expansion in hominid population, the exponential growth in artefact variety, in environmental control, and in political unit size is an unequivocable sign of this. But once again we must remember that this overall trend is a composite of many oscillating, fluctuating and desultory individual cultural developments; no one community has continuously crested this curve of development, indeed the continuously shifting focus of climax development is one of the features of analytical interest.

The multiple factors and their cumulative effect in defining the particular thresholds will be briefly outlined at the beginning of the time segment which they crudely define. The dates attached to these transitional thresholds are merely rough indicators based on radiocarbon dates relevant to Europe; they must be carefully distinguished from the much earlier appearances of similar thresholds and elements in adjacent areas, especially to the south and east.

The most significant thresholds can thus be usefully employed to define six interfingering phases in which the economic patterns (and therefore the trade, technology, and industrial potential) of Europe was cumulatively repatterned.

 I The gathering-hunting-fishing economies, *ca* 1 000 000–6000 B.C.

 II The agrarian economies, *ca* 6000–2000 B.C.

 III The Aegean network and the early bronze technologies, *ca* 2000–1400 B.C.

I. THE GATHERING-HUNTING-FISHING ECONOMIES

The opening threshold for Man in Europe is made increasingly complex by the inappropriate nature of the term "Man" and by the long-term mosaic development which physical anthropologists are now demanding for these creatures even in Europe. It now seems increasingly probable that Mediterranean Europe was actually within the boundaries of the earliest incipient hominid developments – thus already emphasizing the important ecological frontier separating the European interior from the north littoral of the Mediterranean sea. Several varieties of superior ground-apes, the earliest known hominids, now date back into the late Miocene, *ca* 10 000 000 B.C., with an already extensive middle-latitude habitat ranging from the Mediterranean and Africa to India and China. Many of these hominids had developed a bipedal gait and these groups with free hands probably made regular use of unmodified sticks and stones as implements for knocking down fruit and nuts, for digging out roots and for killing insects and small animals; these capacities are even within the range of the abilities of most of the modern apes today (Pilbeam and Simons, 1965).

The middle-latitude distribution of the earliest hominids was no accident – the middle latitudes of the globe are the richest in plant life, the polar regions for sunshine and photosynthesis. This wealth of plant and animal life provided a great diversity of ecological niches from the forest canopy to the undergrowth floor, and from the savanna parkland to the montane grasslands; a diversity of habitat widely reflected in the great variety of early pongid and hominid populations exploiting these micro-environments. The dentition and skeletal structure of the early hominids similarly reflects the agile pursuit of these multiplex resources to provide an omnivorous diet with the emphasis on vegetable matter – basically leaves, shoots, roots, fruits, seeds, nuts, insects and small animals. A diet which could be held to the mouth by the grasping pentadactyl hands of the free forearms, secured in the mouth by unspecialized canines, bitten by chisel incisors and adequately ground by powerful molar teeth of relatively simple structure. Man's first tool-kit included his hands and feet, his nailed fingers and toes, and his mouth with its varied array of equipment. Man's first artefacts were in many respects simple material imitations and extensions of these integral and inherited tools of survival.

The archaeological evidence from the contexts of the fossil hominids does not contradict this dietary pattern, although there is some uncertainty about the quantity and importance of meat in the hominid diet. Several lines of inquiry suggest that meat was much less important than has been assumed and, although it was an important and regular part of hominid diet, it may never have formed either the bulk or the staple of that diet. Modern dietary observations demonstrate that a multiplicity of vegetable elements have probably always formed the bulk of the diet of man and apes in the middle latitudes; it is only in the photosynthetic deserts of near-Arctic or Antarctic conditions that man must rely predominantly on animal and marine foods, and substitute the moss from reindeer stomachs and the plankton from fish gullets for the missing vegetal elements.

The archaeologically bemusing evidence of the big kill sites, with the dismembered carcasses of big herbivores amidst a scattered variety of stone butchering tools, must be set against the missing vegetable, wood and basketry evidence, lost to decay. Vegetable and insect foods hardly require better artefacts than the hands and teeth with the addition of a few wooden sticks and points, whereas a constellation of specialized stone artefacts is necessary for the particular tasks of killing, skinning, gutting, butchering and otherwise processing animal carcasses – especially those of large beasts. Other evidence combines to suggest that stone artefacts may be quite asymmetrically correlated with the special requirements of hunting, butchering and secondary took production, clustering densely around these activities in the hominid spectrum, whilst the more persistently intensive pursuit of leaves, stalks, roots, fruits, seeds, nuts, grubs, insects, rats, snakes and lizards may be sparsely represented, if at all, in the stone artefact record.

A balanced economic assessment has been made even more difficult by the marginal habitat now occupied by vestigial gatherer-hunter-fishers, wherein extraordinary conditions now prevail, as well as by the cultural emphasis on meat, hunting prowess, and domestic animal numbers which often perversely bears no proportional relationship to their dietary importance in the culture concerned. However, the evidence from fossilized human faeces and the rare survivals of wooden digging-sticks, harvesting crooks and clubs combine with the general purpose design of the earliest hand-picks to suggest that grubbing-out roots may have been a more frequent hominid occupation than hunting big game. In order to redress this longstanding misemphasis, we shall adopt the term gatherer-hunter-fishers, rather than the traditionally misinformed categorization of hunter-fisher-gatherers with its questionable emphasis on hunting.

Implement-using and, consequently, a detailed interest in raw materials, probably goes back to such widespread late Miocene hominids as *Ramapithecus punjabicus*. Artefact-making, however, which requires a greater degree of mental symboling and forethought, probably developed more slowly, but also on the widespread basis of modifying natural implements. By early Pleistocene times, *ca* 1 000 000 B.C., several varieties of *Australopithecus africanus* were habitually bipedal, displayed less specialized jaws and developed various refinements in hand structure in addition to an expansion of brain capacity and complexity; in all probability, these changes were coupled with the widespread development of tool-using and tool-making. Australopithecine populations may have partly evolved in the Mediterranean zone of Europe, although centred in the latitudes to the south. Traces of putatively Australopithecine pebble tools have been found at several sites within the Mediterranean zone of Europe, including finds from the Vallonet cave at Roquebrune-Cap-Martin on the Mediterranean coast, Monte-Peglia in Italy, and possibly at other sites in Romania and Spain (Bordes, 1968, p. 48). However, by middle Pleistocene times, *ca* 600 000 B.C., varieties of *Homo erectus* had evolved in populations barely distinguishable from those within the range of variation of contemporary *Homo sapiens*. It was probably bands of *Homo erectus* that first succeeded in penetrating the European interior and thus commenced the infiltration of this marginal environment by reaching peripheral Britain, Germany, France and Hungary from the littoral of the Mediterranean and Black Sea.

This penetration of "outer Europe" was materially affected by the periodic climatic oscillations of the Ice Age, *ca* 1 000 000–10 000 B.C., which in interglacial spasms lasting some hundreds of thousands of years supported a "Mediterranean-like" environment deep within central Europe. Magnolias flowered amidst mixed woods of beech and hornbeam interlaced by lianas and vines, whilst elephants, hippos and rhinos grazed quietly beyond the reach of the puny, baboon-stalking, Australopithecine pygmies, although soon within the regular hunting capacity of robust *Homo erectus* with his more elaborate artefacts and projectiles.

In the intervening and equally long glacial phases, this European middle-latitude "natural habitat" zone for hominids was gradually displaced southwards by the increasingly cold conditions which swept around the expanding northern ice-cap and the converging alpine glaciers. Now, mammoth, woolly rhinoceros and reindeer grazed, whilst musk-oxen stamped on the frosty, moss-covered tundra or tore up the dwarf willows, polar birch and dwarf pine trees; in warmer pockets, bison and horse herds migrated swiftly across bands of sparsely wooded steppe. Initially, at least, the hominids seem to have retreated to the Mediterranean littoral in these severe phases, ecapsulated within their traditional habitat ecology and abandoning the European interior to its new denizens. Latterly, at the end of the Riss glaciation, *ca* 200 000 B.C., and throughout the Würm glaciation, *ca* 80 000–10 000 B.C., small hominid groups seem for the first time to have succeeded in exploiting the alien tundra environment immediately south of the ice sheets of northern Europe. Amongst these frontier groups, hunting must certainly have played an unusually important role and skilful micro-environmental control, employing fur cloaks, fire, communal tented dugouts and screened caves, together enabled them to survive the somewhat less severe climatic rigours of such favourable areas as Atlantic France and periglacial Poland. Full cultural adaptation to steppe and tundra life, including the use of tailored fur clothing ultimately enabled the late Pleistocene hominids to conquer and survive the Würm glaciation *in situ*, in middle Europe, virtually wherever the land was ice-free. The hominids had finally broken through the northern ecological threshold constraining their habitat zone, using the same means with which they were subsequently able to transcend every similar boundary – by cultural adaptation.

During the interstadials of the Würm glaciation, *ca* 40 000 B.C., the variety of Man known as *Homo sapiens sapiens* first became apparent as a population variety of unspecialized Neanderthal stock in the Near East and in eastern Europe. The archaeological record tells us of an accompanying and widespread technological change from making flint tools on flake blanks to making flint tools on blade blanks which could be hafted in composite tool forms. However, these developments took many millennia to materialize and most of the "innovations" accompanying *Homo sapiens* have long antecedent histories. Bone, antler and probably wooden artefacts were more intensively produced but these materials were already used by *Homo erectus*; ceremonial burial with red ochre, food and equipment became a regular feature but had long been practised by *Homo sapiens neanderthalensis*; group hunting of the large herd herbivores was organized on a large scale, but had been practised regularly since Acheulean times; painted and engraved art flourished conspicuously, but may have long existed on wooden objects and the walls of skin tents as the Mousterian painted and engraved objects from Tata in Hungary might suggest (Bordes, 1968, p. 110). Formalized speech communication can hardly be doubted for *Homo sapiens*, but even this development probably stretches back to the time of the appearance of *Homo erectus*. It is only the further intensification of Man's culture, accidents of preservation, our own ethnocentricity and the extremely localized but impressive evidence of elaborate social organizations in a very few advantageous areas, which have cumulatively combined to lay undue stress on the significance of the transition from *Home sapiens neanderthalensis* to *Homo sapiens sapiens*. Nevertheless, this Upper Palaeolithic phase marks the arrival of the genetic diversity of the hominids within the set of variety still to be found within the racial range of modern man.

Hominid group organization over the million years or so of the Pleistocene was probably as varied as the climatic and ecological environments which provided the oscillating context. This mosaic variety in band organization probably diversified progressively with the development of the later hominids, especially with the successful adaptation of peripheral groups to specialized survival within fresh ecosystems such as the temperate forest, steppe and tundra conditions in Europe north of the Mediterranean. Except in very advantageous coastal areas, perhaps including parts of the Mediterranean littoral, these diverse populations must have moved cyclically around large territories in order to take advantage of the seasonal harvests of groups of resources, in turn through the year. Such bands will have varied in social organization, role allocations, economic strategies, territorial areas, rotational schedules and varied in size from tens to perhaps hundreds, both from group to group and from season to season. It is probable that in the richer resource areas and seasons family bands could temporarily come together to form substantial tribes with a developed and elaborate social structure. But these are unusual conditions which seem to have prevailed from time to time in the Dordogne, the Ukraine and in one or two other environmentally favoured areas of middle and Mediterranean Europe. It is not surprising, therefore, to find in these favoured areas and periods many of the material trappings of rank insignia, prestige and display equipment and commodities, and, therefore, a developing system of exchange in rare and attractive materials and resources.

Sea-shells, animal teeth, boars' tusks, fossils and ivory plaques were perforated and sewn in hundreds on the caps and clothing of *élite* individuals, or strung in crescentic spacer-plate necklaces around the fur-caped shoulders of the powerful. The same restricted individuals also displayed their rank in intricately decorated and elaborately finished bone and probably wooden spearthrowers and batons of various kinds; super-elaborate versions of the focal artefacts of the community. Every kind of coloured stone was now collected and their sources noted – including amber, ophite, coloured jasper and quartz crystals, and red, yellow and black ochres. Equipped in his finery of fur and feathers, shells and teeth, his face fiercely painted in reds and yellows, the Gravettian and Magdalenian hunting-chiefs and shamans must have presented a deliberately impressive sight as they performed the ceremonial rituals which enshrined and conveyed their perception of Man's relationship with the world of nature.

Mediterranean and Black Sea shells were carried hundreds of miles inland to the Gravettian sites of the Ukraine, to the Mousterian sites of Hungary, and to many French Aurignacian and Solutrean sites. The Magdalenian culture group of Southern France was especially rich in perforated sea-shell finery – mainly *Dentalium*, *Nerilium*, *Columbella*, *Petunculus* and *Spondylus* shells brought from the Mediterranean and the Atlantic littoral. Utilitarian commodities also circulated within the same limited territories. Distinctive and desirable siliceous raw materials for artefacts were often selectively obtained from particular outcrops and sources. Slovakian obsidian and radiolarite was used, for example, at Polish Aurignacian sistes such as Zwierzyniec. White flecked flint from Świeciechów on the Middle Vistula circulated over an area of some 120 miles radius in Aurignacian and Szeletian contexts. Baltic flint from Silesia was exploited by Gravettian bands from Moravia, occurring at their winter sites 100 miles away through the Carpathian passes to the south (Jaźdźewski, 1965, pp. 37–47). Bitumen from the Styrian tar wells may also have circulated widely in Central Europe for tool hafting and waterproofing. Obsidian from Hungarian Mousterian and Aurignacian sites such as Ballovolgyer and Keckesgalyer seems to have come from the deposits 100 miles away in the Hegyalja range of the Carpathians (Vertes, 1959, pp. 21–40). Grand Pressigny flint was widely distributed amongst the Aurignacian and Gravettian groups of France (Clark, 1952, pp. 182–183). It is therefore quite apparent that the European stone and flint resources were already known in especially minute detail within particular territorial boundaries; as one might expect for the main technological raw material of the period. Doubtless other organic commodites may have circulated to the same limited extent – the furs and feathers of the tundra game, the hides, horns and antlers of the steppe beasts, and the wood, bark and resins of the timber stands.

One consistent pattern emerges from the surviving distributions of shells, pigments, and special stones – with very rare exceptions, the distributions are restricted to a limited area, usually no more than 100 miles in radius, often much less. This strongly suggests that these movements of raw materials and commodities must be placed within the context of mobile gathering-hunting-fishing bands, which of necessity continuously moved around large territories in their annual subsistence cycle. In this context, one resource or quarry outcrop may often simultaneously, yet successively, serve as a focus within the peripheral inter-section of several group territories, which would exploit that resource at different seasons of the year. Since a gathering-hunting-fishing terri-tory of 120 miles radius is not unusual for recent groups of this kind, it is not at all surprising to find a resource distribution unit of a similar dimension operating in Palaeolithic Europe. The rare cases of wider distributions can largely be accounted for in terms of peripheral gift exchanges or by the simultaneous yet successive exploitation of a com-mon resource, by several intersecting groups which would, therefore, on this simple model, be capable of a distribution unit of about 240 miles radius – perhaps in this respect fitting the distribution of Carpath-ian obsidian from the Middle Danube to the Ukraine.

In terms of this territorial model, we can perhaps discern the groups from the Garonne moving into the Pyrenees with the spring migration of bison and returning in the autumn with ophite and minerals from Isturitz (Les Rois B, Mouthiers: (Mouton and Joffrey, 1961)). From the Dordogne valley, other groups will have moved west to fish and seal on the Atlantic coast, returning with skins, shells and salmon verte-brae beads. Some will have followed the northern herds making the spring migration to the freshly exposed pastures of the Loire and Paris Basin in the north and the Auvergne plateau in the east – returning with Parisian fossil shells (Grotte du Renne), Grand Pressigny flint (Fontenioux), and coloured ochres from the rocks of the Auvergne (Leroi-Gourhan, 1961; Pradel, 1952, pp. 413–432). Presumably, other groups centred on the Mediterranean littoral will have carried sea-shells northwestwards into the Cevennes above the Dordogne; perhaps in spring and autumn movements from their Mediterranean winter bases. Much the same pattern may have framed the spring movements of Moravian hunters trekking northwards on to the Silesian plain, with their Czech flint, Styrian bitumen, and Hungarian obsidian artefacts, returning through the Moravian Gates in the autumn with their Baltic flint, amber nodules and northern furs.

In this way, the gathering-hunting-fishing bands will have moved around their territories, exploiting a sequence of material and organic resources in a formalized rotation, changing their group configuration and size in a rhythmic family dispersion and congregation as the resources seasonally permitted. Almost incidentally, raw materials and commodities would have been gathered from one spot and circulated with and amongst the family bands in their annual movements; per-haps, occasionally, some commodities might be exchanged with peri-pheral bands of other groups in largely ceremonial gift exchanges of partly symbolic and partly useful foreign commodities. Naturally, it would be such rare, colourful and exotic acquisitions that *élite* individuals would above all treasure and display as part of their prestige and status insignia. To some extent, therefore, the long-distance movement of desirable commodities will have been directly stimulated by the more elaborate ceremonial and social roles which the economies of the more advantageous areas could support – the chiefs and sub-chiefs, lineage headmen and hunt leaders, shamans and spirit doctors, tribal functionaries and skilled semi-specialists that might operate advantageously in uniting the temporary tribal band gatherings of the Dordogne, Moravia and the Ukraine. In these situations territories rich in natural resources could support unusually elaborate social structures with an unusual variety of social ranks, each requiring distinctive display insignia and therefore together stimulating gift exchange systems to satisfy these needs.

II. THE AGRARIAN ECONOMIES

Postglacial conditions, *ca* 10 000–6000 B.C., reintroduced heavily forested landscapes to middle and northern Europe, largely replacing the grasslands, steppe and tundra and their big, herd herbivores with thick forest vegetation and the mainly small or scattered game associated with these environments. The gathering-hunting-fishing bands responded to these changes with more scattered and less specialized social structures and economies – the agile individual stalking of forest deer with the bow replaced the communal *battue* and the open country spear and spearthrower techniques. In the Mediterranean zone of Europe, these postglacial changes were less dramatic and indeed hardly detectable outside a general trend towards drier conditions and fluctuations in marginal mountain and plateau zones. The Mediterranean gatherer-hunter-fishers therefore show a marked continuity of Palaeolithic techniques in interrelated Epipalaeolithic complexes which remained comparatively densely deployed in advantageous areas of the Mediterranean littoral.

The threshold marking the establishment of the first simple agrarian economies in Europe is, therefore, as complex a series of events and changes as any we have to discuss. Gathering, hunting and fishing continued as vigorously as ever, both beyond the territories of the peasant settlers and, indeed, as a significant subcultural activity within the agricultural communities. Stone technology remained the basis of artefact manufacture, and the Palaeolithic cognitive map of the primary resources of Europe still contributed the main framework for exploitation; everywhere the continuity of the aboriginal gatherer-hunter-fisher communities is to some extent attested.

Nevertheless, from the seventh millennium onwards, southern Europe was increasingly networked by new kinds of sociocultural unit which gradually repatterned the social, economic, religious and psychological configuration of most of the populations of Europe. Within the space of two thousand years, *ca* 6000–4000 B.C., peasant villagers had cut and burnt their way from one end of forested Europe to the other, spreading a lattice of village communities with a population density per square mile hitherto unparalleled in any except the most advantageous aboriginal territories of the continent – and therein quite unmatched for economic stability and potential. The basis for this population deployment was cereal agriculture backed by stock-rearing and balanced by gathering, hunting and fishing as before; the forest-consuming stone adze and fire, the antler and crook-branch hoe, the ceramic pottage bowl and the storage jar were the artefacts of the age. The slow retreat of the Scandinavian ice-cap and the collapse of its peripheral glacial weather system set the context of this threshold in European development. The ensuing postglacial optimum introduced the Atlantic climatic phase in Europe north of the Mediterranean – a warm, wet phase with a mean annual temperature some $2-2\frac{1}{2}$ °C above those now prevailing and lasting almost 3000 years, *ca* 5000–2000 B.C. The period of optimal warmth fell broadly *ca* 4000–3000 B.C. and brought to a climax the dense mixed forest of oak, elm, lime and alder which then stretched almost without interruption from the Carpathians to the North Sea, parted only occasionally by the sinuous highways of the major river systems and the Alpine heights.

The expansion of the agrarian frontier from the Mediterranean littoral to the fringes of the northern coniferous forests was a process of the greatest importance for the subsequent economic development of Europe. The initial foci in which the separate elements of this new and complex set of economic strategies had first appeared was further east – in that elliptical football which encloses the Anatolian and the Iranian plateaus. These two great middle-altitude plateaus, with their rain-trapping mountain rims and their then moderate climate, were for the most part rolling grasslands filled with herbivore herds and scattered belts of oak, cedar and pistachio woodlands. Amongst these wild grasses were the ancestors of the agrarian cereals – emmer, einkorn, barley, millet and oats; amongst the herbivores grazing on these grasses and woodlands were the ancestors of the domestic animals – sheep, goat, pigs and wild cattle. The trees of the plateau parkland also included most of the orchard fruit- and nut-trees – almond, pistachio, wild grapes, figs, apples, pears and others. On the northwestern flanks of this area, the Anatolian wild einkorn cereal spilled into adjacent Mediterranean Balkan Europe and Greece. To the south of the plateaus, emmer and barley

were also to be found in scattered stands along the temperate altitudes
of the Lebanon Range, probably extending as far south as Sinai. It
was in these plateau and peripheral territories that the gathered food
supplies were at first trivially augmented by fencing and resowing small
patches of wild grasses for their seeds, by protecting and propagating
the trees which produced fruit or nuts; other techniques were also developed for capturing female animals and their young alive, to be
penned up against hard times; the simplest way to preserve food
supplies was to keep the staples alive. The gatherer-hunter-fishers in
these limited but diverse territories were thus increasingly able to stabilize their food supply in a run of good and bad years by a little supplementary horticulture and stock-rearing.

The initial mosaic of regional experiments in food regulation took
place between *ca* 10 000–6000 B.C. around and within the primary plateau areas, assisted by the fluctuating desiccations of some of the more
marginal terrain in conjunction with the breakdown of the ice-cap
weather system in northern Europe. The gatherer-hunter-fishers of
these southern areas had already, for many millennia, seasonally harvested and pulverized the seeds, fruits, nuts and legumes of the proto-
domesticates, including – the cereal seeds, alfalfa, ryegrass and flax
seeds, wild caper, almonds, pistachio nuts, acorns, peas, beans, lentils,
Astragalus and *Trigonella*, wild grapes, figs, apples and pears. Over the
same vast inland area, with its negligible river and lake resources, the
wide absence of fish, shellfish and other forms of aquatic protein helped
to emphasize the prolonged and intimate hunting acquaintance of the
gatherer-hunters with the ancestors of the domestic animals – sheep,
goat, cattle and pigs. Retrospectively, it is possible to distinguish
markedly regional and localized gatherer-hunter band economies,
stabilized with idiosyncratic combinations of semi-domesticates –
sheep, goat and barley here, goats, legumes and orchard trees there,
cattle, pigs and einkorn elsewhere. Band contact and interaction coincided with convergent conditions to pool the economic strategies and
staples of the local groups until, by the seventh millennium, these had
stabilized into a limited set of widespread agrarian systems based on
combinations of principle staples – sheep, goat, pig, cattle with emmer,
einkorn, barley cereals, plus peas, beans, lentils and apples, pears and
nuts balanced against continued gathering, hunting and fishing. A
large number of semi-independent regional subsistence props were thus
increasingly and successively integrated within a smaller number of
balanced economic systems, in which the props had become the main
pillars of the new, more extensively mixed strategies. The three-sided
equilibrium triangle of the gatherer-hunter-fisher economies was now
a stabilized polygon with fresh agrarian resource dimensions and a

capacity for the territorially dense occupation of long-term settlement sites producing an annual food surplus.

Around 6000 B.C., perhaps earlier in places, the first definite traces of agrarian settlers are found in Europe. These settlements are restricted to the Balkan Mediterranean zone immediately adjacent to the Anatolian plateau, and tightly confined to the ecological niches already occupied by the wild prototypes of the new domesticates; it is even possible that the territories of this area were fully within the zone of primary developments, but this has yet to be demonstrated. On the fertile plains of Macedonia and Bulgarian Thrace, settlers from northwestern Anatolia extended a growing network of substantial villages of flat-roofed rectangular houses, using ceramic containers for their cereal gruels and stews. The grassy plain of Thessaly, directly linked with southern Anatolia by the island chain from the Gulf of Volos, now began to support numerous small villages in which pottery was still unknown, although emmer wheat, barley, peas, beans and lentils were grown, sheep and goats reared, and the same fruit and nut trees maintained as those found in the Anatolian and Iranian plateau areas.

However, the ecological personality of Europe is not so closely similar to that of the Mediterranean plateaus and littoral to permit a wholesale intrusion without adaptive modification. Geological contortions have contrived to rim the Mediterranean basin on its northern periphery with a semi-continuous chain of formidable mountains which drop precipitately to the narrow littoral plains. The altitude of this chain, together with its consequent rainfall and winter snows, combine to extend fingers of temperate middle European and Alpine ecology to the very edge of the Mediterranean itself. The plains of Bulgarian Thrace, Macedonia and Thessaly are abruptly walled by plateaus and peaks which then carried belts of temperate European deciduous oak forest below an Alpine beech and fir band, the whole populated by elements of middle European fauna – deer, mountain goat, wild cattle, boar, bear and wolf. The indigenous European gatherer-hunter-fisher band territories must already have embraced most of the surface area of the continent, but with these largely mobile populations the occupation density was insignificant, except along the Mediterranean, Atlantic and Baltic littoral zones, where marine and land resources were complementary; in these latter areas, there is every evidence that the ancient populations continued and gradually re-equipped and repatterned under agrarian acculturation.

Northwards again, beyond the Mediterranean outliers of the mid-European ecology, there lay a far more formidable environmental cordon, barring the northwestern exit of the great Hungarian plain in a broad diagonal band, where the Austrian Alps threaten to join the

Little Carpathians, only 40 miles away across the Danube. The formidable character of this natural Maginot line was complicated for the Mediterranean agronomists by the even-wetter-than-present Atlantic climate which prevailed beyond it and by the reinforcing complexity of its separate ecological factors which provided a cumulative defence in depth. Northwest of this band lay the European glacial soils and clays, the long, snowy European winters, the heavy annual rainfall, the short cloudy summers and the primeval deciduous oak forest, in a climax form several millennia old – an uncleared tangle of massive, fallen, dead and decaying trunks 3–10 feet thick, interlaced by the formidable undergrowth which a damp, ungrazed deciduous forest supports. That this primary forest exists nowhere in Europe today is a tribute to generations of peasant farmers and a relentless clearance against which the forest finally capitulated only in late Medieval times. The aboriginal gatherer-hunter-fishers had always lived in and through the forest, their own friendly englobing environment; to the land-using peasant farmer this forest was a hostile ogre which must be felled with the axe and burnt with fire. It is little wonder that European peasant folktales to this day are uniformly dominated by the contrast struck between the friendly open villages and the threatening forest, with its stock of menacing inhabitants – from wolves and bears to magical shamans and bands of little forest people; the socioeconomic significance of the young woodman as a folk-hero was perhaps similar to that now reserved for Russian tractor drivers.

The Mediterranean farming communities simply skirted and outflanked the southernmost European defences, utilizing but not settling the higher zones of the Pindus and Balkan Mountain massifs. The seventh millennium villages therefore extended their network along the rivers and coasts, where important supplementary food supplies were always available and communication was easy. They moved inland around the peripheries of the great ranges, following the fertile valley soils and the Mediterranean micro-environments which extended far up the ascending Danube, Maritsa, Kara Su, Struma and Vardar rivers. By exploiting this deep peripheral penetration of aspects of Mediterranean ecology into lowland Bulgaria and Macedonia, some peasant groups were able to infiltrate the great Hungarian plain without the necessity for drastic cultural adaptation. However, those communities on the northwestern Hungarian frontier and those on the higher headwaters of the Balkan–Serbian plateau rivers were gradually forced into closer and closer mutual adjustment with Middle European fauna and flora in its less dense development. In these transitional areas, an important first acquaintance and elementary knowledge of European resources was gradually established; timber increasingly replaced *pisé* in house construction, ridge roofs were adopted against the wet Atlantic climate, the range of stone axe and adze types proliferated in response to the forest environment. Suitable stone for adzes and arte-facts rapidly became a resource of great importance and, doubtless, some knowledge of the properties of the strange stones, timbers, edible roots, berries, nuts, animals and plants will have been gained from the aboriginal groups into the midst of whom the peasant settlers were moving.

A peasant community of this period may be usefully illustrated by the riverside village at Lepenski Vir, on the Danube east of Belgrade, carbon dated at 4950 ± 150 B.C. The village of 30–35 trapezoidal houses was set on a terraced spur above the whirlpool which has given the site its name. The whirlpool, it materialized, was an important resource in its own right – sucking surface water and food down to the depths where huge sturgeon, catfish and carp permanently hovered and ate their fill, to be netted and harpooned by the villagers. The situation of the village within the steep Danube gorge tightly restricted the agri-cultural land to small garden-size pockets, but this could be set against the advantages of the immediately adjacent river resources and those of the limestone cliffs which soar from 300 to 700 metres above the site. In effect, the limestone canyon concentrated at one locus the separate resource and microclimate zones of the Danube, its shallows, the warm environment of the beach terraces and the village site, the temperate forest and animals of the middle slopes and the cool montane peaks beyond. The strategy of this site location may reflect the relatively small part played by cereal "garden horticulture" in the Lepenski Vir economy and, certainly, the plentiful fish bones, wild boar, wild cattle, deer and small carnivore remains eloquently reflect the natural resources of the vertical hierarchy of resource zones adjacent to the site (Nandris, 1968, pp. 64–70).

By the fifth millennium, similar small village communities were strung along the Mediterranean littoral and islands, from the Aegean and Adriatic to the coasts of Spain, France and North Africa. These coastal communities also relied heavily on the rich harvest of sardine, tunny, shellfish and Mediterranean seals to augment their small patches of cereals and their herds of sheep and goats. Many of these coastal communities seem to represent convergent acculturation and the spread of artefacts and techniques amongst the pre-existing and rela-tively populous, interrelated gatherer-fisher-hunter bands of the Epirote-Adriatic, Franco-Italian and Ibero-Mauritanian Epipalaeo-lithic complexes. The inland penetration of Europe was only slightly slower, the village network rapidly extending to the boundaries of the Hungarian plain by the end of the sixth millennium. Villages strung along the river networks of the Balkans and deployed in chains north from Thessaly and Macedonia, up the river Vardar, down the river Morava to the Danube and thence northwards along the well-drained terraces of the Körös. Along this filigree linkage, large shells from the Aegean *Spondylus* mussel were exchanged from hand to hand in the form of necklaces of cylindrical shell beads, or as bracelets cut from entire shells; the mute surviving traces of what was once probably an intensive two-way exchange of Mediterranean against European commodities.

The infiltration of the Balkan uplands had already acquainted the peasant farmers with some aspects of European fauna and flora in the atypical Mesomediterranean bioclimatic zone. However, the north-western Hungarian threshold to the true mid-European ecology required the relentless peasant persistence of the whole fifth millennium before successful adaptations and mutations amongst the societies, material culture, crops and animals of the farmers enabled them to emerge with a stably integrated cultural format; one capable of pene-trating the mid-European environment – the inner frontier of reinforc-ing glacial soils, thick deciduous forest, sharp winters and wet summers. This pioneer penetration was apparently accomplished by the Danu-bian peasants from the northwestern fringes of the Körös network. Tightly organized in small lineage communities, these pioneers slowly forged a technique of slash-and-burn hoe agriculture in forest clearings on loess slopes, thus exploiting the virgin fertility of the finest, well-drained glacial soils in a rotational schedule around the settlements of neat, large timber longhouses. Cattle and stock were few, and even these were probably stalled for much of the inclement winter in the aisles of the great thatched longhouses. Adzes of carefully selected and widely exchanged tough igneous stones characterize the challenge presented by the forest to these peasants; a challenge successfully overcome only by a careful integration of selected soils, cereals and domestic animals, within a skilful strategy combining settlement stability with the repeti-tive short-term exploitation of fresh loess plots, meeting the forest with socially organized co-operative effort using fire and the adze.

The favoured loess soils were originally precipitated in long narrow bands by the prevailing winds blowing moraine rock dust southwards from the ice face of the long withdrawn Eurasiatic ice-cap. Almost by accident, therefore, these fertile and well-drained soils form a narrow discontinuous fillet of settlement areas, extending from the Ukraine to the Paris Basin in one direction and from Iran to the Hwang-Ho in another. Within the space of little more than 200 or 300 years, the Danubian peasants had multiplied and proliferated their villages along the whole loess chain from the Ukraine to the coasts of the North Sea. Over the same period, other very similar communities, using closely similar economic strategies, dispersed eastwards from northern Iran into northwestern China.

This peasant penetration of continental Europe has often been compared with the European frontier in forested America. The frontiersmen in both situations showed that cultural adaptation was the key to survival and the first European peasants found a very great deal to learn from the spare but minutely adapted indigenous gatherer-hunter-fisher bands. This must expecially have been the case with regard to information on forest craft, gathering-fishing-hunting schedules, local resources and the peculiar properties of the European fauna and flora. The outcrops of hard rocks, decorative coloured ochres and the sharp siliceous stones essential for tool production, were already well known to the local aborigines, as we have seen, and widely distributed within the mobile bands themselves. Now we have a context of a more static village network, supporting a relatively dense population actively engaged in forest clearance; a context which therefore required the intensive exploitation and regular dispersal of the commodities by deliberately adjusted exchange mechanisms operating over far wider fields than the unit band territory and its simple multiples, observed in the preceding phases of European prehistory.

The quarrying of stone, obsidian, flint and coloured ochres had already been extensively practised by some of the gatherer-hunter-fisher bands and, even in these early contexts, it now appears that a limited amount of shallow shaft mining was already practised before the sixth millennium. Szeletian gatherers seem to have quarried a considerable quantity of soft ochre from "paint" mine shafts near Lovas, in Hungary, as early as Wurm I–II, *ca* 35 000 B.C., and comparable workings for a haematite pigment are known from the Kamienna river valley in Poland; significantly, both sites document an intensive Palaeolithic exploitation of coloured pigments in areas where no Palaeolithic painting now survives (Mezaros and Vertés, 1955). The shallow surface quarries for flint at Grand Pressigny and the Belcayre Plateau, in France, were already being exploited by Palaeolithic bands, whilst later gatherer-hunter-fishers extracted quartzite from the quarries at Wommersom in Belgium and flint nodules from the pits at Orońsko in central Poland (de Sonneville-Bordes, 1960; Clark, 1952, pp. 182–183; Jaźdżewski, 1905, p. 56). At the latter site, several hundred pits had been cut some 10 feet deep into the clay to recover the chocolate-coloured flint, the nodules were then worked into rough-outs on extensive surface working-floors, dating *ca* 5600–5000 B.C. It now seems probable that shallow pit and shaft mining had been a frequent practice amongst the large gatherer-hunter-fisher communities of the postglacial north European forests and that the more intensive Neolithic mining over the same territory represents yet one more element in the cultural continuity of this area from late Gravettian, through Maglemose and Ertebølle times, to the early funnel-beaker farmers of the fourth millennium.

However, even the most elaborate quarrying sites of the gatherer-hunter-fisher bands only represent the cumulative consequences of thousands of annual visits, in the course of their enforced movements around the resources of their territories; activities largely, but not entirely, confined to satisfying only the immediate needs of the groups concerned. In contrast, Neolithic mining developed a more advanced semi-specialist status, supported by the increasingly populous agrarian communities and pressured by their voracious demand for axe and adze blades for use in forest clearance. Hundreds of shafts were now successively sunk from 30 to 60 feet through the chalk at focal mining centres, from the Malmö area of Sweden and adjacent Denmark, to Spiennes in Belgium, Grimes Graves and Easton Down in England, to Krzemionki in Poland. In the Mediterranean too, flint was mined from deep tunnels in the limestone at Monte Tabuto, Sicily, and at mainland sites in Apulia; these supplies were also supplemented by limited exchange networks circulating the highly prized obsidian from Lipari, Italy, and the Aegean islands (Clark, 1952, p. 174). In most of these centres of intensive mining, there is evidence of an organization and output superior to that found in the simple pits of the gatherer-hunter-fishers. Special raw materials were gathered from widely distant areas to facilitate the mining operations – hundreds of short-lived antler picks were required, special tough mining axes and mauls were employed, quantities of fat were needed for the dish lamps, not to mention wedges, mallets, shovels and baskets. No less than 244 discarded antler picks were recovered from two of the pits at Grimes Graves, Norfolk. Especially tough igneous stone tools were also imported for the mining activities – Cornish greenstone was employed at Grimes Graves, and picks, hammers, adzes, and mauls of Silesian gabbro and basalt were used at Krzemionki.

The output of such mining centres is likely to have reached many thousands of finished rough-outs per season and, at the Norwegian island quarry of Hespriholmen alone, it has been estimated that some 20 000 boat loads of greenstone had been extracted (Clark, 1965, p. 8). This degree of organization and redistribution is obviously far greater than that necessary to satisfy the requirements of local communities. The periodic exploitation of these resources had clearly been transformed into at least a long annual season of preparation and mining by semi-specialists from nearby villages – probably 20 or 30 men and women successively opening-up four or five deep mines, in the dry season necessary for safe shaft sinking. Although only a few people may have been involved, supplies had to be gathered on a large scale and the mined nodules worked into tool blanks by surface knappers, repetitively employing their special technological skills. Finally, the flint, obsidian or stone ingots had to be distributed over a wide area in exchange for other commodities.

The distribution patterns of these thousands of surplus blades, cores, axes and adzes fully confirm the implications of the more extensive deep mining activities. Whereas the gatherer-hunter-fisher distribution units spanned a hundred or so miles of sparse dispersion, now it is commonplace to find quantities of these "factory" products extending in asymmetrical distribution fans, frequently stretching 200 or 300 miles from the self-same resource centres. It is significant that these factory centres developed a mutually adjusting distribution pattern such that every area could gain supplies from several centres, although one source was usually predominant. This complex distribution outfall could only have been sustained within the context of very active and well-organized systems of interlinked ceremonial gift exchange cycles. These exchange rings will also have circulated other commodities in both directions – pigs, dogs, axes, shells, teeth, boars' tusks, ochres, pitch, furs, feathers, amber, beads, bracelets, pots, obsidian, copper trinkets and display gear, selected artefacts and cereals. The stone axe and copper artefact distribution patterns are, therefore, of the greatest interest mainly as the only surviving skeletal trace of this continuous but swelling traffic in European commodities of all kinds (Clark, 1965).

The premise of "Neolithic self-sufficiency" is therefore only relatively acceptable, if at all. The circulation of European commodities may not have been quantitatively very large, nor very essential in terms of subsistence, but nevertheless the elaborate network of exchange partners, village markets, and resource centres successfully distributed local commodities far beyond the territories within which they had formerly been restricted; the new mobility of commodities thus serving to compensate for the growing requirements of the more static agrarian communities. This traffic incidentally but significantly extended the transmission of many new artefacts and materials, customs and games, stories and religious tenets, and other novel items quite unrelated to the formal commodity content of the exchange networks. The drive in this traffic was the display and consumption of commodities required for the continuous "rites-of-passage" of the tribesman's life-cycle. The circulating machinery for this traffic was the cross-cultural gift exchange network, involving short-distance movements of porters or canoes. The outcome of this traffic was the expanding development of extensive trade networks, linking hundreds of otherwise unrelated communities in the rapid dissemination of innovations and commodities, with mutually beneficial results; a traffic which supported an important rise in the territorial potential of formerly marginal evnironments now coupled multilinearly with various areas of more stable output.

III. THE AEGEAN NETWORK AND THE EARLY BRONZE TECHNOLOGIES

Throughout the fourth and third millennia, the agrarian tribesmen of Europe continued to hoe and weed, hunt and fish, gather and store, whilst the exchange networks serving the settled communities increasingly replaced the old forest trails of the mobile gatherer-hunter-fishers. Even the inhabitants of the northern coniferous forests had adopted limited aspects of the new subsistence patterns, and in the west almost every Atlantic island had become the home of settled communities. Thus, the wide range of European ecology was increasingly reflected in the diversified mosaic of cultures, from the peasant fishermen of the Mediterranean littoral, to the lineage communities collectively cultivating the clearings of the Scandinavian forests, and from the lakeside cabins of the Alpine farmers to the large, timber and pisé fortified villages on the Balkan mounds. However, significant innovations had already begun to appear; restricted to the Balkan and Mediterranean zone at first, but spreading to the inland territories through the intercommunicating village network. Copper metallurgy, including the production of simple arsenical alloys, slowly became an important feature of the Balkan village centres after ca 3500 B.C., although the new mineral remained disadvantageously expensive and rare in middle and northern Europe until the Alpine, Saxo-Thuringian and Bohemian lodes were opened up, after ca 2500 B.C. An innovation with far more extensive repercussions also spread through the same areas, about the same time – the ard, or simple plough. Between ca 2500–2000 B.C. the ard widely replaced the hoe as the primary agricultural tool of the peasant farmers of Europe, rapidly transforming the amount of land one man could bring under cultivation, increasing the demand for land and the surplus from it, and revolutionizing attitudes towards land, property, inheritance and kinship obligations. The complex dissemination of the ard, yoke, ox-traction, wheeled vehicles, the sled, copper alloy technology jointly combined with the drier conditions of the developing Subboreal period cumulatively to transform middle Europe, crossing the threshold ca 2500–2000 B.C.

Meanwhile, major developments in Egypt and Mesopotamia had advanced to a critical stage, affecting the economic and social patterns of their own and immediately adjacent peoples. Sprawling townships began to manifest a higher degree of central organization and an increasing degree of subcultural specialization; urban chiefdoms were developing into regional city states, dependent on the surplus of a penumbra of scattered villages. The enlarging spheres of political interest of these urban centres began to tessellate the countryside and, inevitably, boundary conflicts about peripheral resources became a frequent source of conflict along the great river valleys. In the ceaseless mutual adjustment of conquest and submission, organization and reorganization, larger and larger political units emerged to redistribute the expanding food surplus from the villagers' irrigation and plough agriculture. By *ca* 3500 B.C., the competitive conflict between city and city, nome and nome, had already fully developed; by *ca* 3000 B.C., great states and territorial kingdoms had condensed from this aggregating and segregating process. Menes, the King of Upper Egypt, conquered the delta nomes and ruled the Nile from the first cataract to the Mediterranean; in Mesopotamia, the copper-sheathed phalanxes and battle-wagons of the Kings of Ur, Lagash and Eridu fought for temporary ascendancy until Sargon of Akkad established his short-lived empire in the twenty-fourth century B.C.

The emergence of new social and political units in the valleys of the Nile, the Tigris and the Euphrates had wide repercussions. The rambling tribal towns of Anatolia, Syria and Palestine were already two and three millennia old, but they did not compare in size, degree of organization or potential with the new cities and the new city states; the *civis* and civilization had arrived. The new urban centres were deliberately aimed at the objective of optimal economic output for the greater aggrandizement of the city managers and their state; in this world of competing powers, only the most powerful could remain independent. The focal urban centres drew surplus resources from the countryside on an increasing scale and the central authority organized scribes and officials, with their scripts and seals, to note, count and reallocate the stored surplus to other specialists and artificers, these in turn produced more consumer goods and more complex artefacts. The cities were vast amplifying units plugged into the old Neolithic network of villages, raw materials were sucked in and complex social and material products turned out, but since power and prestige centred in the possession of these complex new products, this output largely remained the restricted property of the temple staff and the king's servants. The temple and the palace were not merely the centres of political and religious power, they were impressive factory centres with whole wings set aside for the reserves of raw materials and magazines of finished products, together with the workshops of the tied artificers; these buildings were simultaneously centres of state, wealth and finance, commercial banks, arsenals, granaries and storehouses for state reserves of all kinds. The palace and temple were the commercial and industrial centres of the revenue state and they survived in these capacities until the collapse of the Byzantine empire and the political elevation of the merchant classes and the self-made capitalists.

These events were seemingly remote from the European tribesmen of the third millennium, but the consequences of these new political organisms, deep in Asia Minor and far across the Mediterranean, reached out to the very borders of Europe, whilst their indirect repercussions sped far beyond direct contacts. The new network of cities and city states expanded over and above the existing lattice of simple villages, which in many ways continued almost unchanged; the new phenomenon was largely a subcultural revolution in which certain restricted castes could benefit from the enlarged revenue extracted from groups of villages. The new political powers therefore depended upon an uninterrupted supply of resources and raw materials. Initially, the bulk of the food requirements could be supplied from local territories, but it was certain strategic raw materials which now necessitated the efficient organization of commodities which had previously trickled in by gift exchange – formal trade was the solution. In the alluvial valleys of the Nile, the Tigris and the Euphrates, the strategic raw materials primarily included big timber for chariots, carts, ships and buildings as well as metals for the tools of production and the weapons of military power. Large and regular quantities of copper were necessary together with the more limited tin supplies later required to make hard bronze. In time, the consignments of tin almost came to assume the strategic importance and political significance that has been attached in modern times to tungsten for steel armour plate and machine tools, or latterly to oil supplies and uranium deposits.

The dynasts of Egypt and Mesopotamia organized increasingly more extensive land and sea networks to supply the raw materials necessary for the maintenance of the state against its rivals. At first, this supply organization was less in the form of continuous flow, two-directional trade as we now understand that term and rather more in the form of annual military expeditions to the resource areas; if the resource area was peripheral to several major states, it would thus become a politically and militarily contested area. Should the population of the resource area prove hostile, they were regularly attacked and looted; if they were more pragmatic, they supplied the expedition's requirements and, in return, the *élite* caste were given rich embassies and treasures and left in peace. Thus, royal gift-exchange became a political and economic procedure for the diplomatic ratification of certain mutual obligations, at the same time linking *élite* castes cross-culturally to an extent often endorsed by intermarriage. Under more peaceful conditions, these expeditions could increasingly be left to professional merchants under armed escort, with regular caravans of pack donkeys and two-wheeled ox carts. These merchants were often required by local rulers to reside only in limited quarters of their towns and such merchant quarters or *karum* then provided all the local facilities of commercial banks and caravanserai. In this way, the local potentates in distant towns were able to take advantage of the routes through their territories to tax and tithe the mechandise passing through, thus materially augmenting the riches and political power of their own dynasty and town.

The proliferating trade networks, therefore, had the general consequence of inducing the formation and agglomeration of many small buffer states and dynasties amongst the already populous tribal townships and chiefdoms of Anatolia and the Levant. Thus, the economic activities of the great states seem to have been instrumental in the rise of the barbarous Hittite kingdom under its earliest dynasts, Pitkhana and Anittas, around their town of Kussura, *ca* 2000 B.C. and in the similar rise of the enriched city states of the Levant: Aleppo, Alalakh, Byblos, Tarsus, Carchemish and Ugarit. Beyond these, the network stretched to the earliest palace kingdoms of Knossos, Mallia and Phaistos on the Cretan plains, and Alasia in copper-rich Cyprus. Even at the most distant boundaries of Anatolia and Europe, the nameless dynasts of Troy II and Dorak seem to have governed small frontier states which may have respectively encompassed Lemnos, Imbros, Tenedos, Gallipoli and the Troad at one end of the Straits, and the Bosporus at the other – barbarous kingdoms with their feet both in Anatolia and Europe. Even beyond these fringes of urban civilization, lay the diminutive but proud halls of the petty Helladic chiefdoms of Lerna on the Gulf of Argos, at Orchomenos on Lake Copais, at Dimini in the Thessalian plain, and at the lesser sites of the Ezero culture in the plains of Bulgarian Thrace. By 2000 B.C. the great imperial powers were focally set amidst an expanding mosaic of vassal kingdoms and free city states, distantly tessellated into a peripheral band of greater and lesser urban and non-urban tribal chiefdoms – a replicating pattern partly precipitated by the organization of the great powers themselves.

It is only when one grasps the scale and dimensions of the new trading enterprises in comparison with the preceding scale of these activities that their indirect importance for Europe becomes apparent. About 2350 B.C., Sargon of Akkad led an expedition northwards into central Anatolia to assist his merchants in the city of Puruskhanda, returning by way of the Silver Mountains (Taurus) and the Cedar Mountains (Amanus). Silmultaneously, the same king could boast that his southern trade network was such that ships lay at harbour in front of his

Mesopotamian palace from Tilmun (Bahrain), Makkan (Persian Gulf) and Meluhha (Gulf of Oman); thus Sargon's network directly drew upon commodities within a radius of one thousand miles and indirectly even beyond that. Caravans of 300 donkeys and a dozen carts travelling 500 miles became a regular occurrence, carrying, on occasion, $12\frac{1}{2}$ tons of tin in a single load – sufficient for 125 tons of hard bronze, or enough to equip the total armoury of a small state. The Pharaohs of the earliest dynasties also regularly sent annual expeditions to Sinai for copper and to Lebanon for timber; in 2650 B.C. alone, the Pharaoh Sneferu brought back 40 shiploads of cedar logs in a single expedition to Byblos. The Levant was rapidly becoming a crucial area of resources simultaneously sought by Egypt, Mesopotamia and Anatolia; only 30 years before the maritime expedition of Sneferu, in 2680 B.C., King Gudea of Lagash had been collecting timber in the same area on his expedition from Mesopotamia. With these intersecting spheres of economic interest, the great powers of Egypt and Mesopotamia were inevitably brought into a military and political involvement which culminated in the Egyptian conquest of the entire Syrian coastline from Sinai to Byblos, under the pharaohs of the XIIth dynasty *ca* 2050–1900 B.C., broadly contemporary with the Sumerian empire of the IIIrd dynasty at Ur, *ca* 2150–2000 B.C.

Beyond the frontier kingdom of Troy, donkey caravans (Zeuner, 1965) may even have trekked annually to the barbaric chiefdoms on the defended mounds of Bulgaria to load woollen cloth, copper, gold, timber and incidental curiosities. More distant still, there now arose tribal chiefdoms scattered along the Danube and in adjacent areas of middle Europe, marked by the rich burials of the chieftains themselves and by the scattered bronze and gold hoards of their personal treasuries. These chiefdoms were the organized consequence of economic surplus, advantageous location and the indirect stimuli emanating from the Aegean, a political precipitate of efficient village agrarian economies using the plough, bronze tools, the cart, the sled and the canoe. The chiefdoms stimulated the exploitation of local copper, gold and tin resources, and organized the exchange networks bringing amber, furs and other products from the north and faience beads, metal vessels and prestige weaponry from the south.

The rise of the middle European Aunjetitz and Tumulus tribal chiefdoms and their short-lived, unstable confederacies were directly related to the rise of intensive European cereal and pastoral agriculture; the more dense population and its more complex economic organization stimulated the redistribution of produce and commodities within more centralized tribal configurations. In this context, and with these early bronze technologies, the metalwork was almost entirely the expensive vehicle for status and rank manifestation: the caste marks of the chief, his kin and his dependent artificers. The showy bronze weaponry and the gold and amber gew-gaws commanded respect and even the few bronze tools only served to produce more equipment to further distinguish the owners of the means of production and to endorse their right to redistribute the communal surplus. The social consequence, although expressed with particular cultural variations, was a cumulative cycle tending to make the *élite* even more wealthy and powerful, stimulating more and more subcultural specialization and differentiation, thus promoting an overall proliferation in cultural castes and social subdivisions.

The intensive plough agriculture produced a surplus for redistribution by the *élite*; the *élite* exchanged the surplus for weaponry, display trinkets and tools for their smiths and artificers; the *élite* became more powerful and took more surplus from more villages and hired more specialists. One man with a plough could free many women from hoeing to specialize in household industries, especially weaving. The surplus cloth joined the surplus foodstuffs, the products of the specialist bronzesmiths and carpenters, and the land ploughed by a man's own efforts, to add to the increased diversity of property. Property itself increased the importance of vertical genealogies and, thus, formalized inheritance patterns within kin groups rapidly became an important and complex machinery for the restriction of property within the bounds of increasingly well-defined complex castes.

Elaborate feuding and hospitality systems probably developed, which at one and the same time could ensure the safe conduct of trade commodities, metal supplies, artificers, merchants and caravans and yet, beyond an invisible line, would permit wholesale piracy, the taking of captives, looting, warfare and murder in pursuit of valuable staples. The increased importance of wealth hoards and the economic desirability of male captives as miners and slaves, or female captives for weaving and handicrafts, would probably have played an important part in a general increase in raiding and, therefore, in the escalation of settlement defences and in weaponry. Indeed, all the traditional elements of the "heroic societies" were now emerging: the increasingly integrated functional developments of intensive economy, metal-using cultures – tribal chiefdoms, socially stratified castes, dependent specialists, elaborate property inheritance, genealogies, feuding and hospitality systems (Goody, 1969). Although doubtless taking many different regional forms, amidst a variety of surviving archaic social patterns, the rise of the European chiefdoms nevertheless witnessed the rise of centrally co-ordinated redistributional societies, in which ceremonial gift exchange as an activity of largely sociological importance was increasingly supplemented by organized trade as an activity of major economic significance (Service, 1966, pp. 143–144).

The elaborate bronze technology and the social apparatus for its maintenance seems partly to have spread through Europe by acquisitive diffusion and internal social reorganization, and partly by tribal movements along the Danube. South of the Carpathian–Sudeten ring, the existing cultures widely adopted the Balkan–Anatolian ceramic and artefact styles of the Proto-Aunjetitz group *ca* 1800 B.C., including plain burnished and metallic ceramics, tin bronze, bivalve moulds, riveted metalwork, rapiers, daggers, helmets, halberds and dress pins. North of this basin, these innovations seem largely to represent the cross-cultural aggrandizement of existing tribal castes, so that "Aunjetitz" metal styles are found widely outside the restricted boundaries of that particular culture. The local chieftains seem quickly to have developed the exploitation of their territorial metal ores and intensive shaft mining, smelting and casting was linked to an efficient redistribution network marked by hoards of copper ingot torques and ingot bars for alloying and reworking in the chief's smithy. In this context, a single hoard from Altenburg on the Austrian border, is reputed to have contained 1000 Aunjetitz copper ingot torques (Childe, 1929, p. 233).

The unsettled conditions developed by the feuding chiefdoms themselves have left us a range of such metalwork caches, from heterogeneous wealth, hoards of weapons, trinkets, scrap, gold, amber, tin and faience to the ingot depots abandoned on the routes radiating from the mining centres. Markedly regional schools of bronze technology quickly emerged and strongly suggest networks of individuals inheriting an occupational caste and trained by an interlinked set of bronze masters. Not only did these regional bronze schools flourish around the mining areas of Iberia, North Italy, the Alps, Bohemia, Moravia, Saxo-Thuringia, Brittany and in the Hiberno-Scottish zone, but the redistributional capacity of the trade network was now such that major bronze schools could be supported in areas without metal ores – notably the remarkable Danish bronze tradition and the Wessex school in Britain.

The period *ca* 2000–1400 B.C. in Europe therefore frames the rise of sophisticated political chiefdoms, a restricted but capable grid of regional bronze technologies, the organization of efficient trade systems carrying many commodities other than the bronzes, and the proliferation of social subdivisions and subcultures. On the Mediterranean, the expansion of the Great Powers proceeded amidst the peripheral development of palace economies and urban chiefdoms, linked by the caravans and carts of the land network and by the sailing ships of the intersecting Aegean, Levantine and Egyptian maritime networks. Along the Mediterranean coastline of Europe the sailed ship for the first time allowed and stimulated direct connection between the eastern and western basins of the Mediterranean through the interlinking triangle of the Tyrrhenian Sea. On the islands and rocky headlands of Italy, Sicily, Sardinia, Lipari and Malta, exotic fortified settlements now sprang up with an evolved copper metallurgy and heterogeneous pottery traditions directly linked to regional wares of Greece, Cyprus, the Cyclades and Crete. These Tyrrhenian centres seem, in turn, to have developed secondary connections with Mediterranean France and Spain, by way of the Balearic Islands and the North African littoral. By this time, the traditional Mediterranean mixed economy combining fishing, sheep and goats, barley plots and olive, vine and fig orchards, seems to have already made its finally integrated appearance and, doubtless, materially helped the more intensive population and exploration of the Mediterranean shores.

Meanwhile, in the rather different environment of middle Europe, the onset of the Subboreal warm climatic phase must have speeded the indigenous mastery of the forested terrain and assisted the more rapid northward spread of Mediterranean innovations. The copper and bronze tools now built effective plank boats, carts and ploughs so that the harnessing of the wind for sail power was hardly less important than the harnessing of oxen for traction purposes. A single boat or cart could carry a cargo of at least one tonne at several miles an hour for long distances, a task which would formerly have required relays of more than 50 porters for each load; now a single ploughman could till, in less than two days, family fields that would have taken a team of women a week to hoe. In Bronze Age Europe, the agrarian communities could, with less manpower, maintain larger fields and produce a greater surplus than their predecessors, freeing man- and womanpower for other specialist pursuits, including the trade of more commodities, further and faster than was within the capacity of their ancestors.

IV. THE MYCENAEAN NETWORK AND THE DEVELOPED BRONZE TECHNOLOGIES

If our frame of reference had not been especially focused on European economic development, there would probably be little or no justification for separating the Mycenaean period from the general context of Mediterranean developments between *ca* 2000–1200 B.C. However, from a European point of view there are several reasons for distinguishing this short phase, if only as a threshold to the events that followed. In this phase, mainland Greece joined the lattice of urban chiefdoms, palace economies and intersecting maritime networks, thus becoming a European centre of civilization in its own right; literate, powerful, and markedly Mediterranean. Politically, there is strong evidence that Greek-speaking Mycenaeans were able to annexe the Cretan kingdom of Knossos *ca* 1450 B.C., introducing a dynasty of aggressive character with strong mainland connections. At Knossos, this transition is marked by the conversion of the old Linear A script to the Linear B idiom for writing Greek and the introduction of the idiosyncratic "Palace Style" in ceramics (Late Minoan II), together with mainland features in fashions, weapons and chariotry. Hereafter, Mycenaean Greek interests not only embraced those of the former Aegean thalassocracy of the Keftiu islanders, formerly headed by the Cretans, but extended their merchant ventures over an area covering the entire basin of the eastern Mediterranean, from the Tyrrhenian to the Black Sea. An urban civilization was thus established on the mainland of Europe with maritime interests stretching from Italy to the Danube delta, and with a strong commercial interest in securing supplies of raw materials from unexplored Europe as an alternative to the very expensive, highly competitive and politically involved markets of the Near East.

Outside Greece, this threshold is marked by the full expansion and developing confrontation of the Egyptian empire, pushing its frontiers to the Euphrates under Tutmosis III (*ca* 1450 B.C.) and the rising power of the Hittite empire under Tudhaliyas II (*ca* 1460–1440 B.C.). Although probably never a politically unified empire in the integrated sense of these great powers, the Mycenaean states nevertheless occasionally seem to have acted together in varying loose federations and they certainly jointly constituted a third major power on the "world" scene at that time – the first European culture to achieve that scale of political significance. In more remote inner Europe, the barbarian chiefdoms and tribes were achieving a rough degree of parity with Mycenaean bronze technology and military equipment, as well as beginning to form unstable political confederations of some size. The fully developed bronze technologies of the Alps, Bohemia and the Carpathians were now based on regular, deep gallery mining which produced a sufficient quantity of copper to extend the previously limited array of display weaponry and restricted tools to a more comprehensive set of bronze equipment, probably available to all higher caste tribesmen. For the first time, bronze displaced stone as the primary raw material for everyday tools and a technical regression in the standards of most flintwork was now accompanied by the contemporary cessation of work at most of the stone axe factories, quarries and mines; important focal resource centres had become unimportant and formerly unimportant Alpine, Bohemian and Carpathian mountain valleys now became centres of radiating bronze networks.

The scale of European bronze production and distribution was accelerating to industrial proportions, although the peak was reached in the ensuing phase, *ca* 1200–900 B.C., under the Urnfield culture group. Already, however, remote mountain lodes were being tunnelled by deep shafts and timbered galleries. The ore was cracked away by fire-setting, followed up by teams of miners using specialist bronze pick-heads, stone mauls and hammers. The debris was dragged to the surface on small sleds, and later by windlasses, where the ore was crushed, milled and separated by flotation in wooden troughs. The ore was then roasted to vaporize impurities and finally smelted in clay crucibles, over charcoal furnaces boosted with skin bellows. It has been estimated that these pit-head activities at some Tyrolean sites would have required some 180 workers or slaves, employed in mining, surface refining processes and cutting timber for props, fuel wood, troughs, pipes, structures and artefact handles. The timber consumption alone would deforest perhaps 19 acres locally every year; an activity which, over a period of centuries must have dramatically augmented the open pasture on the mountain treeline, with a consequent growing stimulus towards the transhumant exploitation of these expanding resources by the valley farmers (Childe, 1955).

From the pit-head, the bronze was taken to the smithies in the form of bun-shaped copper ingots from the crucible bottoms, or recast in bars or rings which have been found in hoards of up to 700 and 1200 pieces (Ebert, 1924). The precious tin was brought by other trade routes to the same smithies, from sources in the Carpathians, Bohemia, Brittany, Cornwall and Galicia. However, very little new tin was needed, except to keep pace with the expanding production and demand, for the scrupulously careful salvage of scrap bronze and worn tools by itinerant merchants served to recover all but a fraction of the original bronze output for recasting. The same merchants bartered the fresh cast tools and weapons on the trip out from the smithing centres, collecting scrap in part exchange to return to the smithy. The hoards therefore often present a seemingly heterogeneous collection of new and old artefacts, not to mention other oddments collected in exchange and perhaps other organic merchandise long since decayed without trace. Smiths themselves seem to have increasingly specialized in the production of particular lines: goldsmiths worked at their delicate anvils with tiny bronze hammers, swordsmiths produced aesthetically superb and functional blades widely traded in bundles, sheet metal-workers skilfully raised and riveted bronze kettles, cans and cauldrons, whilst the village smithy turned his hand to most things, but especially to casting popular lines of axes, sickles, knives, pins, trinkets and to carrying out general repairs. Specialization continued in all spheres of life, and many new "life styles" are marked by the repetitive occurrence of subcultural artefact kits. The capacity of the increasingly organized trade routes widely reflects the use of canoe, sled and cart in the sheer size of the surviving hoards; 200–300 objects are quite common, and some late examples are even larger – 14 800 bronze items and scrap coming from a single cache at Prato di Francesco, Bologna, for example (Childe, 1952). The societies requiring this output, and capable of maintaining these specialists, and sustaining and protecting the vital trade flow, must have included political organizations only slightly less complex than those of the Myceanaean states themselves.

With the emergence of a European society into the comparative light of literacy, one can amplify the purely archaeological record with the evidence of the tablets. The Mycenaean states seem to have covered territories averaging about 25–35 miles in diameter, so that a roughly central capital was never more than a day's march from its own territorial borders and the tributary towns were almost all within a day's march from one another. The state territory was held from these urban sites, which were often fortified, imposing their will upon a network of dispersed villages and themselves loosely controlled from the focally situated seat of the dynastic clan. The kingdom of Pylos, traditionally the seat of the Neleids, encompassed most of Messenia, which was administratively divided into two provinces; a near province of nine tributary towns around the capital at Pylos and a distant province of seven towns around the Messenian Gulf. Similarly, Knossos at this time (ca 1200 B.C.) was apparently capital of the whole of central Crete and lord of more than a dozen towns (Palmer, 1963, pp. 83–102).

The largest burgh would contain the palace-factory of the king (wanax) and the smaller establishments of his immediate kin, all enclosed within a precinct amidst the simple housing of their dependent retainers, grooms, men-at arms, artificers, and slaves, which constituted an outer or "lower" town extending over several acres. Under the authority of the king were the feudal lords (pasireu) of the outlying towns, each of whom would command a retinue and a palace establishment on a lesser scale in their regional capitals. Some of these lords would be kinsmen of the king himself, but others would represent other dynastic families and thus presented a constant source of potential political instability. The king exercised his authority through his commander-in-chief (lawagetas) and his assembled knights (eqeta); here, the legends strongly suggest that the "commander-in-chief" was a senior kinsman of the king, often a brother of the king's father and thus an experienced veteran with the capacity to act as regent in the event of disaster, or on the succession of a young monarch. The "knights" were apparently a war-host of the younger men from the estate-owning families (tereta) who could afford to support the expensive equipage required by their military rank (Palmer, 1963, pp. 83–102, 113–233).

However, the substratum of this state society remained the network of simple villages under village headmen and a caste of craftsmen and serfs, some of whom belonged bodily to the establishment of the king or of the shrines. Some, at least, of this labour force were slaves and captives from border raids, which would accord with their status as the "property" of the captor. Young women were especially prized in this respect, because of their wide variety of skills, for handicrafts, weaving, menial duties and to produce slave offspring. The Homeric picture of noble heroes contending for the fine equipment of a fallen enemy and squabbling over the allocation of particularly fine chariot horses and slave girls seems realistically to enshrine the flavour of this social pattern.

The Mycenaean states represented an important social and economic innovation in Europe at this time, *ca* 1450–1200 B.C. These complex organizations marked the integration of unco-ordinated urban and tribal chiefdoms within centrally organized revenue states which permitted an elaborate cultural development, surpassed only by the metropoli and political empires of the Great Powers. The Mycenaean dynasts appear to have superimposed a system of revenue obligations to a political caste upon earlier patterns of tribal obligations within kinship networks. These archaic tribal patterns continued in peripheral areas of Greece and in the substratum of villages and village headmen, surviving the collapse of the Mycenaean states to re-emerge in the countryside of classical Greece.

The staples of the Mycenaean economy seem to have been barley, wheat, figs, olives and sheep, and from these and other staples the palace industries manufactured and stored olive oil, ewes' milk and cheese, wove and dyed cloth, manufactured unguents with herbs, accumulated reserves of dried foodstuffs, hoarded and reworked metal supplies, amassed stockpiles of imported commodities, maintained an arsenal of weapons and chariot parts, keeping the whole neatly sealed and recorded on the clay tablets and dockets of the quartermaster's stores. Once again, it is the scale of the units recorded in the palace transactions which remind us of the potential of the state economy – 64 580 litres of wheat, 9000 figs, 5520 olives, 10 157 sheep, 300 woollen cloths (Ventris and Chadwick, 1956, p. 214 for Knossos no. 87, p. 219 for Knossos no. 96, p. 198 for Pylos totals, p. 322 for Mycenae no. 288). These mainland products and other commodities were then traded for scarce and foreign goods, especially copper from Cyprus, Assyrian tin from Cilician retailers, Egyptian gold from Crete, ivory from Syria, wine and oil from the islands. Amber too was imported, especially to the Ionian shores; some apparently came from Sicily, some from Scandinavia via the head of the Adriatic, but other amber supplies probably trickled in from Black Sea sources – Buzău in Roumania, Kiev in Russia, and the Caucasus deposits. The importance of the Mycenaean amber trade has been exaggerated, however, to a degree only paralleled by the inflated distortion of the extent of direct Mycenaean intervention in the European Middle Bronze Age as a whole.

The commodities regularly imported by the Mycenaean states seem to have come from a relatively restricted marine network. Almost all the imported goods could have been shipped by seasonal, circular expeditions sailing east through the Cycladic archipelago to the Carian coast, Rhodes, Lycia, Cilicia and North Syria, then returning via Cyprus, Crete and the Peloponnesus; a round voyage of *ca* 1400 miles, probably requiring two or three weeks out from Greece and a similar period for the return. It is precisely along this route that we find Mycenaean commercial and political activity developing, at first in the Cyclades, then in central Crete, next in Rhodes and eventually in Cyprus. A chain of Mycenaean merchant *karum* quarters were set up in restricted districts of the main foreign ports from Carian Miletus, at the foot of the northern Anatolian littoral routes, to Syrian Al Mina at the mouth of the Orontes on the tin and ivory trail. The great hoards of copper ox-hide ingots are strewn along the links of this maritime chain, from shipwrecks between Cape Gelidonya and Kyme harbour in Euboea, and from wayside palace treasuries like those ingots stacked against Syrian elephant tusks in the storerooms of the palace at Kato Zakro, at the easternmost tip of Crete.

Similar ingots and tusks appear on the shoulders of alternating Levantine porters on a copper tripod from Curium, Cyprus (Casson, 1937, pp. 128–129). Indeed, there is considerable evidence that Levantine as well as Mycenaean shipping circulated along this network; the "Phoenicians" of the Homeric epics might therefore equally be restored to this more ancient horizon, together with the Achaeans with whom they are said to have dealt. A motley assemblage of Syro-Cilican seals and Levantine trinkets have appeared in Mycenaean contexts from more than 50 sites, ranging from the sealstones from the Palace at Thebes to the scores of cheap little votive Baal mascots in lead and bronze – good luck mascots for the voyage, perhaps? (Hutchinson, 1962, pp. 311–312; Taylour, 1964, p. 159). The Gelidonya wreck certainly makes patent the risks implied by the storm-god votives and confirms that some of this trade was carried, with the mascots, in Syro-Cilician shipping as well as between the thwarts of the Mycenaean penteconters – a new type of ship traditionally introduced by the Asiatic

Danaus of Argos and, thus, perhaps from the coastal Danaans of Syro-Cilician Adana.

No single find so richly illustrates the nature of the maritime networks at this time as the shipwreck already alluded to. The ship had apparently been driven on Cape Gelidonya by a gale which had turned her broadside on, unable to turn into the wind – a navigational weakness of early galleys, graphically described by St Paul from his own experience off Malta. Cape Gelidonya is the most notorious hazard on the Lycian coast between Rhodes and Tarsus and the wreck was found at its foot by skin-divers who carefully excavated the hulk underwater (Bass, 1966, pp. 134–143). The vessel was a small wooden sailing ship, about 10.5 metres long by perhaps 3.5 metres at the beam, probably carrying a light cabin in the stern. The laden freight included about one tonne of copper ingots, quantities of bronze scrap metal and perhaps 25 kilograms of tin ingots. The cargo was very carefully stowed amidships, the 25 kilogram copper ox-hide ingots and the small tin bars were stacked and wrapped in protective matting, with the scrap bronze and newly cast bronze tools kept separately in wicker baskets; the whole burden was packed around with brushwood bundles to insulate the hull from internal battering in rough weather. The extremely interesting evidence strongly suggests the presence of a smith or smiths on board and this might reasonably be deduced not only from the mixed cargo of pure copper and tin, bronze scrap and untrimmed, freshly cast, bronze tools, but also from a large cushion-stone anvil amidships, together with two stone forging hammers, a bronze swage block, sandstone polishers, whetstones for sharpening and finishing, and a beam balance with weights, perhaps for estimating the weight of tin to copper for the various bronze alloys.

The Gelidonya ship's master probably occupied the small stern cabin, lit with its small oil lamp. The captain carried with him his personal bronze razor and his Syro-Cilician cylinder seal and five scarabs to seal up his cargo against theft, as well as a few chunks of Taurus crystal – perhaps a sample for customers or a private profit-making investment. The rest of the small crew probably slept on deck and one may perhaps attribute to them the knuckle-bone gaming dice and the food bowls with the remains of a meal of fish, fowl and olives. The extensive complement of bronze woodworking tools might suggest that the ship's carpenter was already an essential and specialized craftsman, with his chest of axes, adzes, chisels, gouges, axe-adzes and knives. The bronze spearheads were perhaps part of the ship's armoury against marauders and may even suggest an escort of a marine or two with this rich cargo. Although by no means a treasure vessel by the standards of the time, the Gelidonya galley would certainly have made a handsome prize. A tonne of copper and 25 kilograms of tin would produce something like 50 bronze helmets, 50 bronze corselets, 500 long spearheads and 500 bronze rapiers; sufficient to fully armour the commander-in-chief of Pylos, his sixteen feudal lords and their immediate kin, together with nearly 500 properly equipped knights, the whole war-host of the state of Pylos in fact. By an illuminating chance, the accounts of the Pylos palace preserve a summary of bronze ingot reserves at a time when the state was being put on a wartime alert; these reserves total just over one tonne, or almost exactly the cargo of the Gelidonya wreck (Ventris and Chadwick, 1956, p. 356 for Pylos no. 256).

The observation that one ship might carry the equivalent of the strategic bronze reserves of the palace, and possibly of the state of Pylos, raises other interesting points in this context. We may recall that even by *ca* 1900 B.C. a single Assyrian caravan could re-export $12\frac{1}{2}$ tonnes of Elamite tin on 200 beasts of burden travelling from Assur to Cappadocia. This caravan was part of a regular trade network carrying tin northwestwards to Anatolian Kanish, which in turn re-exported much of this tin westwards to the Syro-Cilician coastal cities, the ports from which the Mycenaean *karum* shipped tin back to the Mycenaean states (Gardin, 1965, pp. 378–391). Now this state of affairs does not suggest that the Mycenaean states would ordinarily find tin in short supply – the absence of Myceneaen bronze hoards proclaims the efficiency of their reutilization system and, furthermore, the $12\frac{1}{2}$ tons of tin from the single Assyrian caravan would probably suffice to stock the tin reserves held by all of the dozen or so Mycenaean states taken together. What this export and re-export trade does suggest is that tin would normally be plentiful but very expensive, and that supplies would be extremely sensitive to the political situation far beyond the Mycenaean sphere of intervention; diplomacy with the Syro-Cilician potentates, often against Hittite interests, must have much exercised Mycenaean political activities.

It would appear that the Mycenaean state economies could, in theory, have been self-supporting except in respect of copper and tin supplies and the many luxury items that a caste society demands to bedeck its ranks and statuses. The sea peoples of the Anatolian and Levantine coasts retailed most of these requisites, but at a price. Mycenaean maritime enterprises, therefore, seem to have increasingly probed the coastline of Europe, from the Tyrrhenian Sea to the Danube delta, for cheaper, more reliable supplies of staples and exotica. The effects of these Mycenaean expeditions were mainly peripheral and indirect in their impact upon middle European cultures, but Mycenaean wine and oil jars regularly found their way to many southern sites on the coasts of metal-rich Italy, whilst rapiers, spearheads and faience beads of Aegean–Anatolian type appear in a few coastal Bulgarian and Romanian hoards.

From the Danube delta, the wealthy chieftains of the intervening chiefdoms of the Wietenberg and Monteoru cultures controlled the reciprocal flow of Middle Danube commodities to the coast and Aegean–Anatolian trinkets and innovations to the cultures beyond the Carpathians. Chariots and chariot harness appear to have been one of the innovations which rapidly passed into the repertoire of the chieftain caste in such central European cultures as the Otomani group. One interesting feature of the chariot harness is the much favoured "rick-rack" motif found on bone cheekpieces, chariot inlays and whip handles from central Europe to the Aegean; perhaps the undulating *roiko* ornament described for similar Mycenaean harness in the tablets (Ventris and Chadwick, 1956, p. 408; Palmer, 1963, pp. 318, 368). The antecedents of this motif are obscure, but they are linked through variations on Otomani and Wietenberg ceramics and bronzes with motifs on Gumelnitsa and Salcutsa artefacts of the southern Balkans, suggesting that the harness form, the motifs and the horses may have reached the Mycenaeans from the famous horse pastures of Thrace, rather than vice versa. Nevertheless, in general one might compare the mercantile activities of the Mycenaean states off the coasts of southeastern Europe with those of the Arab traders along the eastern African coastline from the ninth to the twelfth centuries A.D.

The development and significance of the late Mycenaean maritime network can best be assessed against its general economic and political context. Initially, the Mycenaean chiefdoms were no more than the barbarous beneficiaries of the maritime network linking the Aegean peoples of the islands, the Keftiu, amongst whom Crete had latterly assumed the dominant status, *ca* 1660–1450 B.C. The rise of the urban states of the Greek mainland seems to have culminated with a Mycenaean conquest of Knossos and the subjugation of Crete within an independent Mycenaean kingdom, *ca* 1450 B.C. At about the same time, Mycenaean merchant colonies began to spring up and infiltrate other centres of the former Cretan mercantile network – in Miletus, Rhodes, Tell Atchana, Ras Shamra, Byblos, Gezer, Lachish and in the Nile delta. After *ca* 1400 B.C., Cos and the Dodecanese islands came within the Mycenaean hegemony and more bases were planted on Rhodes and Cyprus, allowing a far more intensive commercial penetration of the Syro-Cilician coastline. The Greek mainland and the islands were thus able to form a reciprocal economic network well equipped to supply the resource deficiencies of individual members and well situated to exploit Levantine and Cypriot commodities to the southeast,

Anatolian and Black Sea trade to the northeast, and Italian and Sicilian resources to the west. It should not be imagined, however, that the expansion of the Mycenaean network was a co-ordinated imperial venture. Initially, at least, it was probably no more than a competitive race for Minoan footholds by the younger sons of various Mycenaean dynasts, only occasionally and temporarily acting in concert in the famous, quarrelsome expeditions of the great epics. Indeed, the Homeric epics, with their fairly exact factual knowledge of the Aegean and their more misty acquaintance with the coasts and islands beyond the Straits of Messina and the Bosporus, seem accurately to embody the navigational experiences of this period and to have drawn upon a corpus of mariner's tales to decorate old and famous stories, in the manner of the Medieval minstrels.

V. THE COLONIAL NETWORKS AND THE LATE BRONZE TECHNOLOGIES

The Mycenaean period marked the extension of the Near Eastern network of interconnected urban, revenue-state economies to the Greek mainland and thus linked the fringe of Europe with the world of the two great powers, the Hittite and the Egyptian empires, and the bustling trading cities of the Levant. The centralized authority and the literate bureacracy of the Mycenaean palace economies represented an important expansion of the frontiers of urban civilization – the world of city states, kingdoms and military empires – and, correspondingly, a slight contraction of the barbarian world of the totemic bands, tribes and tribal chiefdoms of innermost Europe. Nevertheless, the dynasts of the Mycenaean *élite* remained a ruling caste and its subculture, superimposed upon a tribal society surviving in the substratum of villages dispersed in the countryside beyond the burghs; a tribal society which remained a functioning system well into the period of Classical Greece.

The century around 1200–1100 B.C. forms the threshold for momentous events which transformed the then civilized world and stimulated repercussions directly involving the tribesmen of middle Europe. Historically, it would be tempting to represent these changes purely in terms of a sequence of political events, but here, as in other instances, the real threshold integrated a multiplicity of mutually interacting factors, cumulatively made manifest in the political sequence noted by the scribes of the great powers. This century of events witnessed the collapse of the Hittite empire, the disintegration of the Mycenaean states, Imperial Egypt thrown back and attacked on its own frontiers, together with extensive population resettlement from the Troad to Gaza. The eastern Mediterranean was in turmoil and the colonial penetration of the western Mediterranean commenced in earnest with the settlement of whole communities replacing former commercial enclaves.

In middle Europe, the contrasting evidence suggests the development of tribal confederacies and possibly kingdoms of unparalleled wealth and size for the area. In eastern Europe, there are signs that important new socio-economic configurations now emerged with a novel pattern and fresh potential – the rise of the horse-mounted pastoralist societies. Whilst in central, western and northern Europe the late bronze technologies reached a climax of production, providing a full range of metal tools as well as weapons and, incidentally, disseminating the earliest elements of iron metallurgy, released and dispersed by the collapse of the Hittite empire. The exchange networks of these regional bronze technologies now reached to the fringes of the Arctic Circle and deep into the coniferous forest zone of the north and east. At their core, elaborate chiefdoms provided markets, ensured supplies of labour for the deep mines and maintained a flow of carts and porters, canoes and ships, bartering and circulating staples and trinkets. Even at the outermost peripheries, the lives of the hunter-fisher-gatherer bands in the Norwegian forests and the Siberian taiga were increasingly modified in order to exchange furs and skins for bronzes and cereals; the development of full chieftainship, the growth of individual property and territorial ownership, more display equipment and imported finery accompanied the changes in the archaic band organizations.

The principal factors which combined to transform the Mediterranean scene and to modify the cultures of middle Europe at this time, seem to have included climatic trends, the rise of the mounted pastoralist economies, and the coincidence of political circumstances amongst the great powers. These factors are themselves interrelated and were certainly modulated by a far more complex interaction of many other contributing elements. Amongst the Mediterranean states, these developments threatened the restless equilibrium between the *élite* castes administering the sophisticated economies and the peasant substratum beneath. Sequences of unusually severe famine, aggravated by epidemics and by the continuous obligation to supply revenue, could easily stimulate unrest and minor population movements which would in turn contribute to the internal instability. Social unrest of this kind could be seriously exacerbated by external military commitments and inflamed by the conflicting policies of rival dynastic clans within the states, finally erupting into an internal revolt led by an opportunist commander-in-chief, by a brother or an uncle of the ruler, or by a rival faction. The foundation legends of the new colonial towns of the western Mediterranean repeatedly describe such refugees, fleeing to fresh prospects and resources in the "New World" beyond Scylla and Charybdis, to metalliferous and fertile Italy at first but soon to northern Africa, southern France and eventually to the Spanish "El Dorado".

In central Europe, the evidence suggests that external pressures were less important than the internally expanding economic capacity of a growing population, which was throwing up increasingly larger and more complex political organizations. The climatic factors which unsettled the eastern Mediterranean at this time were positively advantageous in central and northern Europe. The barbarian chiefdoms were themselves rapidly converging upon at least incipient state organizations centred on fortified timber townlets, focally placed amidst the scattered agrarian tribal communities. Small political and economic centres of this kind emerged early on in the Lower and Middle Danube basins and soon proliferated on the Upper Danube, amidst the fertile and metalliferous Alpine valleys, in equally rich Bohemia and amongst the lakes and streams of the Baltic Vistula valley. These townlets of the Urnfield culture group covered some 2–15 acres with 200–300 timber houses, holding populations of perhaps 500–2000 persons under the authority of a chief and his retinue, either in a fortified hall in the settlement, or in a separate residence close by. The analogy with the medieval timber towns of the same areas and with the Mycenaean burghs to the south are equally appropriate. Except in degree of organization, overall size and aspects of construction, these Urnfield townlets reflect the foundation of social organizations only slightly less potent than the Mycenaean and continuing in many respects into the medieval pattern. The similarity of these social patterns is made apparent as they emerge into the historical daylight of both the Mycenaean tablets and the medieval chronicles, respectively. One may compare the state of Pylos, already discussed, with the Baltic province of Volhynia in 1219, ruled by five grand dukes from their fortified halls in timber burghs of *ca* 15 acres and administered by sixteen regional dukes from lesser establishments in townlets of 2–10 acres (Gimbutas, 1963, p. 171).

This expanding central European pattern of wealthy chiefdoms and incipient state organizations, or kingdoms, is mainly associated with the regional cultures of the Urnfield culture group, so named from the dense cremation cemeteries adjacent to the settlement sites. The "expansion" of this culture group may probably be best understood as the vector of a number of components – as the spreading material trappings of an expanding social pattern increasingly adopted by similar peoples in similar circumstances, supplemented by tribal population movements and the convergent acculturation of adjacent ethnic groups. The social pattern spread by these processes, the economic systems that they represented and the ethnic groups spreading with them, were responsible for much of the cultural pattern of Europe as it emerged in later history; the historical European scene was set in many essentials *ca* 1200 B.C.

The factors involved in the eastern Mediterranean collapse are therefore mainly of interest for their repercussions amongst the central European cultures and for their colonial consequences in the European littoral of the western Mediterranean and beyond. The climatic factor is the least understood and the most difficult to assess realistically. However, in essence, we may say that the period *ca* 1200–600 B.C. falls at the juncture between the closing phases of the warmer and drier Subboreal climate, *ca* 2000–800 B.C., and the opening Subatlantic phase with its wetter and colder climate, *ca* 800–400 B.C. This transition seems to have been accompanied by short-lived but locally important oscillations, as is so often the case in climatic changes. The evidence is largely circumstantial, uneven and insecure, but its sheer bulk suggests a measure of probability for the general trends involved. The inference is that the inland areas of the Greek and Anatolian peninsulas were subjected to unusually severe and recurrent bouts of desiccation and drought over the period *ca* 1250–1000 B.C., broadly corresponding to a period of unusually mild climate in inland Europe – the setting for the great cultural florescence in that area and perhaps relevant to the rise of the steppe pastoralists. Whether we accept this climatic evidence or not, there is at least supporting evidence for drought in inland Greece and Anatolia in this period, accompanied in some areas by famine, epidemics and small population movements to the more reliable rainfall areas of the littoral (Carpenter, 1966). It must be heavily stressed, however, that this putative evidence is not interpreted as a cause for contemporary events, but merely as one factor amidst many, important in some areas but less important in others.

The second factor cited the rise of the mounted pastoralist economies of the western steppe and their expansive infiltration into a selection of peculiar niches which this freshly integrated economic strategy now permitted. Here again the evidence is incomplete and difficult to interpret, but some clarification is possible. The available evidence suggests that the fertile Pontic prairies were at first occupied by various agrarian village communities practising mixed farming. Domestic animals flourished in the steppe environment and local wild horse herds were certainly domesticated by *ca* 2500 B.C. as merely another variety of "hornless" stock. Between *ca* 2500–1500 B.C., village pastoralist communities from the Caucasus flanks increasingly expanded on to the eastern steppe, apparently controlling large herds from tented ox-wagons and possibly from chariots. In any event, it seems likely that the various communities of the eastern and western steppe practised a stable village economy with subcultural symbiosis between those whose duties operated the stock around the village pastures and those who raised grain and fruit in the fertile soil. This strategy continued until recent times in the Cossack villages and, as Herodotus confirms, there was never a time in which the steppe was occupied only by nomad pastoralists.

The horse was used for chariot traction by *ca* 1500 B.C., but seldom ridden except by grooms or messengers. However, the development of an adequate saddle and bridle harness between *ca* 1500–1200 B.C. seems to have transformed the steppe situation much as the arrival of horse riding transformed some of the Indian prairie farmers into plains buffalo hunters. Given comfortable and controlled horse-riding, the herdsmen on horseback could now manœuvre vast herds with ease and exploit a far wider range of pastures in succession. By a kind of social binary fission, the division of labour between social subcultures now became an independent cultural symbiosis between separately specialized economies; the agrarian villages continued with the pastoralists circulating in their interstices. On the Carpathian fringe, it was apparently some elements of the local Cimmerian, Thracian and Phrygian tribes who increasingly took to the relatively unexploited pastures, which in this dry Subboreal phase extended discontinuously from the Romanian Dobrudja, through Bulgarian Thrace, to parts of Macedonia and Thessaly. Thus, by *ca* 1200 B.C., a group of mounted pastoralist communities deployed amongst their agrarian kinsmen of the plains of Thrace; a militarily formidable but disorganized force poised opposite the closely congruent grasslands of northern Anatolia.

Before pursuing the Phrygian infiltration of northern Anatolia, it is necessary to outline its context, the political circumstances amongst the great powers *ca* 1250–1100 B.C., the third factor in the events which followed. These circumstances follow from the traditional role of the Levantine city states as the direct or retail source of important strategic raw materials, staples and luxuries, tapped in common by successive Egyptian, Mesopotamian and Anatolian dynasts, and now by the Mycenaean princelings. With the floruit of the Hittite empire, between 1460–1220 B.C., the Levant increasingly became the middle ground for the power play between the Hittite kings and the Egyptian pharaohs. This confrontation reached a climax with the indecisive battle of Kadesh *ca* 1286 B.C., in which the Hittite King Muwatallis massed his allies and mercenaries from the Anatolian coastline against the military expedition of Rameses II and his vassals and auxiliaries.

As an effective basis for the pursuit of their southern imperial aims, the late Hittite kings reorganized their empire into two provinces; the home province in the rear included the old Hittite homeland and the capital at Hattusas under the command of a royal governor, whilst the forward province in southern Anatolia was the military base of the armies and the Hittite king, as commander-in-chief. This unbalanced stance assumed that the northern province could be lightly held, whilst the king and his armies pursued a policy of southward expansion. In quick succession, the imperial capital at Hattusas was sacked by northern Kaski tribesmen, the western vassal states of Arzawa and Assuwa came out in revolt with the aid of their Mycenaeanized coastal neighbours in Lydia, Caria and Lycia, and in 1275 B.C. the uncle of the absent king usurped the throne and, after a brief civil war, became Hattusilis III. The new Hittite kings now fought to stabilize the home province with successive expeditions against the rebel areas, including a campaign towards the Troad about the period of the Mycenaean expedition against Troy *ca* 1260 B.C.

Under Arnuwandas IV, the northern and western situation rapidly deteriorated under renewed, and this time partially co-ordinated, attacks from the west by the vassal states and their allies the "peoples of the coastlands", and from the north by the Kaski and also the Mushki – Phrygian horsemen from across the Bosporus, perhaps related to the Kaski themselves. The Arzawa area was seized *ca* 1230 B.C. by a Lydian vassal, King Madduwattas, aided by Attarissiyas, a prince of coastal Ahhiyawa, possibly an Achaean state in Caria centred on Miletus. The more northerly Assuwa area was seized by the Kaski and the Phrygian horsemen, now present in force under a Prince Midas. However, the unprecedented military advantage of the Phyrygian horsemen and the internal dislocation of the Hittite allies soon turned the new force against Arzawa and the Lydian, Carian, Lycian and Cilician peoples of the coastlands; with the arms of Imperial Hatti fighting for survival around Hattusas, nothing could stem the flood of invaders and the turmoil of refugees. Within 100 years of their first foothold, the Phrygian Mushki tribes had consolidated in western Anatolia and had even sallied into northern Syria and Mesopotamia to confront the Assyrian King Tiglath-Pileser I with an army of 20 000 cavalry under five chieftains.

The Hittite empire was smashed and the repercussions for the economically interconnected states of the Levant, Egypt and Mycenaean Greece were only slightly less severe. In 1227 B.C., "northerners from many lands" attacked the Nile delta by boat, including in their number many of the Hittites' former coastal allies from the battle of Kadesh – the Lycians, Ahhiyawans and (possibly) Sardians. This first wave probably represented adventurers from the initially successful revolt by the

coastal peoples of Anatolia, mercenary freebooters armed in the latest
Anatolian-Aegean fashion with tribal variations, crested helmets, plate
cuirasses, Aegean rapiers and the round cavalry and infantry shield;
it is significant that later Greek traditions attributed these military innovations to Caria and Lycia.

However, this first raid was of little consequence by comparison with
the second in 1196 B.C., probably corresponding to the full Phrygian
invasion of coastal Anatolia and their drive down the southwestern littoral. On this occasion, a large fleet of northerners moved down the
Levantine coast, in conjunction with a land army with chariots and
men, women and children in bullock carts – whole peoples were on
the move. The Egyptian scribes noted,

> the coastal peoples joined together, they were displaced from their lands
> and their peoples scattered. No land stood before their weapons, from Hatti
> [the Hittites], Kode, Arzawa, and Alashiya [Cyprus] onwards. They
> camped in Amurru [Syria], they desolated its peoples and its land was de-
> stroyed; they came with fire before them, onwards toward Egypt.

The imperial Egyptian forces retired to the Nile delta and there
Rameses III successfully resisted the invasion, abandoning Palestine
to the invaders. The motley refugees settled the Palestinian coast and
parts of Cyprus, where they became known as the Philistines, after the
Peleseti, the subsequently dominant group amongst the confederation
of Mycenaeanized "sea peoples".

Unfortunately, the Mycenaean collapse is not documented by their
inventory tablets and we must rely on archaeological evidence, eked
out by the oblique indications of the tablets and the later traditions.
However, the archaeological evidence outlines two severe spasms, the
second cumulatively more decisive than the first; one upheaval *ca* 1230–
1200 B.C. and the second *ca* 1130–1100 B.C. In the first spasm, the network of Mycenaean states was severely dislocated by burning and destruction at many of the main citadels, including Mycenae, Tiryns,
Midea, Pylos, Gla, Zygouries, Prosymna, Berbati, Korakou and others,
but with no evidence of any alien invaders. The ceramic distributions
suggest some accompanying population movements outwards from the
interior areas towards the west coasts of the Ionian islands and Epirus,
as well as eastwards to Rhodes and Cyprus; movements which might
link with the growing desiccation of the Greek interior. In this first convulsion, the majority of the political centres show destruction and abandonment, although the citadel of Mycenae survived the destruction of
its outer town. The second spasm, *ca* 1130–1100 B.C., was marked by
the complete destruction of Mycenae, the abandonment of a hastily
built bastioned wall across the Corinthian isthmus and decisive changes

in the culture of the Peloponnesus – no more written records, no more palace bureaucracies, the adoption of Thessalian Protogeometric pottery modes and, apparently, a revival of the underlying substratum of tribal peasant organization. Individual citadels such as Athens survived, but the interdependent network of centrally organized Mycenaean states had been forever destroyed and its administering castes rendered impotent (Carpenter, 1966).

The indications of the late Mycenaean tablets can only be used to infer the kinds of upheaval which might be generically likely in this kind of state system. The Mycenaean state was apparently a fiscal superstructure concentrated in the palaces and towns, financing and organizing trade with other states and empires, in a mutually adjusted international network based on the exchange of revenue for commodities. The village communities of Mycenaean Greece were in many respects beyond the subcultural frontiers of the dynasties which ruled from the great palaces, except for the collection of revenue from the village surpluses. The village network provided the economic substructure of the society and displayed a far greater stability in the face of violent changes. Foreign trade might fluctuate, dynasty murder dynasty, feudal lords plunder townships and palaces, but the village communities farmed on in stoic continuity. The state administration was very little concerned with the organization of the rural communities beyond the extraction of revenue. Tribute was heavy, in times of bad harvests and famine the surplus could be ill-spared; should these times coincide with external unrest and disruption, then the dynasts would tend to levy larger and larger contributions in manpower and commodities to prop up their administration and organize its defence. This in turn would cause further peasant unrest; left with decreasing reserves, on the margins of famine and despair, such a cumulative system of interacting diasters could, if conditions correlated effectively, combine to bring down the state by a combination of civil rebellion and external assault, catalysed by the inevitable opportunist intervention of rival dynastic parties; the same model which seems to outline the general components of the Hittite collapse, already described (Bailey, 1958).

Finally, we can appeal for enlightenment to the epic tales that survived into the Homeric period, although we must remember that, like the *Saxon Chronicle*, their main purpose was to provide a respectable explanation of the ancestry and rise to power of the new Doric upper class. Nevertheless, the tales needed to be entertaining distortions of the truth rather than outright lies, and the picture they extrapolate into the Mycenaean period is wholly reasonable.

Significantly, the epics sketch a period genealogically covering roughly ten generations before the Doric period and, regardless of the particular tale, the frame is always the same – the quarrel between the Perseid clan of "the sons of Hercules" and the upstart Pelopids "the sons of Thyestes and Atreus"; the return of the Heraclids to their rightful domains representing the cue for Doric intervention and the happy ending. In general, the tales portray a ruling caste composed of a relatively few interrelated royal clans, so that the dynasties at various ruling centres were involved in a constantly changing pattern of family alliances and feuds.

The traditions claim that the intrusive Pelopid dynasty became paramount at Mycenae, having dispossessed the Perseids, who thereafter constantly schemed their return to power in the Peloponnesus – the Kingdom of Pelops. True to form, the Pelopid houses of Thyestes and Atreus themselves disputed the succession at Mycenae until the Atreid rival Orestes was banished to the Asiatic coasts of his forefathers, whilst the descendants of Thyestes reigned at Mycenae. The epics then relate a period of great upheaval, separated from a second convulsion by a period of two or three generations dogged by notorious bad luck – the "struggle with the fates" (Erinnyes). The first upheaval is the return of Orestes and his extensive campaign of vengeance against the Perseid strongholds. The sons of Orestes then suffered a period of successive ill-omens, disasters, famine and pestilence, only brought to a close by the triumphant return of the Heraclids with their Thessalian allies the Dorians and the eventual success of their long-drawn-out campaigns against the High King Tisamenes, fortified in the Peloponnesus. The two spasms separated by two or three generations take us back to the two archaeological convulsions *ca* 1230–1200 B.C. and *ca* 1130–1100 B.C., separated from one another by about 100 years and from the historic epics by another 300 years.

We may not trust the ancient epics in any detail, but the tradition seems broadly plausible and corresponds well with the inferences of the tablets, the archaeological record and the general parallel of the Hittite collapse. It seems that some Mycenaean states collaborated in opportunist expeditions in the Troad and perhaps against other parts of the Anatolian coastline, at a time of general disturbance amongst the outer Hittite vassal states and their coastal allies *ca* 1260 B.C. In the absence of these expeditions, political rivals fermented unrest and brought about a coup for the Thyestid house, shortly after the return of the Atreids from their famous exploits overseas. Subsequently, the exiled Atreid contender Orestes returned, recaptured Mycenae and proceeded to campaign against the hostile Perseid citadels; this episode would then correspond with the first major dislocation, *ca* 1230–1200 B.C. This civil war combined with coincidental economic factors and civil disorder to upset the precarious equilibrium of the Mycenaean hegemony, creating a rapidly declining political and economic situation hardly helped by the contemporary collapse of the Hittite and Levantine commercial networks. Perhaps we are also at liberty to attribute the unrest of the Doric tribes around Olympus, and the traditional exploits of the Heraclids against the Centaurs of Thessaly, as the southernmost repercussions of marauding bands of Thraco-Phrygian "horsemen". In any event, dynastic intrigue, economic troubles, civil disorder and famine may thus have conspired to bring down the commercial network of Mycenaean states as quickly as they had disintegrated the Hittite empire.

The collapse of the eastern Mediterranean states broadly corresponds with the period of expansion of the central European chiefdoms and confederacies; in terms of economic surplus, bronze technology, social organization and weaponry, a broad degree of parity now existed between middle and Mediterranean Europe. The flourishing group of Urnfield cultures had already expanded to the Macedonian and Italic fringes of the Mycenaean world; some tribal mercenaries and armourers from these sources even seem to have been involved on a small scale in the closing dynastic squabbles of the Achaeans – apparently carrying their slashing swords, leaf-shaped spears and bossed shields in defence of the Mycenaean kingdoms with western maritime contacts. Beyond the centrally expanding Urnfield peoples was a mosaic of diverse Atlantic and Iberian tribes, a peripheral zone of motley peoples using archaic bronze technologies and weapon fashions long outdated in central Europe. However, it appears that the central developments of the expanding Urnfield network created a situation in which the major metal resources of inner Europe were increasingly devoted to the production and distribution of Urnfield equipment for Urnfield cultures, forming a kind of central "Common Market" area. This situation seems gradually to have forced the heterogeneous maritime cultures of the Atlantic and Iberian littoral into closer and closer interdependence for metal supplies, which increasingly circulated within this outer "Free Trade" area; Britain, Ireland, Brittany, Galicia and Spain thus exchanged trade goods in a network peripherally including Denmark and Sardinia and which mainly exchanged tin, copper, bronze, silver and gold metalwork.

This "Atlantic Bronze Age" first emerges as an economically significant linkage between the western Mediterranean and the Atlantic after *ca* 1000 B.C. and reached its peak with the penetration of its southernmost outlets by the highly organized Phoenician mercantile marine *ca* 900–300 B.C. These later, large-scale commercial dealings in metal supplies, seem to have stimulated the development of "middleman"

Iberian kingdoms, based on redistribution economies, like that of King Arganthonios of Tartessos. The Phoenician trading off the European coastline thus played a significant role in catalysing the development of more complex social organizations in barbarian Europe – just as the Arab and Portuguese slave, ivory and gold trade stimulated the African states of Ghana, Mali, Songhay, Ife, Benin, Zimbabwe, Bakongo and Dahomey.

The Atlantic maritime network probably only moved into effective existence with the introduction of the sail and the keeled galley from the Mediterranean, probably at the hands of the Phoenicians themselves *ca* 900 B.C. The arrival of the sailed ship in southern Atlantic waters now permitted regular, long-distance, two-way commerce on an economically significant scale. Even so, the distribution evidence suggests that the Atlantic maritime network was based on relatively modest, seasonal, short-distance voyages to and fro between adjacent centres – from Britain to Brittany, Brittany to the Garonne, the Garonne to Galicia, Galicia to the Tagus, the Tagus to Gades and Tartessos. It was probably not until the long-distance exploratory voyages of Himilco the Carthaginian, *ca* 450 B.C., and the Massiliote Pytheas *ca* 310 B.C., that any one captain attempted the full length of this trade route.

The nature of the cargoes carried on the Atlantic network is preserved in the distribution of idiosyncratic bronze artefacts and in the records noting the early voyages by Colaeus, Midacritus, Himilco, Pytheas and other earlier and unnamed captains. Apparently, pottery, salt, bronze tableware, oil and wine were traded northwards against Irish copper, gold and bronzework, Cornish and Breton lead and tin, amber and furs reshipped from Heligoland, and cereals, slaves, hides and dogs from various ports. Once again we are fortunate in having the inorganic remains of two ships' cargoes salvaged from different parts of this network. One such cargo is probably represented by the densely packed hoard of bronze tools, weapons and scrap metal dredged from the Odiel estuary at Huelva in southern Spain; a cargo which included bronze swords, axes, spearheads and tools of mainly Iberian origin in association with a few Irish, French and Sardinian types and several Phoenician fibulae of Cypriot type *ca* 700 B.C. The other shipwreck comes from the eastern wing of this same commercial network and has been recovered by divers from Béziers, in the Gulf of Lions near the emporium of Narbo. The vessel contained 760 bronze tools, weapons, and trinkets, together with more than half a tonne of copper ingots, perhaps from the Iberian or Sardinian mines; the whole cargo dating *ca* 800 B.C. (Bass, 1966, p. 87). Irish artefacts, including bronze cauldrons and gold collars, are known from other Atlantic Iberian hoards and Atlantic bronzes from several Sardinian hoards complement the scatter of Sardinian types from Huelva to Hengistbury Head; embossed bronze shields and horned or crested helmets of the same general pattern also link Ireland, Spain, Sardinia and Denmark. The evidence of the wrecks suggests that the shipping was mainly handled by the skilled seamen of native kingdoms, like the Veneti and the Tartessians, but that they were moving freely through areas and into ports from which Phoenician middlemen were also operating. The Phoenician–Iberian trade was thus part of an extensive commercial network which coupled the coastline of Atlantic Europe to the markets of the Mediterranean states and which transported commodities by the tonne load.

The expansion and deployment of the Phoenician colonial network was, therefore, of paramount importance in expanding the development of the Atlantic trade and its social and economic consequences amongst the tribesmen of outer Europe. The Phoenician seamen of the Levantine ports were amongst the most experienced of the ancient world, the inheritors of a maritime tradition as old as the sail itself. The Mycenaeans had nick-named these bronzed traders "red skins" (*phoenikes*) and the Gelidonya wreck reminds us that probably the great bulk of eastern Mediterranean marine traffic was in Levantine hands. The Mycenaeans had their commercial *karum* in Levantine and Cypriot ports, but their marine network was largely complementary to that of the Levantines, centring on the Aegean coast of Anatolia and the Ionian coast of Italy and Sicily, only peripherally exploring European possibilities to the mouth of the Danube, into the Adriatic and into the Tyrrhenian Sea. However, the collapse of the Mycenaean states *ca* 1100 B.C. removed the market, the financial backing and the social environment which had stimulated Mycenaean investment in competitive commercial exploration by the young mercantile princelings, eager to finance the rise to power of their own dynastic clans; it is no accident that the argosies of the epics were crewed by noblemen, or that their ventures should have been a recurrent theme for the dependent court bards. Individual trading by Submycenaean vessels must certainly have continued, but the scale and daring of the enterprises must have diminished with the market which had supported them – the competitive Mycenaean *élite*.

The Phoenician merchants were, therefore, able to exploit the demise of their Mycenaean competitors to the north and west by rapidly deploying into the Aegean markets and through the Sicilian straits already mapped by the Mycenaean mariners. The earliest Phoenician explorations in the western Mediterranean probably date to this phase, *ca* 1100–1000 B.C., gradually plotting the anchorages of the northern African littoral and thus providing the traditional "foundation" dates for Leptis, Carthage and even Gades beyond the Pillars of Hercules. The rapidity of the Phoenician expansion westwards is understandable, given the existing knowledge of the Sicilian channel, the excellent supply facilities of the North African littoral and the pre-existing maritime connections between the peoples of that area and Iberia. By the tenth century, the southern arc of the western Mediterranean was a Phoenician Sea, bounded by new urban and literate settlements on western Sicily, Sardinia and the Balearics, continuing in a chain of ports to the Almerian harbours of Lucentum, Abdera, Malaca and ending at the Atlantic outposts of Gades and Onoba on the coast of Tartessos.

The early Phoenician explorations were by no means confined to the southern arc of the western Mediterranean, which later became the main focus of the Punic league. There is increasing evidence that the subsequent alliances between the Etruscans and the Carthaginians were simply continuing an intimate relationship going back to *ca* 1000–900 B.C. The Phoenicians seem to have retreated from the Tyrrhenian Sea after a very early expansion from the Mycenaean bases in the south to emporia actually on the Etruscan and Latin coastline and on the flanking shores of Sardinia and Sicily. Etruria now emerged from Villanovan tribalism into the federation of incipient state organizations focused on new Italian urban centres, around the Phoenician station of Punicum and other trading ports. The so-called "orientalizing" art styles marking the rise of the Etruscan states from their Villanovan peninsularity are, in fact, the trademark of the ornate, eclectic pastiche of the Phoenician "*art nouveau*", found from the Levant and Cyprus, to Greece and Crete, North Africa and Iberian Tartessos. Phoenician glass, ivories, jewellery, gold and silver bowls, bronze metalware and fibulae appeared in the richer Etruscan chiefdoms which could now pay for them with quantities of copper and iron from the enormously rich mines of Vetulonia and Populonia. The rustic Villanovan chiefdoms rapidly emerged as the twelve states of the famous Etruscan federation and Tyrrhenian thalassocracy *ca* 800–500 B.C. The kingdoms of Etruria and Tartessos were, thus, indirectly the offspring of the mercantile enterprises of colonial expansion into the West Mediterranean and, doubtless, even beyond these coastal states, there were more distant political repercussions of a similar nature.

The Phoenician and later the Greek penetration of the western Mediterranean was a new phenomenon; it was not confined to the establishment of small commercial *karum*, it was the permanent settlement of complete communities in a network of advanced and literate colonial cities. The Phoenician colonists first extended this replicating pattern of urban states to the western Mediterranean shores, established a colonial thalassocracy, and introduced full iron technology and all the concomitants of literate state organization to within range of the European tribesmen of Mediterranean Italy, France and Iberia. The infiltration of the southern end of the Atlantic maritime network by the Phoenicians, *ca* 900 B.C., finally harnessed the economies of outer Europe to the urban markets of the Mediterranean, a process rapidly intensified by colonial Greek settlement and trade with Celtic France and Italic Italy, *ca* 750–600 B.C., and by the colonial Etruscan Alpine trade with central Europe, *ca* 600–300 B.C.

VI. THE COLONIAL EMPIRES AND THE PRE-INDUS-TRIAL IRON TECHNOLOGIES

This closing epoch marks the great acceleration in the progress of the "Mediterraneanization" of Europe, a process which continued until, in recent centuries, the rising economic supremacy of the northern industrial nations reversed this flow of variety. The threshold of this accelerated transformation of European culture was defined by the Subatlantic climatic oscillation, the European adoption of full iron technology, the development of European urban centres, the economic and political intervention of Mediterranean states in European affairs, and the Mediterranean introduction of coinage and cash market economies. Uneven in their distribution and significance, more apparent in the south than the north, these changes nevertheless combined to foretell the end of European tribalism and the rise of the feudal nation states.

The Subatlantic climatic oscillation rapidly displaced the prevailing warm and dry conditions of the Subboreal Bronze Age and introduced our current European climatic pattern. This oscillation opened *ca* 800–400 B.C. with a preliminary extreme phase, even colder and wetter than at present. Beech and hornbeam woods displaced the oak forest in the south, under the more rapidly circulating cool and wet air cover which then made for improved agricultural conditions in middle and Mediterranean Europe. In the far north, however, this oscillation tended to waterlog the rich, valley pastures and killed them with creeping peat bogs; the poorer glacial soils rapidly deteriorated to sandy heathland, and the Atlantic coastal woods were finally deforested. In the mountainous interior of Scandinavia, Britain, and the Alps, the treeline retreated some 200 metres from the summits; thus, in favourable situations, further developing the high grazing meadows available for transhumance or hunting. In the lower lands of middle Europe, the fat loam soils were increasingly liberated from the forest by the iron axe and ploughshare, whilst further north the acid German heaths developed their modern guise, stretching into the zone of inland Hiberno-Scandinavian bogs and meres. As the marginal coastal conditions for Scandinavian farming retreated, the context for intensive hunting, trapping and reindeer grazing enlarged in Norway and in the Scandinavian mountains; everywhere the farmers of the European high valleys increasingly developed the art of the seasonal exploitation of the exposed mountain pastures. In short, the folkways of historic Europe now began to emerge from amidst the more ancient patterns of existence.

Under the Subatlantic climate, the mainly Celtic lands of middle and Mediterranean Europe flourished, whilst the Teutonic area astride the German Sea suffered the unfamiliar constraint of an expanding population and a contraction in the area and quality of available farming land. The agrarian frontier, which had been pushed towards the Arctic Circle itself, now recoiled to a more southerly horizon and the Teutonic tribes were faced with increasingly severe problems in territorial adjustment. Whereas the Celtic tribes expanded westwards into the flourishing lands between the Rhine and the Ebro, and eastwards into the Balkans, the Teutonic tribes sought *lebensraum* to the southeast, pushing beyond the Elbe into the Slav territory of the south Baltic forests. The Slavs were thus pinched between the expanding Teutons, Celts and Scyths and were themselves obliged to erode the territory of their eastern Balt neighbours. The climatic, economic and political factors were beginning to emerge which ultimately combined to stimulate the expansive redeployment of northern populations in the Migration Period.

The rapid adoption of iron technology by the European tribesmen between *ca* 800–500 B.C. contributed to the increasing dislocation of political and economic patterns which had been relatively stable throughout the later Bronze Age; old centres now became peripheral and former peripheral areas became of central importance. The European interior was far richer in high-quality iron resources than the lands of the Mediterranean littoral, with western and central Europe richer in their turn than the Balkans; the broad parity that had already been established with the Mediterranean was now firmly displaced in favour of the centre and west of Europe. The new strategic raw material gave the barbarian territories a far greater economic potential, eventually realized with the rise of coal fuel. Iron and steel now provided cheaper, more plentiful, more durable and sharper weapons and tools, whilst bronze production was released for ornaments and tableware. The expensive flow of bronze artefacts was displaced by a more egalitarian flood of iron and steel implements; even the plough, the mattock and the spade could now be shod with iron, and the cheap iron nail or clamp could be freely employed in more complex structures. Furthermore, the new iron shares and coulters could tackle the more fertile, heavy loam and clay soils of vast untapped areas of glacial Europe, whilst the old Bronze Age centres on the thin chalk and gravel topsoils became of more marginal importance.

The old patronage group of the bronze-equipped *élite* certainly continued as the iron-equipped *élite* of the new societies, but the military and economic capacity of the great mass of ordinary tribesmen was no longer so closely controlled by the chieftain's central role; iron was a more "democratic" raw material than any since the days of the flint and stone technologies. This subcultural shift in the internal balance of tribal power was no less significant than the territorial displacements in the foci of European agricultural and economic importance. Widespread social unrest within the tribes of Europe was thus as significant a factor in these times as the unrest between tribes. Young nobles and warrior-band *impi* could now more easily usurp tribal power, or even detach themselves entirely and wander as marauders and mercenaries to the fringes of the civilized world, to the despair of the pedant palaeologists. Chiefdoms and kingdoms were tending to become oligarchies, detribalization was beginning and the tribally "free man" was now almost a social and economic possibility.

The crucial iron technology spread into Europe along a broad front and after a long period of infiltration as an expensive and peculiar metal, fit for decorative purposes only. Iron would not melt at the available furnace temperatures and, therefore, could not be cast in the mass production technique used for bronze tools – enigmatically, iron could be uselessly soft, or hard and brittle to the point of intractability, sharp and bright or dull and corroded; the operating factors controlling these properties of iron thus required a new understanding. However, the early Anatolians had solved these problems and the Hittites quickly appreciated the stiffness of thin iron blades for daggers and rapiers, which were produced in restricted quantities from before 2000 B.C. down to the collapse of the Empire *ca* 1200 B.C. The Hittite collapse and the dispersal of its border tribes has always been taken as the traditional starting point for the spread of iron technology through the Mediterranean and into Europe. However, modern evidence points to an earlier and more gradual spread of iron with a pronounced lag before its technology was properly appreciated by the rather differently orientated bronze smiths.

A knowledge of iron had certainly reached the eastern Danube by the close of the Middle Bronze Age, as can be seen from the iron-hilted bronze dagger from the Otomani site of Gánovce *ca* 1300 B.C. (Pleiner, 1969). The evidence now points to an early "important phase", in which Anatolian iron objects were sent as gifts to distant potentates and redistributed even beyond these recipients – iron probably appearing in this way in the Balkans, Mycenaean Greece and Crete, the Levant, and Egypt between *ca* 1500–1200 B.C. This initial period of iron imports and the reworking of imported iron introduced iron trinkets and iron wire inlay to the Middle Danube *ca* 1200–1100 B.C. at the same time, or a little earlier, that the same features arrived in the Italian mainland by sea. However, between *ca* 1100–800 B.C. the native production of iron began and increasingly displaced bronze for most weapons and tools, which at first were slavishly copied in the new metal; the Balkans, the Danube valley, Greece and Italy now began to mine and smelt their own iron ores. In the west, the Phoenician trading-posts introduced iron artefacts to the southern Iberian peninsula *ca* 900–800 B.C., whence some slight knowledge of the metal spread into the Atlantic maritime network. Nevertheless, the abundance of local bronze supplies in both the Atlantic west and the Scythian east prolonged the continuing production of some bronze weapons and tools down into the fourth century B.C. in those areas.

The second factor contributing to the political and economic transformation of the European tribal kingdoms was the development of urban centres in Europe itself. One may waste a great deal of energy in arguing the definition of urban units, but, broadly speaking, it is possible to distinguish four categories of early European urban settlements; the first two classes were Mediterranean in style and the latter two categories were partly indigenous native developments and partly the convergent consequence of indirect Mediterranean stimuli – the Timbuctoo and Benin of Europe. In the first instance, we have the instrusive European urban centres of the colonial leagues, the Greek towns of coastal Scythia, Thrace, Italy, Liguria and northern Iberia, the Phoenician towns of southern Iberia, and the Etruscan towns of Alpine Italy. These centres were mainly walled towns of *ca* 50–100 acres with densely packed housing for some 5000–10 000 colonial settlers and their slaves. In the hinterland of these major colonial centres, there developed lesser urban foci, usually around old tribal fortresses; these towns were often unwalled and loose concentrations of terraced housing, extending over 10–50 acres around a central citadel, the inhabitants being local tribesmen and a few merchants. These two urban categories share with those that follow a political and economic importance far greater than their population sizes imply; these sites were focal centres, the seats of major political potentates or their oligarchs, the centres at which peripheral produce was redistributed and integrated in skilled manufacturing processes, the point to which the trade networks converged, the cultural intensifiers of their regions.

In the areas remote from the colonial zone, the earthen ramparts and palisades of the earlier timber townlets proliferated within the tribal areas of Europe, the nodal point of each chiefdom. These occupied hill forts rarely exceeded 25 acres of low-density housing and probably seldom held permanent populations of more than 2000 people, leaving ample room for cattle, refugees and garden plots within the earthworks, which usually enclosed an area roughly double that covered with housing. In the closing centuries of this era, however, there had condensed far more vast timber towns or *oppida*, still with low-density housing but sprawling over 50–200 acres within undulating sites defended by linear earthworks; extreme examples such as Kelheim and Heidegraben on the Upper Danube enclosed 1500 and 3500 acres, respectively. These *oppida* were usually the focus of a confederacy or kingdom and, besides enclosing the royal hall and mint, they might house from 2000–10 000 inhabitants, including industrial specialists of all kinds and often embracing in the outer ward of the fortifications the fields necessary for their support. However, lest one is dazzled with the scale of European urban centres at this time, one must match them not only against the colonial towns but against the many Mediterranean cities, which enclosed 200 acres at high density, and the metropolitan capitals of 400 acres and more, with some 30 000 inhabitants.

The near Eastern urban network now stretched in a continuous economic superstructure over the littoral of Mediterranean Europe and in a discontinuous lattice stretching far out across the European hinterland. At the centre of this network lay the Persian Empire and its metropoli, surrounded in the west by smaller urban confederations and leagues, such as those of the Greeks, Carthaginians and Etruscans, and beyond these again there now extended the native towns of the Iberian, Celtic, Thracian and Scythian tribal kingdoms. As far as peripheral Europe was concerned, one of the most important agents in the coastal colonization was the Greek maritime leagues. The Phoenician and Etruscan thalassocracies continued, but first the Assyrian and then the Persian conquests of the Levant isolated Carthage at the head of the western Phoenician colonies and, at the same time, stimulated the resurgence in Greek colonial activities.

Early Greek colonial activity continued the Mycenaean pattern with the Ionian settlement of coastal Anatolia and coastal Sicily and southern Italy *ca* 750–700 B.C. Again, following the Mycenaean lead, exploratory voyages were made from these two major trading areas northeastwards into the Black Sea and westwards into the western Mediterranean. In the Black Sea, a chain of early colonies was established *ca* 700–600 B.C. in the coastal lands of the Thracians, Getae and Scythians, strategically placed at river mouths conveying staples from deep in the interior, and regularly spaced at one or two days' sail along the coast. The most important centres, Panticapaeum, Olbia and

Tomis, rapidly became wealthy cities with regular trading relation–
ships stretching hundreds of miles into innermost Europe.

Panticapaeum lay in the Crimean wheatlands at the mouth of the
Sea of Azov, with the river Don stretching away into distant Muscovy
and a coastline adjacent to the metalliferous Caucasus. Olbia was
founded at the joint mouth of the rivers Bug and Dnieper, which Herodotus' informants knew intimately for some 40 days' travel inland towards Kiev. As the northernmost port in the Black Sea, Olbia was at
the point where the Baltic trade emerged and where the steppe, deciduous forest and coniferous forest resources are closest to the sea. The
Olbian merchants knew all about the Scythian mare-milkers of the
steppe, the gold-winning Agathyrsi of the Carpathians, the wolfskin-
clad warriors of the Slav Neuri around the southern Polish swamps,
and even something of the distant Fenni fur-trappers of the coniferous
forests. Greek wine, oil, pottery, jewellery and metalware passed
upstream in quantity as far as Kiev, whilst amber, furs, hides, pitch,
gold, slaves, wheat and horses passed to the coast for redistribution by
the maritime network. Similar products were brought to Tomis, the
strategically sited outlet for the entire Danube trade. Avoiding the
dangerous marshes of the Danube delta, the colony of Tomis was cunn-
ingly situated to the south, where the meandering channel of the
Danube comes closest to the coast; thus, an easy portage of 50 miles
to Tomis on the coast cut out 250 miles of perilous delta swamp navigation. By *ca* 300 B.C., the inland trail of Rhodian wine and oil amphorae
was matched by a scatter of silver coins of Thasos, reaching as far as
the Theiss and Maros rivers, although concentrated in the hoards of
the middlemen south of the Iron Gates. Together, these colonies on
the Black Sea regularly supplied the Greek mainland with very large
quantities of important staples, including cereals, salt, iron ingots, hides,
timber, slaves, ship's tar, salted meat, salted sturgeon and tunny fish,
as well as such luxuries as honey, amber, fine furs, Carpathian and
Caucasian gold, and Thracian silver.

In the western Mediterranean, the Greeks fought their way into the
highly competitive market by a mixture of intrigue and violence
launched from the homeland and from the eighth-century footholds
in southern Italy and Sicily. The Carthaginian league already
embraced all the Phoenician cities of northern Africa, western Sicily,
Sardinia, the Balearics and the annexed kingdom of Tartessos, whilst,
from their Iberian bases, the voyages of Hanno and Himilco, respectively, explored the African coast down to Sierra Leone and the European coast as far as Brittany by *ca* 450 B.C. In the north, the Etruscan
confederation was at the height of its power and, both politically and
economically, controlled the area from the Campanian and Adriatic

coasts to the foot of the Alpine passes. The colonial Greeks skilfully usurped the Punic trade with Etruria, whilst at the same time inciting and aiding the Latin tribes against their overlord. The wedge between the Punic and the Etruscan leagues was then driven home by the defeat of their combined fleets at Alalia off Corsica by the Phocaeans in 535 B.C. and by the successful land and sea operations of the successive tyrants of Syracuse over several centuries. By these devices, the Greeks managed to infiltrate the gap between the southern Iberian colonies of the Carthaginians and the western Ligurian colonies of the Etruscans. The Phocaeans quickly founded a major colony at Massilia *ca* 600 B.C. to command the Rhône trade and by 500 B.C. a belt of Greek towns extended from Nice to Alicante under the general patronage of the flourishing Massiliotes. Even earlier, *ca* 640 B.C., Colaeus of Samos had successfully slipped through the Pillars of Hercules and returned with a cargo of Iberian silver. But although other Massiliote captains, like Pytheas in *ca* 300 B.C., repeated the voyage of Himilco to the British Isles, the subsequent Carthaginian seizure of southern Spain forced the Massiliotes to concentrate on outflanking this Atlantic blockade by trading overland to the Atlantic estuaries of the Gironde and Loire and to the headwaters of the Rhône itself.

In general, the Greek settlement of the Gulf of Lions resembled the colonial pattern adopted in the Black Sea – a string of coastal towns carefully placed at the natural outlets of rivers and routes running deep into the interior. The luxuries and manufactured goods of the Mediterranean now flowed inland in exchange for cereals, hides, wool, iron, tin and slaves, ferried in a continuous flow from the distant bounds of the Celtic territories. However, the competitive commercial enterprises of the Massiliote Greeks and the Etruscans seem to have clashed deep in Alpine Europe. The Etruscan expansion to the foot of the Alps intensified the ancient trade with the Celtic tribes of the Upper Danube, importing salt, tin and amber whilst exporting jewellery, bronze wine services, wine and oil. About the same period, the Massiliote merchants appear to have established commercial connection with the same Alpine area from the headwaters of the Rhône valley and a trade war seems to have ensued, on a military footing in the Mediterranean and on a commercial basis in the interior.

The nodal triangle between the headwaters of the Saône, Seine, Rhône, Rhine and Danube, only 100 miles broad, thus became a competitive focus, attracting all the luxuries of the Greek and Etruscan world. Glass, coral, gold, jewellery, fine Italian metalware, wine services, Greek pottery, oil and wine now flowed into the tribal strongholds of this crucial area, whose chieftains controlled the redistribution of British and Breton tin from the Seine, Belgic iron from the Rhine, amber, salt and copper from the Danube valley. One stronghold, at Heuneburg on the Upper Danube, suddenly sported a novel bastioned brick wall in provincial Greek style – surely planned by some Greek adviser; other sites in the same general region have revealed the princely wealth of the chieftains' burials with their Rhodian flagons and southern Italian wine services. However, amidst the riches of Kappel, Vilsingen, Grächwil and Berne, the grave of the Celtic queen at Vix, on the Upper Seine, is the most remarkable. This innominate Boudicca lay on a dismantled wagon with a Graeco-Italian gold torque at her throat, quantities of ornaments of bronze and amber around her and a complete bronze table set of southern Italian origin, with accompanying Attic wine cups. In the corner of the grave there stood an import of regal proportions – a huge bronze volute-krater, $1\frac{1}{2}$ metres tall and magnificently decorated, probably the work of the best Tarentine workshops. The Vix krater, and the accompanying wine service and gold torque may well have been part of a Massiliote diplomatic embassy of especial importance in the commercial rivalry with the Etruscans; a royal gift of prodigious value commissioned and brought from the finest southern Italian *ateliers* to the wharves of Massilia, then laboriously shipped to the Upper Saône and presumably presented by a deputation of merchant ambassadors, anxious to secure the continued flow of trade upon which their livelihood and that of Massilia depended.

A fascinating picture of the Mediterranean penetration of Europe now emerges, with the first definite evidence of Mediterranean merchant-explorers sailing the Atlantic coastline, operating deep in Iberia, following the Rhône to the umbilical communications' centre of Europe, crossing the Alpine passes from Etruria to the Celtic homelands, following the Danube to the Iron Gates, exploring the Dnieper northwards to Kiev and probing the Sea of Azov to the mouth of the Don. These expeditions were not the work of the epicurean Greek literati, who all too rarely allude to their taller stories, but the achievement of largely anonymous freebooters, speculative merchants, mercenary artificers and artisans, renegade riff-raff, outlaws of the frontiers of civilization; the opportunists of the colonial world, destined to remain nameless unless they returned with the fortune which could transform their venality into nobility, as happened to Colaeus of Samos. These hybrid frontiersmen, sparingly literate, clad in the outlandish mixture of Greek and native dress so carefully depicted on colonial works of art, but the joke of the Attic Comedies, these were the men who penetrated the southern flanks of Europe to a depth of some 300 miles and talked with Herodotus of their 40-day journeys inland.

This largely riverine penetration of southern Europe was not a uniform process; on the contrary, the trade goods often show a markedly polarized distribution, in which the largest quantities of the finest products appear mysteriously concentrated at the most distant extremities of exploration. The richest presents and the finest wines were destined for those distant kings and chieftains who could most fundamentally control the flow of desirable European commodities and their redistribution. The very finest products of the civilized world appear in the distant treasuries of the Celtic *élite* at Vix, Mont Lassois, Camp du Château and the Heuneburg, in the hoards of remote Geto-Thracian aristocrats at Craiova and Agighiol, or amidst the wealth of faraway Scythian princes at Chertomlyk and Kul Oba.

Everywhere in the wake of these deep commercial penetrations of middle Europe are found the coins of the Greek colonial cities. At first, these coins were probably accepted as so much convenient gold or silver bullion, but gradually their convenience as a medium of exchange for certain restricted transactions became apparent. The earliest Mediterranean coins were struck by the Lydian kings, *ca* 700 B.C., possibly for the express purpose of paying mercenary soldiers unable to take payment in kind, a purpose for which much early coinage was specifically minted. These early coins were not, however, the first currency — they were merely another medium of exchange circulating in addition to the variegated iron spits, bars and ingots, gold and silver rings and lumps, bronze rings, axes and even arrowheads. The superiority of coins lay in their standardization in convenient units of exchange, visibly authenticated by the stamp of the issuing authority; a cash market economy was now possible. From the Lydian kingdom, the production of coinage rapidly passed to the adjacent Ionian cities and, by *ca* 600 B.C., most of the cities of the Greek maritime leagues were already minting their own coinages. Some especially reliable, plentiful and pure coinages rapidly gained confidence as international currencies — the Persian "archers", the Corinthian "foals", the Athenian "owls" and the Macedonian "Philippi", for example, but the majority of coinages circulated internally within a more restricted group of local markets.

The Iberians, Celts, Geto-Thracians, and Scythians rapidly became acquainted with the coinage of the Greek merchants and coin balances are a frequent find in the European tribal *oppida*. The employment of coinage for military pay, for provisioning armies in the field and for the widespread employment of tribal mercenaries also trailed coinage in the wake of every military expedition into Europe; from the Persian invasion of Dacia and Scythia in 515 B.C. and the expeditions of the Macedonian kings into Bulgaria and Yugoslavia between *ca* 450–350 B.C. to the Celtic mercenaries hired by the Etruscans, Graeco-Italians and Syracusans from *ca* 450–300 B.C. and the Punic forays into central

Iberia *ca* 400–200 B.C. By *ca* 300 B.C., there was widespread familiarity
with money transactions in middle Europe and, soon after this date,
the Celts of France and central Europe began to mint careful copies
of the "Philippus" and the coins of Massilia, whilst the Geto-Dacians
simultaneously copied the coins of Larissa and Thasos as well as the
Macedonian series; likewise, the northern Iberians struck inscribed
coins based on the drachmae of Greek Emporion and the southern
Iberians copied the Punic silver of the Barquidae. These earliest European coinages were initially very close copies of the original Mediterranean models, and even carried intelligible inscriptions either taken
from the original source, or, more significantly, introducing the name
of the issuing dynast or tribe and thus giving evidence of a growing
acquaintance with Mediterranean letters and language. This same evidence also suggests that the earliest tribal coins, with their neat filleted
borders and accurate inscriptions, were designed and produced for the
local chieftains by Mediterranean craftsmen working in native service.
Perhaps the same renegades that helped negotiate with grasping merchants and advised on matters varying from the best wines and tableware
to problems in fortifications, or even those early artificers who stimulated the rise of the great native art-styles with their Mediterranean
embellishments. However, after the art of coin striking was learnt and
the foliate basis of Mediterranean art appreciated, the tribal artificers
took over with their own weird elaborations; neither the coinage nor
the art-styles can be said to degenerate, they are simply transformed.

The native European coinages circulated primarily within the restricted markets of particular tribal kingdoms and their distributions
clearly define the territories belonging to various tribal unions. These
local coinages probably gave a great economic stimulus to the internal
production and retail of goods of all kinds in a market economy, at
the same time tending to accelerate detribalization by their increasing
substitution in transactions formerly fulfilled by mutual obligations. In
many respects, the subsequent emergence of the European feudal state
economies represented the further development of these early changes.
The feudal economies embrace a category of systems employing redistribution mechanisms intermediate between those of the tribal societies
and those of cash economy revenue states. At first sight, the feudal
machinery is apparently based on the minutely detailed, formalized
and institutionalized hierarchy of personal obligations and services in
return for land held. In fact, the minute evaluation and codification
of these obligations can be shown to have evolved largely in order to
convert these theoretical statutory services quickly and conveniently
into pecuniary or other equivalents. Ultimately, the European feudal
systems elaborated an almost ritual formalization of the tribal clientship

system in terms of a calculus of archaic obligations long since superseded, in order to harness an ancient social pattern with an economy
based in reality on revenue, taxes, coinage and manufacturing towns;
a calculus in which "x equals obligation" was substituted by "x equals
cash equivalent".

However, it is unlikely that the earliest European tribal coinages
were used in quite the advanced manner already in vogue throughout
the Mediterranean cash markets. Initially at least, these tribal coins,
struck with mystic tribal insignia at the royal *oppida*, may have served
very restricted and carefully prescribed internal tribal purposes; hence
their restricted distributions. What these various restricted transactions
might have been can only now be guessed, but in northern Europe there
long survived the custom of treating the small issues of tribal coinage
as symbolic wealth medallions in the gift of the chief or king, bestowing
status and approval to the holder, and circulating in society at large
as wealth held for services to the tribe and its royal family, exchanged
for material commodities only when necessary. Perhaps we should take
in this context the curious stories of the *potlatch* ceremonies of Luerna,
the King of the Arverni, who distributed gold and silver coins to his
tribesmen by his own hand from his chariot (Filip, 1960, p. 96). Certainly, the acceptable media of exchange for barter, clientship, blood-
money, bride-price, dowries, tribute and taxes long continued to involve
the traditional commodities – cattle, grain, salt, iron, tools, weapons or
garments, and to what extent coin could be substituted in these transactions we do not know.

Within the span of this closing period, the entire lateral band of
middle Europe was penetrated by the commercial and political agents
of the Mediterranean powers. This infiltration operated at many social
and cultural levels and proceeded on a series of broad fronts from western Punic Iberia, to Greek Celtica, Etruscan Rhaetia, to Greek Illyria,
Thracia and the Pontus. This intensive subcultural interpenetration
nevertheless had repercussions far beyond those limited areas directly
penetrated by Mediterranean merchant-adventurers; the whole area
south of the Rhine and Danube was directly or indirectly exposed to
massive new stimuli, as well as lesser influences in restricted areas even
further to the north. Barbarian mercenaries, artisans and slaves now
served in the armies, factories and cities of the Mediterranean powers.
Conversely, Mediterranean adventurers, advisers and artificers also
entered the service of the barbarian potentates and introduced them
to literacy and other delights and achievements of the civilized world.
At a more direct level, there was outright interaction between the
armies of civilized Persia, Macedon, Etruria, Massilia, Punica and
those of the barbarian Scythians, Thraco-Getians, Celts, Ligurians and

Iberians – battles in which the Scythians and Celts were able to defeat the finest field armies of the ancient world and permanently seized southern France, northern Italy, Anatolian Galatia and the Coastal Pontus, respectively. Even at more indirect levels, the mutual inter-action was a significant factor in stimulating novel social, material, eco-nomic, religious, political and artistic developments that were not en-tirely one-sided. This intensive subcultural ferment extended not only along the entire geographical frontier between Mediterranean civiliza-tion and the tribal kingdoms, but also proceeded in depth, down the whole social frontier from the luxury-loving *élite*, to their dependent artificers, the surplus-producing tribesmen and the mercenary warriors, to the industrial slaves and captives.

It would be quite untrue, however, to portray the economic develop-ment of Europe purely in terms of an increasing degree of Mediter-ranean penetration. The economic development of Europe, like that of historical Africa, was indeed transformed by colonial intervention and its repercussions, but the pattern that was thus transformed was already a European pattern, long before the changes began and long after their withdrawal. The general analogies between the Mediter-ranean impact on ancient Europe and the colonial impact on historical Africa are quite striking, especially in relation to the rise of the tribal chiefdoms, urban development, detribalization and the rise of the native nation states, with their initial instability.

In ancient Europe we can note the transition from a phase in which European products were an economic curiosity for the Mediterranean states, *ca* 2000–1400 B.C., through a period of their increasing but still peripheral importance, *ca* 1400–600 B.C., to a phase in which European commodities were a small but crucial element in the expanding Medi-terranean economies, *ca* 600–0 B.C. This latter phase commences with the full deployment of the urban colonial bases along the southern European coastline and the expansion of their role in the political and economic affairs of tribal kingdoms far beyond their immediate vicini-ties. This external colonial stimulus, aided by the development of coinage and re-distributional cash market economies, catalysed the formation of larger kingdoms and confederate chiefdoms, centred on increasingly more complex *oppida* and townlets. Everywhere, imported objects and artificers stimulated the European development of new but markedly hybrid native art-styles, initially the distinctive livery of the subcultural equipment and insignia of their Mediterraneanized patrons, the tribal *élite*. The parallel inceptions of the Ibero-Punic Tar-tessian, Graeco-Celtic La Tène, Thraco-Getian, and Graeco-Scythian art styles were the artistic offspring of this seminal episode.

It is during this transitional phase, *ca* 600–0 B.C., that Spanish,

French, northern Italian and Carpathian metal resources first became essential to the exponentially expanding requirements of the Mediterranean world. At the same time, the Iberian, Celtic and Scythian supplies of cereals, salted meat and fish, wool, hides and slaves had become only slightly less important reserves for the increasingly industrial and decreasingly agrarian Mediterranean cities. The situation was rapidly approaching the point at which leading Mediterranean powers could no longer afford to allow the flow of such vital European resources to fluctuate at the whim of distant despots and at the risk of interception by political rivals. The European Greeks, however, were more interested in the superior resources and tempting challenge of the Near East, commercially following the conquests of Alexander into India itself, but firmly holding their Celtic and Pontic granaries nevertheless. The Carthaginians and Etruscans began to appreciate and militarily exploit the European trade routes on their immediate borders, in Iberia and northern Italy. But these developments were rudely interrupted by the rise of Rome, the former Italic puppet of the Hellenic league, which now began to exploit its central location and the divisions between its Etruscan, Punic and Greek rivals.

Rome quickly overthrew its Etruscan overlords, with the tacit acquiescence of the Greek colonists of Italy and aided by the devastating raids of the Celts through the Alpine passes *ca* 410–390 B.C. Subsequently, the rapid expansion of the Latin league, headed by Rome, alarmed the Graeco-Italian cities into united action under Pyrrhus, King of Epirus, but, although actions were lost, the new power was not crushed and opportunist Carthaginian activities in Sicily intervened *ca* 278 B.C. The Romans then absorbed Syracusan Sicily and Massiliote Gaul in return for protection against the expanding Carthaginian domain, *ca* 210 B.C. The great duel of the Punic Wars finally culminated in the triumph of the Roman legions, the surrender of Carthage and the Roman occupation of Iberia *ca* 200 B.C. Greece fell next in *ca* 146 B.C. and Mediterranean Europe had finally become a Roman province. From this broad beachhead, the Roman military machine expanded inexorably – Scythia followed in *ca* 70 B.C., northern Gaul *ca* 50 B.C. and, by the reign of Augustus, the Roman legions were deployed on the new Rhine and Danube frontier *ca* A.D. 9. The colonial leagues of the old Mediterranean world were now engulfed in the military empire of a European super-power, the western successor to the eastern empires of Alexander and the Persian Achaemenids. Henceforth, the detribalized but dependent Europeans, south of the Roman frontier, were tax-paying members of one huge revenue state. North of the new Rhine–Danube frontier there now developed a new trade zone and new barbarian chiefdoms competed in unstable perturbation;

to the north, the Germans and Slavs, to the east the Huns and Parthians. The thresholds of the European German empire and the Slav kingdoms, the Medieval feudal nation states, the Renaissance colonial powers and the empires of the Industrial Iron Age were yet to come.

The author is deeply indebted for the help of Andrew Sherratt in reading and discussing the manuscript, and would also like to acknowledge the debt which he owes to Paul Wilkinson for help and advice in preparation of the section on Palaeolithic commodities.

REFERENCES

Bailey, F. G. (1958). *Caste and the Economic Frontier*, Manchester University Press, Manchester.
Bass, G. F. (1966). *Archaeology under Water*, Thames & Hudson, London.
Bordes, F. (1968). *The Old Stone Age*, Weidenfeld and Nicolson, London.
Carpenter, R. (1966). *Discontinuity in Greek Civilisation*, Cambridge University Press, Cambridge.
Casson, S. (1937). *Ancient Cyprus*, Methuen, London.
Childe, V. G. (1929). *The Danube in Prehistory*, The Clarendon Press, Oxford.
   The Cambridge Economic History of Europe, Cambridge University Press, London, Vol. II, Chap. 1.
Clarke, J. G. D. (1952). *Prehistoric Europe; the Economic Basis*, Methuen, London.
Clarke, J. G. D. (1965). Traffic in stone axe- and adze-blades, *Economic History Review*, **18**, 1–28.
Clarke, D. L. (1968). *Analytical Archaeology*, Methuen, London.
Ebert, M. (1924–32). *Reallexikon der Vorgeschichte*, de Gruyter, Berlin.
Filip, J. (1960). *Celtic Civilisation and its Heritage*, Czech Academy of Sciences, Prague.
Firth, R. (ed.) (1967). *Themes in Economic Anthropology*, Tavistock Press, London.
Gardin, J. C. (1965). The reconstruction of an economic network of the second millennium BC, in *The Use of Computers in Anthropology* (D. E. L. Hymes, ed.), Mouton, The Hague, pp. 378–391.
Gimbutas, M. (1963). *The Balts*, Thames & Hudson, London.
Goody, J. (1969). Inheritance, property and marriage in Africa and Eurasia, *Sociology*, **3**, 55–76.
Harding, T. G. (1967). *Voyagers of the Vitiaz Strait*, Manchester University Press, Manchester.
Hutchinson, R. W. (1962). *Prehistoric Crete*, Pelican Books, Harmondsworth, Middlesex.
Jaśdśewski, K. (1965). *Poland*, Thames & Hudson, London.
Leroi Gourhan, A. (1961). Les fouilles d'Arcy-sur-Cure (Yonne), *Gallia Préhistoire*, **4**, 3–16.
Mecaros, G. and Vertes, L. (1955). A paint mine from the early Upper Palaeolithic age near Lovas, *Acta Archaeologica Hungarica*, **5**, 1–34.
Mouton, P. and Joffroy, R. (1956). The Aurignacian site of Les Rois, Mouthiers, *Gallia*, Supplement 9.
Nandris, J. (1968). Lepenski Vir, *Science Journal*, pp. 64–70, January 1968.
Palmer, L. R. (1963). *Mycenaean Greek Texts*, Clarendon Press, Oxford.

Pilbeam, D. L. and Simons, E. R. (1965). Some problems of hominid classification, *American Scientist*, **53** (2).

Pleiner, R. (1969). Iron Age: a notion in history, paper presented at the symposium on "Theory and Methodology in Archaeological Interpretation" at Flagstaff, Arizona, September 1968.

Pradel, L. (1952). Fontenioux, *Bulletin de la Société Préhistorique Française*, **49**, 413–432

Service, E. R. (1966). *Primitive Social Organisation and Evolutionary Perspective*, Random House, New York.

de Sonneville-Bordes, D. (1960). *La Palaeolithique Supérieur en Périgord*, Delmas, Bordeaux.

Taylour, W. (1964). *The Mycenaeans*, Thames & Hudson, London.

Ventris, M. and Chadwick, J. (1956). *Documents in Mycenaean Greek*, Cambridge University Press, London.

Vertes, L. (1959). The Mousterian in Hungary, *Eiszeitalter und Gegenwart*, **10**, 21–40.

Zeuner, F. E. (1965). *A History of Domesticated Animals*, Hutchinson, London.

The Beaker Network — Social and Economic Models

DAVID L. CLARKE

THE THEORETICAL ASPECTS
(OR THE GAMES THAT ARCHAEOLOGISTS PLAY)

The beaker problem is like other problems in archaeology. It appears to be merely a matter of fact, simply requiring more data, a fine classification and a more detailed chronology for its ultimate solution. This promised solution to the beaker "problem" has been imminent for almost half a century now and yet recedes from our grasp. In reality, the problem is not a matter of data but a matter of alternative assumptions and approaches, alternative models and concepts, alternative questions and explanations – in short, a matter of theory. The data that we take is already theory-laden and a product of our selection, modified by the limitations and obscurities of the archaeological record, our methods of recovery and examination, and by our languages of expression. Finally, this contaminated and impure information becomes the victim of archaeological reasoning, classification, interpretative modelling and explanation. Dare we suspect, perhaps, that the beaker "problem" is a philosophical artefact of our own manufacture, an unreal problem, an insoluble problem or perhaps a problem not worth the effort of solution?

The beakers of Europe and North Africa certainly represent a classical problem for traditional archaeology. Within this paradigm the problem becomes one of "origins". Rival hypotheses for beaker origins and dispersion compete one against another in terms of various universal culture historical explanations, operating upon general classifications with simple cultural models. These hypotheses variously arrange the data of the moment to be "judged" or "tested" mainly by the chronological and distribution evidence available at the time; attempts to

Reprinted with permission from *Glockenbechersymposion Oberried 1974* (J. N. Lanting and J. D. van der Waals, eds), Fibula-van Dishoek, Bussum/Haarlem, 1976, pp. 459–477.

explain how, when and where the beaker culture first emerged and spread using the traditional Montelian approach.

This traditional approach to the classical problem of "origins" is by no means without value but there is reason to doubt if much more can now be usefully achieved by using these procedures on our poor data samples with our coarse chronological methods. There are also additional reasons for believing that even within this traditional approach a successful outcome is denied by a combination of semantic confusions (the people who used beakers – the beaker people) and inappropriate assumptions, objectives, models, classifications and explanations. Certainly, little more has been achieved than a bewildering flight of the "area of beaker origins" from one region to another in a shifting and almost cyclical pattern of changing consensus views.

New approaches would wish to begin at a more humble level but aim at more lofty objectives. Within these paradigms the problem of "origins" becomes partly an unrealistic attempt to answer a largely inappropriate question of dubious meaning, and partly in the aspects which can be answered certainly one of secondary importance. They would seek more limited but penetrating explanations for other questions and for smaller parts of the beaker problem, with its imperial dimensions; explanations which seek to understand the cumulative causes of the variability in beaker assemblages within particular contexts and varied ecologies, in both domestic sites and graves, across limited spans of space and time. These problems require a better initial understanding of the functional and idiosyncratic attributes of the beakers and their assemblages, *before* any classification. Then with the aid of such preliminary analyses we can formulate more realistic models of the probable range of social and economic behaviour involved in the manufacture, distribution, usage and deposition of the entire pottery assemblage and its associated artefacts, sites and contexts. Wherever possible scientific and quantitative techniques and appropriately sophisticated models must be used in limited analyses in order to test and assess the significance of these results more stringently. Better explanations may partly follow from the manipulation of more varied and meaningful classifications but meaningful classifications themselves depend upon purpose, and the essential attributes for the purpose depend upon an understanding of the context and background aspects *before* and not after a classification has emerged.

These objectives may sound like the work programme for a ten-year plan – and this is precisely what they are. New paradigms open up fresh routes for advance and map out large areas of work yet to be accomplished; old paradigms age because they have little further to offer beyond their established achievements. It follows that in this intermediate stage no summary article can produce the results of much hard work which still remains to be done. Nevertheless, a useful start has been made in this very Symposium, first by eschewing the overall problem of "origins" and concentrating on the developments in limited regions, second by the valuable probing attacks upon the primary problems of functional variability and social and economic factors (van der Leeuw and Shennan). This paper will try to complement that work, first of all by sketching some of the general weaknesses of the universal explanations and oversimple models within the conventional approaches to the beaker problem and then by exploring some alternatives with an emphasis on the domestic sites and their possibilities.

Even within its own framework the traditional attempts to offer a single comprehensive explanation for the origin and spread of beakers seem doomed to failure. Quite apart from the semantic confusion about whether the explanation relates to the origin and spread of different people who used beakers, one beaker people, merely the beaker drinking vessels or a total cultural assemblage – there remains the fatal tendency to seek single all-embracing explanations for a large, diverse set of phenomena. The favourite explanations have usually been culture historical hypotheses of invasion, migration and diffusion, or genetic explanations of the form that beakers developed out of "X" and into "Y"; explanations in which people and pots have been obscurely fused. Social, economic, ecological and environmental explanations have also been singled out for universal application to the beaker phenomena but with less fervour because their inherent clarity makes them the more easily refutable.

Now this is not to deny that these factors were operating in the beaker case. On the contrary, the point is that it is self-evident that all of them will have operated to some degree in various combinations in particular local circumstances since they merely describe aspects of every human population. The error resides in the attempt to single out one aspect and apply it universally to the beaker phenomena from Norway to North Africa, from Ireland to Hungary, over a time-span which varies regionally from perhaps a century to over half a millennium. A more basic objection is that, at best, these explanations suggest "how" certain circumstances arose but almost none of them move on to "why" scattered communities over vast distances came to take up and later gave up using certain fine pottery and other distinctive artefacts. Fundamentally, the latter question identifies more central and general concern with mechanism and with process than the traditional preoccupations with ceramic "origins", which are to some extent irrelevant to its pursuit.

Beakers present different phenomena in the different areas of their occurrence. In some areas we have thousands of beaker sites (Britain), in other equally well-researched areas there are a few dozen finds (Denmark). In some contexts we have one or two beakers associated with the domestic-material of indigenous Neolithic groups and forming less than a few per cent of the assemblage (Ogna, Rogaland, south Norway; Skjølsvold, 1972). In other contexts there are domestic sites in which no other tradition is present and the fine decorated beakers make-up some 30% or more of the material, numbering some scores of vessels (Molenaarsgraaf, Netherlands; Louwe Kooijmans, 1974). Over and above this crude variation we have areas and assemblages with barbed-and-tanged arrowheads, bracers, buttons, copper daggers and metal trinkets associated with beakers but in others the beakers are associated with only some of these goods and alternatives are used in addition, elsewhere again the same associated artefacts are found with other ceramic assemblages.

Even if by "beaker assemblages" we specify the regular associations of the fine pottery then there are clearly different kinds of beaker presence. The beaker phenomenon is a different phenomenon in different areas and different though related explanations may be required for these differing contexts. A universal, Pan-European, single factor explanation is unlikely to be a realistic hypothesis to account for the variability in local densities, settlement and domestic contexts, association and distribution patterns and varied time depths. The mechanisms which produced thousands of beakers with their own domestic sites interspersed with a relatively dense indigenous Neolithic tradition across the seas in Britain are likely to be rather different from those operating in Denmark or even in the Netherlands, and in the inland areas of Europe. Towards the end of this paper we will try to move a little way towards crudely defining some kinds of beaker presence and offer some tentative sketches for the economic and social models and explanations which might be involved.

However, before we can move on to alternative objectives and alternative models and explanations for particular beaker contexts we can learn some useful lessons from the inadequacies of the simple and often anachronistic models currently in vogue.

The implied assumption underlying many of the conventional models and hypotheses about beaker pottery has been that the pots are merely and exclusively a cheap, functional domestic product made by every housewife. This represents a particular extension of the set of undiscussed and implicit assumptions which underlie so much archaeological hypothesis; a combination of anthropological *naïveté* and anachronistic modern values (e.g., cheap, insignificant domestic pottery) – the output of that conveniently uncomplicated lay figure *Homo archaeologicus* which archaeologists use to make complex archaeological problems simple and determinate. Such an approach gives a quick, convenient and simple answer and what is more important it gives a single answer which does away with the embarrassing problem of testing between many viable alternative possibilities, or at least the problem of handling many viable alternative possibilities. Alas, *Homo archaeologicus* seems to be extrapolated modern, urban Euro-American man in hairier clothes but still basically modern man with none of the alarming habits of the "primitives" – "irrational" behaviour, complicated kinship, and non-optimizing economics which cannot even be separated from social and religious factors.

In relation to decorated beakers in particular, and other prehistoric fine wares in general, the assumption that all such pots were simply cheap and utilitarian functional vessels, made within each household, would now seem improbable in the combined light of the evidence for the contemporary prehistoric exchange networks, the evidence of direct experimental analogies, the evidence of broadly based ethnographic models, and increasingly in the light of the direct physical evidence of the fine beakers themselves and their domestic sites. Of course the situation is complicated, and we shall go on to examine some of the potential complexities, but the probability is that although much of the domestic ware may have been locally made, some at least of the finest beakers, in some contexts, will have been exchanged over considerable distances from their place of manufacture. In short, as an initial working assumption from which to depart, it now seems safer to invert the traditional assumption and wiser to assume that beaker fine wares were major vehicles of rank, prestige, and status display, very expensive to produce both in man-hours and in contemporary value terms, and therefore exchanged for these reasons over considerable distances, between various communities, in a context where their utilitarian and functional values were secondary. Such a combination of local production, exchange and copying of course raises considerable problems for the classical culture concept and simple direct ethnic interpretations and explanations.

What evidence can we produce for such an iconoclastic view? Well, let us start with the simple *a priori* evidence. Contrary to archaeological belief, the finest potting clays have very special qualities and are almost as restricted as other rare mineral resources such as copper and gold ores; this in itself puts a very different complexion on the attractions of such areas and resources in prehistoric times. Moderate and adequate potting clays are of course a good deal less restricted, indeed fairly widespread especially in glaciated areas. However, the local conjunction of *first* quality clays, abundant and suitable fuel and water, adjacent to good land and dense settlement is an uneven and very restricted occurrence (Fig. 3). Against this background, even from the period of the earliest Neolithic ceramics, settlements in poor potting areas would have found it more economical to import good clay or ready-made vessels from a distance, via a simple exchange network (Fig. 1).

Most peasant pottery assemblages from the earliest times onwards embrace a crudely hierarchical range of wares – fine wares, everyday wares and heavy-duty wares (Fig. 2). The fine ware, often of thin, carefully prepared and well-fired first quality clays, is usually elaborately shaped and burnished, and frequently lavishly decorated, encrusted or

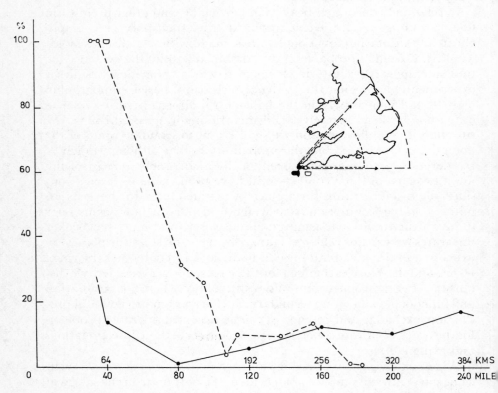

Fig. 1. Neolithic pottery and stone axe exchange from westernmost Cornwall *ca* 3500–3000 B.C. The decrease in the percentage of Hembury "f" ware in contemporary pottery assemblages and the fluctuating density of Cornish Group I axes with distance from Penzance (pottery open circles, axes filled circles). The Group I axes and the pottery of gabbroic clay come from neighbouring sources in the West Cornish area (Mounts Bay and Lizard Head). The maximum range for the distribution of the pottery is *ca* 180 miles radius and for the axes *ca* 350 miles radius (see inset map with radii). Based on original research by Ian Hodder; Clarke, 1965; Peacock, 1969.

painted. Although such fine wares are functional and utilitarian, within that "function" they often clearly, directly and symbolically communicate the large-scale expenditure of energy considerably in excess of merely utilitarian requirements. These are the fine vessels frequently selected for burial with individuals; these are the vessels which are often made by a few seasonally semi-specialist potters within each village or at the optimal clay and fuel areas and then widely copied and exchanged beyond these centres. The everyday wares are usually less elaborate and more closely related to the short-lifetime duties of cooking and food preparation; consequently less energy is wasted in decoration and wherever possible they are produced from locally adequate clays. In some cases, much of the everyday ware represents the undecorated

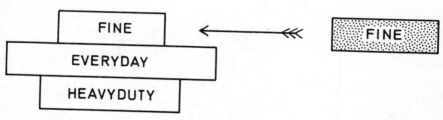

Fig. 2. Model I: A schematic model of the crudely hierarchical set of subassemblages in most peasant pottery assemblages – fine prestige wares, everyday utilitarian wares and heavy-duty storage and special process wares (see text). One fine ware may displace and substitute for another without altering the substratum of local everyday and heavy-duty wares.

or swiftly adorned residue left after selecting the best of each batch for more elaborate decoration; a fossilized stage of production. The heavy-duty wares are usually related to large storage vessels, beer brewing pots, durable vessels for special processes and so forth. Their large size and special use often dictates special engineering and construction qualities, involving large gritting, thick wall diameter, ring construction, strengthening ribs and rustication. Complete beaker domestic assemblages display all of these varieties of wares from the fine burnished, heavily decorated and sometimes encrusted and even painted beakers, through the undecorated or lightly rusticated plain beakers, bowls or "Begleitkeramik", to the huge potbeakers with their heavy plastic rustication and ribbing or large flowerpot or bucket shapes (Clarke, 1966, pp, 181, 183).

This is of course a far too generalized model of pottery assemblages but it is an improvement on many implicit models and it does already begin to explain and predict certain possibilities (Fig. 2). The prestige

and display value of the fine wares and their special production requirements would tend in many cases to make them semi-specialist products for exchange; it would also suggest that they would therefore have
large distribution and replication areas whilst at the same time making
them more volatile to fashion changes and substitution by alternative
fine wares, or indeed by any alternative prestige and display artefacts.

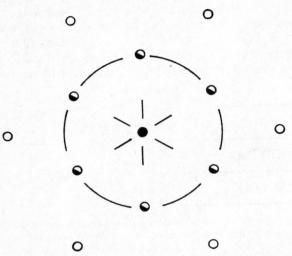

FIG. 3. Model I: The spatial representation of the "simple" situation. Sites close to
good clays produce all their own fine wares and exchange their products within a network of other sites taking part in the reciprocal exchange of commodities. A domestic
mode of production, without full-time professional potters is assumed (see text) within
a reciprocal exchange context.
    ●, Beaker culture sites near good clays, producing all their own beakers and export-
ing (30–20% fine beakers in domestic assemblage); ◑, beaker culture sites on moderate
clays, producing most of their own beakers but importing a percentage (30–20% fine
beakers in domestic assemblage); ○, beaker culture sites on bad clays, importing
all fine ware (10–0% fine beakers in domestic assemblage).

In contrast, the more locally produced, short-lived, everyday wares
would tend to represent more stable and locally long-lived potting
traditions – an old-fashioned and conservative reservoir in some respects but an area of more free innovation in certain others, providing
prototypes for eventual fine wares. The heavy-duty wares would be
somewhat similar although their specialized usages would make them
susceptible to special changes of a technological and functional kind.
    One fascinating implication of this as yet crude and simple model
is that in such situations one might expect to detect assemblages united

over large areas by their common fine ware, obtained and copied within interlinked exchange networks at one level, but differentiated beneath this superficial uniformity by much more regional substrata of local everyday and heavy-duty wares representing the common products of much more directly interrelated communities; although the inverse of this model also represents another real possibility. The attraction of the former model is that this is indeed what we seem to observe with the interregional beaker fine wares and the distinctly regional beaker domestic wares, themselves grouping within larger traditions often both antedating and post-dating the beaker "Horizon" (Fig. 4). These con-

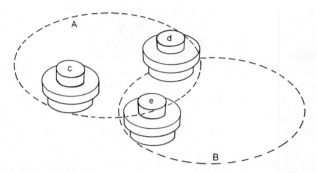

FIG. 4. Model II: A schematic model of the hierarchical set of pottery subassemblages (fine ware, everyday ware, heavy-duty ware) (see Fig. 2) at three domestic sites "c", "d", "e". A common exchanged and copied fine ware is shared by all three sites which are then part of an interregional fine ware "culture/tradition" "A". However, beneath this fine ware uniformity based on exchange and replication are more regional everyday and heavy-duty ware groupings, e.g., "B".

siderations are not of course restricted to beaker pottery and in the earlier Corded Ware/PFB tradition too we can perhaps separate the interregional beaker forms from the distinctly regional ceramics of the localized Vlaardingen and Haffküstenkultur everyday and heavy-duty wares.

Although this theoretical model of pottery assemblages is capable of further development, especially in its sampling implications, it is nevertheless important to point out that it will always be too general-ized for many real situations. To mention but one, it is sometimes the case that the technical requirements of the heavy-duty *pithoi* are quite as demanding in special skill and raw materials as any fine ware. In such cases, there will probably emerge distribution networks for these coarse wares of a larger or smaller area according to local context factors and communication facilities. Clearly, changes in settlement density, social organization, transport technology and changes from exchange networks to market and cash economies will clearly add many other complicating factors.

In respect to the implications for the culture concept we may note that although many commodities, including pottery, will be moving in such networks the cultural constraint in the choice of "what to buy" is not substantially different, as market geographers have found, from the cultural choice of "what to make". In other words, although the culture defined merely in ceramic terms becomes a blurred concept, nevertheless the fact of exchange networks and exchanged commodities merely adds to the various levels of networked interrelationships, of one kind or another, which go to make up these polythetic and many-dimensional entities. What does emerge as a possibility is that the term "network" may perhaps be preferable to the overburdened term "culture" since it directly links the network of settlements on the ground, the network of interrelationships between the people within and between those settlements and the dynamic form of the network – the operational system. Certainly a practical consideration raised by such an appraisal is – what are the factors which cause a population to reorientate its network of relationships from one alignment to another?

So far our evidence for the exchange of beaker fine wares has rested on this simple *a priori* model, and its capacity to fit some of the observations on the ground (Figs 2, 3). This is of course at best merely circumstantial evidence in favour of but one out of many possibilities. However, we can produce some direct archaeological evidence which seems to demonstrate that European pottery was being exchanged over some hundreds of miles radius at least a thousand years before the development of the beaker wares (Fig. 1). At the same time, there is a little direct and some indirect evidence that some beakers at least were also exchanged similar distances in a like manner (see below). Finally, there is the abundant evidence that stone axes, flint, obsidian, amber, callais, copper, gold, ivory, shells were being regularly exchanged over large areas of Europe not only earlier than but in many circumstances in association with beaker settlements. Given the restrictions, on fine clays, fuel, water and appropriate skills it seems unlikely that such a valuable and convenient unit as pottery, especially fine beaker pottery, could fail to be distributed in a similar way within these contemporary networks; especially when an overwhelming mass of ethnographic data from many different continents suggests not only the restricted, repetitive and stereotyped nature of suitable exchange commodities but also confirms the universal role of fine pottery in this capacity (Sahlins, 1974; Dalton, 1971).

Preliminary analyses of some of the fine painted wares of the Balkan and south Italian Neolithic from 5500 to 3000 B.C. seem to indicate a combination of local production and the more widespread exchange of the finest prestige products as early as the Starčevo, Proto-Sesklo and Capri phases, culminating in the elaborate production and distribution networks for the Tripolye, Gumelnitsa, Serra D'Alto and Dimini products (Clarke, 1952, p. 251; Renfrew, 1973, p. 190). Even in the context of the Linearbandkeramik groups on the Rhine we have evidence for the early exchange of pottery along the river network, although there is need to check the old analyses with more modern techniques (Clarke, 1952, p. 251). In all of these cases the pottery is but one element in elaborate cyclical exchange systems involving *Spondylus*, rare and useful stones, attractive raw materials or metal goods and trinkets; a whole range of primitive valuables moving principally by canoe along coastal and riverine networks.

The most clear and direct evidence for early pottery exchange over a distance is only now emerging as the result of the growing programme of thin-section analyses and neutron-activation studies. Perhaps the best example can be taken from Peacock's analyses of British Neolithic Hembury ware, which demonstrates that as early as 3500–3000 B.C. fine wares made near the Lizard in Cornwall were being distributed by boat over a radius of some 160 miles (256 km) (Fig. 1) (Peacock, 1969). Greenstone axes from the Group I axe factories in the same general area of Cornwall display a related but more extensive distribution pattern. Although these distribution patterns vary significantly with the kinds of material exchanged, the order of magnitude of archaeological and ethnographic cases frequently reach distribution radii approaching 150–200 miles (256–320 km).

Unfortunately, although obviously now a rich field for research, the thin-section and neutron-activation studies of beaker sherds have only just begun. Our model (Figs 3, 5) would predict that the majority of beaker ceramics was locally produced but that a small and very important proportion of fine wares should have been more widely exchanged. Indeed, we do have a little evidence for this already in the beaker case. The analysis of a beaker from Chesham, Buckinghamshire, significantly belonging to the Wessex/Middle Rhine typological group, has suggested manufacture from a clay of the Middle Rhine area, whilst there are other indications that the same network may also have circulated Alpine copper, tin bronze, Niedermendig querns and Rhenish jadeite axes in Britain (Clarke, 1970, pp. 84–107). More oblique but probably indicative evidence can be drawn from the occasional occurrence of exotic beakers characteristic of one area quite out of context in other distant beaker assemblages – for example the "Moravian" beakers from

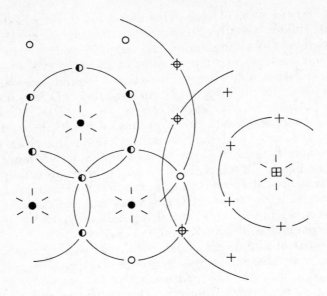

FIG. 5. Model II: The spatial representation of the more "complex" situation (heavily idealized). Once again, sites close to good clays produce all their own fine wares and exchange their products within a network of other sites taking part in the reciprocal exchange of commodities (Model I, Fig. 3); in this case beaker culture sites inter-penetrate non-beaker culture sites operating their own exchange network (circle and cross symbols). However, sites with marginal clay supplies or in locations marginal to the networks may acquire the fine ware of one group whilst maintaining the everyday and heavy-duty wares of another (Fig. 4); with network reorientations through time the position becomes more complicated. The model is *not* to be seen as the *economic* market areas of competing centres of pottery production (anachronistic) but merely the ceramic aspect of complex, *social* exchange systems circulating pots, axes, trinkets, textiles against women, food, metals and other resources. Note the convergence in the marginal zone of beaker and non-beaker assemblages (all up to 10% fine beakers) otherwise distinguished by the rest of their domestic assemblage (sites with open circles and crossed circles).

●, Beaker culture sites near good clays, producing all their own beakers and export-ing (30–20% fine beakers in domestic assemblage); ◑, beaker culture sites on moderate clays, producing most of their own beakers but importing a percentage (30–20% fine beakers in domestic assemblage); ○, beaker culture sites on bad clays, importing all fine ware (10–0% fine beakers in domestic assemblage); ⊞, non-beaker culture sites, producing all their own fine ware and exporting (0% fine beakers in domestic assemblage); +, non-beaker culture sites, producing most of their own fine ware but importing a percentage excluding beakers (0% fine beakers in domestic assemblage); ⊕, non-beaker culture sites, importing all fine ware (0–10% fine beakers in domestic assemblage).

West Overton, Wiltshire, and Harskamp, Veluwe, or the Dutch "Veluwe" beaker from Frankenthal in the Middle Rhineland (Clarke, 1970, pp. 87, 99, 157). Since it now appears that beaker bracers of rare and attractive stones were also items of widespread exchange (Clough and Green, 1972, p. 138) there might be a significant relationship between the Dutch "Moravian" beakers and the exotic Dutch bracers of Bohemian/Moravian purple-brown stone (van der Waals and Glasbergen, 1958).

The validating evidence for the exchange of beaker fine wares must await the detailed results of extensive programmes of thin-section and neutron-activation techniques. However, *a priori* evidence (Fig. 3) suggests that we should expect to find a limited but extensive exchange of beaker fine wares and products over some hundreds of miles as part of exchange cycles in many commodities; networks which existed long before the beaker period and which continued to form an important basis for Early Bronze Age "trade". Certainly, thin-section analyses show that by *ca* 3000 B.C. it was not unusual for limited quantities of fine pottery to move over a hundred miles by sea (Fig. 1). In the later beaker context itself we have definite and unassailable evidence that other commodities were exchanged with increasing vigour and it would therefore be highly surprising if some of these extremely fine vessels had not moved within the same networks, as other ceramics had done both before and after the beaker phase.

To summarize: contrary to conventional archaeological assumptions, for reasons of uneven resource distribution, it would now seem more likely that a small proportion of pots was exchanged between sites from the very inception of pottery making. Later on, more substantial proportions of fine wares were increasingly widely exchanged as but one of many organic and inorganic commodities circulating against one another, where the inorganic commodities of the archaeological record are merely the skeletal trace of this much more comprehensive range of both staples and valuables. Partly because it was less expensive in time and energy to exchange and import fine wares from centres on good clays, near sea or river communications, and partly for social reasons involving personal alliances, prestige, status symbolism and display behaviour – it would be natural for fine pottery to enter these exchange activities. In a period when the best long-distance bulk transport was undoubtedly provided by canoe it is not surprising to see the role of the sea routes and river networks as a major factor in beaker distribution, particularly the Rhine, Rhône, Danube network with their convergent headwaters, and the littoral and island chains of the West Mediterranean and North Atlantic.

The beaker distribution then may not be entirely or even substanti-

ally a distribution of beaker societies so much as groups who wished
to import beakers. In this light the beaker "culture group" would indeed more realistically be called the beaker "network" – certainly the
distribution has more holes than nodes and those areas of contemporary
population which did not participate in the beaker exchange cycle then
become of intense interest in their own right (e.g., the SOM and Grand
Pressigny network). However, we do not wish to commit the very error
of universal single factor explanations which we set out to avoid. In
other words, although exchange networks must surely have been an
important factor in the development of some of the regionally differing
beaker phenomena, none the less regionally many other factors will
also have been involved. Although we may characterize the culture
group as a network and distinguish the people who use beakers from
the beaker people – nevertheless, it remains an important truism that
there will have been a "core" area in which beakers were first developed
together with other aspects of the characteristic beaker assemblage of
artefacts and activities. But before we approach that problem via the
different kinds of regional and domestic beaker presence it would be
as well to complete our rejection of the conventional assumptions that
prehistoric ceramics were simply cheap, utilitarian, functional containers made within each household. This we can best illustrate by a
combination of ethnographic analogy and direct experiment.

ETHNOGRAPHIC AND EXPERIMENTAL MODELS

Before the archaeologist can achieve any really useful interpretation
of prehistoric pottery phenomena he needs to consider on one hand
the known general range of analogous ethnographic situations and on
the other hand the additional range of *a priori* theoretical and experimental models which provide a supplementary range of possibilities
for investigation and test. This procedure helps to prevent the archaeologist making the immediate mistake of interpreting the past purely
in terms of either the restricted variability of the modern present or
the ethnographic sample. However, to do this with rigour would
require a handbook on the ethnography of ceramics and a three- or
four-year research programme. Archaeologists are indeed beginning to
assemble just this kind of data in a series of important studies in ethnographic contexts, beginning at the more "humble" level discussed in
the opening paragraphs of this article. Here, we shall merely borrow
some recent ethnographic data of this kind to illustrate the general
nature of some of the "non-modern" factors which may be operating
in such a setting and at the same time to give some impression of quan-

titative "order-of-magnitude" figures for some of the key steps in pottery production in this kind of context; these figures converge with a little direct experimental evidence gained from trials in beaker manufacture and decoration. However, it must be very severely stressed that we are not taking these few studies as definitive models for the beaker case – they merely identify some relevant factors in a general context, and no more.

First of all, the archaeological data provides an expanding body of evidence for the increasingly vigorous exchange of many commodities between European communities from *ca* 6000–2000 B.C. There is direct evidence that communities using beakers were very actively involved in such exchange networks in regard to a number of products and resources and circumstantial evidence strongly points to the inclusion of some of the fine decorated wares within such cycles. Our first need is to gain some impression of the general nature of networks such as these and this we can glimpse both from studies in archaeology and economic anthropology (Clark, 1965; Sherratt, 1976; Dalton, 1971; Sahlins, 1974; etc.).

The primary point to stress is the multiple purposes of these networks – their social and religious roles were quite as important as their undoubted economic consequences; important both at the time and for the interpretive archaeologist today. Food, artefacts, domestic animals and useful resources circulated in exchange networks but so did sea-shells, feathers and curious arbitrary valuables. Indeed, primitive valuables often had individual names; pedigrees and genealogies of successive holders were treasured and recited, they were not anonymously interchangeable units (Dalton, 1975). Items were often ranked or classed, each grade of valuable recycling in specially defined and restricted systems of social, political, religious and economic transactions and events, such as bridewealth, bloodwealth, fines, reparations, sacrifice, warfare, raiding, ceremonials, alliance formations, and so forth. The acquisition and interchange of primitive valuables often circulated within an *élite* "prestige" cycle as a means of acquiring, symbolizing and displaying status, prerogatives, power, an *entourage* of followers, or superior political, military, judicial and religious roles. Clearly, different items circulated in different ways for different purposes but, for example, if fine beakers were involved in circulation in partly religious and social contexts then the appearance of such vessels in graves and at ceremonial sites may take on a rather different aspect and the substitution and eventual displacement of one such fine ware by another may require new dimensions of explanation (Fig. 2).

The production and exchange of pottery in such contexts is very well documented and we can take the particular cases documented for the

Goodenough Island, Amphlett Group and Wanigela community, all in the Papuan area (Lauer, 1970, 1973; Egloff, 1973). The pots are made by a proportion of the women (*ca* 55%) in the potting villages with access to good clay quarries and even these villages are frequently 2 kilometres (1.3 miles) and up to 4 kilometres from their clay sources (2.6 miles). Clay sources at much greater distances are also exploited if they may be directly approached by canoe. Pot making is a seasonal activity, usually following a regular cycle geared to the breakage and demand rate, the seasonality of travel and raw materials and the competing demands of other activities. Clays are frequently "alloyed" or mixed and prospecting for fresh clay sources is a major activity; if the clay source is at a distance households will store clay "hoards" and the average canoe load will provide 400–600 kilograms of clay. In the Wanigela case suitable timber fuel is only available at a distance and sometimes journeys of more than 6 kilometres (4+ miles) have to be made for fuel alone.

Even if one chooses to ignore the social and religious context of this pottery production then the economics of this activity alone strongly refute the anachronistic "cheap" pottery model and these figures are by no means extreme within the ethnographic range. The following data represent the *average* time spent by a Goodenough housewife in the process of making *a single pot*; the sequence of activities is given on the left (after Lauer, 1973).

Processes	*Time taken for a single pot*

Quarrying clay;
  selective digging,
  transport,
  storage
	1.3 hours

Preparation of clay;
  wetting the clay,
  kneading and cleaning
	0.5

Building the vessel;
  forming rolls,
  rolling strips,
  ring-building the vessel
	1.0

Initial drying;
Smoothing the exterior;
Decorating the vessel;
  lifting, beating, trimming,
  preparing rim,
  decorating,
  scraping and burnishing the interior.
	1.5+

Drying the vessel;
Firing the vessel;
  gathering fuel,
  preparing the fire, } 1.0
  setting the vessels,
  lighting the fire,
  tending and removing vessels

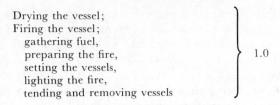

TOTAL = 5.3 hours per vessel

The economics of this activity are striking. Just keeping a small household of six persons in pottery, in the period before modern European containers, required more than 100 work hours or 16–20 days work a year without allowing for the surplus production of pottery for exchange. Even today, in this context, each household produces 4–8 pots a month and pot-making averages 1–2 days a week, depending on the season.

The pots produced in this way are partly used for domestic consumption and partly for exchange within and between villages over considerable distances – especially to villages without good clay quarries. The pots exchange against food, canoes, feathers, shells, cloth and obsidian as well as entering varieties of social and prestige transactions. Busama taro, for example, is traded against southern pottery at a rate of 22.5 kg (50 lb) of taro to one small pot or 70 kg (150 lb) to one large pot (Sahlins, 1974, p. 289). A very large canoe could be obtained by villages without large canoe timber for about 80 pots, or a single piece of bark cloth for a single pot; the value of the pots is high and commensurate with, although not determined by, the time and energy expended in their production. It is significant that the factors which limited the area of dispersal and influence of these ceramics was not determined as in a modern economic situation by competition from other ceramic centres but by problems of transportation and distribution; since for social and prestige reasons exotic pots will penetrate regions which have abundant pots and clays of their own, quite apart from areas without these resources. The reciprocal exchange networks, of which the pottery was merely one commodity, were necessary to maintain and stabilize the pattern of life of settlements both with and without key resources – canoe timber, vegetal foods, domestic animals, axes, textiles, etc. – both in lean years and in good ones. In the Amphlett group alone 3000–3500 kilograms of food were exchanged into the system from outside each *month*; one wonders if site catchment-area analysis takes this kind of factor, probably present from the earliest Neolithic times, sufficiently into account.

How would these "order-of-magnitude" figures and general considerations affect the beaker case? Well, the finest beaker pottery is if anything more carefully made and more heavily decorated than the Goodenough pottery, with the most careful treatment of the clay and control under firing. A heavily decorated late Veluwe beaker or southern British beaker may have between 2000 and 5000 dentated spatula impressions on a single vessel and over and above this may be colour encrusted and wiped, or even painted as we now know. Direct experiment confirms that the Goodenough Island figures of 1.5 hours for clay preparation and vessel building, together with a minimum of a further 1.5 hours for decoration, could hardly be reduced for the heavily decorated beaker fine ware. In short, a period of *ca* 4–6 hours' work would be needed for each fine decorated beaker; everyday vessels left at the undecorated stage or made less carefully from less well-prepared clays would achieve a significant saving and cost *ca* 3–4 hours work, or less if clay and fuel are easily accessible.

What does all of this imply for the significance of the beakers in their own and other contexts? It suggests that the fine decorated beaker was in its context an expensive commodity to produce – expensive in time and energy in an agrarian economy where both were under heavy competitive pressure (e.g., preparation of the daily cereals by grinding and cooking alone will have required several hours a day). By contrast, it costs the average working man in western Europe less than 0.1 hours work to buy a china cup (say 10p) whereas each fine beaker cost *ca* 4–6 hours work, the equivalent of, say £4–6, and even the everyday ware *ca* £3–4 a vessel. Of course this direct equivalence cannot quite be made in this way, but the "order-of-magnitude" difference is quite apparent and the anachronism of extending a modern attitude to cheap utilitarian pottery breakage emerges as not so very trivial; no wonder so many prehistoric pots were so laboriously mended by drilling and glueing.

Prehistoric pottery was worth mending in prehistoric contexts, and in areas with poor local clays or inadequate fuel it will often have been more efficient to import finer and durable products of better clays and with a longer working life than to use exclusively poor local products. The fine decorated beaker then emerges as an expensive chunk of congealed time and energy quite apart from the prestige and status role of its exchange contexts. Judging from the demography of its grave associations the fine beaker was sometimes restricted by age and status; perhaps as a rank symbol it was the funerary equivalent of the elaborate stone battle-axes which it displaced in the Corded Ware assemblages. This in turn raises the interesting cultural question of the causes and the consequences which follow when one set of rank, status and prestige symbols are displaced by another and our archaeological interpretation of these kinds of event.

Certainly the fine beakers were an expensive and prestigious item and we would expect them to fulfil an important role in the beaker exchange cycles already documented for stone axes and bracers, flint axes, copper and bronze daggers and points, copper, gold and silver trinkets, ivory, amber, callais, shells and perhaps salt, textiles, women and pots? The alternating zonal style of beakers and their detailed motif vocabulary have often been compared to those of simple textiles and it is perhaps tempting to speculate that the women, textiles and beakers formed related parts in self-reinforcing regional systems of considerable stability. Thus the economy of beaker-using groups is in many areas associated with a more open environment with greater areas of fallow and grazing and an increased emphasis on stock, including sheep. The more efficient metal axe must have assisted this development and the ard intensified it, releasing increasing quantities of labour from hoeing fields for the growth sectors of shepherding, shearing, wool processing, weaving, dyeing, textile manufacture and the development of dairy products. That these developments had already taken place in some areas before the rise of the beaker phenomenon is certainly implied by the elaborate zoned, geometric motifs and textiles suggested by the Sion, Petit Chasseur menhirs and the Almerian schist "idols", for example.

One could imagine that particular textile weaves and geometric styles might become at first accidentally typical of certain areas, valleys and locations by the limited interchange of women and their motifs within bounded networks and then perhaps self-consciously developed as a group identifying and symbolizing heraldic device in a manner similar to the rise of the tartans of the Scottish clans and the clothing idiosyncrasies of the North American Indians (Clarke, 1968, p. 395). If the women who intermarried wove the textiles and also made and decorated the fine beakers for exchange then it would be easy to understand how each reciprocally influenced the other, leading to a stable and explicit symbolism in both textile and pottery motifs with the remarkable regional and temporal stability and conservatism observed in some of the regional beaker traditions, lasting over half a millennium in some cases. The direct circulation of women by intermarriage, against bridewealth and alliance payment in pots, textiles and other commodities might complete the association picture but this much is speculation, although perhaps ultimately not untestable speculation.

Primarily we wish to make the case that prehistoric pottery was often an expensive domestic necessity as well as a significant social and economic factor in daily life. Over and above this it became, in certain circumstances, a major vehicle for display and symbolism directly communicating to the contemporary casual observer aspects of the social and economic status and alliances of the household; "functional" display far in excess of the merely utilitarian requirements of pots for domestic purposes. Now, this special role and attributes of some fine pottery diminishes if superseded by new alternative age, sex, rank and status display equipment. Within this context, for example, the Late Neolithic across much of Europe seems to reflect the culminating peak in the social importance of painted or decorated pottery for symbolic display – the cumulative ceramic technology of the preceding centuries provided an ample repertoire, the domestic mode of production was still predominant and equally important still socially tied and socially accepted. Perhaps, then, the regionally different but widespread "decline" in potting standards to the bare minimum necessary to do the job, significantly correlated with the onset of the Bronze Age, might be seen as the social displacement of fine pottery from its role as a primary prestige vehicle, by bronze weaponry, metal vessels and gold finery, and the repatterning of the "Neolithic" ceremonial exchange networks involving pots, feathers, obsidian, stones, flints and shells by freshly important incipient trade networks circulating quantities of bronze daggers and axes, pins, torques, gold trinkets and other items (Clarke, 1970, p. 233). Perhaps too, the poor quality of the pottery may represent not a squalid degeneration but the move from the domestic mode of production of a socially important product to the restricted production in kilns of a more utilitarian artefact? At any rate, the change from the realm of the archer "Big Man" with his fine gold-tipped bracer and heraldic beaker to the Bronze Age "Chief" with his bronze axes, daggers, rapiers and metal finery seems to reflect just such a displacement of pottery from a once prestigious niche. The change resembles the devaluation of a currency – in this case a social currency – the devaluation of the ceramic unit of former exchange networks once necessary to maintain the pattern of life of "beaker" settlements in areas without suitable clays, copper or gold sources, adequate flint or stone materials, canoe timbers or whatever.

THE BEAKER PROBLEM

This article began by pointing out that the beaker "problem" for traditional archaeology is in the main the problem of "origins" and that newer approaches would prefer to attack other more limited problems of deeper scope. Nevertheless, even in its own conventional terms the problem of "origins" has been made intractable, in so far as it is at all soluble, by a combination of anachronistic and naive models – the *Homo archaeologicus* of the twentieth-century urban Euro-American academic. It is not claimed that the models sketched here are in any way more adequate but it is felt that they may show where some of the difficulties and inadequacies lie and point the direction in which more sophisticated models, studies and analyses might move. This is after all, a superficial symposium paper and not the end result of a deep and considered research programme. Nevertheless, we may paradoxically whilst pursuing these other objectives yet throw some oblique light on the problem of origins – admitting the truism that everything begins somewhere.

How do the preceding assumptions, hypotheses, models and speculations relate to this aspect of the beaker problem? First, at the general level, we would suggest the following.

1. The need to distinguish between "people who used beakers" and the "beaker people", if such can be said to exist.
2. The need to break down the problem into specific aspects and specific regional problems, especially the evidence for the pre-beaker, beaker, and post-beaker populations, assemblages and their quantitative interrelationships within and between domestic sites.
3. The necessary development of more appropriate and more complex models which may offer explanations for some of the variability observed in this way; these will necessarily involve more sophisticated social, economic and classificatory frameworks.
4. The beaker "problem" will be answered regionally, on domestic sites, and will require more sophisticated analyses (thin-section, neutron-activation, etc.) and a more quantitative approach; the mere presence or absence approach cannot tackle this problem involving different degrees, densities and types of beaker presence.

Then, at the more specific level it would appear that

1. Fine pottery was exchanged over distances of up to 150–200 miles (256–320 km) radius from European Early Neolithic contexts onwards (Fig. 1).
2. Beakers are some of the finest fine wares known in this period in western Europe, and since it is doubtful that all of the finest beakers could have been produced at all of the sites in which they occur, given the distribution of raw materials and skills, then we would expect and are now getting evidence that some beakers at least were circulating within exchange networks, alongside other known circulating beaker commodities.
3. The context of these networks was as much social and religious as economic and therefore interpretation must proceed accordingly.

Rather than leave these suggestions as a set of pious hopes, let us, whilst admitting the premature nature of the escapade, try and look at the direction in which this current evidence is running. First of all we can try to take up the challenge which asserts that the beaker problem will be solved regionally, on domestic sites, and will require a quantitative approach. The sampling problems imposed by the different levels of research and excavation in different areas are indeed severe but let us look and see.

Crudely speaking, inspection of the different kinds of beaker "national" presence seems to identify two artificial poles of density and occurrence.

Type 1 regional presence
A high density and frequency of decorated beaker sites (hundreds of thousands of sites with fine decorated beakers); many domestic sites known (hundreds); considerable local beaker continuity and time depth (C14 300–500 years).

Examples Type 1 presence
Netherlands and Low Countries
West Germany (in parts)
Eastern Britain (in parts)
France (in parts)
Northwestern Iberia (in parts)

Type 2 regional presence
A low density and low frequency of sites with decorated beakers (tens to hundreds); few domestic sites with decorated beakers (tens); considerable non-beaker continuity with little evidence of beaker time depth (C14 100–300 years).

Examples Type 2 presence
Denmark and Norway
Ireland (in parts)
Czechoslovakia, Poland, Hungary, Austria, Italy, southeastern Iberia
West Mediterranean islands, North Africa.

These divisions are of course crude divisions of a complex continuum with many elements involved and the sampling problems are sufficiently severe to threaten to move regions from Type 2 into Type 1 as evidence accumulates. Nevertheless, the startling differences between such well-researched areas as the Netherlands and Denmark suggest that some real underlying trends in density are involved.

In addition to those gross regional differences there appear to be correlated differences in the kinds of beaker "settlement" or domestic site presence. These are subject to the same kind of sampling problems of a no less severe kind.

Type A domestic presence
A high proportion of the vessels in the assemblages are decorated beakers (30–15%); representing a significant number of decorated beakers in contemporary use (tens to hundreds); accompanied by characteristic beaker domestic wares.

Examples Type A presence
Most Dutch domestic sites, e.g., Molenaarsgraaf (30–20%) (Louwe Kooijmans, 1974)

Most eastern British sites, e.g., Belle Tout, Sussex (25%) (Bradley, 1970), America Farm, Northants (30%) (Clarke, 1970, p. 490)

Some Irish sites, e.g., Dalkey Islands ? (Clarke, 1970, p. 529), Ballynagilly, Tyrone (?) (ApSimon, 1969)

Some French sites, e.g., Embusco (?) (Taffanel, 1957)

Some northwestern Iberian sites, e.g., Casa Pia, Belem Montes Claros (?), El Ventorro, Madrid (?)

Type B domestic presence
A low proportion of decorated beakers in the assemblages (1–10%); representing a small number of vessels in use at any one time (one to ten); accompanied by the domestic wares of some other group – Begleitkeramik, VNSP wares, Millaran wares, Protopolada wares, Corded Ware, etc.

Examples Type B presence
Myrhøj, Jutland (2–9%) (Jensen, 1972)

Some Irish sites, e.g., Monknewtown, Co. Meath (2–3%) (Sweetman, 1971)

Most Italian sites, e.g., Monte Covolo (3–5%) (Barfield, 1976)

Most southeastern Iberian sites, e.g., Cerro de la Virgen (5–10%) (Schule, 1976), Zambujal (1%), Vila Nova de S. Pedro (?) (Sangmeister, 1976), Tabernas (1%), Phenha Verde (8–10%)

Most if not all Czech sites (Shennan, 1976)

Most if not all Hungarian sites (Kalicz, 1976)

Most if not all Polish and North African sites.

These domestic sites are impossible to compare accurately; different areas and proportions of these sites have been excavated with varying techniques and sampling biases, even the percentages are not calculated on an identical basis. However, when we compare fifteen beaker sherds amidst a tonne of Almerian/Millaran domestic plain sherds from Tabernas with nearly a thousand decorated beaker sherds, accounting for more than a third of the assemblage at Risby Warren, Lincolnshire, associated with its own beaker rusticated ware, then an "order-of-magnitude" difference does seem likely to be involved. In addition, interesting modifications to superficial impressions are produced: for example, there emerges a virtual absence from Bohemia or Moravia of any beaker domestic sites approaching Type "A" proportions and this combines with the discovery that the dense distribution maps of Czech "beakers" are overwhelmingly composed of undecorated Begleitkeramik and not the much more sparse decorated fine beakers. Thus the hypothesis for an East European origin for beaker pottery would seem to draw little support from this evidence.

What overall conclusions can we draw from these different kinds of regional and domestic site decorated beaker presence? Probably, in the light of the sampling problems it would be most unwise to make any sweeping deductions. However, as a speculative hypothesis we might note the crude correlation between the domestic sites with a high proportion and large numbers of decorated beakers (Type A), with the regions having very high densities of individual decorated beaker find sites (mainly burials), unusually large numbers of beaker domestic sites and evidence for a considerable local beaker ceramic tradition (300–500 years) (Type 1). These Type 1/Type A areas seem to constitute regional foci within some kind of core area embracing Britain, the Netherlands, the Low Countries, West Germany, and more questionably parts of France, Galicia and the Meseta. Beyond this core lies a peripheral "halo" of mainly Type 2/Type B presence – regions having few dispersed sites, with very few beakers in domestic contexts, and even there associated, in extremely small numbers both absolutely and proportionately, with other local non-beaker ceramic traditions; the penumbra of Norway, Denmark, Poland, Czechoslovakia, Hungary, Austria, Italy, Almeria, Valencia and North Africa.

Taken altogether, if this evidence withstands the test of time, it might at first glance suggest a beaker network core area made up of regional nodes or foci with a regular reciprocal, long-lived and intricate exchange of commodities and kin, a cultural grouping presumably embracing the area of beaker origins. Around these nuclei it would be tempting to interpret the peripheral skirt of 150–200 miles (256–320 km) depth as exactly what we would expect from the outward exchange and copying of beaker ceramics within non-beaker networks, as predicted by the models at our disposal (Figs 1 and 5). However, our *a priori* models and the practical realities suggest that the phenomenon is at least a little more complex than this attractive core/periphery model might suggest. In reality, in several areas we have evidence of a complex interfingering situation in which sites of both crude types (Type A and B) are found interspersed within a single region; thus, for example, Monknewtown, Co. Meath, and Ballynagilly, Co. Tyrone, seem to illustrate this kind of dual presence in Ireland as do Cerro de la Virgen and Montes Claros, perhaps, in Iberia. In other words a simple zonal model with outwards distance decay of beaker presence will not suffice and the reasons probably involve the modifying factors of the physical interpenetration of one social network and economy by another, combined with the complicating effects of the differential distribution of suitable clays, fuel, water, communication facilities and other social, economic and environmental elements (Fig. 5).

Although the invocation of movements of people to account for the whole beaker phenomenon has clearly been drastically overdone, nevertheless in some cases explanations based exclusively on the replication of exchange partnerships and changing prestige gear do seem inadequate. Indeed, on the null hypothesis to invoke the opposite assumption "that there were no movements of people or communities in prehistory" would seem both extreme and undesirable. Thus in the case of the Mediterranean and Atlantic islands where miles of open and difficult seas had to be traversed, physical movements must be involved to some degree. In the Mediterranean, between the south of France, Liguria, the Balearics, Sardinia and Sicily this may have been of a limited kind but the extraordinary density of beaker burials, domestic sites and complete material assemblages found in eastern Britain, parts of Ireland and some of the distant Hebrides, for example, seem at least to some extent to require movements of population, albeit small in number, over prolonged periods of time and assuming indigenous continuity. Indeed, it would be quite natural for settlement to follow a period of across-the-sea exchange partnerships, alliances and reciprocal exchange relationships. Perhaps we might think in these "bow-wave" terms of an early period of Low Countries beaker/British Neolithic relationships commencing with a British Neolithic acquisition of a very few beaker goods and artefacts leading to the Grooved Ware tradition (*ca* 2500–2000 B.C.) only subsequently followed by physical beaker settlement from across the North Sea by beaker groups and the commencement of the distinctive, numerous and long-lived British beaker tradition. The regional explanations are likely to be complex indeed and we should resist the temptation to substitute one simple explanation for another. Certainly in Britain the relationship between the communities using beakers and those predominantly using Mortlake,

Fengate, Grooved Ware and Urn ceramics seems likely to become more rather than less complex.

If we permit ourselves to be forced to return to the "origins" problem, then the importance of the "core" area and especially the Rhineland seems to add some weight to the van der Waals and Lanting hypothesis. Such an hypothesis would explain the otherwise surprising density and longevity of beaker ceramics in peripheral Britain. In the same way, it is only the undecorated and rusticated beaker, bowl and potbeaker everyday and heavy-duty wares of this area which seem to represent an indigenous and integral beaker domestic ware. The domestic pottery of the eastern cycle sites, the Begleitkeramik pots and jugs, conspicuously arises from a pre-beaker Carpathian and Balkan background and continues into the Proto-Aunjetitz traditions long after the beaker fine wares have disappeared from circulation; indeed over much of that area beakers were never circulated at all and other fine wares prevailed. In Italy, the proto-Polada/Polada development seems to present a similar and related continuity and in southern Spain the substratum of Almerian/Millaran plain wares march on through the stratigraphies to develop into the Argaric tradition, with Millaran painted and fancy fine wares first substituted by fine beakers and then by fine burnished metallic-looking plain wares (Fig. 2).

But enough of this unwise temptations to move into the disreputable problem of "origins". We still have everything to learn about the domestic, social and economic setting of the fine decorated beakers. We still lack reliable quantitative studies of all kinds and the analyses of beaker clay sources and work on the manufacture and functional aspects of the pottery have only just begun. The physical anthropology of the situation still seems debatable and the relative status of the "people who used beakers" and the "beaker people" is genetically as unclear as ever. The other neglected artefacts in the beaker assemblages still require careful and comprehensive study within an integrated setting embracing the pottery as but one aspect. However, for the time being the small, dispersed beaker settlements with their little family cemeteries, and their need to make or acquire fine beakers, stone axes, bracers, copper daggers and axes, metal trinkets and perhaps interchange women, pots, textiles and foodstuffs all point to a low-density situation in which interconnection and reciprocal support must surely have been vital. A social and demographic situation, in a transitional stone/metal period, in which the alliance role of exchange networks may have been of as crucial importance for the maintenance of the identity and common relationships of scattered groups, as the economic role will have been for reciprocal exchanges in foodstuffs, resources, metal and technology.

REFERENCES

Apsimon, A. M. (1969). An early neolithic house in Co. Tyrone, *The Journal of the Royal Society of Antiquaries of Ireland*, **99**, 165–168.

Barfield, L. H. (1976). The cultural affinities of Bell Beakers in Italy and Sicily, in *Glockenbechersymposion Oberried 1974* (J. N. Lanting and J. D. van der Waals, eds), Fibula–van Dishoek, Bussum/Haarlem, pp. 307–322.

Bradley, R. (1970). The excavation of a beaker settlement at Belle Tout, East Sussex, England, *Proceedings of the Prehistoric Society*, **36**, 312–379.

Clark, J. G. D. (1952). *Prehistoric Europe: The Economic Basis*, Methuen, London.

Clark, J. G. D. (1965). Traffic in stone axe and adze blades, *The Economic History Review*, XVII, 1–28.

Clarke, D. L. (1966). A tentative reclassification of British Beaker pottery in the light of recent research. *Palaeohistoria*, **12**, 179–197.

Clarke, D. L. (1968). *Analytical Archaeology*, Methuen, London.

Clarke, D. L. (1970). *Beaker Pottery of Great Britain and Ireland* (2 vols), Cambridge University Press, London.

Clough, T. H. McK. and Green, B. (1972). The petrological identification of stone implements from East Anglia, *Proceedings of the Prehistoric Society*, **38**, 108–155.

Dalton, G. (ed.) (1971). *Studies in Economic Anthropology*, Basic Books, Washington, DC.

Dalton, G. (1975). Karl Polanyi's analysis of long-distance trade and his wider paradigm, in *Ancient Civilisation and Trade* (J. A. Sabloff and C. C. Lamberg-Karlovsky, eds), University of New Mexico Press, Albuquerque.

Egloff, B. J. (1973). Contemporary Wanigela pottery, *Occasional Papers No. 2, Anthropology Museum, University of Queensland*, pp. 61–79.

Jensen, J. A. (1972). Myrhøj. Three houses with Bell Beaker Pottery. *Kuml*, 1972, 61–122.

Kalicz-Schreiber, R. (1976). Die Probleme der Glockenbercherkultur in Ungarn, in *Glockenbechersymposion Oberried 1974* (J. N. Lanting and J. D. van der Waals, eds), Fibula–van Dishoek, Bussum/Haarlem, pp. 183–216.

Lauer, P. K. (1970). Amphlett Island's pottery trade and the Kula, *Mankind*, **7**, 165.

Lauer, P. K. (1973). The technology of pottery manufacture on Goodenough Island and in the Amphlett Group, SE Papua. *Occasional Papers No. 2, Anthropology Museum, University of Queensland*, pp. 25–60.

Louwe Kooijmans, L. P. (1974). The Rhine/Meuse delta. Four studies on its prehistoric occupation and holocene geology, Thesis, Leiden; also *Oudheidkundige Mededelingen Leiden*, pp. 53–54 (1972–3).

Peacock, D. P. S. (1969). Neolithic pottery production in Cornwall, *Antiquity*, **43**, 145–149.

Renfrew, C. (1973). Trade and craft specialisation, in *Neolithic Greece* (S. A. Papadopoulos, ed.), National Bank of Greece, Athens, pp. 179–200.

Sahlins, M. (1974). *Stone Age Economics*, Tavistock, London.

Sangmeister, E. (1976). Das Verhältnis der Glockenbercherkultur zu den einheimischen Kulturen der Iberischen Halbinsel, in *Glockenbechersymposion Oberried 1974* (J. N. Lanting and J. D. van der Waals, eds), Fibula–van Dishoek, Bussum/Haarlem, pp. 423–438.

Schüle, W. (1976). Die frühmetallzeitliche Siedlung auf dem Cerro de la Virgen in Orce (Granada), in *Glockenbechersymposion Oberried 1974* (J. N. Lanting and J. D. van der Waals, eds), Fibula–van Dishoek, Bussum/Haarlem, pp. 419–422.

Shennan, S. J. (1976). Bell Beakers and their context, in *Glockenbechersymposion Oberried*

1974 (J. N. Lanting and J. D. van der Waals, eds), Fibula–van Dishoek, Bussum/ Haarlem.

Sherratt, A. G. (1976). Exchange networks in prehistoric Europe, in *Problems in Economic and Social Archaeology* (G. de G. Sieveking, I. H. Longworth and K. E. Wilson, eds), Duckworth, London, pp. 557–581.

Skjølsvold, A. (1972). Slettabø i Ogna. Foreløpig orientering om en boplats med bosetning fra yngre stenalder og bronzealder, *Viking*, XXXVI, 5–82.

Sweetman, P. D. (1971). An earthen enclosure at Monknewtown, Slane: preliminary report, *Journal of the Royal Society of Antiquaries of Ireland*, **101**, 135–140.

Taffanel, O. and Taffanel, J. (1957). La station préhistorique d'Embusco, *Cahiers Ligures de Préhistoire et d'Archeologie*, **6**, 53–71.

Waals, J. D. van der and Glasbergen, W. (1958). Een laatneolithische tweeperiodentumulus te Harskamp, *Bijdragen en Mededelingen der Vereniging "Gelre"*, LVII, 1–14.

DISCUSSION

van der Waals   I could not help thinking of a lecture given some 15 years ago by Hélène Balfèt concerning an ethnographical study of pot making in a North African village. There was the seasonal domestic potting of the women in the village, there were travelling potters coming around to satisfy the demands for finer wares, and there were large storage jars imported from coastal factories. She also studied the possibilities of explaining archaeological material in comparable terms (cf. Balfèt, in *Ceramics and Man*, Chicago, 1965, pp. 161–177).

Case   van der Waals mentioned ethnographic parallels. The problem is of course with ethnographic parallels you can prove almost anything as they rather tend to vary. Now I remember talking with Matson. He said he tried to record evidence from places in the world where specialist pottery was still being made and traded. One area in which he found specialist potters still at work was Afghanistan; they were men. He said they were men because they were specialist potters, but I do not know whether this is the kind of argument that follows. These specialist potters would come round the villages at a certain season of the year and would trade pots or make them for you, and they would either trade their own forms of pot made of their own clays, or they would bring their clay with them and make your forms of pot, or make either out of your clays. And then, of course, the women in the villages would imitate the specialists' kinds of pots in their local clays, and so on. The whole picture became enormously confused and if we would have this kind of evidence in the form of archaeological data we would be lucky to interpret it correctly even with the aid of extensive scientific sampling of the fabrics.

Furthermore, the ethnographic parallels that we are seeing now are those conditioned by our own modern society; and they often work through the means of our society. In former years, before Matson got there, the pots were traded on pack animals, and the process of pottery trading was seasonal, as Clarke said. But now the pots are traded in the school buses, in quite a different season – the school holidays.

Clarke Of course, I was being rather careful not to impose a particular ethnographic model. I tried to collect figures on pot making from all the monographs available to me, and the one I cited was the only one which had detailed figures, and the point is that clearly there is a great variety of different ethnographic possibilities which give the kind of pattern we see. But there is a pattern of a certain type. In a sense it does not really matter which of the ethnographic models we take. Potting, for example, in this kind of context is universally seasonal, and it does not matter whether it is seasonal because there is a travelling potter, or seasonal because you have to make it yourself, and it has to fit in with your other things. It is seasonal, that is a pretty general characteristic.

van der Leeuw You mention the value of pots in measure of time. There are quite a few prehistoric pots that have been repaired and used since. A thing that you did not mention is polishing, which is a very laborious and time-consuming task, and that is not necessary if you are going to decorate it.

Bantelmann If you want to determine the value of the pot-making process as expressed in time, it may be useful to know how much time it takes to grind the grain for the need of one man for one day with the grinding stones of that time. It takes considerable time, I think, some three or four hours a day.

Sangmeister Something about the classifying of settlements. I do agree that in the eastern zone of the "Begleitkeramik" we do not know any settlement we could attribute to the bell beaker culture, because there are none with more than a few isolated beaker sherds. So we now tend to think that they all belonged to different groups who did buy the finer and decorated wares. On the other hand, we must not forget that possibly we do not know the bell beaker settlements, because they did not leave any traces.

Clarke Do you have domestic sites with Corded Wares in Germany! I would think you do have Corded Ware domestic sites here in

Germany, but since you mainly find domestic "Corded" Ware in these sites you can put them in other cultures.

Sangmeister The site of Ilvesheim-Atzelberg near Mannheim is considered a domestic site of the Corded Ware Culture, but, I rather think, after your model we should say it is a different culture, with a few Corded Ware elements, that have been bought.

van der Waals In the Netherlands, there can be no question about it: the domestic Corded Ware (= Protruding Foot Beaker) sites are chiefly characterized by the same pottery we find in the beaker graves. There is an admixture of coarse ware with "Short-Wave Moulding" that also turns up as domestic ware in Danish Single Grave context (cf. Becker, *Proceedings of the Prehistoric Society*, **21,** 65–71, 1955). Such "storage vessels" are not found in the graves.

Curiously enough, all beaker culture settlement finds in the Netherlands are confined to special circumstances: namely when they were preserved whilst lying on the surface, underneath sand dunes and clay deposits, and sometimes below barrows. Settlement pits with beaker finds hardly ever turn up in our large-scale surface stripping excavations of urnfields and settlements of later periods, but the flat graves of the beaker cultures do. If we had no dunes and no coastal clay deposits, we would not know that there had been any real beaker settlement sites at all. And, to make sure, on our higher sandy grounds where most beaker graves are found, we have no contemporary culture groups bearing different names that could have deposited their dead in graves with beakers.

A Provisional Model of an Iron Age Society and its Settlement System

DAVID L. CLARKE

Archaeologists are everywhere devoting an increased effort to the location and excavation of settlement sites of all periods. In most cases, the location technology and the excavation methods employed are far in advance of those of the last century. However, in some respects the retrieval, analysis and interpretation of information from these settlement observations remain scarcely more developed today than the intuitive procedures employed by the best excavators of the nineteenth century.

There are many reasons for this state of affairs. Settlement sites preserve an embarrassing wealth of information, an abundance potentially multiplied by the many purposes and many new methods of analysis and classification that may now be applied to a site, its deposits, artefacts, features and context. It has been customary to accord a very uneven treatment to the different categories of information embedded within the observations recovered. Information about the particular numbers, kinds and positions of items is often effectively treated, but information about their mutual relationships and the strengths and covariation of those relationships in a variety of alternative classificatory dimensions is less often fully explored. Even just the spatial relationships between the artefacts, other artefacts, site features, other sites, landscape elements and environmental aspects present a formidable matrix of alternative individual categorizations and cross-combinations to be searched for information. These problems and their rich information content are, alas, artificially simplified and thus easily overcome by the archaeologist's tendency to fit the observations within a single preconceived interpretative model, derived without further discussion from some historical or ethnographic analogue. Whereas the least that these

Reprinted with permission from *Models in Archaeology* (D. L. Clarke, ed.), Methuen, London, 1972, pp. 801–869.

complex observations demand is the erection of a set of alternative models, explicitly justified and derived from many sources, embodying alternative reasonable assumptions and then the explicit testing between the alternatives or their consequences for predictive accuracy and goodness of fit, by using skilfully devised experiments in the field or upon the recorded observations. It may not always be possible for the archaeologist to substantiate various alternatives directly but it is usually the case that he can test between their differing consequences.

This particular study is the interim product of a long-term experimental exercise in information recovery from a selected settlement site of the kind so assiduously sought by the field archaeologist. The exercise is an attempt to meet the mass of observations from a selected site with a set of experimental models and the manipulative capacity of the computer. The model-using approach is essential in such a study if the site observations are to transcend the level of mere descriptive records, since these observations can only release fresh information in relation to some explicitly developed model or models. The computer is not essential but since the characteristic of this kind of problem is the superabundance of information hidden in the many possible dimensions of relationship and requiring very cumbersome data manipulation, then the role of this tool becomes self-evident.

The Iron Age settlement excavated at Glastonbury, Somerset, by Bulleid and Gray at the beginning of this century was selected for this exercise (Bulleid and Gray, 1911, 1917). The objective was simply to explore the old data in a variety of new ways. The question in mind was this – if a site as rich as Glastonbury was excavated in the 1970s, could we retrieve no more information today than was extracted by the excavators 70 years ago? We would inevitably recover a greater *quantity* of observations by virtue of our more advanced technical expertise, but much of this mass of data would be a redundant reiteration of information already registered. Can we not now extract more information from the data of the 1900s or have our analytical and interpretative procedures progressed no further than simply operating upon an increased volume of observations in the same old way?

The overall aims of the long-term experimental exercise are fourfold.

1. To learn about the problems of information recovery from the kinds of site currently searched for but perhaps thankfully not yet found.
2. To produce a series of alternative models, based on differing assumptions, which might then be tested by further experiments.
3. To take *one* interim model towards the limits of its potential to expose the consequences of its chain of assumptions and thus to facilitate testing.

4. To explore as a provisional essay the kinds of information that might be recovered from the spatial relationships involving the site, its artefacts, structures and features as a system within a system or hierarchy of other sites, distributed in an interconnected network over a landscape distorted by distance into a contextual *Chinese Box*, receding from the site locus, its territory, its system catchment area to an englobing region of linked systems and beyond.

Several things must be very carefully emphasized about this exercise. It is merely an experimental exercise on the "simplified" problem presented by the records and observations of an excavation conducted 70 years ago. No archaeological study can be any better than the reliability of the observations upon which it is based and the assumptions that frame the development of its analysis and interpretation. This study is no exception and the observations upon which it is based are patently limited in scope and accuracy. Nevertheless, the data can be understood as merely representing data of its type, so the exercise is not invalidated by the quality of the observations, although the potential of the results must be regarded as limited. The approach, therefore, is simply that of the classical exercise: let us take *a* as given, and assume *b* and *c*, then . . . *x*, *y* and *z* follow. Now, at least, we can substitute alternatives for *b* and *c* and seek to test between the varying *x*, *y*, *z* by selected experiments.

THE SITE: THE POST-DEPOSITIONAL MODEL AND ANALYSES

The Iron Age settlement at Glastonbury is set in the marshland of the Somerset Levels of southwestern Britain, $1\frac{3}{4}$ miles northwest of Glastonbury Tor, between the Mendip and Polden hills, 14 miles from the Bristol Channel (Figs 7–9). This western peninsula region was the political territory of the loose confederation of sea-linked Celtic tribes known as the Dumnonii, where the Mendip hills formed a frontier zone facing the alien Durotriges and Dobunni to the east and the more comparable Silures to the north, on the Welsh coast. This tribal frontier was significantly selected by the Roman army for their military frontier based on the Fosse Way, established by A.D. 47–8 within a generation or so of the abandonment of the Glastonbury site.

The site itself was discovered in 1892, excavated between 1892 and 1907 and published in 1911 and 1917 (Bulleid and Gray). The excavation uncovered a settlement built on adjoining artificial mounds or crannogs of interlaced logs, brushwood, hurdles, peat, clay and rubble set on a raised bog and alluvium promontory at the intersection of a small river and the shore of an extensive rush-fringed mere. An irregular embanked stockade surrounded the site, with one or possibly two gates providing land access in dry weather for carts, wagons, chariots and stock, whilst a causeway to the floodplain gave permanent access by boat from an ingenious deep-water staithe in the river mouth. Within this perimeter lay an "amorphous agglomeration" of 90 clay floors, hearths and timber structures – many of them frequently renewed in a shifting palimpsest as the timber footings rotted or worked loose and the underlying peat dried out, compacted and subsided under the weight and heat of the clay floors (Plate 1). The rubbish sealed in and around the floors and systematically dumped over the palisade for disposal by floods and scavengers produced some 9000 artefacts of wood, antler, clay, bone, stone, flint, iron, bronze, lead, tin, glass, shale and amber, together with more than 12 000 bones of domestic and wild animals and many hundreds of domestic and wild plant remains. It is quite clear that these totals would have been substantially augmented by modern excavation techniques.

Any analysis and interpretation of an archaeological site must rest upon a post-depositional model which accounts for the structure of the site in its modern form (see Daniels, 1972, Fig. 5.1). This vital category of model is all too frequently left unvoiced and often appears to imply that everything on the site lies where it was originally built, used or discarded such that the even continuation of this process over space and through time produces a stratified layercake, preserved in encapsulated form into the present day. Alternatively, if the site is very complex the excavator comfortingly adopts the model that it is a structureless rubbish dump or midden and promptly ceases to search for structure which would at least test the model. The demonstration that uneven accumulation has alternated with erosion and destruction, that much material was burned, removed, or lost beyond the site, whilst the remainder went through many life cycles and suffered a constant "Brownian motion" of buffeting by daily human, animal and plant activity, inevitably leads to the customary archaeological cycle of interpretation and counter-interpretation. The original site structure and activity patterns can only be realistically recoved through the explicit use of a micro-geomorphological model covering the post-depositional period.

The post-depositional situation at Glastonbury is very complex in every respect. Preservation is excellent in the waterlogged and peaty deposits and has produced the hundreds of wooden artefacts but not a single sample of textiles or leather materials. In contrast, the preservation was quite different in the acid clay floors where timber, metal and alkaline materials have been severely eroded or demolished. Ash dumps and partially burned wooden, bone and antler artefacts underline the constant loss of combustible rubbish. Many other artefacts were gathered and dumped in land reclamation projects around the site margins and used for raising the house platforms. Old timbers were re-used, clay floors renewed up to ten times and hearths up to fourteen times at a single spot, leaving unrecorded the completely demolished timbers, floors and hearths. The palisade boundary was continuously extended on different occasions in the different sectors and the river jetty was smashed by unusually heavy winter floods and rebuilt twice. It seems that the daily activities on the site must have eroded and erased both deliberately and accidentally many of the traces of earlier activities and structures.

However, this still only accounts for the first post-depositional phase of scrambling. Eventually, the eastern riverside margin of the site flooded repeatedly, and the site was abandoned and became waterlogged, to be colonized by rushes and embedded in peat. The repeated flooding must have removed and altered many items and features. The inhabitants and their descendants must have salvaged and carried off much that remained useful – only the uneconomic, broken, too heavy or too deeply buried would be ignored. Then 2000 years of restless and relentless burrowing, rooting, subsiding and sliding activity by plants and animals brings us to the excavation. Although the site was almost completely excavated, the sampling characteristics of the excavation suggest that a significant quantity of small or microscopic items was missed. At Glastonbury "time's arrow" left a continuous and destructive trace throughout its 2000-year trajectory (Ascher, 1968).

With a filter of this severity imposed upon the archaeological sampling "window", what position may we legitimately take in the analyses that follow? It is at this point and many later nodes that a range of different assumptions may be made and different models employed in the analyses. However, we should note that the site as it survives is not without pattern; it is not amorphous. Definite house plans survive and in some cases part of their contents has been preserved *in situ* by rebuilding over the rubble of structures frequently destroyed by thatch fires. Almost every surviving quern stone may still be matched with fragments of its original opposing stone in the same geological material. It was even found to be possible to set up a series of simultaneous equation models predicting the expected relationship between numbers of querns, pots, spindle whorls, weaving combs, hut floors and food mass remains, based on the ranked survival capacity of each category and taking the settlement population and duration as common unspecified unknowns. The predicted proportional relationships were shown by statistical tests to deviate insignificantly from those implied by the observed sample. Reversing the situation and quantifying these proportions allowed various estimations of the population and duration to be made.

From these and other pieces of evidence it seems that the surviving material is a fragmentary, smudged and noisy sample of a series of activity patterns which changed with time over the lifetime of the settlement. That some traces of some patterns do survive in the debris from the site could be glimpsed by testing the null hypothesis view – that there is no significant difference between the relationships observed within the site and those that might be expected to arise from random agencies. It is these remaining patterns that the following analyses were designed to search for and prepare for testing.

First, however, we must summarize the position taken and assumptions made in the particular post-depositional model selected for further exploration in this essay (see aim 3).

(a) Many of the relationships observed within the site are indeed no stronger than might be expected from chance factors, but superimposed on this background "noise" level are some patterned relationships well above that threshold – where the particular threshold setting may be discovered by suitable experiments.

(b) Whilst it is likely that discarded artefacts and rubbish have suffered a "Brownian motion" of constant buffeting by animate and inanimate forces, nevertheless it is characteristic of Brownian motion in two dimensions that the buffeted particle will probably remain within a small radius of its point of deposition, given a long timespan (Hersh and Griego, 1969). Even where these continuous random walk processes were overridden by directed human activity, such as gathering and dumping rubbish, we may hypothesize that inertial tendencies would in most cases ensure that the majority of the rubbish collected would probably have been produced by the dumping group itself and gathered by them from the immediate vicinity of their focus of operations. Even the rubbish dumped over the palisade would probably have derived very largely from the sector whose perimeter it formed and in the main from the huts nearest that stretch of the perimeter. It is assumed that there will have been exceptions to these probabilities but that they will not have been sufficiently regularly repeated either to reduce all traces of patterned relationships within the site to the "noise" level or to introduce false patterns; these assumptions may be tested for in the analyses that follow (Clarke, 1972, Fig. 1.6).

(c) Selective sampling and differential preservation have ensured that the available observations are a fragmentary and distorted selection of the observations that might have been recorded immediately after the abandonment of the site. However, the information loss is probably small because of the great repetitive redundancy with which most activities will have been recorded in their extensive artefact kits. This situation is greatly helped by the almost complete excavation of the settlement – further work would in part merely have recovered more spindle whorls, more undecorated sherds, more flints and so on. Fragmentary patterns of strong relationships may still be observed, well above the noise level, although others that must once have existed will have been destroyed or reduced to a level distinguishable from that of chance relationships.

(d) The interpretation of structures on this and comparable complex sites was much confused in the past by a rather exclusive focus upon the clay floors. In this study structures are not simply defined by the clay floors but identified by fragmentary, composite "signatures" recorded by distinct categories of articulated lines and repeated patterns of posts, together with their intersections and stratigraphic relationship with the clay floors, rubble patches and other features, punctuated by a characteristic debris pattern.

(e) It is assumed, on evidence already mentioned, that the site was occupied for many years. Any interpretation must therefore allow for the continuous but uneven and dynamic development of the site and its population, and consequently for an uneven rate of artefact production and deposition. For example, on demographic and preservation grounds, it is probable that the predominant proportion of the artefact sample and detectable activity patterns relate the closing phases of the site.

The initial analyses of the Glastonbury data have been set up for examination against this framework of assumptions or post-depositional model, although it is hoped that the same data can in time be re-examined against alternative models for the site. These preliminary analyses fall into four groups of related experiments pursued in parallel, in order that fresh information gained from any stage of one group might be fed into an appropriate stage of the other analyses. The procedure thus resembles a developing lattice rather than a unilinear string or a set of separate parallel investigations.

The four groups of analyses include:

1. Analyses of vertical spatial relationships
2. Analyses of horizontal spatial relationships
3. Analyses of structural relationships
4. Analyses of artefact relationships.

Analyses of vertical spatial relationships

This group of studies concentrated on the overlapping stratification of the structures, clay floors and hearths and the artefacts that they contained, with the aim of unravelling the sequence of site development. The essential key to the development within and between the different settlement sectors is provided by more than 70 sets of recorded stratigraphic relationships between chains of neighbouring clay floors and structures. Fortunately, the sequence of structures within each sector can be broadly established from these relationships, although correlating the sequences of the different individual sectors derives in part from horizontal spatial adjustments observed during the site's development. The stratigraphic analyses provided the essential framework of the expansion of the settlement, and even in themselves already suggested certain structural and locational regularities which could be scrutinized against the evidence of the other analyses.

The information recovered suggests that the site ended as five interlinked settlement clusters on five crannogs stabilizing the margins of a centrally higher and drier enclosed area (Figs 5, 6). These differentiated clusters were designated *sectors* of the site – the southern, central, eastern, northwestern and northeastern sectors – plus the separately categorized causeway and landing stage. The partially independent and successive development of these site sectors is apparent in the diverging lobed margins of the site perimeter, and is confirmed and documented in detail by the chain of floor stratigraphies, the artefact stratigraphies, artefact typology and marked trends in overall artefact densities. Since some ninety or more structures existed on the site a dynamic portrayal would theoretically require a sequence of not less than ninety successive "frames". However, in practice, the stratigraphic relationships allow no finer a resolution level than the clear representation of four crude "phases" of this continuous site development (Figs 2–5).

Analyses of horizontal spatial relationships

This group of analyses focused upon the non-random, mutually patterned relationships and spatially adjusted locations of the structures, clay floors, hearths and artefacts in order to attempt the recovery of the inherent rules of building followed by the inhabitants. The procedure commenced with the search for repeated locational relationships between structures on the site: a search to recover any locational regularities which deviated strongly from a simply random arrangement – the alleged "amorphous agglomeration" of huts. By this means a building model was cumulatively assembled which it was hoped would gradually begin to converge with the conceptual planning model of the individual builders, suggesting something of the cultural and functional priorities and rules of construction they may have tacitly followed. This procedure employs in reverse the powerful general methods of modern architectural planning and micro-locational analysis. The contemporary discipline of architectural studies embraces a large and powerful array of relevant analytical procedures, dynamic models, computer graphics and simulation models for precisely such investigations in locational problems (March, Echenique *et al.*, 1971).

It is assumed that, although the settlement was developed on a piecemeal and individual basis, and not planned by a central authority, nevertheless each individual in the community would attempt to repeat a culturally accepted building format and similarly optimize the location of his structures within those common severe constraints to satisfy similar common functional, cultural and technological priorities. In this way even the most primitive human and animal settlements display a patently non-random development (Fraser, 1969).

Initially, the building model distinguishes three main elements: activities, building stocks, and the site building potential. The activities refer to those regularly repeated human activity patterns and combinations of activity patterns that make up the day-to-day, week-by-week, season-by-season routines for which the settlement is a principal arena – daily work tasks within and without the site, travelling to and from these tasks, and so forth. The building stock element refers to the built containers of these activities – cleared land, surfaced areas, floor space, transport routes, roads and paths. The site building potential derives from the parameters imposed by the amenity of a particular site to construction, in terms of cost, aspect, micro-climate and micro-environment, together with the ease of connectivity between activity patterns within the settlement and between the settlement and its context. The building model of a particular site then represents the detailed interaction between these various elements and the values given them by the particular set of inhabitants. But the important relationships emphasize the way in which the early activity patterns demand a certain built stock, which, once built, restricts the further development and location of activities and is itself initially restricted by the building potential of the selected site (Figs 2–5; see also Clarke, 1972, Fig. 1.17).

The study commences with an analysis of the stock on the site and the locational relationships between that building stock, including adapted spaces for floors, hard-standing, structures, etc., and channel spaces for transport and communication routes within the site, which must ultimately converge and link to routes running out of the site –

an obvious but powerful constraint. The routes in most cases may be negatively defined as interlinking open spaces without structures or barriers, and so access routes, through routes and linking routes could be distinguished, noting proximity to structural categories, exclusive linkage between structural categories and closure of groups of structures. These observations identified the main access routes (two gates and jetty), through routes (clay or rubble pathways and unbuilt dry spaces between structures), regularities in proximity patterns (distances between structural categories), repeatedly exclusive linkages (nearest neighbour structures directly linked to or facing one another) and deliberate closure patterns (superstructures so positioned as to prevent, according to width remaining, the passage between them of (a) pedestrians and animals and (b) carts and chariots).

The building model then considered the settlement development process at three levels: the choice of this locus as opposed to alternative local sites for the settlement, the layout chosen for this particular locus, and the deliberate allocation of different structural categories to selected relative positions within the site. A separate spatial analysis considered the relative locations of the activity patterns, artefacts and artefact categories in relation both to one another within and across the structural features, and to the overall settlement plan.

The model had to satisfy the very stringent requirement that any building "rule" or constraint postulated from regularities in the relationships observed on the site for any one phase must be substantiated in every succeeding phase of the settlement and not merely satisfy the final arrangement. Thus, within the model, the input parameters of each building phase were specified from the output of the stratification studies and the successive solutions in terms of settlement layout were examined and judged against a series of variable criteria – increase in population, changes in social structure, etc. The results of this appraisal led either to the alteration of the interpretation proposed or to a modified estimate of the parameters. The building model therefore provided an invaluable interactive capacity which enables the experimenter to explore the different consequences of his different estimates, assumptions and hypotheses about the site (March, Echenique et al., 1971).

The interim information already recovered by this group of analyses richly complemented that derived from the stratigraphies. It is apparent that the interlinked estuary, lakes and rivers running from the northern margin of the site will have provided rapid long-distance communications, capable of carrying heavy loads, to the foot of the Mendips three miles to the north and to more distant points. The more seasonal overland access routes appear to have approached the settlement from the south, running along the promontory parallel to the old river bed, from the direction of the Tor and the Poldens (Fig. 7). This directional linkage is shared by the contemporary settlement at Meare, three miles to the west, with trackways of many periods running back from these lake margin settlements towards the low hills behind. This linkage might be expected from a settlement pattern expanding on to freshly accessible, fertile alluvium and peat areas released by the periodically shrinking fen margin to the north.

The land route from the south probably forked around the southern sector of the settlement with an eastern branch hugging the riverside perimeter, serving the east gate and the landing stage, whilst a parallel track followed the western perimeter (Fig. 5). The stratigraphic evidence for these tracks suggests that they were simply broad lines of approach, patched with clay and tipped rubbish. Certainly, during the annual winter flooding of this low relief landscape the riverside branch would have frequently been unusable, which might explain the purpose of the alternative western fork. It may be noticed in passing that the presence of these two routes is strongly supported by the internal development of the built stock and its articulation with the internal transport network. Whilst there were repeated expansions of the settlement margins and palisades on the northern and northeastern waterside perimeters, the western and southeastern margins with admirable dry land were held comparatively rigid by virtue of these adjacent channel spaces. In addition, the internal routes approach the perimeter at these two points, which are marked at the juncture by probable guard huts.

In the final phase the settlement grouped around two open compounds, an *outer compound* entered from the hypothesized western gate, itself opening upon an *inner compound* surrounded by some of the oldest structures to survive into the late phase of the site (Figs 2–5). The inner compound had once been surrounded by its own stockade, broached by routes to the landing stage and to the western approach track. There are also ample traces of elaborate internal stock fences and baffles, especially within the eastern sector and its gateway. The compounds clearly served many different purposes, but they could have provided the occasional capacity to corral more than 1200 Celtic sheep or some 300 head of Celtic cattle.

Within the site the analysis of the clusters of structures linked by pathways, by proximity and by facing doorways, and separated by access closure, produced many interesting and suggestive regularities. A repetitive linkage emerged between certain pairs of structures of the kind that may be noted on other "Celtic" sites, but here there were at least two different categories of linked structures – pairs of interlinked substantial houses and smaller huts linked to subrectangular structures.

Thus each sector of the settlement begins to resemble the varied replication of some kind of modular building unit based on these pairs of
structures and their dependent work floors. At this stage the building
model assumes a far greater significance in terms of the parallel analyses
which had been devoted to structural features and artefact evidence
for activity patterns.

Analyses of structural relationships

This third group of analyses investigated the observations recording
the attributes of the structures and features on the site with the aim
of discovering different categories of structures and features and defining their characteristics. The main structural attributes and dimensions
were reduced to a list of elements which were combined in various ways
by the range of phenomena observed on the site, including size of
structure, shape, total number and types of associated finds, substructure and flooring, frequency of floor renewal, hearth types, frequency of hearth renewal, pattern of marginal posts, pattern of internal
posts, doorway features, porch features. Many structures combined
only a few such elements, some combined all of them. The procedure
was to search this matrix of combinations of structural elements in the
hope of uncovering repeated structural categories with a distinctive
polythetic "signature" which might be identified even when some of
the elements had been dismantled or destroyed, or had gone unrecorded.

These structural element analyses primarly scrutizined four sets of
relationships. The first scheme examined the correlation matrix of the
various states of the eleven multistate structural elements noted above,
producing clusters of correlated structural elements which frequently
recurred together – defining a number of different but recurrent construction categories within a continuum of relationships. The second
and complementary scheme searched for groups of similar constructions by clustering the 100 or so structures on the site in order of
their mutual affinity in terms of shared structural elements – arranging
the observable structures in sets of similar construction. The numbered
structures were also independently grouped in order of their mutual
affinity in terms of the sets of artefact types that they contained. Finally,
a study was set up to research the covariation of structural elements
and artefact types across the 100 structures.

The structural studies so far completed suggest that the number of
associated finds, the size of the structure, and the frequency of renewal,
were especially critical if interdependent variables for this site. Two

thresholds are seemingly important in this respect: structures with less than ten artefacts convey no evidence of residential use and structures with more than forty associated artefacts form a distinct and separate category. It is interesting to note that the causeway and jetty with an area twice or three times that of the other structures produced only twenty items lost or abandoned in its construction and use, thus falling below the "lived-in" threshold for this site. All the structures with more than forty artefacts stand out amongst the continuously renewed and intensively occupied set convergently identified by the locational analyses as substantial house pairs.

Analyses of artefact relationships

Only the preliminary studies have been completed in this fourth group of analyses – the evaluation of the artefact information. Here the variety of different aims of the analyses require different classifications of the same data to be successively employed. However, these include a regression and trend analysis of the different artefact types one with another across the structures, represented as a network of contiguous cells. The artefact concentrations and residuals produced by this approach have already confirmed that the artefacts must be classified experimentally in a number of different ways, each designed for the different dimensions of clearly specified problems, otherwise much information on relationships is lost by the use of insensitive general purpose categorization (Clarke, 1970). The cross-occurrence of different artefact types on the floors of the structures has been set up and scrutinized for correlated clusters of artefact types categorized according to different special purpose classifications. These classifications include groupings defined by material, taxonomy, activity usage, male or female association, and rank-status association, including evidence from beyond the site itself. The information gathered from these studies on kinds and locations of activity patterns conducted within the site was fed back into the building model providing a fresh round of information output.

The detailed typological analysis of selected artefact types in terms of their intrinsic attributes also promises to be a most rewarding field, especially where the artefact is sufficiently abundant to occur frequently in space across the site and vertically in stratigraphies. A cluster analysis classification of the fibulae, bone combs and pottery elements may be expected to provide the basis for the detection of simultaneous spatial and temporal trends on the site, together with locational deviations. It may be noted here that any interpretation of such a pottery analysis must be made in the light of Peacock's important petrological work, which has identified the large-scale importation of fine ware from market sources to Glastonbury and Meare, where it was used alongside locally made utilitarian pottery (Peacock, 1969).

THE SITE: ASSESSMENT AND A STRUCTURAL MODEL

The combined information from the four groups of analyses integrates to define a distinct range of structures repeatedly reproduced on the site and repetitively clustered in such a way that each sector of the site resembles the varied replication of a single kind of modular unit (Fig. 1). This interim assessment rests on the many assumptions developed in the foregoing discussion and itself allows several different interpretations. However, in the interests of brevity the structural categories that have emerged will be listed and described briefly with an attached interpretative label deduced from the total associations of the structure – where these labels should be regarded merely as convenient handling devices.

Seven polythetic categories of construction may be distinguished in terms of their structural attributes, but these broad classes (I–VII) may then be internally subdivided by the intersection of their sets with differing sets of artefact association patterns and the structure's location relative to other structures. This produces thirteen different kinds of repeated built form on this site: major houses (Ia), minor houses (Ib), ancillary huts (IIa), workshop huts (IIb), courtyards (IIc), baking huts (IId), guard huts (IIe), annexe huts (IIf), work floors (III), clay patches (IV), granaries or storehouses (V), stables or byres (VI) and sties or kennels (VII). Since the development of the settlement is a dynamic continuum it must be recognized that structures may successively escalate or descend through these categories – starting as a major house, then becoming an open work floor and then a granary stance, and vice versa. Indeed, an immediate point of interest is the restricted and repeated direction in chains of succession of usages.

Ia. Major house pairs
(*Plate 1, Nos 4–5, 13–14, 29–35, 27–38, 42, 62–5, 74–76–70; the numbers are in Roman numerals on Plate 1*)

There are fourteen major house structures, arranged for the most part in seven pairs (Fig. 1). These large circular houses are distinguished by the relatively substantial nature of their overall construction and

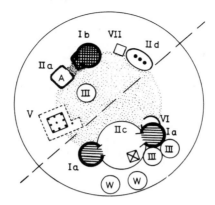

Fig. 1. The modular unit – the social and architectural building block of which the settlement is a multiple. The analyses of vertical and horizontal spatial relationships, structural attributes and artefact distributions convergently define a distinct range of structures (I–VII) repeatedly reproduced on the site. Each replication of the unit appears to be a particular transformation of an otherwise standardized set of relationships between each structural category and every other category. The basic division between the pair of major houses (Ia) and their satellites, and the minor house (Ib) and its ancillaries may be tentatively identified with a division between a major familial, multi-role and activity area on one hand and a minor, largely female and domestic area (see Fig. 6).

Below: the iconic symbols used to identify the structures in the schematic site models, Figs 2–5.

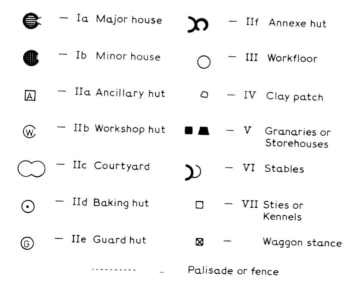

☗	— Ia Major house	ꓷ	— IIf	Annexe hut
●	— Ib Minor house	○	— III	Workfloor
Ⓐ	— IIa Ancillary hut	▱	— IV	Clay patch
Ⓦ	— IIb Workshop hut	■ ▲	— V	Granaries or Storehouses
◯◯	— IIc Courtyard	ꓭ	— VI	Stables
⊙	— IId Baking hut	☐	— VII	Sties or Kennels
Ⓖ	— IIe Guard hut	⊠	—	Waggon stance
· · · · · · · · · ·	—			Palisade or fence

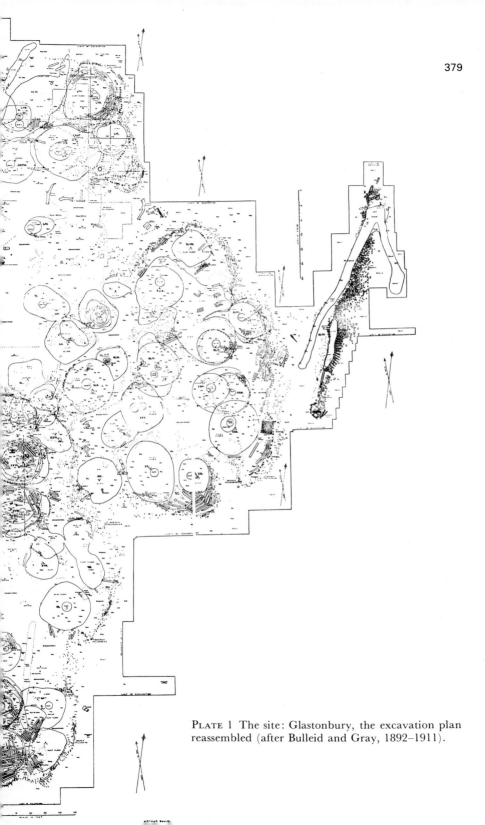

PLATE 1 The site: Glastonbury, the excavation plan
reassembled (after Bulleid and Gray, 1892–1911).

by their lengthy occupation and successive renewal. They were built on individual substructures of interlaced timbers covered by successive clay floors and hearths; the walls were of wattle and daub and the roof was supported by a central post with peripheral subsidiaries. Three distinctive features are the doorways of stone slabs, their porches of diverging rows of posts, which on occasion become an external fenced yard, and their use of split timber plank floorboards above the clay floors.

Average number of associated artefacts   46 (max. 149, min. 12)
Average external diameter in feet   30 (max. 34, min. 28)
Average number of stratified floors   4–5 (max. 10, min. 3)
Average number of stratified hearths   6–7 (max. 14, min. 3)

These major houses are arranged as one pair in each unit, set close together in one half of the unit area, facing on a common yard. Lean-to annexe huts and stables are exclusively attached to this category of structure. Facilities for almost every kind of activity on the site are found represented at these focal houses, including the bulk of the horse and chariot gear, together with most of the weaponry and finery. The abundant artefacts of all types suggest that the full range of male and female activities were either conducted here, or that their artefacts were stored here; in contrast, all other structures on the site contain a specialized selection from this repertoire. Thus, here, workshop activities are represented as but one element amongst many others – bronze smithing, carpentry and lathework, wool combing, spinning, weaving and embroidery.

The distinctive but not exclusive artefact associations are: furnace furniture, crucibles, iron and bronze tools and equipment, slingshot, needles, combs, small ovens, querns, human bones buried in the floor, and the highest ratio of decorated fine wares to undecorated pottery. Some, at least, of these structures had internal radial partitions (No. 65) and many conducted special productive enterprises, iron smelting in one (No. 71), shale turning in another (Nos 62, 64) and finishing imported quern stones in another (Nos 4, 5). These houses were probably the focal repositories for tool chests and equipment that could be taken out into the light of the courtyard and work floors for daily use. In many respects these houses, in addition to their social role, somewhat resemble cottage factories served by hands drawn from the many neighbouring structures within each unit.

1b Minor houses
(*Plate 1, Nos 9, 11, 18, 49, 57, 70, 55, 30, 44*)
There are nine minor house structures, closely resembling the major houses but differentiated from them by features of construction, con-

tents and locations – features made more apparent when taken in relation to their values for neighbouring structures in the unit rather than upon an absolute scale. The minor houses were also substantially built with many of the features of the major houses but on a smaller scale and lacking the funnel porch. Instead these structures approach oval or pear-shaped outlines, a tendency in many cases caused by a transverse wind-baffle extension to the entrance – a feature found on stone huts elsewhere within the breezy Dumnonian territory (Fox, 1964, p. 91).

Average number of associated artefacts	42 (max. 74, min. 12)
Average external diameter in feet	30 (max. 36, min. 24)
Average number of stratified floors	3–4 (max. 9, min. 2)
Average number of stratified hearths	4–5 (max. 10, min. 2)

A single minor house exists within each unit, set in the opposing half of the unit area to the major house pair, at more than twice the distance from that pair than each of its members is from the other (Fig. 1). These minor houses are linked by a short path to, or face directly on, an ancillary subrectangular hut (IIa). Activities are less extensive than in the major houses and all the male activities are missing – no furnaces, no slag, no crucibles, no weapons, no iron workshop tools; whereas the female activities remain – combing, spinning, querning, leather and fur working. Amber, glass and shale beads and bracelets are here positively associated with perforated teeth and boars' tusks, lead and tin spindle whorls, bronze tweezers and human bones buried in the floor – in some cases certainly female and in many cases very young children.

Other finds include iron hogback knives, sickles, a bone necklace and buttons, pigmy cosmetic pots perhaps for the red lead found elsewhere on the site, cereals in open dishes (No. 70), a wooden ladle (No. 9) and perhaps a dresser with its pottery (No. 44). There is a comparative abundance of pottery within this class of structure but the proportion of undecorated domestic ware is greater than in the major houses; six of the twelve perforated ceramic strainers from the site are from these minor houses, the remainder from associated work floors (III) and baking huts (IId). The presence of harness in several minor houses should perhaps be linked with their leatherworking equipment and seen as maintenance and production centres for mending, storing and making reins, leather harness and perhaps shoes and clothing from hides. The overwhelming proportion of female trinkets and gear suggests that these houses were not only foci of female activities but also the especial centres of female residence.

IIa. Ancillary huts

(Plate 1, Nos, 83, 16, 25, 78, 12, 32, 48, 58, 17)

There are nine ancillary huts on the site and possibly examples of one or two more (floor No. 34 and earliest phase No. 38). There is a single ancillary hut in each unit, immediately adjacent to the unit's minor house and granary, and usually linked thereto by a path or clay patch. The ancillary huts appear to be lightly built subrectangular structures made of hurdles and posts with one or two central roof posts and a hearth.

Average number of associated artefacts	15 (max. 31, min. 3)
Average external dimensions in feet	24 by 20 (max. 29)
Average number of stratified floors	2–3 (max. 4, min. 1)
Average number of stratified hearths	2 (max. 4, min. 0)

The ancillary huts have no significant individual substructure, no floorboards, no porch and no doorway slabs. The number of artefacts found in these structures (average 15, minimum 3) runs at a level oscillating about the background noise threshold of scattered rubbish (around ten artefacts per structure). However, the association pattern is consistent and represents in all respects an impoverished version of the array found in the adjacent minor houses – no furnace or smithing equipment, no heavy-duty iron tools, no "male" artefacts, but a sparse scatter of items from the "female" complex: pottery, glass beads, shale trinkets, tin and lead spindle whorls, perforated tusks and teeth, some antler combs and a few immature human bones.

At least two of these huts failed to produce the characteristic black "occupation layer", which marks the intensively occupied houses and possibly derives from a strewn rush floor covering. Flint scrapers, although sparsely represented on the site, were unusually abundant in these ancillary huts. The overall artefact pattern suggests displaced, dumped and abandoned equipment reinforced by the sporadic transference of activities from the linked minor houses. Taken with the structural lightness, the subrectangular form and the locational linkage with the female(?) minor houses, the artefact evidence might suggest that these huts served as milking parlours, foodstores and cowhouses for perhaps one or two milch cows, some milking ewes or goats and their offspring, kept on the site the year round.

IIb. Workshop huts

(Plate 1, Nos 75, 45, 59, 23, 3, 61, 60, 44)

The eight detectable workshop huts are characteristically small, neat circular structures, mostly without any posts supporting the small roof span or cluttering the floorspace. There are one or two contemporary workshop huts in each unit, sited close to the major house pair and set in the same half of the unit area. Some of these workshops are the focus of groups of open work floors (III), presumably the centre of fine weather operations in the unobstructed daylight (floors 59–79, 45–46, 1–3, 73–75).

Average number of associated artefacts	19 (max. 36, min. 9)
Average external diameter in feet	23 (max. 32, min. 21)
Average number of stratified floors	2–3 (max. 4, min. 2)
Average number of stratified hearths	2–3 (max. 9, min. 0)

The workshop huts contrast strongly with the ancillary huts (IIa) in structure, location and the repeated presence of precisely the equipment pattern not found in those structures – crucibles, a stone mould for bronze bracelets (No. 44), iron heavy-duty tools, whetstones, flint flakes, antler, bone and shale production roughouts, waste and splinters, and an absence of floor burials, querns or any significant level of female artefacts. The associated iron tools include files, adzes, a bill-hook, saws, a gouge, nails, together with a bone bow-drill bow, sheet bronze waste and fragments of wooden lathe furniture (? X45, X51, X71). Many broken or unfinished lathe-turned products came from the vicinity of these huts: an unfinished wagon-wheel hub, spokes, wheels, wooden tubs and barrel staves, and the by-products of shale work. The workshops represent selective and more intensive foci of the mending, maintenance and manufacturing activities and skills already noted in the major houses.

IIc. Courtyards

(Plate 1, Nos 33, 28, 73, 63–64, 40–41–26, 1–2, between 13–14)

Seven courtyards are represented by enclosed open spaces or irregular complexes of overlapping clay floors, crudely defining a rectangular area with no substructure, no substantial superstructure but a few scattered posts suggesting light roofing in parts.

Average number of associated artefacts	23 (max. 35, min. 2)
Average dimensions in feet	40 by 20
Average number of stratified floors	2–3
Average number of stratified hearths	2–3

One irregular courtyard area is attached to the major house pair of each of the seven units, either between or adjacent to the houses which may together face on the yard. The splayed porch of the major house is sometimes continued as a fence at one end of the courtyard, a feature found on other Celtic sites and in stone on Galatian *oppida* (Piggott, 1965, p. 224). Other hurdle fencing may open on and traverse the yard and a hearth is usually set asymmetrically at one end of the floor. In some cases a separate rectangular area *ca* 10 by 6 feet is provided with a timber flooring, perhaps as a *wagon stance*. In one instance the courtyard plan is developed into a formalized and almost architectural feature reminiscent of a rustic portico (courtyard No. 63–64, between house pair No. 62–65).

The average number of finds from these yards is equivalent to that of the workshop huts and it is clear from the range of artefacts that many productive and maintenance activities requiring ample space, heat and light were carried out on these partially covered yards, which probably doubled as threshing floors, unloading bays, loom stands, midden dumps and open workshop areas. However, male artefacts are dominant and there is a strong association with horse and wagon gear – harness, toggles, broken linchpins and antler goads. This would accord with the wagon stance platforms and strongly suggests that this is where the wagon and chariots might be accessibly stored under cover and the horses or oxen daily harnessed or unhitched from their gear. That these yards were the primary precinct of the many hunting and sheep dogs is suggested by a complete dog skeleton from one floor (No. 33) and many gnawed bones from others (e.g., No. 73).

IId. Baking huts
(Plate 1, Nos 37, 51, 15, 6, 84, 80, 36)

The seven baking huts are arranged one with each unit, located slightly apart from other structures, perhaps on account of the fire risk, but adjacent to the granary and the small, rectangular, fenced sties or kennels (VII). The baking huts are therefore optimally sited for the daily routine of collecting grain, grinding, preparing and cooking food and dispensing the waste to the pigs. All the baking huts together with most of the granaries are set around the outer margins of the two main compounds (except No. 6). The structural characteristics of the baking huts include an irregular clay floor with a longitudinal array of hearths and ovens covered by a light roof carried on a pair of posts – no substructure, no floorboards, no stone threshold and no porch. Small ovens were also found in some of the major and minor houses and these doubtless served for small-scale daily cooking, whilst the bakehouse seems to have provided a large-scale communal facility for each unit, perhaps mainly concerned with the weekly routine of breadbaking in bulk; analogously focal bakehouses are common in European peasant villages of many periods and areas, including Neolithic examples (Vinča and Aichbuhl; see Clark, 1952, pp. 145–146).

Average number of associated artefacts	14 (max. 37, min. 3)
Average external diameter in feet	22 (max. 25, min. 21)
Average number of stratified floors	2–3 (max. 5, min. 1)
Average number of stratified hearths	5 (max. 9, min. 1)

The artefact pattern is consistent with the use of these structures as centres of female activity. The large dumps of wood and bone ash around the floors contained a relatively large quantity of pottery, with the highest proportion of undecorated decorated wares on the whole site, together with pottery strainers or sieves, glass beads, perforated tusks and teeth, shale trinkets, lead and tin spindle whorls, flint flakes, quern stones, bone needles, gouge pegs and the bones of many fur-bearing fenland mammals, especially beaver. Taken together, the information portrays the baking huts as local centres of female activity, taking grain and provisions from the granary, querning, preparing food, dressing and pegging out skins and furs to dry, gossiping pleasurably in the comfort of this warm and dry micro-environment on a very wet site. The clay ovens and floors acted as ceramic heat stores and radiators and were thus perhaps favourite foci to which to bring many minor tasks, both here and in comparable ethnographic situations.

IIe. Guard huts

(Plate 1, Nos 21, 77)

Location and content are the chief features distinguishing the guard huts from the other classes of hut structure on the site. Hut No. 21 is on the immediate left flank of the eastern gate inturn so that the eastern branch of the perimeter track passes below the hut before swinging in through the seven-feet-wide gravelled gateway, with its smaller wicket gate, hung from pairs of six-inch thick posts. Hut No. 77 is on the immediate right of the probable position of the western gate and is again sited to overlook the western perimeter track before it turned to enter the main outer compound. It would be tempting to see a similar hut facing No. 77 and making a pair, but since the other gate has only a single guard hut and the arrangement is known elsewhere in Dumnonian territory, one should resist this symmetrical restoration.

Average number of associated artefacts	9 (max. 16, min. 2)
Average external diameter in feet	17 (max. 17, min. 17)
Average number of stratified floors	2 (max. 3, min. 1)
Average number of stratified hearths	1 (max. 1, min. 0)

The guard huts are small circular structures with finds below the "residential" threshold and with evidence for only a very light superstructure. The finds from the vicinity are mainly discarded rubbish although a grain bowl is probably *in situ* (No. 21) and one may note the dice box and dice at the eastern gate, a favourite Celtic pastime well suited to guard duty. The location of the western gate itself is inferred not only from the associated guardhouse (No. 77) but from the unique tangenitial contact at this point between the perimeter, the outer compound and the western trackway, backed up by the litter of broken and discarded wheels, spokes and linchpins (X19, X43, X87). Antler harness toggles and a terret also suggest that the adjacent floors, Nos. 20 and 25, may have acted as hard-standing for unloading vehicles parked within the eastern gate and jetty way. Fragments of impaled skulls with sword cuts were found near both gates and elsewhere around the palisade in accordance with Celtic custom. Otherwise the guard huts are defined negatively – the absence of residential debris, querns, weaving gear, tools, beads or productive equipment.

IIf. Annexe huts

(Plate 1, Nos 43, 66)

This type of structure is frequently found on Celtic sites, often attached, as here, to a major house. The two annexe huts are lean-to constructions with a party wall shared with a major house but having a separate entrance. In the northwestern sector annexe hut No. 66 is attached to major house No. 74, and in the central sector, annexe hut No. 43 is joined to major house No. 42; indeed, in many other ways the plan of the major half of the northwestern unit resembles a deliberate reproduction of the terminal layout cumulatively developed in the corresponding area of the central unit based on house No. 42 (Fig. 5).

Average number of associated artefacts	8 (max. 12, min. 5)
Average external diameter in feet	19 (max. 21, min. 17)
Average number of stratified floors	1–2 (max. 2, min. 1)
Average number of stratified hearths	3 (max. 5, min. 1)

The annexe huts are simple, roughly circular structures with hearths but without any other special features. The evidence for the use of these annexes is circumstantial. The negligible level of the finds is below the residential threshold and includes no metal tools or weapons, little pottery and no beads or querns. To this negative artefact evidence we can add the locational and structural resemblance between these rather more substantial annexes and the similar class of smaller lean-to structures found against the other major houses on the site – the stables or byres (Class VI). Annexe hut No. 66 is directly linked with the probable stable No. 85 and contains horse bones buried in its floor, broken linchpins and an antler mallet. Annexe hut No. 43 has horse bones buried in its vicinity, also with linchpins, and, as has already been pointed out, the whole area between these structures and the eastern gate is fenced and stabilized in a manner suggesting service facilities related to traffic through the gate. Finally, these annexe huts may be directly compared with the closely similar stables or chariot sheds at Hod Hill and elsewhere (Richmond, 1968, Figs. 10B, 13).

III. Work floors

(Plate 1, Nos 69, 7, 72, 20, 22, 46, 67, 53, 24, 56, 54, 68)

The twelve work floors are irregular areas stabilized with clay and timber, carrying small hearths and lacking any substantial substructure or superstructure. The absence of walling, doorways and substantial post patterns would imply that these floors were open to the sky or merely covered with lean-to roofs. The floors are peripherally distributed, often close to the palisade, with from one to four floors within each of the five wealthy units, clustered adjacent to the minor house or in the vicinity of the workshop huts.

Average number of associated artefacts	19 (max. 40, min. 8)
Average external diameter in feet	25 (max. 32, min. 15)
Average number of stratified floors	2–3 (max. 5, min. 1)
Average number of stratified hearths	2–3 (max. 5, min. 1)

The artefact association pattern indicates intensive activity on these floors, including both male and female artefact complexes – metalwork, spinning, querning, weaving and much antler and bone work, together with its debris and discards. These multipurpose work floors seem also to have served as convenient store caches or dumps for raw material, especially antler, and in general provided a setting for activities requiring heat, light and space.

IV. Clay patches

(Plate 1, Nos 52, 31, 88, 89, 34, 85, 81, 8, 19, 86, 90, 79, 10, 50, 72, 87, 39)

Seventeen irregular clay patches are scattered around the outer compound and west gate, where some at least are the eroded fragments of the earliest structures on the site attested by stratigraphy. Whilst some patches may be relics of earlier phases, others are merely small areas to provide dry approaches to granaries, stables or sties, which may also be paved with such a clay, rubble brushwood and rush-covered patch; yet others seem simply to patch potholes in access routes.

Average number of associated artefacts	3 (max. 13, min. 0)
Average external diameter in feet	17 (max. 27, min. 6)
Average number of stratified floors	1 (max. 3, min. 1)
Average number of stratified hearths	zero

Few of these patches were renewed, none carried hearths, most of them were below the occupation threshold of around ten artefacts per floor and, together with the causeway, they provide a good example of the noise level underlying the whole pattern of associations – one or two sherds, flints, whorls, antler or bone fragments, only.

V. Granaries or storehouses

(*Fig. 1*)

There are traces of at least 25 granary or storehouse footings on the site – three or four per unit, of which it can be shown that only one per unit existed at any one time. The granary "signature" was usefully sterotyped; in its most complete form an area uniquely devoid of arte-facts, roughly 10 feet by 10 feet, with a scatter of cereals or legumes, is set with nine, six or four regularly spaced sugar-loaf piles driven through mortice holes in horizontal timber groundplates to spread the weight and prevent tilting. The whole complex is usually enclosed within a light fenced area 18 feet square, with a "stepped" perimeter and adjacent patches of clay hard-standing. Most of the granaries are square but some are trapezoidal as on some Durotrigian sites. The size of the granaries is strictly uniform with a single exception, 10 feet by 12 feet, perhaps a communal or chiefly granary – significantly set at the focus of the somewhat elliptical outer compound (Plate 1 between patches Nos 80–82).

The Glastonbury granary "signature" interestingly resembles the features of a so-called Late Bronze Age "ritual structure" recovered from a comparable bog site in the Netherlands at Bargeroosterveld, with similar sugar-loaf piles (Waterbolk and Van Zeist, 1961). It might be plausible to reinterpret that structure as a granary or storehouse and see it as yet another archaic Late Bronze Age element in the Dumnonian Iron Age.

It is possible to gain an impression of the granary structure on the basis of the dismantled granary timbers re-used in the substructure of floor No. 56 and the fragments, including the ladder, from the granary to house No. 29. They appear to have been rectangular frame platforms supporting a square superstructure of hurdles with an open vestibule, reached by ladder, the whole carried on the heads of the sugar-loaf piles perhaps with staddle tops, some three feet or more above the damp ground. The granaries were several times renewed in each sector, some after burning, and it is from these structures that the rectangular timber frame base plates were taken for re-use in the footings of other buildings (X33, X34, X96).

The granaries held barley, wheat and beans and their maximum individual capacity must have approached 500 cubic feet, or about 100 sacks weighing some 20 000 pounds when full, the equivalent of seventeen half-ton wagon journeys each. On a nine-post granary the vertical load per post would thus be more than 2000 pounds, hence the need for the sugar-loaf pile and frame combination to spread the weight and prevent the posts being driven clean through the peat; even so, granary rebuilding was frequently made necessary by fires, rot and tilting.

VI. Stables or byres

(Fig. 1)

One major house in every unit has either an attached annexe (IIf) or a lean-to smaller structure (VI) with the probable exception of the two units on the western side of the inner compound (Houses 13, 14, 29, 35). These lean-to stables(?) are represented by a lobed extension of the house perimeter, *ca* 6 feet by 16 feet, enclosed by an arc of hurdling; on this site, as on others, it is difficult to distinguish between stables and successive reconstructions of the house walls. The stables are tentatively identified by the repeated burial of butchered horse skeletons in and around them and an artefact level below the occupation threshold, suggesting the regular removal of manure and litter to a midden in the yard. The few artefacts associated with these areas include linchpins and cheekpieces from bits.

These stables would only accommodate some four head of horses or draught oxen, although the larger annexe huts might stable up to eight head so that the combined annexe plus stable complex of the northwestern sector unit (Nos 66, 85) has a potential capacity of some fifteen beasts. In winter, this head of stock would generate 4–15 kW of heat, the equivalent of 4–15 single-bar electric fires – a valuable by-product of stalling stock in or against the dwelling.

VII. Sties or kennels

(Fig. 1)

Some small rectangular stake enclosures, *ca* 6 by 5 feet, are found adjacent to the baking huts (IId), granaries (V) and ancillary huts (IIa). Pig bones, otherwise rare on the site, have been noted in the vicinity of these structures (No. 65) but they may at times equally have been used for dogs.

The combined information from all the analyses suggests that the Glastonbury settlement was built and enlarged in terms of the varied replication of a single kind of unit, regularly comprising the same set of different categories of structure (I–VII). Furthermore, these structures were systematically arranged in repeatedly similar relative locational patterns within all the units ever built on the site – presumably a near-optimal pattern adjusted to satisfy the common social, economic and cultural traditions of the inhabitants and the special conditions of the site. Presumably, this pattern had stabilized over long years of cultural development and living and building on similar sites.

On the basis of all the analyses it is possible to idealize the building model of the settlers, to consider its implications and the meaning of individual deviations from it, as well as testing it against comparable sites. For example, many of the puzzling features represented on dry sites by enigmatic complexes of pits, post-holes and irregular hollows are clearly preserved at Glastonbury in forms adapted to the wet environment. The conjectured "amorphous agglomeration" of irregular structures emerges on this and other Celtic sites as a figment of our contemporary rectilinear controlling models. Instead, we now perceive an architectural universe based on rounded structures, laid out in arcs around courtyards and arranged in curvilinear sweeps around compounds, from which new development springs in a series of recurving convolutions significantly analogous to the aesthetic universe of the contemporary La Tène art.

The four peripheral bulges of the southern, eastern, northeastern and northwestern site sectors around the central area can now be seen to relate to the expansion of comparable building units within each sector, based upon four such units deployed around the inner compound. Each of these units allocates a limited number of defined structures to particular relative loci in fixed halves of their respective unit areas (Figs 1–6). In one half of tne unit area stands the pair of major houses (Ia), one of which will have attached stables (VI) and both of which share a courtyard area (IIc) and its wagon stance. In the immediate vicinity are one or two workshop huts (IIb) and open work floors (III). In the complementary half of the unit area a minor house (Ib) is linked to a subrectangular ancillary hut (byre? IIa) and nearby stands a baking hut (IId), pigsty (VII) and granary (V) (Fig. 1).

It follows that alternative interpretations of the Glastonbury settlement will hinge upon the alternative interpretations of the kind of social unit operating behind these building units. The internal evidence shows the units to be discrete organizations, theoretically self-supporting and self-servicing, each with its own housing, bakehouse, granary, stable, work floors and courtyard – apparently a stock-, land- and property-owning modulus accustomed to burying some of their number in the floors of their houses. The three substantial dwellings in each unit – the two major houses and the minor house – do not simply duplicate facilities but complement one another; for example, the minor house seems to be associated with female residence and only one major house in each pair has the attached stable which serves the whole unit. The structural elements emphasize a degree of interdependent reciprocity within a social unit and not merely a repetition of independent elements in a group.

The size of this repeated social unit may be roughly gauged from the floor space of the main dwellings, the number of huts in the unit, and the capacity of the unit granary. The two major houses and the minor house together provide a maximum roofed area of about 200 m², which, according to the deterministic mathematical model of Cook and Heizer (1968) relating residential numbers and floor area, would give a theoretical maximum unit size of around 20 individuals. A parallel model derived from ethnographic data would suggest that on average two to three roofed structures of this size, or their equivalent, are required for each "family" in a food-producing society (Flannery, 1971). Finally, the maximum capacity of the unit granary of 500 cubic feet, allowing one-third of the contents for seed, would support a maximum of some 24 people for one year. But if we allow for supplementary cereal fodder for several chariot ponies and draught oxen, together with a minimal surplus for trade and customary tribal dues, plus a safety margin – then a maximum of 20 individuals is again suggested for these units. Taken altogether the evidence points towards an inturned, internally networked, co-operative social unit averaging perhaps 15–20 individuals including males, females, juveniles and adults, ancestrally linked to the unit houses, jointly owning and inheriting property; anthropologically such a unit would normally be a kin group based on an extended family or lineage system (Murdock, 1949).

THE SITE: INTERPRETATION AND A SOCIAL MODEL

A site occupation unit based on pairs of round houses with varying auxiliaries accords well with the abundant evidence on many other British and Irish Late Bronze Age and Iron Age sites. These settlements include units with "great" houses up to 50 feet in diameter or the more modest 30-foot variety, and they embrace isolated single units and multiple complex units, enclosed and unenclosed settlements (Hamilton, 1968; Piggott, 1965, p. 237). However, it would be a sweeping mistake to assume that the units observed over this wide area of space and time are identical translations of a single social concept – although they may very well represent a family of related transforms of such a concept. The test must come from the detailed consideration of the sizes, shapes, features, relative locations and artefact associations of all these structures. It would indeed be surprising if the variety of tribes and tribal groups throughout Britain's varied environment had not produced some equivalent variety in social and economic activities and ways of housing them and we may look forward to comparative research revealing them.

However, in passing we may note the remarkable parallels between the settlement unit of the twelfth century B.C. at Itford Hill, Sussex, the enclosed unit of the seventh century B.C. at Staple Howe, Yorkshire, and the units reiterated at Glastonbury (Piggott, 1965, p. 152, Fig. 113). The Staple Howe and Itford Hill units have similar structural categories similarly disposed over comparable unit areas, which even include an entrance stock baffle like that glimpsed within the eastern gate of Glastonbury; indeed, if the Staple Howe complex is superimposed upon the northeastern unit at Glastonbury an extremely close fit is obtained. Once again, the survival and continuity of late Bronze Age traditions is stressed in archaic, peripheral Dumnonian Glastonbury.

Within the region of the Dumnonii themselves direct parallels may be drawn with the four pairs of courtyard houses facing one another along the terrace at Chysauster or with the single unit settlement at Goldherring. Particularly striking in these later Cornish sites is the manner in which the structures represented by six or seven clustered floors at Glastonbury are precisely translated into a single nucleated stone structure with the same appurtenances – courtyard, wagon, stance, stable, byre, pigsty, granary, roundhouse rooms. Perhaps even the room structure of the later Romano-Celtic farmhouses with a courtyard between two wings might represent a rectilinear transformation of the same kind of functional unit, or of its Halstatt predecessor (Fox, 1964, Fig. 46; Piggott, 1965, Figs 83, 114).

In any event, the sequential development at Glastonbury can now be pursued in the further light shed by the artefact evidence and interpreted in terms of the social units tentatively linked with the repeated building modulus. Initially, the artefact evidence can be used to test and check the stratigraphic and locational evidence for the site development, to help estimate the length of occupation, and to provide a skeletal frame for a demographic and social sketch model of the community's development. This archaeologically derived model may then be briefly run against the biased but direct information on Celtic society as preserved from contemporary records.

The chain of stratigraphic relationships between the structures has provided a developmental basis which is confirmed by trend analysis studies of the artefacts – both in terms of density distributions and distributions of early and late forms within individual typologies. The overall quantitative trends in the most abundant artefacts found on the site – potsherds and slingshot – fall off dramatically over the northwest and northeast sectors. The trend maps depicting the ratios of early late fibulae, early late pottery, early late comb types, early saddle querns, late rotary querns all reinforce this same pattern – where, it might be noted, the stratigraphies also allow an independent test of earliness or lateness. The same trend is brought out in the distribution of floors and hearths which had been many times renewed. Early cordoned and zoned sherds are heavily focused in the centre and southern sectors, whereas countersunk handle jars of the late Durotrigian model trend heavily to the north, significantly overriding the contrary overall potsherd trend. Clearly, the two units of the northern sectors represent a later expansion towards the lake margin, subsequent to the primary development of the central and southern sectors.

Indeed, it is the northwestern lakeside sector that produces the very latest material on the site – some Romano-Durotrigian sherds left perhaps by fishermen or trappers sporadically reoccupying the lakeside debris of their ancestral home. The overall evidence from the artefact relationships thus heavily endorses the information from the stratigraphies, the locational development and minor points like the apparent reproduction of the final plan of the main central unit (House 42 and complex) in the initial plans of the northwestern and northeastern units.

The length of the occupation sequence at Glastonbury can only be approximately estimated at present by comparing an array of differently based estimates, ranked in order of dependability. The broad dating consensus has long been established for this site and the margin of error from the particular approaches remains virtually unchanged. If we take the most modern information on the typology of the fibulae, fine pottery and other key artefacts, and take the latest find stratified in the earliest floors, and the latest find stratified within the latest floors then an occupation span of about 100 years is suggested, within the period ca 150 ± 50 to 50 ± 50 B.C. This dating is crudely confirmed by pollen analysis, by the 4–5 feet of peat which accumulated during the occupation of the settlement, and by independent chains of assumptions involving the numbers of superimposed hearths and floors, the frequency of house and granary rebuilding, and the sample numbers of surviving fibulae, querns, spindle whorls, potsherds and food debris. Although this chronology could be refined by more detailed pollen analysis, radiocarbon, thermoluminescent and palaeomagnetic estimates, nevertheless the most satisfactory chronology might still be recovered from this site by dendrochronology on timbers from carefully selected contexts in the different sectors. The advantage of this preli-

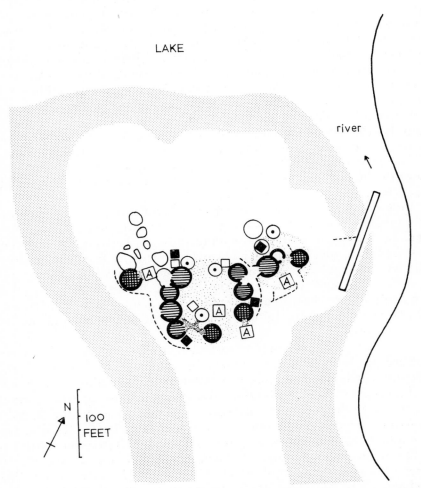

Fig. 2. The site – Phase I; 4 units, 12 houses, estimated population *ca* 60 individuals. This interpretative model and those that follow (Figs 3–6) are "best guess" interpretations of the combined output of all the analyses. These models are schematic and tentative (for iconic key, see Fig. 1).

minary model building is that we can now pinpoint where such samples might best be taken to test the alternative chains of assumptions and interpretations.

With the crude parameters of the site established an interpretative sketch of its sequential development can now be made (Figs 2–5).

Phase O   Some of the scattered floors clustered around the western gateway are amongst the earliest on the site, but no definite plan of this

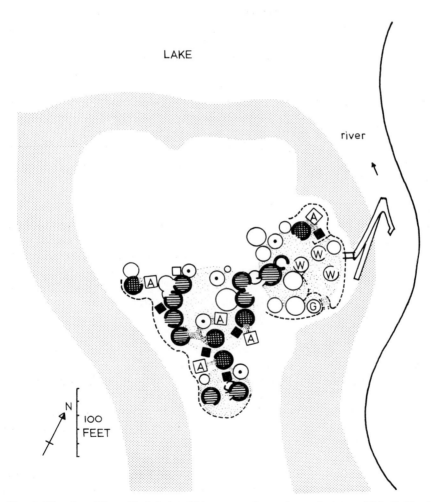

FIG. 3. The site – Phase II: 5 units, 15 houses, estimated population *ca* 75 individuals. The expansion of the site probably under drier conditions, the rebuilding of the jetty.

phase can be recovered – if, indeed, it ever had a separate existence. It is possible that it anticipated the form of the outer compound on a scale appropriate to the embryonic antecedent to the Phase I compound.

Phase 1   4 units, 12 houses, estimated population about 60 people. A roughly circular compound related to the "banjo" class of Iron Age settlements (Bowen, 1969, p. 23). Two units on each side of the compound and traces of an encircling palisade. The units on the western side of the compound have special characteristics which will be discussed later; so too, does the especially elaborate compound around House 42, with its large annexe stable (?VI) and its direct access to the earliest jetty of lias, stone and timber (Fig. 2).

Phase II   5 units, 15 hours, estimated population about 75 people. The inner compound expands on the landward and riverside perimeters, taking up the last "dry" land. The southern sector unit is built. The whole of the area between the central sector and the jetty is remodelled and the eastern sector emerges. The sophisticated landing stage is built, the causeway rebuilt, several workshop huts are erected and the eastern gate and guardhouse complex constructed, all this as virtually an extension of the compound of House 42 (Fig. 3).

Phase III   7 units, 21 houses, estimated population about 105 people. The northern area between the settlement and the lake margin is now reclaimed and occupied by the northeastern and northwestern sectors with their units. This is a spacious and planned development with a degree of architectural symmetry in which the major house pairs face one another and the older compound across the new outer compound with its western gate and guardhouse (Fig. 4).

Phase IV   7 units, 15 houses, estimated population about 120 people. No new units are deployed and the site limits have virtually been achieved, although reclamation and rebuilding continues on the lakeside margin, taking the palisade to its final positions. The fifteen houses have accumulated some twelve auxiliary huts and workshops and these probably shelter a population rather higher than that estimated, if we allow for a packing factor (Fig. 5).

There are too many unknowns to pursue a detailed demographic model for the Glastonbury population but the estimates suggest either a low population growth rate at *ca* 0.5% per annum or a higher rate accompanied by hiving off of the surplus. Some comparable populations grew little, if at all, over long periods of time, especially pastoral ones, and their demography can be understood in terms of Wrigley's model for a community with social customs affecting fertility (see polygyny), a significant infant mortality (marsh environment) and an adult mortality above average (see female deaths in childbirth and warfare casualties from this tribal boundary area) (Wrigley, 1969, model 2, pp, 18–22; Postan, 1966, p. 665). The crucial evidence of the community's

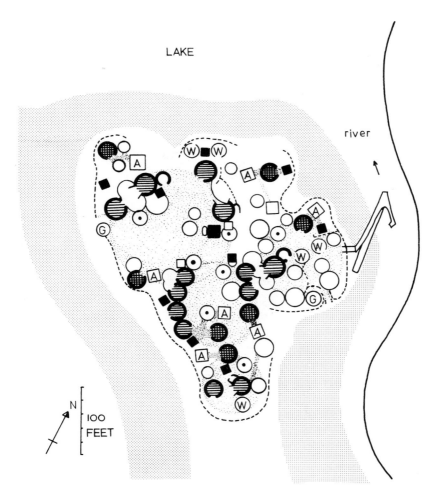

FIG. 4. The site – Phase III : 7 units, 21 houses, estimated population *ca* 105 individuals. Marginal reclamation continues on the unconstrained lake and river sides. The central inner compound is joined by a spacious outer compound.

cemetery is missing – a lacuna which may relate to the scarcity of suitable dry sites in the immediate vicinity. Perhaps the Glastonbury dead
were buried collectively with those of consanguineous fenland communities on a communal sacred "island of the dead" – the traditional
Avalon?

Any social model of the Glastonbury population must derive from
the detailed analyses of the individual settlement units and their arte-

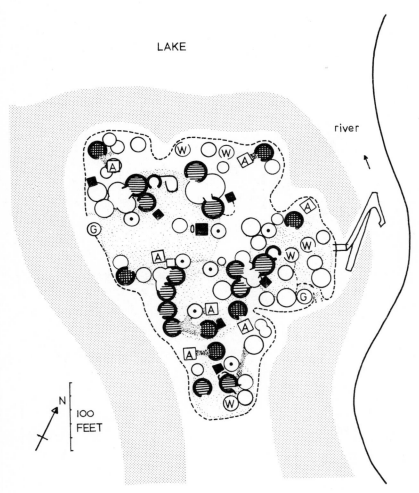

Fig. 5. The site – Phase IV : 7 units, 15 houses, estimated population *ca* 105 plus, perhaps
ca 120 or more with terminal packing within the limits of the site, now achieved in
wetter conditions.

facts. A first examination of the data gives a strong impression of the equality of the units involved. There is no uniquely large house in a focal location. The artefacts do not suggest a great range in the social status of the extended family units nor do they support a great difference in their property and activities – indeed, rather the reverse. Each unit has its granary, its stable of draught animals, its chest of iron tools and its woollen industry and workshops. Sampling problems apart, a poly-thetic picture prevails, a unit marginally richer in one respect is mar-ginally poorer in another and vice versa. If there is a "headman" then he would appear to have been a "first amongst equals", in material terms at least.

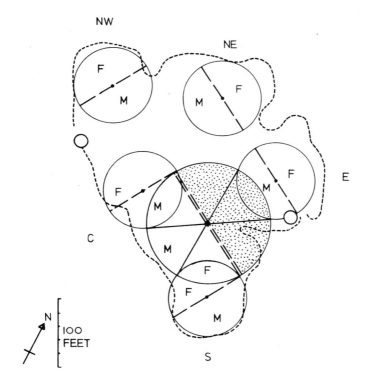

FIG. 6. The site – Phase IV: a tentative social model of the structural pattern of the site. The modular units deployed in each sector occupy closely comparable areas at relatively regularly spaced intervals. Each unit is shown divided, as the evidence suggests, into a major familial section (M) and a minor dependent sector (F). It is suggested that the mega-unit of the original inner compound area itself reproduces this same division at a higher level, with a major sector (shaded) and a minor dependent sector, each composed of several units.

A closer examination discloses deviations from this broadly accurate model. At a finer level of scrutiny the independent units of the north-western, northeastern and southern sectors fit the prediction, but it begins to break down for the four older units arranged around the inner compound in the central and eastern sectors (Fig. 6). If there is a centre of wealth and status in the settlement then the evidence marginally favours the central sector in general and the complex around major House 42 in particular.

The central area of the settlement has produced traces of especial wealth – a hoard including a bronze mirror, tweezers, two dress pins and cosmetic galena, the only coin and currency bar (Z1, Z2), a bronze cup, another mirror fragment, a glass-topped pin, amber beads, the mould for bracelets – all over and above the normal complement of bronze and iron tools, weapons, weapon mounts, bits and harness, beads and shale trinkets. The central area has three other unique features. House 42 contained more weaving combs than any other structure, and whereas the combs of the other units were apparently manufactured independently within each sector and differ accordingly, those from House 42 are drawn from every sector on the site – perhaps drawing female labour in the same way. The minor house of this unit (No. 49) contained the most comprehensive range of fine imported pottery found on the site. Finally, Houses 30 and 42 contained the most extensive variety of bronze fibulae of all periods, including heirlooms. If we add to these observations the central position of the sector, its early foundation and continuous rebuilding, its nodal relevance to the jetty and approach routes, then if there was a Glastonbury "headman" his establishment might be speculatively identified with the inner compound in general and with the precinct of House 42 in particular.

Further analysis reveals an interesting contrast which heightens the preceding observations. The two units on the western margin of the inner compound (Nos 29, 30, 35; 11, 13, 14) are negatively distinguished as against the site norms, whereas those on the eastern margin are positively emphasized (Nos 18, 27, 38, 42, 43, 49). If the precinct around House 42 is marginally the "richest" on the site, then the two complementary units on the western margin are demonstrably the "poorest", notwithstanding the strongly advantageous sampling effect introduced by the latter's outstanding number of superimposed floors (rebuilt up to ten times). The structures of this "poor quarter" are repeatedly reflected as significantly negative residuals when compared with the other units on the site in terms of spindle whorls, weaving combs, loom weights, querns, beads, shale trinkets and finger-rings. The many superimposed floors produced no evidence for the smithy that every other unit possessed, no heavy iron tools, no dependent workshop huts (IIb), no metal or antler harness or vehicle equipment of the many types abundantly scattered throughout the site, and no stables (VI). Yet in every other respect these two units, comprising some twelve structures and totalling 54 superimposed floors, faithfully reproduce the standard building unit features with their pairs of houses with floor burials, minor houses, ancillary hut, baking hut, granary and traces of male and female residence.

The evidence suggests that the two familial units of the western half of the richest sector were the poorest on the site. They were comparable in every respect but two with the five other site units – they lacked independent means of production (iron tools, workshops, draught animals) and the wealth and status that went with that means (warrior equipment and female finery). Although they maintained the capacity to own and presumably to fill their private granaries they were somehow dependent. The labour surplus from the western half of the inner compound must have been invested to the benefit of inhabitants other than themselves – and here we may perhaps legitimately look across the compound to the *enceinte* of the *primus inter pares*, House 42, with its extra large annexe stable (43), the spare plough beam in the yard (X92), the workshops turning wagon parts (X59), and its levy of female weavers from all round the site (54 textile frame pieces came from this sector alone, X65–66). This household seems to have exercised the capacity to export its products via the jetty it controlled, and thus to import the widest range of fine pottery and fibulae and barter for fine mirrors and currency in the Mendip markets.

The design of the inner compound itself lends some support to such an interpretation. The bilateral symmetry of the circle of houses is strongly reminiscent of the division between the minor house half and the major house half of each unit area, so scrupulously repeated in each of the seven units. Perhaps the relationship between the dependent, low-status half of the compound and the rich, high-status half might represent a structural analogue of the relationship between the minor, female half of each unit area and the major, familial half (Fig. 6). Certainly, the circular compound of structures itself appears as a modulus or mega-unit, found either independently, as here in Phase I (Fig. 2), or with penumbral units as in Phase IV (Fig. 5), enclosed or unenclosed, on British and Irish Late Bronze Age and Iron Age sites where they may embody differing versions of the kind of relationship inferred here.

If the individual characteristics of the extended family units and their artefacts are pursued to the limits of their reliability, some tentative information about the social relationships between the units on the site and with the outside world may be gleaned. Relationships between the units may be glimpsed, for example, from the idiosyncratic stylistic affinities between various household assemblages, and from the manner in which they deviate individually or in groups from the overall settlement trends. The differential selection of artefacts or designs exercised between a range of equally suitable alternatives marks out the products and imports of one unit from another – weaving combs with different motif preferences, glass beads of restricted types, imported raw materials, pottery, spindle whorls, and querns selectively acquired from different sources. Single element relationships of this kind are probably meaningless given the sampling problems but here we are dealing with a cumulatively reinforcing web of such relationships.

Some of these inter-unit and extra-unit relationships between artefacts are probably incidental to the circulation and interchange of women both in marriage and in the course of their economic activities. It is exceedingly unlikely, for instance, with the wealth of local material commonly used on the site for making spindle whorls (bone, antler, clay, pottery), that a single unattractive spindle whorl of Exmoor sandstone or Blackdown chalk was traded 20 miles to the site. It is altogether more probable that the occasional spindle whorl, weaving comb, beads and trinkets may have moved in a series, or in single, generational marriage moves. With other classes of artefact other social or economic mechanisms will be more appropriately invoked, including the whole network of customary tribal services. However, it is interesting to note the absence of the otherwise abundant finger-rings from the "poor" half of the central compound in comparison with their universal distribution across all the other units. It may be tempting to interpret the rings as symbols of married and adult status exchanged only between individuals of a certain standing. Certainly, the strong pattern of idiosyncratic relationships discretely shared between the extended family units and their artefact characteristics, together with the restricted pattern of trivial exotics from beyond the settlement's territory, does suggest a degree of settlement inter-unit endogamy and extra-settlement exogamy. We are thus forcibly reminded that the site can only be meaningfully modelled against a network of related and different sites within an interrelated system.

The same class of evidence suggests that the different kindred units may also have maintained slightly different degrees of economic and social contact with different areas of the outside world, at this microlevel. The contrast that emerges with the appropriate classification is between the "new" units in the northwest and northeastern sectors on one hand and all of the remaining "older" units on the other. The foreign exotics amongst the spindle whorls and imported pottery are here reinforced by a mass of circumstantial information.

Pottery and raw materials imported from the Mendip hills are com-

mon to all the units, but the southern unit combines an especial abundance of north Mendip pottery from the Dolebury area (Peacock
Group 3) with fine ware from the south Mendip and Maesbury area
(Peacock Groups 2, 4), as well as lias and sandstone whorls from the
same localities, and maintaining the unique workshop turning out
querns from blanks of Maesbury old red sandstone and andesite (Fig.
7). In contrast, the two northern sector units supported the workshop
turning Dorset shale imported from the territory of the Durotriges in
cylinders and discs. Furthermore, these northern units have produced
a quite exclusive range of exotics – whorls of sandstone and chalk from
south and west Somerset, the only exotic pottery from Cornwall (Group
I) and the Exeter regions (Group 5), most of the countersunk handle
"Durotrigian" jars, and pyramidal loom weights and glass beads, also
best paralleled at Hengistbury, a major Durotrigian *oppidum* and port.

This range of evidence suggests that the northwestern and northeastern units maintained especially strong connections with the trade
routes extending to the southern seaways – the routes by which the
settlement's tin and shale may have been imported – whereas the southern and central units preserved unusually strong ties with the Mendip
range, a region with which the marsh villages were closely interdependent, and which was the main source of lead and iron (Figs 7–
8). Thus the exotic spindle whorls and female items would seem to indicate a measure of settlement exogamy perhaps related to the varied
external connections of the individual kin units within the settlement.
If this is taken with the evidence for the within-settlement exchange
of women between the extended family units we have an impression
of a settlement community of closely related exogamous lineages linked
by bonds of settlement endogamy balanced with some settlement
exogamy. This model is supported by the physical anthropology of the
skeletal remains from the house floors, which imply "one unmixed
group of families", and is analogous to the social structure of comparable communities (Bulleid and Gray, 1917, p. 681; Murdock, 1949).

The consensus of information derived from the site and its artefacts
therefore enables us to erect a very tentative social model for this fenland settlement. The social unit of the community appears to have been
the patrilocal extended family, averaging some 15–20 persons, embracing an older man, his wife or wives, his unmarried children, his married
sons and their wives and children. This community will necessarily have
contained extended family lineage units from several different agnatic
clans who might thus intermarry within the settlement, creating community ties. The three lineage generations of each unit, including the
nuclear families of father and sons, apparently lived in clusters of
adjacent dwellings in which a female house served every pair of major

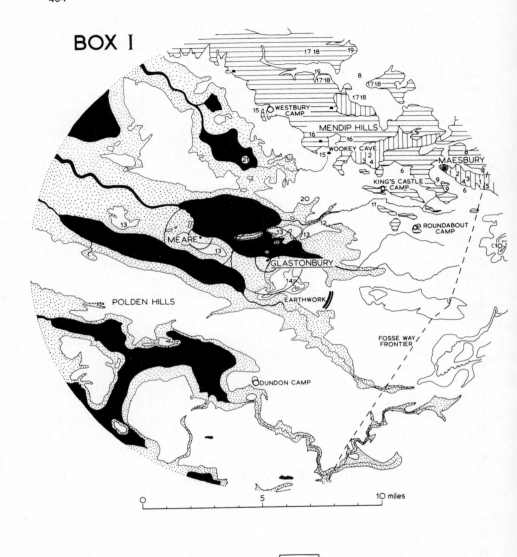

BOX I

17 18   19

19
1718

8

1718

15   WESTBURY CAMP

1718

MENDIP HILLS

16

16

WOOKEY CAVE

15

MAESBURY

KING'S CASTLE CAMP

11

ROUNDABOUT CAMP

20

MEARE

13

GLASTONBURY

EARTHWORK

POLDEN HILLS

FOSSE WAY FRONTIER

DUNDON CAMP

0   5   10 miles

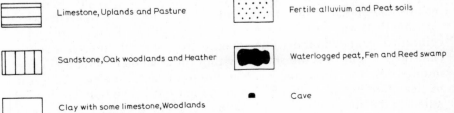

Limestone, Uplands and Pasture	Fertile alluvium and Peat soils
Sandstone, Oak woodlands and Heather	Waterlogged peat, Fen and Reed swamp
Clay with some limestone, Woodlands	Cave

familial houses. These co-operative kin groups were of broadly equal status, with the exception of the two "dependent" units on the west side of the inner compound, and were potentially self-supporting and self-servicing – hence the existence of the single unit settlement type (Fig. 1). However, the evidence suggests that the community was not acephalous and that a "headman" may have existed to focus community activities and co-ordinate the competing requirements of the

FIG. 7. The territory – Box 1: analysis of imported and exported materials from the site suggests, by the distribution of their sources, a site exploitation territory of *ca* 10 miles radius. This exploitation territory has a radius appropriate to the sophisticated pack-horse, cart, wagon and boat transport at the disposal of the community; the territory will have been exploited by overlapping sites (e.g., Meare) and should not be confused with the exclusive agricultural territory of each site (see the 0.5 mile radius infield and 1.5 mile radius outfield suggested on the map).

The territory depicted is a segment of the fenland running to the Mendip rim of limestone and sandstone hills, up to 1000 feet high. The site's exploitation territory runs from the major multivallate hill fort of Maesbury, from whose vicinity so many of the site's resources stem, to the Roman Fosse Way in the east, a later frontier which perhaps followed an earlier tribal boundary. Four smaller "hill forts" within the area – Dundon Camp, Roundabout Camp, King's Castle Camp and Westbury Camp – may have been related within the Glastonbury and Meare settlement systems. For the wider setting of the territory see Figs 8 and 9.

The details of the waterlogged areas on the map are speculative. The key to the resources exploited by the site community (below) indicates a particularly intensive relationship with the nearest sector of dry highlands between Westbury Camp and Maesbury (Maes is Celtic for upland field; Celtic fields are known from this area).

1 Clay sources for Peacock's Group 2 fine wares.
2 Oak forest source for heavy timber – dugout canoes, etc.
3 Probable main source for shed red deer antlers – the Old Red Sandstone ecology.
4 Quernstones of Old Red Sandstone.
5 Quernstones of Andesite lava.
6 Quernstones of Croscombe Lias.
7 Gannister clay for smelting crucibles.
8 Harptree chert for whetstones, etc.
9 Lower Limestone shales for hammers, whetstones, whorls, etc.
10 Fuller's earth from Maes Down.
11 Flint nodules from Dulcote gravels.
12 Flint nodules from Coxley gravels.
13 Alluvial clay sources for local coarse wares.
14 Upper Lias clay and rubble for floors, jetty, whorls, etc.
15 Draycott Triassic dolomitic conglomerate for hearthstones.
16 Closest area of upland limestone pastures and fields.
17 Lead ore sources.
18 Coloured lead ochre sources for paints, cosmetics, etc.
19 Iron ore sources, low quality, abundant limestone flux.
20 Chert from the Green Marls.
21 Estuarine and brackish water lake resources – shoals of shad, etc.
22 Freshwater fen resources – fowl, fish, fur-bearing predators.

family units. These units were in any event united by kinship linkages one with another within the settlement and also with clan kinsmen in neighbouring settlements, forming a consanguineous network extending through agnatic clans and tribal sections, to regional tribes within the loose tribal confederation of the Dumnonii (Fig. 9).

However, this social model must be a dynamic one. The settlement's ancestral community included perhaps sixty people in four extended families, living around a circular compound with two "dependent" families on one side and two "independent" families on the other (Fig. 2). This early settlement became the constantly renewed nucleus of a community which expanded from four to seven extended family groups and from perhaps 60 to more than 120 people over some 100 years.

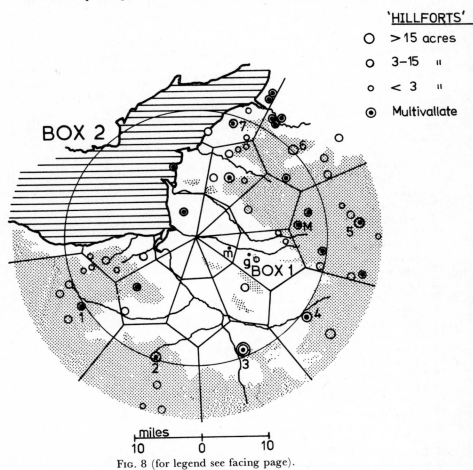

FIG. 8 (for legend see facing page).

It is perhaps significant that the settlement was abandoned at exactly the point at which it had generated a population surplus equal to its own initial size – 60 persons. Perhaps 120 people represented a critical size at which the community could maintain itself no longer at this maximal density, and simultaneously represented the minimal size to generate two communities of viable size in this demanding environment, suggesting an almost cyclic pattern of settlement development through a hierarchy of categories (Phase I to Phase IV to two Phase I's ... etc., 60 to 120 to 60 plus 60 ...). If this dynamic model is acceptable it might prove possible to study the different hierarchy of site categories in different areas and establish their different critical thresholds in different environments. Certainly, it reminds us that settlement "types" may only be phases in the life-cycle of a community and not necessarily independent classificatory taxa, and this in turn uncovers the important criterion – that *certain* settlement forms may *not* be derived from or ancestral to certain other forms simply by growth transformation.

In conclusion, this tentative social model derived from the archaeological evidence may briefly be compared with the historical information on Celtic society preserved in the records of the classical authors and in the Irish vernacular tradition. There we learn that the Celtic tribal unit (*túath*) was usually ruled by a chieftain or king (*rí*) who was served by his client nobles, men of rank distinguished by the capacity

FIG. 8. The area – Box 2: the Glastonbury territory (Box 1) is but one tessera of a mosaic of territories running from the encircling hills down into the undrained fenland basin. Contiguity, common resources and the drainage system converging on the Bristol Channel preform this area of *ca* 20 miles radius (Box 2) into a related settlement system.

The artificially regular tessellation suggested in this model is derived from a Thiessen polygon analysis of the major fortified site distribution; the relationship between this interpretative model and reality is envisaged as comparable to the relationship between reality and the model in Fig. 11. The analysis suggests a ring of large upland territories associated with central major earthworks:

1	Castle Hill	5	Tedbury
2	Castle Neroche	6	Maes Knoll Camp
3	Ham Hill	7	Cadbury Congresbury
4	Cadbury Castle		

This outer tier of territories dips to the fen edge and encloses a second tier of fenland/estuarine territories centred on isolated hills and island sanctuaries. Although the hill forts may not be exactly contemporary, they nevertheless are the man-hour insignia for considerable populations who both pre-existed and post-existed their construction.

g = Glastonbury
m = Meare
M = Maesbury Camp, here seen as perhaps a lower order site of the Tedbury hierarchy.

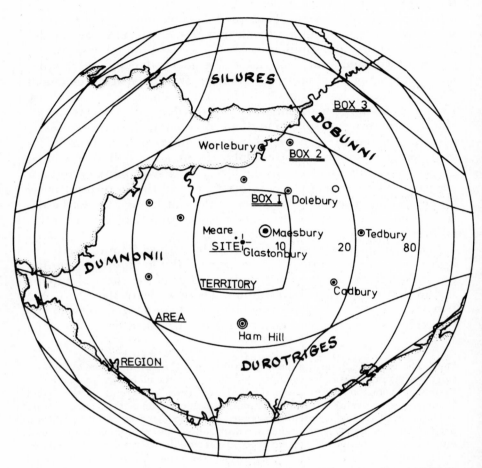

Fig. 9. The region – Box 3, a logarithmic transformation: the Dumnonian tribal region and the Chinese Box model of the Glastonbury site within its territory, area and regional systems (Boxes 1, 2, 3 – Figs 7–9). A logarithmic transformation of distance is used to show that the significance of distant areas for Glastonbury falls away according to the volume of activity occurring between them; a prior correction allocates land transport and distance twice the value of the speedier sea transport. These transformations show the way in which sea transport united the Dumnonian region. The significance of regional and interregional trade is confirmed by the Cornish tin, fine pottery from Maesbury, Dolebury, Cornwall and Lyme Bay areas (Groups 1–6), Nailsea sand(?) glass, Forest of Dean high-grade iron, Dorset shale and Scandinavian amber – all found on the Glastonbury site.

to own, maintain and equip one or more chariots – the *equites* of Caesar, the "chariot" men (*eirr*) of the Irish epics. The noble grade were themselves supported by their client retinue of companions (*ceile*), warriors (*gaiscedach*) and charioteers. These were drawn from the non-noble freemen (*boaire*) who were cattle- (*bo*) and property-owning commoners, Caesar's *plebs*; they were farmers, who might possess their own simple chariot and cart and carry arms, and whose skills included those of the craftsmen and smith. The druids, magicians and bards (*drui, faith, bard*) served the spiritual needs of the noble grades from whom they were recruited, whilst below all came the unfree, propertyless men, without the status of arms: tenants, labourers, inferior craftsmen, indebted clients, slaves and handmaidens who laboured to the economic advantage of their masters (Jackson, 1964; Powell, 1959).

Of course, Celtic society varied through time and from tribe to tribe. Yet, everywhere, the web of Celtic kinship seems to have been crosscut by broadly comparable grades, often elaborately distinguished by the almost heraldic significance of the subcultural artefact insignia appropriate to each status. The fabric of Celtic society appears to have derived its strength from kinship interwoven with allegiance. The Irish Laws confirm this and are much concerned with what property a man may be allowed to hold in keeping with his rank, carefully differentiating between the property of the ordinary freeman (*boaire febsa*) and a serior freeman who might be a local headman or magistrate (*boaire mruigfer*). We may appropriately compare their property, households and stock holdings with those of the Glastonbury units – and in particular compare their "seven roofs" or "houses" with the seven structures in each Glastonbury unit (I–VII) (Fig. 1).

Boaire febsa Twice seven cumals of land; a house of 27 feet with an outhouse of 15 feet; a share in a mill [quern?], so that he grinds for his family and his companies of guests; a kiln [bakehouse?], a barn, a sheepfold, a calf fold, a pig sty. These are the *seven roofs* in respect of which every *boaire* is paid for injury. He has twelve cows, a half share in a plough ... a steer is his customary due ...

Boaire mruigfer Land of three times seven cumals he has. He is *boaire* of adjudication, the senior *boaire* of his lineage, with all the artefacts of his house in their proper places; a cauldron with its spits and supports; a vat in which a boiling [of ale?] may be brewed; a cauldron for ordinary use, utensils including irons, trays, mugs, a trough, bath, tubs ... knives for cutting rushes, ropes, an adze, an auger, a saw, shears, a trestle, an axe; tools for use in every season ... a whetstone, mallets, a billhook, a hatchet, a spear for killing cattle; a fire always alive ...

a cask of milk and a cask of ale ... he has three sacks always in his house ... a sack of brewing barley, a sack of sea salt against the cutting up of joints of his cattle, a sack of charcoal for the irons. *Seven houses* he has, a kiln, a barn, a mill – his share therein so that he grinds in it for others, a dwelling of 27 feet, an outhouse of 17 feet, a pig sty, a calf fold, a sheepfold. Twenty cows, two bulls, six oxen, 20 pigs, 20 sheep, 400 hogs, two brood sows, a saddle horse with an enamelled bridle. Sixteen sacks [of seed] in the ground [stored?]. He has a bronze cauldron in which a hog fits. He owns pasture in which there are always sheep without [need to] change ground. He and his wife have four changes of dress. His wife is daughter of his equal in grade ... three companions [*ceile*] are his retinue in the tribe [*túath*] ... he protects his equal in grade ... a cow is his tributary due.

In contrast, the tribal chieftain (*rí*) was entitled to a house of over 30 feet to sleep up to seventeen persons and encircled on occasion by a "ditch of vassalage" (*drecht gialnai*) (*Crith Gablach*, Binchy, 1941; Hamilton, 1968, p. 72).

Now the finest artefacts from Glastonbury are of good quality but they are not abundant and they are never of the highest quality found elsewhere in this region – there is no enamelled harness comparable to the suite for a noble equipage of some seven chariots buried five miles away in the Polden hoard, no torques like those from Clevedon or Wraxall, no fine shield mounts, no coral, gold or silver like the material from Cadbury. There is no evidence in artefacts or house size of nobility; the Glastonbury craftsmen were skilled part-time operators making lower order goods and providing comparable services – they were village smiths, not master craftsmen (Fig. 12).

There is, however, clear evidence at Glastonbury for the presence of independent wealth on a small scale and the possession of property, weapons, chariots, horses and stock, together with abundant evidence for skilled craftsmen in carpentry, lathework and elementary smithing. These attributes of the free man are precisely those redundantly repeated for all five of the independent lineages whom we might tentatively identify as the extended families of non-noble freemen (*boaire febsa*) and their dependants. The exceptions are the two "dependent" units on the west side of the inner compound and the enclosure of the "headman" on the east side. Perhaps here we might infer the presence of the senior man (*boaire mruigfer*) of the senior lineage served either by two unfree families or dependent clients.

Now, by chance, Caesar records as an interpolation in his narrative a fragmentary "ethnology" of those parts of Britain best known to merchant adventurers before the Roman invasion – principally, the territories of the Dumnonii in the west and the Cantii in the east (Caesar, V. 1; Warner, 1960, pp. 94–95). In this "ethnology" a brief description is given of the social organization of local Celtic communities, including the observation: "women are held in common between groups of ten or twelve men, particularly between brothers or between fathers and sons; but the children born from these unions are considered to belong to the man to whom the woman was married first."

This terse observation of the first century B.C. presents a condensed but intelligible record of an important complex of functionally inter-related Celtic social customs found together in many analogous societies – the patrilocal extended family, fraternal polygyny, and levirate (Murdock, 1949, pp. 23–41). Furthermore, the Celtic custom of fosterage, often historically viewed as a barbaric eccentricity, is a frequent element in the same recurrent set of customs (Murdock, 1949, p. 35). The classical authors and Irish evidence confirm that, although monogamous unions will have numerically prevailed, Celtic society was polygynous by rank and status, with a single principal wife (*cétmuinter*) in addition to others of subordinate rank (Powell, 1959, p. 84). All of these customs recur together where women have great economic impor-tance and where the most efficient unit for economic co-operation is larger than the nuclear family. Certainly, the kindred units at Glaston-bury seem to approach these conditions and one might dare to see the hypothesized units of 15–20 men and women, in residential units such that each pair of familial houses holds in common a minor "female" house, as a structural analogue of the social convention noted by Caesar (Filip, 1960, p. 94).

Economic and other factors predispose a society to move towards a limited set of viable family structures and residence patterns. The economic advantages of plural wives may be critical in circumstances where the numbers of an extended family must be maintained and where many hands are required for weaving, milking, shepherding, field work, light manufacturing and food production. The reproductive and working capacity of a single wife will often be too precarious, especially when she may be sterile or at best regularly incapacitated by pregnancy. These pressures towards an extended family form are redoubled wherever substantial time and co-operative effort have been locked up in the capital of animal herds, ditched, diked and manured fields, permanent structures or localized and interlocking resources such as fishing, fowling, trapping or grazing rights. Then property fac-tors promote the development of extended family patterns and inheri-tance mechanisms of the levirate type (Murdock, 1949, pp. 36–40; Goody, 1969).

The type and size of family and tribal units may be modelled as a response surface varying with the mandatory or permissive constraints of the territorial area, within the range allowed by technology and the society's antecedent social pattern. The categories and sizes of site developed by the society in its settlement system or hierarchy, and even the numbers and structural organization of elements like the lineages, will be limited and controlled by the nature of the territory and its segmentation (Evans-Pritchard, 1940, p. 248). At Glastonbury, then, we have several patrilocal extended families of non-noble freemen farmers, united by kinship ties, and a system of allegiance through a headman, supported by a range of dependants or clients. We may suppose that the combined mechanisms of the patrilocal extended family, fraternal polygyny, levirate, clientship and fosterage may here have served to support and bind these co-operative kin groups within a most effective structural response to the uniquely burdensome group tasks required by their demanding but rewarding marshland home – clearing, ditching, diking, draining, building crannogs and tracks, droving, shepherding, manufacturing and exporting – a high risk but a high yield strategy.

THE SITE: AN ECONOMIC MODEL AND ITS LOCATIONAL CONTEXT

The preliminary analyses of the mass of information embedded within the site observations have enabled us to establish some crude parameters, to discuss social models for the Glastonbury community, and to compare both with indirect historical information. But no model for such a site can be complete without a consideration of the locally critical relationships between the community's ethology, economy and environment. Some attempt should be made to isolate the critical variables in the nexus of relationships between this community and its behaviour patterns and those of other communities, together with the mutual exploitation of their loci, territories, areas and regions. No site is, or was, an isolate and no site may be comprehended without a consideration of its possible or probable roles within a network of contemporary sites; whether or not those contemporary sites may still be identified is immaterial.

Once again, such a study logically leads to an array of alternative models to be tested against information from other sources. In the interests of brevity the most plausible and momentarily most powerful model will be outlined to show the significance that observations made beyond the site must have for interpretation within any site.

The area surrounding Glastonbury forms a geological bowl with a rim of limestone and sandstone hills barely five miles from the site (Fig. 7). The gravels at the feet of these hills merge into a succession of peats, clays and alluvium, which forms the fenland bottom, cleft only by the low spit of the Lias Polden hills running between the rivers Brue and Parrett. The limestone uplands carried open forest and rich pasture whilst the sandstone pockets supported acid soils with fine oak stands and patches of heather – an area rich in deer and pig herds. Below, the oak and ash woods of the sheltered gravels petered out amidst the many miles of shallow freshwater meres, reed swamps, sedge moors and fen carr, wooded with willow, alder, thorns, birch, dwarf oak and ash and interspersed by richly grassed herbaceous clearings in the summer drought. To the west, brackish waters came within 5 miles of the site and estuarine conditions within 10 miles, each with their own rich and diverse ecology. Within the fen the occasional island offered hospitality in the maze of interlinked and sluggish waterways – so hostile to the newcomer, so rewarding to those with sufficient specialized knowledge of this rich but treacherous environment.

The "Green Island" (*Ynys Glas*) at Glastonbury was just such a refuge: a small, verdant, conical peninsula of sand and clay defended on its landward eastern margin by an Iron Age earthwork, Ponter's Ball. Similar refuges and sacred sites presumably existed on comparable islands around the fenland bowl, serving the many focal purposes for the lowland communities around them that the more obvious hill forts similarly provided on the Mendip hills. The settlement at Glastonbury, like the broadly contemporary settlement at Meare, three miles to the west, was set amidst the fens close to the rich river silt and the alluvial flats exposed by the periodic contractions of the vast Meare pool. Probably every such island and peninsula supported several similar consanguineous communities scattered in a shifting but mutually adjusted distribution around their margins.

This sheltered, low-lying lakeside area occupied one of the warmest and driest climatic niches in the Dumnonian regions famed for their Atlantic warmth, wetness and mild winters. The location carried many other special advantages – the high-quality alluvial and peat soils, the level surfaces, the availability of water, the year-through richness of fenland wildlife resources, the long-distance bulk-carrying and inter-communication permitted by boat, and the contiguity within a small radius of a great diversity of ecological habitats, ranging from estuarine marshes through freshwater fens to gravel terraces and geologically variegated hills (Figs 7, 8).

However, this locality shared the many disadvantages and the basic paradox posed by most fenland sites. An excess of water is a handicap to farming – the stock become prone to foot rot, parasites and insect diseases, and the co-operative labour requirements of draining and diking are severe but essential if the root systems of the crops are to be kept from waterlogging in the crucial weeks of the growing season. Furthermore, the severe annual flooding will have been disastrously exacerbated from time to time by concurrences of high tides, Atlantic gales and heavy rainfall in the hills, and from period to period climatic and sea level oscillations rendered most of this area temporarily uninhabitable.

If water and fen resources were abundant in the marshes there were other important staples that had to be imported – flint, stone, clay, metals and large timber. It is in this context that a marsh location close to the hills becomes an optimal solution on the Weberian model (Chorley and Haggett, 1967, pp. 362–417). Nevertheless, these advantages and disadvantages are almost trivial against the background of the fundamental paradox of this flat terrain – that in the course of every annual cycle two-thirds of the little dry land available was inundated. The annually dependable dry land area, to which all permanent settlement was confined by the wet season, was less than one-third of that richly grassed alluvium available during the summer drought; a dearth of land in winter, an unexploitable superabundance in summer. Thus the territory presented a high-risk area for farmers, perhaps unacceptably high for small farming units below a critical labour level and outside a reciprocally supporting settlement network. But the territory also represented a potentially high-yield terrain with easily worked rich soils and the rich wild resources.

In the periods before technology could attempt the drainage of the whole fenland basin this territorial paradox could be solved in only two ways.

1. By adapting social organization and economy to the special conditions and resources of the fenland environment and accepting the flood constraint to semi-independent, small-scale, low-density communities, with a low level of economic and political organization.
2. By adapting to the special conditions and resources but rejecting the flood constraint by establishing a system of territorial segmentation with the contiguous hill areas such that reciprocal, interdependent and symbiotic relationships would allow the ebb and flow of people and commodities to mutual advantage. This solution not only allows but demands community interdependence and reciprocal specialization over large areas, with larger scale, higher density society requiring a high level of economic and political organization.

In each solution the unique environment requires an adaptive response extending from social and political organization, through technology to economic strategies with an emphasis on special crop, stock and wild resource management patterns. However, the second higher level solution requires some degree of sophistication and is simultaneously the more risky. We should certainly not make the mistake of ordering these two solutions in an evolutionary and chronological succession. Quite apart from the oscillating conditions of the fenland through time, it is evident that these two solutions are alternatives and communities of the first type might coexist amidst a society of the second category, although the more complex category of organization may only have been viable in "dry" periods in the fenland – in Middle Late Neolithic, Middle Late Bronze Age, Middle Late Iron Age and Later Roman periods. Thus, when similar conditions returned similar responses re-emerged with a slight technological advance; parallel conditions with similar sequences may also be observed for the East Anglian fenlands (Darby, 1940; Godwin and Dewar, 1963).

The information recovered from the site at Glastonbury and from the broadly contemporary sites of the surrounding territory points firmly to the existence of interdependent and reciprocally specialized communities of the second category, networking the fenland settlements to those of the surrounding hills and vice versa. It should be noted that this interdependence is not merely postulated on theoretical grounds, nor conjured from the hypothetically analogous Medieval transhumance patterns found both here and in East Anglia (Darby, 1940, Fig. 13), but is demonstrated by the extensive range of items reciprocally exchanged between a limited area of the Mendips and the Glastonbury settlement (Fig. 7) and by the otherwise insupportable degree of idiosyncratic affinity between the artefact assemblages of the fenland and the Mendip slopes.

The material evidence points to an especially intensive volume of activity between the *locus* of the Glastonbury site and an exploitation *territory* of about 10 miles radius – with an especial emphasis on the segment of Mendip between the large hill fort at Maesbury and the leadworkings at Charterhouse, above Cheddar Gorge (Fig. 7). There is evidence of a less intensive but pronounced volume of activity relating Glastonbury and this Mendip territory to a wider settlement *system catchment area*, some 20 miles radius from the site, itself apparently but one tessera within a mosaic of catchment areas running orthogonally across the resources from the Mendip rim to the fenland bowl (Fig. 8) (Clarke, 1968, p. 505). At a still more related level similar evidence relates this site and the Somerset area network as a tribal sept within the 80 miles radius of a putative Dumnonian septarchy or tribal group (Fig. 9).

The Glastonbury site and its contents therefore relate to a series of successively wider networks or regional frames – from a local territory, through an incorporating area, to an englobing region. However, in activity terms land surface is far more complex than a homogeneous plane over which activity volume diminishes steadily with distance. The volume of activity focused on the Glastonbury site in reality falls away logarithmically in intensity over distance in a series of concentric but asymmetric frames, with an important major distortion – distance by sea appears to be less than half the impedance of distance overland, a distortion that in itself almost accounts for the existence of the Dumnonii as a regional unit (Fig. 9).

The successive frames may be arbitrarily named, crudely defined and subject to sampling problems, but they still seem to reflect zones of changing degrees of relationship with the site. The site exploitation territory maps an activity zone apparently related to the effective daily range of man, animal, canoe, cart and chariot load movements in and out of the site; it is interesting to note that the advanced technology and water transport give a larger site exploitation territory than elsewhere (see Jarman, 1972). The 20 miles radius area of the site system to which Glastonbury belongs represents the complex accumulation of the preceding factors for a large number of unknown sites interacting with ecological, economic, demographic and political elements within the network of adaptively located settlements of the Somerset bowl. Then, finally, the regional unit of the Dumnonii is represented by a tract of some 80 land miles radius but perhaps only ten sea hours sailing time, within which some six or seven area systems were interlinked by communication, reciprocity and common political, ethnic and linguistic constraints.

However, it is at the local territorial level that the most intensive connections demonstrate the interdependence of the Glastonbury fenlands and the Maesbury highlands. The exotic resources brought into the site from this territory include hundreds of tons of Upper Lias clay and rubble from the Tor, iron, lead and red lead ochre from Charterhouse, hearthstones from Draycott and flints from the Coxley gravels (Fig. 7). The immediate vicinity of Maesbury Camp, and its probable predecessor at Blacker's Hill, contributed Old Red Sandstone, Andesite and Croscombe Lias quern stone roughouts, doorsteps, hammerstones, whetstones, spindle whorls, fine pottery (Peacock's Group 2), special Gannister crucible clay from Oakhill, fuller's earth from Chewton and miscellaneous stones from the Lower Limestone shales, Dolomitic conglomerates and Harptree chert. The same Mendip slopes probably supplied the Glastonbury community with the many hundreds of feet of shed deer antler, the large oaks for canoes, but above all the potential of some 25 square miles of sheltered, well-drained winter browse and grazing at a season when the flooded fenland islands could measure their dry area in square feet. Conversely, when the summer droughts exposed acres of freshly-deposited alluvium in the fens, the Mendip pastures would have been grazed to the ground and dried by the sun.

The archaeological evidence from this segment of the Mendips reciprocally supports the evidence from within the Glastonbury site. The Wookey Hole caverns, 5 miles away at the foot of the hills, have produced a wide range of artefacts, which are not only broadly contemporaneous but closely match the Glastonbury assemblage in a broad spectrum of structured idiosyncrasies which suggest that we are dealing with the material culture of communities from a common society. Many similar caves scattered along the limestone escarpment clearly show regular use at this period as seasonal base camps for transhumant shepherds and their flocks, as bivouacs for seasonal mining, smelting and smithing activities and in some cases as druid sanctuaries (Dobson, 1931, pp. 112–115). Wookey Hole alone produced many cubic feet of sheep and goat dung interspersed with fragments of milking pots, weaving combs and lathe fragments, and burials including one with an iron billhook, knife, dagger, latch-lifter and stalagmite ball closely comparable to those from Glastonbury.

Perhaps the most convincing evidence linking the Glastonbury settlement with the Maesbury fortified site is provided by the detailed concurrence between Peacock's petrological analyses of the Glastonbury and Mendip area pottery and the evidence from the petrology and taxonomy of the Glastonbury community's quernstones. Peacock has been able to show that fine pottery was being "mass produced" in localities with suitable clays and suitable *in situ* demand and then marketed over wide areas (Peacock, 1959). Glastonbury, for example, was importing fine ware from north and south Mendip markets (Groups, 2, 3, 4) as well as acquiring the odd vessel from as far afield as Cornwall (Group 1) and Devon (Group 5), all within the Dumnonian region. Now Peacock has been able to trace the most likely source of the Glastonbury Group 2 wares to clays of the Sandstone deposits between Maesbury and Beacon Hill, near Shepton Mallet (Peacock, 1969, p. 46). These same deposits are the very source of the Glastonbury querns of Old Red Sandstone and Andesite which the settlement was importing in roughout form. Furthermore, the closest parallel to the peculiar Glastonbury quern type found outside the site itself comes from this source locality (Bulleid and Gray, 1911–17, pp. 610–611). It seems highly probable that the large-scale quarrying and dressing of quernstones and the manufacture and kilning of fine pottery were connected with the location of the largest local hill fort at Maesbury, dominating as it does the central Mendip resources of timber, pasture, lead, coal, iron and a variety of stone resources. We may hypothesize, and subsequently test by excavation, that it was from this centre that Glastonbury imported much of its raw materials and to which it exported its own products. It was around this centre that the nearest hill pasture lay and it was perhaps to this centre that Glastonbury owed its political allegiance and thus its customary tribute.

It is only against this locational context that the internal site information on the economy of the Glastonbury, community can now be intelligibly assembled. It is only against the context of the summer surplus of fine fenland pasture and the Mendip surplus of dry winter grazing that we can understand both the choice of sheep as a fenland staple and the large numbers in which they were kept. Upon this in turn rests the community's textile industry and the critical significance of the numbers of women who could be gathered and held together within polygynous extended families or the number of brothers who could be released for droving and shepherding for months in the year. Once again the information will bear several alternative chains of interpretations that must be tested, but at least the data on the settlement's domestic animals, crops and fenland resources now permit us to review the most likely pattern for their integrated management (Clarke, 1972, Figs 1.10–1.12).

Only a sample of the animal bones from the site have survived contemporary destruction by burning and dogs, only a sample of these were recovered and only a sample of this sample was analysed by species (Bulleid and Gray, 1911–17, p. 641). Precise calculations are therefore impossible and the range of estimates can only be accepted as indicating the rough scale of the activities. Nevertheless, arguments based on the estimated human population, sampling evidence and the relatively complete excavation suggest from the quantity of bones discovered and from the settlement span that the Glastonbury herds may have ranged from some 200–1000 sheep of Soay type, perhaps 20–30 small oxen and cows of Kerry type, 10–20 Celtic ponies and a few dozen pigs and dogs, expanding from the lower figure towards the higher figure over the 100 years of settlement expansion (Phases I–IV, Figs 2–5). These figures receive a crude confirmation from estimates separately derived from the expanding stable, byre and sty facilities of the settlement and the developing capacity of the inner and outer compounds to corral when necessary up to some 1200 head of stock. This complement of livestock would be sufficient for the meat and milk needs of the estimated population with a sufficient surplus for safety, breeding, wastage, tribute and exchange purposes. Tacitus reminds us, for example, that the customary gift annually due to men of rank was an important economic mechanism at this time—"it is the custom that each tribesman shall give the chieftain presents either of cattle or of part of his harvest. These free gifts are marks of respect, but they also supply the needs of those who receive them" (Postan, 1966, p. 273).

The main crops grown at Glastonbury were two-rowed and six-rowed barley, wheat and the small Celtic bean. Large quantities of threshed grain and beans were found around the granary stances and it is interesting to note that although beans and wheat often occurred together in the debris the barley usually appeared alone. This slight evidence might suggest the separate sowing of winter barley in the restricted dry area around the settlement and a main crop of wheat and beans sown in late spring over a wider expanse of fertile alluvial flats, river floodplain and burned-off peat and reed beds. These tactics resemble the Medieval practice in the Somerset levels and in this archaic form amount to a variety of infield–outfield system, which long survived in the peripheries of the Celtic fringe (van Bath, 1963, pp. 58, 246, 263).

The infield, here defined by the winter floods, usually occupied less than one-third of all the arable but was kept under continuous tillage by burning off, ashing and fertilizing annually with high phosphate and potash hearth debris (estimated site output *ca* 4000–7000 cubic feet per annum) plus manure and fouled sedge litter from the stables and byres (estimated site output *ca* 100 000–200 000 pounds per annum) and direct manure from grazing on the stubble fields after harvest. The alluvial and peat soils are also natural phosphate and nitrate reservoirs and, with the manuring and the nitrogen-fixative legumes, there should have been no difficulty in maintaining an infield permanently under the plough, without fallow.

On the outfield, cereals and legumes would be grown around a wider radius until the yields were no longer rewarding, after which the patches would be fallowed and used to fold stock. After this enrichment the land could again be sown annually for 5 years and then the cycle repeated. The "waste" areas of sedge and reed flats beyond the outfield might be annually reclaimed by slashing and burning to provide land for short-term cultivation and by natural succession to rich pasture of sheep's fescue (*Festuca ovina*) and purple moor grass (*Molinia caerulea*). In this way three concentric zones of agrarian activity will probably have expanded and contracted around the settlement with the waxing and the waning of the fenland floods (Fig. 10).

Under these conditions yields would have been high but subject to severe annual fluctuations introduced by unusually wet years—a high return for high risk and heavy capital investment. Certainly part of this investment in labour time, plant and capital must have taken the form of extensive ditching. The fenland soils cannot be exploited without the diking and draining that allow the crop roots the minimal period without waterlogging essential for their growth. We do not know which of the many simple forms of drained-field cultivation the Glastonbury community used, but the infield and much of the outfield areas

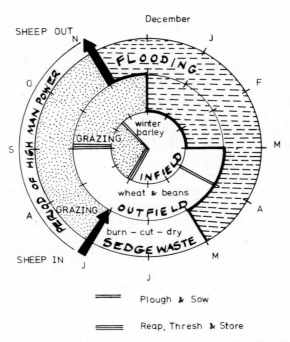

Fig. 10. A hypothetical economic cycle model for the Glastonbury settlement. The site is imagined at the centre of the diagram, in the middle of three zones of agrarian exploitation – the infield, outfield and sedge wastelands. The decisive factor in this strategy is the annual flooding of most of the outfield and sedge areas in winter and the superabundance of grazing in high summer. This inequality is defeated by moving large herds and flocks in and out of the area at key seasons. In actuality, the settlement's agrarian area occupied a semicircular radius forced by the lake margin to the north (see Fig. 7).

must have possessed extensive systems of small open ditches. Aerial photography and extensive excavation would test this assertion and there is already some evidence that small, squarish, ditched fields may have been in such contexts (Denevan, 1970; Bowen, 1969, Plate 1.3; Norman and St Joseph, 1970, p. 67, Figs 38, 39). On this assumption the Glastonbury cropland can hardly have required the digging and regular cleaning of less than 15 miles of ditches – yet another activity in which the regular, co-operative and periodically intensive labour of kin groups will have been essential for the common good, firmly tying the community to the capital investment of its fields.

The Somerset tribes were no novices in wet farming, both the local and Celtic traditions inherited some 3000 years of successful agrarian experiment on lake margins, in marshes, on crannogs and islands. The perimeter of the Glastonbury site was, for example, ingeniously stabilized and repeatedly extended by a subtle reclamation technique in which pairs of converging banks dug in the drought were closed in a pincer and then levelled with dumped rubbish (Bulleid and Gray, Plates XXIX, XXXIII). Banks and ditches dug with iron-shod oak spades were fundamental elements of Iron Age technology and it is significant that broken spade handles are amongst the more common artefacts found at Glastonbury, together with the sedge farmer's iron billhooks (Dobson, 1931, p. 118; Bulleid and Gray, 1911–17, pp. 319, 366).

The iron plough share (Z3) and the plough beam roughout (X92) from Glastonbury show that a light two-oxen plough of the Donnerupland type was in use (Bowen, 1961, p. 8). If we accept the analogy between the Glastonbury residential units and establishments on the scale of the Irish freemen (*boaire febsa*) then we might expect one such plough and two draught oxen for each free unit – totalling perhaps two ploughs and four oxen in Phase I to five ploughs and ten oxen in Phase IV (Figs 2–5). These draught oxen and the other settlement stock will have derived essential winter fodder from the bean plants during the crucial wet months, although both oxen and ponies will also have required a small supplementary ration from the cereal surplus.

Estimates of the cereal yield and area cultivated from the site can be very crudely approached from the separate evidence of the storage capacity of the granaries and from the minimum yield necessary to feed the population estimated from the site's structures. These lines of inference are in broad agreement with one another and with information from analogous sites in comparable circumstances. This evidence suggests that the ploughland in annual use would have risen over 100–200 acres (Phases I–IV), requiring a minimum total outfield area rising between 150 and 300 acres. Since the area north of the site was standing water the outfield area will have crudely extended over a half circle with a minimal radius of between 0.5 and 1 mile from the site. Beyond this outfield will have extended the zone of sedge farming and the extensive pasture confirmed by pollen analysis, and to these minimal calculations must be added a substantial factor for inlying pockets of untillable terrain (Godwin, 1960; Godwin and Dewar, 1963).

All in all, it would be difficult to estimate the outer radius of plough-

land, pasture and waste regularly exploited from the site at less than
ca 1½ miles. The significance of this figure becomes apparent when we
note that the related site at Meare, 3 miles to the west, then emerges
as a nearest neighbour site with a contiguous zone of activities on the
same lake shore (Fig. 7). Taken further, the same chain of inference
allows us to guess the most likely loci for other contemporary settlements
in this area – and within its crude limits the model becomes predictive
and testable.

No sketch model of the Glastonbury economy can legitimately ignore
the vast resources offered to the settlement by the fenland itself – the
shellfish, fish, water plants and rhizomes for food and fodder; hazel
nuts, light timber and the finest smelting charcoal from the buckthorn
and the carr, with willow for baskets and hurdles, reed and sedge for
thatch, bedding and flooring, peat turf for fuel, fen mammals for fur,
and wild fowl in superabundance. Fish, fur and fowl were the traditional fenland staples.

The lead net weights and bones confirm that fish were netted in the
meres. A prolific variety of ducks, geese and swans were taken as eggs
in the nest or on the wing with hunting dogs and slingshot from the
margins of the site itself. The fur-bearing mammals – beaver, otter, fox
and wild cat – were extensively taken and caches of their bones discarded from skinning were repeatedly found near the baking huts,
where their pelts were perhaps dried and treated before stitching to
the fine embroidered woollen cloaks. The seasonal fenland resources
certainly contributed in no small measure to stabilizing the precarious
agrarian regime of the settlement.

However, this static sketch model must be set into dynamic motion
if the integrated management pattern for this complex of interdependent resources is to be simulated and ultimately quantified (see
Thomas, 1972). The very complexity and seasonality of the many competing elements witnessed in the evidence imposes the limiting restrictions which make such an input–output study possible and an energy
system model conceivable.

Waterlogging seasonally reduced the dry land area around the settlement by two-thirds. Grazing was therefore virtually non-existent in the
vicinity of the village for flocks of any size until the summer months,
when there would have been a superabundance by late summer with
the first flush of grass colonizing the alluvial flats and banks, purple
moor grass dominating the burnt and cut sedge areas, the long stubble
left after harvesting the entire infield and outfield with sickles, plus the
extensive herbaceous browse of the waterside. In contrast, the better
drained limestone and sandstone hillsides would have provided admirable over-winter and spring grazing but would have become too dry,

overgrazed and nutritionally too poor to support very large flocks at the critical period when the ewes and lambs require their highest plane of nutrition in June and July (Large, 1970, Fig. 1; Hurst, 1970).

Thus the fenland bowl provided its peak of surplus pasture of the very highest quality in exactly the months when the Mendip slopes would have been exhausted. The sheep were therefore most probably driven up to Mendip as the autumn became wetter and the outfield flooded, to return to the fenland settlements late the following summer as the maximum grazing became available and the crops safely harvested. In this way the sheep-carrying capacity of the upland–lowland system was far greater than could have been sustained by the individual component territories acting independently (Fig. 7).

Given this situation, the agrarian cycle of the community would have moved into operation as the spring floods receded, with the preparation, ploughing and sowing of the outfield (March–April) and any residual parts of the infield not already sown with winter barley the previous year (October–November) (Fig. 10). The community may have been short-handed at this time if many of the young men accompanied the flocks to the Mendip slopes, but once the spring sowing was completed the season would have been appropriate for egg collecting, fowling and fishing and it is at this time (May–June) that the big shoals of marine shad (*Clupea finta*) must have been netted as they came up to spawn in the brackish meres three miles distant (Fig. 7).

By June–July the winter-sown infield crops might be harvested, threshed and carted to the granaries and later the sedge would be dry enough to cut for thatch and litter or ready for burning in preparation for pasture. With the maximum land area exposed for grazing the flocks could be driven down from Mendip with their three-month-old lambs now able to travel, just weaned and requiring the fresh nutritious pasture immediately available on the alluvial flats and the infield stubble. In July–August the fleece of the Soay sheep "moults" and would be ready for pulling, perhaps using the antler "weaving" combs and iron knives (Wild, 1970). This would be a busy time, with one harvest in, another to reap and up to 1000 sheep to fleece, but the community's full manpower would be available.

In August or September the main crop in the outfield would be ripe for harvesting, leaving yet more grazing to augment the freshly grassed sedge areas. When this harvest was in, there would remain a useful month or more of dry autumnal weather and full manpower when building and reconstruction tasks could be undertaken, land reclaimed by diking, ditches cleaned and extended and obligatory tribal works undertaken. This timing is confirmed by the discarded debris of lunches of hazel nuts left by the builders in the foundations of huts under construction at this fruitful season of nuts, hunting and wildfowling (Bulleid and Gray, 1911–17, pp. 70, 148).

By the close of October the rams would have served the ewes and the grazing around the village would have neared exhaustion, but the ewes would then have required a high plane of nutrition for the first four weeks after mating, if lambing was to be successful (Hurst, 1970). With the early November rains threatening to flood the fen pasture and close the trackways the shepherds would have gathered their flocks and left for the slow drive up on to the fresh Mendip pastures from nearby Shapwick, via the Sheppey valley, to Shepton and Maesbury (from Sheep-village, along Sheep-island valley to Sheep-town). Back in the fen it would be time to prepare, plough and sow the infield so recently manured by grazing stock and in general to prepare for the winter.

In the early winter the waterways and meres would have been restored to their fullest navigable extent by the rains and journeys by canoe were thus made the more effective. The presence within the settlement of sea-shore pebbles, sea-shells, cormorant and puffin bones suggests trips to the important saltings at the mouth of the river Brue to trade for "a sack of seasalt against the [winter] cutting up of joints of his cattle" and perhaps for salted sea bird carcasses harvested from the famous Bristol Channel island sanctuaries. Winter itself will have brought the return of the thousands of migrant ducks, geese and swans flying back to their fenland refuge and the fur-bearing mammals will have been sleek in their new winter coats – the time for hunting fresh non-salted meat and trapping desirable pelts. For the women there still remained between 200 and 1000 pounds of wool to be combed, cleaned, washed, dyed, spun and woven – enough for 40–200 fine blankets or cloaks fit for heroes, trimmed with fur, embroidered with the bronze needles on the special wooden frames found in the settlement (Bulleid and Gray, 1911–17, Plate LV; compare *Objets et Mondes*, vol. VIII, No. 1, 1968, p. 56, Fig. 12). Such Celtic woollen cloaks were a famed export from this area of Britain to the Roman empire and may have been the principal output of the Glastonbury community (Wild, 1970; Powell, 1959, p. 71).

This preliminary sketch of the economic model in its annual cycle immediately suggests that the annual movements of shepherds and flocks between the fenland settlements and the Mendip slopes may have provided the context and mechanism by means of which Mendip raw materials, antlers, querns, pots, lead and timber were collected and brought down to Glastonbury and the fenland products taken up to Wookey, Maesbury and the other caves and hill forts. Indeed, the extraction of local iron and lead deposits might also have been part of seasonal small-scale mining expeditions from the transhumant base camps. It is tempting to identify these winter base camps and stock corrals with the chain of smaller, univallate "hill forts" distributed at intervals of a few miles along the escarpment, both here and elsewhere.

Such camps may presumably have been erected and held in common by consanguineous groups of lowland communities like Meare and Glastonbury and may either have been devoid of permanent habitation or held only a small resident group. These camps are ideally sited and constructed for the seasonal marshalling of the large united herds from the lowlands and as bases from which to graze these units in rotation on the adjacent sheltered valleys or on the more distant upland pastures commanded by convenient limestone caves. On the comparable escarpment around the East Anglian fenland, analogously sited camps are entirely lacking and there is some suggestion that the same problems there were solved by the exact converse of the Mendip solution – the major residential population of agrarian farmsteads and hamlets centred on the hills with a movement of stock down to seasonally occupied lowland camps amidst the fen pastures (Arbury Camp: Alexander and Trump, 1972).

All in all, an idealized model of the settlement pattern and area site system to which Glastonbury belonged can be assembled and, as with ideal gas models, although it may be unreal it provides a basis for prediction and thus for testing the degree of its reality or unreality. The landscape probably contained a mixed pattern of single extended family farmsteads comparable to the individual Glastonbury units and hamlets of co-operative clusters of such units – the former more abundant on Mendip and the latter the rule in the fenland. However, the status of the settlement in either category might be radically altered by the "embedded" presence of noble establishments, with a great house (over 30 feet), attached clients and perhaps even a "ditch of vassalage" (Kingsdown Camp, Somerset: Dobson, 1931, p. 202) (Fig. 12).

With the markedly uneven distribution of permanent and seasonal resources over the area and effective means of intercommunication, the settlements would inexorably tend to become reciprocally specialized and mutually supporting within an area network embracing segments of fen and the Mendip slopes. A few "centres" would be still further specialized, producing higher-order complex manufactured goods and providing higher-order services. These goods and services would in some cases be so costly or so restricted to rank that they must depend upon and serve a far wider population than that of the immediate area, distributing instead to a small portion of a larger market. Thus the individual areas themselves become mutually interlinked within a region

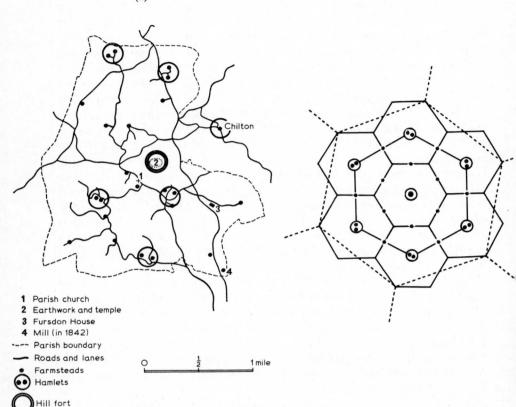

(a)   (b)

Chilton

1 Parish church
2 Earthwork and temple
3 Fursdon House
4 Mill (in 1842)
-·-- Parish boundary
— Roads and lanes
● Farmsteads
◉ Hamlets
◯ Hill fort

0   ½   1 mile

FIG. 11. The parish of Cadbury, Devon (after Hoskins, 1967). A Dumnonian multivallate hill fort of *ca* 3 acres, its territory and settlement hierarchy (*a*); an idealized model
of the system (*b*).

(*a*) Special circumstances have probably preserved in this area a "fossil" impression
of a fully developed late Celtic settlement pattern—five multilineage hamlets, twelve
single lineage farmsteads and a central hill fort with a Romano-Celtic shrine. The constraint of the massive boulder early field boundaries allowed minimal reorganization
of the pattern, established before the eleventh century, in an area which remained
Celtic and Celtic-speaking even after Saxon penetration in the eighth century (Hoskins,
1967, pp. 15–21).

(*b*) The model generalized from the Cadbury "fossil" suggests a settlement pattern
of $k = 7$ type, developed to a third order of settlement (farmsteads, hamlets, hill fort).
Christaller showed that this type of "administrative principle" system develops where
firm central administrative control is important, such that all the dependent places
owe allegiance to the central place (hill fort and cult centre) without divided loyalties.
A Dumnonian network of this order is also supported by nearest-neighbour studies
(Clarke, 1968, Fig. 115).

for the supply of items such as fine mirrors, swords and pottery over and above the everyday requirements satisfied by each area's own internal network. Whether these market "centres" can in all cases be simply and exclusively identified with the populations concentrated in or around the larger multivallate hill forts, like Maesbury, remains an arguable matter, open to test (Fig. 12).

Now, a rise in income, production and intensive employment in one group of economic activities in a site, territory, area or region stimulates the comparable expansion of other groups, through an increased demand from the former group for the goods and services of the latter (positive feedback). This process is expressed in economics as a Multiplier Model and it is already apparent that replicating processes of this kind lurk behind the "spread" of many archaeological phenomena that are more usually "explained" by diffusion, especially where the spread involves complexes of rather generalized elements (e.g., spread of redistribution economies, chieftainship, etc., in the European Early Bronze Age, or the spread of the Urnfield complex including settlement patterns with hill forts). The multiplier model may act between social segment and social segment as an internal economic multiplier within settlements, or as an external economic multiplier between adjacent or interlinked areas. In the Glastonbury area of the Dumnonian region multiplier analysis provides a valuable starting point for considering models of spatial variation and locational specialization in economic and settlement pattern (Chorley and Haggett, 1967, p. 275).

At the regional level there is ample evidence of reciprocity and specialization in adjacent areas of the Dumnonian system correlated with a growing volume of trade and the emergence of the settlement hierarchy required to manufacture, handle, redistribute and market the goods. Mendip lead and pottery products circulated against Cornish fine wares, silver, tin, copper and domestic products; high-quality iron, gold, shale and glass were redistributed from external sources; perishable staples like dairy products, salt, corn, stock, wool and slaves moved overall (Fox, 1964, pp. 111–135). Although the primary production and manufacturing units were the settlements scattered throughout the region, the movement and organization of exports soon concentrated in certain centres optimally located with respect to a number of resources and at important links in transport routes, like the port of Mount Batten. As the export activity expanded the operation of the multiplier process will have stimulated the development of dispersed, locally oriented service industries feeding the system – pottery, textiles and metal industries, for example. The locational consequence of this development was the growing role of handling centres for collection and redistribution because of the economies of supply offered by their

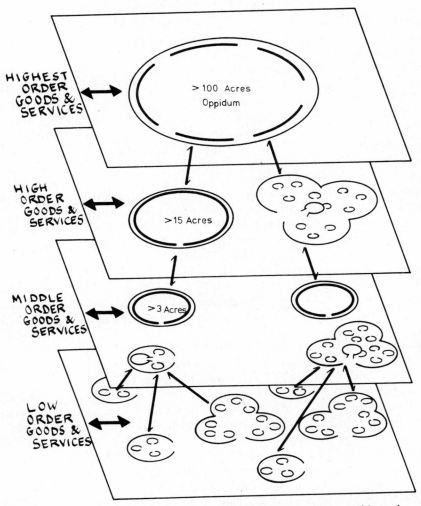

HIGHEST ORDER GOODS & SERVICES

> 100 Acres
Oppidum

HIGH ORDER GOODS & SERVICES

>15 Acres

MIDDLE ORDER GOODS & SERVICES

> 3 Acres

LOW ORDER GOODS & SERVICES

FIG. 12. A schematic model of a late, fully developed, Celtic settlement hierarchy suggesting the nature of its integration with the social hierarchy and grades on one hand and an economic hierarchy on the other. Evidence suggests that settlement patterns of the two lowest orders had widely developed during and because of socio-economic changes of the Early–Middle Bronze Age (see Sherratt, 1972). The "high-order" tier developed in the Late Bronze–Iron Age, as in the Glastonbury area. The Glastonbury area system did not fully develop a "highest-order" centre of the *oppidum* type, although Ham Hill may have latterly approached that status (Fig. 8, No. 3). The ditched-and-banked enclosures lumped together as "hill forts" are seen as having different but overlapping functions; at the higher levels the settlements may be within or adjacent to these enclosures; for clarity only the latter case has been sketched. The model is generalized and speculative but presents a form which may be fully specified, tested and elaborated for particular areas by field work, excavation and aerial photography.

location, partly because of their strategic role as distribution centres, plus their growing importance as markets. These embryonic centres were thus increasingly able to attract a large proportion of the domestic-ally oriented manufacturing and a large proportion of regional trade and service employment for the production of luxury goods. These centres would have grown comparatively rapidly with the growing aggrandizement of the chieftains who controlled the redistribution sys-tem and by population influx from the surrounding countryside – a con-text in which tribal allegiance, obligatory labour, fosterage and client-ship will have been accelerating social mechanisms. The net result of the cumulative pattern of regional and locality specialization and inter-dependence was the transformation of a settlement system into a settle-ment hierarchy (Fig. 12).

The categorizing factors in the distinct settlement hierarchy of which Glastonbury was a lowly member include not merely absolute popula-tion size or ground area but also the order of services and products produced, their internal format, their distance from comparable sites, and the rank and status of the inhabitants. There emerges a progression from lower-order settlements to those of higher order, where the lower-order goods, services, skills and products would be repeated in the higher-order sites but with the *addition* of distinctive, specialized activi-ties which might act as classificatory indicators – enamel and glass workers, master craftsmen and armourers, coin and currency bar mints, workshops either producing *élite* goods or mass producing common goods, and marketing extra-regional materials like amber, coral, gold and shale. The higher-order functions and products for high-status in-dividuals required a greater population for their support and thus the range of the famous products of the Mendip school of La Tène master craftsmen included the entire Dumnonian peninsula (Fig. 9) (Fox, 1964, Fib. 40, pp. 33–34).

As far as the evidence goes, Maesbury would fall into this category of higher-order centre for the Glastonbury area, comparable to sites like Cadbury Castle and Ham Hill (Fig. 8). One can see that the later introduction of *oppidum* sites of an even higher order still, with yet richer services and even greater political and economic range, is an indicator with considerable implications for the network and hierarchy support-ing that order of site, with its almost international scale of operations.

To return to the particular segment of the Mendips to which the Glastonbury settlement relates, we might tentatively identify a settle-ment hierarchy with a broad base of a few noble and numerous non-noble first-order family farm units scattered amidst second-order ham-lets of groups of such units, like Glastonbury and Meare. In the fens the emphasis may of necessity have been on the larger co-operative second-order units, whereas on Mendip a more varied pattern may have prevailed amidst the abundant Celtic fields and upland pasture. If the earlier interpretation is accepted, the fenland communities independently or in conjunction with resident Mendip groups may have jointly maintained the small third-order ditched base camps on sheltered spurs of the foothills. These simple hill forts would be the annual resort of the fenland drovers and may have served as territorial centres for the exchange of lower-order goods, stock and women, as well as acting as unifying foci for the scattered communities that had co-operatively undertaken their construction.

These base camps, served by their own first- and second-order sites and satellite caves, were perhaps dependent upon the highest fourth-order market centre at Maesbury, 15 acres in extent, the multivallate "citadel of the mining district" (Dobson, 1931, p. 202). Fenland sheep, stock, textiles, salt fish, fowl, furs and other products and services will have flowed as exchange and tribute through this network to Mendip, whence political protection and the first-order products of the famous local school of master smiths, enamellers, weapon and mirror makers will have trickled back in return, where appropriate by rank, together with currency, ingots of imported and local raw materials, fine ware from the local kilns, and perhaps ponies, cattle, pigs and cereals when necessary (Fig. 12).

CONCLUSION

At this stage, the particular and merely interim conclusions of this study should be put on one side, bearing in mind the experimental nature of the exercise emphasized in the opening section of this chapter. Instead, it would be more appropriate to underline the critical role of the model-using approach in relation to studies of this kind. Settlement sites encapsulate a wealth of latent information involving both within-site and without-site relationships. This information remains latent and often unsuspected until the descriptive observations are selectively regrouped and scrutinized against an explicit model or a series of alternative models based on differing assumptions. Then experimental tests suggested by the predictive aspects of the different models may be used to discriminate between them as rival possibilities.

In this particular study the points at which branching series of alternative models might equally fit the range of variability of the data have been merely noted, in order that a chain of "most plausible" interim models might here be pursued towards the limits of their potential. This provisional procedure usefully exposes the full consequence of the cumulative chain of assumptions for further testing, but it is in no way a substitute for the necessary testing between models.

It is important to note the many different kinds of model necessarily involved in a study of this kind, ranging from the post-depositional site model, through structural and building models, reconstruction models, social models, demographic models and economic models to locational and settlement hierarchy models. The models deployed here are but crude and elementary preliminaries but they suggest at once the ways in which they might be tested and the directions in which they must be refined. Thus the inferences based on the spatial trends are directly susceptible to statistical tests of significance and confidence. Field survey, limited excavation, dendrochronology, skeletal analysis and perhaps aerial photography may test the predictions about the location of comparable sites, the length of occupation, the site's social organization, and the claimed use of ditched field agriculture. The economic input–output sketch model is potentially quantifiable and might be used to simulate the system with a variable range of inputs and conditions to reveal the critical "bottlenecks" in the economy. In these various ways a preliminary set of models and estimated parameters may serve to identify the target areas for the second and successive cycles of research within the project.

REFERENCES

Alexander, J. and Trump, D. (1972). Arbury Camp, *Proceedings of the Cambridge Antiquarian Society*, 1972.

Ascher, R. (1968). Time's arrow and the archaeology of a contemporary community, in *Settlement Archaeology* (K. C. Chang, ed.), National Press, Palo Alto, Calif.

Bath, B. H. S. van (1963). *The Agrarian History of Western Europe A.D. 500–1850*, Arnold, London.

Binchy, D. A. (1941). *Crith Gablach*, Stationery Office, Dublin.

Bowen, H. C. (1961). *Ancient Fields*, British Association for the Advancement of Science, London.

Bowen, H. C. (1969). The Celtic background, in *The Roman Villa in Britain* (A. F. L. Rivet, ed.), Hutchinson, London, pp. 1–48.

Bulleid, A. H. and Gray, H. St G. (1911 and 1917). *The Glastonbury Lake Village*, Vols I and II, Glastonbury Antiquarian Society, Wessex Press, Taunton.

Chorley, R. J. and Haggett, P. (eds) (1967). *Models in Geography*, Methuen, London.

Clark, J. G. D. (1952). *Prehistoric Europe: The Economic Basis*, Methuen, London.

Clarke, D. L. (1968). *Analytical Archaeology*, Methuen, London.

Clarke, D. L. (1970). Analytical archaeology: epilogue, *Norwegian Archaeological Review*, **3**, 25–33.

Clarke, D. L. (1972). Models and paradigms in contemporary archaeology, in *Models in Archaeology* (D. L. Clarke, ed.), Methuen, London, pp. 1–60.

Cook, S. F. and Heizer, R. F. (1968). Relationships among houses, settlements areas and population in aboriginal California, in *Settlement Archaeology* (K. C. Chang, ed.), National Press, Palo Alto, Calif.

Daniels, S. G. H. (1972). Research design models, in *Models in Archaeology* (D. L. Clarke, ed.), Duckworths, London, pp. 201–230.

Darby, H. C. (1940). *The Medieval Fenland*, Cambridge University Press, Cambridge.

Deneven, W. M. (1970). Aboriginal drained-field cultivation in the Americas, *Science*, **169**, (3946), 647–654.

Dobson, D. P. (1931) *Somerset*, Methuen, London.

Evans-Pritchard, E. E. (1940). *The Nuer*, Oxford University Press, London.

Everson, J. A. and Fitzgerald, B. P. (1968). *Settlement Patterns*, Concepts in Geography Vol. I, Longmans, London.

Filip, J. (1960). *Celtic Civilisation and its Heritage*, Czech Academy of Sciences, Prague.

Flannery, K. V. (1971). The origins of the village as a settlement type in Mesoamerica and the Near East: a comparative study, in *Man, Settlement and Urbanism* (P. Ucko, R. Tringham and G. W. Dimbleby, eds), Duckworth, London, pp. 23–53.

Fox, A. (1964). *South West England*. Thames & Hudson, London.

Fraser, D. (1969). *Village Planning in the Primitive World*, Studio Vista, London.

Godwin, H. (1960). Prehistoric wooden trackways of the Somerset levels, *Proceedings of the Prehistoric Society*, **26**, 1.

Godwin, H. and Dewar, H. S. L. (1963). Archaeological discoveries in the raised bogs of the Somerset levels, *Preceedings of the Prehistoric Society*, **29**, 17.

Goody, J. (1969) Inheritance, property and marriage in Africa and Eurasia, *Sociology*, **3**, 55–76.

Hamilton, J. R. C. (1968). *Excavations at Clickhimin, Shetland*, Ministry of Works Archaeological Report No. 6, HMSO, edinburgh.

Harvey, D. (1969). *Explanation in Geography*, Arnold, London.

Hersh, R. and Griego, R. J. (1969). Brownian motion and potential theory, *Scientific American*, **220** (3), 66–74.

Hoskins, W. G. (1967). *Fieldwork in Local History*, Faber, London.

Hurst, D. (1970). Feeding the lowland ewe, *Country Life*, 23 April.

Jackson, K. H. (1964). *The Oldest Irish Tradition: A Window on the Iron Age*, Cambridge University Press, Cambridge.

Jarman, M. R. (1972). A territorial model for archaeology: a behavioural and geographical approach, in *Models in Archaeology* (D. L. Clarke, ed.), Methuen, London, pp. 705–734.

Large, R. V. (1970). Getting the most out of your sheep, *New Scientist*, 9 July.

March, L., Echenique, M. *et al.* (1971). Models of environment, *Architectural Design*, **41**, 275–320.

Murdock, G. P. (1949). *Social Structure*, Collier-Macmillan, London.

Norman, E. R. and St Joseph, J. K. S. (1970). *The Early Development of Irish Society: The Evidence of Aerial Photography*, Cambridge University Press, Cambridge.

Peacock, D. P. S. (1969). A contribution to the study of Glastonbury ware from southwestern Britain, *The Antiquaries Journal*, **49** (1), 41.

Piggott, S. (1965). *Ancient Europe from the Beginnings of Agriculture to Classical Antiquity*, Edinburgh University Press, Edinburgh.

Postan, M. M. (ed.) (1966). *The Cambridge Economic History of Europe: The Agrarian Life of the Middle Ages*, Cambridge University Press, Cambridge.

Powell, T. G. E. (1959). *The Celts*, Thames & Hudson, London.

Richmond, I. A. (1968). *Hod Hill, Vol 2: Excavations 1951–58*, Trustees of the British Museum, London.

Sherratt, A. G. (1972). Socioeconomic and demographic models, in *Models in Archaeology* (D. L. Clarke, ed.), Methuen, London, Chap. 12.

Thomas D. H. (1972). A computer simulation model of Great Basin Shoshonean subsidence and settlement patterns, in *Models in Archaeology* (D. L. Clarke, ed.), Methuen, London, Chap. 17.

Warner, R. (1960). *War Commentaries of Caesar*, New American Library, New York.

Waterbolk, H. T. and Zeist, W. van (1961). A Bronze Age sanctuary in the raised bog at Bargeroosterveld, *Helinium*, **1**, 5–19.

Wicken Fen (1964) (anon.) *Wicken Fen Guide*, National Trust, London.

Wild, J. P. (1970). *Textile Manufacture in the Northern Roman Provinces*, Cambridge University Press, Cambridge.

Wrigley, E. A. (1969). *Population and History*, Weidenfeld & Nicolson, London.

Towns in the Development of Early Civilization

DAVID L. CLARKE

Ideas about the early stages of urbanism – as about many aspects of prehistory – are often distorted by too limited a set of models, derived from the better-known but atypical situations of the present day. It is especially tempting to create a simplified and pseudo-historical succession from the existing types, beginning with the simplest and progressing to the more complex, and then to assume that this exemplifies an inevitable tendency towards a pinnacle of evolutionary development in modern urban civilization. Such assumptions begin to merge with political and ideological judgements about the value of economic growth and the criteria of "progress".

Archaeology offers an escape from this circularity by providing a vast and continuous time-depth of evidence for study, which stresses the great variety and variability of what have been called "towns". One example, and a classic instance of a "Big Surprise" when its early layers were exacavated, is that of Jericho; an urban site which began 10 000 years ago in a pre-metal, pre-market and perhaps even pre-domestication context, and was occupied more or less continuously for more than 8000 years (Kenyon, 1957). With its vast time-depth and global scale, therefore, archaeology provides a massive array of urban forms, functions and contexts, many representing largely extinct patterns of activity – a body of evidence which ought to demolish at a blow most

---

This paper was originally developed as a lecture and presented to a conference on towns organized by the historical magazine *Past and Present* in 1976.

The first few paragraphs have been rearranged in accordance with David's stated intention (letter to E. A. Wrigley, 10 November 1975) and have been converted from their original note form into continuous prose. After the first few pages, however, David wrote out the lecture in full, and the rest of this paper is in his own words, except for references which have been added where appropriate.

Other papers presented at this conference are now available in Abrams, P. and Wrigley, E. A. (eds), *Towns and Economic Growth, Past and Present*, New York, 1978.

unilinear and monocausal explanations of urbanization and economic development.

Instead, this evidence emphasizes that the development of urban settlement systems was a complex and multilinear *process*, and not an *event*; a process whereby an increasingly substantial proportion of the population of a settlement system came either to live in a central place, or to be involved in a variety of ways in the activities of a central place. This process is closely, though not inevitably, associated with the Neolithic subsistence revolution; and the "Neolithic Revolution" and the "Urban Revolution" of Gordon Childe (1954) can best be regarded as one continuous process, and not a sequence of events.

There are thus many degrees and forms of urbanization, and many routes into the form of an urban system. This multiplicity of urban forms and functions represents a multidimensional structure which, while it may be collapsed into one dimension, arranged linearly and dichotomized endlessly, can only be done so with great arbitrariness, and loss of information, to produce a classification useful only for limited purposes.

If urban forms and functions cover a complex continuum, it is more important initially to adopt a comprehensive definition which brings together and does not falsely divide closely related phenomena. Archaeologically, the most useful definition of the continuum of urban forms and functions is outlined by three dimensions.

1. Large-scale residential population at a site.
2. Numbers of specialists who do not produce their own food.
3. Elaboration of within-site and beyond-site functions as a political, religious, economic or military centre for other sites in its catchment system.

The definition is quantifiable, but relative to particular contexts – an urban settlement is an area which contains a relatively large number of residents, relatively densely settled and in which a proportion of the population is non-food producing. Such a definition allows relationships with concentration camps, prisons, fortresses, barracks, monasteries and palaces in one direction and with aerodromes in another – but these relationships are real, and that is as it should be.

When we turn to the archaeological evidence for these processes, we find that there have been dramatic changes of interpretation in recent years. The old archaeological picture may be characterized as follows. Food-production is a superior form of economy which was first invented in the Near East *ca* 5000 B.C. and diffused outwards. The production of surplus by the new subsistence techniques, the plough, multiple-cropping and irrigation gave rise to urbanization, first in Mesopotamia *ca* 3500 B.C., and then in Egypt, India and China. Urbanization reached Europe by Greek colonial settlement; separate development took place in America but very late, with the emergence of the Maya and the Incas and Aztec urban systems in the Medieval period.

The new archaeological picture looks more like this. Food-production is a more demanding and more labour-intensive way of feeding a population than hunting, fishing and gathering. Plant and animal domestication developed initially within the narrow sub-equatorial belt around the globe (between 0 and 45° N) in the immediate postglacial phase from *ca* 10 000 B.C. onwards, as ecological conditions within that belt deteriorated and population pressure on wild resources became too great. Elsewhere hunting-fishing-gathering continued, in some areas to the present day. The earliest known food-producing communities emerged in the Near East by 9000 B.C. and the earliest urban concentrations are scarcely later, having appeared in a limited area by 8000 B.C. In Palestine, Jericho and Mureybit in the ninth millennium B.C. covered 4 hectares and 3 hectares, respectively, while by the mid-seventh millennium the central Anatolian site of Çatal Hüyük covered 15 hectares (Mellaart, 1975). Similar early developments are now suspected elsewhere, probably in Egypt, India, southeast Asia and China by 4000 B.C. Urbanization developed *in situ* in Mediterranean Europe by *ca* 3000 B.C. – for instance at Los Millares in Spain, covering some 10 hectares – and in Temperate Europe by 500 B.C. (and perhaps in some areas as early as 1500 B.C.), in the form of timber-built hill forts and *oppida* (Piggott, 1965). Urbanization in America, in both a nucleated form and in the form of ceremonial centres, had emerged by the mid-second millennium at sites like Las Haldas in Peru and San Jose Mogote in Mexico (Lanning, 1974; Marcus, 1976); and this type of urbanization probably extended in some form over much of Colombia, Ecuador and Peru. In Africa, we now know that large tribal urban and ceremonial centres flourished before European settlement in Ethiopia, Nigeria and perhaps Rhodesia between 700 and 1200 A.D.

The most striking feature of the archaeological record is the variety of urban forms and functions. There have been towns of stone and brick, and towns of timber, earth and thatch; there have been towns based on tropical root agriculture and towns based on cereals, towns with domestic animals and traction transport and towns without significant animal domesticates or transport facilities. Archaeology suggests that some of the earliest urban concentrations may still have been based on hunting-fishing-gathering; that with Jericho and Mureybit we have towns before domestication. There have been towns with only stone tools, towns with metallurgy, towns with coinage and full market economies and towns with gift exchange; towns with writing and numerals and towns without them (Millon, 1973).

These combinations and permutations themselves correlate with immensely variable ranges of social structure, kinship and land tenure systems. The oft-quoted incompatibility of tribal organization and urban systems, for example, does not seem to be supported by archaeological and historical evidence in which urban systems have frequently been an integral part of tribal organizations for many thousands of years from Africa to Mesoamerica. Only certain restricted categories of urbanization seem to be the social solvent so universally invoked; only certain restricted contexts of urbanization seem to be positively correlated with massive economic and industrial growth. Generalization in this continuum is not impossible, but it is difficult and it must proceed from large numbers of analyses to substantiated generalizations and not by extrapolation from a few, unspecific examples.

A large variety of urban forms and urban functions has existed in a diversity of regional, climatic, social, technological and economic settings. This spectrum of urban systems cannot be divorced from the contexts and settlement networks of which they were once an integral part, with their varying urban catchment areas, social parameters and so forth. Urbanization is the emergence of site *systems* with urban *elements* and we must study and classify the development process of these systems as a whole and not just their most conspicuous urban nuclei. These contexts clearly have to do with the form and stability of the towns themselves. Urban centres and their external settlement systems are interdependent for population supply and resources, but once again it is only amongst certain restricted categories of urban system that there is the tendency to try and control outlying resources and to reorganize and restructure the urban fields of influence ("raid following trade") often associated with the emergence of city states, nation states, colonial and industrial empires (Flannery, 1972).

At the moment, there is a strong temptation to typologize from above, to attack the variability beneath the urban continuum by surface classifications emphasizing form and morphology, using lists of physical attributes and then erecting evolutionary "chest-of-drawer" models in which there is a succession of discrete categories. This will not do. Complex systems cannot be specified by laundry-lists of attributes, whether physical or organizational, any more than a watch can be understood from a list of its parts. Urban systems must be analysed as working systems in a context so that comparisons between such systems may reveal analogous and homologous structures, and, hence, a structural classification involving the flow of variety. Morphological generalizations from categories of physical form seem to have severely limited possibilities. Instead, there is a need for the limited comparison and categorization of systemic structures with similar roles. This implies the seeking-out of isomorphic system features – different features with the same contextual behaviour, and similar features with different contextual behaviour.

At the moment, then, archaeological evidence suggests that the process of urbanization was an equifinal solution to many different but related problems and stimuli connected with postglacial changes in ecology which affected different regions at different speeds and in different ways – in some areas not appearing at all, in others only very recently. Globally it would seem that the stimuli, pressures and courses towards urban systems were different but analogous. The same solution, urbanization, solved many differently formulated regional problems, emphasizing that a common category does not necessitate a common cause. Postglacial changes and ecological disequilibrium are certainly a common factor but single causes are clearly insufficient and probably we are involved with the interaction between long-term global trends of evolutionary and ultimately astronomical scale, with regional medium-term cyclical and oscillatory trends (population cycles, ice ages, etc.) and with short-term local fluctuations (technical innovations, local ecology and culture, etc.). Urbanization appears wherever such complexes of interacting factors did correlate in certain ways and did not appear where these factors were absent or took a different regional pathway.

By and large hunting-fishing-gathering economies required a low labour intensity for subsistence but only in unusual circumstances did they allow large, relatively stable population aggregates, as at Jericho. The development of food-production itself was therefore an enforced response to regional ecological disequilibrium and postglacial subsistence difficulties, that required a heavier labour intensity for subsistence, but both allowed and in some cases forced the appearance of large centralized population aggregates with their advantages (and disadvantages) of scale. Urbanization was in some cases mandatory, in other cases merely a new stochastic possibility. (This is but one aspect of a general division in human group behaviour, between mandatory and permissive groupings – the concentration camp or the football crowd, the forced co-operative winter hunting necessary for survival amongst the Netsilik eskimos or the permitted jamborees of aboriginals in times of plenty.) Mandatory urbanization was the main early adaptive solution in areas of growing postglacial aridity, loss of fertile land and ecological degradation. Voluntary urbanization, often therefore less stable in the long term, appeared contagiously wherever it provided a marginally more adaptive prospect than other social and economic forms; we must not forget that mobile hunting-fishing-gathering is still preferred to this day wherever conditions allow and most areas of the globe avoided the urban response until the last three millennia.

A mode of subsistence based on domestication and food-production was a response to regional postglacial difficulties. Urban settlement systems also were a mandatory response wherever these difficulties were especially severe, or a voluntary response later – and rather more slowly and erratically – for complex reasons. Urbanization, having been forced to develop in one class of situations, gradually displayed advantages that emerged in other, rather different, situations. After all, urbanization is not fundamentally a stable or unstable, reversible or irreversible, change; it is stable or unstable in a certain range of contexts, reversible or irreversible in certain others. In fact, although cities do not diffuse, nevertheless they do give rise to a kind of creeping subversion – a horizontal or spatially multiplying contagion. This is because urban systems depend upon and effect communities and resources beyond their immediate bounds, thus often creating in those areas the conditions which brought themselves into being in their own locality – urbanization is a replicative and autocatalytic process, whose occurrence at one point increases the probability that it will occur at another point (note the relevance of long-range transport for exporting to great distances the conditions for urbanization).

Urbanization certainly has advantages – advantages largely from economies of scale, cumulative interaction, co-operative effort and reciprocal specialization. Urbanization also has very special advantages for hierarchical regulation, control and amplification (concentration of resources in unstable settlement networks). These combined advantages were decisive in certain postglacial environments where settlement systems had to smooth out spatial and temporal unevenness in resources – manpower, raw materials and food. By means of settlement systems with urban nuclei, the population carrying-capacity of an area as a whole might approach and surpass the capacity of networks of unco-ordinated individual settlements at their maximum productivity; a result of the strategy of extreme reciprocal specialization which would be quite impossible if each area merely supported its own population (Sherratt, 1972). The scale of efficient settlement size increased with time as technical, economic and organizational expertise improved and raised the level of scale economies and raised the lower threshold of the efficient operation of units; but his efficiency was always relative to particular contexts and it did not increase linearly or irreversibly but in a series of curves with marked oscillations by period and area. Nevertheless, within agricultural communities at certain regional population levels, and in certain demanding environments, urban settlement systems ensured the highest population-carrying capacity and the highest chances of survival for the population as a whole. It was the most adaptive system – even though it might mean shorter lives for some, unhealthy social and medical conditions, supply problems and individual overspecialization – the corresponding disadvantages of scale. However, for the population and settlement network as a whole it became advantageous for large nodal settlements to exercise specialized administrative, regulating, governing, controlling and amplifying (supplementary) functions to the benefit of the whole.

After 10 000 B.C., food production provided the increased possibility of large population concentrations but of itself gave no impetus towards urbanization. Hunting-fishing-gathering still gave the best subsistence for the least effort over most of the globe for many millennia to come. Large population concentrations first arose to survive scarcity of resources in certain restricted contexts and then multiplied both by the contagion of analogous conditions and elsewhere to take advantage of economies of scale in contexts of plenty. In essence, the advantages and disadvantages of urbanization work to the law of the square: interaction (and therefore the spread of ideas and disease) goes up as the square of the population, but the area of an urban field needed for residence or food supply only goes up as the square of the radius – a little increase in radius providing a large increase in accessible new land surface.

Urbanization is certainly synonymous with increased specialization in social, economic and settlement roles, and increased specialization is synonymous with growth in variety, composite innovations and inventions. New social and economic organizations must be developed to cope with the fresh scale of activity and a new world view elaborated to symbolize the new order for its inmates. The growth and redistribution of this variety in urban networks was certainly greatly aided by the inevitable unhealthiness of towns with population from outlying settlements providing an important resource to the urban centres, the population recycling both to maintain urban population levels and for periodic events and ceremonies. This daily, seasonal and annual migration into and out of the urban field circulated and increased the flow of variety and innovations. Although many technological innovations were made in the countryside it was often as part of the urban field. This increased development of variety is certainly synonymous with urbanization and takes the amplifying positive feedback pattern suggested by Pred's model (Pred, 1966). However, the bulk of this dramatic expansion of variety need not be predominantly economic and technical – this is a special modern facet – in other urban societies at other times social, religious and conceptual innovation frequently predominate, and even retard economic and technological change. Everything depends on the context and the nature of the existing variety – where a man's activities were restricted by rank, status and religion and not by ability and wealth, then the increased innovation was largely social, religious, political and symbolic and less frequently economic and technological. Where every man was potentially equal and the accumulation of wealth an equalizer then every man was a potential *entrepreneur* and innovative variety was largely technical, industrial and economically orientated. There is a clear connection between urbanization and florescence curves of civilizations, but the connection is always context-dependent.

To return, then, to the theme on the relationships between towns and economic growth in pre-industrial and in industrializing countries; the archaeological evidence over ten millennia seems to suggest two main conclusions. The first is that urbanization is a reversible but auto-catalytic process – sometimes mandatory and sometimes voluntarily employed to smooth out spatial and temporal unevenness in resource distributions in certain contexts and within certain thresholds. The second is that urbanization is synonymous with growth in variety, but this is not necessarily channelled into a growth in economic variety. Urbanization is only synonymous with economic growth within certain social and economic contexts. Such contexts occur only where vertical social mobility is effective and status may be freely acquired by wealth and economic activity. (One might contrast urban societies with hereditary roles on one hand or rotatory, short-term office holding like the American Indian cargo systems.) These situations are most common where ecological and economic disequilibrium (caused by population boom or environmental change) has become endemic and semi-continuous, necessitating a continuous and cumulative technological and economic response, more intensive methods of exploitation, export trade and colonialization, and increasingly involved productive processes with more demanding energy requirements and longer working hours.

In this light, the urban systems of western Europe in the last few centuries are atypical but not unique, and their agricultural and industrial revolutions were aided but not caused by their urban pattern.

REFERENCES

Childe, V. G. (1954). *What Happened in History*, Pelican Books, Harmondsworth, Middlesex.

Flannery, K. V. (1972). The cultural evolution of civilizations, *Annual Review of Ecology and Systematics*, **3**, 399–426.

Kenyon, K. M. (1957). *Digging up Jericho*, Bonn, London and Praeger, New York, 1964.

Lanning, G. P. (1974). The transformation to civilization, in *Prehispanic America* (S. Gorenstein, ed.), Thames and Hudson, London, pp. 110–123.

Marcus, J. (1976). The size of the early Mesoamerican village, in *The Early Mesoamerican Village* (K. V. Flannery, ed.), Academic Press, New York, pp. 79–90.

Mellaart, J. (1975). *The Neolithic of the Near East*, Thames & Hudson, London.

Millon, R. (1973). *Urbanisation at Teotihuacan*, University of Texas Press, Austin, Texas.

Piggott, S. (1965). *Ancient Europe*, Edinburgh University Press, Edinburgh.

Pred, A. R. (1966). *The Spatial Dynamics of U.S. Urban Industrial Growth*, MIT Press, Cambridge, Mass.

Sherratt, A. G. (1972). Socioeconomic and demographic models, in *Models in Archaeology* (D. L. Clarke, ed.), Methuen, London, Chap. 12.

Technical Studies in Archaeological Method

STEPHEN J. SHENNAN

INTRODUCTION

This section spans the full range of David's working career, from the matrix analysis and remanent magnetism papers of 1962 to the paper on spatial information published in 1977. The ten-year gap between this latter paper and the most recent of the others in this section makes for a very obvious division between them. Indeed, in this sharp juxtaposition, without considering the books and articles published in the intervening years, it is hard to believe they were written by the same man; in some respects the difference between them is a measure of the progress which has been made in archaeology within this period, in which David played a crucial part. The studies in archaeological method of 1962 are small-scale technical studies concerned with the minutiae of European prehistory, that of 1977 is a sketch of the basis of a unified theory of spatial information in archaeology, intended to have relevance wherever archaeologists work.

The development of David's interest in spatial questions which culminated in "Spatial information in archaeology" is, however, easy to trace back to the "New Geography" of the mid-1960s. As Hodder (1977) notes, spatial analysis receives considerable attention in *Analytical Archaeology* and again in the introduction to *Models in Archaeology*, while the study of Glastonbury in the same volume is a superb example of what can be done in the way of obtaining information from spatial relationships, and draws attention to David's particular contribution to spatial studies in archaeology, intra-community analysis based on models derived from architecture. "Spatial information in archaeology" is not a substantive analysis of this type but a very wide-ranging and highly stimulating review of the different levels of resolution in spatial analysis and the models appropriate to them, showing an impressive command of all these different aspects. It is difficult to view it in the same way as the others in this section since it has not had the time which they have had to fall into some sort of historical perspective, but it seems not unreasonable to predict that it will form one of the foundations of future attempts to build up the body of *archaeological* spatial theory, transcending that derived from other disciplines, which David rightly sees as vital to the future development of archaeology.

As we have already suggested, it is a considerable jump from this paper to the three following it in this section, which represent different aspects of David's attempts to solve the problems which came up in his thesis as he tried to make sense of the British beakers. In some respects these articles do not stand up on their own: they are stop press reports from the research frontier which only make sense when read in conjunction with the dissertation itself or with the published beaker pottery volumes. It then becomes clear, for instance, why the beaker reclassification paper was placed in this section rather than the preceding one on substantive problems in European prehistory, which might initially seem more logical.

The dissertation was an attempt at a new historical interpretation of the British bell beakers. The old interpretations were based on inadequate and ever more oversimplified classifications of the material. A new approach involved a new classification which had to be closer to human cultural reality: the beaker groups were intended to be "groups or assemblages of beaker pottery and artefacts believed to reflect a group of people or a social tradition over several generations" (Clarke, 1966, p. 183).

The techniques which David had available to him for this purpose were the traditional methods of archaeology which he lists in *Beaker Pottery of Great Britain and Ireland* (Clarke, 1970, p. 4): typology, stratigraphy, associations, distribution and absolute chronology, and of the last of these little existed in 1960, when he started. The intractable nature of the data with which he was working led him to the conclusion that these methods were inadequate for the problem in hand and that new ones would have to be devised. With typical imagination, David identified two possibilities, the application of the Robinson–Brainerd method of chronological seriation, and the use of remanent magnetic dating, which seemed to him to offer the chance of producing classifications independent of those obtained by traditional means and especially useful from the point of view of chronology. All three, the traditional and the two new methods, were seen as experiments in classification, the aim being to "define a limited area of 'truth' by as many differing aspects of approach as is feasible" (Clarke, 1966, p. 182). It should perhaps be said that he did not put equal weight on all three: the new methods he looked on as experimental. The general beaker classification was not based on the matrix analysis, as many people still seem to think, but on the traditional procedures listed above; the fact that the two methods produced strongly convergent conclusions confirmed to him the general validity of his results.

With these points in mind, it is possible to turn to the individual papers themselves, passing quite briefly over the article on remanent magnetism which, from a 1977 perspective, seems the least significant. Although the application of the technique was a good idea, the results it produced were not particularly helpful and only succeeded in confirming well-established archaeological conclusions, albeit by entirely independent means. The article states that experiments with the technique are continuing, but these were never published and it is interesting to note that no weight is given to this approach in the published beaker pottery volumes: remanent magnetism receives only a very brief mention.

The matrix analysis paper is a very different matter. Its publication in 1962 was undoubtedly a milestone in the development of archaeology in Britain, not because of the technique itself, or the conclusions drawn from it, but because of what it symbolized. This first application of quantitative and computer techniques to later periods marked the beginning of a change in attitude towards European prehistory. It was made even more scandalous by the fact that it dealt with beakers, a subject at the heart of traditional British archaeology. Similar experiments with the Palaeolithic did not attract half as much attention.

The battles which raged around this paper and the criticisms which it generated are now a thing of the past and there is no point here in going through them yet again. It must be acknowledged that the method published in this paper was not the most appropriate for the aim which David wished to achieve, which was really the definition of trait clusters rather than a seriation; furthermore, the use of raw counts rather than a measure of association between the traits was also unsatisfactory, although, as Cowgill (1972) has shown, neither of these criticisms mean that trait clustering or trait seriation are meaningless, a point of view which seems to be taken by some authorities. It should be added, too, that at the time when the work was carried out the cluster analysis procedures which are now so widely available were still in their infancy.

David's own assessment of this early work in the beaker pottery volumes (Clarke, 1970, p. 24) seems to me to remain valid. He rightly noted the advances in multivariate methods and their application which had occurred since the matrix paper appeared, but suggested that his initial beaker analysis had at least played a historic role in developing interchange between statistical analysis and archaeology.

In fact, David's experiments with such techniques were not restricted to the much-criticised matrix analysis. Both in his reply to Matthews (Clarke, 1963, pp. 790–792) and later, in the beaker pottery volumes and again in *Analytical Archaeology*, he refers to work carried out using other methods, including other ways of trait clustering and item clustering of the beakers themselves. Unfortunately, these were never published, no doubt at least partly because David's interests had already moved to other things, but all the techniques, he says, produced a large measure of agreement: "the conclusions have not been significantly modified by the succession of more rigorous techniques the author has been able to employ since" (Clarke, 1970, p. 24). To anyone who has experimented with such methods themselves, this statement will probably come as no surprise. Structure in archaeological data, when it exists, is often very robust and will be revealed by all sorts of techniques, including inappropriate ones, although that is no reason for using them.

The matrix method, then, was an attempt to solve the classification problem by statistical means. Once the attributes had been selected, with the aim of providing a satisfactory description of the variation present in the beakers, they were all treated equally, in a deliberate rejection of the use of *a priori* assumptions as to their relative value for the classification. As we have already mentioned, however, David also tackled the problem using the traditional weapons of the archaeologist's armoury, including typology, and accepted the practice of weighting traits differently, according to some *a priori* scheme. In most cases, the reasoning behind the weighting barely rises to the level of the archaeologist's consciousness, but David presented a reasoned argument for the view that, in contrast to the basis of earlier classifications, the greatest importance should be attached to the decoration and its arrangement, and that beaker shape should be regarded as of secondary importance. Nevertheless, he did not think that any single category of variation was adequate for the purpose of a classification whose divisions would correspond to "ancient social traditions" (Clarke, 1966, p. 180).

This approach, and the results largely derived from it, although taking account of the matrix analysis, were first published in the paper on the reclassification of British beaker pottery. It was really superseded by the eventual publication of the two volumes of *Beaker Pottery of Great Britain and Ireland* in 1970, but remains of interest for a number of reasons. First, it provides a convenient summary of David's views on beaker classification for those who are daunted by the full publication. Secondly, it enables one to see in an early form, developing out of beaker problems, some of the ideas which were later to be fully developed in *Analytical Archaeology*. One of these is the emphasis on using all the available attributes of objects for their classification, since otherwise it "can only have partial and rather muddled validity"; nevertheless, David is not yet arguing for the virtues of general purpose classification as such since, as we have seen, his beaker taxonomy has the stated aim of "reflecting a group of people or a social tradition over several generations" (Clarke, 1966, p. 183). Further embryonic ideas are seen in his preliminary conclusions on the dynamics of change in pottery assemblages, which had resulted from his examination of the material from beaker domestic sites.

Inevitably, however, any estimate of the success of this paper, apart from the renewed interest in beaker problems which the work created, must depend on an evaluation of the classification itself. The full version presented in the book and the dissertation, which has to be the basis for any such evaluation, has, of course, been the subject of detailed criticism by Lanting and van der Waals (1972), who find fault with it for a number of reasons and propose their own alternative. David, unsurprisingly, was not happy with their version and, if he had been writing this introduction himself, would no doubt have had much to say on the subject of what he used to call Lanting and van der Waals' "seven clockwork phases".

What is interesting to note, as Neustupný (1976) has observed, is that these disagreements lie largely at the level of initial assumptions and not in the conclusions drawn from analysis. These initial assumptions are of varying kinds, some purely theoretical and some concerning the factual basis on which David's analysis was built. The disagreements too are correspondingly varied and it seems worthwhile to consider them here in some detail, although the account which follows will necessarily presuppose some knowledge both of David's scheme and of Lanting and van der Waals' review.

The theoretical objections of the Dutch, relating to the cultural significance of vessel shape and the relative importance of different attributes in classification do not, I believe, need to be taken too seriously. The points they raise concerning the weights which should be placed on the attributes are at least debatable, while their advocacy of tree-type typology, which is by no means as universally accepted as they imply (see Doran and Hodson, 1975), seems to me largely irrelevant to their argument.

More important are their objections to some of the substantive assumptions which David made at the start of his analysis. It seems to me that their criticisms concerning the lack of homogeneity of two of his motif groups are entirely justified: the evidence which Lanting and van der Waals provide is conclusive on this point and the central European data too confirm it. Equally convincing in my view is their

documentation of the unsatisfactory nature of David's view of the continental connections of British beakers, but, as they point out, much
of the evidence with which they refute him has been discovered since
his work. These points do make a difference to the conclusions which
follow, and, in particular, Lanting and van der Waals' demonstration
of the lack of coherence of the hypothetical continental ancestors of
many of the supposed invading beaker groups does give a measure of
empirical support to their assertion that the continental links, which
both sides acknowledge, should be seen largely as representing "influences" rather than the result of "invasions". If it were not for this,
choice between the two would indeed be based, as Neustupný (1976)
points out, entirely on "paradigm preference". This still plays an important role, particularly as it affects the interpretation of motifs: Lanting and van der Waals correctly point out the difference between
David's view of motifs as the best indicators of human group tradition
and their own belief in regarding them as elements easily transferred
and therefore as potential proofs of inter-group contact. It is, in contrast, interesting to note the considerable measure of agreement
between the Clarke and Lanting–van der Waals schemes on the subject
of chronology; there is much more obviously just one correct answer
to the question of whether one event precedes or follows another.

What the Dutch see as the crux of the matter, however, is the procedure of classification adopted by David to achieve his aims, which
they criticize for not including the attribute of geographical location.
They regard it as incorrect "to deal with all British Beakers in one classificatory process according to uniform criteria", and on this basis they
produce their own alternative scheme based on a number of different
regional sequences.

This Lanting and van der Waals view seems to me to be unsatisfactory for a number of different reasons. Their focus areas with greater
beaker densities certainly owe as much to the differing intensity of past
archaeological activity as to any once-existing reality. Furthermore,
their argument that the recurrence of certain so-called "densely
settled" areas on the distribution maps of beakers of several different
types means that there was a continuity of development in these areas
is undoubtedly open to question. Most unconvincing is the chest-of-
drawers approach to regional and chronological classification. The
countryside is neatly partitioned, with all "distorting effects" removed,
and it is assumed that this division corresponds to some sort of beaker
social reality. Inevitably, with location forming one of the main bases
of the classification, the possibilities of actually testing such an assumption are extremely restricted and are, in fact, hardly even mentioned.
Moreover, the highly complex distribution patterns of British Late Neo-

lithic pottery styles should warn us against such neat distributional schemes. Similar criticisms may be levelled against the Dutch treatment of the chronological dimension, which is simply intended to illustrate a continuity which is assumed rather than documented. The series of mechanical steps shows no awareness of the complexity of change in pottery, no concept of a complex of interdigitating ceramic modes such as David was at pains to emphasize.

In fact, the revision of the British beaker classification proposed by Lanting and van der Waals is merely a sketch. It would be a great pity if the question of beaker classification were merely left there, and worse still if there were a return to the safe reductionism of considering only whether beakers are early, middle or late, a practice which was in part responsible for David's initial attempt at reclassification. It is to be hoped that in the not too distant future there will be a reworking of the British beaker material, taking into account the Dutch criticisms and making use of the new computer methods and the techniques of spatial analysis which have been developed over the past decade.

The final paper in this section is David's earliest on a subject unconnected with the British beakers. His thesis phase was over, but, as we have seen, it had provided specific instances of the more general archaeological problems which David went on to explore in the writing of *Analytical Archaeology*. This examination of the use of cumulative curves with Professor Kerrich is the first published indication of the move to more general interests and it was obviously prompted by the appearance of the papers by the Binfords and by Doran and Hodson which are cited.

There is much justification behind the criticisms made, some of which are relevant to a much wider range of archaeological analyses than simply the use of cumulative percentage frequency graphs. The comments were apposite at the time and have remained largely valid to the present, but in as much as they are essentially negative the paper seems to me to be of less interest than those in which David goes on from his criticisms to construct his own alternative approach. It does, however, show that he was by no means the uncritical user of statistical techniques which he has often been accused of being. On the other hand, unlike the vast majority of his British contemporaries, he was himself an innovator and his attitude to innovation in archaeology was correspondingly positive as he makes very clear at the end of this paper:

The new frontier is even now producing an increasing flow of novel and daring attempts to use the latest techniques for archaeological analysis. This frontier is not without its dangers and much will be learned by the mistakes of those willing to risk its difficulties in the pursuit of information and not content to mull safely around parochial puddles (Clarke, 1967, p. 69).

David's work was constantly at this frontier and he occasionally felt that his own pioneering role with its inevitable mistakes was insufficiently appreciated; but he was never accused of mulling around parochial puddles!

REFERENCES

Clarke, D. L. (1963). Matrix analysis and archaeology, *Nature*, **199**, 790–792.

Clarke, D. L. (1966). A tentative reclassification of British beaker pottery in the light of recent research, *Palaeohistoria*, **12**, 179–198.

Clarke, D. L. (1970). *Beaker Pottery of Great Britain and Ireland*, Cambridge University Press, Cambridge.

Cowgill, G. L. (1972). Models, methods and techniques for seriation, in *Models in Archaeology* (D. L. Clarke, ed.), Methuen, London, pp. 381–424.

Doran, J. E. and Hodson, F. R. (1975). *Mathematics and Computers in Archaeology*, Edinburgh University Press, Edinburgh.

Hodder, I. R. (1977). Preface in *Spatial Archaeology* (D. L. Clarke, ed.), Academic Press, London and New York.

Kerrich, J. E. and Clarke, D. L. (1967). Notes on the possible misuse and errors of cumulative percentage frequency graphs for the comparison of prehistoric artefact assemblages, *Proceedings of the Prehistoric Society*, **33**, 57–69.

Lanting, J. N. and van der Waals, J. D. (1972). British beakers as seen from the Continent, *Helinium*, **12**, 20–46.

Neustupný, E. F. (1976). Paradigm lost, in *Glockenbechersymposion Oberried 1974* (J. N. Lanting and J. D. van der Waals, eds), Fibula-van Dishoeck, Bussum/Haarlem, pp. 241–247.

Spatial Information in Archaeology

DAVID L. CLARKE

This essay is an attempt to pull together the implications of several levels of spatial studies outside archaeology and the momentarily miscellaneous and disconnected archaeological studies involving spatial analysis, at various scales, on diverse material in several different archaeological schools or traditions. The main claim will be that the retrieval of archaeological information from various kinds of spatial relationship is a central aspect of the international discipline of archaeology and a major part of the theory of that discipline wherever it is practised. Certainly, part of this archaeological spatial theory may be reduced to the existing spatial theories of human behaviour developed in economics, geography, architecture and ethology—it would be surprising if it were not so. However, although rightly emphasizing the significance of this body of theory for the archaeologist, this common ground is but a small part of archaeological spatial theory which must deal with a more comprehensive range of hominid behaviour patterns, using data with the special characteristics and sampling problems of the archaeological record. Within this paradigm, individual manifestations of archaeological spatial analysis, whether settlement archaeology, site system analyses, regional studies, territorial analyses, locational analyses, catchment area studies, distribution mapping, density studies, within-site and within-structure analyses or even stratigraphic studies, are all particular forms of spatial studies at particular scales and in particular contexts (Clarke, 1972a, p. 47).

1. HISTORICAL INTRODUCTION

In essence, there is a very evident expanding and convergent interest in archaeological spatial information in all the contemporary schools of archaeology, from the Russian to the Australasian. This interest has

Reprinted from *Spatial Archaeology* (D. L. Clarke, ed.), Academic Press, London and New York, pp. 1–32.

of course a respectable antiquity within each tradition, but there have been marked differences in emphasis and only now is the full significance and generality of archaeological spatial analysis being grasped and disconnected studies integrated around this important theoretical focus. In Europe, archaeology was from the first much concerned with inferences from spatial distribution and the ties with geography were strong, if intermittent. In particular, the important Austro-German school of "anthropo-geographers" (1880–1900) developed the formal mapping of attributes and artefacts in order to distinguish and explain culture complexes as well as extending this approach to mapping correlations between prehistoric settlement patterns and environmental variables; often publishing in the *Geographisches Zeitung* (Gradmann, 1898; Ratzel, 1896; Frobenius, 1898). Certainly, by the turn of the century the comparative analysis of archaeological distribution maps had become a standard if intuitive procedure within European archaeology.

The same movements more or less directly affected British archaeology where they impinged on an existing tradition which taught that ancient and historic settlement patterns were conditioned by landscape and geography (Williams-Freeman, 1881; Guest, 1883; Green, 1967). These various ideas were combined and developed further by Crawford, an archaeologist who trained as a geographer at Oxford in 1909, and also by Fleure, Professor of Geography at Aberystwyth, in a series of archaeological papers to the Royal Geographical Society and elsewhere (Crawford, 1912; Fleure, 1921). It was from this background that Fox later elaborated a technique combining series of archaeological and environmental distribution maps to cover a region or a country changing over several millennia, in a remarkable contribution which was widely followed in the 1930s (Fox, 1922, 1932; Childe, 1934; Grimes, 1945; Hogg, 1943; Woolridge and Linton, 1933). After an interval in which "economic" interests dominated British prehistory, the "spatial" approach reappeared in a revised form ultimately stemming from the direct stimuli of the Cambridge School of New Geography (Haggett, 1965; Chorley and Haggett, 1967) and the neighbouring research centre of the School of Architecture (Martin *et al.*, 1974) – in one respect as a development in theoretical models in archaeology (Clarke, 1968, 1972*a*) and in another as the development by Vita-Finzi and Higgs (1970) of the "catchment area" concept from Chisholm (1968).

The American approach to spatial archaeology also shared something of the nineteenth-century tradition of the "anthropo-geographers" but it increasingly emphasized social organization and settlement pattern rather than artefacts and distribution maps; the anthropological dimension became stronger and the geographical aspect diminished. Jeffrey Parsons (1972) suggests that Steward's key studies on prehistoric regional and community patterns in the North American Southwest (Steward, 1937, 1938) are distantly related to the earlier studies of Morgan (1881) and Midenleff (1900) on the sociology of architectural remains and settlement development. Steward's work certainly stimulated a series of major field researches concerned with locating and mapping archaeological sites on a regional scale with the express purpose of studying the adaptation of social and settlement patterns within an environmental context: notably the lower Mississippi Valley survey carried out by Phillips *et al.* between 1940–7 (Phillips *et al.*, 1951) and the more influential Viru Valley survey undertaken by Willey (1953). Willey's project was so full of innovations that, rather like Fox's *Archaeology of the Cambridge Region* (Fox, 1922), it had widespread repercussions and tended to fix the form of spatial interest in settlement pattern studies (Parsons, 1972).

The proliferation of archaeological settlement pattern studies in America culminated with the publication in 1956 of *Prehistoric Settlement Patterns in the New World* (Willey, 1956), by which point large numbers of archaeologists in America and elsewhere had slowly become more fully aware of the significance of settlement pattern and settlement system analyses (Winters, 1967, 1969). Field projects multiplied on the regional settlement survey model of the Viru Valley – Adams's project in the Diyala region of Iraq, 1957–8, Sanders' in the Teotihuacan Valley of Mexico, 1960–74 and Willey's Belize Valley in British Honduras project, 1954–6 (Parsons, 1972). At the same time, investigations into spatial patterns and social organization began to move from conventional categorization (Chang, 1958, 1962) to new analytical approaches and spatial variability in archaeological data (Binford and Binford, 1966; Wilmsen, 1975; Longacre, 1964; Hill, 1966; Cowgill, 1967; Wright, 1969). However, in most of these studies the sociological, economic or ecological objectives remained the dominant archaeological consideration and the role of spatial information, spatial structure and spatial variability was merely ancillary; spatial archaeology remained a secondary consideration.

Related developments in the spatial aspects of archaeology are equally to be found in most of the other schools of archaeology, with an anthropological and exchange system emphasis where "primitive" populations have survived (Chagnon, 1967; Campbell, 1968), and a geographical, marketing or economic emphasis in "developed" areas (Skinner, 1964; Stjernquist, 1967). In France, the older geographical approach has been joined by a swiftly growing interest in spatial distributions, especially at the micro-level, exemplified by the work of

Leroi-Gourhan (1972), at the Magdalenian open site of Pincevent, and similar studies elsewhere. Russian archaeology, with its early Marxist emphasis on settlement and social structure, pioneered many aspects of detailed large-scale settlement excavation and regional settlement pattern study, from Gravettian open sites to complete Medieval cities – a lead which certainly had direct repercussions in western European settlement studies (Biddle, 1967). In Oceania, Australasia and Africa there has also been a particularly stimulating interaction between local anthropological approaches, American settlement pattern archaeology and British ecological catchment area studies with very promising developments (Parsons, 1972, p. 134; Buist, 1964; Green, 1967, 1970; Groube, 1967; Shawcross, 1972; Bellwood, 1971; Cassells, 1972; Schrire, 1972; Parkington, 1972).

This expanding interest in archaeological spatial information in all the contemporary schools of archaeology has become an increasingly explicit but fragmented common development. Attention has been strongly focused on only limited aspects developed within each school – notably distribution analysis, locational analysis, catchment studies, exchange and marketing systems and regional settlement pattern projects. These specializations clearly relate to local interests and local school histories and, in particular, several complementary developments can be noted in which, for example, integrated settlement pattern studies were an early focus in the United States, whereas an interest in the formal extraction of information from detailed distribution mapping and the full impact of modern geographical methods first emerged in European studies.

It has, therefore, been as characteristic of this area of archaeological disciplinary development as any other that important steps in the retrieval of information from spatial relationships in archaeological contexts have been dispersed, disaggregated and dissipated: dispersed regionally and lacking developed cross-cultural comparisons; disaggregated by scale and context, severing within-site studies from between-site analyses, Palaeolithic spatial studies from Medieval and catchment studies from locational analyses; dissipated by slow communication between schools of archaeology at a general theoretical level and aggravated by a persistent reluctance to see beyond parochial manifestations of problems to their general forms throughout archaeology. In addition, the analyses of spatial information in archaeology for a long time tended to remain either inexplicit, intuitive, static and typological, or at best a secondary aspect of studies devoted to other objectives. However, it is not argued here that spatial studies in archaeology are more important than other objectives but merely that it is time that the major role of archaeological spatial information was recognized and its common assumptions, elements, theories, models, methods and problems explicitly investigated and systematized.

2. PAST, PRESENT AND FUTURE STATES

Although every archaeological study, past and present, has some spatial component, nevertheless the archaeological discovery and conquest of space has only recently begun on a serious scale. Of course, spatial archaeology was one of the twin pillars of traditional Montelian archaeology – the central pillars of the typological method and distribution mapping; the study of things, their classification into categories and the study, interpretation and explanation of their distributions (Clarke, 1973, pp. 13–14). However, as with artefact typology and taxonomy, it can now be seen that the intuitive analysis of spatial form both "by inspection" or "eyeballing" is no longer sufficient nor an end in itself. It has slowly emerged that there is archaeological information in the spatial *relationships* between things as well as in *things* in themselves.

Spatial relationships are of course only one kind of relationship for archaeologists to investigate and the current interest in spatial relationships is thus merely part of the current ideological shift from the study of things (artefacts) to the study of the relationships between things (variability, covariation, correlation, association, change and process) (Binford, 1972). It is also part of the wider realization that archaeologists are engaged in information retrieval and that which constitutes archaeological information depends on a set of assumptions combined with some theories or hypotheses as well as some observations; archaeological observations are not only theory-laden but they only provide information at all in so far as they are constrained by assumptions and led by ideology. The collection and ordering of information, therefore, presupposes a theoretical frame of reference whether tacit or explicit – "all knowledge is the result of theory, we buy information with assumptions" (Coombs, 1964). The clear implications of this for spatial archaeology are that assumptions are honourable and necessary and theory is intrinsic and essential, with the reservations that assumptions and theory must be explicitly brought out, they must be flexible and not dogmatic and they must be subject to continual reappraisal against reality. To conceal or deny the role of archaeological assumptions and theory is merely to remove the possibility of gaining fresh information as well as to delude ourselves.

So the explicit scrutiny of spatial relationships and the sources of spatial variability in archaeology, together with their underlying assumptions and alternative theories, are all part of the current reformation in archaeology. Every archaeological school has long realized in its own intuitive and tacit manner the information latent in archaeological spatial relationships – this much is clear from the otherwise unwarranted precision of many maps and groundplans going back into the eighteenth century and the early intuitive manipulations of distributions or the meticulous three-dimensional location of artefacts in some early excavations. This mass of unliberated information, information gathered at a level more refined than the capacity for explicit analysis at the time, signals the intuitive recognition of the information hidden in spatial configurations, whilst at the same time these studies still present us with the valuable possibility or recycling old observations, maps, plans or reports for the extraction of new information (see Glastonbury, Clarke, 1972). Perhaps problem focused research and rescue excavation should bear in mind the possible capacities of future techniques and make some altars of observations to unknown technological gods. The choice is, after all, not between the impossibility of recording everything for unspecified purposes and recording only observations relating to specific problems but a skilful gamble somewhere in between, recording as many supplementary observations as time, money and primary objectives will allow.

To summarize, then, at the present time it is widely realized that there is archaeological information embedded in spatial relationships and there is much scattered individual work on settlement patterns and settlement archaeology, site systems and activity patterns, catchments and locations, exchange and marketing fields and population areas and territories. But with honourable exceptions, these projects still tend to be static, disaggregated studies involved in typologies of sites, patterns, distribution, as things; we get bits of individual clocks but no account of working systems and their structural principles. The only major books available are either confined to restricted archaeological aspects (Willey, 1956; Ucko et al., 1972; Chang, 1958) or come from other disciplines (Haggett, 1965; Chorley and Haggett, 1967; Abler et al., 1971; Martin and March, 1972). With the exception of the important and complementary research work by Hodder and Whallon, spatial analyses in archaeology are still either largely intuitive or based on an inadequately discussed statistical and spatial theory and unvoiced underlying assumptions (Hodder, 1974, 1977; Whallon, 1973–4). Thus archaeology has accumulated many scattered individual spatial studies at particular scales, usually with narrowly limited horizons and employing only single spatial techniques; in very few studies are the mutually essential within-site and between-site levels integrated and the many appropriate techniques brought together in an harmonious analysis (for sketches in this direction see Moundville and Peebles, 1975; Glastonbury and Clarke, 1972*b*; Hammond, 1972).

Spatial archaeology, therefore, needs the elaboration of a common range of useful elements, assumptions, theory, models, methods and problems to be tested, reassessed and extended in dynamic and integrated case studies. Only now is the full significance of archaeological spatial analysis being grasped and a common integration of theory and methods beginning to emerge from slow internal development and scattered contacts with territorial ethology, regional ecology, locational economics, geographical studies, ekistics, architectural theory and proxemics – the spatial social sciences. Certainly, these theories and methods represent an ill-assorted ragbag of miscellaneous and abused bits and pieces, but this is to be expected on the boundaries of archaeological research where the exercise is not the retrospective description of a completed field of perfected inquiry but rather the exploration of a difficult uncharted and expanding dimension. Equipped with a growing amalgam of spatial theory and methods, integrating small-scale and large-scale aspects, and appropriately transformed for the special problems of our data, archaeological spatial exploration can move forward and accurate mapping can commence.

The integration of archaeological spatial theory is, therefore, an enterprise which has hardly begun in a formal manner. The archaeologist must develop his own models and theories where possible or adopt and adapt suitable models and theories from the spatial sciences wherever they may prove appropriate. An early step towards this end should therefore include some appraisal of the common assumptions, theories and methods of the spatial techniques in other fields, in order to see how appropriate or inappropriate they are for archaeological purposes and how they may be adapted, modified and translated for archaeological data. Another early requirement must be to seek clarification about which spatial assumptions, theories and methods are appropriate at particular levels of study, within-structures, within-sites and between sites, and which have a powerful generality at several levels or a special restriction to more limited scales and form of problem.

However, this fresh expansion of archaeological theory is not just important in itself, for it is interlinked with implications for field techniques, analyses and interpretation. These theoretical developments have, after all, been partly brought about by and inevitably imply a revision of field techniques and excavation ranging from field research strategies (Struever, 1968*b*, 1971), to the more general three-dimensional recording of excavation data (Brown, 1974; Biddle, 1967) and detailed physical analyses of raw materials and artefacts to trace sources and movements as well as the increasing use of sophisticated surface and aerial surveys of all kinds. Spatial information comes not only from knowing the locational relationship of various items but also from tracing their relative movements and flow – the dynamic aspect. These sorts of requirements in turn necessarily focus attention on basic archaeological assumptions about the deposition and disposition of items in the archaeological record and in particular on sampling and simulating their spatial movements and spatial significance at every scale (Binford, 1972; Clarke, 1972a). This feedback between theory and practice, practice and theory, is an important reminder of the inter-active nature of disciplinary development in archaeology.

Archaeology needs integrated and dynamic spatial studies because information comes from the interplay of different fields of observation and because, in archaeology, systems have no existence except in their proximity, flow and contact pattern; the restricted flow of activity within and between structures, sites and resource spaces – the clock-working. This gives us the basis for a rough definition of spatial archaeo-logy and at once specifies its clear links with behavioural studies and the analysis of activity patterns. In the section that follows a purely preliminary and tentative attempt will be made to outline spatial archaeology, some of its common elements, relationships, theory, models and methods as well as highlighting the underlying assumptions and problems in practice.

3. SPATIAL ARCHAEOLOGY

Spatial archaeology might be defined as – the retrieval of information from archaeological spatial relationships and the study of the spatial consequences of former hominid activity patterns within and between features and structures and their articulation within sites, site systems and their environments: the study of the flow and integration of activi-ties within and between structures, sites and resource spaces from the micro to the semi-micro and macro scales of aggregation (Fig. 1). Spa-tial archaeology deals, therefore, with human activities at every scale, the traces and artefacts left by them, the physical infrastructure which accommodated them, the environments that they impinged upon and the interaction between all these aspects. Spatial archaeology deals with a set of elements and relationships.

The elements principally involved are raw materials, artefacts, features, structures, sites, routes, resource spaces and the people who ordered them. The sites selected for study are *not* confined to settlements and include cemeteries, megalithic tombs, caves, shelters, mines, quarries and centres of resource extraction, indeed any centres of human activity; spatial archaeology, therefore, englobes but is not synonymous with settlement archaeology. The technical term "resource space" is introduced here as a valuable recognition that one area of space may be a resource in its own right and much used, whilst another neighbouring space may not have been used or visited at all – at the micro-level the areas around a fire or cooking range or in the lee of a house are resource spaces and so are zones of good agricultural soil, grazing pastures or mineral resources, at a different scale.

An important additional step is the recognition that archaeological maps, plans or section drawings are all "graphs" and that archaeological elements on maps or plans have all of the qualities which are more familiarly associated with graphical displays:

Elements on maps have distributions which may be statistically summarized

Elements on maps have qualitative and quantitative values

Elements on maps may have structure (statistical non-randomness or geometrical regularity)

Elements on maps may have associations or correlations with other sets of elements within and beyond the system at hand.

The next step is to identify the principal elements at a selected scale of study and the particular relationships between them. By definition we are interested in the spatial structure of the system – the way in which the elements are located in space and their spatial interaction. The analysis of the spatial structure of the system of elements is the stage at which appraisal by a swift intuitive glance must in most cases be replaced by the surprisingly complex search for distribution shapes, significant trends and residuals in quantitative and qualitative values, patterns of association and correlation and locational structure or geometrical regularity. Having discovered the strength and nature of any significant distribution patterning, trends, correlation or spatial structure within the elements in the system, other information from the system can be brought in to try to model, interpret and explain the activity patterns involved and their relationship to the dynamics of the system under study.

Spatial structure at the levels of the site system, the site and the built structure can then be described as the non-random output of human choice processes which allocate structural forms, activities and artefacts to relative loci within sites and within systems of sites and environments. The aim of this kind of study is the search for and explanation of spatial regularities and singularities in the form and function of particular patterns of allocation, in order to gain a fuller understanding of the

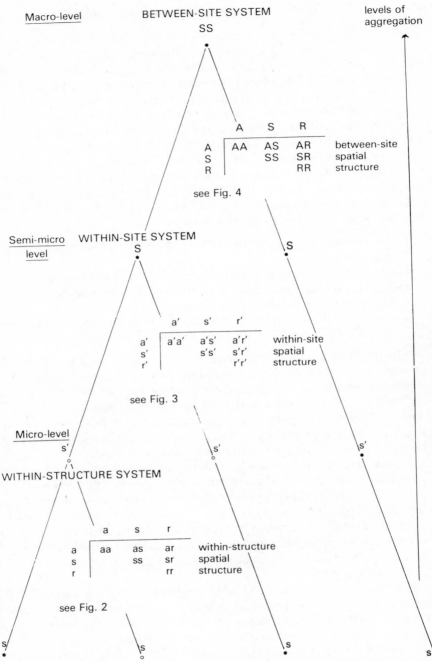

FIG. 1. Levels of resolution of archaeological spatial systems. Each level aggregates the output of the levels below and above as internal and external inputs into that system level. See Figs 2, 3, 4 for key to the symbols.

adaptive role of particular systems at work and a better knowledge of the underlying causes of archaeological spatial variability in general.

The level of resolution of these studies, sometimes called the level of aggregation, can and should be deliberately varied. Each element in the system can be considered itself to be a subsystem which contains a new set of elements (Fig. 1). Each level aggregates the output of the levels below and above as internal and external inputs and, therefore, no elements can be understood without investigating the competing requirements of its individual compound structural units and the constraints imposed by the wider system of which it is merely a part. Three main levels or scales of spatial structure in this continuum of spatial relationships can be arbitrarily defined, each level with its appropriate scale of assumptions, theory and models. However, as we have already pointed out, the three levels are not separate and one of the attractive possibilities of spatial archaeology is that the problem, theory, models and methods of one level may be found useful at others within a spatially unified field theory (Echenique, 1971).

4. LEVELS OF RESOLUTION OF SPATIAL ARCHAEOLOGY (FIG. 1)

A. Micro-level

The micro-level is within structures; proxemic and social models are mainly appropriate (Hall, 1944, 1966; Fast, 1970; Watson, 1972). At

Within structure

Spatial relationships
between

		Artefacts a	Features s	Resource spaces r
Artefacts	a	aa	as	ar
Features	s		ss	sr
Resource spaces	r			rr

FIG. 2. Matrix of the spatial relationships which must be searched for archaeological information at the within-structure micro-level.

this level of personal and social space, individual and cultural factors largely dominate economic ones. Locational structure here comprises the non-random or reiterative allocation of artefacts, resource spaces and activities to particular relative loci within the built structures. A structure is any small-scale constructed or selected unit which contained human activities or their consequences; "structures" may therefore include, for example, natural shelters, rooms, houses, graves, granaries or shrines (Fig. 2).

B. Semi-micro-level

The semi-micro-level is within sites; social and architectural models are mainly appropriate (Lévi-Strauss, 1953; Sommer, 1969; Douglas, 1972; Alexander, 1964; Martin and March, 1972; March and Steadman, 1971). At this level of communal space, social and cultural factors may outweigh most economic factors but economic location looms

Within site
Spatial relationships
between

	Artefacts a'	Structures s'	Resource spaces r'
Artefacts a'	$a'a'$	$a's'$	$a'r'$
Structures s'		$s's'$	$s'r'$
Resource r' spaces			$r'r'$

FIG. 3. Matrix of the spatial relationships which must be searched for archaeological information at the within-site, semi-micro-level.

larger. Locational structure is again the non-random or reiterative allocation of artefacts, resource spaces, structures and activities to particular relative loci within the site. A site is a geographical locus which contained an articulated set of human activities or their consequences and often an associated set of structures; sites may be domestic settlements, ceremonial centres, cemeteries, industrial complexes or temporary camp locations (Fig. 3).

C. Macro-level

The macro-level is between sites; geographic and economic models are largely relevant at this level (Haggett, 1965; Chisholm, 1968; Chorley and Haggett, 1967; Clarke, (ed.) 1972, pp. 705–959; Renfrew, 1974). Because of the scale involved and the friction effect of time and distance on energy expenditure, economic "best-return-for-least-effort" factors largely dominate most social and cultural factors at this level. Locational structures here comprise the non-random or reiterative allocation of artefacts, resource spaces, structures and sites to particular relative loci within integrated site systems and across landscapes. A site system is a set of sites at which it is hypothesized that the interconnection between the sites was greater than the interconnection between any individual site and sites beyond the system; the flow or flux between the sites embracing reciprocal movements of people, commodities, resources, information and energy. Studies at this scale embrace all large-scale archaeological distributions dispersed across landscapes as well as the integrated site systems that generated them (Fig. 4).

Between site

Spatial relationships between

		Artefacts A	Sites S	Resource spaces R
Artefacts	A	AA	AS	AR
Sites	S		SS	SR
Resource spaces	R			RR

FIG. 4. Matrix of spatial relationships which must be searched for archaeological information at the between-site, macro-level.

It will immediately be apparent that these levels of resolution are arbitrary horizons determined by the scale at which we wish to conflate related phenomena in a continuum of related phenomena; the levels and entities are merely summarizing terms-of-convenience and may be altered at will in particular studies by further subdivision or the choice of other specific scales and criteria. In the limiting case, the "structure" converges with the "site" and the "site" with the "site system"; the large rock shelter moves from the status of a structure to that of a site, the Minoan palace is a structure at a scale which converges upon the properties of sites of village or factory calibre, and a large settlement site may resemble and may even once have been a closely spaced system of smaller separate sites. The scale of definition and resolution is a matter of choice for the purposes of the particular study in hand.

It may also be noted that any partition of factors into personal, social, cultural, economic or geographic is similarly arbitrary, a modern retrospective separation of aspects of a whole into subsystems of convenience. It is, therefore, a truism that personal, social, cultural and economic factors count in spatial patterning and variability at every level. However, one utility of this truism is the realization that, at the small scale, the "cost" of being uneconomic is negligibly small and may therefore be overruled by the factors which we distinguish as personal, social, cultural or religious factors. At the large scale, the converse becomes true; although social and cultural factors always remain present, they may be dominated by economic and geographic constraints. A large religious or ceremonial centre with a permanent population must be sited so that its "cost" is tolerable to the supporting society, in relation to the expenditure of human energy involving other sites already in existence, as well as local resources and environment. However, the tolerable "cost" in energy expenditure is relative to particular societies and is obviously in part a culturally conditioned threshold as much as a purely economic one (viz., the cost of the Pyramids, Stonehenge, Avebury or Teotihuacan).

5. THE MATRIX OF SPATIAL RELATIONSHIPS

Spatial archaeology is especially concerned with the information latent within the spatial relationships between elements – the spatial structure. A large range of classes of archaeological elements is potentially involved and there exists, therefore, a vast number of possible mutual spatial relationships to explore for information; so vast that the archaeologist is often unaware of all but a few. The aim of spatial archaeology is to make the archaeologist aware of the vast matrix of spatial relationships and the many kinds of information which it contains for recovery by the proper methods. In real studies, this vast matrix of potential information-niches is only partially filled for recovery – the particular archaeological situation may preserve few artefacts, no structures and sparse external information. But this dilemma only emphasizes more clearly the need for the systematic extraction of what information there is and the greater priority that ought to be given to situations and sites which are known to be more richly endowed in this sense; if we are seeking more and new information we should not squander our limited resources on sites with little or only redundant information to yield, with certain exceptions.

It is impossible to illustrate the potential scale of the matrix of archaeological spatial relationships because the number of classes or elements is infinitely variable within alternative classifications, but using the arbitrary elements that we have already distinguished, we can at least sketch its outline (Figs 1, 2, 3, 4). At each of our three arbitrary levels of resolution, the need to search for information in the spatial structure, the non-random reiterative or geometric spatial relationships has to be indicated.

(a) At the within-structure level: Spatial relationships between artefacts and other artefacts (aa), artefacts and features (as), artefacts and resource spaces (ar), features and features (ss) and resource spaces and other resource spaces (rr) (Fig. 2).

(b) At the within-site level: Spatial relationships between artefacts and other artefacts (a'a'), structures and structures (s's'), structures and resource spaces (s'r') and resource spaces and other resource spaces (r'r') (Fig. 3).

(c) At the between level: Spatial relationships between artefacts and other artefacts over landscapes (AA), artefacts and sites (AS), artefacts and resource spaces (AR), sites and other sites (SS), sites and resource spaces (SR) and resource spaces and other resource spaces (RR) (Fig. 4).

This arbitrarily simplified and terse matrix identifies six sets of different spatial relationships for examination and search at each of three levels, outlining eighteen coarse information niches which are potentially rich in archaeological information in any area with sites, structures and artefacts (Fig. 1). All of the existing studies in spatial archaeology can be identified as sitting within some of these individual niches – activity pattern analysis (aa, as, ar), structural module analysis (a'a', s's'), locational analysis (SS), market and exchange analysis (AR), catchment area analysis (SR), etc. The point is that existing studies tend, with exceptions, to explore only one or two such information niches ignoring the others which are not only present but essentially and reciprocally interrelated.

However, the position has already been taken here that the archaeological information within our spatial matrix is not simply a collection of raw observations but rather a selection of observations which will only yield information when arranged in terms of a theoretical background, given certain assumptions (Coombs, 1964). What, then, are the theories in terms of which the archaeologist tackles his spatial analyses? Well, most spatial archaeology rests either upon unstated but implicit archaeological spatial theory, as in the case of the great studies by Fox (1922, 1932) and Willey (1953), or upon theory borrowed from the spatial sciences (Clarke, 1968, 1972a; Vita-Finzi and Higgs, 1970). The contemporary dilemma for the archaeologist is the choice between an archaeologically appropriate but inexplicit theoretical foundation for his analyses, or an explicit theory derived from another field, based on assumptions that may or may not be reasonable for the archaeological context. However, the solution is in the archaeologists' hands and the gap between the individual theories of the spatial social sciences is not so great that particles of common or potentially common theory and dependent common models and methods are not already visible, however unsatisfactory they may be. Let us look briefly at some of the main theoretical approaches to spatial problems, noting in particular the archaeological acceptability of their assumptions and their ideological and metaphysical background. In this way, we can hope to see the way in which ideological and metaphysical assumptions directly affect our theories, explicit or implicit, and thence filter through to our common models and techniques, finally colouring the information we draw from our observations.

6. COMMON SPATIAL THEORIES

A theory, in this sense, may be defined as a system of thought which through logical, verbal or mathematical contents supplies an explanation of archaeological spatial forms, variability and distributions – how they arise and function, their basic structure and how they develop in processes of growth and change. It is usual to distinguish between "complete" and "incomplete" theories. Complete theories are those formal and comprehensive networks of defined terms or theorems which may be derived from a complete set of primitive and axiomatic sentences by deduction and tested against reality (e.g., Euclidean geometry). However, most theories in the social and behavioural sciences belong to the group of incomplete theoretical networks and they are often only "quasi-deductive" or "non-formal" theories. Archaeological theory in general, and spatial archaeological theory in particular, is in the main only quasi-deductive and largely non-formal. The theories are quasi-deductive in the sense that there are difficulties, some of them intrinsic, in establishing precise primitive terms in the initial stages of theory formation and thus a consequent weakness in the deduction process.

The same theories are also non-formal since there are often difficulties in testing the theory and its models empirically because of vagueness and ambiguity, limited data, limited capacities for controlled experiment, severe sampling problems and a general lack of suitable evaluation techniques (Harvey, 1969, pp. 96–99; Riquezes, 1972, p. 83). However, this state of affairs makes it the more important for archaeology to move as far as possible in reforming its theories towards as complete, formal and deductive a form as may be possible, together with appropriate modelling and experimental testing in order that we may be clearer about the size and nature of any archaeological residue, if any, which cannot be treated in this way.

So archaeological spatial theory is represented by some loose, informal general theories, ultimately extended from anthropology, economics, biology or statistical mechanics, and by an incomplete series of localized and fragmentary subtheories and their dependent models, mainly derived from the spatial sciences and social sciences. The explicit subtheories are firmly linked to the general theories but the entire network is invisibly completed by important areas of yet unspecified archaeological subtheory, implicit in what many archaeologists do.

Four general theories underlie most of the detailed spatial archaeological studies that have attempted to move beyond description to the explanation of the relationships which occur in archaeology. These theories are not mutually exclusive alternatives but related and intersecting approaches whose differences arise from differing underlying assumptions and often a preoccupation with a particular scale of study. The four theories may be loosely labelled as follows.

1. Anthropological spatial theory.
2. Economic spatial theory.
3. Social physics theory.
4. Statistical mechanics theory.

Anthropological spatial theory has long been the traditional background for archaeological speculations and it has taken many changing forms over the years – from the direct equation of archaeological spatial relationships with social, tribal and ethnic ties to the more recent structural and behavioural approach (Lévi-Strauss, 1973; Binford, 1972). The essence of the more recent versions of this theory rest on the proposition that archaeological remains are spatially patterned as the result of the patterned behaviour of the members of an extinct society, thus the spatial structure is potentially informative about the way the society organized itself. The deep structure of social grammar is believed to generate different spatial surface manifestations and spatial moieties; elements of social structure are present in spatial structure, especially at the micro-level. In practice, this approach has concentrated upon the functional interpretation of spatial clusterings of artefacts and the social interpretation of spatial patterning amongst ceramic attributes (Longacre, 1968; Speth and Johnson, 1974). The first step is usually to define patterning of the archaeological remains by quantitative methods and then to offer testable hypotheses based on anthropological or mathematical analogy as to the organization of the society and the associated patterns of individual and group behaviour behind the spatial patterning observed.

Economic spatial theory is perhaps the most common theoretical approach to spatial problems, especially at the macro-scale. This theory makes the assumption that over a span of time and experience, people move to choices and solutions which minimize costs and maximize profits; originally conceived in economic and monetary terms, the theory is now seen as a special case of the general ecological theory of resource exploitation and usually interpreted in terms of choices which minimize energy and information expenditure and maximize energy and information returns. The theory underlies many geographic subtheories, notably the "least cost" location theories of Von Thünen, Weber, Christaller and Chisholm and archaeological extensions of these, e.g., the catchment area and territory approach of Vita-Finzi and Higgs (1970). The underlying theory has been criticized as too ideal in its disregard for non-economic factors and the fact that "cost" is at least in part a culturally conditioned and relative threshold, as noted earlier.

Social physics theory goes back to nineteenth-century speculations that although individual human actions may be unpredictable, nevertheless the resultant of the actions of large numbers of individuals may form predictable empirical regularities which the researcher may utilize. Here the analogy is being drawn between the behaviour of large numbers of human beings and large numbers of physical particles, with successful early physical laws, such as the Gas Laws, providing the stimulus. In its spatial form the researcher does not ask why archaeological spatial patterns occur but merely observes them and tries to find some empirical regularity in the process which will enable him to simulate their occurrence (Echenique, 1971). In trying to describe these empirical regularities, physical and electrical analogies have proved very helpful in formulating models, as in the case of the "gravity models" for predicting the interaction between places and populations – an analogy based on Newton's theory of gravity which had already been developed in the nineteenth century and appearing in several archaeological studies (Hodder, 1974; Tobler and Wineburg, 1971; Clarke, 1972a, p. 49). While the social physics approach has produced surprisingly good results for the simulation of spatial phenomena, it has been conceptually unsatisfactory because of its essentially descriptive flavour (Harvey, 1969, p. 110).

Statistical mechanics theory, in its spatial context, represents an interesting elaboration of the missing statistical and stochastic background behind the social physics approach and the analogy between the behaviour of large numbers of people and particles. This statistical theory of spatial distributions is largely the work of Wilson (1967, 1971) extended by subsequent development; the theory represents a limited but significant breakthrough by linking the social physics approach with the logic of statistical inference and the Likelihood Law (Hacking, 1965). In its original form, the theory was expressed using the intermediate concepts of statistical mechanics, thermodynamics and information theory but it may now be reduced to more fundamental Likelihood terms.

The basis of this statistical theory is that the most probable state of any system at a given time is the one which satisfies the known constraints and which maximizes its entropy, where maximum entropy is achieved by that state which can be arrived at in the maximum number of ways. The advantage of Wilson's approach is that the system can successfully be described as a whole without having to know or describe the detailed behaviour of individuals. This follows the pattern of the statistical solution to the mechanics of gases which the Newtonian approach, attempting to sum the co-ordinates and velocities of each particle, found insoluble. Statistical theory gives the probable state of the gas by simpler means; by maximizing its entropy where the concept of entropy may be given as the expected log probability of the states of a thermodynamic system. In the case of human spatial behaviour, it is similarly impractical to determine all the factors which governed individual decisions and dispositions, especially prehistoric ones, but it is possible, by means of this theory, to describe an overall system of spatial structure and to explain why particular equation models should be applicable to spatial structures for which certain assumptions are valid (Martin and March, 1972, pp. 175–218; Echenique, 1971).

In the practical approaches to particular spatial problems, the informal general theories which we have just outlined are usually expressed in the form of a subtheory restricted to a limited class of phenomena. There are many of these scattered subtheories and their dependent models, but the most important are the macro-location subtheories of von Thünen, Weber and Christaller and their within-site applications to site spatial structure (Haggett, 1965); all of these have now been applied in archaeological situations. It will be noted that many of these subtheories originated in nineteenth-century economics before their later elaboration in geography and subsequently in architecture, anthropology and archaeology, cascading from the senior social science down to those with less developed theoretical underpinnings. In the same way, the classical pattern of development can be observed, in which descriptive models based on broad analogies and empirical regularities may be upgraded to mathematical models of deterministic form but with deeper powers of explanation, eventually themselves being replaced by more comprehensive statistical and stochastic theoretical models (social physics models, gravity models, Wilson's statistical models). However, from the narrow archaeological point of view the current application of models and subtheories from this limited background has certain inherent dangers and drawbacks, especially at the micro-level of within-site studies.

A. von Thünen's location subtheory

In his major work *Der isolierte Staat* in 1826, the economist Von Thünen developed a model recognizing the relationships between the spatial distribution of activities and land-use around a centre and the law of diminishing returns with distance. The underlying theory of this model states that concentric zones of land-use and activity pattern tend to develop around "isolated" site centres. Although originally expressed in monetary terms, the theory is most powerfully developed in terms of time and energy input and maximizing the returns for least effort, given the friction effect of distance. The concentric zones of land-use and activity pattern may then be directly derived from the competing rate of increase in energy expenditure for particular activities with increasing distance from the centre: the less intensive the land-use, the further away from the centre.

Von Thünen's basically descriptive and limited model was extended into a normative theory by Lösch and Chisholm (1968) and developed for archaeological use by Vita-Finzi and Higgs (1970) as the catchment area approach to agrarian and hunter-fisher-gatherer sites. At the same time the theory has been successfully applied to concentric zone patterns at the within-site level in archaeology and geography and even at the micro-level the concept of interacting concentric activity zones around artefacts (artefact association spheres) and structures (structural catchment areas) also has clear potential (Raper, 1977; Hammond, 1972). It is important to recollect that von Thünen specifically considered the case of the idealized, *isolated* agrarian site and therefore made important assumptions about:

1. The site considered in isolation from its network with no resources coming in and no produce going out to other sites or markets

2. Uniformity of surrounding land and one main means of transport
3. Rational (i.e., modern economic) behaviour to maximize returns from the application of minimum efforts (economic spatial theory).

These assumptions make it clear that the subtheory is very useful but unsatisfactory when extended beyond its simple limits. In archaeology its weaknesses are fairly apparent when foodstuffs and commodities appear to have moved between sites in significant quantities certainly from the beginning of the Neolithic and in hunter-fisher-gatherer contexts there is a clear need for more appropriate special expressions of the subtheory.

B. Weber's location subtheory

In his economic text *Uber den Standort der Industrien* (1909), Alfred Weber put forward a model in part complementary to that of von Thünen. Instead of considering the pattern of land-use around an isolated site, Weber considered the location of a site in terms of its outward connections and the movement of resources. The central proposition of Weber's theory, further developed by Isard, was that sites would be selected so as to minimize unnecessary movement; sites represent minimum-energy least-cost locations. The location of a site will, therefore, depend on the distance to and from external resources, the weight of the material to be moved, and the effort or competitive cost of all movements (see Foley, 1977).

Weber's subtheory of optimum site location clearly rests upon the acceptance of the underlying economic spatial theory combined with some particular assumptions.

1. The sites mainly in mind were modern industrial sites at which methods of "rational" economic planning might be assumed.
2. The sites are considered purely in terms of their outward locational constraints, ignoring internal factors.
3. Weber took the limiting cases of stable, unchanging resources, sources, transport and technology. Isard has pointed out that transport costs are convex and increase with distance (Haggett, 1965, pp. 142–152).

Weber's subtheory has a number of theoretical and practical drawbacks but still provides a useful starting point. The subtheory has largely been ignored in explicit archaeological discussions although its ideology clearly underlies many archaeological discussions of "optimal site locations". With modifications the technique could be applied to hunter-fisher-gatherer site locations in relation to resources but an obvious and better fitted case would be its use to explain the pattern of locational development of the major European Bronze and Iron Age workshop traditions in relation to their metal or clay sources, markets and distribution areas – a changing situation which Weberian analysis fits quite closely and upon which it throws many insights. The technique can also be applied to "optimum locations" of structures at the within-site semi-micro-level of aggregation where it clashes interestingly with social models derived from anthropological spatial theory, the Garin-Lowry activity location model from social physics and the stochastic models derived from statistical spatial theory (Echenique, 1971, pp. 279, 293, 306; Clarke, 1972a, p. 48). Once again the weaknesses of the underlying assumptions for archaeological cases are readily apparent but may be met by the development of more appropriate archaeological and anthropological developments of the subtheory.

C. Christaller's central place subtheory

Walter Christaller, a German geographer was the first to successfully model the relationships between the area served by sites, the sites' functions and the network of sites, moving from the isolated site level of von Thünen, through the sites and resources level of Weber to the level of aggregation of site systems as a whole. Christaller started by considering a network of sites packed in an undifferentiated landscape and introduced the notion of a hierarchy of sites in which some sites provide resources or services for others; clearly referring to relatively sophisticated communities. Assuming static sites and circulating resources, Christaller employed an analysis of demand to determine the "range" of goods, resources and services in terms of distance distributions from sites, in order to define an optimal least-cost organizational structure of sites within the network. From these assumptions and this analysis, Christaller showed that the sites in the network are likely to adopt a hexagonal territorial tessellation of space which may be varied by changing the orientation of the hexagonal net, the size of each territory and thus the number and variety of sites served by each site; he also showed that some solutions were much more likely to occur in reality than certain others (Haggett, 1965, pp. 118–125).

In 1941, Lösch exploited the problem of site location within a wider scope and produced a synthesis of Christaller's central place hierarchies, industrial location networks and the distribution structure of service areas. The basic features of this developed model are listed.

1. Concentration of sites into sectors separated by less dense sectors.
2. Sites increase in size with distance from central large sites.
3. Small settlements are located about halfway between larger ones.

The subtheory has been further strengthened by later workers and there has been some convergence of marketing "spheres of influence" work with movement studies to develop areas of subtheory on general patterns of element dispersal in diffusion, exchange, trade, marketing and migration situations, with the emphasis on the pattern dynamics rather than upon individual locations (Haggett, 1965).

Central place models have been very widely developed in archaeology, especially in urban contexts with sophisticated economies, for example in Hodder's (1974) work on Romano-British towns and Johnson's (Ucko et al., 1972) study of early dynastic Mesopotamian settlement patterns in Iraq. Whether the assumptions about site hierarchies may be wilfully extended backward with tombs, temples and camps beyond the urban threshold and quite how the central place model can be reorganized to cope with less "optimizing" societies has yet to be explicitly worked out. As with the preceding subtheories, central place models may also be used at the within-site level and certainly Lösch's sector model has interesting settlement applications, notably in urban sector development (Hoyt, 1939).

D. Site spatial structure subtheory

The subtheories which have tried to cope with the spatial structure of elements within sites have a much more miscellaneous background. At each stage it has been noted that the macro-location models of von Thünen, Weber and Christaller can have a micro-application at the within-site level but with only moderate success, and that mainly at the largest micro-scale possible with the greatest economic constraints – in urban sites. Architectural models too have concentrated on urban sites with the same large scale and economic qualities, either using the Lowry within-place location model or statistical and stochastic models (Echenique, 1971, pp. 279, 293, 306). Anthropological models of site spatial structure ought to provide a major contribution for non-urban sites at this scale, dominated by social and proxemic factors but, alas with the anthropological neglect of explicit spatial theory, we are only provided with the retrospective analyses of particular sites (Douglas, 1972). Indeed, it seems probable that an awakening interest in the general importance of spatial patterning as opposed to kinship calculi may first reach anthropology from the trials and errors of the archaeologists in this area. In the meantime, the archaeologist is driven back to argument from selected ethnographic spatial analogies to support his archaeological inferences in the absence of the necessary general spatial theory in anthropology, or to developments of the most appropriate economic, geographic or architectural spatial models.

The Lowry within-site location model, for example, starts with the tasks which have to be performed to maintain the site and shows the relationships by which the correlated quantity of adult workers themselves generate a number of dependents (families, children, old people, domesticates) who in turn generate an additional number of service tasks and workers. Potentially, the new service and maintenance employment may generate more residents who in turn demand more services and so on. The iterative structure, however, approaches a state of equilibrium for a given input of adult worker-residents in a given environment. Garin improved this structure by explicitly representing the relationships within the site as flows, thereby taking into account the between-structure traffic. The Garin–Lowry model shows that the relationship between primary tasks and residents is the collective distribution of the journeys to the service areas. These models have been largely developed for architectural studies in urban contexts but once again they illustrate the general shape that analogous anthropological models might take and identify some of the positive and negative analogies between these different situations (Echenique, 1971, pp. 278–279).

The remaining within-site spatial structure subtheories represent micro-location extensions of the von Thünen, Weber and Christaller theories to underpin otherwise purely descriptive models. The concentric zone model put forward by Burgess in 1927 suggests that a site will develop a series of concentric zones of residence type, up to five in a large urban site, and each zone will migrate outwards into the territory of the next in a radial expansion through time (Haggett, 1965, p. 178). The main features of the Burgess models are based on von Thünen's theory of radial solutions to competing land-use and costs; the model assumes an expanding population and that accessibility declines with equal regularity in a radial manner. Nevertheless, the Burgess model or an analogous concentric zone model approaches the archaeological structure at sites as diverse as the Mayan ceremonial centre at Lubaantun and the Graeco-Roman city of Pompeii (Hammond, 1972; Raper, 1977).

Alternatively, Hoyt put forward a "sector model" in 1939 which suggested that internal site structure tends to organize itself in wedges of different usage radiating from the centre with the main routes (Haggett, 1965, p. 178). The model is largely descriptive but appears to rest on the micro-application of Lösch's sector development of Christaller's central place theory (Haggett, 1965, p. 123); the approach improves on the concentric model by considering the direction of locations from the centre as well as the distance.

A more elaborate "multiple nucleus" model was put forward by

McKenzie (1933) and developed by Harris and Ullmann (1945). This in effect constitutes a multiple Burgess approach with a number of competing growth centres with the individual site, with the consequent interference of their radial repercussions. These inlying centres may have begun as neighbouring small sites. When the areas in between later become occupied with intensive settlement, then the whole unit is restructured in order to function as a higher-order site; an interesting possibility for the agglomerated temple mounds of many Meso-American centres and historically documented for a number of early urban centres elsewhere (e.g., Rome). However, the multiple "ward" or "tribal" centres can also arise or elaborate after the initial growth by virtue of the many locational forces which cluster some functions but scatter others (Haggett, 1965, p. 180).

The four alternative within-site spatial structure models (Lowry, Concentric Zone, Sector, Multiple Nucleii) and their underlying theory are not mutually exclusive; they select different aspects to model, at different scales, making different but related theoretical assumptions. In Raper's study of Pompeii, for example, the concentric zone and radial expansion model fits quite well for the town as a whole, but at the level of individual building blocks a multiple nucleii pattern accounts for many of the residuals (Raper, 1977).

The archaeological drawback with most of the spatial models drawn from the "economic" background, even at the macro-level, is that they are largely based on spatial theory generalized from consciously optimizing, post-industrial revolution European and American case-studies; most of these are large-scale settlement systems with urban components. These models and theories, therefore, make assumptions that rarely fit the archaeological situations very closely, although they still remain useful tools, pointing to the kinds of model and theory which must replace them and at the same time suggesting important information by the very deviations of the archaeological cases from the "economic" ideals. Nevertheless, there clearly is and has been a far wider variety of archaeological and anthropological spatial patterning than these models and theories comprehend, of which not the least important and most intractable are those traces of extinct systems which became maladaptive and nowhere survived into the recent ethnographic or geographic sample.

The theory and models that should be most useful to the archaeologist, especially at the within-site level, are those to be developed from anthropological spatial theory. However, as we have seen, anthropological spatial theory has been even more neglected than archaeological spatial studies. There are many scattered, individual studies and insights but the determination with which anthropologists have resolutely mapped all the variability of their data on the arbitrarily selected dimension of kinship relations has reduced spatial patterns of individual and group behaviour to the level of mere dependent variables, rather than the complex resultant of interaction between spatial, kinship and many other relationships. After all, distance is equally likely to affect economic and blood relationships and vice versa. When general anthropological spatial theory is contrasted with the limited but explicit theories of the economic, social physics or statistical approaches no comparably explicit models, mathematical or empirical, are found but only vague generalizations and inexplicit insights. Indeed hopefully, it is likely that the incompetent and naive attempts of the archaeologists to model "primitive" human spatial behaviour will be a primary stimulus towards creating a greater interest in theories of anthropological spatial variability, as well as making a direct contribution to the elaboration of that theory.

In conclusion, archaeologists may make considerable use of existing spatial theories, subtheories and models derived from ethology, sociology, architecture, geography, economics and anthropology. But in the end, archaeology must develop its own related range of spatial theory, capable of simulating extinct situations, suitable for dealing with the difficult but not impossible spatial characteristics of archaeological samples and, in its various branches, able to embrace non-settlement site data from linear, sectored, spiral, multiple nucleii cemetery spatial patterns to three-dimensional stratigraphic spatial clusters. We are certainly only just beginning to explore the possibilities of archaeological spatial theory at a sufficient level of generality to make it cross-cultural, cross-time and cross-specialization to the degree necessary for a respectable international set of disciplinary theory. New developments in methodology, from computer pattern recognition procedures to the source analysis of raw materials, now provide us with new kinds of information on spatial relationships, movements and connectivity, whilst even old observations may with care be pressed to new purposes. The interdependence of theory and method, method and practice is constantly ensuring that new possibilities in spatial archaeology are continuously developing for widespread use, but the archaeologist needs to be able to perceive the wider field to which particular spatial examples may relate, as well as a capacity to integrate, amend and systematize these developments within an explicit body of spatial archaeological theory.

REFERENCES

Abler, R., Adams, J. S. and Gould, P. (1972). *Spatial Organisation: the Geographer's View of the World*, Prentice-Hall, Englewood Cliffs, New Jersey.

Adams, R. M. (1965). *Land Behind Baghdad: A History of Settlement on the Diyala Plains*, University of Chicago Press, Chicago.

Alexander, C. (1964). *Notes on the Synthesis of Form*, Harvard University Press, Cambridge, Mass.

Bellwood, P. (1971). Fortifications and economy in prehistoric New Zealand, *Proceedings of the Prehistoric Society*, **37**, part 1, 56–95.

Biddle, M. (1967). Some new ideas on excavation, Research Seminar Paper, London Institute of Archaeology, December 15th 1967.

Binford, L. R. (1972). *An Archaeological Perspective*, Seminar Press, London and New York.

Binford, L. R. (1973). Interassemblage variability – the Mousterian and the "functional" argument, in *The Explanation of Culture Change* (C. Renfrew, ed.), Duckworth, London, p. 242.

Binford, L. R. and Binford, S. R. (1966). A preliminary analysis of functional variability in the Mousterian of Levallois Facies, *American Anthropologist*, **68**, 238–295.

Brown, J. A. (1974). Stratigraphy and regression analysis, *Proceedings of the XLI International Congress of Americanists, 1974*, Mexico.

Buist, A. (1964). *Archaeology in North Taranaki, New Zealand*, New Zealand Archaeology Society Monograph 3.

Campbell, J. M. (1968). Territoriality among ancient hunters: interpretations from ethnography and nature, *Anthropological Archaeology in the Americas* (B. Meggers, ed.), Anthropol. Soc., Washington, DC, pp. 1–21.

Cassells, R. (1972). Human ecology in the prehistoric Waikato, *The Journal of the Polynesian Society*, **81**, (2), 196–248.

Chagnon, N. (1967). Yanomamo social organization and warfare, in *War: The Anthropology of Armed Conflict and Aggression* (M. Fried, M. Harris and R. Murphy, eds), Natural History Press, Garden City, pp. 109–159.

Chang, K. C. (1958). Study of Neolithic social groupings: examples from the New World, *American Anthropology*, **60**, 298–334.

Chang, K. C. (1962). A typology of settlement and community pattern in some circumpolar societies, *Arctic Anthropology*, **1**, 28–41.

Childe, V. G. (1934). Neolithic settlement in the west of Scotland, *Scottish Geographical Magazine*, **50**, 18–25.

Chisholm, M. (1968). *Rural Settlement and Land Use*, 2nd ed., Hutchinson, London.

Chorley, R. J. and Haggett, P. (1967). *Models in Geography*, Methuen, London.

Clarke, D. L. (1968). *Analytical Archaeology*, Methuen, London.

Clarke, D. L. (1972a). Models and paradigms in archaeology, in *Models in Archaeology*, (D. L. Clarke, ed.). Methuen, London, pp. 47–52.

Clarke, D. L. (1972b). A provisional model of an Iron Age society and its settlement system, in *Models in Archaeology* (D. L. Clarke, ed.), Methuen, London, pp. 801–870.

Clarke, D. L. (ed.) (1972). *Models in Archaeology*, Methuen, London.

Clarke, D. L. (1973). Archaeology: the loss of innocence, *Antiquity*, **47**, 6–18.

Coombs, C. H. (1964). *A Theory of Data*, Wiley Interscience, New York.

Cowgill, G. (1967). Evaluacion preliminar de la aplicacion de metodos a maquinas computadoras a los datos del mapa de Teotihuacan, in *Teotihuacan: Onceava Mesa Redonda*, D. F. Soc. Mex. de Antro, Mexico, pp. 95–112.

Crawford, O. G. S. (1912). The distribution of Early Bronze Age settlements in Britain, *The Geographical Journal*, August and September 1912, pp. 184–217.

Daniel, G. E. (1952). *A Hundred Years of Archaeology*, Duckworth, London.

Douglas, M. (1972). Symbolic orders in the use of domestic space, in *Man, Settlement and Urbanism* (P. J. Ucko, R. Tringham and D. W. Dimbleby, eds), Duckworth, London, pp. 512–521.

Echenique, M. (1971). A model of the urban spatial structure, *Models of Environment: Architectural Design*, May, pp. 277–280.

Fast, J. (1970). *Body Language*, Evans, New York.

Fleure, H. J. (1921). *Geographical Factors in History*, Macmillan, London.

Foley, R. (1977). Space and energy: a method for analysing habitat value and utilization in relation to archaeological sites, in *Spatial Archaeology* (D. L. Clarke, ed.), Academic Press, New York and London, pp. 163–187.

Fox, C. (1922). *The Archaeology of the Cambridge Region*, Cambridge University Press, Cambridge.

Fox, C. (1932). *The Personality of Britain*, National Museum of Wales, Cardiff.

Frobenius, L. (1898). *Der Ursprung der Kultur*, Forschungsinstitut für Kulturmorphologie, Berlin.

Gradmann, R. (1898). *Das Pflanzenleben der Schwäbischen Alb*, Badischen botanischen Vereins, Stuttgart.

Green, J. R. (1881). *The Making of England*, Macmillan, London.

Green, R. C. (1967). Settlement patterns: four case studies from Polynesia, *Asian Pacific Archaeology Series*, **1**, 101–132.

Green, R. C. (1970). Settlement pattern archaeology in Polynesia, *Studies in Oceanic Culture and History*, **1**, 12–32.

Grimes, W. F. (1945). Early man and soils of Anglesey, *Antiquity*, **19**, 169–174.

Groube, L. M. (1967) Models in prehistory: a consideration of the New Zealand evidence, *Archaeology and Physical Anthropology in Oceania*, **2**, 1–27.

Guest, E. (1883). *Celtic Origins and Other Contributions*, Macmillan, London.

Hacking, I. (1965). *Logic of Statistical Inference*, Cambridge University Press, Cambridge.

Haggett, P. (1965). *Locational Analysis in Human Geography*, Arnold, London.

Hall, E. T. (1944). Early stockaded settlements in Governador, New Mexico, *Columbia Studies in Archaeology and Ethnology*, 2(*i*).

Hall, E. T. (1966). *The Hidden Dimension*, Bodley Head, London.

Hammond, N. D. C. (1972). Locational models and the site of Lubaantun: a Classic Maya centre, in *Models in Archaeology* (D. L. Clarke, ed.), Methuen, London, pp. 757–800.

Harris, C. D. and Ullmann, E. L. (1945). The Nature of Cities, *Annals of the American Academy of Political and Social Science*, **242**, 7–17.

Harvey, D. (1969). *Explanation in Geography*, Arnold, London.

Hill, J. N. (1966). A prehistoric community in eastern Arizona, *Southwestern Journal of Anthropology*, **22**, 9–30.

Hodder, I. (1974). Some applications of spatial analysis in archaeology, unpublished PhD thesis, Cambridge.

Hodder, I. (1977). Some new directions in the spatial analysis of archaeological data at the regional scale (macro), in *Spatial Analysis in Archaeology* (D. L. Clarke, ed.), Academic Press, New York and London, pp. 223–351.

Hodder, I. and Orton, C. (1976). *Spatial Analysis in Archaeology*, Cambridge University Press, Cambridge.

Hogg, A. H. (1943). Native settlements of Northumberland, *Antiquity*, **17**, 136–147.

Hoyt, H. (1939). *The Structure and Growth of Residential Neighbourhoods in American Cities*, Federal Housing Administration, Washington, DC.

Leroi-Gourhan, A. (1972). Fouilles de Pincevent, *Gallia Préhistoire*, Supplement VII.

Lévi-Strauss, C. (1953). Social structure, in *Anthropology Today* (A. Kroeber, ed.), University of Chicago Press, Chicago, pp. 524–553.

Longacre, W. A. (1964). Archaeology as anthropology: a case study, *Science*, **114**, 1454–1455.

Longacre, W. A. (1968). Some aspects of prehistoric society in east-central Arizona, in *New Perspectives in Archaeology* (S. R. and L. R. Binford, eds), Aldine, Chicago, pp. 89–102.

McKenzie, R. D. (1933). *The Metropolitan Community*, McGraw-Hill, New York.

March, L. and Steadman, P. (1971). *The Geometry of Environment*, RIBA Pubs, London.

Martin, L. and March, L. (1972). *Urban Space and Structures*, Cambridge University Press, Cambridge.

Martin, L. *et al.* (1974). *Land Use and Built Form Studies*, Working Papers 1–70, 1967–1974, University of Cambridge School of Architecture, Cambridge.

Mindeleff, C. (1900). Localization of Tusayan clans, *19th Annual Report of Bureau of American Ethnology*, pp. 639–653.

Morgan, L. H. (1881). *Houses and House Life of the American Aborigines*, Contributions to North American Ethnology 4, US Department of the Interior, Washington, DC.

Parkington, J. (1972). *Seasonal Mobility in the Late Stone Age*, Circulated Research Paper, University of Cape Town, South Africa.

Parsons, J. R. (1972). Archaeological Settlement Patterns, *Annual Review of Anthropology*, **1**, 127.

Peebles, C. S. (1975). *Moundville: The Organisation of a Prehistoric Community and Culture*, University of Windsor, Windsor.

Phillips, P., Ford, J. A. and Griffin, J. B. (1951). Archaeological survey in the Lower Mississippi Alluvial Valley, 1940–1947, *Papers of the Peabody Museum of Archaeology and Ethnology, Harvard University*, **25**.

Raper, R. A. (1977). The analysis of the urban structure of Pompeii: a sociological examination of land use (semi-micro), in *Spatial Archaeology* (D. L. Clarke, ed.), Academic Press, New York and London, pp. 189–221.

Ratzel, F. (1896). *Anthropogeography – the Application of Geography to History*, J. Engelhorn, Stuttgart.

Renfrew, C. (1974). *Before Civilisation: The Radiocarbon Revolution and Prehistoric Europe*, Cape, London.

Riquezes, J. (1972). Operational research and the social sciences: with special reference to urban and regional planning, LUBF research thesis, Cambridge.

Sanders, W. T. (1965). *Cultural Ecology of the Teotihuacan Valley*, Pennsylvania State University Department of Sociology and Anthropology.

Schrire, C. (1972). Ethno-archaeological models and subsistence behaviour in Arnhem Land, in *Models in Archaeology* (D. L. Clarke, ed.), Methuen, London, pp. 653–670.

Shawcross, W. (1972). Energy and ecology: thermodynamic models in archaeology, in *Models in Archaeology* (D. L. Clarke, ed.), Methuen, London, pp. 577–622.

Skinner, G. W. (1964). Marketing and social structure in rural China, Part I, *Journal of Asian Studies*, **24**, 195–228.

Sommer, R. (1969). *Personal Space*, Prentice-Hall, Englewood Cliffs, New Jersey.

Speth and Johnson (1974). Problems in the use of correlation for the investigation of tool kits and activity areas, *Proceedings of the XLI International Congress of Americanists*, Mexico City.

Steward, J. H. (1937). Ecological aspects of southwestern society, *Anthropos*, **32**, 87–104.

Steward, J. H. (1938). *Basin-Plateau Aboriginal Sociopolitical Groups*, Bureau of American Ethnology Bulletin 120.

Stjernquist, B. (1967). Models of commercial diffusion in prehistoric times, *Scripta Minora* 1965–66, **2**, 5–44.

Struever, S. (1968*a*). Problems, methods and organisation: a disparity in the growth of archaeology, in *Anthropological Archaeology in the Americas* (B. Meggers, ed.), Anth. Soc., Washington, DC.

Struever, S. (1968*b*). Woodland subsistence-settlement systems in the Lower Illinois Valley, in *New Perspectives in Archaeology* (L. R. and S. R. Binford, eds), Aldine, Chicago, pp. 285–312.

Struever, S. (1971). Comments on archaeological data requirements and research strategy, *American Antiquity*, **36**, 9–19.

Tobler, W. R. and Wineburg, S. (1971). A Cappadocian speculation, *Nature*, **231**, 39–41.

Ucko, P. J., Tringham, R. and Dimbleby, G. W. (eds) (1972). *Man, Settlement and Urbanism*, Duckworth, London.

Vita-Finzi, C. and Higgs, E. (1970). Prehistoric economy in the Mount Carmel area of Palestine: site catchment analysis, *Proceedings of the Prehistoric Society*, **36**, 1–37.

Watson, O. M. (1972). Symbolic and expressive use of space. An introduction to proxemic behaviour, *Current Topics in Anthropology*, **4**.

Whallon, R. (1973–4). Spatial analysis of occupation floors, I (1973), II (1974). *American Antiquity*, **38** (3), 266–278 and **39** (1), 16–34.

Willey, G. R. (1953). *Prehistoric Settlement Patterns in the Viru Valley, Peru*, Bureau of American Ethnology Bulletin 155.

Willey, G. R. (ed.) (1956). *Prehistoric Settlement Patterns in the New World*, Viking Fund Publications in Anthropology, 23.

Willey, G. R. *et al.* (1965). Prehistoric Maya settlements in the Belize Valley, *Paper of the Peabody Museum of Archaeology and Ethnology, Harvard University*, **54**.

Williams-Freeman, J. P. (1881). *An Historical Geography of Europe*, Macmillan, London.

Wilmsen, E. N. (1975). Interaction, spacing behaviour and the organisation of hunting bands, *Journal of Anthropological Research*, **29**, 1–31.

Wilson, A. G. (1967). Disaggregating elementary residential Location Models, *Centre for Environmental Studies Working Paper No. 37*, London.

Wilson, A. G. (1971). *Entropy in Urban and Regional Modelling*, Pion, London.

Winters, H. D. (1967). *An Archaeological Survey of the Wabash Valley in Illinois*, Illinois State Museum Report and Investigation, **10**.

Winters, H. D. (1969). *The Riverton Culture*, Illinois State Museum Monograph, 1.

Woolridge, S. W. and Linton, D. L. (1933). The loam-terrains of southeast England and their relation to its early history, *Antiquity*, **7**, 297–310.

Wright, H. T. (1969). *The Administration of Rural Production in an Early Mesopotamian Town*, Anthropology Paper 38, University of Michigan Museum of Anthropology.

Remanent Magnetism and Beaker Chronology

DAVID L. CLARKE and G. CONNAH

INTRODUCTION

Recent work on archaeomagnetism has been concentrated in two main fields, first, detection of sites with magnetic anomalies using instruments like the proton magnetometer, and secondly the construction of a dated graph of the Earth's magnetic field with the ultimate aim of providing an absolute chronology for fixed fired sites, mainly kilns and hearths. Important work in a third field, using the changing angle of inclination of pottery to provide a relative chronology for a series of vessels entirely independent of archaeological means, has fallen out of fashion despite the efforts of the pioneers of archaeomagnetism and more recently the researches of Mr R. M. Cook on Corinthian pottery at Cambridge and Dr M. J. Aitken on Chinese porcelain at Oxford.[1] It is with this third method of approach that the present article is concerned and its application to a series of British beakers.

When a clay vessel is fired its temperature is usually raised well above the Curie-point, about 500–600 °C.; at this point the magnetic elements in the clay will begin to orientate themselves with the prevailing Earth's magnetic field rather as though they were myriads of minute compass needles. Upon cooling, this uniform orientation will remain "fossilized" and under normal conditions a permanent record of the Earth's magnetic field at the time and place of firing. However, the finished vessel will then be used and removed from its firing position, thus for ever removing any chance of comparing its angle of declination (or compass bearing) with that now existing, since their positions relative to geographic north cannot be determined. If it can be shown that the vessel was fired in a vertical position the angle of inclination (dip) is still recoverable for comparison with the modern angle and with that preserved in other similar vessels. Since the angle of inclination alters a

Reprinted with permission from *Antiquity*, **36**, 206–209, 1962.

little every year (non-linearly) – it should be theoretically possible to arrange them in relative order of firing or date, thus providing an invaluable relative chronology.

Before the method can hope to succeed some evidence must be provided that the crucial condition of firing in a vertical (or very closely so) position was fulfilled. This can partly be provided by testing a series of the vessels on a magnetometer and showing that their inclinations have a non-random distribution confined to a relatively narrow set of limits and partly by archaeological data, in that fine, thin-walled vessels with precise horizontal rims and bases together with elaborate handles, glaze or decoration would normally be fired in a vertical plane. Unfortunately neither of these criteria can be taken as independently conclusive of vertical firing position but should both conditions be fulfilled the probability is strongly in favour of a preferred vertical firing position. For these reasons then it is not surprising that investigators have concentrated on fine wheel-made pottery like Corinthian ware and Chinese porcelain. The results of these experiments were enlightening but a little disappointing from the point of relative chronology. The general conclusions showed that these pots represented an industrial approach, a specialist potter producing the maximum quantity of well-made vessels for minimum labour and firing as many vessels as his kiln would hold at a single firing. It was clear that in most cases the pots were stacked one upon the other until the kiln was full; thus individual vessels from a single firing might have had angles of inclination varying more than 10° from each other, making any chronological observations too vague for such well-dated products.

For these reasons the present authors turned their attention to a period and pottery that would not suffer from these industrial refinements. A prehistoric pottery series was chosen not wheel made, probably made in small numbers by members of a household for that household, very fine thin rims and fabric, well fired, bearing elaborate easily smudged decoration, occasionally with handles, decoration on the rim and usually with stable flat bases. The pottery fulfilling these rigorous conditions is of course the well-known beaker pottery of the British Late Neolithic and Early Bronze Age.

THE EXPERIMENTS

A sample of thirty-eight beakers from East Anglia and Kent was collected, for which we would particularly like to acknowledge the help given by Dr G. H. S. Bushnell, Mr G. C. Dunning and the Curator and staff of Colchester museum. Initial experiments suggested that beakers would have been unstable if tilted much more than 5 ° from the vertical and the uniform oxidation of the external and internal surfaces suggested free access of air during firing, consistent with firing upright. Each beaker was packed in a standard box with sawdust and then measured on the Astatic magnetometer at the Museum of Classical Archaeology, Cambridge, in exactly the same manner as the cubical plastered kiln samples, that is to say measuring the angle of the mag-

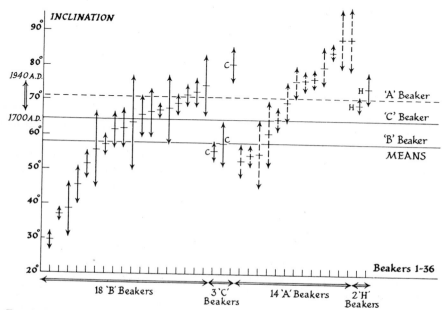

FIG. 1. The magnetic angle of inclination measured for a series of 36 beakers from East Anglia and Kent.

netic component and then computing the inclination and standard deviation. In order to compare the results with archaeological hypothesis it was recorded whether each sample belonged to the "bell" (B), "short-neck" (C) or "long-neck" (A) varieties as at present recognized. Readings were thus obtained for eighteen "bell" beakers (including the B2 variant), three "short-neck" beakers, thirteen "long-neck" beakers and two handled beakers; only two vessels gave erratic results (one the famous Bottisham handled beaker) both interestingly leached by long immersion in river deposits. All the results excepting the erratic samples (two) are plotted (Fig. 1) with their standard deviations, grouped under "A", "B", "C" and "H" (handled) in order to see if this supposedly cultural–chronological division accords with the independent grouping by inclination.

THE RESULTS

(*a*) The beakers have a remanent field which is easily measurable on the Astatic magnetometer; indeed they are so strongly magnetic that a comparatively coarse torsion fibre was necessary.

(*b*) The mean readings of inclination for the three groups in increasing order were

$58.6°$ for "bell" beakers (B)
$64.5°$ for "short-neck" (C)
$71.0°$ for "long-neck" (A)

A test for the significance of the difference of the (A) and (B) means was of the order of 1%, i.e., the difference is significant. The sample of three "C" beakers is of course inadequate for comparative purposes but has been included for general interest. The two examples of handled beaker were treated as "long-neck" as their archaeological associations confirm.

THE TENTATIVE CONCLUSIONS

It must at once be admitted that the sample as a whole and by varieties is too small to admit of any but the most tentative conclusions. However it might be argued that the sample is comprehensive and has the advantage of coming from a restricted geographical area. The work as a whole has been no more than an initial test of an untouched field carried out on a small experimental scale. The authors still feel that these interim results are worth recording before more detailed treatment is possible. The following conclusions suggest themselves.

(*a*) It appears that beaker pottery was particularly well fired above a temperature of about $600°C$. This suggests some greater refinement of technique than just open hearth firing (perhaps controlled draught in a pit?).

(*b*) If the mean readings are accepted then:

1. They are consistent with a two ("A" and "B") and possibly threefold ("A", "B", "C") grouping of the pottery, the two examples with handles apparently correlating with the "long-neck" beakers ("A").

2. Since the mean values increase from "bell' (B) to "short-neck" (C) to "long-neck" (A) they are also consistent with a chronological separation in time (though probably overlapping) in that sequence or the reverse.

3. The mean inclinations lie between 58.6° and 71.0°, suggesting that this component of the Earth's field was not very far removed from that observed over the last two centuries from about 74.3° to 67.0°.

4. Radiocarbon dating suggests a floruit for the beaker culture between about 2000 and 1500 B.C. This would give 500 years for the cycle 58.6° to 71.0° (12.4° in 500 years). This accords well with the modern change from 74.3° in 1700 A.D. to 67.0° in 1940 A.D. (7.3° in 240 years).

Whilst none of these conclusions suggests any startling change in the accepted views on beaker development it must be realized that the above results were entirely independent and therefore a valuable check upon conclusions reached by archaeological methods. Further investigations are proceeding to assess whether the individual inclinations of the vessels can be used to place them in chronological order relative to one another, i.e., an independent check on typology. It is of interest to observe at this stage that amongst the lowest (therfore possibly earliest?) angles of inclination at 37.0° is an all-over corded beaker of the type confirmed by radiocarbon as amongst the earliest classes of beaker ware.

NOTE

1. See *Archaeometry*, **1,** 16–20, 1958.

Matrix Analysis and Archaeology with Particular Reference to British Beaker Pottery

D. L. CLARKE

INTRODUCTION

After more than a century of work in the field, a wealth of archaeological material has been recovered for analysis and interpretation by the prehistorian in his continuous attempt to understand the cultural traditions and relationships of his own ancestors. A varied array of analytical methods have grown to aid him in his task of defining ancient cultural groups. In many cases these methods have grown without their underlying principles being perfectly understood or clearly stated: they were used first and understood later. A typical example of this process has been the changing implications of the "three age system". Curiously the position often taken today seems to suggest that no principles underlie the study of prehistory, since when these are defined they are never used and those used are rarely defined. This position is contrary to the observations of social anthropology and ethnology and the pioneer work of the late Professor Childe. Wherever human actions or their fossil results, the artefact, can be studied they show distinctly non-random action conditioned by the peculiarly human attributes, namely foresight and transmitted culture. In other words they obey certain limiting principles. The present position in the study of prehistory is similar in many ways to the position of the emergent natural sciences in the seventeenth and eighteenth centuries; data has been amassed, but the principles remain dimly perceived or are even denied existence.

The most important criteria used today to evaluate and test archaeological data are:

(1) Stratigraphy
(2) Typology
(3) Associations
(4) Distribution
(5) Absolute chronology.

Reprinted with permission from *Proceedings of the Prehistoric Society*, **28**, 371–383, 1962.

Within recent years, however, particular strides have taken place in an additional field, the application of simple statistical methods in the form of graphs, histograms and numerical notations, especially in Palaeolithic studies. The reasons for their application in the earliest prehistoric period are not difficult to see: the quantity of material is great, the number of variable factors relatively small, the "human" element less overawing and above all Palaeolithic specialists have often been trained in geology, botany or zoology, disciplines in which statistical methods have been a useful tool for almost half a century. However, in the later field of prehistoric studies statistical methods have hardly emerged. One of the main reasons is the greatly increased complexity of later cultures, the very great number of variable factors to be analysed, pottery, bronzes, flints, houses, etc., which often means that specialists each concerned with a single aspect divide the material and so arbitrarily break up its entity. Simple graphs and histograms cannot cope effectively with many more than four variables on a single diagram and it is in this respect that a multifactorial system capable of dealing with almost unlimited variables of all materials on a single page would be immensely valuable in giving objectivity to an otherwise intuitive analysis. Matrix analysis is just such a system.

Before going into the details of one particular system, it would be as well to consider briefly just how relevant statistical methods are to the elucidation of prehistory and their position relative to the more traditional techniques. An answer can best be discerned if we examine the definitions of artefact and culture, the real basis of our attempt to understand the prehistoric past. One artefact is distinguished from another by its possessing one consistently recurrent group of humanly imposed traits as opposed to another differing selection; in this way we can differentiate between axes and scrapers, beakers and urns, even though these classes have perhaps more traits in common than they have apart. Similarly an archaeological culture is normally defined as a consistently recurrent group of contemporary artefacts within a limited geographical area. The important point to note in these definitions is that the phrase "consistently or frequently recurrent", or some alternative, forms the key condition. These terms are basically statistical, they refer to the number of times "A" occurs with "B" occurs with "C" etc., and cannot be accurately expressed without the proper use of statistical methods. So it can be seen that statistical methods are not peripheral to the subject but vital to the proper understanding of significant or non-significant archaeological groupings. General Pitt Rivers shrewdly observed that the archaeologist should primarily be concerned with features that were common, or frequent, and less so with the rare though perhaps beautiful.

MATRIX ANALYSIS

Matrix analysis is then a system of multifactorial analysis for examining archaeological or other material for signficantly recurrent groups of traits. The general principles of the method were proposed by Dr W. S. Robinson in conjunction with Dr G. W. Brainerd at the University of California in 1948. The following is a brief summary of the theoretical background.

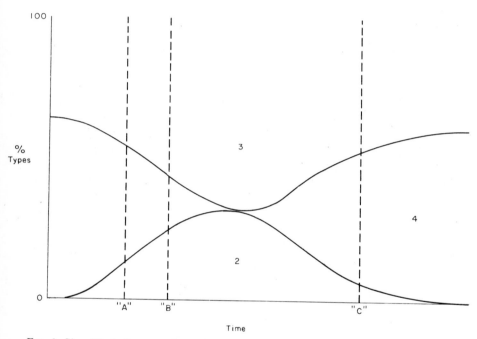

Fɪɢ. 1. Simplified diagram of a cultural assemblage of type artefacts "1", "2", "3" and "4", changing with time.

First, let us consider a hypothetical archaeological situation as shown in Fig. 1, in which a culture represented by an assemblage of types is shown changing with time. The types or traits are expressed as a percentage of the total assemblage and individual types are conceived, become popular and then die out, to be replaced in turn by others. At any one particular time, e.g., at time "A", the culture will be typified by the relative percentages of the various types, e.g., at "A" by 60% of type 1, 10% of type 2, 30% of type 3 and so on. A little later in time the proportions will have changed slightly, as at "B", 20% of type

1, 40% of type 2, 40% of type 3, etc. At a much later date "C" the change compared with "A" will be even more marked, e.g., at "C" 5% of type 2, 55% of type 4 and 40% of type 3. If we create an "index of correlation" – between the sections cut at different periods "A", "B" and "C" etc., then section "B" would have a higher index of correlation with "A" than would section "C". This would seem to be a basic feature of this type of variation: the closer the sections are in time, the higher their index of correlation in terms of the percentages of traits or types. Conversely the greater the time passed after section "A" the smaller the index of correlation becomes. Thus if faced with a series of assemblages of a culture from different sites or different levels of the same site, by arranging these samples in decreasing order of their index of correlation one should be able to produce the probable chronological sequence entirely from the internal evidence.

Let us imagine arbitrarily then that the highest order of correlation be called 7, and that a series of sections or samples "A–G" are taken from cultural material increasingly later than "A". We can then proceed to fill in the correlation table Fig. 2; the correlation of "A" with itself (and "B" with "B", "C" with "C", etc.) will be the highest possible therefore will be index 7, the correlation of "A" with "B" will be a little less say 6, "A" with "C" index 5, "A" with "D" index 4, and so on until each row has been evaluated. It will be seen at the close that Fig. 2, which should represent the general position for any culture during passing time, possesses a definite pattern. Conversely, if archaeological culture material can be sorted into a pattern of this type, then

	A	B	C	D	E	F	G
A	7	6	5	4	3	2	1
B	6	7	6	5	4	3	2
C	5	6	7	6	5	4	3
D	4	5	6	7	6	5	4
E	3	4	5	6	7	6	5
F	2	3	4	5	6	7	6
G	1	2	3	4	5	6	7

FIG. 2. Correlation table for consecutively adjacent sections "A" to "G" in time through a changing cultural assemblage.

the sequence from left to right should be chronological. This then very briefly is the basis of matrix analysis, given a large sample of archaeological material from a culture, varying in any number of characteristics, materials, etc., it can be tested for the basic pattern of the type shown in Fig. 2, if it does not possess this pattern or if random material is fed in no amount of operation can produce the pattern but if it does then the conclusions follow. Only if the material does represent an assemblage changing in time will it produce this type of pattern; if it does then the arrangement gives detailed information on the types and their probable chronological sequence.

THE BEAKER PROBLEM

The author's interest in this method was aroused in the course of research into the grouping and definition of the beaker culture in Great Britain. The ordinary research methods available seemed unlikely to yield as much information as one would have liked because of the absolute rarity of stratified sites and useful associations. This does not mean that these methods have not been applied, only that the present article is concerned primarily with matrix analysis as a technique of much wider applications. In this case the main interest was the pottery, other associations being so infrequent as to need separate treatment. Each beaker, and pottery in general, possesses four major variable qualities:

(1) Shape   (3) Position of decoration
(2) Decorative motifs   (4) Paste and firing.

It was found that each of these could only be defined by larger groups of variables, thus:

Shape   Unfortunately the shape of a vessel or artefact cannot easily be defined by a single equation or factor. The most feasible system is to express the proportions of the vessel as a ratio in terms of a common factor: in this case the diameter at the waist was chosen. A series of five ratios expresses the basic shape, each subdivided into ranges determined by plotting all the ratios against the number of vessels and dividing the resulting graph accordingly. To these sixteen variables another seven are added to describe rim shape, curvature, etc., allowing 23 variables in all to define the shape of the vessels.

Decorative motifs   Beaker decoration motifs are very numerous but can be treated under ten main categories. Some, like comb-impressed decoration, can usefully be omitted, since it could be seen that 90% of the material possessed it – i.e., it was so constant as hardly to be variable.

Position of decoration   The position of the decoration motifs on the vessel represents an important and often neglected feature and six broad decorative styles can be distinguished. The sorting of these variables allows a useful independent assessment of "zone contraction" as a chronometer.

Paste and firing   The paste and firing of beakers was found to be remarkably consistent, the differences being largely a matter of local geology; therefore this factor was omitted.

We are thus left with a minimum of 39 variables, each occurring one with the other to define individual vessels. This means that the number of possible combinations and permutations of these features is of the order of many millions. The analysis of this vast array is usually done in the archaeologist's brain, a remarkable feat of mental arithmetic.

Although the general principles of matrix analysis had been suggested, some time was spent evolving more delicate and accurate analytical details with expert advice. The resulting method was accepted as a dissertation at the Faculty of Mathematics at Cambridge in the spring of 1960. The major advance was the use of the electronic brain EDSAC II, one of the finest in Europe, for the actual sorting and testing of the material. In 1960–1 a fairly complete corpus of full-scale drawings and measurements of British beakers was compiled, amounting to more than 760 complete or completely reconstructable beakers, beside many thousands of sherds. The variables defining each complete beaker were punched out on tape and fed into the electronic brain which then stored all the information. The first stage was to produce an unsorted matrix diagram (Fig. 3): that is the matrix was merely filled in with the frequency correlations of all the factors in numerical order. This diagram is already of great value since on it all the relevant data describing the beakers is available; the number of times any factor occurs with any other factor can be checked directly on the diagram. Relative terms such as "rare" and "common", which have cloaked so many archaeological mysteries, are replaced by the actual figures available. However, this is only the first rather crude step. The next stage is to feed a detailed programme tape to the computer with directions to test the material for the sort of pattern already described. This was a crucial point: since it was clear archaeologically that the material should show some such

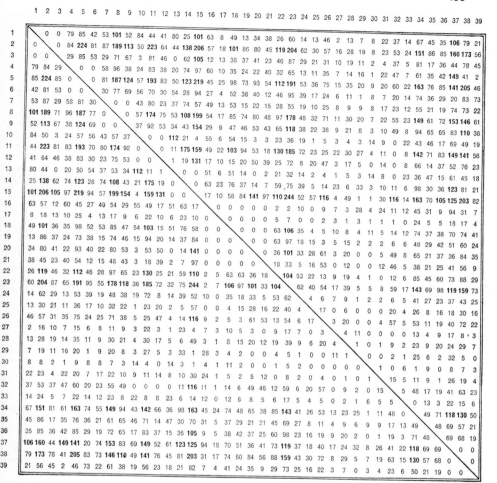

Fig. 3. Unsorted matrix, showing the frequency correlation of traits in British beaker pottery. For key to traits 1–39, see p. 501–2.

pattern; but it remained to be seen whether the method would reveal it.

In the sorting process the vertical and horizontal columns representing the variables are continuously rearranged in an effort to bring the higher frequencies into closer association: this it may be emphasized is virtually an impossible task by hand since it must be realized that when one column is shifted the overall pattern is changed. The final result of this sorting process was matrix diagram Fig. 4, in which it

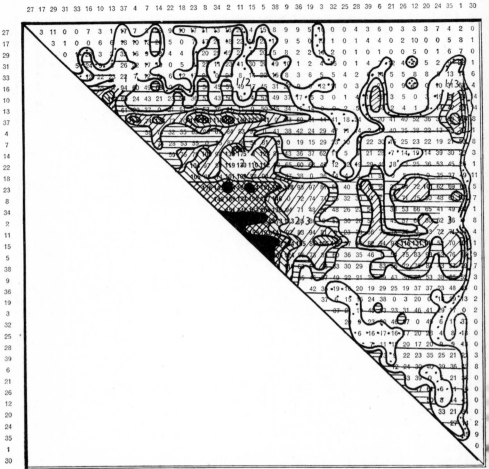

FIG. 4. Sorted matrix, showing the grouping of traits within British beaker pottery. The overlay shows the pattern in three dimensions with the main complexes numbered. (In the original publication the overlay was on a separate transparent sheet.)

can be seen that some sort of pattern has emerged with the high frequencies congregating around the diagonal.

Once the material has been sorted it is useful to treat the frequency diagram as a contour map so that high-frequency groupings stand out as peaks or plateaux and their relationship shown by the linking contours. The fully sorted diagram Fig. 4 shows quite clearly that the ideal of three or more distinct and separate groups, A, B, C beakers, etc., is not a reality. Rather, a continuous spectrum of combinations of traits is presented, but with very distinct trends and concentration about certain properties. This of course portrays a long recognized situation that the archaeological "type" is an abstraction from reality; on the experience of drawing more than 800 beakers it was clear that perhaps only 300–400 would fit comfortably the Abercromby type series, mainly because that series and all its more recent embellishments are based on shape alone with the decoration tailored by judicious cutting to fit.

The result is that "types" in the old sense are of limited utility and, in the interpretive diagram (Fig. 5), "ranges" of shape and decoration are used to show the main trends within the diagram. The important suggestion of the results is that at any one time a range of shapes and decorations prevailed, not single categories of each; and that as time passed the ranges of shape and decoration shifted gradually in well-defined trends. The absence of any large isolated assemblage of traits intruding into the diagram strongly suggests that the development was largely an internal matter except for the early stages. Of the ranges isolated only groups 1, 1/2, and 2, have close European parallels and the fact that they commence the diagram confirms the underlying principle that the vertical and horizontal axis represent chronological time. Another interesting feature is that group 1 is very largely compiled of all-over cord beakers (B3), a type well known on the Continent and the earliest of the bell beaker series dated by C14. Although there is no room to cite all the evidence here, the details of stratigraphy and association so far available confirm this diagram even in its unexpected details.

One interesting inference of the diagram is that the "A" beaker class, so often said to be of intrusive European origin, appears here only as a development and agglomeration of traits already present very early in the system. The interesting riddle of how long a neck a short-neck beaker may have before falling into the long-neck class, and the converse, is given a quantitative value, but the main lesson is that no single trait is sufficiently dominant to define the groupings with reality. The important question of whether classes like the "AC" beakers represent genuine groups, or just hybrids of two categories, is an example of the value of this form of analysis. If the type was a mere hybrid appearing only in the adjoining zone of two "types" "A" and "C", then one would hardly expect it to be present in numbers as large as both. The number of artefacts in an arbitrary group is a reasonable test of its validity, e.g., are Ó Ríordáin's halberd classes I (three examples) and II (nine examples), real groups in a sample of 143? This is after all an important question because it is on these classes that the Irish origin of halberds entirely depends. The evidence concerning the "AC" beakers offered by the diagram suggests that they are largely equivalent to group 2/3, which appears intermediate in time and qualities between

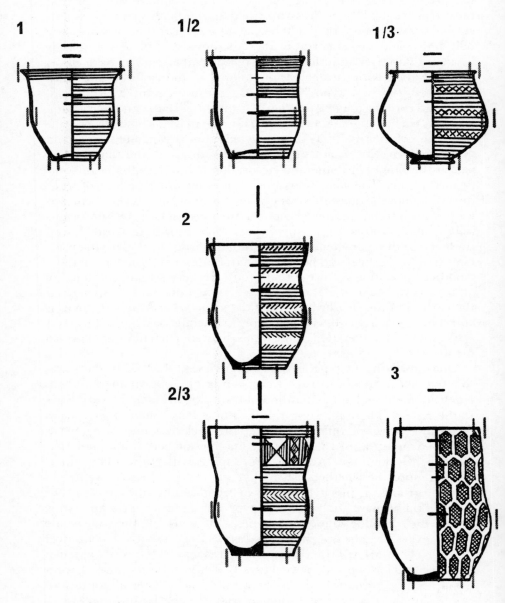

FIG. 5. The main beaker groupings defined by the sorted matrix (Fig. 4). The short
lines represent the limits within which the group is defined; the decoration shows only
one format of the range typical of each group.

group 2 (roughly "C" beakers) and group 3 (roughly "A" beakers). Two major trends of development are apparent in the diagram which represent a reality not sufficiently stressed:

(i) that represented by the development 1–1/2–1/3 (roughly "B" to "B2" to extreme "B2");

(ii) development 1–2–2/3–3 (roughly "B"–"C"–"AC"–"A").

Briefly, trend (i) represents the development of beakers with increasingly narrow mouths, increasingly globular bodies and high waists just below a rolled-over rim. Trend (ii) shows the developing "wide" mouth series culminating with the long everted neck. The information on the diagram suggests that these two series were contemporary developments sharing decoration motifs and their arrangement, both series culminating in slack biconical shapes. Therefore, either the two series represent developments in two separate geographic areas or two series of domestic vessels within a single developing assemblage, i.e., functional varieties. External evidence must decide, but at the moment this seems strongly in favour of the latter argument, or a compromise.

Although a great deal more useful information can be gleaned from the sorted matrix, this must await a subsequent article in which all the aspects of the beaker culture can be considered using all the collateral and equally important methods. On this occasion we are mainly concerned with the wider applications of the method of matrix analysis and the rather swift treatment of the results concerning beakers must be excused. Two general observations can perhaps be made: firstly the great asset of an analysis like Fig. 4, which allows practically all the information available to be shown on a single diagram, rather than on a host of little graphs and histograms. Secondly, the value of the technique as an independent test for relative chronology and the typology of archaeological material.

WIDER APPLICATIONS

The possibilities for the wider application of matrix analysis are impressive, since it is the only method available for dealing adequately with large quantities of material varying in many characteristics. Even with the most primitive artefacts or assemblages it is clearly not sufficient to plot graphs of two or four characteristics and make wide deductions, when the material possesses perhaps 15–20 traits which go unnoticed and unrelated. Are the length/breadth correlation graphs for Acheulean hand-axes from Hoxne, Swanscombe and the Atelier Commont really sufficient to equate the industries represented? What about the other variables involved – thickness, shape, technique, retouch, etc.? The later the period in time, the more complex the culture, the more variables involved and the greater the need for a method of this type. The ultimate aim must be to produce such a diagram for each culture, incorporating as it can stone, bone, metal and house types – indeed all the cultural paraphernalia. Each culture, if it has real identity, should produce a distinctive and directly comparable diagram providing a basis for interpretation and argument. One salutary comment on our present field technique is that with the beaker culture as with most others we have almost no information to analyse other than the pottery from burials. Surveying the possibilities period by period, we may summarize as follows.

Palaeolithic Matrix analysis could provide useful diagrams for comparison for most Palaeolithic assemblages. Particular problems which leap to mind are the detailed comparison of Acheulean and Chellean assemblages with the hope of gaining some insight to what extent the various types of hand-axe were contemporary or successive variants. In the Upper or Advanced Palaeolithic the method provides an ideal tool for coping with the larger variety of types and materials. Thus it would be possible to take all the sites, open or cave, from Europe and Asia, believed to be for example Aurignacian and directly compare them, with internal evidence suggesting a chronology.

Mesolithic Similarly, the well-known Mesolithic assemblages, Maglemosian, Sauveterrian, Tardenoisian, etc., could be directly compared with one another *in toto* on single diagrams without recourse to yards of histograms.

Neolithic and Bronze Ages Assemblages from open sites could be closely compared and some conclusions reached on the real associations of types of artefacts in the settlements, e.g., to what extent do vessels with food-vessel characteristics occur as part of the beaker domestic assemblage? It would be straightforward to produce detailed analyses for the Wessex barrows or the German Tumulus graves treating all the data, barrow type, burial, rite, bronzes, amber, faience, etc., and directly compare the English and Continental series. It would not be necessary with matrix analysis to make any assumption of the type "inhumation is earlier than cremation", since if this observation were in fact true then the material would fall into the twofold division appropriate to it.

Bronze typology based on the associations of types in hoards and graves could be based objectively on matrix diagrams, of which one would be sufficient to portray the whole Bronze Age associations for Britain; information from metallurgical analysis could be included as traits. The diagram also has the advantage of showing the actual available frequency of occurrence including those types which never occur together. Ideas like the "Ornament Horizon" or the "Carps-tongue Sword Complex" could quickly be tested out.

Iron Age – Saxon period   Again, open-site material and pottery could be analysed, but one interesting exercise would be the grave group analysis of graves in large cemeteries believed to show horizontal stratigraphy. A matrix analysis of the material from the cemetery would reveal any changing assemblage or grouping; these could then be plotted on the plan or alternatively location in a grid could be used as a trait.

CONCLUSION

In order to convey the basis of the method and its very wide applications much of the detail has had to be treated superficially. In particular the full details on the beaker analysis have had to be kept to a minimum, a deficiency it is hoped to correct at a later date. It must be stressed that matrix analysis provides a new tool relevant to the very basis of archaeological analysis, but that it in no way replaces the established methods with which it should be used to provide a range of probes of varying delicacy for enlightening the prehistoric past.

Key to the thirty-nine variable traits sorted in the matrix*

Shape and Size:			
	1.	Rim/waist diameter ratio, range	0.90–1.10
	2.	Rim/waist diameter ratio, range	1.10–1.20
	3.	Rim/waist diameter ratio, range	1.20–1.40
	4.	Belly/waist diameter ratio, range	0.90–1.10
	5.	Belly/waist diameter ratio, range	1.10–1.20
	6.	Belly/waist diameter ratio, range	1.20–1.50
	7.	Foot/waist diameter ratio, range	0.40–0.60
	8.	Foot/waist diameter ratio, range	0.60–0.70
	9.	Foot/waist diameter ratio, range	0.70–0.90
	10.	Rim height/waist height	1.00–1.20
	11.	Rim height/waist height	1.20–1.52
	12.	Rim height/waist height	1.52–1.72
	32.	Rim height/waist height	1.72–2.00
	13.	Extremely recurved or rolled over rim	
	14.	Externally straight/concave neck and rim	
	15.	Externally straight/convex neck and rim	

33. Stand-ring base
34. Dished base
35. Squeezed-out foot
36. Prominent internal boss on the base
37. Rim height/waist diameter   0.80–1.42
38. Rim height/waist diameter   1.42–1.72
39. Rim height/waist diameter   1.72–2.35

Position of Decoration:
16. All-over decoration, no zones
17. Multiple equal width zones, alternately filled and unfilled
18. Broad filled zones, often of paired/trebled narrow zones
19. Fully contracted zones, grouped at the rim, belly and foot occasionally with the intermediate spaces filled
20. Neck totally filled, Belly alternately zoned
21. Neck totally filled single waist zone, totally filled belly

Decorative Motifs:
22. Fringe decoration, pendant from the zones
23. Complex zone fillings based on hatching between fringes
24. Deeply grooved neck, giving overall ribbed effect
25. Panels or metopes
26. Positive/negative designs in which filled patterns float in and contrast with plain burnished areas
27. Internal rim decoration
28. Decoration on the rim surface
29. Cord-impressed decoration
30. "Barbed-wire" cord-wrapped stamp-impressed decoration
31. Finger-pinched "rusticated decoration"

---

* The numeration of the traits is arbitrary, the disconformities being due to changes made as the work proceeded.

A Tentative Reclassification of British Beaker Pottery in the Light of Recent Research

DAVID L. CLARKE

The history of the analysis and classification of British beakers between 1807 and 1960 is too well known to need any lengthy restatement here. This complex "tradition" has been summarized and restated in a more modern guise by Professor Piggott in his recent paper (1963). All that I wish to do at this stage is to emphasize four salient features underlying the current classification of British beaker material:

(*i*) Abercromby's scheme of "A, B, C" beaker groups (Abercromby, 1912, p. 18) was based on the "excellent" system of division by shape variation devised by Thurnam (1871). The British beakers were basically separated into three groups according to their shape alone – "ovoid cups with recurved rims", "low brimmed cups" and "high brimmed cups". Thurnam's "α,β,γ" groups became Abercromby's "A, B, C" and eventually Piggott's "long-neck, bell and short-neck" beaker groups. In these schemes the decoration, motifs and zonal styles of the beakers are not integrated into the process of classification, merely being described for the classes already defined by shape alone. This fact makes these schemes, or rather this scheme, completely at variance with modern ethnological/archaeological thought.

Beakers and pottery in general display variation usefully noted under the headings – decorative motifs, arrangement of the decoration (zonal styles), shape, paste and firing. Any one of these facets can be, and has been, used to classify and define groupings in prehistoric pottery. However, each classification based on but a single aspect, such as shape alone, can only have partial and rather muddled validity. Indeed, if one was forced to choose a single aspect by which to analyse a prehis-

Reprinted with permission from *2nd Atlantic Symposium, Gröningen, April 1964*, 1967, pp. 179–198.

toric pottery group then decoration would probably be the most valid basis, since the shape of pottery vessels is at least in part limited by functional considerations and the paste and firing of the vessels can be only partially controlled by the potter's will. The decorative motifs and their arrangement on the pot are, in contrast, a deliberate aesthetic and non-random selection of elements from an inherited *corpus* of social tradition. The number of motifs and arrangements possible are infinite, the number used in practice is relatively small and limited in range. It would seem that if forced to choose a single aspect, then decoration would have been the most compatible with the attempt to define ancient social traditions.

Clearly then, the current classification of British beaker material is ill-based although partially valid. On the arguments advanced above, the decoration and zonal styles of the beakers would be a better alternative and form the backbone of most advanced studies of beaker classification today (van der Waals and Glasbergen 1955). The best alternative of all, however, would surely be an analysis integrating shape, motif, style, paste, firing, associations, distribution, etc., etc. This is the alternative course that I have followed in my attempt to detect pottery traditions and groups within British beaker material. Groups can be defined by a limited range of vessel shapes, motifs, styles, etc., although the space available prevents the full definition of the group characteristics here. The practical difficulties of applying the Thurnam/Abercromby/Piggott scheme have long puzzled the curator and the student when in practice classifying beakers by the presence of large areas of floating lozenges or hexagons, or by the multiple groups of narrow zones with simple motifs, rather than by physically measuring the neck length. There are, unfortunately, "long-neck" beakers with "short-neck" beaker decoration and vice versa; many "long-neck" beakers even have necks of the same proportions as those on "short-neck" vessels. The uncomfortable but demonstrable fact remains that the current British beaker classification is a classification by shape alone, inherited from the nineteenth century.

(*ii*)   Abercromby was the first and last scholar to make a reasonably full, illustrated *corpus* of the beaker material available (then *c*. 300 vessels); upon this basis he divided the vessels into groups.

(*iii*)   Most of the schemes devised since 1912 have been based largely upon Abercromby and have mainly been minor modifications of that scheme. A recent trend has been to steadily simplify Abercromby's intially complex analysis. In this way we seem to have lost all trace of Abercromby's A/B, A/C, B/C; Fox's Bl(*a*), and Crichton Mitchell's C(A),

C(B), beaker groups. Were these beaker groups completely unreal; if not how are we to label them under the simplified classification at present in vogue? Could it be that the further we get away in time from the original piece of detailed research the more easily we can ignore the complexity of the real beaker situation?

(*iv*) No illustrated *corpus* of British beaker material has been made since 1912, although it was known even then that Abercromby's *corpus* was incomplete. Probably in this one fact the germ of the confusion lies, that the material has never been properly gathered together and examined objectively.

The four points listed above have led me to attempt an entirely new classification of British beakers starting from first principles and based on a new *corpus*. This fresh *corpus* now includes more than 1944 beaker finds from England, Scotland, Wales and Ireland; 800 beakers are complete or completely restorable and nearly 100 beaker domestic sites are now known, each yielding many hundreds of sherds. This *corpus* of drawings and details reveals that the Abercromby classification was based on less than 16% of the material now available for study. This fresh *corpus* itself can hardly represent all the material in existence but in attempting a 100% cover I hope effectually to have embraced around 90–95%, a more than sufficient sample for a fresh classification and study. The analysis and interpretation of this new body of data has formed the basis of the classification that I shall outline in the latter half of this paper. The analysis itself has been designed to try and avoid the rather narrow approach this sort of problem has received in the past.

Most of the intact beaker material in Britain comes from burials, but the proper environment of these specially selected vessels was in the domestic assemblages, now surviving only in thousands of sherds. In these domestic assemblages the beaker form was the common general purpose food and drink container but other forms were also in use, including the giant storage vessels up to 60 cm high, various hemispherical and conical bowls and many rusticated vessels. Comparative study of the sherds from domestic sites of various beaker groups demonstrate a roughly common breakdown into three varieties of vessels. The most common variety, perhaps accounting for half the number of vessels present on each site, is always the normal beaker form with decoration impressed by comb or cord. These vessels have given their name to the cultural assemblage as a whole and seem to have been the multipurpose container, selected examples being buried in the graves. However, roughly a quarter of the domestic beaker assemblage appears to have consisted of similarly shaped small beakers but with rusticated designs in finger-nailing, finger-pinching or stick impressions, or sometimes entirely undecorated; in fact a kind of second-best ware. The remaining quarter of the vessels used were also rusticated but this time comprise thick sherds up to 2 cm across and coming from giant storage beakers often with cordoned or collared rims; these represent the heavy-duty containers. In essence then, the beakers from the graves reflect only the fashions of the "fine-ware" aspect of the assemblage, only partially matched by the fashions of the "second-best" and "heavy-duty" domestic wares.

Any scheme of beaker classification must be based principally on the fashion fluctuations of beaker fine ware but should nevertheless aim at tying these fashions in with the contemporary assemblages of domestic vessels. Indeed in some cases it is possible to demonstrate that the domestic assemblages provided a pool of minor innovations and inventions, some of which were only later integrated into the finer and more conservative wares.

In the previous approaches to beaker classification, and indeed in many related problems, it seems that the direction of approach of the particular prehistorian more or less predetermined the solution eventually arrived at. The problem is rather similar to a man walking the plank; having once decided the direction of the goal, walking the plank brings one to an inevitable end. In practice, it seems much more likely that an observer can arrive at equally valid but different aspects of his objective from any one of many angles. In this way the Abercromby beaker shape classification certainly has partial validity. Surely, the best method of ascertaining the nucleus of a problem is not by using a single approach or even the intersection of two approaches but rather by defining a limited area of "truth" by as many differing aspects of approach as is feasible. It is therefore necessary to approach the problem of British beakers from as many different bases as possible and then resolve their conclusions into a coherent whole.

I have attempted to integrate separate and partially independent conclusions based upon stratigraphy, typology, material and ritual associations, statistical tests, distribution and absolute chronology. There are from Great Britain at least 124 sites in which beakers have been recorded in stratigraphical relationship to other beakers, providing invaluable evidence of sequence in particular areas. In addition to these there are more than 88 cases of direct or probably direct association of groups of two or three beakers in individual graves. Other material associations have been found with another 239 beakers, including metal daggers, bracers, buttons, awls and flint arrowheads, themselves susceptible to an independent typology. These latter finds have provided an independent ordering of the beakers associated with them. Statistical tests have been used to supplement typology as far as is possible and sensible in terms of the material. Distribution maps have played a crucial part in suggesting the complementary or successive nature of the groups already defined, as well as inferring whether groups are sensible in terms of human cultural activity. In the case of absolute chronology we have a small but precious group of carbon-dated beaker finds from Britain and western Europe which also throw light on the successive development and sequence of the beaker groups. It is then on the basis of the detailed integration of all these aspects of British beakers that the tentative reclassification has been attempted.

Before I proceed to outline the proposed scheme for British beakers, I must emphasize one or two points. The first and most important point is that this article is a tentative preliminary sketch, not a definitive work. Pressure of work on the main thesis, the length of this article and the problem of illustrations combine to prevent any other solution in the time available. That this sketch has been produced at all can solely be attributed to the debt that I owe my Dutch colleagues for material help and stimulus. My second point is the nature of the beaker "groups" that I am about to discuss. In an attempt to devise a classification close to human cultural reality I have used the term "group" to define a group or assemblage of beaker pottery and artefacts believed to reflect a social tradition or group of people over several generations. The type fossil of each group is the typical fine-ware beaker which usually makes up half the domestic assemblage. Nevertheless, an attempt has been made, and must in future be developed, to define the other vessels in each beaker group as well as the distinctive burial rites and associations.

Detailed analysis of the beaker domestic sites has revealed interesting information on the "mechanics" of innovation and change in pottery styles. This can only approximately be expressed in words but might be roughly paraphrased as follows: apparently, contemporary assemblages of beakers from individual domestic sites can be separated into three categories. Perhaps about 80% of each assemblage of fine beakers reflect the same general shape, motif assemblage and zonation, thus enabling typology and zone contraction ideas to have some reality. However, about 10% or so of the beakers still carry "archaic" motifs, shapes or zonation, inherited from preceding phases, whilst yet another 10% exhibit "prototypical" variations, *some* of which will become "typical" of the ensuing generations of pottery in that group. In the process of change within the beaker group the sequence can be crudely said to follow a progressive cycle, in which the "typical" beaker type of a given phase becomes the "archaic" variant of the succeeding assemblage, which is then typified by the dominance of a formerly "prototypical" element accompanied by yet another set of new experimental innovations. If we extend this picture to each vessel form of the beaker assemblage and admit from the outset that even the "type" in vogue has a considerable range of variation, then we begin to approximate

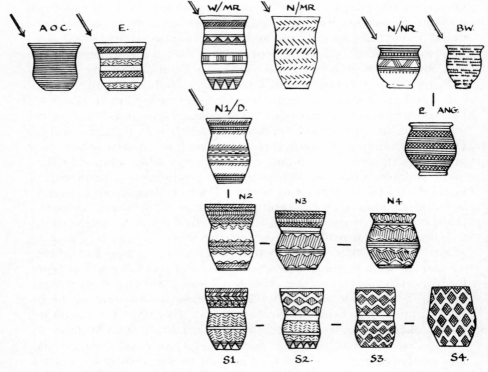

FIG. 1. A diagrammatic sketch of the evolving beaker traditions of Great Britain, using the new group classification. The intrusive groups from the Continent are indicated by the oblique arrows and the three main indigenous traditions are linked by lines. The diagonal from top left to bottom right represents passing time from *ca* 2000–1450 B.C. The diagram underlines the pattern independently established by the matrix analysis of British beaker data (*Proc. Prehist. Soc.*, **28**, 1962, p. 378, Fig. 5; wherein Group 1 comprises AOC, E; Group 1/2 comprises W/MR, N/MR; Group 1/3 comprises N/NR, BW, E. Ang; Group 2 comprises N1/D, N2; Group 2/3 comprises N3, S1, S2; Group 3 comprises N4, S3, S4).

to the many dimensions of change present in evolving pottery assemblages. Against this background the value of the typology of individual pots is strictly limited and of doubtful significance. Comparative safety only lies in treating real assemblages or in their absence by treating large numbers of similar, individual vessels. Each of my beaker "groups" must then be understood as parts of a dynamic assemblage frozen at convenient points and defined by a limited assemblage of vessel types, with particular emphasis on the narrow range of shape, motif and zonal decoration in vogue on the principal beaker form.

After some consideration, it seemed that algebraic and alphabetical labels for beaker groups were undesirable since they would undoubtedly be confused with previous classification systems and in any case they produce a misleadingly mechanical sense of succession. Similarly, a nomenclature based on type sites is not yet feasible, if only because of the absence of properly excavated beaker domestic sites. Therefore, wherever a beaker group has an internationally agreed name such as "All-Over-Cord" and "Barbed-Wire" beakers, I have thought it sensible to extend it to the British material. Apart from these examples, I have adopted regional names based on the name of the area in which the beaker group is centred, in the manner of the "Severn–Cotswold", "Clyde–Carlingford" nomenclature. When the beaker group being discussed is intrusive in Britain, I have used compound labels broadly indicating the area of origin in Europe and the area of settlement in Britain, thus: the Wessex/Middle Rhine beaker group. Exceptions to this rule are the labels already noted as internationally accepted.

In Great Britain, I propose to distinguish a minimum of seven beaker groups or assemblages intruding into Britain from various parts of western Europe at various times. These include the All-Over-Cord, the European Bell Beaker, the Wessex/Middle Rhine, the Northern British/Middle Rhine, the Northern British/North Rhine, the Barbed-Wire, and the Primary Northern British/Dutch, beaker groups. From these main waves of beaker settlers there evolved in Britain three long-lived and competing regional beaker traditions of a purely insular character. These three "native" beaker traditions comprise the Northern British tradition centred north of the Wash, the Southern British tradition centred south of the Wash and finally the East Anglian tradition centred on the littoral strip of East Anglia and the Thames estuary. The picture is one of complex and notably regional development contrasting strongly with the ever more simplified pattern extrapolated from Abercromby's admirable early work. In the sections that follow, I will briefly discuss each beaker group in approximately chronological succession. Unfortunately, space and time prevent my putting the evidence in detail in this interim report, which must take the form of a summary.

THE ALL-OVER-CORD BEAKER GROUP (AOC)

Probably in the century around the year 2000 B.C., groups of All-Over-Cord beaker settlers began infiltrating the east coast of Britain from the Rhine Delta and the areas immediately to the north. These peasant farmers and fishermen settled principally in centres around the Upper Thames, the Wash, the Humber and the eastern coast of Scotland. Subsequent expansion took them to the Bristol Channel in the south and the west coast of England and Scotland in the north. From these points, All-Over-Cord beakers ultimately reached northern and southern Ireland, respectively, but in very small numbers restricted to coastal sites. The pottery assemblage consisted of mainly low, broad, bell-shaped beakers, including some with narrow mouths and cordoned or collared rims. The distinctive feature is the normally total decoration with fine two-strand twisted cord applied in short but overlapping spiral lengths sometimes extending inside the rim. The domestic assemblage included quantities of undecorated beakers and small bowls, possibly used as lamps. Rusticated ware was already present but at this stage is normally decorated with non-plastic single and paired finger-nailing, supplemented by bone impressions. The group seems to have been formally Neolithic although having some knowledge of, and probably importing, a few copper and gold trinkets. The normal burial rite was crouched inhumation, often under barrows. The detailed study of the pottery and burial idiosyncrasies strongly support the Rhenish/North German connections of the British group and show no positive evidence of Breton connections.

THE EUROPEAN BELL BEAKER GROUP (E)

The chronological evidence is uncertain, but at least one stratigraphy and several carbon dates suggest that the "true" comb-impressed beaker assemblage reached Britain contemporarily with, or even later than, the main All-Over-Cord beaker settlement. This beaker group is usually associated with the initial explosive expansion of beaker assemblages to western, central and eastern Europe. The so-called Pan-European or Maritime beaker appears to have been only a single decorative variant in a much wider assemblage. Hence, I have chosen the name "European" Bell beaker to embrace the early beakers of Britain that share the same basic shape and motif assemblage as their cousins from most of Europe. In Britain the distribution of the European Bell beaker group partially overlaps, but is mainly complementary to, that of the All-Over-Cord beaker folk; the centre of gravity being in southern

England as opposed to the All-Over-Cord preponderance, or survival, in the north.

The early European Bell beakers preserve the low, broad bell-shaped silhouette and display a range of cordoned and collared forms. The domestic assemblage follows the established pattern of undecorated beakers, small bowls and larger vessels in non-plastic rusticated techniques. Once again the only metalwork certainly associated with the group are gold trinkets and copper awls. It is particularly significant and striking that the early Bell beaker groups of Britain and possibly of much of western Europe, were apparently formally Neolithic and unacquainted with either tanged copper daggers, bracers or "V" perforated buttons, the so-called beaker type objects.

The main centres of European Bell beaker settlement in Britain were Wessex, the East Anglian coast, the Yorkshire Wolds and the Scottish eastern coast; subsequent expansion reaching the Bristol Channel and southern Ireland, as well as to western Scotland and northern Ireland. The pottery and burial rite idiosyncrasies once again point mainly to the Rhine delta and even Lower Saxony rather than to any significant Breton influx. This holds true for the Irish material which can best be paralleled in Britain and the Rhineland.

The decoration on the European Bell beakers normally consists of multiple narrow zones of decoration, although quite often the zones are joined in pairs, or are of double breadth. The repertoire of motifs is comparatively small, but already included variations on the filled triangle and lozenge. Comb-impressed decoration is normal but occasional cord-defined zones and internal rim cording betray the strong connections with the All-Over-Cord beaker group. The tendency for increasingly tall and slender vessel shapes begins to appear in both of the earliest beaker groups, presumably reflecting the influence of the Protruding-Foot beakers of the Rhineland. This feature is particularly noticeable amongst some of the Maritime beakers and becomes a constant feature in some of the following beaker groups from the Rhineland.

THE WESSEX/MIDDLE RHINE BEAKER GROUP (W/MR)

This intrusive beaker group is one of the most important and clearly defined waves of beaker settlers to reach Britain; an important forerunner of events later to shape the full Bronze Age of Wessex and Brittany. The assemblage defining this group centres around tall slender, or biconical, beaker forms. The absolute range in size is much greater than amongst the preceding groups and is accompanied by a new range of motifs and motif preference. Principal amongst these distinctive motifs is the extreme emphasis on narrow lattice, ladder, chequer and ermine zones, frequently accompanied by filled triangles. Especially distinctive is the introduction of the arrangement of filled triangles around the beaker base giving the impression of a flower's calyx or a band of "flames". Equally distinctive and surprisingly consistent is the bright burnished "sealing-wax" red fabric, strongly recalling burnished copper. Cord decoration and internal rim decoration have both entirely disappeared from the assemblage. The domestic assemblage remains generally the same, including as before plain beakers and bowls and non-plastic rustication. The zonal arrangement is now predominantly in broad or paired decorative zones with the occasional vessel anticipating full zone contraction. Similarly, some beakers already display the sharpened neck profile typical of the later Dutch beakers.

The available dating evidence points to the arrival of this group in Britain around 1800–1750 B.C. The group as an assemblage has no close parallel in the Netherlands, with the important exception of one or two vessels of which the Odoorn beaker may be an atypical example. The only area in which the British vessels are paralleled, and indeed can be shown to have evolved, is in the Middle Rhineland, particularly in the beaker foci around Koblenz and Mainz, at either end of the Rhine Gorge. The early beaker groups of this area appear to have developed a particularly rich and flourishing economy, based in part on the strategic trading position of their territory. The area dominates the confluence of the rivers Rhine, Neckar, Main, Lahn and Moselle, bringing direct contact with the metope beakers of Saxo-Thuringia to the northeast and the Straubing/Singen groups to the south. These various areas contributed many of the features transported by the Wessex/Middle Rhine group to England, notably polypod bowls, metope patterns, bone belt rings, bracers and a flourishing copper and copper alloy metallurgy. The metalwork includes raquet head pins, tanged and simple riveted daggers, tubular beads, large awls, gold-capped "V" perforated buttons and probably thick butted axes made from sulphide ores. The earliest and rare examples of tin bronze occur in both the German and British aspects of this beaker assemblage.

The Wessex/Middle Rhine beaker group appears to have emigrated almost directly from the Middle Rhine to southern England. At first sight a long leap, but one should remember that they were following in the immediate footsteps of their own ancestors, the European Bell beaker folk, and that the Rhine will carry an unpowered boat from Mainz to the Channel in one or two days. Scattered outliers of the group reached the Wash, the Thames valley and the Sussex coast but over 80% of the total group are clustered within sixty miles radius of Stonehenge, hence the choice of the Wessex/Middle Rhine label. Some of the sherds and the metope decorated bowl from Lough Gur, Co. Limerick in southern Ireland, belong to this beaker group, making it very probable that the Wessex/Middle Rhine beaker group was responsible for the early bronze and copper sulphide ore metallurgy of Ireland. This early Irish metalwork was apparently traded back to Wessex where graves of this group contain daggers of Irish copper and trinkets of gold (Coghlan and Case, 1957). Thick butt copper axes may also have been introduced by this group.

For the first time, tanged copper daggers, flint daggers, bracers and probably "V" perforated buttons appear as part of the British beaker assemblage. Five or possibly six rich burials, with tanged copper daggers and other equipment of Straubing/Adlerberg and Irish origin, have been found with Wessex/Middle Rhine beakers[1] in the Wessex area (Coghlan, 1957). Almost all of these early "dagger" burials occur in the triangle between the Upper Thames, the Bristol Channel and North Wessex. Clearly the importance of the Wessex area as an economic centre linking Irish, Rhenish and Breton trade had already been anticipated; controlling the Thames headwaters to the east, the Bristol Avon to the west and the Wiltshire Avon to the south. In Brittany too there appears to have been a less numerous intrusion of the same Middle Rhenish beaker group accompanied by similar equipment and a similar boom in copper and early bronze metallurgy. In this way the links between Ireland, Wessex, Brittany and the Middle Rhineland, which become so apparent in the full Bronze Age, had already been anticipated by the Wessex/Middle Rhine beaker group and its wealthy aristocracy.

THE NORTHERN BRITISH/MIDDLE RHINE BEAKER GROUP (N/MR)

This beaker group was closely allied to the Wessex/Middle Rhine group, being roughly contemporary and coming from the same general region with similar material equipment. The difference lies mainly in their different origins and pottery and different distribution in Britain. Whereas the Wessex/Middle Rhine group was a fairly pure development from the early European Bell beaker settlement along the Rhine, the Northern (British)/Middle Rhine group reflects the integration of contemporary Bell beaker folk with Sangmeister's Westdeutsche Becher groups on the surrounding hills. These Westdeutsche Becher were a late Single Grave group whose slender beaker forms were decorated with horizontal herringbone impressions made with a stick or spatula, burying their dead under barrows with central timber structures and palisade ring (Sangmeister, 1951, p. 64, Taf.X–XI, XVIII–XIX, Karte 18). The amalgamation of the two populations, in the area immediately adjacent to the Wessex/Middle Rhine area of origin, led to a series of beakers of mixed traditions and similarly mixed material and ritual associations. Typical features of the pottery are once again a tall slender curvilinear or biconical profile decorated with zones of horizontal herringbone either impressed by a spatula or a dentated comb. Some of the vessels preserve the Single Grave feature of leaving the lower half of the vessel undecorated and this can be seen on some typical English specimens, e.g., at Linch Hill, Oxon (Grimes, 1943/4, pp. 34–35).

The distribution of this beaker group in Britain is roughly complementary to the contemporary Wessex/Middle Rhine group but overlapping in the Thames valley, the probable common access route. The Northern British/North Rhine group clusters in small foci along the east coast of Britain north of the Thames valley and stretches into Lowland Scotland. The tanged copper daggers from these regions were perhaps introduced by this group but are unfortunately without pottery associations. Nevertheless, a distinctive association with this beaker group are the various forms of bone belt rings or buckles derived ultimately from the Single Grave background of the Westdeutsche Becher. At Sittingbourne, Kent (Jessup, 1930, pp. 96, 115), such a bone belt ring was associated with a single rivet dagger of the early tanged variety and a two-hole bracer;[2] at Melton Quarry, Yorkshire,[3] with another two-hole bracer and an undecorated beaker (bowl?) rim sherd. Such a belt ring was found *in situ* in the well-known archer's grave at Linch Hill, Stanton Harcourt, Oxford, with a typical Northern British/Middle Rhine beaker and an inhumation in a coffin. The related Northern/Middle Rhine beaker from Talbenny, South Hill, Pembrokeshire, Wales, came from under a barrow with a timber post circle in typical Westdeutsche Becher tradition (Fox, 1943).

THE NORTHERN BRITISH/NORTH RHINE BEAKER GROUP (N/NR)

The particular interest of the Northern/North Rhine group and its close cousin the Barbed-Wire beaker group, is that both groups only just scrape within the definition of beakers of the Bell beaker tradition. Both the Northern/North Rhine and the Barbed-Wire beaker groups comprise traditions of mixed Late Corded Ware and peripheral Bell beaker origin. This mixture of traditions can be recognized in the squat, protruding foot, ovoid body beakers with recurved rims, incised or grooved decoration with a poor repertoire of basic beaker motifs and a Neolithic poverty of grave associations. To these factors can be added the occasional use of cremation burial rite in a small grave with the beaker beside the cremation heap, and a number of vessels without decoration below the belly.

The Northern/North Rhine beaker group then is represented by the small squat or globular vessels with protruding feet. The decoration frequently consists of heavy grooving below the rim with crude or carelessly incised zones on the body, including metopic motifs. The typical motif is the multiple outlined triangle of the diagnostic form common throughout the Corded Ware tradition and entirely alien in the Bell beaker motif assemblage (Struve, 1955, p. 136). The origin of the group seems to lie in the similar assemblages found immediately north of the old Rhine delta and along the hinterland of the Frisian coasts. The Dutch examples of this group have been partially defined by Modderman (1955) but the type is centred across the border in coastal Germany.[4] In this area it would appear that late and devolved Corded Ware groups integrated small bands of beaker settlers producing a pottery assemblage of hybrid character.

These folk, with their strong non-beaker background, apparently crossed the North Sea in a series of small bands somewhere around 1700 B.C. or slightly later. The settlers clustered in three foci based on the North Sea coast: around the Moray Firth, in the Border counties and on the Yorkshire Wolds. The domestic assemblage included both undecorated and non-plastic rusticated ware. The main importance of these settlers from across the North Sea lies in the subsequent integration of certain of their pottery features with the later Dutch beakers of the Veluwe type, giving rise to regional insular variations such as the beakers with short, angular, all-over-grooved necks.

THE BARBED-WIRE BEAKER GROUP (BW)

The Barbed-Wire beaker group represent another wave of settlers of mingled Late Corded Ware and Bell beaker ancestry. The group that settled in Britain came from the area immediately south of the Northern British/North Rhine group with whom they share many minor characteristics, based on their common background. The immediate and closest parallels of the British vessels are with the Barbed-Wire vessels of the Lower Rhineland. From this area the Barbed-Wire beaker settlers seem to have moved into the East Anglian littoral and penetrated along the Thames valley as far as the Bristol Channel and even into north Devon and South Wales. In this way they occupied the interface of the territories of the Northern British/Middle Rhine and Wessex/Middle Rhine beakers, whilst simultaneously holding the North Sea coast in the area immediately south of their North Rhine cousins (N/NR).

The Barbed-Wire beaker pottery varies over a considerable range of shapes including archaic bell forms, prototypical short-neck forms and various hybrids with Wessex/Middle Rhine beakers. However, the typical form appears to have been a small, curvilinear profile, ovoid-bodied beaker with protruding foot and recurved rim. The decoration is stereotyped and with a minimal repertoire of Bell beaker motifs, mainly simple hatched or lattice-filled zones. The outlined triangle and grooved neck features of the Northern/North Rhine beakers are also occasionally found. The decorative zones are usually broad and sometimes contracted to the salient points of the vessel profile; archaic all-over motifs and decoration within the rim is preserved on a few vessels. The decoration is typically applied by a thread-wound stamp with supplementary decoration added by jabbing, incision and grooving. The normal beaker comb was occasionally used and some vessels entirely decorated with comb impressions certainly belong to this group, others used both techniques together.

The domestic material of these beaker settlers has been admirably illustrated by Dr Isobel Smith in her initial publication of this pottery assemblage (Smith, 1955). The assemblage includes large and small Barbed-Wire beakers and bowls, large and small rusticated beakers and some comb-impressed or incised vessels. The larger rusticated vessels attain sizes of up to 60 cm high with small peg-like bases of the Fengate type. Some of these larger vessels have been found inverted over cremation burials in Britain and on the Continent.

The Barbed-Wire beaker group appears to have been numerically small and rapidly became assimilated with beaker traditions already settled in Britain. The corrected radiocarbon dates and stratigraphy suggest that the Barbed-Wire beaker infiltration started around 1700–1650 B.C. The area of settlement is roughly complementary to the territory of the preceding Middle and North Rhenish beaker groups (W/MR, N/MR, N/NR). Nevertheless, the area infiltrated still contained a residual European Bell beaker population and the integration of the two traditions partly led to the rise of the distinctive East Anglian beaker group.

THE EAST ANGLIAN BEAKER GROUP (E. ANG.)

The origins of the East Anglian beaker tradition are typical of the processes of regional integration leading to the three main insular beaker traditions. The East Anglian littoral was a centre of European Bell beaker settlement second only to Wessex itself. The predominant regional decoration of this European Bell beaker focus was the All-Over-Comb impressed variant. Exactly as in the domestic assemblages of all the European Bell beakers, the range included a variety of narrow-mouthed vessel forms. The integration of elements from the Mildenhall Ware Neolithic population of the area, especially the rolled-over rim, led to the evolution of a new beaker tradition. The vessels are small, with biconical or globular profiles symmetrical about a prominent belly axis. The base and rim diameter are roughly equal and the rims are characteristically rolled over and rounded (roughly Abercromby's B2 beakers). The decoration is often simply All-Over horizontal comb or incision but finer examples have broad or paired zones with lattice or some other simple filling. Certain aspects of the decoration point to the absorption of some of the small outlying pockets of Wessex/Middle Rhine settlement around the Wash.

The slow evolution of the East Anglian tradition outlined above occupied the period between *ca* 1900 and 1700 B.C. In the half century following this phase, the Barbed-Wire beaker group began landing up and down the East Anglian littoral strip and the two traditions confronted one another. The result appears to have been the steady integration of the Barbed-Wire tradition into the larger, locally evolved group with a resultant loss of identity. However, the East Anglian beaker group itself became changed by the intrusion, adopting many of the Barbed-Wire beaker characteristics. The revitalized East Anglian tradition now commenced to consolidate its control of the Fen Basin and the East Anglian coast, whilst simultaneously expanding into the Thames estuary and along the Kent and Sussex coast. This coastal territory, linked by the sea, remained complementary to the established and flourishing Wessex/Middle Rhine group to the west.

East Anglian beaker domestic sites repeat the same characteristics as those of the Barbed-Wire beaker group. Large and small rusticated vessels are common and for the first time begin to develop a ribbed or plastic finger-pinched surface. This feature is still rare and may be tentatively equated with the arrival of the first Primary Northern/Dutch beaker settlers. Undecorated vessels are now uncommon in this and the contemporary beaker domestic assemblages, consequently rus-

PRIMARY NORTHERN BRITISH/DUTCH BEAKERS
(N1/D)

The evolution in the Netherlands, particularly in the Veluwe, of a specifically Dutch beaker type with a specific motif assemblage, zonal range and short-necked profile, has been demonstrated by van der Waals in the classic paper with Professor Glasbergen (1955). In the century between 1700 and 1600 B.C. it would seem that the Dutch beaker folk of the Veluwe began to settle the opposing coast of Great Britain. These beakers, corresponding exactly to van der Waal's 2^{Ic} group, make up my Primary Northern/Dutch beaker group (N1/D).

These new arrivals found southern Britain already in the hands of at least two or three alien and flourishing traditions (W/MR; BW; E. Ang.). The north of Britain was far more sparsely held by beaker groups of small size (N/MR, N/NR, and AOC surviving in Scotland). Nevertheless, the new wave of Dutch settlers consolidated small bridgeheads in the south, securing the shortest crossing from the Veluwe to Norfolk. Other small foci appear on the Fen Margins, the Lincolnshire and Yorkshire Wolds, in the Border counties, and along the enticing, thinly populated east coast of Lowland Scotland. The distribution noticeably clusters around the large estuaries and inlets with all the find spots within 25 miles of North Sea tidal waters.

The domestic assemblage of this and the succeeding Northern British beaker groups is very poorly represented. However, there appear to have been large and small rusticated short-neck vessels ("potbeakers") with the new development of plastic finger-pinching in alternate horizontal and vertical bands imitating the contemporary zonal styles in use on the fine ware. Undecorated beakers are absent; collared or cordoned rims are rare, being entirely restricted to the rusticated pottery. The fine beakers are identical with the Dutch beakers described by van der Waals (1955) under his 2^{Ic-d} phases. The vessels are typically small but slender with a straight or concave neck profile above a sharply defined waist. The decoration is especially distinctive and introduces a new array of motifs which form the basis of the Northern British tradition lasting for many centuries. The distinctive feature of this new motif tradition is the assemblage of "fringe" decorations that can be attached to zone borders; not all the vessels, however, have fringe motifs. The typical zone arrangements tend towards groups of three or more narrow zones separated by undecorated areas. A system of three groups of three zones was much favoured, emphasizing the main shape elements; some of these vessels show full zone contraction as in the Veluwe beakers.

THE NORTHERN BRITISH BEAKER TRADITION (N1, N2, N3, N4)

The intrusive beaker group, represented by the Primary Northern/ Dutch folk, rapidly settled, consolidated and expanded their territory in Britain. This Primary group established a beaker tradition that was to continue to evolve in northern Britain for at least another two centuries. I propose to divide the beakers of the subsequent Northern British tradition into a series of four consecutive assemblages or groups, each of which represents a successively later phase in the tradition. Needless to say these assemblages or groups are only phases in the coherent development of a single social tradition and must be assumed to overlap considerably. In addition to the Primary Northern group (N1/D), just discussed, I propose to distinguish a Developed Northern group (N2), a Late Northern group (N3) and a Final Northern group (N4), each defined on the basis of the evolving motif assemblage and shape variation that separate the increasingly insular Northern British tradition from its divergently evolving Veluwe ancestor. There is, however, some evidence of continued contact with the Netherlands up to, and including, a few beakers and associations of van der Waals' 2^{Id} group. The available evidence points to the continued links with the Veluwe as the source of the single-rivet and notched rhomboidal knives and also as the stimulus for more extensive metallurgy in northern Britain.

The confines of this paper are too small to allow the detailed description of the successive phases of the Northern British beaker tradition. However, I wish to underline one or two aspects. By the Developed Northern beaker phase *ca* 1600 B.C. this tradition was the dominant beaker tradition in Britain. Regional centres of the tradition evolved regional shape and motif preferences within the body of the main tradition. These areas included extensive settlements around the Fen Margin, in north Wessex, on the Yorkshire Wolds, in the Border counties and along the Scottish east coast. This chain of settlement areas along the North Sea coast clearly maintained its commonly evolving tradition by sea traffic. Consequently, the central area of Yorkshire originally played a crucial axial role in linking the other groups one to another. With the subsequent expansion of the Southern beaker tradition, the centre of distribution within the Northern tradition retreated into the Scottish counties with consequent expansion of related groups to the west Scottish coast and ultimately to northern Ireland. One crucial feature needing special emphasis was the relatively heavy settlement of Northern British beakers (N2, N3) around the fen margin of East Anglia and more sparsely, in north Wessex.

The situation in Britain *ca* 1600 B.C. sees the Developed Northern

Beaker tradition (N2) occupying most of Britain north of the Wash. The remnants of the earlier beaker settlers were integrated into the new tradition but gave rise to regional styles within the tradition (groups absorbed include N/MR, N/NR and some AOC, W/MR). Meanwhile, in southern Britain the Wessex/Middle Rhine group itself absorbed the earlier European Bell beaker population and consolidated its territory in central and south Wessex. The Upper Thames had by then been partially infiltrated by Developed Northern beaker folk from Yorkshire and the fen margins. To the east, the East Anglian beaker group retreated from the Fenlands in the face of Developed Northern beaker expansion. Sheltered by the forested East Anglian clay belt, the local beaker group still held the littoral strip, the Thames estuary and the coast of Kent and Sussex. It is about this stage that new developments slowly begin to emerge amongst the Developed Northern beaker groups of the Fen Margin, foreshadowing the evolution of the third major beaker tradition native to Great Britain, the southern British beaker tradition.

THE SOUTHERN BRITISH BEAKER TRADITION (S1, S2, S3, S4)

The fully evolved beakers of this tradition display a preference for longer-necked profile and a new motif assemblage based partly on reserved motifs, ultimately stemming from filled lozenges and triangles (E & W/MR), and partly on motifs common on Developed Northern beakers (N2). In addition to these features, two new zonal arrangements were developed that were unknown amongst the repertoire of the Dutch beakers, although based indirectly upon them. These include the filled neck/zoned belly style and a little later, the filled neck/filled belly style. These two styles allow extra broad areas of decoration and thus stimulated the evolution of new motifs including floating patterns of various kinds.

In the Primary Southern beaker assemblage (S1) the neck length is often the same or slightly longer than of normal Developed Northern beakers. The motifs used clearly show the fusion of the simple reserved triangle and lozenge motifs of local Wessex/Middle Rhine and European Bell beaker origin, intermingled with Developed Northern British (N2) motifs. This mixed motif assemblage now appears on beakers with the medium/short neck length and sharp neck profile of the Developed Northern beaker group. It would seem that locally strong elements of Wessex/Middle Rhine and perhaps late European Bell beaker groups had become integrated with the Developed Northern beaker settlers of the fen margin, and to a less extent, of the Yorkshire Wolds and the Derbyshire Peak. In short, the fen margin regional form of the Developed Northern beaker assemblage represents the beginnings of the first phase of the Primary Southern British beaker tradition. In a sense, the reason why long-neck beakers and their motifs evolved in the south and not the north of Britain is because in the north the Northern British/Dutch beaker settlers were imposed on a feeble scatter of earlier beaker groups. Whereas, the Northern British/Dutch settlers of southern Britain had to integrate large populations of earlier beaker settlers, principally the Wessex/Middle Rhine and late European Bell beaker groups.

The association evidence of the Primary Southern beaker group completely confirms the dual cultural background of the group. From the Wessex and Northern/Middle Rhine groups the Primary Southern tradition inherits an array of equipment including "V" perforated buttons, flint daggers, polished bone spatulae and jet belt rings (in the so-called "pulley" form). Associations derived from the Developed Northern beaker group include the knowledge of latest bronze metallurgy, "V" perforated buttons of Whitby jet and northern amber, flint strike-a-lights with pyrites nodules as a standardized male kit, and bone awls.

The Southern British beaker tradition is as long lived as the parallel Northern British beaker groups. Once again successive phases of the Southern beaker tradition can be isolated in terms of the evolving motif assemblage, zonal styles and shape variations. These phases I have labelled in a similar fashion to the Northern pattern, defining a Developed Southern (S2), Late Southern (S3) and a Final Southern (S4) series of assemblages. The Developed Southern beaker assemblage expanded to the south and west, engulfing the late Wessex/Middle Rhine centre around Stonehenge, ultimately reaching southern Wales and Ireland. A parallel expansion from the fen margin and the borders of the Wolds and Peak pushed northward into former Northern beaker territories. Yorkshire and the Peak were overrun; with western expansion into north Wales and northern Ireland balanced by northern settlement as far as the Scottish Lowlands. The territory of the Northern British beaker tradition was steadily usurped and the Northern beaker groups confined to Scotland and northern Ireland.

Apparently at the height of Developed/Late Southern beaker expansion *ca* 1550 B.C. the first elements of a new and alien warrior aristocracy entered Wessex with their dependent bronze and gold artificers. The intrusive Wessex I aristocracy with its new range of prestige weapons and accoutrements gradually aligned itself with the non-beaker population of indigenous Late Neolithic origin, perhaps as a genuine political move against the economic and social status of the beaker groups. Whatever the cause, the Late Southern beaker group abandoned the crucial Wessex area to the powerful intruders. Consequently the Late and Final Southern beaker distribution is markedly complementary to the centres of Wessex I affiliation, with a compensating expansion or retreat northwards. In the Final phase, the slack biconical Final Southern beakers are carelessly decorated with blade incised lines and comb impression is abandoned. The beaker features of the pottery become increasingly less evident, especially when compared with convergent development of adjacent Collared and Biconical Urn groups. The new bronze weapons and Wessex personal trappings scarcely reach a single beaker grave whilst the indigenous Collared and Biconical Urn traditions become expensively re-equipped and expand their territories into former beaker areas. The British beaker tradition gradually becomes a scatter of devolved and engulfed groups slowly losing coherence, ultimately to be reintegrated into the birth of new traditions.

The domestic pottery of the southern British beaker tradition continued and developed the plastic finger-pinch rusticated ware developed by the Northern British/Dutch tradition. The domestic assemblages include large and small rusticated beakers, some of colossal biconical proportions, also apparently large rusticated and comb-impressed conical bowls. Heavy plastic ribbing strengthened the larger beaker domestic vessels but at the same time continued to follow the zone styles in vogue on the finer ware. The overall trend follows the fine beaker tendency to simple biconical profiles.

In conclusion, I must once again stress that this paper is a preliminary sketch prepared with serious limitations of space, time and illustration. I have deliberately avoided specific reference to the Middle and Late Neolithic Cultures of Britain, many of which must be drastically reinterpreted in the light of the beaker evidence. To include this topic and related facets such as food-vessel origins and handled beaker development would take many chapters of detailed argument. Nevertheless, I hope in the not too distant future to publish more fully these aspects of the beaker problem. In the meantime I would like to tender this paper as a small token of the great debt that I owe my Dutch colleagues for stimulus, advice and material help.

NOTES

1. For W/MR beakers see Coghlan (1957), Fig. 3, top.
2. Sittingbourne, Kent – Inhumation in flat grave with a two-hole bracer, bone belt ring and single-rivet tanged dagger, *Proceedings of the Society of Antiquaries of London*, **10**, 1884, p. 29.

3. Melton Quarry, Yorkshire – beaker rim sherd, bone belt ring, two-hole bracer with four imperforate pits, human bones – probably a disturbed grave, unpublished, by courtesy of Hull Museum.

4. For the beakers related to the British N/NR group see Modderman (1955), Fig. 4, Nos 9, 10; Fig. 5; Fig. 7.

REFERENCES

Abercromby, J. (1912). *A Study of the Bronze Age Pottery of Great Britain and Ireland and its Associated Grave Goods*, Vol. I, Clarendon Press, Oxford.

Coghlan, H. H. and Case, H. (1957). Early metallurgy of copper in Ireland and Britain, *Proceedings of the Prehistoric Society*, **23**, 91–123.

Fox, C. (1943). A beaker barrow, enlarged in the Middle Bronze Age, at South Hill, Talbenny, Pembrokeshire, *Archaeological Journal*, **99**, 1–32.

Grimes, W. F. (1943/4). Excavations at Stanton Harcourt, Oxon., 1940, *Oxoniensia*, **8/9**, 19–63.

Jessup, R. F. (1930). *The Archaeology of Kent*, Methuen, London.

Modderman, P. J. R. (1955). Late beaker-ware decorated with impressions made by a thread-wound stamp, *Berichten van de Rijksdienst voor het Oudheidkundig Bodemonderzoek*, **6**, 32–43.

Piggott, S. (1963). Abercromby and after: the beaker cultures of Britain re-examined, in *Culture and Environment. Essays in Honour of Sir Cyril Fox* (I. Ll. Foster and L. Alcock, eds), Routledge and Kegan Paul, London, pp. 53–91.

Sangmeister, E. (1951). *Die Glockenbecherkultur und die Becherkulturen*, Schriften zur Urgeschichte III, Bernecker, Melsungen.

Smith, I. F. (1955). Late beaker pottery from the Lyonesse surface and the date of the transgression, in *Eleventh Annual Report of the Institute of Archaeology*, University of London, pp. 29–42.

Struve, K. W. (1955). *Die Einzelgrabkultur in Schleswig-Holstein und ihre kontinentalen Beziehungen*, Wachholtz, Neumünster.

Thurnam, J. (1871). On ancient British barrows, especially those of Wiltshire and the adjoining countries, *Archaeolgia*, **43**, 285–552.

Waals, J. D. van der and Glasbergen, W. (1955). Beaker types and their distribution in the Netherlands, *Palaeohistoria*, **4**, 5–46.

Notes on the Possible Misuse and Errors of Cumulative Percentage Frequency Graphs for the Comparison of Prehistoric Artefact Assemblages

J. E. KERRICH and DAVID L. CLARKE

For many years archaeologists interested in the study of the Palaeolithic in North Africa and Eurasia have been using cumulative percentage frequency graphs for the comparison of prehistoric artefact assemblages. For examples we refer to Bordes (1954), Sonneville-Bordes (1960) and Tixier (1963). However, it is perhaps time carefully to review this technique and its future utility.

Statistical techniques and mathematical models are slowly infiltrating and reshaping the discipline of archaeology – increasing the power and depth of both analysis and synthesis. It is perhaps already possible to distinguish the cumulative advance of these techniques in archaeology from the initial role of demonstrative aids and methods of data display towards an increasingly powerful analytical role with a capacity for predictive inference. In the ranks of the first generation we have the early use of graphs, frequency polygons and histograms for mapping severely limited numbers of percentages or attribute ratios. In the second generation of statistical techniques the impact of the computer is felt for the first time and archaeology is developing an array of exploratory attempts to integrate the probing capacity of such methods as factor analysis, matrix analysis and principal component analysis. Now the cumulative percentage frequency graph and its use for the comparison of prehistoric artefact assemblages has probably been the

Reprinted with permission from *Proceedings of the Prehistoric Society*, **33**, 57–69, 1967.
The section on "ordering errors" was written by Professor Kerrich; the remainder of the article is almost entirely the work of David Clarke.

single most successful and useful contribution of the first generation of statistical techniques in archaeology. However, it is the point of these notes to suggest that this technique is no longer adequate for the detailed analysis and comparison of artefact assemblages because of its inherent susceptibility to dangerous errors which warp interpretation. This warning is especially relevant to recent attempts to employ the methodology or typology appropriate to cumulative curve studies in hybrid conjunction with more modern techniques (Binford and Binford, 1966; Doran and Hodson, 1966).

The dangers and errors that may arise in this kind of analysis have been increasingly voiced over the last decade. Particularly important in this respect have been a number of papers by Professor J. E. Kerrich and Dr R. J. Mason which clearly emphasize the problems involved (Kerrich, 1957; Mason, 1957, 1962).

In these notes we discuss the dangers of the cumulative percentage frequency curves under five main headings:

> Sample errors
> Percentage errors
> Ordering errors
> Typological errors
> Perceptive errors

Some of these errors, or bases for error, are not restricted to cumulative curve studies – sample errors for example. However, by far the most serious fields for error – the aspects which might become perpetuated – are the ordering and typological components. Taken point by point and error by error these five headings may seem small considerations, but taken cumulatively they confirm the impression that the limits of usefulness of the technique have already been reached and that further development hybridized with modern techniques will seriously prejudice the interpretation of results.

SAMPLE ERRORS

Sample errors seem the obvious point to start the discussion, although these are not confined to studies based on cumulative curves. Consequently, these errors are only mentioned in passing as possible sources of hazard.

Nature of the sample – the assemblages plotted on the cumulative curves are analysed samples from archaeological sites. As samples they immediately raise several important questions which may perhaps be impossible to answer but which nevertheless must be allowed for in comparative interpretation. Does the sample assemblage represent the site population fairly? What is the inevitable margin of error relating the sample percentages to the site population percentages and by what similar margin is the range of variation of the parent cultural assemblage defined? Some assemblages have come from the complete excavation of a site stratum of many square metres, others have come from localized shafts of a few square metres – even though modern excavations have proved the operation of strong locational trends in specific artefact types within domestic floors (Movius, 1966). Some again are samples from thin and well-defined strata and yet others are from thick, ill-defined and possibly long-forming layers. Problems of this general kind can be tackled in suitable cases with a properly organized sampling plan, but in many cases one is left with an assemblage spectrum in which crude presence/absence is a preferable measure of affinity between assemblages than the comparison of percentages with an unvoiced margin of error of an order close to the percentage itself. Sample statistics should never be accepted as representing population parameters without a careful assessment of the samples background and credentials.

Size of sample – the assemblages plotted on the cumulative curves are samples of very varied size, from a hundred or so artefacts in some cases to several thousands in others. It must at once be said that most Palaeolithic studies using cumulative curves have been very careful to avoid using samples that were too small – but not all are beyond reproach and sometimes the search for large samples has driven the analyst to use assemblages with poor credentials.

PERCENTAGE ERRORS

Percentages are a most dangerous statistic. Percentages are inward-looking and have reference to the internal structure of a certain assemblage, of a certain size, with a certain error in relation to a site and cultural assemblage population. It follows that percentages are especially untrustworthy in comparative studies designed to assess the affinity between assemblages.

Since the assemblages plotted on the cumulative curves are samples of varying size the component percentages are virtually never equivalent although the system shows them as equivalent and uses this factor in marking similarity. A 10% step in an assemblage of 1500 artefacts represents 150 artefacts; a 10% step in an assemblage of 500 artefacts represents 50 artefacts – one 10% is three times larger than another 10%. This factor may be less gross in most practical assemblage comparisons but there is *always* an error of this kind on *every* entry in the cumulative frequency curves and these errors are cumulatively added one to another right through the range of components – as indeed is every error that appears in this kind of graph.

Percentages are interdependent statistics and their changes of differences may not be as easily related as at first appears. A percentage change in one artefact type may alter all the other individual percentages. If there is a simple assemblage with 50% of type A and 50% of type B, then a decrease in type A to 49% will automatically increase type B to 51%. The actual change in each set of artefacts is only 1%, but the changes are in opposite directions, giving a 2% difference between A and B. This may happen even if the actual number of artefacts of type B does not alter at all.

The role given to 0% in cumulative curves is most curious. If an artefact type or group of types are represented in the curves as 0% then we know – within a margin of error – that these types are absent in comparison with a range in which they might have appeared. A number of 0% values for four or five artefact types may be scattered through the cumulative curve and yet they will make little or no difference to the "apparent" shape of the curve when compared with that of an assemblage having these artefact types in small percentages. On archaeological grounds, assemblages which are dissimilar to the extent of differing in numbers of unshared artefact types are usually to be separated on these grounds even though they may share 13.2% of type X and 17.5% of type Y (where these percentages, as we have seen, may represent very diverse numbers of artefacts). If the aim of cumulative curve studies is the comparative assessment of affinity or dissimilarity between sets of assemblages, surely presence or absence of numbers of artefact types should not be obscured by chance matches in a few percentages. It must also be emphasized that the difference between 3% and 2% is not at all of the same nature as that between 1% and 0%; 0% is not one degree less than 1% and, furthermore, 0% is the least detectable and most important relation in cumulative curves, wherein 0% makes minimal change. Numerical taxonomy evaluates affinity and dissimilarity in assemblages on quite the opposing basis and would noticeably give a quite different classification of assemblages at present clustered by percentage matching (Sokal and Sneath, 1963; Escalon de Fonton and De Lumley, 1955).

Percentages tend to hide significant aspects present in the original data and are no substitute for the actual data as a basis for analysis and synthesis.

ORDERING ERRORS

Ordering, or the arbitrary arrangement of the sequence of artefact types along the horizontal axis of the frequency graph, has a most serious affect upon the shapes of the resulting cumulative curves and consequently upon our assessment of the similarity or dissimilarity of artefact assemblages. This aspect can best be illustrated by some examples.

A basic arrangement of statistical data consists of the frequency distribution of observations of a statistical variable. An example is given in Table I.

TABLE I

Number of boys in families with 5 children x	Number of families f	Percentage of families $\%f$	Percentage of families with x or fewer boys $c\%f$
0	5	2	2
1	35	14	16
2	75	30	46
3	80	32	78
4	45	18	96
5	10	4	100
	$n = 250$	100	

In this table, $x =$ number of boys in families with five children and is an observable quantity which varies from one family to the next and hence is termed a statistical variable. It is a natural countable characteristic of each individual family.

In this example, a random sample of 250 families from a certain well-defined community has been examined and the frequency with which each value of x occurred in the sample has been noted. Thus, 5 families contained no boys (and five girls), 35 contained one boy (and four girls) and so on.

These two columns together constitute the so-called observed frequency distribution of x.

Since it is simpler to compare two percentages than it is to compare two ratios, the third column has been added, giving the percentage of families, $\%f$, which showed each value of x.

Finally, by successive additions of the percentage frequencies, a fourth column of cumulative percentage frequencies, $c\%f$, has been added which gives the percentage of families with x or fewer boys for each value of x.

The basic method of representing a percentage frequency table graphically is by means of a bar diagram.

The bar diagram for the data in Table I is shown in Fig. 1. In Fig. 1 for each value of x the height of the corresponding bar represents the percentage of families showing that value of x.

Another method of representing the information given in Table I is by means of a cumulative percentage graph as shown in Fig. 2. In Fig. 2, the height of a point above the x axis gives the $c\%f$ associated with the corresponding value of x. The bars that join the points serve to carry the eye from one piece of information to the next but have no physical significance whatever.

Both Fig. 1 and Fig. 2 contain exactly the same information, expressed in different ways. Given *either* Fig. 1 *or* Fig. 2, then you can immediately draw the other figure, and do it in one way only.

Often, useful information which is latent in Fig. 1 can be obtained more rapidly from Fig. 2, especially when many more values of x can occur than in the example given.

It will be seen from Fig. 1 that in this sample there is a tendency for families to have more boys than girls. Suppose now that a similar sample is drawn from a different community and shows a tendency for families to have more girls than boys. Immediately, sociologists, geneticists, anthropologists *et al.* would become wildly excited and demand to know why and to what extent the two *communities* differ.

The first point to be noted is the possibility that both *communities* have exactly the same characteristics and that the observed differences in the samples have arisen by chance. (This possibility is termed the "null hypothesis".) The first step to be taken is to test this null hypothesis. A standard statistical test exists for doing this. (The chi-square test.) The result of the test will advise you to do one of two things: "accept" the null hypothesis or "reject" it.

If the result advises you to "accept" the null hypothesis, then you are warned that the partial information contained in these two *samples* is not sufficient to enable you to form a sound judgement as to whether or not the *communities* have different characteristics.

(Of course, you may be able to combine the information contained in these two samples with other cognate data and examine the combined data, but at this point we are confining our attention to these two samples only.)

If the result advises you to "reject" the null hypothesis then you are told that the evidence in the *samples* does suggest quite strongly that

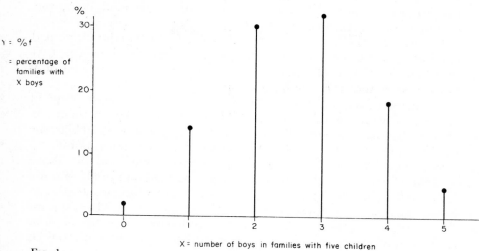

$Y = \%f$

= percentage of families with X boys

X = number of boys in families with five children

Fig. 1

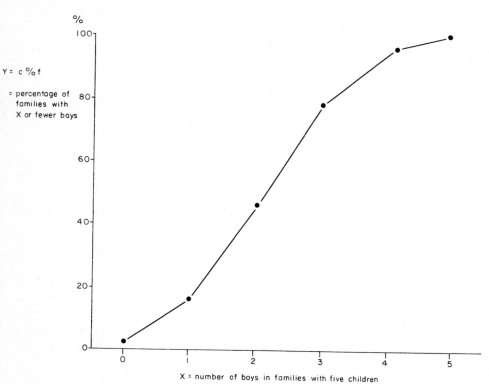

$Y = c\%f$

= percentage of families with X or fewer boys

X = number of boys in families with five children

Fig. 2

the *communities* have difference characteristics, provided it can be assumed that the samples are random samples.

In this case, the next step to be taken is to estimate the numerical value of certain aspects of these differences. Remember, however, that by means of *samples* information concerning the *communities* can only be estimated and never determined exactly.

Remember also, that the results of these tests and estimates depend on the *size* of the samples as well as on the percentages in them. As always, the *total* amount of information that is available affects the quality of the judgements that can be based on that information.

It is impossible, in an article of this nature, to expound the above ideas any further. But they are basic ideas, founded on sound common sense, and archaeologists are urged to consult basic statistical textbooks and make themselves thoroughly acquainted with them. The result for certain types of data should be to make archaeologists more cautious in their judgements and get rid of much dogmatism and acrimonious argument in their literature. Why should archaeologists remain forty years behind their colleagues in medicine, sociology, psychology, etc., in their use of statistical sample theory?

Now examine the archaeological data given in Table II which gives two samples, one from Site A, the other from Site B.

TABLE II

Reference number x	Class of artefact	Number of artefacts		Percentage of artefacts		Cumulative percentages	
		Sample A	Sample B	Sample A	Sample B	Sample A	Sample B
1	Hand axes	96	44	32	22	32	22
2	Sidescrapers	84	76	28	38	60	60
3	Cleavers	57	18	19	9	79	69
4	Endscrapers	36	44	12	22	91	91
5	Long flakes	21	0	7	0	98	91
6	Short flakes	6	18	2	9	100	100
		300	200	100	100		

The basic information contained in the two samples is given by the percentages. They can easily and simply be represented by means of two bar diagrams (see Fig. 3), with corresponding bars for each class of artefact drawn just next to each other. Alternatively, we can draw cumulative percentage graphs as shown in Fig. 4, in the manner fol-

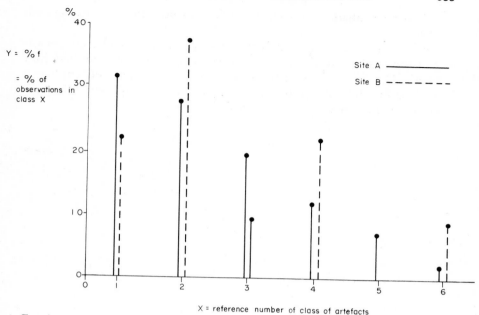

Y = % f

= % of observations in class X

X = reference number of class of artefacts

Fig. 3

lowed by Bordes (1954), Sonneville-Bordes (1960) and Tixier (1963). Just what useful information can we read from Fig. 4 that cannot be more easily obtained from the bar diagrams or the tables of percentages?

There is no sarcasm in this question. One can see certain immediate advantages of Fig. 4 over Fig. 1 such as "Fig. 4 shows at a glance that for both samples 91% of observations fall in the first four classes".

TABLE III

Reference number x	Class of artefact	Percentage of artefacts		Cumulative percentage	
		Sample A	Sample B	Sample A	Sample B
1	Sidescrapers	28	38	28	38
2	Endscrapers	12	22	40	60
3	Short flakes	2	9	42	69
4	Long flakes	7	0	49	69
5	Cleavers	19	9	68	78
6	Hand axes	32	22	100	100
		100	100		

It is more difficult to obtain this information from the bar diagrams in Fig. 3.

But for the statement in inverted commas to be completely meaningful the reader must know what the contents are of "the first four classes". Contrast this with the statement "In a sample of families of five children 96% of families had four or fewer boys", which is completely meaningful as it stands. (See Fig. 1.)

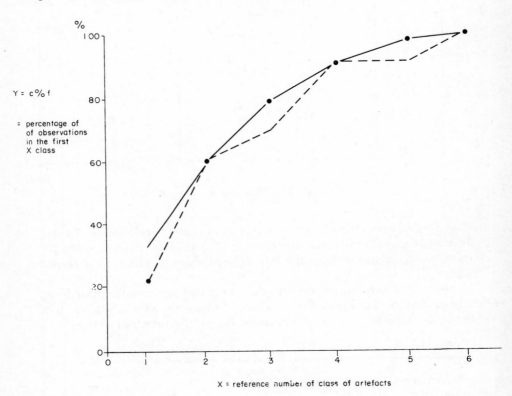

Fɪɢ. 4

Now, surely the classes given in Table II can be rearranged in many quite sensible ways. For instance, the authors can see no logical reason why the data should not be rearranged as shown in Table III.

From the cumulative percentages in Table III we obtain the cumulative graphs shown in Fig. 5.

Remembering that Fig. 4 and Fig. 5 contain the same type of graph and represent *exactly the same information*, which do you prefer and why?

Worse is to follow, because the six classes of artefacts can be arranged in $6 \times 5 \times 4 \times 3 \times 2 \times 1 = 720$ different ways, so that there are 720 possible diagrams of which Figs 4 and 5 are only two. Which of the 720 would you choose?

Does not the danger exist that if you make the subjective judgement that the two samples are "very much alike" you would choose a dia-

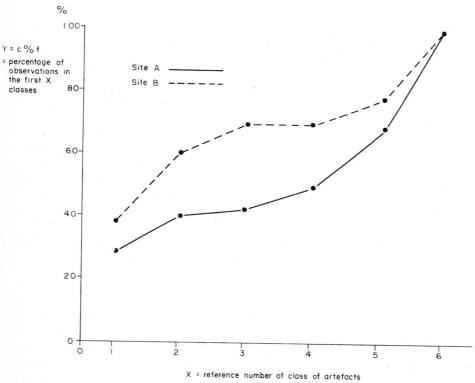

Fig. 5

gram like Fig. 4, while if you considered that the samples were "very different" you would choose one like Fig. 5?

If—as has occurred in practice—a table of artefact percentages contains 112 items, then some 1.972×10^{182} different cumulative frequency diagrams can be drawn for the same data, all containing the same information!

What has happened can be seen by comparing Table I with Table II. In Table I, where x = number of boys in families of five, each value of x is associated with *one particular* natural phenomenon, while in Table

II, where x = reference number of a class of artefacts, it can be arbitrarily associated with *any one* of a large number of classes of artefacts. Thus, in this case, x is itself an artefact.

Until all archaeologists can agree on one standard method of arranging their classes of artefacts they will be well advised to regard cumulative percentage graphs with a certain amount of grim suspicion.

Even if this happy state of agreement could be arrived at within such a body of sturdy individualists, would it not be advisable for the subjective impressions gained from any diagram to be tested and measured by means of the objective methods provided by certain standard modern statistical techniques?

TYPOLOGICAL ERRORS

Taken in conjunction with the ordering problem just discussed, typological errors provide the other major source of uncertainty in cumulative graphs and their use for the comparison of artefact assemblages. Furthermore, the basis of this source of error is at present being carried over into the second generation of statistical techniques with serious consequences for their otherwise powerful dissection of archaeological data.

The problem stems from the proper definition of artefact types as sets of artefacts with a precise range of attribute dispersion and variation, and in addition from the inherent treatment of assemblage analysis in terms of these types.

The importance of developing an adequate definition for artefact types and then applying the definition with all possible rigour cannot be overestimated. Many Palaeolithic studies make great play with variation from artefact assemblage to assemblage of the relative percentages of a given set of artefact types. Some of the most elegant and powerful of modern statistical methods have recently been applied to this kind of data (Binford and Binford, 1966; Doran and Hodson, 1966). However, hardly any of these studies define their artefact types on other than an intuitive and arbitrary basis of debatable adequacy and these categories are certainly not sufficiently comprehensive or sufficiently well defined in terms of attributes and attribute ranges.

The consequent danger is that an alternative or conflicting definition of the artefact types within such assemblages would radically alter the much discussed relative percentages and correspondingly alter their meaningful interpretation. Such a procedure immediately undermines the power and elegance of the techniques used in the recent analyses and most of the objective virtues of the diagrams and cumulative curves of such intuitive types. Surely, it is an incongruous anachronism to use powerful modern techniques to build up an impression of the upper levels of prehistoric entities when the lower levels and foundations are certainly inadequate and unsafe – one cannot build sound structures from doubtful components.

If elaborate techniques are to replace cumulative curves in the higher levels of interpretation then the entities of the lowest level must be similarly defined. The distaste generated by the thought of having to so define each of the artefact type categories must be swallowed if undue haste and the pursuit of quick returns are not to spoil the quality of the results of much time-consuming and expensive analysis.

Inadequate typology gives rise to the inconsistent analysis of even the same sample assemblage and renders the cross-comparison of cumulative graphs, or their more modern counterparts, quite impossible. As examples of the typological confusion hidden beneath the undiscussed type headings one can point to such greatly varying typologies as those for Upper Palaeolithic endscrapers in which three studies since 1954 variously suggest four endscraper types at one pole or eleven at the other (Sackett, 1966). On a similar basis it becomes impossible to compare meaningfully the cumulative curves for say the Mousterian of Hungary with the Mousterian of France – the artefact types not being similarly defined, cannot be compared. Perversely, the answer to this dilemma rests with the more accurate definition of the artefact types in terms of their attribute range and distribution by means of precisely those multifactorial clustering techniques rushed into application on the sadly unsatisfactory arbitrary typologies. Thankfully, some archaeologists have fully appreciated this factor and have set to work on this essential task using the latest methods.

A major source of uncertainty in cumulative graph comparisons therefore resides in the inconsistent results obtained by different workers analysing even the same sample. Careful training will only bundle together the individual's personal inconsistency into a consistent group-inconsistency and will not solve the problem – to show that one's assistants' results are all within a 4%–10% band is merely to demonstrate the consistency of the teaching. Tests with real Palaeolithic data reported in cumulative curves have revealed personal differences ranging between 4% and 50% in the attribution of certain artefacts to certain type categories – and these are differences between trained experts (Mellars, 1967). Errors or differences of this kind are of course cumulatively and additively carried through from type to type in the cumulative graph.

Finally, it is to be noted that there are two other sources of typological error or uncertainty. The first of these are the "overlap" types wherein two intuitive artefact types merge into one another and possess a zone of common membership. Here again which type category the artefact goes into is an arbitrary decision which may differ drastically between analyst and analyst—once more altering the cumulative percentages. There remains the residual rag-bag of "divers" types often inserted as a type category defined by the "left-overs" from the preceding typology—this of course is an additional hazard to the implications of the existing percentages.

Once again, until archaeologists can agree on a valid procedure and definition for artefact types they will be well advised to regard their cumulative expression with suspicion—however sophisticated the method of clustering the assemblages of arbitrary types might be.

PERCEPTIVE ERRORS

Perceptive errors may appear wherever different people are asked to compare and contrast lines or curves and to state something about the figures' similarity one with another. This is quite a minor factor but it nevertheless adds one more difficulty to the cross-comparison of cumulative curves. Differential psychology suggests that people form a continuum from "synthetic perceivers" at one pole to "analytic perceivers" at another (Anastasi, 1965). When presented with complex lines the individual may tend to perceive an integrated whole with little detail, and compare whole curve with whole curve on this basis, or the individual may concentrate on the precise perception of isolated detail and compare local detail with local detail. The comparison of cumulative curves provides a nice study in comparative perception. What is being compared—the affinity of whole shape with shape, the detailed pattern of steps in the ascending curve, or the difference between percentage step and percentage step? One thing is certain, given the same pair of curves some observers might find them to be quite similar and others might find them quite dissimilar.

CONCLUSION

The development and use of the cumulative percentage frequency graphs mark the single most stimulating contribution of the first generation of statistical techniques in archaeology. Those archaeologists that have contributed towards this important attempt at objectivity are to be congratulated as pioneers in a quest of primary importance in the development of archaeology as a discipline.

However, the steady development of statistical techniques and the wide availability of the computer are ushering in a fresh generation of methods and models of much improved power and penetration. The new frontier is even now producing an increasing flow of novel and daring attempts to use the latest techniques for archaeological analysis. This frontier is not without its dangers and much will be learned by the mistakes of those willing to risk its difficulties in the pursuit of information and not content to mull safely around parochial puddles. In this perspective we must highlight the dangers of extending the cumulative percentage technique and its corresponding typology too far into a dangerous and incongruous future.

One final remark. Archaeologists are warned that although certain statistical techniques will provide useful tools to help them to think clearly and arrive at sound judgements, these techniques will not automatically do all their thinking for them. The final onus of ensuring that their research is sound rests on the archaeologists themselves.

REFERENCES

Anastasi, A. (1965). *Differential Psychology; Individual and Group Differences in Behaviour*, Collier, Macmillan, New York. Reference to p. 354 of 3rd ed.

Binford, L. and Binford, S. R. (1966). A preliminary analysis of functional variability in the Mousterian of Levallois Facies, *Amercian Anthropologist*, **68** (2), part 2, 238–296.

Bordes, F. (1954). Les limons quatemaires du Bassin de la Seine, *Arch. Inst. Pal. Hum.*, **26**.

Doran, J. E. and Hodson, F. R. (1966). A digital computer analysis of Palaeolithic flint assemblages, *Nature*, **210** (5037), 688–689.

Escalon de Fonton, M. and De Lumley, H. (1955). Quelques civilisations de la Mediterranée septentrionale et leurs intercurrences, *Bull. Soc. Préhist. Française*, **52**, 379–390, Table.

Kerrich, J. E. (1957). Statistical note, *South African Archaeological Bulletin*, **12** (48), 137.

Mason, R. J. (1957). The Transvaal Middle Stone Age and statistical analysis, *South African Archaeological Bulletin*, **12** (48), 119–143.

Mason, R. J. (1962). *Prehistory of the Transvaal*, Witwatersrand University Press, Johannesburg, p. 224.

Mellars, I. (1967). Unpublished PhD thesis, University of Cambridge.

Movius, H. L. (1966). The Harths of the Upper Porigorchay and Aurignacian horizon at the Abri Pataud, Les Eyzies, *American Anthropologist*, **68** (2), part 2, 216–325.

Sackett, J. R. (1966). Quantitative analysis of Upper Palaeolithic stone tools, *American Anthropologist*, **68** (2), part 2, 356–390.

Sokal, R. R. and Sneath, P. H. A. (1963). *Principles of Numerical Taxonomy*, Freeman, San Francisco and London.

Sonneville-Bordes, D. (1960). *Le Paléolithique supérieur en Périgord*, 2 vols, Delmas, Bordeaux.

Tixier, J. (1963). Typologie et l'epipaléolithique du Maghreb, *Mem. C.R.A.P.E.*, Alger.

Index

STUDIES IN ARCHEOLOGY

Consulting Editor: Stuart Struever

Department of Anthropology
Northwestern University
Evanston, Illinois